RACE, RACISM, AND INTERNATIONAL LAW

RACE, RACISM, AND INTERNATIONAL LAW

EDITED BY

DEVON W. CARBADO,
KIMBERLÉ WILLIAMS CRENSHAW,
JUSTIN DESAUTELS-STEIN, *and*
CHANTAL THOMAS

STANFORD UNIVERSITY PRESS
Stanford, California

Stanford University Press
Stanford, California

© 2025 by the Board of Trustees of the Leland Stanford Junior University. All rights reserved.

No part of this book may be reproduced or transmitted in any form or by any means, electronic or mechanical, including photocopying and recording, or in any information storage or retrieval system, without the prior written permission of Stanford University Press.

Library of Congress Cataloging-in-Publication Data
Names: Carbado, Devon W., editor. | Crenshaw, Kimberlé, editor. | Desautels-Stein, Justin, editor. | Thomas, Chantal, editor.
Title: Race, racism, and international law / edited by Devon W. Carbado, Kimberlé Williams Crenshaw, Justin Desautels-Stein, and Chantal Thomas.
Description: Stanford, California : Stanford University Press, 2025. | Includes index.
Identifiers: LCCN 2024040333 (print) | LCCN 2024040334 (ebook) | ISBN 9781503630161 (cloth) | ISBN 9781503640993 (paperback) | ISBN 9781503641006 (ebook)
Subjects: LCSH: International law--Social aspects. | Critical race theory. | Racism.
Classification: LCC KZ1249 .R33 2025 (print) | LCC KZ1249 (ebook) | DDC 341.089—dc23/eng/20240830
LC record available at https://lccn.loc.gov/2024040333
LC ebook record available at https://lccn.loc.gov/2024040334

Cover design: Bob Aufuldish, Aufuldish & Warinner
Cover photograph: Courtesy of the author
Typeset by Newgen in 10.25 pt/13.25 pt Garamond Premier Pro

The authorized representative in the EU for product safety and compliance is:
Mare Nostrum Group B.V. | Mauritskade 21D | 1091 GC Amsterdam | The Netherlands |
Email address: gpsr@mare-nostrum.co.uk | KVK chamber of commerce number: 96249943

CONTENTS

Acknowledgments ix

List of Contributors xi

Introduction 1
(Devon W. Carbado, Kimberlé Williams Crenshaw, Justin Desautels-Stein, and Chantal Thomas)

PART I *Histories and Structures*

1 Race and Empire in International Law 27
(E. Tendayi Achiume and Aslı Bâli)

2 A Racist International Law: Domination and Resistance in the Americas of the Nineteenth Century 45
(Arnulf Becker Lorca)

3 Racial Panics and the Making of (White) International Law 76
(Frédéric Mégret)

4 A "World Problem": Apartheid, International Law, and the Domestication of Race 105
(Christopher Gevers)

5 From Metaphor to Memory: Remembering Dantès Bellegarde and W.E.B. Du Bois in the Legal Definition of Slavery and Forced Labor at the League of Nations and the International Labor Organization 124
(Adelle Blackett)

6 Transforming the Racialized International System: Intellectual and Political Challenges 144
(Rogers M. Smith)

PART II *Peoples, Places, Perimeters, and Powers*

7 Human Rights, COVID-19, and Global Critical Race Feminism 173
   (Adrien K. Wing)

8 Law and Epidemiology in the Making of Guantanamo 193
   (Aziza Ahmed)

9 White Health and International Law 203
   (Matiangai Sirleaf)

10 Race and Politics in International Criminal Law: 240
   Case Studies from the Arab World
   (Wadie E. Said)

11 Ukrainian Racial Contracting and the Geopolitics of 255
   Welcome in International Refugee Law
   (Marissa Jackson Sow)

12 Unsettling the Border 277
   (Sherally Munshi)

13 Race as a Technology of Global Political Economy 306
   (Chantal Thomas)

14 Barbarians at the Gate: The NIEO and the Stakes of 325
   Racial Capitalism
   (Vasuki Nesiah)

15 Race Consciousness and Contemporary International Law 338
   Scholarship: The Political Economy of a Blind Spot
   (Akbar Rasulov)

16 An Unreliable Friend? Human Rights and the 365
   Struggle Against Racial Capitalism
   (Ntina Tzouvala)

PART III *Critical Race Theory and International Law*

17 Postracial Xenophobia: An Abbreviated History of Racial Ideology in International Legal Thought
 (Justin Desautels-Stein) — 383

18 Toward a Transnational Critical Race Theory: Black Radicalism across the Oceans
 (Joel Modiri) — 402

19 Shades of Ignorance: A Critique of the Epistemic Whiteness of International Law
 (Mohsen al Attar and Claire Smith) — 429

20 A Critical Race Theory of Global Colorblindness: Racial Ideology and White Supremacy
 (Michelle Christian) — 452

21 The Post-Racial Universalist Framework: Colonial Logic in International Law and Relations
 (Kehinde Andrews) — 478

22 Critical Race Theory Meets Third World Approaches to International Law
 (E. Tendayi Achiume and Devon W. Carbado) — 494

Index — 529

ACKNOWLEDGMENTS

The list of people who played some role shaping the contours of this book is too long to articulate. They include not only the people whose chapters you will read, but also the scholars in the fields of CRT and TWAIL with whom we have been in conversation for many years now about precisely the interface this book effectuates. We will dispense with the normal practice of listing names because inevitably such projects leave people out. We do, however, want to explicitly thank our respective institutions—UCLA School of Law, the University of Colorado Law School, Cornell Law School, and Duke Law School—for providing support for this project.

LIST OF CONTRIBUTORS

Editors

Devon W. Carbado is the Elihu Root Professor of Law at NYU School of Law and Distinguished Research Professor of Law at UCLA School of Law. He is the author of *Unreasonable: Black Lives, Police Power, and the Fourth Amendment* (2022).

Kimberlé Williams Crenshaw is Professor of Law at Columbia Law School and UCLA School of Law. A pioneering scholar and writer on civil rights and critical race theory, she is a founding coordinator of the Critical Race Theory workshop and a co-founder of the African American Policy Form.

Justin Desautels-Stein is Visiting Professor of Law at Duke Law School, and Professor of Law and Founding Director of the Center for Critical Thought at the University of Colorado. His most recent book is *The Right to Exclude: Racial Ideology, Borders, and the Global Legal Order* (2023).

Chantal Thomas is Professor of Law at Cornell Law School, where she also directs the Clarke Initiative for Law and Development in the Middle East and North Africa. She has published in *Law & History Review*, *Cornell Law Review*, and *American Journal of Comparative Law*, among many others.

Contributors

E. Tendayi Achiume is Professor of Law at the UCLA School of Law, and a research associate of the African Center for Migration and Society at the University of Witwatersrand. Her scholarship has been published in the *Stanford Law Review*, *Vanderbilt Journal of Transnational Law*, and *Minnesota Law Review*.

Aziza Ahmed is Professor of Law at Boston University School of Law. Ahmed's scholarship has appeared in the *University of Miami Law Review*, *American Journal of Law and Medicine*, *University of Denver Law Review*, *Harvard Journal of Law and Gender*, and *Boston University Law Review*.

List of Contributors

Mohsen al Attar is a Reader in International Economic Law and Associate Dean for Learning and Teaching at Xi'an Jiaotong–Liverpool University. His scholarship has appeared in *Law & Critique*, *Journal of International Economic Law*, and *Asian Journal of International Law*.

Kehinde Andrews is Professor at Birmingham City University and co-chair of the Black Studies Association. He is the author of several books including *The Psychosis of Whiteness: Surviving the Insanity of a Racist World* (2023) and *The New Age of Empire: How Racism and Colonialism Still Rule the World* (2021).

Aslı Bâli is Howard M. Holtzmann Professor of Law at Yale Law School. Bâli currently serves as co-chair of the Advisory Board for the Middle East Division of Human Rights Watch and President of the Middle East Studies Association of North America.

Arnulf Becker Lorca is Visiting Professor of Law at Harvard Law School and Chair in Public International Law at European University Institute. He is the author of *Mestizo International Law: A Global Intellectual History, 1842–1933* (2015), which won the 2016 Book Prize of the European Society of International Law.

Adelle Blackett is Professor of Law and Canada Research Chair in Transnational Labour Law at McGill University. She is the author of *Everyday Transgressions: Domestic Workers' Transnational Challenge to International Labor Law* (2019), which won the Canadian Council on International Law Book Award.

Michelle Christian is Associate Professor of Sociology at the University of Tennessee-Knoxville. She is the author of *The Global Journey of Racism* (2025).

Christopher Gevers is a Lecturer at the University of KwaZulu-Natal School of Law and Senior Fellow at Melbourne Law School. His research focuses broadly on critical approaches to international law, legal history, and legal theory.

Marissa Jackson Sow is Associate Professor at University of Richmond School of Law. Her scholarship focuses on the areas of contracts, constitutional law, international law, human rights, and rhetoric, and has recently appeared in *University of California Irvine Law Review*, *California Law Review*, and *Michigan Law Review Online*.

Frédéric Mégret is Professor of Law at McGill University, where he is also co-Director of the Centre for Human Rights and Legal Pluralism. He is co-editor of the second edition of *The United Nations and Human Rights: A Critical Appraisal* (2014) with Philip Alston.

Joel Modiri is Associate Professor and Head of the Department of Jurisprudence at the University of Pretoria. His main research focus areas are critical race theory, African jurisprudence, law and identity, feminist political philosophy, Black political thought, legal education, and critical pedagogy.

Sherally Munshi is Professor of Law at Georgetown Law School. A recipient of the Program in Law and Public Affairs/Perkins Fellowship at Princeton University, her areas of scholarly interests include property law, immigration law, and critical legal theory.

Vasuki Nesiah is Professor of Practice at New York University and is one of the founding members of the Third World Approaches to International Law (TWAIL). She is a co-editor of *Bandung, Global History, and International Law: Critical Pasts and Pending Futures Law* (2018).

Akbar Rasulov is Professor of International Law at the University of Glasgow School of Law and the director of the LLM program in International Economic Law. His research interests include international economic law, international legal theory, and post-Soviet legal studies.

Wadie Said is Professor of Law at the University of Colorado Law School. He is the author of *Crimes of Terror: The Legal and Political Implications of Federal Terrorism Prosecutions* (2015, 2018).

Matiangai Sirleaf is Assistant Professor of Law at the University Pittsburgh School of Law, where she was awarded the Chancellor's Distinguished Research Award in 2019. She is the editor of *Race and National Security* (2023).

Claire Smith is a PhD candidate at the University of Amsterdam.

Rogers M. Smith is Christopher H. Browne Distinguished Emeritus Professor of Political Science at the University of Pennsylvania. He was elected as an American Academy of Arts and Sciences Fellow in 2004 and a Fellow of the American Academy of Political and Social Science in 2011.

Ntina Tzouvala is Associate Professor at the School of Global and Public Law, University of New South Wales and a Global Fellow at the Centre for International Law at the National University of Singapore. She is the author of *Capitalism as Civilisation: A History of International Law* (2020).

Adrien K. Wing is the Associate Dean for International and Comparative Law Programs and the Bessie Dutton Murray Professor at the University of Iowa College of Law, where she has taught since 1987. Professor Wing has advised the founding fathers and mothers of three constitutions: South Africa, Palestine, and Rwanda.

RACE, RACISM, AND INTERNATIONAL LAW

INTRODUCTION

Devon W. Carbado, Kimberlé Williams Crenshaw,
Justin Desautels-Stein, and Chantal Thomas

In 1973, Derrick Bell published the first edition of his now classic textbook, *Race, Racism, and American Law*. Sweeping in its historical analysis and doctrinal exegesis, Bell's book helped set the foundation on which the movement that would become known as Critical Race Theory (CRT) was built. *Race, Racism, and American Law*, along with the rest of Bell's oeuvre, encouraged an emerging cohort of critical thinkers to place race at the center of scholarly inquiry. In the context of doing so, Bell challenged not only conservative approaches to race, but also dominant liberal paradigms—and he invited other scholars to do the same. Bell's "call" in that regard was met with a CRT "response." Indeed, as Kimberlé Crenshaw, Neil Gotanda, Gary Peller, and Kendall Thomas explain in their seminal text on CRT, the oppositional stance Bell's scholarship took with respect to racial equality discourses writ large became a point of departure for CRT.[1]

From the beginning, CRT's target was the field of law and legal thought, in part to demonstrate how law constituted, and not merely reflected, racial power.[2] At the same time, CRT sought to expose a realm of racial power that lay beyond the regulatory boundaries of antidiscrimination law. This "remainder" of racial power was not located in the traditional sites of racial subordination; counterintuitively, it lived instead at the very center of liberal institutions and foundational liberal ideas that were otherwise lined up in favor of "racial reform." For example, and as Crenshaw and her colleagues note, liberals have long framed racial remediation efforts as "racial preferences."[3] Under this view, policies like affirmative action are necessary to "achieve diversity," notwithstanding that they are otherwise racially discriminatory.[4] This "apologetic" approach "testif[ies] to the deeper ways that civil rights reformism has helped to legitimize the very social practices—in employment offices and admissions departments—that were originally targeted for reform."[5] Crenshaw and her colleagues rightly contend that by framing affirmative action as a form of discrimination that departs "from otherwise legitimate selection processes, liberal race rhetoric affirms the underlying ideology of just deserts, even as it tolerates limited exceptions to meritocratic mythology."[6]

Of course, law has never been, and nor should we expect it to ever be, the only means through which to entrench racial hierarchy. Other disciplines certainly naturalize structures of thought and action that constitute patterns of racial domination and subordination.[7] But at least during the 1980s, law was on the frontlines of retrenchment, in part because the relationship between losing particular legal battles and suffering particular material losses was readily visible.

Yet the high visibility of law as a domain for staging a racial critique was perhaps also due to law's putatively apolitical status and the corresponding claim that, as a modality of thought, "reason" could distinguish "truth" from "ideology." CRT vigorously contested these ideas.[8] That contestation was a part of a broader claim about the distribution of racial power both in the law broadly speaking, and in academic institutions that researched and taught the law. To wit, no neutral concept of merit justified the lack of professors of color at elite law schools, and no neutral process of legal analysis—which is to say, "reason"—could justify the racialized distribution of power, prestige, and wealth in the United States.

CRT's illustration of the ways in which both merit and claims to neutrality were racially invested was directly linked to that field's engagement with "colorblindness" and the "perpetrator perspective," concepts that collaborated across broad swaths of United States constitutional law to entrench rather than disrupt patterns of racial inequality. Consider first colorblindness, or the notion that race is and/or should be irrelevant to governmental decision-making and in society more generally. In the abstract, there's nothing per se problematic about that view. But against the backdrop of a nation whose very constitutional foundation was predicated on racism (for example, slavery and dispossession) and whose constitutional principles expressly legitimized racism (for example, Jim Crow racial segregation), colorblindness is not racially neutral; it is a way of turning a blind eye to how race continues to structure our identities, as well as the material conditions of social life. That is why the hegemony of colorblindness in United States law is so troubling. Across multiple doctrinal regimes, colorblindness functions as a juridical mechanism not only to "not see" all the places in which racism resides, but also to render constitutionally suspect efforts to address those manifestations of racism.

As Devon Carbado has argued, part of what is particularly pernicious about colorblindness is that it has helped to create a body of United States constitutional doctrine that treats Black people and racial remediation efforts to address Black subordination as "suspect," but treats the existence of racial inequality as a natural and ordinary feature of society.[9] The work colorblindness performs in that regard is one reason that Critical Race Theorists have described the ideology as a disciplinary device that both elides racial inequality and restricts or prohibits race-conscious civil rights initiatives to eliminate that inequality.[10]

The "perpetrator perspective" compounds that problem.[11] To appreciate how, it's helpful to unpack what we mean by the "perpetrator perspective." Once again, we turn to Crenshaw and her colleagues' groundbreaking text for guidance. They write:

> The construction of "racism" from what Alan Freeman terms the "perpetrator perspective" restrictively conceived of racism as an intentional, albeit irrational, deviation by a conscious wrongdoer from otherwise neutral, rational, and just ways of distributing jobs, power, prestige, and wealth. The adoption of this perspective allowed a broad cultural mainstream both explicitly to acknowledge the fact of racism and, simultaneously, to insist on its irregular occurrence and limited significance. As Freeman concludes, liberal race reform thus served to legitimize the basic myths of American democracy.[12]

To put what Crenshaw and her colleagues are saying another way, the default under the perpetrator perspective is that, but for a few bigoted individuals ("perpetrators"), the United States is a colorblind society. That is the sense in which colorblindness and the perpetrator perspective are traveling partners or collaborators in an overarching projecting to obscure and entrench extant racial hierarchies.

Still, it would be a mistake to conclude that "colorblindness" and the "perpetrator perspective" are particular instances of an "American exceptionalism" confined to United States constitutional law. Both have analogs that traverse the domestic/international dichotomy. Indeed, part of the project of this volume is to expose and interrogate juridical iterations of "colorblindness" and the "perpetrator perspective" in international law, including in global contestations over the abolition of the slave trade.

A useful starting point for understanding the nexus between colorblindness and slavery is the lyric: "I once was blind, and now I see." So rings the famous verse of the hymn "Amazing Grace." Penned by John Newton, a former trafficker in enslaved persons who later renounced the slave trade and became an abolitionist, the hymn became one of the great civil rights anthems of the twentieth century.[13] For Newton, "blindness" was a condition that allowed the participation in and profit from the slave trade by himself and so many others who, "Christians although we are called, ... exceed in wickedness all the heathen nations that ever existed upon the earth."[14]

In considering the role of "blindness" in facilitating the slave trade, it is important first to establish the centrality of the slave trade, and the broader age of European imperial conquest, to creating the world as we know it today. Slavery wasn't just a "peculiar institution"[15] that took away people's rights and "propertized" them, to borrow from Cheryl Harris.[16] Slavery was also a critical component of multiple systems of moving people, goods, and capital through global mechanisms of resource extraction and commodity production that implicated the intersection of race and empire, wreaking genocide, dispossession, and dehumanization in their wake. These globalized matrices of subordination required a vast set of legal frameworks that both traded on and transcended domestic juridical structures.

Traditional historical narratives rarely represent slavery in this way. Instead, they portray the global transformations wrought by industrialization and modernization as phenomena that emanated from the global North outward. On such accounts, the practices of slavery and colonialism represented unfortunate backward-looking vestiges of pre-modern or feudal sensibilities. Contemporary social histories, however, increasingly articulate a different story. Central to that story is an account of the pivotal role that racialized global extraction and exploitation played in fueling the rise of modernity. In this telling, global racial domination constituted one of the processes through which modernity came into being.

Returning to the metaphor of blindness, the role of blindness in allowing the slave trade to persist, in the singular telling of the hymn noted above, deserves our contemplation for at least three reasons. First, "blindness" is celebrated as one of the great tropes of justice in liberal legality—and certainly *the* dominant juridical racial trope in United States constitutional law. Second, interrogating "blindness" in relationship to slavery suggests how the metaphor functions as a technique for denying, disavowing, and disattending a crucial driver of capitalism and empire. And third, marking the role "blindness" performed in the legitimation of the slave trade suggests that "blindness" is potentially a productive on-ramp scholars can take to examine how international law collaborates with domestic law to instantiate racial inequality.[17] We elaborate on these points below.

In both the domestic and global arenas, the trope of "colorblindness" has served to legalize various forms of "white ignorance," in Charles Mills's formulation,[18] in the dispensation of justice. At the most basic level, colorblindness effectively calls for an intentional perpetuation of ignorance. Indeed, even where a race-conscious understanding is wholly available, colorblindness exhorts that it must be actively rejected. The simultaneous availability—and rejection—of race-consciousness as an intervention is precisely the sense in which racial ignorance and "colorblindness" noxiously reinforce each other, including in the law. Which is to say, the legibility and deployment of colorblindness in law is predicated on a willful ignorance about the role race plays in structuring injustice. Thus, even if one is fully aware of how racial difference shapes social hierarchies, one must proceed "as if" racial difference did not exist. In that sense, colorblindness—within and across national borders—is a foundational legal fiction. That legal fiction renders any form of racial awareness both normatively and juridically suspect.

The role colorblindness plays in the production and legitimization of racial subordination, so powerfully articulated by CRT vis-à-vis US law, also operates, this volume asserts, in the international legal arena. Yet Critical Race Theorists have not fully employed critiques of colorblindness to challenge the racial investments of international law. Indeed, it is fair to say that, by and large, there has been comparatively little CRT engagement of international law, even as that framework might be useful to efforts to expose and disrupt the racialized world international law helps to make and sustain. As Crenshaw and her colleagues observed more than three decades ago, "Critical Race Theory might bring a useful perspective... [on the] liberal and left debate in the US over the proliferation of economic, political, social relations across national borders which has come to be known as globalization."[19] Central to their thinking is the view that the "left-liberal approach to globalization has yet to generate an adequate account of the connections between racial power and political economy in the New World order. Instead, generalized references to the 'North' and 'South' figure as a metaphorical substitute for serious and sustained attention to the racial and ethnic character of the massive distributive transformations that globalization has set in motion."[20]

Needless to say, in offering the foregoing example, Crenshaw and her colleagues did not mean to exhaust the scope of interventions CRT could make in the international arena. Their point was to stress that CRT could be a part of broader efforts to foreground the degree to which globalization has long functioned to create what we call a "racialized world order." Given CRT's potential intervention in this context, it is worth pausing to ask why, for the most part, that intervention has not fully materialized.

Part of the explanation might be that the covert elements of the contemporary international racial order are simply more difficult to define than were the overt racisms of the nineteenth and early to mid-twentieth centuries. Motivating this view is that idea that, by the 1960s, and contemporaneously with US civil rights legislation, the international legal system formally prohibited racial discrimination and formally endorsed racial equality. That shift in legal consciousness, the argument runs, reinforced a tendency to view racism as a problem of *individual prejudice*, and no longer a problem of the interstate *system*.[21] Without controversies like formalized chattel slavery, formalized apartheid, or formalized Jim Crow to organize the field, today's blend of racism and xenophobia appears too vague, too "amorphous" to serve as predicate for a robust racial engagement with international law.

Though the preceding explanation is not without merit, it might prove too much. After all, one of CRT's aims is to expose the places in law—outside of explicitly formalized racial regimes—where racism performs its subordinating (and superordinating) work. That effort includes illustrating how systems of putative formal legal equality entrench racial inequality. Indeed, it is precisely CRT's investment in that unmasking project that is the basis for its critique of the "perpetrator perspective," a perspective that, as we have already discussed, obscures the many layers of structural racism.

A second possible explanation pertains to an ongoing preference in international legal theory, and even within its more critical strands, to focus on ethnicity, language, religion, or culture as bases for the colonial encounter and as sites for exposing and interrogating domination and subordination, rather than race.[22] The emphasis on ethnoculture instead of racism might in turn rest on the premise—and it is a correct premise—that race is not biologically determined but rather a function of a number of social processes of which culture and ethnicity are the meaningful parts.

Yet CRT challenges precisely the same naturalistic accounts of race. CRT has long argued that the social constructedness of race does not render it any less socially material. From a CRT perspective, eliding a racial analysis in favor of a focus on ethnicity or culture treats race as an epiphenomenon to culture and ethnicity in ways that promote the idea that problems of race ought to be solved through the prism of the latter two social formations. Such an approach not only obscures how ethnicity and culture are themselves socially constructed and contingent, but also the ways in which these formations are intertwined and should thus be analyzed through an intersectional framework.

Perhaps a third explanation for CRT's minimal engagement with the international arena is the rise of what has since become known as anti-essentialism. As Crenshaw and her colleagues noted early on, this critique emerged most forcefully in response to legal scholar Patricia Williams's now-classic account of being racially profiled "shopping while Black" in New York.[23] Critics challenged the frame of race as a container for the story, querying how "race" could possibly hold together the account of an elite African American woman's encounter at a swanky New York store with, say, an everyday encounter of an Indian woman in New Delhi.[24] Packaged within this claim was the idea that for race to have any explanatory force in the context in which it was invoked, it should presumably find a fixed expression across space and time.

The problem of essentialism in domestic debates about race could explain the limited application of CRT to international law discourses. For if it seemed mistaken to "essentialize" or "totalize" race and racism across various lines of difference within the United States, how much more so if we begin to look at racism as a problem stretching across the world of international law?

But here, too, one might question the power of this "anti-essential" explanation. Thick debates developed in CRT about how to manage the essentialism critique so as not to jettison altogether the notion of group formation as a basis for both naming and disrupting social (including racial) hierarchies.[25] Those debates could be mobilized to position racial formation alongside other highly contingent and socially constructed formations within international law—such as the nation-state. The point would be that if the state can function as a unit for analysis, a basis for political organization, and a predicate for collective identity, why not race?

A final plausible reason for the absence of robust CRT engagements with international law could derive from the currency of international law's somewhat self-congratulatory idealism, which extends to pronouncements of racial egalitarianism. From the international abolition of the slave trade, to the adoption of the 1964 treaty against racial discrimination, to various instrumentalities against racism and xenophobia in the present-day context, international law has presented itself as being on the right side of history, and as a harbinger of human rights. This view provides at least a partial explanation for why international law functions as the juridical archive to which people turn as a resource for contesting domestic expressions of racial oppression.[26]

Yet the reality of international law is decidedly more complex. International law has not only failed to displace powerful structures of racial subordination, but also fallen short of producing a full analysis of how that subordination persists. This shortcoming renders the field a target of opportunity for, not a barrier to, a race-conscious engagement.

Whatever the reason for the limited space concerns about "the international" occupy in CRT, it is clear to us that the global arena is a crucial one for taking up questions of race. That observation invites us to ask a corollary question to the one we posed about why Critical Race Theorists have not taken the "global turn:" Why have concerns about race remained relatively marginal to both mainstream and critical theories of international law?

In raising the foregoing question, we are not claiming that international law scholars have neglected concerns about the contemporary reach of colonial domination, for that is clearly not the case. Scholars in the Global South, for example,[27] have long challenged the role international law has played in producing and sustaining a global world of "have" and "have not" nations, as well as "have" and "have not" peoples. In particular, those scholars have exposed and critiqued international law's normalization of empire by, among other things, highlighting how formal equality has functioned in international law to instantiate a range of global inequalities. These critical interventions were important in their own right, but they also helped create conditions of possibility for the emergence of Third World Approaches to International Law, or TWAIL, a formation that, at least to some extent, initially operated vis-à-vis international law the way CRT operates vis-à-vis US constitutional and antidiscrimination law—as a kind of outsider jurisprudence.

TWAIL developed as a self-identified intellectual formation in the late 1990s, roughly a decade after CRT. Whereas TWAIL focused mostly (though not entirely) on empire, CRT, as already discussed, focused mostly (though not entirely) on race. Thus, while each school of thought built trenchant methods of analyzing each of these forms of oppression—race and empire—the two discussions remained mostly parallel, a parallelism that may reflect aspects of the subordinating discourses in each domain—an American exceptionalism that is less interested in connections between the United States and the rest of the world, and a domestic and international erasure of race from the terms of legal discourse.[28]

A significant point of departure for TWAIL is the claim that domination was built into the very fabric of international law (which tracks the CRT claim that racial domination was built into the very fabric of US constitutional law). Antony Anghie, for example, advanced this argument by showing how sovereignty, a foundational concept in international law, was promulgated against the backdrop of and acquired legibility through the colonial encounter.[29] This assertion upended the typical progressionistic narrative of international law—namely, that Europe developed the concept of sovereignty internally, and then in encounters with other territories discovered other peoples who did not live up to the "standard of civilization" sovereignty presupposed.

Anghie theorized otherwise. In painstaking detail, he demonstrated how the concept of sovereignty was developed as a way of differentiating European peoples from others and thereby justifying domination. Put another way, sovereignty did not always already exist outside of and separate and apart from the globalizing hierarchies the concept helped to create and sustain. Sovereignty came into being through its production and legitimization of those hierarchies.

More generally, TWAIL scholars have been committed to demonstrating how international legal rules simultaneously could claim lofty ideals of sovereign equality and human rights while justifying and reinforcing structures that perpetuated the oppression of colonized peoples. This idea, too, has its corollary in CRT: As we have already observed, lofty ideas such as "due process" and "equal protection" in United States constitutional law have comfortably coexisted with, and perpetuated and justified, the oppression of people of color.

While as a body of work TWAIL did not completely ignore questions of racialization, it is also fair to say that the "race problem" of international law was infrequently theorized. In this sense, the absence of overt reference to race in some of the TWAIL literature mirrored, at least to some extent (though with very different normative sensibilities), the absence of race in international law more generally. We have already provided a partial explanation for this absence/marginalization, including the hegemony of colorblindness in international law discourses, the conceptualization of race as less real and less contingent than other markers of difference, and the dominance of the prejudice model—which is to say, an iteration of the "perpetrator perspective"—in international law. But another explanation that bears articulating pertains to the jurisdictional boundaries of CRT itself.

As we indicated earlier, at its inception, Critical Race Theory was explicitly focused on US systems of racial domination. Indeed, its founders defined CRT as a school of thought that "challenges the ways in which race and racial power are constructed and represented in *American legal culture* and, more generally, in *American legal society* as a whole."[30] That framing raises at least a question mark about the extent to which CRT techniques could be applied in the international sphere. Indeed, it is precisely that uncertainty that motivated Ruth Gordon, more than two decades ago, to organize a symposium that set itself the "difficult task of discerning whether CRT can assist in understanding, and possibly transforming, the international system, and ascertaining how an international dimension might enrich the Critical Race critique of race and rights."[31]

Gordon was clear-eyed about the main features complicating such an inquiry: the question of whether an analysis formulated in the United States context could aptly capture international dynamics; the relative muteness of discourse on racial justice in international law scholarship up to that point; and yet the often striking parallels between the political and economic marginalization of the "colored world" within the US and the "colored world" on the international plane.[32]

For many, the connections were importantly illuminated in the context of the struggle against apartheid in South Africa, and for the liberation of Southern Africa more generally. The role of the international legal community, both formally in instruments of the United Nations and decisions of the International Court of Justice, and in broader civil society in the anti-apartheid boycott and sanctions efforts, was crucial in condemning the racial violence of apartheid and in pressing the cause for self-determination. For scholars and activists focused on racial justice in the United States, the parallels between racial segregation in the US and apartheid in South Africa were clear.

Yet questions emerged as to whether a Black American perspective on international law could be said to exist, and what it would entail if so. Hank Richardson answered that question in the affirmative and argued for a robust understanding of this perspective.[33] Richardson's intervention was predicated on three important sensibilities: (1) that international law should be deployed to support Black Americans' domestic civil rights claims; (2) that Black Americans' contestation of US racism should be viewed through the prism of the international law of self-determination, and (3) that Black Americans' understanding of racial history in the US offered a perspicacious lens not only on the liberation struggles of peoples of color globally, but also on the role international law could play supporting or suppressing those efforts.[34] While this book does not internationalize race discourse precisely the way Richardson suggests, it joins Richardson's project of rejecting hard dichotomies between "the domestic" and "the global" vis-à-vis problems of race and empire. Indeed, central to our book is the view that disrupting the domestic/global dichotomy clears the ground for an understanding of how constructs of race, and the social dynamics of racial valuation and hierarchy, played a significant role in the colonial project and in empire-building more generally.

It bears emphasizing that "modern discourse[es] of racial difference and hierarchy" mediated and obfuscated a transnational and global phenomenon—"the exclusions built into modern notions of citizenship, sovereignty, representation, and the rule of law."[35] Elaborate systems of "racialized classifications" facilitated—within and across nation states—"legally sanctioned regimes of discipline and control."[36] Undergirding the particulars of this global dynamic lay a "racialized concept of the standard of civilization"[37] that was normatively white and Western. In that regard, asking the "race question" vis-à-vis the legalization of colonial domination and exploitation opens the door to an exploration of how constructs of racial difference traveled reliably with assertions of cultural difference across and within national boundaries, even as the particulars of racialization varied widely in each context.

Part of the aim of this book is to name the preceding racial realities, excavate their historical underpinnings, and expose their contemporary manifestations. In so doing, *Race, Racism, and International Law* steps into a space that, by and large, neither CRT scholars nor international law scholars have fully engaged—the racial construction of the global order. In that respect, one might think of this volume as staging a *global intervention* into CRT and a *racial intervention* into international law. These interventions will not only reveal the epistemic invisibility of race within international law doctrines and discourses, but will also identify the various mechanisms through which the production of racial ignorance functions as a handmaiden of racial oppression and domination.

Motivating our interventions is the claim that international law has been crucial to the design and enforcement of what Charles Mills called the "racial contract." As we discussed earlier, part of what Mills means to foreground with the concept of the "racial contract" is the epistemological condition of white ignorance that accompanies structures of white supremacist domination. In the same way that traditional social contract theory provided a heuristic lens through which to distill core political commitments as understood by the foundational philosophers of the liberal age, Mills redeployed the social contract frame to consider the centrality of white supremacy, racial hierarchy, and racial dispossession. Mills asserted that no social contract can accurately describe Western history without accounting for the reality that the traditional Western polity was a "racial polity." That racial polity was formed either through "white settler states" or through "white presence and colonial rule over existing societies."[38] The latter created conditions of citizenship that depended on a "preliminary conceptual partitioning and corresponding transformation of human populations into 'white' and 'nonwhite.'"[39]

Yet, the reality of that subordination, and the corresponding social, political, economic, cultural, and legal technologies and institutions of racialized governance through which it was accomplished, has been (and continues to be) overwritten and obscured by a set of ostensibly neutral governing social principles and practices to which Western society nominally adheres. This creates a critical term and condition in Mills's racial contract—"an agreement to misinterpret the world." According to Mills:

> So here, it could be said, one has an agreement to misinterpret the world. One has to learn to see the world wrongly, but with the assurance that this set of mistaken perceptions will be validated by white epistemic authority.... Thus in effect, on matters related to race, the Racial Contract prescribes for its signatories an inverted epistemology, an epistemology of ignorance, a particular pattern of localized and global cognitive dysfunctions ... producing the ironic outcome that whites will in general be unable to understand the world they themselves have made.[40]

Fundamental to Mills's formulation, then, is a conceptualization of law as a foundational frame for enforcing a racial contract predicated on a collective agreement among Western states to be ignorant about the very material conditions the racial contract was producing and instantiating—white racial domination. It is that willful ignorance—about the various ideological, discursive, and juridical ways in which racial domination is produced, legitimated, and elided in the global arena—that this volume puts into sharp relief.

Animating *Race, Racism, and International Law* is the claim that the concept of racial difference sits at the foundation of the legal, political, and social structures of hierarchy that shape our contemporary global order. Cumulatively, the chapters spotlight the historical role race has played in mediating the contradiction between universalistic claims to equality and liberty, on the one hand, and fundamental practices of domination and oppression, on the other. The expansion of the West unfolded in dependence not only on the conquest of other peoples and their lands, but also on the theft of other people's labor, resources, and their very humanity. Racialization was a critical technique through which all of this was effectuated and legitimized.

Significantly, in describing racialization as a "technique," we are not saying that, in the global arena, racialization was monolithically expressed across space and time. That was certainly not the case. As will become clear from our summary of the chapters, as in the context of "the domestic," racialization on the international stage is far from static. It moves back and forth between "text" and "subtext," between law and culture, between the formal and informal, and between reform and retrenchment.

Race, Racism, and International Law marshals together many of the themes we have rehearsed in this introduction and offers diverse vantage points, case studies, and analytical styles to unpack the stories those themes tell about race, racism, and international law. Together, the chapters illuminate how international law helped to produce a racially hierarchical world order. Many of the chapters foreground how international law performed this work explicitly, including through imperial domination. Others focus on the racially constitutive dimensions of international law. Central to these chapters is the idea that racial categories did not preexist international legal regimes but rather were partially constituted by them through what Chantal Thomas calls "technologies of global economic governance"[41] and Justin Desautels-Stein refers to as structures of ideological production.[42]

An additional set of chapters explores the historical mechanisms of racialized hierarchy in particular national settings as a way of demonstrating how contemporary international law perpetuates inequality by failing to undo inequalities of the past. And still other chapters make clear that while exposing the failure to undo feature of international law is important, it can also legitimize the idea that the *current* international legal system is egalitarian and that the problem facing the global order is the effect of *historical* discrimination and domination. Accordingly, these chapters highlight and contest the "here and now" racial investments of international law.

Many of the ideas these chapters present grew out of a collaborative effort that began in 2018 between UCLA and the University of Colorado, in which Tendayi Achiume and Justin Desautels-Stein organized a conference in Boulder titled "International Law and Racial Justice." That event was followed two years later by a symposium in Los Angeles titled "Transnational Legal Discourse on Race and Empire," hosted by Tendayi Achiume and Aslı Bâli, just before COVID arrived and changed the face of collective dialogue. The essays collected in this volume are the fruits of the discussions that have been evolving over the past seven years, and many of the authors have been involved from the start.

The volume is divided into three parts: "Histories and Structures," "Peoples, Places, Perimeters, and Powers," and "Critical Race Theory and International Law." These divisions are not intended to be hard thematic boundaries, but rather soft rubrics to crystallize not only the multiple ways in which "race" and "racism" have functioned as foundational features of international law, but also the role international law has played producing and anchoring both. The chapters included in part I focus primarily on the relationship between international law and the historical development and deployment of racial structures in the global context. Part II gathers a collection of case studies to examine particular manifestations of race and racism in specific fields of international law. Finally, part III foregrounds the question of CRT's applicability beyond the United States, and not only as a comparative enterprise, but as a distinctive approach to international law and international relations.

Below we offer a summary of the chapters and their relationship to the foregoing themes. Cumulatively, the chapters demonstrate not only how race, racism, and empire have been co-constitutive, but also how a CRT/TWAIL analysis can illuminate that longstanding and intersectional arrangement.

The book opens with a chapter by Tendayi Achiume and Aslı Bâli that explicitly trades on insights from both TWAIL and CRT to explore the international law frameworks Western actors have applied in Libya for more than a decade, including humanitarian law, counter-terrorism, and migration control regimes. They argue that the workings of these international instruments cannot be fully assessed absent an explicit engagement with empire and race. Central to their chapter is an engagement of mainstream and official analyses of NATO's intervention into Libya. By and large, those analyses described that intervention as one in which humanitarian responders attempted to address a crisis not of their own making. Achiume and Bâli contest that reading by illustrating that a racialized framing of Libya—and its subordination to imperial prerogatives—proved critical to the international governance regimes Western actors mobilized to manage that country and its peoples.

Arnulf Becker Lorca's chapter tracks the rise of race as an argument in international law. According to Lorca, race as a marker of civilization or the lack thereof helped to cement both Anglo-supremacism vis-à-vis the emerging nations of Latin America and those nations' suppression of indigenous populations in their territories.[43] To tell that story, the chapter retrieves the different ways international law traded on race to manage the Americas. The chapter reveals that the attributed racial character of Latin America did not emerge in a vacuum, but rather against the backdrop of international law's construction of white, African, and indigenous racial identities.

Frédéric Mégret's chapter denotes the Haitian Revolution as the original "racial panic" in international law—a generative moment in which the Haitians' revolutionary claims engendered consolidation of Western powers to mobilize efforts to ensure that the Haitian revolution did not overturn the racial ordering of the world.[44] Mégret maintains that the perception of the dangers incidental to racially subordinated peoples exercising true sovereignty generated important developments in international law. These include, but are not limited to: the rise of neoliberalism in international economic law, the emergence of the responsibility to protect as a basis for territorial intervention in international humanitarian law, the development of extraterritorial tribunals to adjudicate questions of criminal justice (among other areas of law), the shift from explicitly racialized border control mechanisms to "postracial" ones, and structural changes in international economic law.[45] According to Mégret, the preceding developments in international law were all designed to manage the threat of individual and collective expressions of non-white sovereignties.

Chris Gevers's contribution discusses the role international law has played domesticating racial domination.[46] Gevers employs contestations over South African apartheid as a point of departure to articulate that account. His central claim is that South Africa has operated as both an "exception" to an otherwise race-neutral world order and as a model for how race should be juridically, normatively, and politically managed. Gevers problematizes the precedential role South Africa has played in that regard and urges a re-conceptualization of racial injustice and domination as a "world problem" in which international law is (and has long been) deeply implicated.

Adelle Blackett's intervention describes CRT as an act of memory. Under this formulation, CRT is constantly in motion as both a framework and a movement that insists on knowing a past that does not and cannot remain in the past. Blackett maintains that because CRT elucidates slavery's afterlives in ways that challenge both racialization and legal liberalism, it is a productive analytical tool to problematize how the metaphorical deployment of slavery in international law has functioned to erase the Black Atlantic. To concretize her argument, Blackett revisits the League of Nations' Slavery Convention, which was organized and run primarily by colonial administrators. Not only did those administrators focus their attention largely on practices in "Abyssinia" and Liberia (rather than Europe), they carved out Forced Labor as a matter that should be addressed by the International Labor Organization (ILO) via separate, progressive regulation. In telling this story, Blackett recuperates articulations of anti-Black racism as global (and not simply a domestic) intervention through the figure of W.E.B. Du Bois, whose entreaty to the ILO was unequivocal: No labor would be free until Black labor was free.

Rogers Smith's contribution rounds out part I. According to Smith, a significant "intellectual challenge" confronting international law theorists today is imagining realizable alternatives to our real world, a world predicated on nation-states having absolute sovereignty, "including plenary power to control migration on any grounds that a nation sees as in its self-interest." Smith posits this problem as a challenge because "conservative, often authoritarian nationalisms are resurgent in many parts of the world, opposing all movements for constructive transformations in the prevailing nation-state system, including bans on racially biased immigration policies." Smith's concern is that efforts to challenge this conservatism often flatten the histories, complexities, experiences, and perspectives of both the colonized and the colonizer in ways that undermine our ability to reimagine and transform the world. The chapter's injunction is that people seeking to change the current state of international affairs should adopt more nuanced approaches to history and be ready to translate theoretical frameworks like CRT into normative and rhetorical registers that have the capacity to reach multiple and sometimes skeptical audiences.

Part II, "Peoples, Places, Perimeters, and Powers," opens with a chapter by Adrien Wing. Broadly articulated, Wing's aim is to employ a Global Critical Race

Feminist (GCRF) framework to demonstrate the impact of the COVID pandemic on women of color. In addition to providing an overview of the intersectional impacts of COVID-19, the chapter proposes legal solutions that tap into various dimensions of the international legal apparatus. In trading on the remedial possibilities of international law, Wing is not denying the ongoing ways in which international law instruments are implicated in regimes of racial and gender oppression. Her project is reconstructive: to mobilize an "intersectional praxis" to spotlight and ameliorate the social, economic, and political harms COVID inflicted on women of color across the globe.

Aziza Ahmed's chapter also centers on the relationship between health-related epidemics and racialized global governance. Ahmed's specific focus is on a still-underexamined moment of border management that implicates the racial construction of diseases—the detention of Haitians living with HIV in Guantanamo in the 1990s. Drawing explicitly on both CRT and TWAIL, the chapter illustrates how race and otherness were baked into not only how Haitians were imagined, but also how HIV was understood. Ahmed contends that this co-constitutive relationship between disease and race has roots in both colonial history and neocolonial power and provided precisely the kind of normative predicate that justified and normalized the detention of a racially marginalized group.

Matiangai Sirleaf's chapter engages similar themes, with a particular focus on how questions of global health are connected to and themselves shape concerns about racial inequality. Her chapter surfaces how international law, through both omission and commission, structures and reifies racialized hierarchies of care and concern. Sirleaf explores the connections, legacies, and important disjunctions between tropical medicine and global public health. She argues that the primacy given to "White health" is one of the animating purposes behind the emergence of the global public health regime. "White health," Sirleaf maintains, is part of a broader problem that she refers to as the "racialization of diseases," a phenomenon that attaches racial meaning to illnesses based on racial group membership. That racialization, in turn, structures which racial bodies are perceived to be deserving of what forms of health interventions. The chapter demonstrates not only how international law facilitates a racially globalized dispensation of health, but also the role "White health" plays in that arrangement.

Wadie Said's chapter shifts the site of intervention to international criminal law. But here, too, the concern is with how international law creates juridical economies in which bodies are differentially racially valued. Adopting a "case studies" approach, Said draws a nexus between the differential racialization of "peoples" and the differential applications of international criminal law. Said unpacks the effects of this dynamic in three important contexts: the Special Iraqi Criminal Tribunal's prosecution of deposed Iraqi President Saddam Hussein; the Special Tribunal for Lebanon's trial of the murder of former Lebanese Prime Minister

Rafik al-Hariri; and the International Criminal Court's indictment of former Sudanese President Omar al-Bashir. His analysis shows how the legal and ideological justifications for each of these tribunals rested on a dismissal of the validity of the origin states' legal systems as a basis for dispensing criminal justice. Although the particulars of each context differed and played out in various ways, Said argues that Arab racialization shaped how criminal violence was addressed in each of the preceding settings.

Marissa Jackson Sow continues the theme of racialization in international law, this time to contest the idea that racialization in the international arena is a thing of the past. In her account, international law is a domain in which racialization is actively maintained and reconstituted. To substantiate this claim, Jackson Sow analyzes how the UN system and the international community more generally responded to the plight of refugees from the Ukraine in ways that coded Ukrainians as white. In the context of telling that story, Jackson Sow articulates a broader critique of the racialized structures of international humanitarian law and demonstrates how those structures rest on racial logics of race and colonialization.

Sherally Munshi's chapter focuses on the relationship between "domestic" law and contemporary manifestations of race and empire. According to Munshi, race, nation, and empire shape contemporary regimes of territorial border governance. Munshi's chapter unsettles and excavates the normative tenets of border nationalism and demonstrates the work they perform providing the logic for the contemporary immigration controls powerful nation-states so tenaciously apply.[47] To do so, Munshi offers a history of the O'odham peoples, who inhabit an area that crosses the US–Mexico border, as an example of resistance to the logics of border control and an illustration of the conquest and dispossession those logics can produce. Intertwining histories of "territorial expansion, Indigenous removal, and immigration policies," Munshi shows how the border supremacy that underwrites expressions of sovereignty in the contemporary moment "leaves wholly unexamined a global racial order shaped by centuries of colonialism and empire."[48]

The final four chapters of part II explore the intersection of race, political economy, and international governance. How was it, these authors ask, that a global order that permitted human trafficking, and that relied upon forced and exploited labor, could also proclaim itself dedicated to human betterment and salvation? Chantal Thomas's chapter takes up this question by explicating the political economy of racial governance. Her chapter describes how race was deployed as a technology that helped shape global regimes of commodity production and labor exploitation. The chapter argues that critiques of racial hierarchy should include an analysis of not only the historical contingency and underpinnings of that hierarchy, but also how that hierarchy perpetuates—in "colorblind" terms—materially harmful global law and policy. Such an approach, Thomas reasons, is critical to identifying how a racialized political economy structures contemporary international economic law in ways that protect—in the *present*—the wealth extraction and dispossession empire effectuated *in the past*.

Vasuki Nesiah's contribution focuses on efforts to challenge precisely the dynamics Thomas's chapter describes.[49] Her chapter pays particular attention to the resistance those efforts have historically encountered. In Nesiah's account, interventions to rewrite rules of international law to achieve greater global equity have been both backward- and forward-looking. To illustrate this, Nesiah situates her analysis in the context of examining the New International Economic Order (NIEO), which she describes as an apex of attempts on the part of decolonizing states to re-envision international law in order to advance substantive equality. The chapter details the resistance NIEO encountered and explains how that resistance converged with and was expressed through the rise of neoliberalism. Understood in this way, Nesiah writes, neoliberalism "was not just a set of economic policies that majority white countries advanced; rather, neoliberalism was itself an expression of white supremacy." According to Nesiah, "the neoliberal marketplace was the final defense against the movement of 'colored peoples . . . towards Bethlehem' in greater and greater numbers."[50]

Akbar Rasulov's chapter brings a focus to the political economy of knowledge production and, more particularly, the mechanisms through which knowledge production is embedded and transmitted.[51] Rasulov asserts that training in critical methods, as an element of legal education, is available at a small number of globally elite institutions—reproducing a relationship of hegemony to the rest of the world that is reflected in the power structure those methods are designed to expose. This arrangement, Rasulov argues, creates a dilemma for scholars who are situated outside of Anglo-European-Australian hegemony. The dilemma is that these scholars often feel that they must choose between being a "specialist local informant" or a "token other."[52] Rasulov's account of this fraught positionality suggests that the logics of colonization are at play even in projects designed to contest the legacies of colonization. In that sense, the chapter is a reminder that the interplay between racism and international law this volume seeks to contest is not just "out there" in some legal regime or governance policy, but also "in here," the very spaces in which we are staging our interventions.

Ntina Tzouvala's chapter closes out part II with another indication that racialization in international law is not an historical relic. Tzouvala offers a bracing critique of how human rights law has been applied in the context of international investment tribunals. Her chapter highlights how these tribunals functioned to protect the property white landowners acquired in the era of colonial expropriation.[53] According to Tzouvala, part of what drives this white-centered protectionism is a racial logic that was essential to the entire edifice of colonization—namely, that white property ownership signifies civilization and progress, and non-white property ownership signifies uncivilization and backwardness. The account

Tzouvala provides is a compelling illustration of how racism can function to reinforce—and bring forward into the present—the historically marginalizing practices on which race and empire were built.

Part III, "Critical Race Theory and International Law," includes chapters that directly take up the question of how scholars might mobilize CRT in the global arena. Our starting point is a chapter by Justin Desautels-Stein that follows an intellectual line he associates with the work of Cheryl Harris, Kim Crenshaw, Denise Ferreira da Silva, and Nahum Demetri Chandler. His aim is to shift attention away from the regulatory spaces of the international legal order to the deeper intersection of sovereignty, property, and white supremacy.[54] More precisely, the chapter explores the structure of racial ideology in international legal discourse, as it developed between the eighteenth and twenty-first centuries, culminating in what he calls "postracial xenophobia." According to Desautels-Stein, these structures of racial ideology have shored up the sovereign's right to exclude and at the same time mystified the ways in which international law continues to produce systems of racial hierarchy.

Joel Modiri's chapter also explicitly engages with CRT, but he does so to contest the tendency on part of some scholars to overly particularize and discipline the potential reach of CRT. The chapter takes the generative relation between the Black Radical Tradition and CRT as a starting point for articulating a "critical race approach to international law" (CRAIL).[55] Grounded in a globalist, internationalist, transnational vision of the Black radical tradition, Modiri urges a view of CRT that transcends understandings of that framework as relevant only to the United States. To do so, the chapter directly responds to what Modiri calls the "incommensurability thesis" about CRT according to which CRT is "a largely an American import that is, for reasons of history, incompatible with other parts of the Black world." While acknowledging the real danger of "unidirectional" cultural exchange between Black Americans and, for example, South Africans, the chapter nonetheless argues that CRT is deeply informed by and is an iteration of the Black Radical Tradition. Rearticulating CRT in that way, Modiri contends, clears the ground for a more capacious understanding of CRT that, rather than artificially restricting the application of the theory, would facilitate the entrance of CRT onto the global stage to engage different geopolitical, disciplinary, and political contexts.

In some ways, Mohsen al Attar and Claire Smith's chapter is an illustration of precisely what Modiri means. Their chapter locates white ignorance as an epistemic feature of international law. The chapter maintains that white ignorance plays an enormously important role absenting concerns about race from international law. Al Attar and Smith view that absence as a "deliberate" choice to "advance ... an epistemic project," namely Eurocentrism. Situating racial thinking as a cornerstone of international law, al Attar and Smith argue that far too much of international law scholarship is normatively colonial and far too many international legal thinkers conceal their epistemic racial investments. In addition to exposing these aspects of the international legal order, al Attar and Smith offer analytical means for repudiating them.

Michelle Christian's chapter describes what she calls a "Critical Race Theory of Global Colorblindness." In doing so, Christian offers a synthesizing account of how core components of liberal legality were initially used "*in conjunction to race* to justify an evolving colonial enterprise" that fused together conceptions of legality, civilization, and whiteness.[56] Christian reasons that this fusion remains a core dimension of international law, albeit in less overt ways. To substantiate her claim, Christian theorizes global colorblindness along the following interrelated axes: (1) racist erasure; (2) the global expression of colorblindness through neoliberal policies and practices; (3) racial interactions that create varying geographic colorblind political cultures; (4) a stable global racial hierarchy; and (5) the authority and currency of white racial knowledge production. The chapter's takeaway rehearses a central CRT idea about the nexus between colorblindness and the law—namely, that colorblindness functions at the transnational level (and not just the domestic level) to naturalize and solidify the globalization of white racial power.

Kehinde Andrews's chapter contributes to the growing body of scholarship detailing how foundational universalist conceptions of liberal legality explicitly incorporated racialized exclusion in their logics of universalism.[57] For example, the work of Immanuel Kant, often understood as a precursor to modern human rights theory, is expressly predicated on racial hierarchy. Andrews contends that Kant articulated a conception of universal equality that positioned peoples racialized as non-white beyond its reach. Contradictions of this sort, Andrews reasons, were also manifested in newly emerging expressions of equality law under English common law. Here, too, Black people were beyond the reach of those equality-conferring structures. According to Andrews, this contradiction—between universalist commitments to equality and legalized forms of inequality—obtains with respect to international law as well. Which is to say, rather than representing a break with the colonial order, international law has merely shifted from being openly imperialistic to being benevolently colonial.

Part III concludes with a chapter by Tendayi Achiume and Devon Carbado, who argue that, for the most part, CRT and TWAIL have existed in separate epistemic universes. The chapter contends that the borders between these two fields are unwarranted. Specifically, Achiume and Carbado articulate six parallel ways in which CRT and TWAIL have exposed and challenged the racial dimensions of United States law and international law, respectively. According to Achiume and Carbado, both CRT scholars and TWAIL scholars have: contested the legalization of white supremacy; marked and problematized the degree to which regimes of inclusion can operate as mechanisms of exclusion; staged important if non-identical critiques of colorblindness; engaged and repudiated neoliberal, racialized claims about the social responsibility and agency of Black people and African nations; confronted perceptions that CRT and TWAIL exist outside the boundaries of the presumptively neutral scholarly conventions of constitutional law and international law; and remained invested in reconstruction and transformation of and within law, while staying clear-eyed about the limits and costs of such engagements and the need to effectuate change in other arenas, such as social movements. In many ways, the chapters in this volume track the parallel lines between CRT and TWAIL that Achiume and Carbado describe.

In closing, we should be careful to note that in providing the preceding summary of the chapters that comprise this book, we do not mean to suggest that the chapters cover the entire terrain of race and international law. No single volume could do that, nor was that our aim. In soliciting these very different chapters that traverse very different dimensions of the global landscape, our goal was to construct a space in which to subject international law and its various discourses and logics to a sustained racial critique.

As we have already said and want to repeat here, this racial critique is not intended to be the final word on the matter. On the contrary, notwithstanding the breadth and depth of the chapters and the critical interventions they perform, there's more that needs to be said. Indeed, one of the reasons we published this volume was precisely to generate more: more interrogations of the elisions of race from international law, more unpacking of the role colorblindness plays in that elision, and more analyses of not only how race and empire—and racism and colonialism—are co-constitutive, but also of the ways in which international law has instantiated that racially hierarchical arrangement.

It bears emphasizing—again—that the racial ordering of the world and its peoples is not a "natural" state of international affairs; it is a geopolitical and legally contingent one. From that vantage point, "First" and "Third" World nations did not exist a priori. Which is another way of saying: "First" and "Third" World nations were not born that way. They were made "First" and "Third" World nations through, among other "structural adjustments," the conscription of international law to legalize and maintain racial domination. That is the story this volume tells. It is a story in which race and racism—and colonialization and empire—are not peripheral dimensions of international law, but rather defining features of it. *Race, Racism, and International Law* is our effort to shed light on that enduring reality.

Introduction

NOTES

1. Kimberlé Crenshaw et al., *Critical Race Theory: The Key Writings that Formed the Movement* (New York: New Press, 1995), xx.
2. Crenshaw et al., *Critical Race Theory*, xxv.
3. Crenshaw et al., *Critical Race Theory*, xv.
4. Crenshaw et al., *Critical Race Theory*, xv.
5. Crenshaw et al., *Critical Race Theory*, xv.
6. Crenshaw et al., *Critical Race Theory*, xv.
7. Kimberlé Crenshaw, *Seeing Race Again: Countering Colorblindness Across the Disciplines* (Oakland: University of California Press, 2019), 22, 153–54, 267–68.
8. To be sure, there is a rich tradition of ideology-critique in the history of American legal thought that preceded the emergence of Critical Race Theory, and that developed contemporaneously. For discussion, see Justin Desautels-Stein and Akbar Rasulov, "Deep Cuts: Four Critiques of Legal Ideology," *Yale Journal of Law and the Humanities* 31, no. 2 (2021): 435.
9. See generally, Devon W. Carbado, "Strict Scrutiny & the Black Body," *UCLA Law Review* 69, no. 1 (2022): 2–79.
10. See generally, Devon W. Carbado and Cheryl I. Harris, "The New Racial Preferences," *California Law Review* 96, no. 5 (2008): 1139–214; Neil Gotanda, "Our Constitution is Colorblind," *Stanford Law Review* 44, no. 1 (1991): 1–68.
11. Alan David Freeman, "Legitimizing Racial Discrimination through Antidiscrimination Law: A Critical Review of Supreme Court Doctrine," *Minnesota Law Review* 62, no. 6 (1978): 1049–120; Alan David Freeman, "Antidiscrimination Law: The View From 1989," *Tulane Law Review* 64, no. 6 (1989–1990): 1407–42.
12. Crenshaw et al., *Critical Race Theory*, xiv.
13. "The Creation of 'Amazing Grace,'" Library of Congress, accessed June 13, 2024, https://www.loc.gov/collections/amazing-grace/articles-and-essays/creation-of-amazing-grace/.
14. Joseph Benson, *A Sermon, Preached at the Methodist Chapel, in Hull, on Wednesday, the 7th of March, 1798, Being the Day Appointed for a National Fast* (Sacramento, CA: Creative Media Partners, LLC, 2018), 21.
15. Joseph E. Inikori, "Atlantic Slavery and the Rise of the Capitalist Global Economy," *Current Anthropology* 61, no. S22 (2022): S159–70; Gavin Wright, *Slavery and American Economic Development* (Louisiana State University Press, 2006).
16. Cheryl I. Harris, "Whiteness as Property," *Harvard Law Review* 106, no. 8 (1993): 1707–91.
17. Justin Desautels-Stein, *The Right to Exclude: A Critical Race Approach to Sovereignty, Borders, and International Law* (New York: Oxford University Press, 2023), 265–312.
18. Crenshaw et al., *Critical Race Theory*, xxx.
19. Crenshaw et al., *Critical Race Theory*, xxx.
20. Crenshaw et al., *Critical Race Theory*, xxx.
21. On the "prejudice approach" associated with international human rights law, see E. Tendayi Achiume, "Beyond Prejudice: Structural Xenophobic Discrimination Against Refugees," *Georgetown Journal of International Law* 45, no. 2 (2014): 323–82.

22. Luis Eslava et al., "The Spirit of Bandung," in *Bandung, Global History, and International Law: Critical Pasts and Pending Futures,* ed. Luis Eslava et al. (Cambridge University Press, 2017), 3–32.

23. Crenshaw et al., *Critical Race Theory,* xv–xxxii.

24. Kimberlé Crenshaw, "Twenty Years of Critical Race Theory: Looking Back to Move Forward," *Connecticut Law Review* 43, no. 5 (2011): 1294.

25. Devon W. Carbado and Cheryl I. Harris, "Intersectionality at 30: Mapping the Margins of Anti-Essentialism, Intersectionality, and Dominance Theory," *Harvard Law Review* 132, no. 8 (2019): 2213–14; Kimberlé Crenshaw, "Close Encounters of Three Kinds: On Teaching Dominance Feminism and Intersectionality," *Tulsa Law Review* 46, no. 1 (2010): 180–81.

26. Carol Anderson, *Eyes Off the Prize: The United Nations and the African American Struggle for Human Rights* (United Kingdom: Cambridge University Press, 2003). In her trenchant critique of the NAACP for not appealing to international human rights law, Anderson fails to include a critique of international human rights and its shortcomings. For more discussion see Chantal Thomas, "Racial Justice and International Law," in *Oxford Handbook of Race and Law in the United States,* ed. Khiara Bridges et al. (Oxford University Press, forthcoming), SSRN: https://papers.ssrn.com/sol3/papers.cfm?abstract_id=4110161.

27. Antony Anghie, "The Evolution of International Law: Colonial and Postcolonial Realities," *Third World Quarterly* 27, no. 5 (2006): 739–53; Christopher Gevers, "Unwhitening the World: Rethinking Race and International Law," *UCLA Law Review* 67, no. 6 (2021): 1652–85; James Thuo Gathii, "Imperialism, Colonialism, and International Law," *Buffalo Law Review* 54, no. 4 (2007): 1013–66; Aslı U. Bâli and Aziz Rana, "Pax Arabica: Provisional Sovereignty and Intervention in the Arab Uprisings," *California Western International Law Journal* 42, no. 2 (2012): 321–52; John Reynolds, *Empire, Emergency and International Law* (United Kingdom: Cambridge University Press, 2017); Mohammad Shahabuddin, "Minorities and the Making of Postcolonial States in International Law," *TWAILR: REFLECTIONS* (May 13, 2020), https://perma.cc/BS3M-9LS7.

28. James Thuo Gathii, "Beyond Color-Blind International Economic Law," *AJIL Unbound,* no. 117 (2023): 61–65.

29. Antony Anghie, *Imperialism, Sovereignty and the Making of International Law* (United Kingdom: Cambridge University Press, 2004).

30. "Critical Race scholarship . . . [is] unified by two common interests. The first is to understand how a regime of white supremacy and its subordination of people of color have been created and maintained in America and, in particular, to examine the relationship between that social structure and professed ideals such as 'the rule of law' and 'equal protection.' The second is a desire not merely to understand the vexed bond between law and racial power but to change it." Crenshaw et al., *Critical Race Theory,* xiii.

31. Ruth Gordon, "Critical Race Theory and International Law: Convergence and Divergence," *Villanova Law Review* 45, no. 5 (2000): 829.

32. Gordon, "Critical Race Theory and International Law: Convergence and Divergence," 829–31.

33. Henry J. Richardson, III, *The Origins of African-American Interests in International Law* (Durham, NC: Carolina Academic Press, 2008); Henry J. Richardson, III, "Afro-America and International Law," *Black Law Journal* 5, no. 2 (1977): 204–7; Henry J. Richardson, III, "Permissible Measures and Obligations for Outside States and Internal

Peoples Toward Minority Rule in South Africa," *American Society of International Law Proceedings*, no. 80 (1986): 308–10.

34. Richardson, III, *The Origins of African-American Interests in International Law*; Richardson, III, "Afro-America and International Law," 204–7; Richardson, III, "Permissible Measures and Obligations," 308–10.

35. Tayyab Mahmud, "Colonialism and Modern Constructions of Race: A Preliminary Inquiry," *University of Miami Law Review* 53, no. 4 (1999): 1219.

36. Mahmud, "Colonialism and Modern Constructions of Race," 1219; Judith Surkis, *Sex, Law, and Sovereignty in French Algeria, 1830–1930* (Ithaca, NY: Cornell University Press, 2019).

37. Ralph Wilde, *International Territorial Administration: How Trusteeship and the Civilizing Mission Never Went Away* (United Kingdom: OUP Oxford, 2010), 317.

38. Charles W. Mills, *The Racial Contract* (Ithaca, NY: Cornell University Press, 2014), 12.

39. Mills, *The Racial Contract*, 13.

40. Mills, *The Racial Contract*, 18.

41. Chantal Thomas, "Race as a Technology of Global Political Economy," in *Race, Racism and International Law*, ed. Devon W. Carbado et al. (Stanford University Press, 2025), 306.

42. Justin Desautels-Stein, "Postracial Xenophobia," in *Race, Racism and International Law*, ed. Devon W. Carbado et al. (Stanford University Press, 2025), 383.

43. Arnulf Becker Lorca, "A Racist International Law: Domination and Resistance in the Americas of the Nineteenth Century," in *Race, Racism and International Law*, ed. Devon W. Carbado et al. (Stanford University Press, 2025), 45.

44. Frédéric Mégret, "Racial Panics and the Making of (White) International Law," in *Race, Racism and International Law*, ed. Devon W. Carbado et al. (Stanford University Press, 2025), 76.

45. Mégret, "Racial Panics and the Making of (White) International Law," 76.

46. Christopher Gevers, "A 'World Problem': Apartheid, International Law, and the Domestication of Race," in *Race, Racism and International Law*, ed. Devon W. Carbado et al. (Stanford University Press, 2025), 105.

47. Sherally Munshi, "Unsettling the Border," in *Race, Racism and International Law*, ed. Devon W. Carbado et al. (Stanford University Press, 2025), 277.

48. Munshi, "Unsettling the Border," 277.

49. Vasuki Nesiah, "Barbarians at the Gate: The NIEO and the Stakes of Racial Capitalism," in *Race, Racism and International Law*, ed. Devon W. Carbado et al. (Stanford University Press, 2025), 325.

50. Nesiah, "Barbarians at the Gate," 325.

51. Akbar Rasulov, "Race Consciousness and Contemporary International Law Scholarship: The Political Economy of a Blindspot," in *Race, Racism and International Law*, ed. Devon W. Carbado et al. (Stanford University Press, 2025), 338.

52. Rasulov, "Race Consciousness and Contemporary International Law Scholarship," 338.

53. Ntina Tzouvala, "An Unreliable Friend? Human Rights and the Struggle Against Racial Capitalism," in *Race, Racism and International Law*, ed. Devon W. Carbado et al. (Stanford University Press, 2025), 365.

54. Justin Desautels-Stein, "Postracial Xenophobia: An Abbreviated History of Racial Ideology in International Legal Thought," in *Race, Racism and International Law*, ed. Devon W. Carbado et al. (Stanford University Press, 2025), 383.

55. Joel Modiri, "Toward a Transnational Critical Race Theory: Black Radicalism Across the Oceans," in *Race, Racism and International Law*, ed. Devon W. Carbado et al. (Stanford University Press, 2025), 402.

56. Michelle Christian, "A Critical Race Theory of Global Colorblindness: Racial Ideology and White Supremacy," in *Race, Racism and International Law*, ed. Devon W. Carbado et al. (Stanford University Press, 2025), 452.

57. Kehinde Andrews, "The Post-Racial Universalist Framework: Colonial Logic in International Law and Relations," in *Race, Racism and International Law*, ed. Devon W. Carbado et al. (Stanford University Press, 2025), 478.

PART I
Histories and Structures

CHAPTER ONE

RACE AND EMPIRE IN INTERNATIONAL LAW

E. Tendayi Achiume and Aslı Bâli

I. RACE AND EMPIRE IN INTERNATIONAL LAW AT THE INTERSECTION OF TWAIL AND CRT

Within TWAIL, the "Third World" is a "counter-hegemonic discursive tool that allows us to interrogate and contest the various ways in which [geopolitical] power is used,"[1] and it is an "anti-imperial and anti-racist project."[2] It is a category that enables fundamental diagnosis and critique of international law and its operation. Additionally it acts as a "subaltern epistemic location" and a site of knowledge production about international law that aims to disrupt dominant approaches, which explicitly and implicitly treat the West as the only legitimate and plausible source of international legal knowledge.[3] TWAIL also unifies a diverse set of scholars who share the foundational premise that international law cannot be understood or analyzed apart from its mutually constitutive relationship with empire and its enduring contemporary legacies.[4]

Similarly, Critical Race Theory proceeds from the premise of race as a social construction, according to which physical features and lineage are imbued with social, political, economic, and even legal meaning.[5] CRT has its origins in the study of US law,[6] but it has traveled far outside the borders of the United States.[7] CRT analyses demonstrate the degree to which law is implicated in racial subordination, rather than existing outside of the problem, merely as solution. CRT scholars have mapped the mutually constitutive relationships among race, racial subordination, and the law; and they have examined law's historical and contemporary role in the construction of race and racial subordination.[8] Understandably there is growing momentum among TWAIL scholars to engage with CRT and to center race as analytically productive in analysis of empire. CRT, as well, could benefit from greater engagement with TWAIL.

Below, we approach NATO's intervention in Libya and its aftermath as an example of what is possible through an approach that brings CRT to bear on TWAIL.[9] The Libyan case demonstrates how humanitarian intervention, counterterrorism, and migration control regimes in international law cannot be fully assessed absent engagement with empire and race. By utilizing a CRT lens in tandem with TWAIL, we aim to center race as the critical analytical category for understanding the operation of contemporary global governance regimes structured by empire. Though TWAIL scholars already implicitly operate at this intersection,[10] we take an explicit approach as a way of forging links between TWAIL and CRT, which remain largely siloed.

II. LIBYA AND INTERNATIONAL LAW: A RACE AND EMPIRE ANALYSIS

In considering the case of Libya, we challenge the conventional international legal analyses of NATO's intervention, particularly from the perspectives of humanitarianism and counterterrorism on the one hand, and the laws and policies governing migration on the other. Mainstream and official analysis casts the international system and its hegemonic actors in the role of humanitarian responders to a crisis not of their making. Our analysis centrally implicates these hegemonic actors as the architects of the conditions that made intervention possible and who sustained the dysfunction that followed. We argue that the dual and contingent nature of Third World sovereignty—a mainstay in the modern international system[11]—is at work here, and race is a part of this story, too. Our conception of race in this analysis is grounded in a CRT approach that treats race as a social construction that imbues morphology and ancestry with meaning—including through law and legal processes[12] that determine how rights and privileges are allocated.[13]

A TWAIL-CRT approach exposes the ways that Third World sovereignty is formally asserted or vitiated in the international system on terms set by First World nation-states.[14] We also explore how different bodies of international law function and thrive as systems of racial governance, where racial governance refers to the different ways that race creates a means of ordering bodies and territories transnationally on a hierarchy according to which imperial exploitation can occur.[15] Race, here, functions as a technology of empire. In the case of Libya, we demonstrate how the racial framing of Libya proved critical to the international governance regimes for managing the country from 2011 to the present.

First, by framing Libya as an Arab—not African—state, First World countries sidelined the African Union's efforts at mediation to defuse the conflict and presented military intervention backed by the United Nations (UN) as enjoying regional legitimacy by virtue of the Arab League's endorsement. Second, the later framing of Libya as an Arab state awash in jihadis situated the country in a familiar racialized script of Arab and Muslim violence[16] enabling ad hoc, unilateral applications of force in the territory at the discretion of First World militaries wielding counterterrorism doctrine. Ironically, as Libya became the privileged theater of operation for experimentation with new counterterrorism techniques, it became the territorial locus for consolidating a new operational command structure for the US military to "secure" Africa. Third, treating Libya as an Arab "transit" state for Black Africans—racialized as definitionally non-Libyan—enabled vast interdiction operations using race as a proxy for unauthorized migration and establishing a European "racial border"[17] on Libyan soil. Libya therefore highlights how international law structures regimes of racial governance in line with Reynolds's pithy formulation: "racist, reactionary, legal."[18]

A. INTERVENTION, RACE, AND STATE UNMAKING

The UN-authorized intervention in Libya was both remarkable and unexceptional. On the one hand, Libya was the first time that the "responsibility to protect" (R2P) was invoked as the basis for coercive action under chapter VII of the UN Charter.[19] The United Nations Security Council (Security Council) licensed an armed intervention against a state not because of an act of aggression or a threat to its neighbors but ostensibly to protect its own civilian population.[20] On the other hand, this unprecedented authorization is better understood as continuous with a longer tradition of colonial and postcolonial military interventions in the Third World justified by appeals to humanitarianism. The critical question missed in almost all of the international law analyses of the Libya intervention is how the country could in a matter of weeks become the object of an international consensus that set aside all considerations of sovereignty in favor of a massive bombing campaign purportedly to protect civilians. To answer this question, it is essential to center race and empire in the analysis.

Sovereignty doctrine reflects the colonial origins of international law. Sovereignty is a concept that was developed to manage and justify unequal relations between European states and the non-European world.[21] Decolonization and the emergence of formerly colonized societies as independent, sovereign states were often presented as the end of formal empire in the international system and the beginning of a postcolonial era of sovereign equality.[22] Yet, as the R2P doctrine makes particularly explicit, Third World sovereignty remains highly contingent. The possibility that the Libyan regime might put down a popular uprising by force was sufficient grounds to set aside Libyan sovereignty in the name of an asserted universal interest in humanitarianism.[23] The racial and imperial character of the governance arrangements that facilitate intervention in some contexts and exempt others reflects the dual nature of postcolonial sovereignty. Third World sovereignties that serve First World interests—either because of patronage relations or the need to solidify borders to manage migration flows—are impermeable. Protesters in countries like Saudi Arabia and even Syria would have been mistaken to expect humanitarian considerations to result in international intervention in their favor. But—as Libya shows—where First World geopolitical interests dictate setting sovereignty aside, it is readily cast off whether in the name of humanitarianism or the pursuit of other interests.

Libya was distinctive in several respects—the country was a member of both the League of Arab States and the African Union.[24] But unlike the majority of Arab authoritarians facing uprisings, Muammar Qaddafi did not have longstanding partnerships with powerful states outside of the region or counterparts in the Arab world.[25] Indeed, Qaddafi's strongest relationships were with counterparts in the African Union, not the Arab world.[26] Qaddafi honed his pan-Africanism as part of a strategy of self-promotion and geopolitical posturing in his own right.[27] Prior to 2011, Libya's regional role was firmly in Africa and not in the Arab world. But for the purposes of isolating the regime and laying the groundwork for intervention, Libya's Arab rather than African identity proved salient in 2011.[28]

Qaddafi's investment in a pan-African orientation for Libya was due both to his strained relations with other Arab leaders and to seize on the opportunity to use Libyan oil wealth to gain strategic leverage on the African continent.[29] Additionally, the nomadic tribes of Libya's Fezzan region range into neighboring countries to Libya's south, and a significant minority of the Libyan population identifies primarily as African.[30] For better or worse, Libyan foreign policy was deeply invested in African affairs,[31] with the Qaddafi regime supporting a variety of actors from the African National Congress party in South Africa[32] to insurgents and later dictators in countries such as Sierra Leone and Liberia.[33] Libya was also one of the largest contributors to the African Union itself.[34] The African Union, in turn, supported mediation to find a negotiated solution to the Libyan uprising.[35] None of this suited the purposes of intervention by the Security Council, with powerful states looking for a regional partner to endorse the necessity of armed action rather than mediation. In order to elevate a regional voice amenable to First World intervention, the Arab League was presented as the appropriate regional organization, and Libyans themselves were racialized as exclusively Arab at the UN by Western states arguing for the legitimacy of intervention.[36]

The Arab League, for its part, closed ranks against Qaddafi while continuing to support authoritarian crackdowns against protesters elsewhere among its members. Libya was suspended from the League on February 22, 2011,[37] and within three weeks the League issued an endorsement of a UN no-fly zone over Libya.[38] The Arab uprisings underscored that the League was little more than a club for dictators—many busy suppressing uprisings in their own capitals—but one suddenly empowered by the First World to offer regional support for an international strategy of intervention, something the African Union declined to do. At the United Nations, Arab League action in support of Qaddafi's ouster was treated as evidence of the legitimacy of intervention in the eyes of regional, non-Western powers.[39] Meanwhile, efforts by the African Union to pursue a negotiated settlement between the regime and protesters in Libya were studiously ignored.[40]

Within less than a month of the start of protests,[41] the Security Council issued Resolution 1973, citing ongoing human rights violations as a basis to authorize member states to take "all necessary measures" to "protect civilians" under threat of attack.[42] The rhetoric employed to justify the urgent imperative to intervene echoed calls from earlier centuries demanding Western action against barbarism.[43] Two days after Resolution 1973 was passed, the United States, the United Kingdom, and France formed a coalition to carry out airstrikes against military targets in Libya, initiating an operation that would be taken over by forces under the command of the North Atlantic Treaty Organization (NATO).[44] By October 2011, with NATO support, Libyan militias fighting against the Qaddafi regime gained control of the capital, captured and killed Qaddafi, and were recognized as part of a "transitional" authority deemed by the United Nations as the legitimate government of Libya.[45] Retrospective criticism of Security Council action in Libya focused largely on its implications for future great power cooperation and the association of R2P with regime change.[46] What is missing from such analysis is a forthright account of how and why Libya could so easily become the object of an international consensus setting aside sovereignty considerations.

The humanitarian argument in favor of regime change intervention in Libya reprised the logic of an earlier century's civilizing mission.[47] The country's civilians were portrayed as victims almost from the start of demonstrations and the Qaddafi regime as savages, with NATO ultimately styled a humanitarian savior.[48] But not all civilians' humanitarian welfare was treated alike. For civilians supportive of the Qaddafi government, a combination of NATO airstrikes and rebel attacks resulted in untold infrastructure damage and a significant proportion of the Libyan civilian death toll in 2011.[49]

NATO evinced little sense of humanitarian obligation in the aftermath of its aerial campaign, particularly as related to rebuilding.[50] Far from assisting with repairing the country's damaged infrastructure, the countries most involved in the NATO airstrikes against Libya maintained a freeze on the assets of the Libyan state held in international bank accounts.[51] Those assets—frozen by the Security Council in February 2011—remain in a sort of virtual trust held by Western banks[52] to be made available to Libya only upon satisfaction among the great powers on the Security Council that a legitimate successor government has been established in Libya.[53] The aftermath of the Libyan intervention brings to mind Partha Chatterjee's reflections on the persistence of "imperial privilege in a world without colonies."[54] In the Libyan case, intervention, destruction, and asset seizure raise obvious parallels with histories of colonial intervention and plunder. The familiar logic of First World intervention in the name of universal humanitarianism against Third World savagery make plain the workings of race and empire duly authorized under international law.

After 2011, the original logic of intervention gave way to new imperatives of counterterrorism and migrant management. More than a decade after the UN-backed regime change, the infrastructure and institutions of the Libyan state remain dismantled and the country is gripped by a civil war fueled by continuous external intervention.[55] One scholar of Libya has described the country's experience over the last nine years as a "globalized process of state unmaking."[56] To understand this globalized process requires an analysis that centers the racial and imperial logics that once underwrote intervention and now require ongoing policing of Libya's borders and its interior.

B. LIBYA AS A COUNTERTERRORISM LABORATORY

When the intervention's military operations concluded, the eastern portion of Libya was left in the hands of the militias armed and supported by NATO.[57] During the intervention, these militias were portrayed by Western powers as heroic freedom fighters in a struggle against an autocratic tyrant.[58] But in the predictable aftermath, particularly following the September 2012 attack on a US compound in Benghazi,[59] the militias were reframed as extremist jihadis—consistent with racialized portrayals of the Arab world.[60] At this point, the international law practitioners and scholars moved from a reckoning with the doctrine of R2P to developing innovative counterterrorism[61] doctrines of drone airstrikes, targeted abduction, and killing.

From 2011 to the beginning of 2020 three foreign-backed attempts to wrest control of the country failed. During this period, overt and covert external assistance to various factions in Libya dismantled what was left of the state. In 2014, a UN-sponsored political process sought to create a transitional authority for the country known as the Government of National Accord (GNA).[62] Even this attempt was largely a rushed affair to produce a transitional political body that could serve as a partner for Western counterterrorism strategies.[63] The GNA was never able to consolidate control over the country, with eastern Libya refusing to recognize the Tripoli-based government.[64] While the international community, through the United Nations, remains nominally committed to supporting the country's political transition,[65] the actions of the states that undertook the 2011 intervention speak to a different set of priorities. Their emphasis has shifted from concern for civilians and human rights to "stabilizing" the country and containing the threat of terrorism at what is sometimes described as "Europe's Southern frontier."[66]

The need for stability in Libya is crucially tied by European analysts and policymakers to the imperative of securing Europe against terrorism and migration.[67] Thus the fallout of NATO's intervention effectively set the stage for new counterterrorism and migration regimes to manage Libya. First World interests once presented as aligned with Libya's liberation now required instead that all identified threats be contained within that country's borders. The paramount international objective of the post-intervention was to prevent spillover from Libya's unraveling reaching First World shores. The now ascendant logics of counterterrorism and migrant interdiction, in turn, produce further support to favored militias deemed capable of imposing stability at the borders by force.[68]

The imperial logic of ongoing intervention and management of the Libyan territory have a complex legal relationship to Libya's purported sovereignty. The international legal analysis of counterterrorism operations in Libya center on whether Libyan authorities "consent" to operations on their territory.[69] Yet the First World international backing for the GNA may be understood in part as designed to produce a partner[70] capable of providing such consent. This speaks to the contingent nature of Libyan sovereignty. Moreover, where consent cannot be manufactured, even this formality may be waived[71] in favor of novel concepts positing forms of "confidential"[72] or "secret"[73] consent despite protestation from Libyan officials to the contrary.[74]

A review of US and European Union policies toward Libya from the end of 2011 to the present reveals the extent to which Libya has become a laboratory for counterterrorism innovation with little regard for the country's sovereignty. The 2012 attack on the US diplomatic compound in Benghazi[75] resulted in a series of special forces operations to detain and render those suspected of being responsible for the attack.[76] Post-Benghazi, Libya became a central testing ground for both military and law enforcement operations that trump considerations grounded in sovereignty.[77] American intelligence operations to seize, capture, detain, and render suspected terrorists, together with drone strikes and targeted killings, are justified by arguments invoking self-defense and counterterrorism.[78] Libya retains a kind of "ephemeral sovereignty" from the perspective of interveners.[79] The privileging of the security interests of the First World intervener over the consent and sovereignty of the Third World state against which force is deployed exemplifies the role of international law in sustaining logics of imperial governance.[80]

Even when Third World consent is sought, as with the US operation to which the internationally backed Libyan GNA gave its support, the scale and scope of destruction visited on the territory in the name of counterterrorism knows little proportionality. In 2016, US special operation forces provided "direct, on-the-ground support" to Libyan fighters in a massive attack intended to eliminate the Islamic State (ISIS) from the coastal city of Sirte.[81] The intense military air campaign to dislodge ISIS from Sirte took place in a densely populated city and involved nearly five hundred airstrikes.[82] Deemed a counterterrorism success, the air assault left the city of Sirte "deeply scarred physically and psychologically" with "whole neighborhoods... flattened."[83] From a counterterrorism perspective, the operation was a success, with American officials citing the battle of Sirte as a model to be replicated in Iraq against ISIS.[84] But the consequences for the affected civilian population were excluded from this calculation of success. The presentation of Libya as an Arab state beset by terrorist actors uses a racial shorthand to naturalize the crisis in the country without the slightest recognition that international actions produced the conditions of possibility under which these fighters are now present on the territory.

Following the fall of Sirte, US counterterrorism analysts noted that "Sub-Saharan Africans have had a progressively stronger presence in the Islamic State in Libya with the group taking advantage of its links to human trafficking networks to recruit from among migrants attempting to reach Europe."[85] The convergence of the counterterrorism and migration agendas in Libya features a racialized account both of the identity of migrants as non-Libyan and of sub-Saharan Africans as ready recruits to the ranks of the Islamic State. The predominantly African framing of the threat is reflected in the command structure for American operations in Libya as well. US strategy for Libya is shaped by the relatively newly formed Africa Command (AFRICOM), a combatant command structure created in 2007 for the American military with the objective of "promoting greater security in Africa."[86] The intervention in Libya and its aftermath was the "watershed event for interagency integration at AFRICOM."[87] A US Army War College assessment of AFRICOM concluded that the Libyan operation provided a theater for the nascent combatant command to develop "lessons learned," improve its military operations, and complete the bureaucratic process of becoming integrated in the broader American military command structure.[88] In short, Libya served as the testing ground for the United States to consolidate its new operational command structure for securing Africa.

In less than a decade, Libya went from locus of humanitarian concern to an incubator of racialized threat that provides a central site for new operational and organizational structures to oversee the securing of African territories. Humanitarian intervention dismantled the Libyan state and armed the very militias that must now be targeted for counterterrorism ends. Counterterrorism imperatives to secure Europe from threats emanating from Libya, in turn, justify further intervention. In each case, international law furnishes a legitimating framework while working assiduously to obscure the international sources of destabilization and violence that generate the imperative of intervention. Mainstream international law—and the predominantly Western legal scholars preoccupied with doctrinal justifications of humanitarian intervention and legitimating frames for the prerogatives of counterterrorism—has more often been a handmaiden than a critic of the imperial and racial logics of "securing" Libya.

C. RACE AND LIBYA'S "SOVEREIGN" BORDERS

If one half of our legal analysis focuses on racialized intervention, including through the counterterrorism prism, the other half relates to border or migration governance. Here, too, legal reckoning cannot be complete without analysis that accounts for race and empire, yet official analysis tends to obscure both. We critique conventional accounts of legal liability for human rights violations within Libya and on its shores as partial—both incomplete and biased. They obscure the complicity of powerful external states and regional bodies with imperial interests in Libya. These accounts also neglect analysis of migration or border control as a form of racial governance that is similarly only comprehensible through an imperial lens, which reveals the crucial role of international legal doctrine in sustaining this state of affairs.

For example, in 2019 an airstrike in Libya hit the Tajoura Detention Center (Tajoura). This airstrike resulted in, according to the United Nations, fifty-seven migrants and refugees being killed during the strike, six of whom were children.[89] Other reports cited larger numbers of detained and injured—600 and 130, respectively—comprising "at least 17 nationalities, *mainly African*."[90] In interviews following the attack, migrants and refugees reported their routine torture and ill-treatment by Tajoura personnel, as well as forced labor.[91] In 2020, the UN published a report attributing the airstrikes to the Libyan National Army (LNA) led by Khalifa Haftar—the major militia group in conflict with the UN-backed government.[92] The report attributed liability to Libya as the sovereign nation bearing the sole responsibility for the loss of life, conditions of detention, and the attendant violations of international law.[93] It includes no analysis or acknowledgment of the racialized nature of the violations, and no analysis of First World contributors to the violations. The result is an incomplete accounting of the harm and of the liability for the harm. Formal sovereignty, in the conventional legal analysis, treats Libya's political and territorial borders as fully within the control of the Libyan nation-state. But this formal account belies the contingent and greatly vitiated nature of Libyan nation-state sovereignty discussed above. It also masks the ways in which race shapes Libya's borders, and how these borders have differential racial impacts on terms set by imperial hegemons in the international order. With respect to political control of Libya's territorial borders in particular, this control, historically and in the present, remains at best shared with and at worst largely in the hands of external sovereign interests.

Libya's borders have played and continue to play a crucial role in a longer-term project to keep Africans out of Europe, specifically Black Africans[94]—a project to which racial governance is central.[95] Among EU member states, Italy forged the strongest migration governance partnerships with Libya, in part on account of the historical colonial entanglement of the two nations.[96] Beginning in the late

1990s, Italy sought to strengthen its capacity to prevent migration to its shores via the Mediterranean, and the externalization of its borders to African territory was an essential feature of its strategy.[97] In December 2000, Italy and Libya signed a cooperation treaty that included a commitment to combating undocumented migration.[98] In 2004, then Italian Prime Minister Silvio Berlusconi reached another agreement with Qaddafi to stop irregular migration to Italy, according to which Libya allegedly committed to the deportation of unauthorized Black African migrants and to closing its southern borders.[99] Libya also agreed for the first time to readmit "illegal" migrants from Italy,[100] a category that is undeniably racialized.[101] Eventually, the EU also agreed to lift its arms embargo, which then allowed Libya "to import (semi-)military equipment officially destined for improving border controls."[102] Italy also funded law enforcement training and the construction of immigration detention camps in Libya, as it worked closely with that country "in concerted expulsions of thousands of undocumented migrants from Italy via Libya to their alleged origin countries."[103] In 2008, Libya and Italy signed a Partnership Treaty between the two in which funding to Libya (including to prevent African migration to Europe) was astonishingly framed as a quasi-reparations gesture.[104]

A closer look at Qaddafi's engagement with Europe on migration governance shows how Qaddafi exploited European anti-Black racial anxiety, and used an inflated specter of unauthorized migration across the Mediterranean via Libya to leverage his bargaining power with Europe.[105] His regime went so far as having Black Africans put on boats and sent to Italy "to unleash an unprecedented wave of illegal migration into Europe," and as a threat to the European Union.[106] Europe, on the other hand, poured financial and human resources into building capacity for racial migration governance in Libya, which included barely mitigated racial borders—border regimes undergirded by international doctrine, regional and bilateral legal, and policy agreements with intended racially disparate effects.[107] This history speaks to a long relationship between the former Libyan dictator and Europe, a relationship that is essential to explaining the existence of facilities such as the Tajoura Detention Center, and the predominantly Black African population detained there. Finally, within a year of the NATO intervention, Italy signed an agreement with the Libyan authorities in order to resume migration cooperation, including the training of Libyan police and coastguards, and the construction of detention centers and migrant interdiction infrastructure.[108]

In 2012, the European Court of Human Rights found that Italy had violated its non-refoulement obligations by intercepting a group of African migrants and refugees headed for its shores in the Mediterranean, and returning them to Libya where they faced risk of torture and cruel, inhuman, and degrading treatment.[109] *Hirsi* affirmed the extraterritorial application of the European Convention on

Human Rights on the basis that Italian authorities had exercised effective control over the migrants and refugees. But this judgment did not name or critique the EU's racialized regional containment project. Italy and Europe's response was to invest more resources into embedding its borders within the front of Libyan sovereignty. If *Hirsi* represents an international human rights law attempt to disrupt Europe's violent externalization of its borders, it proved no match for Europe's evasion through the more robust public international law doctrine of formal sovereignty, according to which Libya now bears liability for this externalization as manifest in the UN analysis of Tajoura.

With respect to migrant interdiction, rebuilding Libyan capacity to carry out this task was a successful means both of keeping Africans out of Europe and of evading liability under the bodies of international law that *Hirsi* would have enforced. Rebuilding this capacity meant first and foremost establishing an effective "Libyan Coast Guard" to take responsibility for interdiction efforts at sea, invoking Libyan sovereign rights in its territorial sea.[110] Should European forces themselves carry out such interdiction efforts, they might generate obligations to render humanitarian assistance or adjudicate asylum claims. As a consequence, shoring up Libyan sovereignty as the basis for a Libyan-led interdiction effort served the European purpose of insulating their own territory and forces from contact with migrants. Ironically, even as Libya's sovereignty was being perforated for counterterrorism purposes the legal fiction of its sovereignty had to be reinforced to enable the territory to host an externalized version of Europe's borders—borders especially hostile to Black bodies.

The Libyan Coast Guard (LCG) that was put in place is an EU-funded and trained force that has become one of the most efficient means of blocking migrants from reaching European soil.[111] The LCG is staffed by militias that had previously been engaged in smuggling migrants; the creation of the Coast Guard allowed the EU to remove one network of smugglers while employing their skills to disrupt other networks that facilitate seaborne migration. In the year 2017, the LCG reportedly intercepted twenty thousand migrants at sea and likely facilitated the drowning deaths of hundreds if not thousands more.[112] When migrants stranded at sea make contact with European officials, those officials contact the Libyan Coast Guard to "rescue" them. As Europe abandoned its earlier rescue efforts at sea in favor of reliance on the Libyan Coast Guard, deaths in the Mediterranean soared while arrivals to Europe declined precipitously.[113] Whereas the United States has collaborated with Libyan militias in pursuit of counterterrorism objectives, the EU has worked with another set of militias to pursue goals in a related domain—that of migration "management." With respect to migration management, the militias are subcontracted to interdict and detain migrants seeking to transit through the Libyan land mass and territorial sea en route to Europe.[114]

D. CONCLUSION

In sum, the EU and its member states (albeit to varying degrees) bear significant responsibility for the refugees and migrants who were injured and killed in the Tajoura Detention Center, and for the detention of these groups in the first place. And these deaths and injuries are racial injustices as they are the product of efforts of racialized exclusion from the European Union. None of this analysis appears in the UN reports accounting of responsibility—the legal analysis identifies Libya as solely liable, the sovereign that is not a sovereign—and speaks of an international community that ought to encourage Libya to close these detention facilities. The border controls, deportations, and deaths in the desert and at sea, together with drone strikes, aerial bombardment, and renditions, reveal how the states of the Global North use law, targeted intervention, territorial boundaries, and militarized security structures to promote and ensure a particular hegemonic racial order. A race-centered TWAIL analysis enables identification of the imperial and specifically racial logics embedded in global counterterrorism and migration governance, which remain largely ignored in mainstream and conventional international legal scholarship. Without a CRT-TWAIL analysis, both the operation of international law and the mainstream approaches to its study risk entrenching these logics and deepening the structural subordination of communities across the Global South. Making visible and contesting the imbricated logics of race and empire are prerequisites for developing global and regional governance mechanisms that operate on more equitable terms.

NOTES

1. See Balakrishnan Rajagopal, "Locating the Third World in Cultural Geography," *Third World Legal Studies* 15, no. 2 (1999): 1, 19.

2. John Reynolds, *Empire, Emergency and International Law* (Cambridge University Press, 2017), 21.

3. James Thuo Gathii, "TWAIL: A Brief History of Its Origins, Its Decentralized Network, and a Tentative Bibliography," *Trade Law and Development* 3, no. 1 (2011): 26.

4. For background on TWAIL see, e.g., Gathii, "TWAIL: A Brief History"; Makau Mutua, "What Is TWAIL?," *Proceedings of the ASIL Annual Meeting* 94 (2000): 31, 31–32; Obiora Chinedu Okafor, "Critical Third World Approaches to International Law (TWAIL): Theory, Methodology, or Both?," *International Community Law Review* 10 (2008): 371; Karin Mickelson, "Rhetoric and Rage: Third World Voices in International Legal Discourse," *Wisconsin International Law Journal* 16, no. 2 (1997): 353, 355–62; and Luis Eslava, "TWAIL Coordinates," *Critical Legal Thinking*, April 2, 2019. For bibliographies of TWAIL scholarship, see, e.g., Gathii, "TWAIL: A Brief History"; and James Thuo Gathii, "The Promise of International Law: A Third World View," Grotius Lecture, 2020 Virtual Annual Meeting of the American Society of International Law, June 25, 2020, https://ssrn.com/abstract=3635509, 28–66. For new works on TWAIL, see Laura Betancur-Restrepo, Amar Bhatia, Usha Natarajan, John Reynolds, Ntina Tzouvala & Sujith Xavier, "Introducing the TWAIL Review: TWAILR," *TWAILR: Extra*, August 30, 2019.

5. Ian Haney López, *White by Law: The Legal Construction of Race,* 10th ed. (NYU Press, 2006), 7. For a review of definitions of race and racism within CRT, see Ruth Gordon, "Critical Race Theory and International Law: Convergence and Divergence," *Villanova Law Review* 45, no. 5 (2000): 827, 838n45.

6. For an overview of Critical Race Theory (CRT), see generally Devon W. Carbado, "Critical What What?," *Connecticut Law Review* 43, no. 5 (2011): 1593; and Kimberlé Crenshaw et al., *Critical Race Theory: The Key Writings that Formed the Movement* (New York: New Press, 1995).

7. See, e.g., Debito Arudou, "Japan's Under-Researched Visible Minorities: Applying Critical Race Theory to Racialization Dynamics in a Non-White Society," *Washington University Global Studies Law Review* 14 (2015): 695; Adelle Blackett, "Follow the Drinking Gourd: Our Road to Teaching Critical Race Theory and Slavery and the Law, Contemplatively, at McGill," *McGill Law Journal* 62, no. 4 (2017): 1251; Laura Carlson, "Critical Race Theory in a Swedish Context," *Juridisk Tidskrift* (20121): 21–49; Tanya Kateri Hernández, "The Value of Intersectional Comparative Analysis to the Post-Racial Future of Critical Race Theory: A Brazil-US Comparative Case Study," (2011): 1407; Joel Modiri, *The Colour of Law, Power and Knowledge: Introducing Critical Race Theory in (Post-)Apartheid South Africa, South African Journal on Human Rights* 28, no. 3 (2012): 405; Esther Ojulari, "The Social Construction of Afro-Descendant Rights in Colombia," in *Contemporary Challenges in Securing Human Rights* ed. Corinne Lennox (University of London, 2015), 19.

8. See generally "Commentary Critical Race Theory: A Commemoration," *Connecticut Law Review* 43, no. 5 (2011): 1253–701.

9. Our analysis in this chapter draws heavily on our article previously published by the UCLA Law Review. E. Tendayi Achiume and Aslı Bâli, "Race and Empire: Legal Theory Within, Through and Across National Borders," *UCLA Law Review* 67 (2021): 1386.

10. See Aziz Rana, *The Two Faces of American Freedom* (Harvard University Press, 2010), 3. See also Adelle Blackett with Alice Duquesnoy, "Slavery Is Not a Metaphor: US Prison Labour and Racial Subordination Through the Lens of the ILO's Abolition of Forced Labour Convention," *UCLA Law Review* 67 (2021).

11. See generally Antony Anghie, *Imperialism, Sovereignty and the Making of International Law* (Cambridge University Press, 2005). See also Siba N'zatioula Grovogui, *Sovereigns, Quasi Sovereigns and Africans: Race and Self-Determination in International Law* (Minneapolis: University of Minnesota Press, 1996), 2.

12. See Haney López, *White by Law*.

13. See Anibal Quijano, "Coloniality of Power, Eurocentrism, and Latin America," *Nepantla* 1, no. 3 (2000): 533.

14. See Aslı Bâli and Aziz Rana, "Pax Arabica?: Provisional Sovereignty and Intervention in the Arab Uprisings," *California Western International Law Journal* 42, no. 2 (2012): 321.

15. Quijano, "Coloniality of Power."

16. See Carolina Mala Corbin, "Terrorists Are Always Muslim but Never White: At the Intersection of Critical Race Theory and Propaganda," *Fordham Law Review* 86 (2017): 455; see also Neil Gotanda, "The Racialization of Islam in American Law," *The ANNALS of the American Academy of Political and Social Science* 637, no. 1 (2011): 184; Sudha Setty, "Targeted Killings and the Interest Convergence Dilemma," *Western New England Law Review* 36 (2014): 169, 178.

17. See, e.g., Nicholas De Genova, "Europe's Racial Borders," *Monitor Racism*, January 2018; Ian Law, "The Mediterranean Expulsion Machine," in *Mediterranean Racisms* (Palgrave Macmillan London, 2014), 123; Martin Baldwin-Edwards and Derek Lutterbeck, "Coping with the Libyan Migration Crisis," *Journal of Ethnic and Migration Studies* 45 (2019): 2241, 2441–43, 2251–53.

18. John Reynolds, "Emergency and Migration, Race and the Nation," *UCLA Law Review* 67 (2021).

19. Andrea Carati, "Responsibility to Protect, NATO and the Problem of Who Should Intervene: Reassessing the Intervention in Libya," *Global Change, Peace & Security* 29, no. 3 (2017): 293.

20. "Security Council Authorizes 'All Necessary Measures' to Protect Civilians in Libya," *U.N. News*, March 17, 2011.

21. Anghie, *Imperialism, Sovereignty and the Making of International Law*, at 3.

22. See, e.g., Robert Jackson, *Quasi-States: Sovereignty, International Relations and the Third World* (Cambridge University Press, 1990), 16–18.

23. Anghie, *Imperialism, Sovereignty and the Making of International Law*, at 238.

24. Charter of the Organization of African Unity, September 13, 1963, 479 U.N.T.S. 39.

25. See Michael Slackman, "Dislike for Qaddafi Gives Arabs a Point of Unity," *New York Times*, March 21, 2011; Gavin Cordon, "Muammar Gaddafi: A 40-Year Thorn in the West's Side," *Independent*, October 20, 2011, 13:29.

26. James Kirchik, "South Africa Stands with Qaddafi," *Atlantic*, September 6, 2011.

27. See Adekeye Adebajo, "Gaddafi: The Man Who Would Be King of Africa," *Guardian*, August 26, 2011.

28. See Phillip Apuuli Kasaija, "The African Union (AU), the Libya Crisis and the Notion of 'African Solutions to African Problems,'" *Journal of Contemporary African Studies* 31, no. 1 (2013): 117, 127–28.

29. Adebajo, "Gaddafi: The Man Who Would Be King of Africa."

30. "Official Figures: 11 Percent of Libya's Population Is Mostly African Immigrants," *Al-Arabiya*, August 5, 2018. See also Frederic Wehrey, *Insecurity and Governance Challenges in Southern Libya* (Carnegie Endowment for International Peace, 2017), 4–6. See also Judith Scheele, "The Libyan Connection: Settlement, War and Other Entanglements in Northern Chad," *Journal of African History* 57, no. 1 (2016): 115–17.

31. See, e.g., "Libyan Aid and Investment Projects in Africa," *Reuters*, November 24, 2010.

32. See Lyn Boyd-Judson, "Strategic Moral Diplomacy: Mandela, Qaddafi, and the Lockerbie Negotiations," *Foreign Policy Analysis* 1, no. 1 (2005): 73.

33. See e.g., Douglas Farah, "An 'Axis' Connected to Gaddafi," *Washington Post*, November 2, 2001.

34. See Robert Nolan, "The African Union After Gaddafi," *Journal of Diplomacy* (blog), December 5, 2011.

35. See Alex DeWaal, "The African Union and the Libya Conflict of 2011," *Reinventing Peace* (blog), December 19, 2012. See also "African Union Mediators Call For an 'End to Hostilities' in Libya," *Deutsche Welle*, April 10, 2011.

36. See Siba N. Grovogui, "Looking Beyond Spring for the Season: An African Perspective on the World Order After the Arab Revolt," *Globalizations* 8, no. 5 (2011): 567, 569.

37. "Arab League Suspends Libyan Delegation," *Reuters*, February 22, 2011.

38. See Richard Leiby and Muhammad Mansour, "Arab League Asks U.N. for No-Fly Zone Over Libya," *Washington Post,* March 12, 2011.

39. Security Council, "Security Council Approves 'No-Fly Zone' Over Libya, Authorizing 'All Necessary Measures' to Protect Civilians, by Vote of 10 in Favour With 5 Abstentions," press release SC/10200, March 17, 2011. The press release also cited statements by the representative of China indicating that "China had not blocked the action with a negative vote in consideration of the wishes of the Arab League."

40. See DeWaal, "The African Union and the Libya Conflict of 2011."

41. "'Day of Rage' Kicks off in Libya," *Al Jazeera,* February 17, 2011. See also "Timeline: Libya's Uprising Against Muammar Gaddafi," *Reuters,* August 22, 2011.

42. Security Council, "Security Council Approves 'No-Fly Zone' Over Libya."

43. See, e.g., Tom Malinowski, "Too Little, Not Yet Too Late," *Foreign Policy*, February 22, 2011.

44. SC Res 1973, UN Doc S/RES/1973, March 17, 2011; David Kirkpatrick, Steven Erlanger, and Elisabeth Bumiller, "Allies Open Air Assault on Qaddafi's Forces in Libya," *New York Times,* March 19, 2011.

45. See Mehrdad Payandeh, "The United Nations, Military Intervention, and Regime Change in Libya," *Virginia Journal of International Law* 52, no. 2 (2012): 355, 378–80.

46. See, e.g., Justin Morris, "Libya and Syria: R2P and the Spectre of the Swinging Pendulum," *International Affairs* 89, no. 5 (2013): 1265, 1274–79.

47. See Makau Mutua, "Savages, Victims, and Saviors: The Metaphor of Human Rights," *Harvard International Law Journal* 42 (2001): 201, 204–5, 209–19 (discussing the "civilizing mission").

48. Katherina Fallah & Ntina Tzouvala, *Deploying Race, Employing Force: 'African Mercenaries' and the 2011 NATO Intervention in Libya*, 67 UCLA L. Rev. 1580 (2021).

49. "Libya: Displaced Population Can't Go Home," *Human Rights Watch,* January 24, 2019. See also "Unacknowledged Deaths: Civilian Casualties in NATO's Air Campaign in Libya," *Human Rights Watch,* May 13, 2012. See also Michael Birnbaum, "NATO Launches Largest Airstrike Against Gaddafi Regime," *Washington Post,* May 23, 2011.

50. See, e.g., Ethan Chorin, "NATO's Libya Intervention and the Continued Case for a 'Responsibility to Rebuild'", *Boston University International Law Journal* 31 (2013): 365.

51. "Libyan Assets Held by Leading Global Banks," BBC, May 26, 2011.

52. See Sophie Quinton, "The Quest for Libya's Frozen Assets," *Atlantic*, August 26, 2011.

53. See Karin Strohecker and Tom Finn, "Exclusive: Libyan Wealth Fund to Hire Auditors in Push to Unfreeze Assets," *Reuters,* November 22, 2018.

54. Partha Chatterjee, "The Legacy of Bandung," in *Bandung, Global History, and International Law: Critical Pasts and Pending Futures,* ed. Luis Eslava, Michael Fakhri, and Vasuki Nesiah (Cambridge University Press, 2017): 657, 674.

55. See, e.g., Emadeddin Badi, "Russia Isn't the Only One Getting Its Hands Dirty in Libya," *Foreign Policy,* April 21, 2020. See also Ramy Allahoum, "Libya's War: Who Is Supporting Whom," *Al Jazeera,* January 9, 2020.

56. Jacob Mundy, "The Globalized Unmaking of the Libyan State," *Middle East Report* (Spring 2019): 3, 4.

57. Mahmoud Habboush and Ali Shuaib, "Militias May Drag Libya into Civil War: NTC Chief," *Reuters,* January 3, 2012. See also Barak Barfi, "Who Are the Libyan Rebels?," *New Republic,* April 29, 2011.

58. See David Brunnstrom, "NATO Worried by Libya Armed Groups, Offers Security Help," *Reuters*, September 27, 2012.

59. See Erica Ryan, "Chronology: The Benghazi Attack and the Fallout," NPR, December 19, 2012. See also, e.g., James Risen et al., "US-Approved Arms for Libya Rebels Fell into Jihadis' Hands," *New York Times,* December 5, 2012.

60. See, e.g., Andrew McGregor, "Europe's True Southern Frontier: The General, the Jihadis and the High-Stakes Contest for Libya's Fezzan Region," *Combating Terrorism Center Sentinel* 10, no. 10 (2017): 19; Risen, "US-Approved Arms for Libya Rebels."

61. See Wadie Said, "The Destabilizing Effect of Terrorism in the International Human Rights Regime," *UCLA Law Review* 67 (2021).

62. "Libya's Faltering New Government," *IISS: Strategic Comments* 22, no. 7 (2016).

63. Elham Saudi et al., "The US Is Focusing on Counterterrorism in Libya, at Human Rights' Expense," *Just Security,* March 21, 2018.

64. Ayman al-Warfalli, "Libya's Eastern Parliament Votes Against U.N.-backed Government in Tripoli", *Reuters*, August 22, 2016.

65. See Francesco Mancini and Jose Vericat, "Lost in Transition: UN Mediation in Libya, Syria, and Yemen," *International Peace Institute,* November 30, 2016.

66. See, e.g., McGregor, "Europe's True Southern Frontier."

67. See Thomas M. Hill and Emily Estelle, "Libya's Migrant Crisis Isn't Just a European Problem," *United States Institute of* Peace, November 9, 2018.

68. See, e.g., "Libya Militias Rake in Millions in European Migration Funds: AP," *Al Jazeera*, December 31, 2019); Peter Bergen and Alyssa Sims, "Airstrikes and Civilian Casualties in Libya," *New America* (2018): 33.

69. See, e.g., Robert Chesney, "Do We Care Less About Air Strikes When Pilots Are in the Cockpit? The Droneless Air War in Libya," *Lawfare,* September 1, 2016. See also Kristina Daugirdas and Julian Mortenson, "United States Justifies Its Use of Force in Libya Under International and National Law," *American Journal of International Law* 110, no. 4 (2016): 804, 808.

70. Saudi, "The US Is Focusing on Counterterrorism in Libya."

71. See Ntina Tzouvala, "TWAIL and the 'Unwilling or Unable' Doctrine: Continuities and Ruptures," *AJIL Unbound* 109 (2016): 266, 266–68.

72. See Tom Ruys, "The Meaning of 'Force' and the Boundaries of the *Jus Ad Bellum*: Are 'Minimal' Uses of Force Excluded From UN Charter Article 2(4)?," *American Journal of International Law* 108, no. 2 (2014): 159, 169.

73. See Ashley Deeks, "A (Qualified) Defense of Secret Agreements," *Arizona State Law Journal* 49 (2016): 713, 763.

74. Jomana Karadsheh et al., "Wife: Captured 'Most Wanted Terrorist' al Libi Had Left al Qaeda," *CNN*, October 7, 2013. Al Libi later died in US custody in 2015. Jomana Karadhseh, "Alleged al Qaeda Operative Abu Anas al Libi Dies in US Hospital, Family Says," *CNN,* January 3, 2015.

75. John Bacon, "Five Things to Know About the 2012 Benghazi Attack," *USA Today,* June 17, 2014.

76. See, e.g., Karen DeYoung et al., "US Captured Benghazi Suspect in Secret Raid," *Washington Post,* June 17, 2014. See also Adam Goldman and Eric Schmitt, "Benghazi Attacks Suspect Is Captured in Libya by US Commandos," *N.Y. Times,* October 30, 2017.

77. See Wolfram Lacher, "Drones, Deniability and Disinformation: Warfare in Libya and the New International Disorder," *War on the Rocks*, March 3, 2020.

78. See, e.g., Marty Lederman, "The Legal Basis for the Abu Khattalah Capture," *Just Security*, June 19, 2014. See also Deborah Pearlstein, "The Raids in Somalia and Libya—Theories of Self Defense?" *Opinio Juris*, June 10, 2013.

79. See Katharine Hall Kindervater, "Drone Strikes, Ephemeral Sovereignty, and Changing Conceptions of Territory," *Territory, Politics, Governance* 5, no. 2 (2017): 207.

80. See, e.g., Kevin Jon Heller, "Analysing the US Invocation of Self-Defence Re: Abu Khattallah," *Opinio Juris*, June 20, 2014. See also Colum Lynch, "The US Makes Case for Libya Abduction at the UN," *Foreign Policy*, June 18, 2014. Several months later, the Libyan government registered its objection to the operation. "Libyan Condemns US 'Violation' of Its Sovereignty," *Middle East Eye*, February 12, 2015.

81. Missy Ryan and Sudarsan Raghavan, "US Special Operations Troops Aiding Libyan Forces in Major Battle Against Islamic State," *Washington Post*, August 9, 2016.

82. Jim Michaels, "How US Drones Helped Win a Battle Against ISIS for First Time in Libya," *USA Today*, April 17, 2017.

83. Sudarsan Raghavan, "A Year After ISIS Left, a Battered Libyan City Struggles to Resurrect Itself," *Washington Post*, January 8, 2018.

84. Michaels, "How US Drones Helped Win a Battle Against ISIS."

85. Lachlan Wilson and Jason Pack, "The Islamic State's Revitalization in Libya and Its Post-2016 War of Attrition," *Combating Terrorism Center Sentinel* 12, no. 3 (2019): 22, 28.

86. David E. Brown, *AFRICOM at 5 Years: The Maturation of a New US Combatant Command* (Carlisle Barracks, PA: US Army War College Press, 2013), 1. Prior to the creation of AFRICOM, the US military command structure located responsibility for Africa with its European Command. Brown, *AFRICOM at 5 Years*, at 5.

87. Brown, *AFRICOM at 5 Years*, at 49.

88. Brown, *AFRICOM at 5 Years*, at 50.

89. Brown, *AFRICOM at 5 Years*, 50, at para. 6.

90. Lisa Schlein, "UN: Release All Refugees, Migrants from Libyan Detention Centers," *Voice of America*, July 5, 2019.

91. UN Support Mission in Libya and Office of the UN High Commissioner for Human Rights, "The Airstrikes on the Daman Building Complex, Including the Tajoura Detention Centre, 2 July 2019," (January 27, 2020), para. 7, 13, https://reliefweb.int/sites/reliefweb.int/files/resources/UNSMILOHCHRReport_AirstrikesTajoura%203.pdf [https://perma.cc/J9JU-CTZF].

92. UN Support Mission in Libya and Office of the UN High Commissioner for Human Rights, "The Airstrikes on the Daman Building Complex," at para. 29–31.

93. UN Support Mission in Libya and Office of the UN High Commissioner for Human Rights, "The Airstrikes on the Daman Building Complex," at para. 32. The legal analysis and findings focus squarely on Libya's international law obligations, and violations by Libyan authorities and armed groups. UN Support Mission in Libya and Office of the UN High Commissioner for Human Rights, "The Airstrikes on the Daman Building Complex," at para. 34–35.

94. See Ziad Bentahar, "Continental Drift: The Disjunction of North and Sub-Saharan Africa," *Research in African Literatures* 41, no. 1 (2011): 1, 3–4. See also Jemima Pierre, "Race in Africa Today: A Commentary," *Cultural Anthropology* 28, no. 3 (2013): 547.

95. See De Genova, "Europe's Racial Borders."

96. See, e.g., Antonio M. Morone, "Policies, Practices, and Representations Regarding Sub-Saharan Migrants in Libya: From the Partnership with Italy to the Post-Qadhafi Era," in *Eurafrican Borders and Migration Management,* ed. Paolo Gaibazzi et al. (2017), 129, 130.

97. Morone, "Policies, Practices, and Representations Regarding Sub-Saharan Migrants in Libya," at 138.

98. Hein de Haas, "The Myth of Invasion: The Inconvenient Realities of African Migration to Europe," *Third World Quarterly* 29, no. 7 (2008): 1305, 1310.

99. de Haas, "The Myth of Invasion."

100. de Haas, "The Myth of Invasion."

101. See De Genova, "Europe's Racial Borders."

102. De Genova, "Europe's Racial Borders."

103. De Genova, "Europe's Racial Borders."

104. Gregor Noll and Mariagiulia Giuffré, "EU Migration Control: Made by Gaddafi?," *Open Democracy,* February 25, 2011.

105. Noll and Giuffré, "EU Migration Control," at 129.

106. Morone, "Policies, Practices, and Representations Regarding Sub-Saharan Migrants in Libya," at 143.

107. The term racial borders refers "to territorial and political border regimes that disparately curtail movement (mobility) and political incorporation (membership) on a racial basis, and sustain international migration and mobility as racial privileges," in the service of empire. E. Tendayi Achiume, *Racial Borders*, 110 Georgetown L. J. 445 (2022). For a legal analysis of international refugee law as one regime that affects racial borders so defined, see E. Tendayi Achiume, "Race, Refugees and International Law," in *Oxford Handbook of International Refugee Law,* ed. Cathryn Costello et al. (Oxford University Press, 2021), https://papers.ssrn.com/sol3/papers.cfm?abstract_id=3636518 [https://perma.cc/U4DG-GEZF]. For an insightful analysis of Europe's borders as racial borders, see Nicholas De Genova, "Europe's Racial Borders." In this Symposium Issue, John Reynolds's contribution maps the manner in which emergency law and crisis responses further consolidate Europe's racial borders, calling special attention to the "racialized regional nationality" that the EU has produced. Reynolds, "Emergency and Migration, Race and the Nation."

108. Reynolds, "Emergency and Migration, Race and the Nation," 144–45.

109. Hirsi Jamaa v. Italy, 2012-II Eur. Ct. H.R. 97, 131–32.

110. Benjamin Bathke, "When Helping Hurts—Libya's Controversial Coast Guard, Europe's Go-To Partner to Stem Migration," *InfoMigrants,* July 24, 2019.

111. Bathke, "When Helping Hurts."

112. Bathke, "When Helping Hurts."

113. Bathke, "When Helping Hurts."

114. See, e.g., Paul Hockenos, "Europe Has Criminalized Humanitarianism," *Foreign Policy*, August 1, 2018.

CHAPTER TWO

A RACIST INTERNATIONAL LAW

*Domination and Resistance in the
Americas of the Nineteenth Century*

Arnulf Becker Lorca

INTRODUCTION

What is the relationship between race, racism, and international law? International lawyers, as this volume shows, are now confronting this question. This is not an entirely new question, but it is one that has gained centrality as legal scholars explore the intersection between Critical Race Theory and Third World Approaches to International Law—the intersection between CRT and TWAIL, which might perhaps be labeled "CR•TWAIL."[1]

For more than four decades, CRT scholars have not only argued that race is a social construct, but they have also demonstrated the constitutive role of race in the law, as well as in the reproduction of racial hierarchies within a neutral, color-blind legal order.[2] These and other CRT insights have been well-received and have inspired TWAIL scholarship. In turn, TWAIL, in the span of two decades, emerged as one of the most important disciplinary trends in contemporary international law.[3] Foregrounding the lived experiences of the peoples of the Third World in their relationship to the international legal order, TWAIL scholars have tirelessly excavated the colonial origins of international law. And like CRT scholars who study the reproduction of racial hierarchies, TWAIL scholars examine international law's colonial legacies, the perpetuation of colonial relations in a postcolonial order, that is, an international legal order that ostensibly no longer discriminates between peoples based on their religion, civilization, or race.

TWAIL's postcolonial critique of international law raises an important question in the context of the present volume. If a critique of international law's colonial constitution is also a racial critique, then what accounts for the demand that there be greater engagement with and examination of the relationship between race, racism, and international law? Why has recent scholarship called for greater collaboration between CRT and TWAIL, if TWAIL was already on the case? Why did a new generation of international legal scholars (many close to or within TWAIL) feel that the question about the relationship between race and international law must be asked again?[4] Is the underlying premise that earlier TWAIL critiques of international law's eurocentrism, like my own, were insufficiently attentive to dynamics of race and racism?[5]

I can only offer preliminary answers pointing towards an interest in understanding not only the role of race as an extralegal force structuring international law, but also the role that race and racism play from *within* international law. I approach answers to these questions through the example of a case study, in the form of a very specific exploration of the history of international law in the Americas. In the Americas of the early nineteenth century, and likewise in other regions and periods of international law's history, racism played a central, though implicit, role in the formation and interpretation of international rules and doctrines. That is, racist politicians, international lawyers, and diplomats produced racist interpretations of international law norms and doctrines. At the same time, however, in the Americas of the nineteenth century, race irrupted as a term in international legal argumentation. Race became not only a criterion to recognize and deny sovereignty, but also a source of international legality. Race became, together with older terms like sovereignty, people, or nation, a category in legal discourse. Just like Americans from the United States who understood international law to be the law of the Anglo-Saxon race, Spanish-Americans (that is, citizens from the nations that had recently become independent after the end of Spanish rule) called for the unity of the "Latin race" and its place in the enactment of a Latin-American international law.

In the United States, race was invoked to justify American continental expansion over the continent's "vacant lands" as well as to delimit the scope of that expansion. When expansion collided with "non-white races" in Mexico, Central America, or the Caribbean, Americans argued for segregation. Newly independent states of the American continent and the Caribbean, as they were populated by non-white inhabitants, were not to be conquered but disciplined—through diplomatic protection and military intervention. A racialized international law defined the contours of an expansionist, segregationist, and interventionist America.

Spanish-Americans of the mid-nineteenth century realized that the greatest threat to the independence of their Republics was neither Spanish recolonization nor the neocolonial adventures of European monarchies, like the French invasion of Mexico, but rather that it was Anglo-American expansion and intervention.

Turning points in this realization were the private filibuster expeditions in Baja California and Central America by William Walker and others, and, more specifically, the Watermelon Riot in Panama. This realization called for both the unity of the Latin race and the enactment of a continental public law reflecting values such as continental solidarity and respect of sovereignty—what later became a Latin-American international law with non-intervention at its center.[6]

The idea of a Latin race confronting the Anglo race fitted well within the lager nation-building project of the nascent Spanish-American Republics. Abolition of slavery in the first constitutions after independence reflected Spanish-American elites' liberalism and republicanism. But extending governmental control over the new Republics' territory occurred at the expense of indigenous peoples, who were redefined as either citizens or members of "uncivilized races," and in both cases to be civilized by assimilation, or by subjection to the coercive enforcement of the Republic's law when resisting the advance of "civilization." Latin-Americanism was born as an anti-hegemonic project vis-à-vis Anglo-America. It was a project of domination in relation to the indigenous peoples of the continent.[7]

WHY CR·TWAIL?

Exploring the rise of a racialized international law in the Americas is relevant to questions about the intersection between CRT and TWAIL—CR•TWAIL. As an academic movement denouncing international law's participation in the domination of the peoples of the Third World, TWAIL has focused on these lived experiences as a powerful means for discovering colonial origins and legacies. International law was born in the colonial encounter not only to justify and regulate colonial expansion, but also to gift sovereignty to the colonizer while withdrawing it from the colonized. Colonial origins became legacies when the patterns of legal argumentation established in the colonial encounter failed to disappear with decolonization; they rather mutated. As TWAIL scholars have demonstrated, international law has used different notions—religion, civilization, economic development—to ground formal unequal treatment and thus differentiate colonizers from colonized, "civilized" from "uncivilized," First from Third World.[8] However, through the "civilizing mission," international law offered ways to overcome these differentiations and the formal inequalities associated to them. Then again, TWAIL argues that the gap—between colonizer and colonized, developed and developing world—is never closed but managed, as differences are recast in new technical legal forms. When the standard of civilization, for example, was reinstated as a standard of statehood, inequalities were not abrogated but shifted from cultural requirements to requirements linked to governance.[9]

And now to return to the question from above: Does this type of postcolonial critique offer a *racial* critique of international law? Is race at the center of this analysis? I think it is, conceived as an extralegal structuring force. Although many of its basic doctrines—discovery, occupation, standard of civilization, statehood—are not formally racial, international law is a racialized order. For TWAIL conceives a racial continuity underlying these doctrines, as they reproduce a differentiation between polities enjoying sovereignty and polities whose sovereignty is disavowed, which ultimately reflects the distinction between and hierarchical ordering of the white and non-white races.[10]

Take for example Antony Anghie's work. More than two decades ago, writing in the first symposium on CRT and TWAIL, Anghie argued that race is "the most powerful and obvious marker of difference."[11] He was referring to the abovementioned difference international law establishes between peoples having sovereignty and peoples regarded as incapable of exercising sovereignty, between the colonizer and the colonized. Anghie, however, noted also that based on race as a "self-evident foundation . . . more elaborate ideas of difference—focusing on culture, on 'civilization,' on economic backwardness—may be constructed."[12] Anghie concluded that although race became "central to the very definition of international law," race then "transmuted into the more comprehensive notion of 'civilization.'"[13]

On this account, race was too crude and rigid to remain a long-term formal marker of difference and inequality. This is because in consonance with its universal vocation and aspiration to govern interstate relations globally, international law adopts abstract and neutral forms. As a result, race mutated into culture, civilization, human rights, or democratic governance. Anghie and others have studied the profound transformations experienced by international law in roughly the century between the 1860s and 1960s. An international law that around 1860 used race as a marker of differentiation became in a relatively short period a formally universal legal order—after the abolition of slavery, after decolonization was triggered by the recognition of self-determination, and after the proscription of racial discrimination. If modern international law originally linked colonialism and race explicitly, the mutation of race into abstract legal forms, for example by making self-determination conditional on a standard of statehood, left race in a murky background.

Thus, from a TWAIL perspective, when the postcoloniality of international law is examined, tracing links between colonial origins and postcolonial legacies, race surfaces indirectly, in the emergence, design, or implementation of formally neutral international legal terms (like sovereignty and statehood), operated by (explicitly or implicitly) racially motivated international legal actors to produce racialized outcomes. In this vein, one could therefore describe the relationship between race and international law as one in which race, as an extralegal force, shapes international law from the outside.[14]

The TWAIL perspective has become mainstream.[15] Why has a new generation of scholars become dissatisfied with the way in which TWAIL presents race and racism infecting international law from the outside? And what would something like CR•TWAIL offer to respond to this dissatisfaction? To some, it may look that TWAIL became uninterested in race when it focused the attention on international law's deployment of formally deracialized and color-neutral legal doctrine. Let us consider Christopher Gevers's work as an example of this view. Gevers, on the one hand, convincingly shows the profound racist views exposed by the founders of the modern discipline of international law, "the men of 1873," not just in the obvious case of James Lorimer, but also in relation to other prominent figures like John Westlake and Johann Kaspar Bluntschli.[16] However, Gevers, on the other hand, warns not to overparticularize and exceptionalize their racism, as to reduce the role of race in international law to the individual racism of its practitioners.[17] Instead, Gevers argues for viewing the role of race in international law in structural terms, in Charles Mills's vein, as part of a multidimensional system of domination, as a global "racial contract."[18]

But if we accept the invitation to look for racism structurally, Gevers also warns not to under-historicize the role of race, not to conflate it with other non-corporeal differentiations—in particular, not to misread or read down "assertions of racial difference as cultural difference (or the conflation of biological racism and cultural racism)."[19] Gevers therefore understands the TWAIL approach to race as under-historicizing the role of race: as "a shorthand history of international law and its unspecified Others, in which the non-European 'savage' becomes the 'uncivilized,' then the 'non-sovereign,' then the 'undeveloped,' then the 'unlawful combatant,' and so on."[20] Not only are differences between each of these periods flattened, but the racial dimension is missed.

Gevers sees Mills offering again guidance to escape under-historicization. Many of the "literal 'racial contracts' implicate international law," Gevers explains, pointing out that from papal bulls to European discussions of discovery, occupation, and colonial administration, racial contracts impose burdens and privileges along the color line dividing Black and white races.[21] Gevers thus understands structural racism as the transhistorical pattern that justifies not losing sight of race and racism. Implicated in the drafting of the racial contracts, international law has been, across time, implicated in the imposition of Black burdens and the granting of white privileges. International law, as Gevers notes, contributed to making the international and the world a white international, a white world.[22]

This commitment to remain focused on race is welcome. In my case, I have studied the history of international law as product of the colonial encounter, and like TWAIL, I have left race in the background. Although I used racial terminology to describe the international law that emerged from the encounter as a mixed race—*Mestizo*—international law, the racial dimension is only to be found in the background of the story.[23] At the same time, this commitment not to lose sight of race and to find a transhistorical racial structure poses further questions regarding the effort to understand the relationship between race and international law.

If investigating global racial contracts one would find race and racism as an outcome in which international law is implicated, the relation between racism and international law would be one of ends to means. When working as means, international law has resorted to a variety of legal resources to draft the racial contracts that have imposed Black burdens and granted white privileges. Only during certain periods has international law resorted to formal racial terminology and reasoning; in others it has not, using instead color-blind terminology. It makes sense not to lose sight of race and racism and thus study racial contracts and the imposition of racial burdens and privileges when international law is formally free of racial terminology and reasoning. In consequence, international lawyers have, as mentioned before, studied the transition from a formally racist to a formally color-blind international law.

However, comparatively less work has been done on the rise of a formally racist international law.[24] And maybe it is because here there is a difficult problem to decipher. How to understand the drafting of racial contracts, for instance, in the early modern period, when arguably race had yet to become a concept and racism was a pervasive social phenomenon—as in the case of the legal justifications for conquest, occupation, and slavery in the New World? And how to understand the shift from a formally pre-racist to a racist international law? It may turn out that race and racism were all over the place in these examples and the clock to find a pre-racial law must be turned back to before the rise of the early modern law of nations. Nevertheless, these questions about the rise of a racist law of nations persist.

When international lawyers foreground race as an extralegal force structuring a formally color-line and color-blind international law, they may overlook a central CRT insight—the social construction of race. If race is socially constructed and if the social construction of race occurs only in practices outside international law, it would mean that international law is epiphenomenal and that all there is to study is how international law is structured from the outside. But if the opposite is true, if race and racism are not ontological categories, we may find pigmentation-based or other phenotypical-based terms entering international law while race and racism were socially crystalizing. We may therefore be interested in looking at race and racism as structuring from *within* international law.

This chapter focuses on a period when and a place where race irrupted within international law. This focus on the Americas of the nineteenth century may start closing a gap in our knowledge about international law's history. As mentioned, much of TWAIL and current new thinking focuses on racial continuities in postcolonial international law, that is, in the law that after decolonization and the prohibition of racial discrimination purged race from formal law. We know less about the irruption of race in formal law. This chapter studies race from within the international legal structure, race as an indigenous element in legal argumentation.[25] The beginning of that story unfolds in the Americas.

THE WATERMELON INCIDENT, PANAMA 1856

In 1848, Gold was discovered in California. That same year, the Treaty of Guadalupe Hidalgo ended the Mexican–American War, sanctioning the annexation of California by the United States. The gold rush that followed transformed not only North America, but also Central America.[26] Before 1869, before the completion of the second transcontinental railroad in U.S. territory, Panama City, then part of New Granada (nowadays Colombia and Panama), was the main transit point connecting the East and West coasts of the United States. The geopolitical importance of the Isthmus of Panama gave rise to diplomatic negotiations between the United States and New Granada, culminating in 1846, with the signing of a Treaty of Peace, Amity, Navigation, and Commerce.[27]

The treaty included rights and obligations recognized under general international law, such as the rights of each other's citizens to transit, dwell, and trade; and obligations of both states such as the protection of foreign persons and property.[28] But the treaty granted also special rights of transit to the United States' government and citizens, "across the Isthmus of Panama, upon any modes of communication that now exist, or that may be, hereafter, constructed." New Granada extended to U.S. citizens the "exemptions, privileges and immunities, concerning commerce and navigation" enjoyed by Granadian citizens. In exchange, the U.S. not only granted equal and reciprocal treatment as well as most-favored-nation treatment to New Granada and its citizens, but also recognized and guaranteed New Granada's sovereignty over the Isthmus.[29]

In 1855, with the opening of a railroad connecting Panama's Atlantic and Pacific coasts, Panama became the fastest route, and thus the main route, for travelers bound to California. It was then common to see large numbers of Americans roaming Panama City while waiting for the train or ship to continue their journey. On April 15, 1856, a couple of drunken American travelers who had ventured outside the train station into La Ciénaga, a poorer peripheral neighborhood, got into an altercation with a fruit vendor, José Manuel Luna, after one of them took a slice of watermelon without paying. Luna demanded payment, reminding the American traveler that he was not in the United States. The scuffle that erupted turned later into a wholesale riot when a crowd of Panamanians that formed in *La Ciénaga* turned against the American assailants. By the next morning, the riot had left a dozen Americans killed and property of the American-owned Panama Railroad destroyed.[30]

Amos Corwine, the special commissioner appointed by the U.S. State Department to investigate the riot, drafted a report. The *incidente de la tajada de sandía*, as it was known and is remembered in Spanish, becomes in Corwine's report the "Panama Massacre," and Luna becomes "a negro who had a large knife... and was demanding a dime... in payment of a watermelon." Corwine added: "The negro spoke English and used violent language towards the American party."[31] Compensation claims filed by American citizens with the State Department led to lengthy diplomatic negotiations. The United States, exercising diplomatic protection of its citizens, sought to settle all claims by a comprehensive convention based on the obligation of New Granada's 1846 treaty obligations "to maintain peace and good order in the interoceanic route of the Isthmus of Panama."[32] Under the American diplomats' proposal, in addition to monetary compensation, New Granada would relinquish sovereignty over some islands where the U.S. would install a naval basis, and from which it would have the right to intervene in order to protect the railroad and city ports.[33] In exchange, New Granada "releases herself from her obligation to protect" the interoceanic route.[34]

The American proposal was not exceptional, but rather reflected the global legal architecture that emerged in the nineteenth century to regulate relations between people at different "stages" of "civilization." This might be why diplomatic relations broke off when New Granada rejected American demands. New Granada's authorities refuted responsibility over damages inflicted by a mob, rejecting the cession of sovereignty as treasonous. Negotiations then restarted and continued until a convention for the settlement of claims was signed in 1857 and ratified in 1860.[35]

New Granada's authorities first noted that troops were promptly dispatched to reestablish public order. Then, they explained that the riot responded to rumors spreading around the city, including not just news of the initial scuffle, but also news about the presence of filibusters arriving from California. The minister of foreign affairs, Lino de Pombo, argued that locals sought to protect the city from an external attack by Americans, like those that had occurred before in Baja California and Nicaragua. De Pombo's fears were not unfounded. William Walker, an American adventurer who organized filibuster expeditions into Baja California and Central America, got entangled in Nicaraguan internecine conflicts that saw him becoming President of Nicaragua in 1856, then ousted and, in a later expedition to Honduras, executed.[36]

More specifically, authorities from New Granada defended the denial of responsibility based on the argument that the riot responded to a spontaneous reaction of locals against the "insolence and attacks of the immigrants."[37] The version of Luna, the street vendor, supporting this account was published in Panama's official gazette. When Luna demanded payment, the American responded: "Don't bother me, kiss my ass." Luna replied: "Careful, we are not in the United States here, pay... and we are settled." The American pulled a pistol and told Luna that he would pay him with a gunshot, to which Luna retorted: "If you have your pistol, I also have my knife."[38]

Lino de Pombo, in a letter to the U.S. Secretary of State, points at these attitudes to understand the incident, describing Americans as "ignorant and immoral, quarrelsome and intemperate men, without any God other than gold." Americans—De Pombo continues—claim to "to be civilized" but have not "shaken off the most hostile prejudices." Not entirely free of prejudices of his own, de Pombo concludes: Americans "look in contempt" at the "native population," even those of "Spanish origin"; for them, people "with African blood, are unworthy of any consideration." The only thought they have when arriving "to a foreign shore, is the thought of '*annexionism*.'"[39]

FROM INDIVIDUAL PREJUDICE TO A RACIST INTERNATIONAL LAW

The Watermelon Incident is full of racial overtones that were neither new nor remarkable to the nineteenth century. Racial animosity had been brewing for a long time between Black Panamanian citizens and American residents in Panama, which as part of New Granada, let us not forget, had both abolished slavery and instituted male universal suffrage.[40] But racial acrimony spread beyond interracial relations in Panama, into interstate relations between the United States and New Granada. Consider, for example, how Corwine, the American diplomat proposing the treaty settlement ceding sovereignty to the U.S., justified his recommendations:

> The interest our countrymen have here are too great to be neglected, and left at the mercy of an ignorant, brutal race, such as infest the Isthmus, and who can neither be restrained nor subdued by the authorities of the country. Nor are they driven hence by the enactment of oppressive, arbitrary laws, in violation of their rights guaranteed by treaty. They need the protecting arm of our government, and I feel a confident assurance that it will be extended to them.[41]

Amos Corwine's report may suggest a turning point. The report exemplifies the irruption of race in international legal discourse to articulate differences between and the hierarchical ordering of peoples in the American continent. Before, since the arrival of the Spanish, differences between them and indigenous peoples as well as ideas about the inferiority of the latter were framed in the language of religion or civilization, rather than on pigmentation or other phenotypical-based notions. Even if differentiation and hierarchical ordering of people concealed an underlying racial impetus, the point is that race was not explicitly used as a term in international legal argumentation justifying order, hierarchy, and its legal manifestations, such as withdrawal of sovereignty or unequal treatment.

Let me offer a more specific contrast between early-nineteenth-century negative views of Spanish-Americans, in which race does not play an explicit role, and mid-century views, where race irrupts explicitly in legal argumentation. In

1815, in letters considering his work as diplomat in Europe, John Adams discussed Spanish-American independence and the efforts by Venezuelan revolutionary Francisco de Miranda to gather support in Europe from France and Britain. Comparing Miranda to the similar quest faced by American revolutionaries, Adams regards Benjamin Franklin and others as having been legitimate representatives of the American people. Miranda had nothing to show—Adams claims: "No delegation... from any original power, any physical force, any animal strength much less from any regular assemblies of people." The reasons for Miranda's shortcomings were for Adams clear:

> The people of South America are the most ignorant, the most bigoted, the most superstitious of all the Roman Catholics in Christendom.[42]

It was also clear for Adams that Miranda's plan to establish free governments "among such a people" was "as absurd as similar plans... to establish democracies among birds, beasts and fishes."[43]

John Adams's son shared the views of his father. John Quincy Adams, as secretary of state, opposed recognition of the new republics of Spanish-America. Adams noted that leaders of independence like Simón Bolivar and Bernardo O'Higgins talk about an American system uniting all the republics of the continent in contrast to monarchic Europe. "But there is no basis for any such system"—Adams objected.[44] If there is one, it is not the system Spanish-American leaders envisioned, for Adams asserts: "We have it; we constitute the whole of it; there is no 'community of interests or of principles between North and South America.'"[45]

Adams, however, had to accept that the U.S. could not remain in total isolation. Territories of the former Spanish Crown would pose a security threat if non-hemispheric powers would use them as base to attack the United States. Because of national security, but also because of the need to open markets for U.S. producers as well as because of American demand for products from Spanish-American nations, Adams recognized that formal contact with these nations was necessary.[46] Establishing diplomatic relations followed American self-interest.

Historians of U.S.–Latin American relations, like Lars Schoultz, have argued that American foreign policy towards Latin America has been consistent, not because of Washington's consistent behavior, but because it has always been motivated by the same pursuit of self-interest. Even if the policy focus has shifted—from the protection of U.S. citizens residing in Latin America, to the protection of their investments, to hemispheric security, anti-communism, or economic development—what makes self-interest the only relevant concern is a "pervasive belief that Latin Americans constitute an inferior branch of the human species."[47]

Around the mid-nineteenth century, this sentiment of American superiority and Latin-American inferiority started to be formulated in racial terms and began appearing in international legal argumentation. Historians have noted the changes in public discourse between the early and mid-century, when "American expansion" came to be viewed "as evidence of the innate superiority of the American Anglo-Saxon... race."[48] The idea of America's "manifest destiny" captured the belief that America had a special mission to fulfil in world history, a mission that was expressed not only in the settler expansion across the North American continent, but also in a sense of superiority when coming into contact with non-Anglo peoples, understood as lower civilizations in need of help and discipline.[49]

Both dimensions intersected directly with international law. America's manifest destiny was for John O'Sullivan (originator of the term) and others, as we will see, a legal title to continental expansion. Treaties enabling commerce—like the abovementioned 1846 treaty signed with New Granada—and doctrines establishing responsibility for injuries suffered by foreign residents and establishing diplomatic protection—as invoked in relation to the Watermelon Riot—were relevant to manage commercial contact with peoples regarded as belonging to lower civilizations. Mid-nineteenth-century international law became racist when it embraced race as a term or category in legal argumentation about continental expansion or the rights of foreign residents.

EXPANSIONIST AMERICA

The "agitation for expansion" that besieged mid-nineteenth-century Anglo-America had dramatic consequences for Spanish-America in general and Mexico in particular.[50] In 1845, American President James Polk made an offer to the Mexican government to purchase disputed territory. When the Mexican President Antonio López de Santa Anna rejected the offer, Polk ordered troops to advance into the disputed territory. Americans were attacked by Mexican forces who were understood to be repelling troops that had crossed into Mexican territory. A large-scale conflict ensued—the 1846–1848 Mexican–American War—which, after thousands of deaths on both sides, ended with American troops occupying the Mexican capital.[51]

American expansion at the expense of Mexican (and indigenous) territory was not a military enterprise without justification. The war declaration passed by U.S. Congress referred to the Mexican attack as *causa bellum*.[52] Moreover, it explicitly declared the war not to be a war of conquest, but only a war of indemnity, that is, a war in which territorial acquisitions were meant to pay off compensation claims by the United States and its citizens.[53] However, the Mexican–American War served to promote another justification that exceeded the narrower legal arguments about a first aggression and indemnity. Only a few years before, in the context of the annexation of Texas and Oregon, "manifest destiny" had become a justification for American continental expansion. The war against Mexico popularized manifest destiny.[54]

In 1845, John O'Sullivan, a lawyer, editor, and later adventurer and ambassador, coined the term. Writing about the annexation of Texas, O'Sullivan declared, "Texas is now ours"—presenting annexation as a fait accompli, as it "became peopled with an American population." The time for opposition to annexation must cease, O'Sullivan protested, condemning the "hostile interference" of foreign powers attempting to "limit our greatness and checking the fulfillment of our manifest destiny to overspread the continent allotted by Providence for the free development of our yearly multiplying millions."[55] A year later, manifest destiny entered U.S. Congress discussions on the termination of the joint British–American occupation of Oregon, but only to be described as a ridiculous title.[56] In the aftermath of the Mexican–American War, however, manifest destiny became intertwined with general ideas justifying expansion as well as more specific ideas about legal title, both dimensions informing treaty-making as the legal tool sanctioning America's expansion through territorial annexation and purchase, in relation to Spanish and then Mexican territory, from the Adams–Onís Treaty of 1819 to the Treaty of Guadalupe Hidalgo of 1848.[57]

As ideology, manifest destiny captured an idea about Anglo expansion that was well entrenched before the annexation of Texas and the war. Since the beginning of the American Republic, it was understood that any neighboring people that had achieved self-government, by compact or by revolution, would be allowed to join the United States.[58] The assumption was that neighboring peoples would be of the same Anglo root that had formed the Union. Manifest destiny captured this inevitability, that as Anglo-Saxons were bound to spread, the United States was meant to expand. Thus, as an ideology, manifest destiny did not limit the scope of expansion. However, linked to arguments about legal titles, manifest destiny provided guidance to the question about which peoples were ready and qualified for self-government. As a discourse about titles, manifest destiny worked together with ideas about occupation and vacant land to delimit the scope of legitimate expansion of the Union westward across north America from the Atlantic to the Pacific.[59]

"Imbecile and distracted, Mexico never can exert any real governmental authority over such a country."[60] The country was California, and the statement by John O'Sullivan moves from the already secured annexation of Texas to a future independence of California. Expanding into Texas and California, at the expense of Mexico, and into Oregon, at the expense of Britain, the United States possessed the only "true title"—O'Sullivan affirmed.[61]

The annexation of Texas, Oregon, and then California and other states in the aftermath of the war against Mexico generated profound public debate about American expansion. O'Sullivan is far from unique, as in Congress and the press, annexation and the war were endlessly debated. But O'Sullivan is particularly relevant, as he intervened, not only coining a term—manifest destiny—that captured the "agitation for expansion," but also advancing arguments that linked the expansionist ideology to more concrete legal justifications. O'Sullivan was of course not the first to rationalize distinctions between peoples understood to be capable or not of occupying land and claiming territorial sovereignty.

In O'Sullivan's America as well as in Spanish-America, the treatise by the renowned Swiss diplomat Emer de Vattel contained the most influential arguments about expansion and occupation. Vattel provided not just an answer, but one that was specific to North America. "More industrious nations" may take possession of territories from "those who still pursue this idle mode of life," Vattel argued in reference to indigenous tribes, clarifying that while "the conquest of the civilized empires of Peru and Mexico was a notorious usurpation," the establishment of "many colonies on the continent of North America might . . . be extremely lawful."[62] Since the "earth belongs to mankind in general,"[63] and thus the "whole earth is destined to feed its inhabitants, every nation is then obliged by the law of nature to cultivate the land that has fallen to its share."[64] In consequence, "erratic nations" that "ranged through" rather than inhabit a territory, that is, cultivate and settle, cannot claim "true and legal possession." The "people of Europe . . . finding land of which the savages stood in no particular need . . . were lawfully entitled to take possession of it, and settle it with colonies."[65]

These arguments are rooted in an old legal tradition.[66] Where others, in this legal tradition, had used civilization, or the ability to constitute a well-organized polity, and where Vattel used cultivation of land to rationalize distinctions, O'Sullivan used race. Later in the century this became also common. In the mid-nineteenth century, O'Sullivan and others used race in legal argumentation in two contexts: in debates on expansion by occupation, and in relation to the continental distribution of races.

FROM OCCUPATION TO MANIFEST DESTINY: A YANKEE, RACIST INTERNATIONAL LAW?

"A population will soon be in actual occupation of California, over which it will idle for Mexico to dream of dominion."[67] Before and then during the Mexican-American War, John O'Sullivan defended Texan annexation and American expansion into California with arguments that echoed Vattel's distinction between nations—that are able to settle and cultivate land—and tribes—that only range through the land they inhabit. O'Sullivan, however, shifts Vattel's argument from nations to the Anglo-Saxon race and from indigenous tribes to Mexicans, to finally argue that it is not actual occupation, but destiny to spread over the continent that defines Anglo-America's ultimate title.

Echoing Vattel, O'Sullivan affirms that "only immigration can develop" California's "capabilities and fulfil the purposes of its creation." But rather than a nation, the population that O'Sullivan is expecting to soon occupy California is the Anglo-Saxon race.[68] "Anglo-Saxon . . . armed with the plough and the rifle, and marking its trail with schools . . . courts and representative halls, mills and meeting-houses. . . . will necessarily become independent."[69]

Whereas Vattel's argument was specifically responding to the legality of taking possession of lands inhabited by "wandering tribes," or those pursuing an "idle mode of life," O'Sullivan's shift to race allows him to extend the argument from indigenous people to Mexicans:

> The Mexican race now see, in the fate of the aborigines of the north, their own inevitable destiny. They must amalgamate and be lost, in the superior vigor of the Anglo-Saxon race, or they must utterly perish.... While the Anglo-Saxon race have overrun the northern section, and purged it of a vigorous race of Indians, the Spaniards have failed to make any considerable progress at the south.

The lack of progress O'Sullivan was highlighting was the "failure to driving back the Indians, or annihilating them as a race." It "has yet to be gone through at the south"—O'Sullivan insists.[70]

Finally, where Vattel identifies cultivation as the marker rendering possession of land just, describing its underlying basis on the pressures of European expansion to feed the world's growing population and ultimately on mankind's common ownership of the earth, O'Sullivan constructs a wider marker, including cultivation, and more broadly, exploiting Mexico's mineral and agricultural wealth and as we saw "marking the trail" with civilizational signs, as schools and political organs. But here, plough, rifle, and a trail of civilization mark a natural racial flow ordained by Providence as America's ultimate title. It is the hand of Providence that leads our race, as O'Sullivan announced in his first editorial.[71] The "descent of the northern race... by the occupation of Texas,"[72] or the "natural flow of events" by which Anglos "pour down upon" California, reflect a predestined right:

> The right of our manifest destiny to overspread and possess the whole of the continent which Providence has given for the development of the great experiment of liberty and federative self-government entrusted to us.[73]

O'Sullivan places his argument about manifest destiny as a title squarely within international law by contrasting it with Mexico's formal sovereignty. Anglo-Saxons in California "will have a right to independence—to self-government—to the possession of the homes conquered from the wilderness... a better and truer right that the artificial title of sovereignty in Mexico a thousand miles distant."[74] Not only ridiculing traditional legal titles—"all these antiquated materials of old black-letter international law"—but also confidently calling for their dismissal—"away, away with all these cobweb issues of rights of discovery, exploration, settlement, continuity, etc."[75] O'Sullivan defines manifest destiny as a new legal title.

In the press and specially in Congress, Whig representatives were not convinced. They objected to invoking international law. Whigs opposed expansionist democrats, from Andrew Jackson to James Polk, who embraced manifest destiny. Polk supported Texan annexation to win the presidency; once elected, he advocated for obtaining full control of Oregon by putting an end to the joint occupation with Britain, and he ultimately steered the country to war with Mexico. O'Sullivan's manifest destiny became a useful justification, not just as ideology, but as title. This double aspect did not remain unnoticed to Whig critics.

When Congress discussed ending the joint British–American occupation of Oregon, the representative of Massachusetts, Robert Winthrop, opposed the measure and manifest destiny. Not without irony, Winthrop calls the view exposed "in a leading Administration journal," as inaugurating "a new chapter in the law of nations; or rather, in the special laws of our own country; for I suppose the right of a manifest destiny to spread will not be admitted to exist in any nation except the universal Yankee nation!"[76]

Winthrop argued for compromise, for titles on both sides are "too confused and complicated to justify any arbitrary and exclusive assertions of right ... vague traditions of settlement, musty records of old voyages, conflicting claims of discovery, disputed principles of public law, acknowledged violations of the rights of aboriginal occupants."[77] Similarly, Caleb Smith of Indiana opposed the measure, criticizing manifest destiny: "Vattel and Grotius, as well as all other writers upon the law of nations, will be searched in vain for evidence of the existence of such a title.... I have too much confidence in the strength and justice of our claims ... to consent to base our title upon pretensions so ridiculous and absurd."[78]

Opposition to a title based on Providence's role given to the Anglo race reinforces the idea that manifest destiny was a legal argument within a political debate about American expansion. The argument provided cover to Polk, but in Congress a Whig majority opposed manifest destiny. The result was compromise and a combination of arguments shaping and justifying annexation of Texas and Oregon and the war against Mexico, including, as mentioned, a first attack, indemnity, and manifest destiny. Political controversy shifted after the war, when expansion into territories inhabited by non-whites was disputed. Manifest destiny emerged then to justify a continental distribution of races in the form of a continental segregation of Anglos from other races. But if the territorial expansion of the United States came to an end, commercial expansion did not. The United States would protect its citizens residing in foreign countries to advance industry and trade; expansionism was replaced by a policy of intervention to protect American interests.

THE CONTINENTAL DISTRIBUTION OF RACES: FROM A SEGREGATIONIST TO AN INTERVENTIONIST AMERICA

Expansion is in principle boundless,[79] unless Anglos enter territories of "mixed and confused blood,"[80] because the "virtues of the Anglo-Saxon race make their political union with the degraded Mexican-Spanish impossible."[81] As the question about annexation became entangled with slavery, namely with the problem of keeping the balance between free and slave states, these statements by O'Sullivan offered manifest destiny as a criterion for delimiting expansion and for a future solution to the end of slavery by a continental redistribution of Anglos and non-whites.

First, O'Sullivan described Mexico as a territory, where because of the racial composition of its inhabitants, self-government is impossible. Describing the political sentiment shared across American towns as the sentiment on which Federal government and democracy depend, O'Sullivan warns there is not such sentiment when inhabitants are "*Gachupins, Gambucinos* and *Mestizoes.*" O'Sullivan affirms that their wishes must be disregarded, "govern them instead of permitting them to govern themselves."[82]

Second, since the cost of imposing such a government would be for the Anglo too high,[83] O'Sullivan argues instead that all races deemed not capable of self-government—including U.S.-American Blacks,[84] in an "eventual voluntary abolition of slavery"—should be removed and left together in the Americas south of the border: "the only receptacle capable of absorbing that race."[85]

This aspect of O'Sullivan's manifest destiny shows white supremacy and race used in international legal argumentation intersecting. In its segregationist facet, manifest destiny halted expansion by treaty. In its interventionist facet, it became one of the underlying bases for the development of an international law of intervention and diplomatic protection.

After the Gadsden Purchase of 1845, further attempts to expand by treaty purchase failed. The 1859 McLane–Ocampo Treaty with Mexico, which would have ceded to the U.S. rights of transit from the Atlantic to the Pacific at the Isthmus of Tehuantepec, was defeated in the U.S. Senate. It was blocked by disputes over the disruption in the balance between free and slave states and by the sense that there was no more land worth acquiring, for unlike territories appropriated in the Guadalupe-Hidalgo treaty, the rest of Mexico was densely inhabited by Mexicans. In 1859 the pre-American-Civil-War drive for expansion into Mexico came to an end.[86]

Although the idea of a territorial boundary matching a racial boundary between the U.S. and Mexico predated the war, with the outbreak of war it regained relevance. This idea was brought to the fore by those opposing the war and southward expansion:

> The stupendous deserts between the Nueces and Bravo rivers are the natural boundaries between the Anglo Saxon and the Mauritanian races. There ends the valley of the West. There Mexico begins. Thence, beyond the Bravo, begin the Moorish people and their Indian associates . . . to whom Mexico properly belongs. . . . While peace is cherished, that boundary will be sacred. Not till the spirit of conquest rages, will the people on either side molest or mix with each other; and whenever they do, one or the other race must be conquered, if not extinguished.[87]

Given that the racial boundary had been breached by the war, it was time now for American troops to retreat. John Calhoun, then southern senator and former vice president and secretary of state, stated in Congress: "You are tied at present, as it were, to a corpse. My object is to get rid of it as soon as possible."[88] Before the war, as secretary of state, Calhoun had supported the annexation of Texas, to avoid the dilution of power of Southern slave states and because of manifest destiny. As far as the war was fought to right Mexican wrongdoings, and as far as seeking indemnity was limited to acquiring sparsely populated territory, Calhoun supported President Polk's war against Mexico. Otherwise, Calhoun was against annexation because "we have never dreamt of incorporating into our Union any but the Caucasian race—the free white race."[89] Calhoun concluded his speech in Congress redefining the purposes of the war: it will "accomplish that all-important consideration, the extrication of ourselves and the country from this entanglement with Mexico."[90]

While territorial expansionism required distinctive international legal arguments—manifest destiny as preordained occupation—seeking disentanglement from Mexico could be simply pursued by relying on the rights ordinarily recognized to any sovereign state to protect its borders. This facet of manifest destiny did not require much legal argumentation, which was not the case for the policy of interventionism.

Extrication did not mean isolation, for American economic interests did not leave Mexico or the rest of Spanish-America and the Caribbean. In fact, it was the opposite. American economic penetration increased after the war, especially with the political stability achieved in the late nineteenth century during the rule of Porfirio Díaz. Under a political and legal environment hospitable to foreign capital, Mexico became prime destination for U.S. investment.

The spread of American capital in Mexico and the Americas was part of a larger nineteenth century trend that saw Americans opening Japan to trade, while European states and in particular Britain had opened much of the world to commerce; from China to Spanish-America, their merchants and investors establishing themselves in city ports across the world. An emerging international division of labor was enabled and regulated by international law.[91]

Protection of Western interests abroad relied on the development of an international legal regime conferring rights and protections to foreign residents—through diplomatic protection and the settlement of disputes by claim commissions, for example. The American continent was one of the places where a regime to protect interests of Western nationals in peripheral countries evolved. To the extent that protection of American interests turned into extraterritorial action, as in the case of punitive expeditions into Mexican territory, the United States used international legal arguments to sustain their legality, to protect nationals abroad, to punish violations of their rights, or to force collection of debt.

European and American international lawyers, during the second half of the nineteenth century, argued that foreign residents enjoyed international rights that the host state had to respect. These were not just any residents, but citizens of "civilized states," of states of "European blood," that is, white citizens. Host states were also a particular kind of state. Some nations, although without "European blood," like the Spanish-American republics, had been recognized as states, acquiring in consequence the duty to secure for white foreign residents a standard of civilized life.

International law's minimum standard of treatment reflected the minimal conditions for white life. Under the threat of foreign intervention in case of violation, respecting the standard of treatment became a matter of survival.[92] However, as Edwin Borchard, a renowned American expert in diplomatic protection, recognized: "the standard of conduct by which a state must be guided in its treatment of aliens . . . is incapable of exact definition."[93] Here is where race entered in the formulation of the standard.

The content of the minimum standard did not emerge from agreement between host states and foreign residents, but, as Borchard explains, it emerged from the "common practice of civilized nations," which throughout the eighteenth and nineteenth centuries coalesced in "fundamental principles from which no nation can depart."[94] The content of the standard thus developed out of customary law, informed by state practice that was uniform, not universal. It was the practice of states belonging to the exclusive club of civilized nations, again in Borchard's words, from "the uniform practices of the civilized states of the western world who gave birth and nourishment to international law."[95] It was the practice of nations of the "Western European type" refusing to accept that their nationals in "some weaker countries of the world" have only the rights granted to them by local law.[96]

Here we have arrived to the late nineteenth century, when, as Gevers has shown in relation to Westlake and others, civilizational markers were at the same time, if not preeminently, corporal-based racial markers.[97] The same could be said about Borchard. Discussing the rights of sovereigns to exclude foreigners, Borchard notes however that the society of states depends on "international intercourse." Thus, a right to admission of foreigners has emerged product of the "network of commercial treaties by which the states, of the white race at least . . . are bound together," establishing "freedom of international intercourse."[98] Then, Spanish-American countries found themselves not only with the obligation to protect foreign residents, but also with the obligation to allow them in, for as Borchard explains, exercising the "right to exclude . . . would violate the spirit of international law and endanger its membership in the international community."[99]

CONFRONTING THE ANGLO RACE: AN INTERNATIONAL LAW FOR THE LATIN-AMERICAN RACE

Towards the mid-nineteenth century, Spanish-American republics were able to secure recognition of their formal sovereignty, excluding the more extreme forms of inequality—like extraterritoriality, the exemption in favor of foreigners of the operation of local law and courts—to which non-Western states in other regions of the globe were subjected. Again, in Borchard's words, in "oriental countries" or in "semi-barbarous states," and because of their "deficient civilization ... and fundamental differences in law and social habits," alien residents from "countries of European civilization" enjoyed not just a minimum standard of protection, but extraterritorial jurisdiction.[100] International law writers would draw up lists of states belonging to this category, based on the conclusion of unequal treaties, on the constitution of protectorates, or based on where Western consuls exercised extraterritorial jurisdiction. The Spanish-American republics were in general not included in these lists, though only conditionally so.[101]

That aliens are subjects to the same law and protections applicable to nationals "is conditional upon the fact that its administration of justice satisfies the standard of civilized justice established by international law."[102] And this conditionality, as Borchard noted, is assessed by the Western state: "foreign states ... undertake to judge for themselves as to the local state's compliance with the international standard."[103] Thus, for non-Western states, respecting an international standard of civilized organization, which was crucial for their claim to formal sovereignty, was at the same time a reason for limiting substantive sovereignty, regarding the treatment of alien residents.[104]

This international regime facilitating and legitimizing Western imperialism fundamentally shaped hemispheric relations. Substantive sovereignty of states depended on the respect of the minimum standard of treatment regarding foreign residents and foreign capital. Independent from substantive sovereignty to regulate and govern domestic life, a minimum standard imposed limits, not just regarding individual rights to life and freedom, but also to property.[105] Latin-American states could neither invoke substantive sovereignty, namely autonomy to enact administrative and legislative regulation, to justify a limits to the minimum standard.[106] Nor could they discharge the obligation to protect foreign residents by granting them the same treatment given to nationals.[107]

These limits on substantive sovereignty became also a threat to formal sovereignty. When a state was unwilling or unable to offer protection to foreign residents, or when it refused to offer adequate compensation, the United States was entitled to pressure diplomatically, and the U.S. did so. In Latin America and beyond, gunboat diplomacy meant that when routine diplomatic pressures were not enough, exceptionally but not unfrequently Western states intervened militarily to protect nationals or to secure compensation. Then, the difference in rights and legal status between states considered formally sovereign, like Latin-American states, and states considered semi-civilized, like those under unequal treaties and extraterritoriality, disappeared. This happened because now both types of states were subject to military interventions, not only for the protection of nationals and for recovering debt and securing compensation, but also to be punished for wrongdoing.

The history of the Latin-American international law that emerged between the late nineteenth century and 1933 to challenge the international regime of intervention and diplomatic protection, by enacting a principle of non-intervention and limiting state responsibility with national treatment, among others, is well known.[108] However, at its roots, this Latin-American legal tradition did not emerge just to counter interventionism. Latin America was born as a reaction to an expansionist Anglo-America.

In 1856, Francisco Bilbao, a mid-nineteenth-century Chilean liberal publicist, gave a speech to a group of Spanish-American intellectuals living in forced or voluntary exile in Paris. Prompted by news of the Watermelon Incident in Panama, the diplomatic incident mentioned at the beginning of this chapter, Bilbao addresses the audience:

> We see empires trying to renew the old idea of domination of the globe ... Yesterday, Texas, after, the North of Mexico and the Pacific greets a new master. Today, the guerilas that advance wake up the Isthmus [of Panama] ... here is the danger. Is there so little awareness of ourselves, so little faith of the destinies of the Latin-American race? (p. 10–11).[109]

With this speech, Bilbao becomes one of the first to coin a new term, "Latin America," to respond to a crisis that he conceived as deeper than U.S. interventionism.[110] For Bilbao and others, it was not just that the U.S. Army was intervening like Europeans intervened to collect debt or protect their citizens' property and expand territorially when possible.[111] The threat was deeper. Bilbao believed that the American continent harbored the promise of overcoming the mistakes of the old world, thus realizing freedom and justice. It is this promise that is threatened by the rise of the United States as an imperial force. The threat is deeper because American expansionism resulted in a racial continental confrontation.

> I do not believe that history presents us with a more transcendental spectacle, than the one presented today by the American continent ... it has never been seen a vast continent dominated by only two races, with two languages, with only two religions and one political form... (p. 7)

> Today we witness the vastest arena of two races, two ideas in the world's largest field to dispute territorial sovereignty and the empire of the future. (p. 25)[112]

Bilbao also understood that the Anglo threat called for unity. When questioning the little faith in the destinies of the Latin-American race, he answered:

> I don't think so, the time has come ... for the unity of the America of the South. (p. 11)

> We have to develop our independence, to preserve the natural and moral borders of our homeland, we have to perpetuate our American and Latin race. (p. 13)[113]

We have seen John O'Sullivan's manifest destiny combining ideas about a sense of mission in the world and the superiority of the Anglo-Saxon race with arguments about the legality of Anglo expansion throughout the continent. If O'Sullivan provided racial-ideological as well as legal fodder to the United States' liberal imperialism, Bilbao retorted in kind. Bilbao proclaimed the Latin race of America to embody a higher ideal of personality and freedom that stands as counterpoint to "Yankee individualism."[114]

For Bilbao, notwithstanding the rejection of European monarchic servitude by both Anglo and Latin America, it was the latter's deeper notion of freedom that offered real emancipation. Bilbao affirms that even though America has become wealthy, rather than abolishing slavery, protecting their heroic indigenous, and pursuing universal causes, it has pursued only narrower interests, the interests of the individualistic Saxon.[115] Only in realizing its role in universal history—Bilbao argued—would America's Latin race find unity and complete the first wave of independence against Spain, with a second wave establishing a Latin-American confederation.[116]

Like O'Sullivan, who had combined racial ideology with legal argumentation to justify U.S. continental expansion, Bilbao's emancipatory role given to the Latin races of the Americas was accompanied with the proposal of a [Latin] American Congress charged with codifying international law, eliminating tariffs, creating an international tribunal, and gathering forces from member states to go to war or embark on other great tasks for the future of the continent.[117]

José María Torres Caicedo, a Colombian lawyer and writer who served as a diplomat in Paris, was present when Bilbao delivered his 1856 speech, published soon after a poem about the confrontation of the Anglo and Latin races of the Americas, which has been recognized as one of the first writings where the term Latin America was used.[118]

Torres Caicedo was important not only because of the impact caused by his poem, but also because, as a lawyer and diplomat, he used the term again in 1865, advocating for political unity and the codification of American international law, specifically in relation to the problem of diplomatic protection of foreign residents.[119] Torres Caicedo explicitly criticized manifest destiny as a misinterpretation of the Monroe Doctrine. It is in this work, among others, where ideas about the primacy of national jurisdiction over foreign claimants started to take form, ideas later formulated as the Calvo and Drago doctrines.[120] It is on the basis of the tradition initiated by Bilbao, Torres Caicedo, Calvo, and others that today we use "Latin America" to describe the states, peoples, and nations of the Americas and the Caribbean that share a common history characterized by formal and informal colonialism, and a common history of resistance through, among other means, international law.

It would be tempting to end here on a note where race as a term in legal argumentation was used for anti-hegemonic purposes—Latin-Americans using international law to resist Anglo-Saxon continental supremacy. However, as already mentioned, Latin-American international law was part of a larger nation-building project that turned hegemonic in the process of subjugating indigenous peoples conceived as members of the uncivilized races. Studying the role of international law and legal discourse in the dispossession of indigenous peoples of the Americas, and specifically the role of race in that process, is a task not only greatly exceeding the scope of this chapter, but also that is only now starting to be asked in relation to specific indigenous peoples.[121]

CONCLUSION

This chapter examined, in relation to one continent—the Americas—the rise of race as an element in international legal argumentation. Americans from the United States understood international law itself to be the law of the Anglo-Saxon race, justifying not only American expansion over the continent's "vacant lands," but also the limits of that expansion. Americans argued for segregation, when expansion ran into "non-white races." Newly independent states of the Americas were not to be conquered but disciplined—through diplomatic protection and military intervention. Spanish-Americans, realizing that the greatest threat to the independence of their Republics was no longer European recolonization, but Anglo-American expansion and intervention, called for both the unity of the Latin race and the enactment of a continental public law, what later became a Latin-American international law with non-intervention at its center. But using the idea of a Latin race confronting the Anglo race to sustain the former's claim to sovereignty redefined indigenous peoples as "uncivilized races" to be civilized by assimilation or war. If Latin America was born as an anti-hegemonic project of resistance vis-à-vis Anglo-America, a racialized international law enabled not only Anglo-American continental domination but also dispossession of indigenous peoples by Latin-American states.

This story of the Americas of the nineteenth century may contribute to our understanding of the relation between race and international law. It suggests examining race and racism not only as a force that structures international law from the outside, determining a transhistorical continuity defined by the distinction between white and Black races and the imposition of burdens and privileges accordingly. But also, as a formal legal term, structuring international law from within.

From O'Sullivan to Bilbao, we saw the mid-century irruption of race, a trend that later consolidated when prominent founders of the modern discipline—remember Bluntschli and Westlake, among many others—identified international law with the law of the white race.

That race irrupted within international law in the middle of the nineteenth century, when racism had become a powerful extralegal ideology, may suggest that international law's racism was structured from the outside. This could be the case. However, this chapter also shows that at least during the first half of the nineteenth century, as an element of legal argumentation, race sustained not only the project of racial differentiation and subordination, but also other projects, such as expansion, segregation, intervention, non-intervention, dispossession, and resistance. This chapter thus suggests that when race irrupted in international law, it could be articulated towards different purposes because race may have not been fully established as an extralegal ideology. This may mean that we, international lawyers, should examine in greater detail earlier historical periods to trace the rise of other formal, racial legal terms or doctrines—especially in the context of slavery, like *asiento de negros* among many others—in order to better understand international law's role in the social construction of race and racism. We may then find international law's implication in global racial contracts producing domination and resistance, and maybe find other ambiguous outcomes, where winners and losers do not perfectly fit into the racial binary.

While this work would reveal the gradual end of a pre-racial international law, this chapter reveals the rise of a racist international law. The international law that had race as an element in formal legal argumentation lasted at least a century, from the 1860s to the 1960s. At times we forget that it lasted well into the twentieth century. Remember W.E.B. Du Bois, at the First Pan-African Conference meeting in London in 1900, challenged the color line, not as a metaphorical line, but as the formal legal line separating whites from Blacks globally. Remember, at the First Universal Races Congress meeting in 1911 at the University of London, Walther Schücking argued that international law has become universal because states from all races could now be members of the international society. Race before 1945 was an element in legal argumentation, and this continued until decolonization and the proscription of racial discrimination, which began the transition from a color-line to a color-blind international law.

NOTES

1. James Gathii, for example, argues that it would be productive for CRT to take into account TWAIL's emphasis on tracing the racial dimension at the global context at 1642. James Thuo Gathii, "Writing Race and Identity in a Global Context: What CRT and TWAIL Can Learn From Each Other," *UCLA Law Review* 67, no. 6 (April 2021): 1610.

See, among others, E. Tendayi Achiume and Devon W. Carbado, "Critical Race Theory Meets Third World Approaches to International Law," *UCLA Law Review* 67, no. 6 (April 2021): 1462.

2. Particularly important to this chapter is CRT's effort to construct a *"race-conscious and at the same time antiessentialist account"* that uncovers *"how law was a constitutive element of race itself: in other words, how law constructed race."* Also important to this chapter is the idea that *race is both socially constructed and real, "in the sense that there is a material dimension and weight to the experience of being 'raced'... a materiality that in significant ways has been produced and sustained by law."* Kimberlé Crenshaw et al., eds., *Critical Race Theory: The Key Writings That Formed the Movement* (The New Press, 1995), xxv–xxvi.

3. Antony Anghie, "Rethinking International Law: A TWAIL Retrospective," *European Journal of International Law* 34, no. 1 (2023): 7.

4. E. Tendayi Achiume and James Thuo Gathii, "Introduction to the Symposium on Race, Racism, and International Law," *AJIL Unbound* 117 (2023): 26–30. See also other contributions to the symposium.

5. Arnulf Becker Lorca, "Eurocentrism in the History of International Law," in *The Oxford Handbook of the History of International Law*, ed. Bardo Fassbender and Anne Peters (United Kingdom: Oxford University Press, 2012).

6. Arnulf Becker Lorca, "International Law in Latin America or Latin American International Law-Rise, Fall, and Retrieval of a Tradition of Legal Thinking and Political Imagination," *Harvard International Law Journal* 47 (2006): 283.

7. Arnulf Becker Lorca and Amaya Alvez Marin, "Turning International Law Against Indigenous Peoples," in *Latin American International Law*, ed. Alejandro Chehtman et al. (United Kingdom: Oxford University Press, forthcoming).

8. Antony Anghie, *Imperialism, Sovereignty and the Making of International Law* (New York: Cambridge University Press, 2005).

9. Anghie, *Imperialism, Sovereignty and the Making of International Law*; Rose Parfitt, *The Process of International Legal Reproduction: Inequality, Historiography, Resistance* (United Kingdom: Cambridge University Press, 2019).

10. James Gathii, for example, argues that the discourse of civilization was a racialized discourse predicated on white supremacy. Gathii, "Writing Race and Identity," 1641. See also Antony Anghie and B. S. Chimni, "Third World Approaches to International Law and Individual Responsibility in Internal Conflicts," *Chinese Journal of International Law* 2, no. 1 (2003): 85, stating that *"race has played a crucially important role in constructing and defining the other."*

11. Antony Anghie, "Civilization and Commerce: The Concept of Governance in Historical Perspective," *Villanova Law Review* 45, no. 5 (2000): 887.

12. Anghie, "Civilization and Commerce," 887.

13. Anghie, "Civilization and Commerce," 887.

14. In addition to TWAIL, CRT scholars who have ventured into the global domain agree. Francisco Valdes and Sumi Cho, for example, believe that international law originated by the "structural need of (white) colonial elites to control and exploit their (non-white) colonies." International law reproduces the "racial and material project of the (white-identified) Global North and West in which the (colored) Global South is the object of material control and political rule." Francisco Valdes and Sumi Cho, "Critical Race Materialism: Theorizing Justice in the Wake of Global Neoliberalism," *Connecticut Law Review* 43, no. 5 (July 2011): 1567, 1569.

15. For example, in his comprehensive study on the Global South's struggle for racial equality, the renowned human rights scholar William Schabas follows TWAIL, arguing that international law's distinction between civilized peoples and others "was imbued with racist perspectives." William A. Schabas, *The International Legal Order's Colour Line: Racism, Racial Discrimination, and the Making of International Law* (New York: Oxford University Press, 2023), 6. On TWAIL as mainstream, see Arnulf Becker Lorca, "After TWAIL's Success, What Next? Afterword to the Foreword by Antony Anghie," *European Journal of International Law* (December 2023).

16. Christopher Gevers, "'Unwhitening the World': Rethinking Race and International Law," *UCLA Law Review* 67, no. 6 (April 2021): 1658–9. On the view of the "men of 1873" criticized by Gevers, see Martti Koskenniemi, *The Gentle Civilizer of Nations: The Rise and Fall of International Law 1870–1960* (United Kingdom: Cambridge University Press, 2001).

17. Gevers, "Unwhitening the World," 1657–60.

18. Charles Wade Mills, *The Racial Contract* (Ithaca, NY: Cornell University Press, 1997).

19. Gevers, "Unwhitening the World," 1663.

20. Gevers, "Unwhitening the World," 1662.

21. Gevers, "Unwhitening the World," 1660.

22. Gevers, "Unwhitening the World," 1661; Christopher Gevers, "'Land[s] beyond the White World': (Re)imagining the International through Fiction," *Law & Literature* 35, no. 3 (January 2023): 1.

23. Arnulf Becker Lorca, *Mestizo International Law* (United Kingdom: Cambridge University Press, 2014).

24. For example, the book by William Schabas, one of the few monographs on race and international law, focuses on the struggle for racial equality, leaving the rise of a racist international law mostly unstudied, as it follows from the distinction between the civilized and uncivilized. Schabas, *The International Legal Order's Colour Line.*

25. For a structural approach to racism in international legal argument, see another of the few monographs on the topic: Justin Desautels-Stein, *The Right to Exclude: A Critical Race Approach to Sovereignty, Borders, and International Law* (United Kingdom: Oxford University Press, 2023).

26. Aims McGuinness, *Path of Empire: Panama and the California Gold Rush* (Ithaca: Cornell University Press, 2008).

27. Peace, Amity, Navigation and Commerce Treaty, U.S.–New Grenada (Colom.), Dec. 12, 1846, 9 Stat. 881, 18 Stat., T.S. No. 54.

28. Peace, Amity, Navigation and Commerce Treaty, article 13.

29. Peace, Amity, Navigation and Commerce Treaty, article 35.

30. McGuinness, *Path of Empire.*

31. *The Panama Massacre: A Collection of the Principal Evidence and Other Documents, including the Report of Amos B. Corwine, Esq., U.S. Commissioner, the Official Statement of the Governor and the Depositions Taken before the Authorities, Relative to the M. Panama* (New Granada: Star and Herald, 1857): 4. A local bystander that disarmed the drunken traveler, who had shot a fire, is described as a "light-colored native."

32. David Hunter Miller, ed., *Treaties and Other International Acts of the United States of America* (Washington, D.C.: U.S. Government Printing Office, 1931): 667.

33. In Panama and Colón, the ports in the Pacific and Atlantic, independent and neutral municipalities would be created, having jurisdiction over a strip of land each side of the railroad connecting both cities. *Nueva Granada i los Estado Unidos de America, final controversia diplomatica con relacion a los sucesos de Panamá del dia 15 de abril de 1856* (Bogotá: Imprenta del Estado, 1857), 2.

34. *Nueva Granada i los Estado Unidos de America*.

35. *Peace, Amity, Navigation and Commerce Treaty*.

36. Michel Gobat, *Empire by Invitation: William Walker and Manifest Destiny in Central America* (Cambridge, MA: Harvard University Press, 2018).

37. Miller, ed., *Treaties and Other International Acts*, 735.

38. José Manuel Luna, "Declaración de José Manuel Luna," *Gaceta del Estado*, April 26, 1856.

39. Miller, ed., *Treaties and Other International Acts*, 735.

40. In 1851, the liberal government of New Granada granted freedom to slaves, a decision that was then confirmed by the Constitution of 1853, which also eliminated the literacy requirement and introduced universal male suffrage.

41. *The Panama Massacre*, 21.

42. John Adams, *The Works of John Adams, Second President of the United States: with a Life of the Author, Notes and Illustrations*, ed. Charles Francis Adams, vol. 2 (Boston: Little, Brown and Co., 1856). See also John Adams, "To James Lloyd, Quincy 27 March, 1815," in *The Works of John Adams*, vol. 10, 144.

43. Adams, *The Works of John Adams*, vol. 10, 145.

44. John Quincy Adams, *Memoirs of John Quincy Adams, Comprising Portions of His Diary from 1795 to 1848*, ed. Charles Francis Adams, vol. 5 (Philadelphia: J. B. Lippincott & Co., 1874–1877), 176.

45. Lars Schoultz, *Beneath the United States: A History of U.S. Policy toward Latin America* (Cambridge, MA: Harvard University Press, 1998), chap. 1.

46. Schoultz, *Beneath the United States*, chap. 1.

47. Schoultz, *Beneath the United States*, xv. See also Frederick Merk and Lois Bannister Merk, *Manifest Destiny and Mission in American History: A Reinterpretation* (Cambridge, MA: Harvard University Press, 1995), 3.

48. Reginald Horsman, *Race and Manifest Destiny: The Origins of American Racial Anglo-Saxonism* (Cambridge, MA: Harvard University Press, 1981), 1.

49. Anders Stephanson, *Manifest Destiny: American Expansion and the Empire of Right* (New York: Hill and Wang, 1996); Amy S. Greenberg, *Manifest Manhood and the Antebellum American Empire* (New York: Cambridge University Press, 2005); Schoultz, *Beneath the United States*, xvi.

50. Merk and Merk, *Manifest Destiny*.

51. Gene M. Brack, *Mexico Views Manifest Destiny, 1821–1846: An Essay on the Origins of the Mexican War* (Albuquerque: University of New Mexico Press, 1975).

52. "Whereas, by the act of the Republic of Mexico, a state of war exists between that government and the United States." James K. Polk, "A Proclamation. By the President of the United States of America," May 13, 1846, California Historical Society Digital Library, Broadsides, Vault B-056, accessed January 29, 2023, https://digitallibrary.californiahistoricalsociety.org/object/2694.

53. Polk, "A Proclamation. By the President of the United States of America."

54. Julius W. Pratt, "The Origin of 'Manifest Destiny,'" *The American Historical Review* 32, no. 4 (July 1927): 795.

55. John O'Sullivan, "Annexation," *United States Magazine and Democratic Review* 17, no. 1 (July–August 1845): 5–10.

56. "Appendix," *The Congressional Globe*, 29th Congress, 1st Session, House of Representatives (Washington: Blair & Rives, 1845–1846), 10.

57. Before the war and before Mexican independence from Spain, America expanded into the Viceroyalty of New Spain by treaty. In the Adams–Onís Treaty of 1819, the United States purchased from Spain East and West Florida. In 1845, after Mexican independence but before the war, American expanded into Mexican territories through the annexation of Texas, which had declared independence from Mexico. The peace treaty ending the war, the Treaty of Guadalupe Hidalgo of 1848, sanctioned the outcome of the war and American expansion up to the Rio Grande/Río Bravo, annexing California and Nevada, most of Arizona and Utah, and parts of New Mexico, Wyoming, and Colorado. Finally, the United States pushed southwards the Arizona and New Mexico borders with Mexico, adding a strip of land purchased by the treaty of 1853, the Gadsden Purchase, known in Mexico as the Venta de La Mesilla.

58. Merk and Merk, *Manifest Destiny*.

59. Merk and Merk, *Manifest Destiny*, 24.

60. O'Sullivan, "Annexation," 9.

61. John O'Sullivan, "The True Title," (editorial) *New York Morning News*, December 27, 1845.

62. Emer de Vattel, *The Law of Nations, or, Principles of the Law of Nature, Applied to the Conduct and Affairs of Nations and Sovereigns,* book I, chapter VII, §81; and book I, chapter XVII, §209.

63. de Vattel, *The Law of Nations*, book I, chapter XVII, §203.

64. de Vattel, *The Law of Nations*, book I, chapter VII, §81.

65. Also here Vattel makes reference to Anglo-America: "We do not, therefore, deviate from the views of nature, in confining the Indians within narrower limits. However, we cannot help praising the moderation of the English Puritans who first settled in New England; who, notwithstanding their being furnished with a charter from their sovereign, purchased of the Indians the land of which they intended to take possession. This laudable example was followed by William Penn, and the colony of Quakers that he conducted to Pennsylvania." de Vattel, *The Law of Nations,* book I, chapter XVIII, §209.

66. Andrew Fitzmaurice, *Sovereignty, Property and Empire 1500–2000* (New York: Cambridge University Press, 2014).

67. O'Sullivan, "The True Title."

68. "The Anglo-Saxon foot is already on its borders." O'Sullivan, "Annexation," 9.

69. John O'Sullivan, "Territorial Aggrandizement," *United States Magazine and Democratic Review* 17, no. 88 (October 1845): 243–48.

70. "Idle Spaniards have but poorly fulfilled their mission. They have neither civilized nor christianized the people . . . The native Indians have been allowed to remain in their passive state of idleness." John O'Sullivan, "The War," *United States Magazine and Democratic Review* 20 (February 1847): 100.

71. In 1837, in the inaugural editorial for the Democratic Review, O'Sullivan writes: "Under the banner of the democratic principle, which is borne onward by an unseen hand

of Providence, to lead our race toward the high destinies of which every human soul contains the God-implanted germ." John L. O'Sullivan, "Introduction," *The United States Magazine and Democratic Review* 1 (1837): 1–15, 9.

72. O'Sullivan, "The War," 100.

73. O'Sullivan, "True Title," and similarly "Annexation," 5.

74. O'Sullivan, "Annexation," 9.

75. O'Sullivan, "True Title."

76. Winthrop continued: "Manifest destiny reminds me of the titles invoked by Spain and Portugal in the 16th c. to North America to which Francis I replied asking to the see the clause in Adams's Will," Winthrop adds, "maybe the Oregon clause can be found in the cave where the Mormon Testament has been discovered, if so he would withdraw his opposition." "Appendix," *The Congressional Globe*, 29th Congress, 1st Session, House of Representatives, 99–100.

77. "Here we have as the bone of our contention, a vast and vacant territory, thousands of miles distant from both countries, entirely capable of division . . . a territory the sovereignty of which might remain in abeyance for a half century longer without serious inconvenience or detriment to anybody." "Appendix," *The Congressional Globe*, 29th Congress, 1st Session, House of Representatives, 99.

78. "Appendix," *The Congressional Globe*, 29th Congress, 1st Session, House of Representatives, 10.

79. "The representative system as practically enjoyed in this country, will admit of an indefinite extension of territory." O'Sullivan, "Territorial Aggrandizement," 244.

80. O'Sullivan, "Annexation," 7.

81. O'Sullivan, "The War," 100.

82. O'Sullivan, "Territorial Aggrandizement," 245.

83. "How should we estimate the fitness of the Mexican people to enter into the enjoyment of our political institutions . . . are they a valuable acquisition to us in any respect? . . . Mexican vote would be substantially below our national average both in purity and intelligence. The Mexican people are unaccustomed to the duties of self-government, and for years to come must travel up through numberless processes of political emancipation before they can dispense with restraints which the Saxon family threw off more than three hundred years ago." O'Sullivan. "Territorial Aggrandizement," 243–48, 245.

84. "Attempt to raise [Blacks] to a political equality with the white race, has not succeeded in practice in the States where it has been carried into effect in theory." O'Sullivan, "European Views of American Democracy-No. II," *The United States Magazine and Democratic Review* 2 (July 1838): 337–57, 352.

85. O'Sullivan, "Annexation," 7. The incendiary bigotry of the whole paragraph might be worth quoting:

"Much gained for the cause of the eventual voluntary abolition of slavery, that it should have been thus drained off towards the only outlet which appeared to furnish much probability of it the ultimate disappearance of the negro race from our borders. The Spanish-Indian-American populations of Mexico, Central America and South America, afford the only receptacle capable of absorbing that race whenever we shall be prepared to slough it off . . . to remove it from the midst of our own. Themselves already of mixed and confused blood, and free from the 'prejudices' which among us so insuperably forbid the social amalgamation which can alone elevate the Negro race out of a virtually servile degradation even though legally free, the regions occupied by those populations must strongly attract the black race in that direction; and as soon as the destined hour of emancipation shall arrive, will relieve the question of one of its worst difficulties, if not absolutely the greatest."

86. Schoultz, *Beneath the United States*, 46–47; Richard Griswold del Castillo, *The Treaty of Guadalupe Hidalgo: A Legacy of Conflict* (Norma, OK: University of Oklahoma Press, 1990), 3.

87. The statement in the context of Texas by Charles Jared Ingersoll, representative for Pennsylvania as chairman of the committee of foreign affairs (February 3, 1845), was quoted many times during debates on the Mexican–American War, see, e.g., to argue that the intention was never to reach Rio Grande. "Appendix," *The Congressional Globe*, 29th Congress, 1st Session, House of Representatives, 949.

88. John C. Calhoun, "Speech on the War with Mexico," in *The Papers of John C. Calhoun, Volume XXV, 1847–1848*, ed. Clyde N. Wilson et al. (Columbia, SC: University of South Carolina Press, 1999), 71.

89. Calhoun, "Speech on the War with Mexico," 64.

90. Calhoun, "Speech on the War with Mexico," 95. Regardless of political differences in this regard Whigs were similar, opposing expansion, especially when Mexico was in question. Merk and Merk, *Manifest Destiny*, 39. For example, Millard Fillmore opposed expansion as it involved the expansion of slavery, justifying the opposition to the incorporation of Cuba as bringing a population of a different national stock. Schoultz, *Beneath the United States*, 51.

91. Becker Lorca, *Mestizo International Law*.

92. "The individual abroad find himself in legal relation to two countries, the country of which he is a citizen, and the country in which he resides or establishes his business.... The common consent of nations has established a certain standard of conduct by which a state must be guided in the treatment of aliens." Edwin Borchard, *The Diplomatic Protection of Citizens Abroad, or, The Law of International Claims* (New York: Banks Law Publishing Company, 1915), v.

93. Borchard, *The Diplomatic Protection of Citizens*, v.

94. Borchard, *The Diplomatic Protection of Citizens*, v.

95. Edwin Borchard, "The 'Minimum Standard' of the Treatment of Aliens," *Proceedings of the American Society of International Law at Its Annual Meeting (1921–1969)* 33 (April 27–29, 1939): 53.

96. Borchard, *The Diplomatic Protection of Citizens*, v.

97. Christopher Gevers, "Unwhitening the World."

98. Borchard, *The Diplomatic Protection of Citizens*, 46.

99. Borchard, *The Diplomatic Protection of Citizens*, 46.

100. Borchard, *The Diplomatic Protection of Citizens*, 102–4.

101. "We are unfortunately too familiar with complaints of the delay and inefficiency of the courts in the South American republics. We must, however, continue to repose confidence in their independence and integrity, or we must take the broad ground that these states are like those of oriental semi-civilized countries." "Note from Mr. Seward, Secretary of State, to Mr. Burton, Minister to Colombia (April 27, 1866)," in *A Digest of International Law: As Embodied in Diplomatic Discussions, Treaties and Other International Agreements*, John Bassett Moore and Francis Wharton (Washington: Government Printing Office, 1906), 660.

102. Borchard, *The Diplomatic Protection of Citizens*, 106.

103. Borchard, *The Diplomatic Protection of Citizens*, 106.

104. The weakness of peripheral states' formal sovereignty was not the weakness of international law in front of material power, but a legal attribute of peripheral sovereignty, in which formal sovereignty as autonomy depended on the respect of international limits to jurisdictional independence, limits to a peripheral state's substantive sovereignty.

105. See Borchard, "The 'Minimum Standard' of the Treatment of Aliens," 54. And in general Borchard, *The Diplomatic Protection of Citizens*, 105.

106. "A State, when charged with a breach of its international obligations with regard to the treatment of aliens, cannot validly plead that according to its Municipal law and practice the act complained of does not involve discrimination against aliens as compared with nationals. This applies in particular to the question of the treatment of the persons of aliens. It has been repeatedly laid down that there exists in this matter a minimum standard of civilization, and that a State which fails to measure up to that standard incurs international liability." Lauterpacht Oppenheim, *International law*, vol. I, 5th ed. (New York and London: Longmans, Green & Co., 1937), 283.

107. Renowned French international lawyer Georges Scelle, for example, discussing the involvement of the League of Nations Council in the controversy around the expropriation by the government of Rumania of land owned by Hungarian optants noted that the Permanent Court had in analogous cases decided that "foreigners have right to better treatment than nationals every time that they are treated contrary to a common law." Georges Scelle, "Le litige roumano-hongrois devant le conseil de la Société des nations," Genève: s.n., 1927. That Scelles is only one among many other continental Europeans with similar views shows this was not a specifically American or Anglo view but a view shared among Western international lawyers.

108. Becker Lorca, *Mestizo international law*.

109. See Francisco Bilbao, *Iniciativa de la América: idea de un congreso federal de las repúblicas* (Paris: Impr. de d'Aubusson y Kugelmann, 1856), 33 and 35. In a "Post-Dictum" Bilbao explains that the published text was presented to a group of citizens of the Republics of the South [of the Americas] clarifying that the idea of the Confederation of the America of the South and the values it embodies will make Yankee individualism retreat in Panama.

110. On the threat of the United States of America and Bilbao, I am following: Arturo Ardao, *Génesis de la idea y el nombre de América latina* (Caracas, 1980); Miguel Rojas Mix, "Bilbao y el hallazgo de América latina: Unión continental, socialista y libertaria," *Cahiers du Monde Hispanique et Luso-Brasilien-Caravelle* 46 (1986): 35–47; and Aims McGuinness, "Searching for 'Latin America': Race and Sovereignty in the Americas in the 1850s," in *Race and Nation in Modern Latin America,* ed. Nancy P. Appelbaum et al. (Chapel Hill and London: University of North Carolina Press, 2003), 87–107. See also Álvaro García San Martín, "Francisco Bilbao, entre el proyecto latinoamericano y el gran molusco", *Latinoamérica: Revista de Estudios Latinoamericanos* 56 (January 2013): 141–62.

111. Before the *intervención norteamericana*, the American intervention as the Mexican–American War is known in Spanish, there was the First French Intervention in Mexico, the Pastry War, and after the Mexican–American War there was the Second French Intervention. On the war, see Josefina Vázquez, *La intervención norteamericana, 1846–1848* (Mexico City: Secretaría de Relaciones Exteriores de México, 1997).

112. Bilbao, *Iniciativa de la América*, 7 and 25.

113. Bilbao, *Iniciativa de la América*, 11 and 13. "The Andean mountain range is the image of the future colossus...[it] will rise higher than the volcanoes not only the traveler's lighthouse, but the splendor of justice. Such an image, such a destiny, such is our duty,

Americans ... it is the pure inheritance of history ... the destiny of the freed man, that should move us to manifest a moral creation yet to be known, worthy of having this continent as a pedestal." Bilbao, *Iniciativa de la América*, 7–8.

114. "The United States ... aspires to ... the domination of Yankee individualism." Bilbao, *Iniciativa de la América*, 10–11 and 36.

115. Bilbao, *Iniciativa de la América*, 15.

116. Bilbao, *Iniciativa de la América*, 11, 13, and 16.

117. Bilbao, *Iniciativa de la América*, 26–8.

118. José María Torres Caicedo, "Las dos Américas," *El Correo de Ultramar* 16 (París: X. de Lasalle y Mèlan, February 15, 1857).

Mas aislados se encuentran, desunidos,	But they are isolated, disunited,
Esos pueblos nacidos para aliarse:	Those peoples born to ally:
La unión es su deber, su ley amarse:	Union is their duty, their law to love each other:
Igual origen tienen y misión;	Equal origin they have and a mission;
La raza de la América latina,	The race of Latin America,
Al frente tiene la sajona raza,	In front it has the Saxon race,
Enemiga mortal que ya amenaza	A deadly enemy that already threatens
Su libertad destruir y su pendón.	To destroy its liberty and its banner.

119. José María Torres Caicedo, *Unión latino-americana, pensamiento de Bolívar para formar una liga americana; su origen y sus desarrollos y estudio sobre la gran cuestión que tanto interesa a los estados débiles, a saber: ¿Un gobierno legítimo es responsable por los daños y perjuicios ocasionados a los extranjeros por las facciones?* (Paris: Rosa y Bouret, 1865).

120. For a history of these doctrines see Jorge Esquirol, "Latin America," in *The Oxford handbook of the history of international law*, ed. Bardo Fassbender and Anne Peters (United Kingdom: Oxford University Press, 2012), 578–603.

121. Becker Lorca and Alvez Marin, "Turning International Law Against Indigenous Peoples."

CHAPTER THREE

RACIAL PANICS AND THE MAKING OF (WHITE) INTERNATIONAL LAW

Frédéric Mégret

INTRODUCTION: FEARING RACE/RACIALIZING FEAR IN INTERNATIONAL LAW

One of the crucial questions to be addressed in the contemporary study of how race continues to structure international law is how that ordering role maintains itself despite international law's clear, even if superficial, commitment to an anti-racist agenda. Following the work of the likes of Musab Younis, this chapter is thus part of a broader interrogation on "how we arrived at our contemporary legal order—officially equalized, yet deeply stratified in ways that reflect its colonial origin."[1] The intuition is that the intersection of CRT and Third World Approaches to International Law (TWAIL)[2] provides a key bridge to better understand the racializing components of continued imperial projects and the colonial dimension of racial ordering.

The chapter's thesis is that the relative invisibility yet pervasiveness of race in international law lies in the fact that, whilst race cannot truly be articulated in contemporary international law, it simultaneously continues to subtly manifest itself in its structures through what I describe as "racial panics." The notion of racial panics borrows from the work of Stan Cohen on "moral panics," which itself drew on the sociology of deviance and social control. For Cohen, writing in the '60s in the UK, "mod" and "rocker" youth subcultures created a moral panic understood as occurring when a "condition, episode, person or group of persons emerges to become defined as a threat to societal values and interests."[3]

The notion of a "racial panic discourse" has since been proposed by Brian Gabrial to describe the nineteenth-century "partisan press era." The basic idea in Gabrial's framework is that "elites, including editors and white slave owners, consciously and unconsciously exacerbated or diminished the threat of slave revolt as a means to maintain power."[4] It is part of a broader strand of scholarship in cultural theory, sociology, or political science that has long emphasized the centrality of white anxiety and its encouragement as a fundamental building block of racist structures.[5] A racial panic is a form of moral panic that specifically focuses not so much on deviance as on race, although the two are often mutually reinforcing. Not all moral panics have a racial element and not all racial panics exhibit elements of moral panic, but the two often subtly overlap. Portraying what are really racial panics as moral panics, in fact, helps to obfuscate the former's fundamental nature, whereas emphasizing the racial element shows how moral panics often coincide with a construction of deviancy as racialized.

A racial panic, then, crystallizes anxiety about the challenge that the rise of certain racial groups creates for dominant groups, especially when it is mediated by demands for equality. Abolitionism was arguably the original racial panic, prompting fears of violence and insecurity stoked by anti-abolitionists and extending all the way to the twenty-first century.[6] The emancipation of African Americans has since been historically met by racial panics specifically directed at the Black cultural repertoire, including most notoriously blues and jazz or the use of marijuana.[7] Fear of crime has often been triggered as part of thinly veiled racialist agendas that emphasize the insecurity of law-abiding citizens.[8] Post-9/11, one witnesses elements of both a moral panic (the fear of terrorism as an absolute danger) and a racial panic (the terrorist is not just the terrorist, they are the racialized Islamic peril), such that terrorism ends up disproportionately setting domestic and international agendas. More generally, immigration has provided a seemingly endless source of moral and racial panics, against the background of recurring fears about demographic "replacement."[9]

The connection between racial panics and the law is not immediately obvious, and the latter, operating at some distance from political pathos, may appear removed from the effects of fear. Yet, as this chapter will argue, the law is constantly called upon to amplify or resist racial panics. This is because, under liberal conditions, the law's racial blindness, entrenching as it does historical patterns of discrimination, makes it one of the last refuges of the maintenance of the status quo. The force of racial panics, specifically, is that they operate in a liminal space, allowing law to proclaim its innocence of the stigma of racism whilst continuing to mediate demands for racial ordering through the continued inertia of legal structures. Instead of "moral panics," in fact, one might speak of "legal panics," understood as the sense among the legal establishment that the law is going to be overturned by new racial upstarts, unaware of its delicate balances and committed, even, to shredding it apart. Legal panics aim to reassert not so much any particular content of the law, as a sense of the ultimate authority in society to ascertain and assert its content.

Finally, whilst the history of moral and racial panics has typically been a domestic one, many moral panics and particularly those with racial overtones have often espoused transnational lines,[10] thus further inscribing the register of fear in the construction of the "international community" and international law. Lauren Benton and Lisa Ford, in particular, have emphasized the law's "uneven tempo" as making "the lived experience of colonial and imperial power Kafkaesque," whilst producing "legal panics" that manifest themselves suddenly in "the exercise of arbitrary legal authority in colonies (fast justice)" to counter the perceived breakdown of metropolitan authority, notably in relation to slavery.[11] Although this approach concerns itself with quite a different configuration, it echoes the basic intuition that international law is often made to play catchup in knee-jerk fashion when its authority is contested. It suggests that, even in what Benton and Ford describe as its local-despot restraining modality (e.g., limiting "excessively" harsh punishment of slaves), imperial law was constantly engaged in a sort of race against time to ensure that change did not occur on terms other than its own.

Racial panics, then, should be understood as describing the context within which international law has occasionally operated and which it has periodically been asked to mediate. No straightforward or linear relationship will be suggested between racial panics and international law: sometimes racial panics will have been at the forefront of international legal conversations; sometimes they will have formed more of an unstated background that helps to understand its evolution and its role; and sometimes they will have been on everyone's mind as, literally and unapologetically, a conversation about race. But their unmistakable imprint lies in their ability to overdetermine certain international legal developments in ways that, crucially, maintain the racial status quo when it might be on the brink of being overturned. They do so notably by distracting from the specific role of race in harm;[12] abandoning certain issues to the vagaries of a domestic law deeply tainted by projects of racialization;[13] or more straightforwardly continuing to foment projects of paranoia as in the case of the so-called "war on terror," ongoing anxieties about the global migration legal architecture,[14] or the fight against the new "pirates."[15]

I will argue that the Haitian Revolution is the very original racial panic in international law, but also suggest that these have emerged at remarkably regular intervals and allowed for the reimposition of the basic ideological conditions under which international law exists by speaking to a sense of white vulnerability. The aim of this chapter is less to engage each of these instances in historical depth than to excavate what they have in common and, in the process, to question how international law can be simultaneously thoroughly anti-racist and thoroughly racist (perhaps along the lines of what Ritu Mathur describes as the "sly civility of . . . racial etiquette").[16]

This chapter suggests that three major racial panics have historically structured the rise of international law: fears about "racialized sovereignty" (the notion that racialized peoples will master their own political destiny and participate as such in the international system); fears about "racialized violence" (that in the process and as a result they will access the violent resources of the state and use these to challenge the racial status quo); and fears about "racialized mobility" (that, in addition, they will migrate and disrupt majority-white nationhood). These are distinct but are also intimately bound together and activate deep-seated anxieties about how international law might undo its racist legacies without undoing itself entirely; or, rather, how international law might continue to be committed to forms of white privilege whilst being seen to proclaim racial equality. The fear at the heart of racial panics, then, is not the fear of the racially oppressed but, crucially, the fear of the racially oppressing, those whose racial positioning relies most on the maintenance of the international legal order as it is.

This chapter is thus a contribution to the broader effort in identifying the deep complicity of international legal institutions with racialization, beyond the better known cases of slavery, colonialism, or apartheid.[17] Rather than relying on what might be described as "racial formalism" (the tendency to take international law at its word in matters of race), the chapter will resort methodologically to a form of "racial realism," understood as an effort to capture international law not only from the perspective of what it says but also what it actually expresses about race. I conclude by discussing briefly how, in late modernity, the traditional conservative effort to maintain the racial status quo gradually gives way to a radical anxiety about the whiteness-decentering propensities of new and racially disruptive international legal practices.

HAITI AND THE FEAR OF RACIALIZED SOVEREIGNTY

Haiti provides an early parable for a deep and abiding fear, that of racialized sovereignty, which structured international law in the nineteenth century and beyond. The access to sovereignty of slaves constituted as a republic crystallized early anxieties about the near-monopoly of "whiteness" over sovereignty. The French and many others in the Western world were genuinely shocked by the manifestation of political agency of slaves, an agency that they had deemed racially impossible. This original fear of racialized sovereignty would extend later on to a more general wariness with broader racialized participation in international affairs as well as concerns about the ability to perpetuate Western economic domination that was typically framed in racial terms.

THE TRANSNATIONAL DIMENSIONS OF HAITIAN INDEPENDENCE

The independence of Haiti must be read against the background of the French Revolution and the short-lived emancipation it gave rise to. This was a case where freedoms briefly granted were quickly withdrawn, creating an intense feeling of aggravation among the slaves of the French Empire. In 1804, Haiti eventually proclaimed its independence after years of slave revolts. The event was of historic proportions. It created a ripple of fear not only among slave owners in Santo Domingo, Guadeloupe, and Martinique,[18] but also in the US.[19] However, twenty years later, France had still not recognized that independence, and other countries refrained from doing so as well. The failure to recognize Haiti rendered it vulnerable to an invasion by France. It also hurt Haiti's "dignity."[20] Lengthy but fruitless negotiations ensued.[21]

A few things are worth underscoring about this process. First, France was relentless for decades in its wish to reestablish the plantation system including slavery and, failing that, to recognize Haiti only in exchange for it becoming a protectorate. Former plantation owners argued vociferously that the racial composition of Haiti barred it from responsible sovereignty. Second, despite conditions of enmity or at least imperial rivalry prevailing at various times, France, England, the US, and Latin American republics were very much united in initially not recognizing Haiti and acknowledging the primacy of France's claim to it. In fact, the US under George Washington had, alongside France and other European powers, actively participated in the suppression of slave revolts on Saint-Domingue as early as 1791.[22] Third, the long failure to recognize Haiti was in contrast to the fact that the Latin American republics and the US itself had promptly been recognized upon acceding to independence.

The racial implications of Haiti's independence, moreover, were not lost in the US, a republic founded on slavery. The emergence of Haiti, just as it acted as a beacon in the Black diaspora, "sparked furious white range and inspired an unrelenting fear of a sovereign Black republic."[23] A source of inspiration for slaves and free African Americans, the celebration of its example nonetheless remained a sporadic and dangerous affair.[24] The peril to the US model of slave-based capital accumulation was obvious. Thomas Jefferson warned that a Haitian victory would lead to the expulsion of whites from the West Indies as part of an early-nineteenth-century hysteria in which Republicans "could not countenance the possibility. Free black people having their own country and trading with the United States."[25] As Senator George Logan put it, "Is it sound policy to cherish the black population of St. Domingo . . . whilst we have a similar population in our Southern states?"[26] Similar warnings were heard in England, where the independence of Haiti came to be seen as threatening the prosperity of the region.

International law was no doubt mobilized in the ensuing debates. It was invoked by third states both to shun and engage Haiti but in ways that were ultimately wary of normalizing its sovereignty. The argument of Republicans, as portrayed by one of its Federalist opponents, Senator Samuel White, was that "the people of St. Domingo can be considered only as revolted slaves, or at best, as French subjects now in a state of rebellion; that they are nationally in no respect separated from France;

that to trade with them is a violation of the laws of nations, and that we have no right to do so."[27] In fact, the argument suggested that the Blacks of Santo Domingo were not like previously emancipated Latin American colonies but rather "a totally new, unprecedented case, and in this manner ... out of the humane provisions of the laws of nations."[28] Contra this argument, White invoked Emer de Vattel to the effect that the Haitians were belligerents in a civil war and not merely rebels leading an insurgency, who fought for a cause that rightly divided them from France and which should allow the US to trade with them.[29] Although the Federalists argued in favor of trade with Haiti, therefore, they hardly did so out of solidarity with slave emancipation—wary as they were of the effects it might have on slavery at home—but on the basis of a pragmatic understanding that trade with the new republic could be advantageous, that it would occur within the US's natural sphere of competence, and that there was no reason to do France's bidding.

These arguments foreshadowed subsequent reservations about recognizing a by then clearly independent Haiti that had overthrown the French yoke. The case for the US not even contemplating recognition was made by one senator from Missouri: "We buy coffee from her, and pay for it; but we interchange no consuls or ministers. We receive no mulatto consuls or black ambassadors. And why? Because the peace of eleven states in this Union will not permit the fruits of a successful Negro insurrection to be exhibited among them."[30] Despite many petitions in favor of the recognition of the young republic and considerable bilateral trade, repeated initiatives in the US to send a chargé d'affaires to Port-au-Prince were rebuffed. European countries, including France and the United Kingdom, were somewhat quicker in recognizing Haiti (respectively in 1825 and 1838), but it was only by 1860 that most Western powers had grudgingly entered diplomatic relations (1864 for the US).[31] Even on the cusp of recognition, one Kentucky senator insisted that "if a full-blooded negro were sent in that capacity from either of those countries [note: Haiti and Liberia], by the laws of nations he could demand that he be received precisely on the same terms of equality with the white representatives from the Powers of the earth composed of white people."[32]

For the most part, the independence of Haiti was subsequently not only occulted from the broader historiography of international relations, but its implications for international law have been systematically ignored. Haiti existed as an incongruity in the nineteenth century within an international system devoted to further colonialism, notably in Africa. International law did not prohibit its recognition, but it certainly did not require it. Contemporaries recognized clearly that its failure to obtain prompt recognition was a function of it having been liberated by Black rather than Creole populations.[33] France ensured that Haiti was at best "manumitted" in exchange for repayment of its "debt," effectively re-enslaving it as a commercial colony as the price to pay for its formal "independence."[34] Despite all its efforts to prove that it satisfied the "standard of civilization" (notably its willingness to abide by international law including when it came to treaties), Haiti was, unlike the US and the Latin American republics after their own independence, repeatedly consigned to the status of a quasi-state. This was evidence that "civilization" was effectively equated with "whiteness."[35]

Going forward, the sovereignty of Haiti would be "upheld" only at the cost of its occupation, notably by the US, reproducing a pattern inaugurated from the outset through France's merely conditional recognition.[36] Haiti heralded a series of technologies (mandates, trusteeship, conditionality, the "Washington consensus," or the "shock doctrine"), all embedded in international law, whose net effect has been to simultaneously constitute and immediately qualify the sovereignty of racialized peoples. Although other states such as Japan and China may have fared better in terms of the promptness with which their full sovereignty was eventually recognized, there is no doubt that their accession to sovereignty was also met by disbelief and a renewal of white anxieties about displacement of the West's centrality.[37] Yet others like Abyssinia witnessed the continued hold of racialized ideas about the "standard of civilization" relied upon (notably through the invocation of their supposed continued ties to slavery) to delay and minimize their full recognition as members of the international community.[38]

ANXIETIES ABOUT PARTICIPATION IN INTERNATIONAL AFFAIRS

A particular variant of this concern with racialized sovereignty arose in relation to the growing prospect that it would afford an opportunity for participation in international affairs, especially in a context of emerging international organizations. This concern was expressed on the fringe of what would gradually emerge as an irresistible movement of participation following decolonization, but it long crystallized a lingering ressentiment about this evolution. Although the admission of Ethiopia was a remarkable development in itself, for example, the British foreign secretary had complained privately that "if Abyssinia is admitted there will be no future ground for excluding anybody."[39] He further noted that one had to take into account "the level of public opinion in each of the Member States" on the question of whether "Abyssinia was in a position to make a worthy contribution to the League."[40] Sir Joseph Cook, head of the Australian delegation at the League, was worried that Abyssinia's presence might create "anomalies . . . if the countries whose internal conditions are similar to those territories under the mandates were called upon to sit on a footing of equality with the members of the responsible administration of the mandated territories."[41]

Japan did fight for the "racial equality" clause in Versailles, but it fought largely for itself (in the same way India after the Second World War fought first and foremost for the Indian minority in South Africa).[42] When it failed to obtain what it had hoped for, it quickly settled for its status as a quasi-Western power.[43] What consideration there was for Japan, moreover, was hardly extended to other, particularly African, states at the League, against the background of emerging fears that non-white states might resist US influence.[44] In 1919, Senator Reed emphasized that:

> When the members of the League of nations meet about the council table there will 15 men representing white nations and 17 men representing black, brown, yellow, and red races; and that among the nations classified as dark the average of the dark-skinned people compared with the total population is nearly 9 to 1. It is also shown that among these races the degree of illiteracy is astonishingly high.[45]

Reed reserved particular scorn for Liberia "that is a vote equal to the vote of the United States":

> Here, then, we have a total population of 50,000 civilized or semicivilized negroes against which is to be balanced 1,950,000 savages ... The Republic from the first has been a joke nation. ... No better commentary on the absurdity of the right of such a nation to sit in the council of the world ... can be found than the fact that, although the American negroes have been frequently importuned to emigrate to that country, they have consistently refused.[46]

The senator then repeatedly addressed "men of the South," emphasizing the deep incompatibility between the treatments of Black people in the South and the idea that Liberia would be given a voice in the world's destiny.

Notably, the response by pro-League senators was that in effect both Haiti and Liberia were already "practically under the protection of the United States, being financed by the United States, coming into the League, it is not likely that we will suffer very much from them."[47] This was hardly a principled defense of their equality as states. Indeed, US administrations, as Robert Knox has shown, were happy to uphold Haiti's membership of the League on the understanding that it was little more than a client state anyhow whose sovereignty was at America's discretion.[48]

Hints of how racism subtly and not so subtly influenced the treatment of racialized participation in international debates can be gathered throughout the history of the League of Nations. Italian fascists described their conquest of Ethiopia as part of an effort to bring (fascist) civilization to an African backwater; when Haile Selassie came to denounce the aggression of his country at the League of Nations—an aggression specifically vindicating the designs of a racist regime that engaged in pogroms and racial segregation—he was loudly booed by Italian delegates; and the League itself then denied him a loan to finance a resistance movement, even as it quickly scaled back sanctions against Italy.

Although harder to come by in an era in which racism had become increasingly taboo (aside from Western support for the South African apartheid regime), lingering concerns with the direction in which a more racially diversified UN membership might take international law can be detected below the surface. A subtle exclusionary drive is evident in the marginalization of early claims made at the United Nations by African Americans,[49] the lack of success of Liberia and Ethiopia in pressing claims against South Africa's mandate in Southwest Africa,[50] or the evisceration of the colonial edge in the notion of "jus cogens" or "erga omnes" norms,[51] all of which suggest the reassertion of who, ultimately, should have a say in the governance of world affairs. It may be, although this is a difficult argument to prove, that wariness with the increasingly diverse racial composition of the General Assembly has gradually precipitated its irrelevance, whether through resort to the Security Council or to parallel ad hoc global governance organs.

FEARS FOR WESTERN ECONOMIC INTERESTS

A third theme related to fear about racialized sovereignty is its strong relatedness to the security of Western investments, despite this dimension being consistently obscured.[52] Recall that the supposed unwillingness of natives to exploit the land[53] or engage in open commercial relations[54] with newly arrived European colonizers had historically been a key justification for colonization. The perceived inability of the indigenous populations of Africa in particular to make the most of the wealth beneath their feet was excoriated by early colonialists. As the famous explorer Henry Morton Stanley put it about the Congo, in an appeal that would eventually be heard by his powerful patron, King Léopold II of Belgium:

> A five-mile march across that intervening stretch of plain between Kinshasa and Kintamo may cause our Europeans to reflect upon the prodigious waste which this madcap population by whom they are surrounded is guilty of. Eight hundred muscular slaves, retainers, followers of the nine Kintamo chiefs, absolutely doing nothing. Nay, they are almost starving, only one day from it at least, and here, round about them, are nearly 50,000 square acres of the richest alluvium it would be possible to find in any part of the world![55]

As the West's colonial stranglehold eventually weakened, inversely, so did concerns about the perennity of racialized exploitation as an economic venture. International law was called upon to ensure that the sovereignty of newly decolonized states was, specifically, not exercised to the detriment of large-scale investments in the Global South. These demands, in turn, often operated against the background of racist tropes and reactivated racial panics about spoliation at the hands of former slaves.

Haiti remains perhaps the starkest illustration of the fear that independence of racialized colonies would be ruinous for the nations of the North. On July 11, 1825, fourteen French ships and their squadron of five hundred cannons threatened Haiti and forced its president, Jean-Pierre Boyer, to sign a treaty with Charles X, King of France. The latter recognized the independence of the old colony in exchange for a colossal 150 million gold franc indemnity. The indemnity was meant to compensate plantation owners deprived of their lands. In effect, it sent a very stern signal that decolonization, especially by slaves, would occur, if at all, at a steep cost. The indemnity would be used as a pretext by the US and Latin American states to refuse to recognize Haiti. It is important to note that France in this context did not so much recognize Haitian independence as it "granted" it.[56]

Importantly, the Haitian government and some of its officials invoked the vernacular of international law to try and make the case against onerous reparations.[57] But international law was certainly very much deployed to make the case for the perennity of Haitian debt. When it came to the very principle of onerous compensation for the losses of slave owners, French officials insisted that although the French state itself could divest itself of its sovereignty on Saint Domingue, "les principes les plus élémentaires du droit des gens interdisaient de toucher à des droits privés." (the most elementary principles of the law of nations forbade touching private rights)[58] This was even justified as being in the interest of encouraging Haiti to, henceforth, respect international treaties as part of the standard of civilization. It essentially reproduced the fundamental structure of slavery by suggesting that slaves had never rightly "owned themselves" and therefore Haiti was liable for their self-emancipation.

Beyond the special circumstances of Haitian independence, a consistent theme since has been the reaction to expropriations of Western investments by the newly independent nations of the South. The fear, expressed early notably vis-à-vis Mexico, was that revolutionary violence, often with a strong anti-imperialist outlook, would forcefully dispossess American and European nationals of their property, creating waves of panic among capitalist entrepreneurs in Latin America. Throughout, US oilmen in Mexico, for example, who "valued the Mexican mestizos about as little as the African Americans back home,"[59] sustained a continuous campaign to encourage the US government to intervene. Although more senior captains of industry were reluctant to publicly agitate for such intervention, "those in the field were like colonialists. They despised the Mexicans. They thought them weak and bumbling, incapable of resisting American fighting men, and in great need of being bossed around by the Anglo race."[60]

In 1916, to justify the continued presence of US troops on Mexican territory to fight Pancho Villa,[61] the US officially complained that "vast properties developed by American capital and enterprise have been destroyed or rendered nonproductive."[62] In turn, the American government "requested in the strongest terms that the de facto Government . . . furnish the protection, which international obligation imposes, to American interests."[63] The international law of the protection of aliens thus emerged in part as a commitment to protect the perennity of Western investments. It would impose a continued burden of racial condescension on nations in the semi-periphery replicating, when it came to investments in commodities, the fundamental structure of Haitian debt bondage, to which was added contempt for local legal systems and their ability to provide worthwhile remedies.

In the decolonization era, major corporate interests such as Belgium's Union Minière du Haut-Katanga (UMHK) would continue to work actively to fend off the inevitable and delay independence, often on the basis or for the purpose of racist policies. The UMHK even encouraged secession in newly independent Congo with a view to create a quasi-apartheid state to secure its investments.[64] Similarly, the Anglo-Iranian Oil Company, an extremely profitable corporation, behaved as effectively a segregated "state within the state" and consistently refused demands for the Iranization of personnel based on "a strong sense of their own superiority and the incapability of the Iranians" and the feeling that "if they allowed greater Iranian participation, then no one would be able to work the heating in the AIOC's offices, let alone operate the oil industry."[65] In other words, the possibility of decolonization was held up by initiatives emphasizing both the need to protect investments and the general unworthiness of locals to take their economic fate in their own hands.

When preventing nationalization became all but impossible, imperial interests turned to exacting the most onerous possible compensation, a position powerfully mediated by international law despite decolonization.[66] Local judicial systems were typically frowned upon as incapable of guaranteeing the sort of "minimum standards" required by the West. This early era can be seen as having laid the basis for future developments in the international protection of investments.[67] Hints of the impact of racial attentions can also be garnered from the reaction to the promotion of such radical agendas as the New International Economic Order or even the notion of "common heritage of mankind" in the law of the sea, and the subtle disqualification of such efforts. The legacy of such anxiety is visible in the occasional episode where repressed racism resurfaces, such as Zimbabwe's attempted seizure of white-owned farms and the ensuing von Pezold award that "equate[s] whiteness with productivity, prudence, and also vulnerability while conceptualizing blackness as inherently violent, chaotic, and destructive" in order to secure forms of violent investment protection that further embed racial capitalism.[68]

"SAVAGES" AND THE FEAR OF RACIALIZED VIOLENCE

The decisive victory of Japan against Russia in the Russo-Japanese War of 1905 elicited grudging respect, but also inflamed fears about a newfound military ascendancy of a non-European peoples.[69] There is little doubt that Japanese victory at the time was viewed very much in geopolitical but also racialized terms. As Sidney L. Gulick put it:

> Japan's amazing victory over Russia has raised doubts among white nations. The despised Asiatic, armed and drilled with Western weapons, is a power that must be reckoned with. In the not distant future Asia, armed, drilled, and united, will surpass in power, they aver, any single white people, and it is accordingly a peril to the rest of the world.[70]

That episode, which is often presented as pivotal, is in fact revealing of what were long-term anxieties about displacement of a Western military supremacy and even monopoly of "legitimate violence," and with it the ability to dominate far-flung locations, as well as fears of resort to violence by "savages," understood as existing outside the realm of European international law.

SUPPRESSING RACIALIZED REBELLION

Early colonization of Africa and the Caribbean was met by violent resistance that sometimes proved a lasting obstacle to settler projects.[71] Both colonization and slavery subsequently created very concrete fears for white security. Slave rebellions, particularly in Haiti, were "burned indelibly on the consciousness of slaveowners everywhere," notably in Louisiana where "white refugees from that holocaust were available in numbers to remind the nervous Louisianians of their potential powder keg."[72] Memory of massacres of whites in Haiti arguably had an impact on Confederate justifications for secession. This meant that "the specter of black insurrection was a constant reality in the minds of whites" and that "white fears were reflected time and again in reports of conspiracy or rumor of slave unrest."[73]

Governments were therefore reluctant to encourage racialized insurrection even when it might serve their military objectives against other states. Abraham Lincoln for example stopped short of inciting slaves to rebel in the South, and instead exhorted freed Southern slaves to "abstain from all violence, unless in necessary self-defence" and, where possible, "labor faithfully for reasonable wages."[74] At best, those who escaped were to be incorporated in the military forces of the Union, and Lincoln proclaimed that "[US] military and naval authority ... will do no act to repress [slaves], or ... any efforts [the slaves] may make for their actual freedom."[75] Even emancipation only emerged as a goal later in the war as a result of military necessity and certainly not because of any sense of compulsion from international law.[76]

International law had relatively little to say, in fact, about slave revolts, unless they spilled onto the international stage. The issue did acquire a recurring international dimension in the context of US history. The newly independent US republic reproached King George III for having "excited domestic insurrections among us."[77] A century later, the US's attitude to emancipation but also to the potential armed rise of slaves in the South stood to have ripple effects. In Lincoln's desire to not repress freedom-seeking slaves, "Europeans heard . . . an infamous invitation to servile insurrection, which at once made the Union cause appear desperate and ruthless."[78] According to Howard Jones:

> What developed was not an expected debate over the morality of slavery but a deep fear among British leaders that the president's move would stir up slave rebellions. The result, they predicted, would be a race war that crossed sectional lines and, contrary to Lincoln's intentions forced other nations to intervene [in America's Civil War].[79]

As the French minister to Washington Henri Mercier put it:

> The Union's expected demand for immediate emancipation would spark a race war that disrupted the southern economy and stopped the flow of cotton. Such a conflict would spread beyond sectional boundaries and drag in other nations.[80]

In short, there was much wariness with the possibility that slave emancipation in one country might encourage slave revolts in another (and vice versa), and reliance on arguments about international order militating for the status quo or at least an attention to the potentially violent consequences of emancipation.

This early wariness with the violence of slaves would be replicated to some extent in the decolonization era, even if in more coded racial terms. The apartheid regime repeatedly raised the specter of a civil war to defer reforms and make its case to the US and the UK. Confronted with the sentiment that, as Frantz Fanon put it, "decolonization is always a violent phenomenon"[81] and claims by the Third World that foregrounded the legitimacy of violent racialized resistance to continued occupation and imperialism, the West reacted with heightened concern at what it saw as a liberation of such violence. For example, it voted against what it perceived to be the more inflammatory General Assembly resolutions, or opposed developments in the Geneva Conventions seen as upgrading wars of national liberation to international armed conflicts. The US in particular argued that according a special status to such wars would "inject subjective and politically controversial standards into the issue of the applicability of humanitarian law" and legitimize terrorism.[82]

DISARMING RACIALIZED SUBJECTS

A more specific chronic fear was that of the natives being armed. This was not incompatible, perhaps paradoxically, with arming slaves or colonial subjects or even occasionally tolerating their own quasi-military organization—at some risk, obviously, but only for the purposes of maintaining white domination. Hence both the British and French Empires recruited locals as auxiliaries in their troops, including to repress colonial insurrections. Treaties had earlier been concluded with maroon communities in Jamaica, only on the understanding that they would catch runaway slaves.[83]

Outside this very limited use of locals as guarantors of the racial order, however, ensuring that racialized subjects were disarmed was a constant in both slavery and colonization,[84] with clear international ramifications. In the heyday of the transatlantic trade, the traffic in arms and in slaves were heavily correlated, as the manufactures of Birmingham poured rifles into Africa.[85] From the early nineteenth century onwards, as the emphasis shifted on colonization, the endemic presence of weapons emerged to complicate the designs of European powers. Local African resistance often managed to access weapons by taking advantage of imperial rivalries even once colonization had been officially established. This became perceived as perhaps the single biggest obstacle to the *oeuvre* of colonization. Writing to the Earl of Rosebery in 1888, the British Consul General at Zanzibar noted:

> The great question is that regarding the import of arms and ammunition into East Africa. This trade has now assumed proportions of which your Lordship may possibly be unaware.... Unless some steps are taken to check this immense import of arms into East Africa the development and pacification of this great continent will have to be carried out in the face of an enormous population, the majority of whom will probably be armed with first-class breech-loading rifles.[86]

The origins of the international law of disarmament, in this context, lie in efforts to ensure that the trafficking of weapons in Africa was suppressed. The resulting "arms control as governmentality" led to "mechanisms of proscription and permission [that] operate as technologies of social control designed to manage which populations can legitimately use what kinds of weapons"[87] that emphasized "European norms of racial superiority and imperialism."[88] Control of the arms trade was justified simultaneously by the need to disrupt the slave trade and the Berlin Act's assumption of benevolent obligations towards indigenous populations. But it also served the not incidental purpose of ensuring that Africans would not be in a position to resist ongoing colonization efforts.[89] The Treaty of Brussels (1890) thus sought to bring an end to the trading of weapons with natives, noting that:

> The experience of all nations who have intercourse with Africa has shown the pernicious and preponderating part played by firearms in slave trade operations as well as in intertribal wars, and has clearly proved that the preservation of the African populations is a radical impossibility unless restrictive measures against the trade in firearms and ammunition are established.[90]

The main reason why arms contraband persisted is inter-imperial rivalry and the fact that both British and French businesses had an interest in selling rifles in the other country's possession.[91] But, under the guise of suppressing slavery,[92] international law contributed to effectively suppressing what might have been a key means of African resistance. As has been since noted, the regulation of the arms trade, notably small arms, continues to this day to perpetuate imperial and race relations, despite its humanitarian claims.[93] Not even the nuclear order is immune from its own underlying racialized economy.[94]

STIGMATIZING "SAVAGE" VIOLENCE

The laws of war have long been structured by racial prejudice.[95] European powers tended to treat use of force by "natives" with contempt. After Haiti, characters such as "Bras-Coupé" were consistently invoked to "to engage, recalibrate, and perpetuate American anxieties of black empowerment, masculinity, and rebellion."[96] "Indians" in the US were portrayed as particularly cruel and thus legitimately the object of hate of colonizers. Muhammad bin Abdullah, the leader of a proto-nationalist rebellion in Italian Somaliland, was described as the "Mad Mullah." Italian defeat in 1896 was ascribed to Ethiopian "trickery" and backwardness. Discussion of violence on white subjects continues to this day to be occasionally represented in ways that suggest some kind of equivalency with the enterprise of colonization.[97]

The resulting use of imperial violence was justified on the basis of discursive practices quite different than the ones applicable between "white nations." The Declaration of Independence emphasized that King George III "has endeavoured to bring on the inhabitants of our frontiers, the merciless Indian Savages, whose known rule of warfare, is an undistinguished destruction of all ages, sexes and conditions."[98] "Small wars" or "Indian wars" had the object of subjecting unruly racialized bodies to punishing measures. As the work of Helen Kinsella has shown, Francis Lieber's General Order 100 was deeply immersed in native extermination and exaltation of the Caucasian "master race" in that it excluded settler colonial violence from the ambit of the laws of war.[99]

International law throughout has not necessarily been the driving force in encouraging similar moves, but it has often appeared endlessly pliable when confronted with racist violence and deeply compromised in the colonial ethos.[100] In Ethiopia, the Italians used mustard gas wantonly in an effort to discourage local resistance by civilians, justifying this use under the international law doctrine of reprisals.[101] In Kenya, the British engaged in a conscious effort to make sure that the lessons of Nuremberg were not applicable to the repression of the Mau Mau rebellion. Even as late as the early 1950s, a "permissive legal environment" made it relatively easy for them to do so, despite the adoption of the Geneva conventions (including common article 3) and the European Convention on Human Rights.[102] International law's gray zones were exploited by the French to argue that the Algerian War was a domestic affair not eligible to the higher protections available to international armed conflicts.[103]

THE "YELLOW PERIL" AND THE FEAR OF RACIALIZED MOBILITY

Finally, a recurring racial panic concerns the possibility of racialized mobility across borders, particularly in ways that might affect "white nations." The idea of the "Yellow peril" emerged in the late nineteenth century based on fears in Europe and the US that Asian peoples would surpass the "white race" and displace its domination. Although activated by anxieties concerning Japanese militarism and Chinese demographics, it is mostly in the immigration realm that it was felt. There, what had until then been very liberal international legal assumptions about the liberty to immigrate need to be assessed against the background of "white only" policies in settler states, that would provide the blueprint for a more generalized tolerance of racialized borders.

AMBIGUOUS LIBERAL BIASES IN FAVOR OF FREEDOM OF MOVEMENT

Freedom of movement was once the default assumption in international law. It was hardly obvious to international lawyers, in particular, that states even had a right to exclude aliens from their territory. The Institut de Droit International (IDI) notably advocated explicitly for a presumptive right to immigrate. As an 1897 IDI resolution put it: "Contracting states recognise the freedom to emigrate and immigrate to individuals in isolation or *en masse*, without distinction of nationality. This liberty shall only be restrained by a duly published decision by the governments and within the rigorous limits of the necessities of social order and politics."[104]

Even if states could ultimately exclude from their territory, then, they could not do so arbitrarily or capriciously but only for "very serious reasons." Exclusion had to be justified, for example, "for reasons of public interest and extremely grave motivations."[105] Arbitrary denial of the right to enter another state's territory was sufficient grounds for the state of nationality to intervene and protest such an exclusion. The IDI went as far as to claim that expulsion for the "protection of national work" would not be permissible. Moreover, the seamless movement of persons across borders was to be secured through appropriate protections and the continued recognition of rights across borders via private international law.

It is unclear what the influence on actual international mobility of these early international lawyers was.[106] But in part their liberal commitment represented an elite liberal sensitivity that was largely swept away by the First World War. More significantly for our purposes, their commitment to equal treatment was already significantly constrained by a certain understanding of the limitations of racial mixity that might be brought about by immigration. The tremendous tolerance for mobility, it turned out, largely operated on the basis of expectations that it was members of the "white race" who were mobile and whose mobility should be welcomed.[107]

This was combined with a stigmatization of states that had historically sought to resist white immigration. China, for example, was particularly criticized for its pulling back from the society of nations. Civilization, by contrast, entailed freedom of movement for the purposes of trade and diplomatic intercourse. As Ernst Isay put it in his Hague Course of 1924, "It is contrary to the law of peoples that a State which is a member of the international community, build a great wall of China. China and Japan, as long as they remained systematically closed to foreigners, could not become parties to this community."[108] Thus the backward character of the non-European world was what justified its colonization or imperial subjection and, concretely, the unfettered mobility of white settlers to far-flung territories.[109]

In many cases, then, white mobility was closely associated with the "white man's burden," a transfer of population that would bring with it civilization and development. By contrast, members of non-white races who invoked international law's presumed commitment to mobility for their benefit often encountered considerable resistance. For example, a group of Chinese nationals complained to the Victoria government that, as a result of the resentment of white workers, they were discriminated against in Australia, despite their high degree of "civilization." They cited Vattel's support of mobility rights and the fact that these rights should be honored by "British dependencies" on the basis of reciprocity and on account of their belonging to the Chinese Empire.[110] Such protests did little to alter the "white Australia" policy, as the Australian dominion increasingly opposed to such demands, in response, its rights as a self-governing community.

THE RACIALIZATION OF THE BORDER

Empires had at least been marked by a certain tolerance of intra-imperial mobility. Both France and Great Britain allowed movement from their colonial territories to the metropolis, in theory. At the same time, this intra-imperial mobility was contested. This was most noticeably in the British case by settler elites who tied claims about dominions' emancipation to demands for control over their borders, demands that were very much oriented towards maintaining white majorities. Fears were raised that had hygienic or eugenic bases but whose unmistakable focus was "mongreling" and loss of national character, or even of young "white" nations being overwhelmed by the disproportionate demographic advantage of Asia.[111]

In the US in the late nineteenth century, fears crystallized around the perception that Chinese immigrants would take jobs leading to a number of racial riots in California. "The Chinese must go!" was a widespread rallying cry. The Chinese Exclusion Act, which was adopted in 1882 and in force until 1943, prevented Chinese laborers from entering the country and becoming American citizens and was complemented by strict quotas to Asian immigration. The Tydings–McDuffie Act ensured that even within the US empire, Filipino emigration, associated with mixed blood and perceived as wholly incompatible with American civilization, was significantly restricted. The Japanese would eventually take over in the national psyche as the minority to most urgently keep at bay, in a context in which "scholarly theories of race conflict and change were developed in response to perceived threats and were then used as evidence by agitators."[112]

The publication of Madison Grant's *Passing of the Great Race*[113] and his protégé Lothrop Stoddard's *The Rising Tide of Color* (1920)[114] inflamed concerns about the multiplication of the "yellow and brown races" overwhelming "white world supremacy."[115] The Immigration Restriction League organized to make sure that Italians and Jews would be kept out, leading to the Immigration Quota Act of 1924. The latter was heavily influenced by eugenics and concerns with "racial admixture" resulting from migration, and particularly targeted the immigration of Japanese laborers. Racial constructions were therefore endemic to the delineation of immigration policy through the deployment of nativist ideology and as part of efforts to maintain white privilege.[116]

These US concerns were intimately tied to the country's history of slavery and more generally the policing, including by the courts, of its racial stratification.[117] But they were hardly limited to the US. Indeed, all settler societies, ironically themselves the beneficiaries of earlier untrammeled privileged mobility, have been characterized by fears over racialized migration. Australia led the way with its "White Australia policy" aimed at preventing Asian immigration. In Canada, a $50 head tax was introduced in 1885 for Chinese immigrants upon arrival in the country, the only racial group to be targeted by such a measure. Legislation was also adopted to prevent Chinese men from employing "white" women.[118] In due course, these countries would coalesce to oppose the Japanese proposal for a racial equality clause in Versailles, seeing it as potentially providing a legitimization of Asian migration.

The dismantling of European empires led to a renewed commitment to police borders along racial lines. Newly independent states were asked to relinquish any claim that their nationals might have a right to emigrate to the old metropolis. Although the needs of former European colonial powers for labor meant that this reality would remain hidden for decades, it set the stage for later policies aimed at significantly curtailing immigration and the rights of migrants. These policies contributed to its reification of the sovereign "right to exclude" and have gradually normalized enduring anti-immigrant discourses as a subtle proxy for racism.[119]

INTERNATIONAL MIGRATION LAW'S RACE NEUTRALITY?

This shift against freedom of movement had primarily domestic, including constitutional,[120] sources. It thus arose largely in the shadow of international law, but not always without it. For example, the problem of Japanese immigration to California was dealt through the "Gentlemen's Agreement" of 1907 between the US and Japan, an international agreement by which the former agreed to not discriminate against Japanese immigrants only on the condition that Japan would block further emigration. Nor was this racializing shift in domestic immigration laws particularly opposed by pliant international lawyers.[121] In fact, international law's superficial commitment to cross-border mobility was confirmed as largely resting on hidden assumptions that it was Europeans who were the privileged subjects of that mobility. Freedom from discrimination in immigration, in particular, was imagined as flowing from the "network of commercial treaties by which the states, of the white race at least, are bound together."[122]

Moreover, a significant concern when it came to inward mobility to the European world was the need to limit mixity and its attendant dangers. In fact, among the "extremely grave motivations" suggested by the relatively liberal IDI already in 1892 to justify restrictions to mobility had been "a fundamental difference of mores and civilisation or . . . a dangerous organisation or accumulation of aliens who would turn up en masse."[123] This was compromise language because some members of the Institut had specifically opposed non-admission based on race, but in recognition that the US had already done exactly that by banning Chinese migrants. Paul Fauchille, a leading turn of the century international lawyer, argued that although it was dubious whether "for its own preservation, a state might wish to prevent a fusion of races which might alter its ethnic character or obliterate its national culture," that would not be the case if "this race belonged to an absolutely different civilisation and its members wished to enter the territory of the state in large numbers."[124] One early twentieth-century American scholar cited for legitimate exclusion from the territory "alien races considered inferior or not capable of assimilation" such as "Chinese and certain Japanese laborers in the United States and many of the British colonies, the gypsies in many European countries, and Turks in Panama."[125]

By the mid-1920s, in fact, a nominal liberal conception to open borders had gradually given rise to a recognition that control over immigration was part of states' *domaine réservé*.[126] International human rights law eventually took over where the necessities of international life or imperial citizenship had once occupied the center stage, but in ways that consolidated rather than disrupted the consensus. As with previous versions of liberal freedom of movement, the impact of human rights was ambiguous and certainly did not challenge the definitive entrenchment of state power when it came to immigration. Attempts to challenge discrimination in immigration have for the most part faltered despite its tendency to replicate white supremacist tropes.[127]

CONCLUSION: INTERNATIONAL LAW AND THE FEAR OF WHITE DECENTERING

This chapter has sought to contribute to our understanding of what it termed broadly "racial panics" but, in the process, more generally to how racial hierarchies are structured, whiteness is produced, and the edifice of international law is maintained in a permanent state of "racist anti-racism" marked by the continuity of imperial politics, the colonial gaze, and policing of the "color line." Contra the emphasis on the building and justification of imperial/racist policies in statu nascendi when a smug good conscience, outright racism, or the force of arms will suffice, it has insisted on the importance, as part of a broader arc of race structuring, of *moments of decline*. It is when the implicit racial order is threatened that panic sets in and that racist fears, both real and as a stratagem to whip up the troops in the service of further racism, emerge with renewed intensity.

The chapter has thus argued for a more complex story than the bland narrative of international law's redemption through its linear move to an anti-racist stance. Racial panics, it suggests, occur typically and somewhat counterintuitively at times of fundamental change and at least superficial progress towards racial equality. They are episodes in which fears are stoked, explicitly and implicitly, about the possibility of forces fundamentally challenging the racial status quo, notably in its socioeconomic dimensions. They are directed at ensuring that whatever change is conceded is nonetheless limited and contained. Ultimately, they ensure that existing structures of domination—sovereignty, the monopoly of legitimate force, and control over borders—are reconducted by drawing on the anxieties of dominant groups. Emphasizing racial panics in this chapter makes it possible to connect the politics of racialization to a parallel lineage of the "politics of fear" that has long emphasized the instrumentality of fear-mongering in maintaining power,[128] as well as its constitutive character in fostering forms of "racial authoritarianism."[129] Fear conveniently fashions "victims" of or among dominant groups (as in the infamous case of "white slavery"[130] or "white genocide"[131]) and emerges as a central tool of social control.[132]

The idea of racial panics thus hopes to be a contribution to unraveling the "mystery" of how international law has occasionally been all about race even when it was not explicitly about race at all, by foregrounding international law's underlying economy of fear(s). Contemporary international lawyers have long kept a sort of studied distance from race,[133] which often features only indirectly through various proxies: as geography, as culture, as civilization, as ethnicity, as intimations of "difference" that are never fully explicated. Questions of race were long symbolically consigned to the domestic sphere and thus naturally presented as beyond the purview of international law. Yet the continuities between domestic and international law, the extent to which international law has made possible domestic legacies of racism or been influenced by them, and the circulation of elites between both spheres lay waste to any notion that international law might not be tainted by some of the racialized legalities it simultaneously enabled.[134]

Racial panics, in this context, often brusquely reveal a racial *refoulé*—the exact moment when international law's abstract liberal good intentions are caught up by the weight of accumulated racial prejudice. Fear of the racialized "other" is intimately connected to neo-social Darwinian ideas foregrounding recurring anxieties about "white decadence," the "clash of civilizations," and the "great replacement."[135] It emphasizes at different times different imagined racial others: Africans, Asians, Muslims, Latinxs. Its racialized nemesis could be a soldier, a migrant, a spy, a mother, a terrorist, or a tradesperson. Tellingly, instances of racial panic often arise in the very moment of liberal inflection towards greater racial reckoning: when reform or adaptation to insistent demands for racial equality suddenly lay bare the depth and breadth of compromises that the moment might require if one were truly committed to a de-racializing agenda rather than one of merely anti-racism. That moment is, more often than not, one of transition from mere formal/liberal equality to structural/critical equality, the moment not merely of inclusion but of dismantling the structures of discrimination. Paradoxically, racial panics then help buttress liberal internationalist projects, understood as civilizational bulwarks against racial rebalancing in favor of the "lower races" that seek to limit "internecine conflict that might lead to the decline of the race."[136]

Racial panics, then, suggest the potency of forms of racial ordering that merely need to hint at the risk of radical equality to leverage certain effects. Where the study of international law and the racial question have been centered largely on the hypocrisy of the "civilizing burden" (liberal racism) or the influence of more explicitly racist ideas (scientific racism, for example), the emphasis on racial panics suggests the importance of a politics of fear around the perceived threat that racialized peoples portend for the international legal order. It thus connects the familiar critique of international law's imperialism as expressed in tolerance for slavery and support for colonization, with themes that have been explored in the context of settler societies' racist constitutions. It also suggests a significant space for the "cultural" production of racism somewhere between its formal liberal denial and its suspicion of its material determinants.

In the complex debate on whether racism is motivated by ignorance, hate, interest, or fear, therefore, the chapter will lean towards highlighting the peculiar significance of fear, but a fear at least as much instrumentalized for specific and interested ends than one that is genuinely "already there." And in the petty crucible of racist political passions, fear—a sort of collective racial angst—provides a powerful and sometimes the only mobilizing force. Where the *mission civilisatrice* is too passé and where scientific racism is too pseudo-intellectual, it offers a racist emotion for the masses, particularly the *petits blancs* enlisted in the project of colonial and racist exploitation, whose social position has most to lose from a brutal realignment of racial opportunities. In that, racial panics bear more than a passing resemblance with the rise of fascism as a reaction to a form of perceived *déclassement*. As liberal elites rightly and relentlessly condemn racism, but with little thought to how it might impugn their privilege, the burden of decentering is felt unequally, with potentially powerfully destructive consequences for liberal democracy.

International law is neither the main cause nor the sole consequence of these developments; but it typically provides a pliable normative environment, neither condoning explicit racism nor having the force to turn against structural racism. In the end, the at least residual structural racism of international law bears more than a passing resemblance to actual, manifest racism.[137] White supremacy is both literal and allegorical. One of the classic recourses of racial panics, for example, is their potential for inversion and white victimhood. A typical example in international law is the orientalist fear of "la traite des blanches."[138] Another more recent manifestation is "anti-white racism," a question that began to be raised at the same moment that the extreme right agitated the threat against the white minority in Rhodesia and that Stokely Carmichael invoked Black Power.[139]

The study of racial panics, then, connects the *longue durée* of racism with the current populist moment, including as it designates racial mingling in the metropolis as a threat of white annihilation. This powerfully reactivates latent fears about miscegenation and *mestizaje*, particularly in the heart of a superpower largely constructed on the basis of racial hierarchies, and in a European *mittelmacht* that struggles to conjure its imperial ghosts.

NOTES

1. Musab Younis, "Race, the World and Time: Haiti, Liberia and Ethiopia (1914–1945)," *Millennium: Journal of International Studies* 46, no. 3 (2018).

2. E. Tendayi Achiume and Devon W Carbado, "Critical Race Theory Meets Third World Approaches to International Law," *UCLA Law Review* 67 (2020): 1462.

3. Stanley Cohen, *Folk Devils and Moral Panics: The Creation of the Mods and Rockers* (Routledge, 2011), 1.

4. Brian Gabrial, "From Haiti to Nat Turner: Racial Panic Discourse during the Nineteenth Century Partisan Press Era," *American Journalism* 30, no. 3(2013): 336. Also Brian Gabrial, "'Alarming Intelligence': Sensationalism in Newspapers after the Raids at Harpers Ferry, Virginia, and St. Albans, Vermont," in *Sensationalism*, ed. David B. Sachsman and David W. Bulla (Routledge, 2017).

5. Christopher L. Robinson, "Bernard Rose's Candyman and the Rhetoric of Racial Fear in the Reagan and Bush Years" *Journal of the Fantastic in the Arts* 32 (2021): 404; Shawn E. Fields, "Weaponized Racial Fear," *Tulane Law Review* 93 (2018): 931; Winsome

M. Chunnu and Travis D. Boyce, "Toward a Post-Racial Society, or a 'Rebirth' of a Nation?" in *Historicizing Fear: Ignorance, Vilification, and Othering*, ed. Travis D. Boyce and Winsome M. Chunnu (University Press of Colorado, 2020).

6. Fields, "Weaponized Racial Fear," 931.

7. William T. Hoston, "The Racial Politics of Marijuana" in *Race and the Black Male Subculture* (Palgrave Macmillan US, 2016).

8. Jennifer Carlson, "Moral Panic, Moral Breach: Bernhard Goetz, George Zimmerman, and Racialized News Reporting in Contested Cases of Self-Defense," *Social Problems* 63 (2016): 1.

9. Peter Brimelow, *Alien Nation: Common Sense about America's Immigration Disaster* (Random House, 1995).

10. Durowaiye Babatunde Emmanuel, "Globalization: Cohen's Theory and the Moral Panic," *Afro Asian Journal of Social Sciences* 5, no. 3 (2014): 1; Kenneth Paul Tan, "Neoliberal Globalization, Authoritarian Populism, and Moral Panics," in *Singapore's First Year of COVID-19: Public Health, Immigration, the Neoliberal State, and Authoritarian Populism* (Springer, 2022).

11. Lauren Benton and Lisa Ford, "Legal Panics, Fast and Slow: Slavery and the Constitution of Empire," in *Power and Time: Temporalities in Conflict and the Making of History*, ed. Dan Edelstein et al. (University of Chicago Press, 2021), 297.

12. Ariela J. Gross and Chantal Thomas, "The New Abolitionism, International Law, and the Memory of Slavery," *Law and History Review* 35 (2017): 99.

13. Catherine Dauvergne, *Making People Illegal: What Globalization Means for Migration and Law* (Cambridge University Press, 2008).

14. Nandita Sharma, "White Nationalism, Illegality and Imperialism: Border Controls as Ideology," in *(En)Gendering the War on Terror* (Routledge, 2008), 126.

15. Jatin Dua, "Privateers and Public Ends: Piracy as Global Moral Panic," in *Panic, Transnational Cultural Studies, and the Affective Contours of Power* (Routledge, 2018).

16. Ritu Mathur, *Civilizational Discourses in Weapons Control* (Springer Nature, 2020), xii.

17. Achiume and Carbado, "Critical Race Theory Meets Third World Approaches"; Christopher Gevers, "Slavery and International Law," *American Journal of International Law* 117 (2023): 71; Chantal Thomas, "International Economic Law and Racialized 'Others,'" *American Journal of Internation Law* 116 (2022); Christopher Gevers, "'Unwhitening the World': Rethinking Race and International Law," *UCLA Law Review* 67 (2020): 1652; Vasuki Nesiah, "The Law of Humanity Has a Canon: Translating Racialized World Order into 'Colorblind' Law" *PoLAR: Political and Legal Anthropology Review* 15 (2020); E. Tendayi Achiume, "Racial Borders," *Georgetown Law Journal* 110 (2021): 445; Frédéric Mégret, "Droit International et Esclavage: Pour Une Réévaluation," *African Yearbook of International Law/Annuaire africain de droit international* 18, no. 1 (2010): 121–83; Vasuki Nesiah, "Crimes Against Humanity: Racialized Subjects and Deracialized Histories," in *The New Histories of International Criminal Law: Retrials*, ed. Immi Tallgren and Thomas Skouteris (Oxford University Press, 2019).

18. Lothrop Stoddard, *The French Revolution in San Domingo* (Houghton Mifflin, 1914), 93–5.

19. Alyssa Goldstein Sepinwall, "The Specter of Saint-Domingue: American and French Reactions to the Haitian Revolution," in *The World of the Haitian Revolution*, ed. Norman Fiering and David Geggus (Bloomington: Indiana University Press, 2009), 317.

20. Julia Gaffield, *Haitian Connections in the Atlantic World: Recognition after Revolution* (UNC Press Books, 2015), 185–6.

21. François Blancpain and Bernard Gainot, "Les négociations des traités de 1838" *La Révolution Française* 16 (2019), accessed November 3, 2021, https://journals.openedition.org/lrf/2757.

22. Timothy M. Matthewson, "George Washington's Policy Toward the Haitian Revolution," *Diplomatic History* 3 (1979): 321.

23. Leslie M. Alexander, *Fear of a Black Republic: Haiti and the Birth of Black Internationalism in the United States* (University of Illinois Press, 2022).

24. Mitch Kachun, "Antebellum African Americans, Public Commemoration, and the Haitian Revolution: A Problem of Historical Mythmaking," *Journal of the Early Republic* 26 (2006): 249.

25. Paul Finkelman, *Slavery and the Founders: Race and Liberty in the Age of Jefferson* (Routledge, 2014), 181.

26. Cited in James Alexander Dun, *Dangerous Neighbors: Making the Haitian Revolution in Early America* (University of Pennsylvania Press, 2016), 227.

27. United States Congress, *The Debates and Proceedings in the Congress of the United States: With an Appendix, Containing Important State Papers and Public Documents, and All the Laws of a Public Nature; with a Copious Index . . . [First To] Eighteenth Congress.--First Session: Comprising the Period from [March 3, 1789] to May 27, 1824, Inclusive. Comp. from Authentic Materials* (Gales and Seaton 1852) 121.

28. United States Congress, *The Debates and Proceedings*, 124.

29. United States Congress, *The Debates and Proceedings*, 127–8.

30. Cited in Charles H. Wesley, "The Struggle for the Recognition of Haiti and Liberia as Independent Republics," *The Journal of Negro History* 2 (1917): 369, 373.

31. Wesley, "The Struggle for the Recognition of Haiti."

32. Cited in Jonathan W. White, *A House Built by Slaves: African American Visitors to the Lincoln White House* (Rowman & Littlefield, 2022), 53.

33. Ernest Nys, *Le droit international: les principes, les théories, les faits* (Brussels: A. Castaigne, 1904), 88 ("Si (la souveraineté d'Haiti) eût été proclamée en faveur des créoles, l'autonomie de l'île ne serait dans l'histoire moderne qu'un phénomène secondaire . . . mais les rebelles d'Haïti qui avaient forcé leurs anciens maîtres à reconnaître le fait accompli sont des noirs, des esclaves et fils d'esclaves, êtres considérés jadis par les blancs orgueilleux comme trop abjects pour appartenir à l'humanité").

34. Liliana Obregón, "Empire, Racial Capitalism and International Law: The Case of Manumitted Haiti and the Recognition Debt," *Leiden Journal of International Law* 31 (2018): 597.

35. Julia Gaffield, "The Racialization of International Law after the Haitian Revolution: The Holy See and National Sovereignty," *The American Historical Review* 125 (2020): 841; Younis, "Race, the World and Time."

36. Robert Knox, "Haiti at the League of Nations: Racialisation, Accumulation and Representation," *Melbourne Journal of International Law* 21 (2020): 245.

37. Enze Han, "Racialised Threat Perception within International Society: From Japan to China," *The Chinese Journal of International Politics* 15 (2022): 272.

38. Jean Allain, "Slavery and the League of Nations: Ethiopia as a Civilised Nation," *Journal of the History of International Law* 8 (2006): 213.

39. Cited in Megan Donaldson, "The League of Nations, Ethiopia, and the Making of States," *Humanity: An International Journal of Human Rights, Humanitarianism, and Development* 11 (2020): 6.

40. Cited in Allain, "Slavery and the League of Nations," 221.

41. "Abyssinia," *Tweed Daily*, September 24, 1923, accessed January 15, 2024, http://nla.gov.au/nla.news-article190179289.

42. Lorna Lloyd, "'A Family Quarrel': The Development of the Dispute over Indians in South Africa," *The Historical Journal* 34 (1991): 703.

43. Margaret MacMillan, *Paris 1919: Six Months That Changed the World* (Random House Publishing Group, 2003), 337.

44. William Dameron Guthrie, *The League of Nations and Miscellaneous Addresses* (Columbia University Press, 1923), 55.

45. United States Congress, *Congressional Record: Proceedings and Debates of the . . . Congress* (Washington, D.C.: US Government Printing Office, 1919), 236.

46. United States Congress, *Congressional Record*, 237.

47. United States Congress, *Congressional Record*, 238.

48. Knox, "Haiti at the League of Nations."

49. Tim Kies, "Liberalism Meets Radicalism: Eleanor Roosevelt and the Internationalization of the Black Liberation Struggle," in *Eleanor Roosevelt's Views on Diplomacy and Democracy: The Global Citizen*, ed. Dario Fazzi and Anya Luscombe (Springer International Publishing, 2020).

50. Teresa Barnes, "'The Best Defense Is to Attack': African Agency in the South West Africa Case at the International Court of Justice, 1960–1966," *South African Historical Journal* 69 (2017): 162.

51. Sarah Riley Case and Frédéric Mégret, "The Colour of Jus Cogens," in *Emancipating International Law: Confronting the Violence of Racialized Boundaries*, ed. Mohsen al Attar et al. (Oxford University Press, forthcoming). https://papers.ssrn.com/sol3/papers.cfm?abstract_id=4779577.

52. Olabisi D. Akinkugbe, "Race & International Investment Law: On the Possibility of Reform and Non-Retrenchment," *American Journal of International Law* 117 (2023): 535.

53. Mario Prost, "'One Vast Gasoline Station for Human Exploitation': Sovereignty as Anthropocentric Extraction," in *The Routledge Handbook of International Law and Anthropocentrism*, ed. Vincent Chapaux et al. (Taylor & Francis, 2023).

54. Antony Anghie, "Francisco de Vitoria and the Colonial Origins of International Law," *Social & Legal Studies* 5 (1996): 321.

55. Henry Morton Stanley, *The Congo and the Founding of Its Free State: A Story of Work and Exploration* (Harper & Brothers, 1885), 393.

56. Ordonnance de S. M. le Roi de France, concernant l'indépendance de l'île de St. Domingue, du 17 avril 1825, Article 3 ("Nous concédons, à ces conditions, par la présente ordonnance, aux habitants actuels de la partie française de Saint-Domingue, l'indépendance pleine et entière de leur gouvernement").

57. B. Vendryes, *De l'indemnité de Saint-Dominique considerée sous le rapport du droit des gens, du droit public des Français et de la dignité nationale* (1839).

58. France Chambre des députés, *Procés-verbaux de la chambre des députés* (1840), 248.

59. Jonathan Charles Brown, *Oil and Revolution in Mexico* (University of California Press, 1993), 87.

60. Brown, *Oil and Revolution in Mexico*, 244.

61. "Correspondence Between Mexico and the United States Regarding the American Punitive Expedition, 1916," *The American Journal of International Law* 10 (1916): 179.

62. "Papers Relating to the Foreign Relations of the United States, With the Address of the President to Congress December 5, 1916 - Office of the Historian," accessed July 27, 2022, https://history.state.gov/historicaldocuments/frus1916/d755.

63. "Papers Relating to the Foreign Relations of the United States."

64. Neil Munshi, "Belgium's Reckoning with a Brutal History in Congo," *Financial Times*, November 13, 2020.

65. Edward Henniker-Major, "Nationalization: The Anglo-Iranian Oil Company, 1951 Britain vs. Iran," *Moral Cents* 2 (2013): 16, 28.

66. Ruth Gordon, "Critical Race Theory and International Law: Convergence and Divergence Racing American Foreign Policy," *Proceedings of the ASIL Annual Meeting* 94 (2000): 260.

67. David Schneiderman, "The Global Regime of Investor Rights: Return to the Standards of Civilised Justice?" *Transnational Legal Theory* 5 (2014): 60.

68. Bernhard von Pezold and Others v. Republic of Zimbabwe, ICSID Case No. ARB/10/15; Ntina Tzouvala, "Full Protection and Security (for Racial Capitalism)," *Journal of International Economic Law* 25 (2022): 224.

69. Ram Prakash Anand, "Family of 'Civilized' States and Japan: A Story of Humiliation, Assimilation, Defiance and Confrontation," in *Studies in International Law and History* (Brill Nijhoff, 2004).

70. Sidney L. Gulick, *The American Japanese Problem* (Charles Scribner's Sons, 1914), 225.

71. Hilary McD. Beckles, "Kalinago (Carib) Resistance to European Colonisation of the Caribbean," *Caribbean Quarterly* 38 (1992): 1.

72. James H. Dormon, "The Persistent Specter: Slave Rebellion in Territorial Louisiana," *Louisiana History: The Journal of the Louisiana Historical Association* 18 (1977): 389, 391.

73. Dormon, "The Persistent Specter," 392.

74. Abraham Lincoln, *Preliminary Emancipation Proclamation* (1862). Pdf. https://www.loc.gov/item/scsm000950/.

75. Lincoln, *Preliminary Emancipation Proclamation*.

76. Antonio F. Perez, "Lincoln's Legacy for American International Law," *Emory International Law Review* 28 (2014): 167.

77. Thomas Jefferson, et al, July 4, *Copy of Declaration of Independence* (1776). Manuscript/Mixed Material. https://www.loc.gov/item/mtjbib000159/.

78. Mark E. Neely, "Review of *Abraham Lincoln and a New Birth of Freedom: The Union & Slavery in the Diplomacy of the Civil War* by Howard Jones," *Journal of the Illinois State Historical Society* 93 (2000): 336, 337.

79. Howard Jones, *Blue and Gray Diplomacy: A History of Union and Confederate Foreign Relations* (University of North Carolina Press, 2010), 120.

80. Cited in Jones, *Blue and Gray Diplomacy,* 146.

81. Frantz Fanon, *The Wretched of the Earth* (Grove/Atlantic, Inc., 2007), 1.

82. Message from the President of the United States, 100th Congress, 1st Session, Treaty doc. 100–2 (Washington, D.C.: US Government Printing Office, 1987).

83. Ruma Chopra, *Almost Home: Maroons Between Slavery and Freedom in Jamaica, Nova Scotia, and Sierra Leone* (Yale University Press, 2018), 21.

84. See, e.g., Brennan Gardner Rivas, "An Unequal Right to Bear Arms: State Weapons Laws and White Supremacy in Texas, 1836–1900," *Southwestern Historical Quarterly* 121 (2018): 284.

85. J. E. Inikori, "The Import of Firearms into West Africa 1750–1807: A Quantitative Analysis," *The Journal of African History* 18 (1977): 339.

86. Cited in R. W. Beachey, "The Arms Trade in East Africa in the Late Nineteenth Century," *The Journal of African History* 3 (1962): 451, 453.

87. Neil Cooper, "Race, Sovereignty, and Free Trade: Arms Trade Regulation and Humanitarian Arms Control in the Age of Empire," *Journal of Global Security Studies* 3 (2018): 444, 445.

88. Cooper, "Race, Sovereignty, and Free Trade," 456.

89. SANE Sokhna, *Le contrôle des armes à feu en Afrique occidentale française 1834–1958* (KARTHALA Editions, 2008).

90. Article 8, General Act of the Brussels Conference, 1890.

91. James J. Cooke, "Anglo-French Diplomacy and the Contraband Arms Trade in Colonial Africa, 1894–1897," *African Studies Review* 17 (1974): 27.

92. Henry de Montardy, *La traité et le droit international* (V. Giard & E. Brière, 1899), 169.

93. Anna Stavrianakis, "Small Arms Control and the Reproduction of Imperial Relations," *Contemporary Security Policy* 32 (2011): 193.

94. Mathur, *Civilizational Discourses in Weapons Control*.

95. Frédéric Mégret, "From 'Savages' to 'Unlawful Combatants': A Postcolonial Look at International Humanitarian Law's 'Other'" in *International Law and Its Others*, ed. Anne Orford (Cambridge University Press, 2006).

96. John K. Bardes, "The Notorious Bras Coupé: A Slave Rebellion Replayed in Memory, History, and Anxiety," *American Quarterly* 72 (2020): 1.

97. See, e.g., John T. Bennett, "The Forgotten Genocide in Colonial America: Reexamining the 1622 Jamestown Massacre within the Framework of the UN Genocide Convention," *Journal of the History of International Law / Revue d'histoire du droit international* 19 (2017): 1. For a response, see Aoife O'Donoghue and Henry Jones, "The Jamestown Massacre: Rigour & International Legal History," *Critical Legal Thinking*, August 24, 2017, accessed December 6, 2022, https://criticallegalthinking.com/2017/08/24/jamestown-massacre-rigour-international-legal-history.

98. Declaration of Independence, July 4, 1776.

99. Helen M. Kinsella, "Settler Empire and the United States: Francis Lieber on the Laws of War," *American Political Science Review* (2022): 1.

100. Mégret, "From 'Savages' to 'Unlawful Combatants.'"

101. Simone Belladonna, *Gas in Etiopia: I crimini rimossi dell'Italia coloniale* (Neri Pozza Editore, 2015).

102. Huw Bennett, *Fighting the Mau Mau: The British Army and Counter-Insurgency in the Kenya Emergency* (Cambridge University Press, 2012).

103. Françoise Perret, "L'action Du Comité International de La Croix-Rouge Pendant La Guerre d'Algérie (1954–1962)," *International Review of the Red Cross* 86 (2004): 917, 927–8.

104. Justitia et Pace Institut de Droit International, "Principes Recommandés par l'Institut, en vue d'un Projet de Convention en Matière d'Émigration," Session de Copenhague (Rapporteurs: MM Ludovico Olivi et CF Heimburger, 1897), art 1 (my translation).

105. Institut de Droit International, "Règles Internationales sur l'Admission et l'Expulsion des Étrangers," Session de Genève (1892) (my translation).

106. Philippe Rygiel, "Does International Law Matter?: The Institut de Doit International and the Regulation of Migrations before the First World War," *Journal of Migration History* 1 (2015): 7.

107. Frédéric Mégret, "The Contingency of International Migration Law: 'Freedom of Movement,' Race, and Imperial Legacies," in *Contingency in International Law: On the Possibility of Different Legal Histories*, ed. Ingo Venzke and Kevin Jon Heller (Oxford University Press, 2021).

108. Ernst Isay, "De La Nationalité," *RCADI* IV (1924): 451, accessed October 14, 2016, http://referenceworks.brillonline.com/entries/the-hague-academy-collected-courses/de-la-nationalite-005-ej.9789028604223.425_488.2#1.

109. Antony Anghie, "The Evolution of International Law: Colonial and Postcolonial Realities," *Third World Quarterly* 27 (2006): 739.

110. Lowe Kong Meng et al., *The Chinese Question in Australia, 1878–79* (FF Bailliere, 1879).

111. Marilyn Lake and Henry Reynolds, *Drawing the Global Colour Line: White Men's Countries and the Question of Racial Equality* (Melbourne University Publishing, 2008).

112. Fred H. Matthews, "White Community and 'Yellow Peril,'" *The Mississippi Valley Historical Review* 50 (1964): 612, 613.

113. Madison Grant, *The Passing of the Great Race: Or, The Racial Basis of European History* (Charles Scribner's Sons, 1918).

114. Lothrop Stoddard, *The Rising Tide of Color Against White World-Supremacy* (Good Press, 2019).

115. Stoddard's early work had been on the Santo Domingo revolution and the threat it had represented to "the ideals of white supremacy."

116. Tanya Kateri Hernandez, "The Construction of Race and Class Buffers in the Structure of Immigration Controls and Laws Symposium: Citizenship and Its Discontents: Centering the Immigrant in the Inter/National Imagination: Part II: Section Three: Rethinking Agency: Global Economic Restructuring and the Immigrant," *Oregon Law Review* 76 (1997): 731.

117. Gabriel Jackson Chin, "Dred Scott and Asian Americans," *University of Pennsylvania Journal of Constitutional Law* 24 (2022).

118. Constance Backhouse, "The White Women's Labor Laws: Anti-Chinese Racism in Early Twentieth-Century Canada," Law and History Review 14 (1996): 315.

119. Roxanne Lynn Doty, "Racism, Desire, and the Politics of Immigration," *Millennium* 28 (1999): 585.

120. Gabriel J. Chin, "Segregation's Last Stronghold: Race Discrimination and the Constitutional Law of Immigration," *UCLA Law Review* 46 (1998): 1.

121. Mégret, "The Contingency of International Migration Law."

122. Edwin Borchard, *The Diplomatic Protection of Citizens Abroad: Or, The Law of International Claims* (Banks Law Publishing Company, 1915), 46.

123. Institut de Droit International, "Règles Internationales sur l'Admission et l'Expulsion des Étrangers."

124. Institut de Droit International, "Règles Internationales sur l'Admission et l'Expulsion des Étrangers."

125. Borchard, *The Diplomatic Protection of Citizens Abroad*, 47.

126. L. Varlez, *Les Migrations Internationales et Leur Réglementation* (1927).

127. Frédéric Mégret, "Is Discrimination in Immigration Racist?" in *Global Systemic Racism,* ed. Kristen Barnes et al. (forthcoming).

128. Barbara Loomis Jackson, "Race, Education, and the Politics of Fear," *Educational Policy* 22 (2008):130.

129. Christopher Sebastian Parker and Christopher C. Towler, "Race and Authoritarianism in American Politics," *Annual Review of Political Science* 22 (2019): 503.

130. Mary Ann Irwin, "'White Slavery' as Metaphor: Anatomy of a Moral Panic," *Ex Post Facto: The History Journal* 5 (1996).

131. James Pogue, "The Myth of White Genocide: A Secessionist Movement Brews in Northern California," *Harper's Magazine,* March 2019, accessed January 16, 2024, https://harpers.org/archive/2019/03/the-myth-of-white-genocide-in-south-africa/.

132. David Altheide, "Notes towards a Politics of Fear," *Journal for Crime, Conflict and the Media* 1 (2003): 37.

133. E. Tendayi Achiume and James Thuo Gathii, "Introduction to the Symposium on Race, Racism, and International Law," *American Journal of International Law* 117 (2023): 26.

134. Mégret, "Droit International et Esclavage: Pour Une Réévaluation."

135. François Pavé, *Le péril jaune à la fin du XIXe siècle: Fantasme ou réalité?* (Editions L'Harmattan, 2013).

136. See, e.g., Michael Odijie, "The Fear of 'Yellow Peril' and the Emergence of European Federalist Movement," *The International History Review* 40 (2018): 358.

137. Mégret, "Is Discrimination in Immigration Racist?"

138. Eileen Scully, "Pre–Cold War Traffic in Sexual Labor and Its Foes," in *Global Human Smuggling: Comparative Perspectives,* ed. David Kyle and Rey Koslowski (Johns Hopkins University Press, 2001), 74.

139. Emmanuel Debono, "Chapitre 14. Un procès pour racisme anti-blancs. L'affaire Nidoïsh Naisseline," in *Le racisme dans le prétoire* (Presses Universitaires de France, 2019).

CHAPTER FOUR

A "WORLD PROBLEM"

Apartheid, International Law, and the Domestication of Race

Christopher Gevers

> The most significant fact of the opening century [is] that the Negro problem in America is *but a local phase of a world problem.*
> —W.E.B. DU BOIS (1905)

I. INTRODUCTION

The formal demise of colonial apartheid in South Africa in the 1990s and the adoption of a liberal, "non-racial" Constitution is commonly figured as the triumph of international law over the last vestige of White Supremacy.[1] At the time, however, Cedric Robinson warned against narratives that produced a "closed text" in which "apartheid was a unique, localised, aberrant ... phenomenon," narratives that sought to "preserve an international order by providing sacrificial lambs."[2] From 1948 onwards apartheid South Africa had been used by Western states and international lawyers to do just that: to "domesticate" race and racial domination literally (i.e., "localizing" it within a statist frame)[3] and metaphorically (i.e., to "tame," "adapt," or "make ... acceptable").[4] The latter taking place through (i) *de-politicizing* the operations of race as aberrant, individual "racism" or "racial discrimination," disconnecting it from (settler-)colonialism and transnational structures of political, economic, and social *domination* (or the sociopolitical system of White Supremacy),[5] and (ii) *de-historisizing* racial domination (and "racism") as eternal and universal, and specifically *not* a "Western thing."[6] This set the stage for the triumph of *liberal* White Supremacist legal orders in the 1990s—both in

South Africa and "internationally"—that silence and evade "race" while maintaining White Supremacy.[7] As Lewis Nkosi put it: "What ... changed [in 1994] is the *physiognomy* of white power, which allows a white minority to maintain its hegemony under the guise of non-racialism."[8]

The continued operations of this domesticating move in the West[9] was evident in the Human Rights Council's "Urgent Debate on Racially Inspired Human Rights Violations" in June 2020, following a petition from relatives of George Floyd, Breonna Taylor, Philando Castile, Michael Brown, and others.[10] In response, African states (finally) took up Malcolm X's "humble plea"—made over a half-century ago to the first Ordinary Session of the Assembly of the Organisation of African Unity (OAU) in 1964—to "bring the United States government before the United Nations," and the (then) Commission on Human Rights in particular, for "violating the human rights of 22 million African-Americans."[11] Malcolm X did so on the understanding that "[i]f South African racism is not a domestic issues, then American racism also is not *a domestic issue*," rather—he insisted—it is "a world problem."[12]

In the resulting Human Rights Council debate, representatives of Western states repeatedly sought to displace the United States (and the West or "White World" more generally) from the scene of the racial violence under discussion, by simultaneously *universalizing* and *domesticating* it.[13] One after another, Western states *universalized* racism and racial violence as a "global problem" ("not limited to one country in the world," as Germany put it), which took place everywhere (such that "no country can claim to be free of the scourge of racism," as Belgium insisted) and in no place or region in particular (especially not Europe).[14]

At the same time, racism and racial violence was *domesticated* by Western states, albeit selectively. First, when it came to addressing "racially inspired human rights violations," "open, liberal democrac[ies], governed by the rule of law"[15] (presumably the United States and its Western allies) were positioned as "much *better placed* to ensure that incidents regarding possible human rights abuses ... [were] investigated" *domestically*, through their "democratic institutions"[16] and "transparent justice systems."[17] By implication, racism and racial violence were only *international* issues—and, more importantly, only the business of the Council—when they occurred in "other" places (i.e., non-Western countries).

Second, by framing the response in criminal justice terms, these states adopted a liberal, individualized account of racial violence[18]—and racial justice—rather than one that recognized it as a manifestation of "institutionalized white power."[19] As a result, not only was racial violence, domination, and injustice de-historicized as not "a Western thing," the suggestion was that it was (today) mostly a non-Western thing, at least when it came international law's role in addressing it. As such, the Council's gaze was redirected—institutionally and conceptually—away from not only the site of the racial violence and injustice that gave rise to the debate (i.e., the United States), but away from the origin point of modern racial violence and injustice: the West.

Throughout the debate Third World states—and in particular those with direct experience of the centuries-long racial violence and injustice of enslavement, colonialism, and apartheid—refused these attempts at evasion and domestication, not only holding the gaze on the United States but connecting the present to the longer arc of Global White Supremacy, historically and theoretically. For example, the representative from Botswana connected the killing of George Floyd to "the horrors of slavery, colonialism, apartheid"; while that of Jamaica placed their concerns with "its long history of slavery," as did South Africa, underscoring the Council's duty to "descendants and victims of the transatlantic slave trade."[20] The South African representative insisted that to "minimize," "generalize," or "diminish" the issue—we might say to *de-politicize, de-historicize,* or *domesticate* it—was "a form of racism in itself."[21]

This Western project to domesticate racial domination in and through international law—and the resistance of Third World states, intellectuals, and social movements to it[22]—runs throughout the twentieth century. The Human Rights Council debate explicitly recalled Malcolm X's efforts over half a century ago to get the OAU to "internationalize" Black Americans' "freedom struggle above the domestic level of civil rights";[23] it implicitly recalled the efforts of the Pan-African Congress *almost half a century before that* to establish "a special commission [in the League of Nations] to hear not only of the African, but the facts as to the American Negro problem" as well (as W.E.B. DuBois optimistically put it at the time).[24]

This chapter traces how, from the 1960s onwards, these competing projects converged on and around the place of apartheid South Africa in the White international order: understood as either an exception or, conversely, an exemplar; as either a relic of the past, or its refiguration in the present; as out of time, or seemingly timeless.[25] In order to do so, part II sets out how modern international law was founded in the late nineteenth century as an explicit racial contract,[26] but the ongoing racialized operations and violences of international law have been rendered "conceptually invisible"[27] by the discipline's domestication of race. In contrast, Critical Race Theorists have shown how Global White Supremacy is a planetary system of sociopolitical domination that gave rise to slavery, colonialism, and apartheid, and ensured their afterlives through racial capitalism.

To begin to recover and re-constellate these shards of critique in a way that centers what Robbie Shilliam calls the "other sciences of blackness,"[28] part III returns to the efforts of Third World states in the 1960s—and newly dependent African states in particular—to re-politicize and re-historicize "race" *as* White Supremacy, and place it in its global context, and to make concrete the relations between slavery, colonialism, neo-colonialism, and apartheid. It shows how apartheid South Africa became a persistent site for both the domestication of race by the West *and its refusal* by actors from the Global South.

The conclusion suggests how re-conceptualizing racial injustice and domination as a "world problem" might work against these evasions and domestications in international law. Not only as a "world problem" in terms of its scale—at once national, transnational, international—but a "world problem" in the sense that Global White Supremacy is a *worldmaking* project,[29] premised on the fabrication, circulation, and sedimentation of what Charles Mills called the "invented delusional world, [and] racial fantasyland" of whiteness: the epistemological dimension of the *racial contract* and the founding fiction of modern International Law.[30]

II. INTERNATIONAL LAW AND RACE: SILENCE AND EVASION

Modern international law was founded on a racial contract.[31] One of its "Founding Fathers"—of whom, remarked another, "every living [international] jurist is [a] pupil"[32]—repeatedly made this plain. In 1894 John Westlake defined international law as "the rules which are internationally recognised between white men," which governed *both* the "international society of the white race" and its relations with "other civilisations with which the white race is compelled to be in contact."[33] Crucially, for Westlake this "white [international] society" (or "White World" as he sometimes called it) *preceded* and *exceeded* the international legal order that it produced—or, as he put it in 1904, the "treaties by which the white world is bound together."[34] In the process, men, states, and the international were co-constituted as *white*, made "white by [international] law."[35]

The resulting "(White) International Order"—consecrated (and constituted) by the League of Nations—was precisely that, an order or, better yet, an *ordering*: with "white" persons and states at the top and "non-white," sub-person "Others" below, with Africa and its descendants "placed . . . at the bottom of the European-inspired universe"[36] in what Frantz Fanon called the "zone of non-being."[37] If race was the ordering principle of late-nineteenth-century international law,[38] the poetics of this racial regime were biological: the global color line was written in blood (figurative and literal). International law's "racial grammar"[39] shifted over the century that followed (as it had in the preceding centuries)[40] to geographical, temporal, and cultural markers, but the "biological trace" remained.[41]

From John Westlake's time to the present, however, within international legal scholarship (as with other disciplines) the subject of race has consistently been met with "silence and evasion."[42] As James Thuo Gathii notes, "issues of race and identity have so far been underemphasized, understudied, and undertheorized in mainstream international law";[43] a silence well-illustrated by the fact that the flagship *American Journal of International Law* has "published little on race in over 100 years" (a little over 1 percent of its published works substantially engages with "race").[44] As Gathii insists, this "racial *aphasia*" demands an explanation;[45] along with a reckoning with the ongoing whiteness of international law, both demographically and conceptually.[46]

Charitably, this silence and evasion results from the predominance of a liberal, "colorblind," or "eliminativist" discourse on race, in terms of which—as Toni Morrison puts it—"ignoring race is understood to be a graceful, even generous gesture," as "to notice [race] is to recognize an *already discredited* difference."[47] However, aside from adopting a perpetrator-based view of race (i.e., as *racism*) that seeks to "redeem white identities,"[48] Critical Race Theorists have long since insisted that ignoring race will not make it go away; rather it simply (re-)enforces racial hierarchy by "defer[ing] to the unseen shape of things."[49] As Morrison put it, "the act of enforcing racelessness . . . is itself a racial act."[50] Moreover, this charitable account glosses over the politics, and the mechanics, of the shifts in how race is articulated, and not.

For this reason placing "race" back on international law(yer)'s research agenda is necessary but not sufficient; one also needs to re-conceptualize how race has been understood in international legal scholarship, to *re-think* race in a different sense. Only then can we account for how race is "evaded" in and through accounts of international law, including "critical" ones; how its articulations have been rendered "conceptually invisible"[51] by the adoption, circulation, and sedimentation of a *domesticated* account of "race" and racial domination.

As Critical Race Theorists have shown, race can be evaded *even when it is mentioned*, most commonly when its operation is reduced to "racism" understood *as individual prejudice* rather than as a system or structure of domination;[52] an "institutionalized politico-economic structure" for which "racist" "ideas, values, and attitudes are an ideological accompaniment."[53] The result is a *depoliticized* (or "horizontalized") account that separates race and politics.[54] According to Mills, this *depoliticization* "has the theoretical disadvantage of making it possible for everybody to be 'racist' . . . thereby deflecting attention from the massive power differentials actually obtaining in the real world between nonwhite individuals with bigoted ideas and *institutionalized white power*"[55] (which Fanon decried as "the habit of considering racism as a mental quirk, as a psychological flaw").[56]

This *depoliticization* also takes place through "the horizontalization . . . of race into ethnicity" (or culture); reducing the study of race to "a harmless social science of ethnic categorization"[57]—based on differences or *preferences* of "attitudes and beliefs, religion, language, 'lifestyle,'" and even "cuisine" that are chosen, rather than biological or "corporeal markers of identity and difference" that are *imposed*[58]—and, once again, "extricat[ing] them from inherited hierarchies of power."[59] As a result, "supremacist hierarchy" is conceptually reframed as "non-hierarchical diversity."[60] As Shilliam notes, this "depoliticiz[es] the meanings of the sufferers' cultural complexes and complexions, extricati[ng] them from inherited hierarchies of power."[61] According to Shilliam, "the majority of critical work in the humanities and social sciences engages primarily with" this depoliticized account of race; belying a "consistent implied preference for the master's science to set the epistemic grounds of debate, propelled ... by a particular anti-racism that is obsessed with the question of whether the master can clean up his own rubbish and make good."[62]

Against this, Critical Race Theorists have conceptualized race *structurally*, and in particular understanding White Supremacy as a "sociopolitical system" of domination that is, at once, political, legal, moral, social, economic, and epistemological.[63] In recent times scholars, including of international law, have paid particular attention to the relationship between structures of economic and racial domination, oftentimes through the lens of "racial capitalism."[64] By bringing (and holding) together these *articulated* structures of domination,[65] this scholarship illustrates how one of the ways in which race is de-politicized is through its de-*materialization*, in both "the standard liberal and the standard Marxist analyses" in which race is "seen as irrelevant to the ontology of the liberal individual or the class membership of workers and capitalists."[66]

Related to this, race is *de-historicized* when modern racism and structures of racial domination are de-linked from "the West," and the slave trade and colonial imperialism in particular.[67] The move to *de-historicize* "race" is related to its depoliticization as individual prejudice: by insisting not only that anybody can be racist but that *everybody has been racist* and therefore "racism" and racial domination is not a "Western thing," or as W.E.B. Du Bois insisted, the "culture of *white folk*."[68] As Frank Füredi has shown, this de-historicizing shift was an explicit project of diplomats and academics in the West from at least the 1930s onwards, who sought to ensure that the problem of racism and racial domination was "eternalized"; such that it was "a problem for which everyone [bears] responsibility," thereby "implicat[ing] everyone and *no one in particular*."[69] This move to eternalize, and thereby de-historicize, "the problem of race" was made explicit by UNESCO's Alfred Metraux in 1950, when he insisted that while "race prejudice has so far been analysed almost exclusively as exemplified by white people though it cannot be said to be their preserve."[70]

These two *metaphorical* domestications of race, in turn, enable its *literal* domestication: where race is understood as operating in distinct domestic spheres, separated off from one another; as opposed to being understood *transnationally* or *globally*.[71] This domestication of race is, on its face, counterintuitive (and a remarkable intellectual feat) as "race" is axiomatically a *global* idea (and "perhaps the ... global idea of our age").[72] Moreover, White Supremacy was a *global* project, "involving a tectonic shift of the ethicojuridical basis of the planet as a whole, the division of the world ... between 'men' and 'natives.'"[73] As Mills notes:

> White supremacy was global, not merely in the aggregative sense of an assembly of white-dominated polities, but to a significant extent in transnational patterns of co-operation, international legislation, common circulating racial ideologies, and norms of public policy (slave codes, indigenous expropriation, colonial governance) in which white rulers in different nations learnt from each other.[74]

This domestication of race—or, the ongoing inability to (un)think race internationally, or transnationally—is transdisciplinary, and overdetermined.[75] It is significantly enabled by the de-politicization of "race" as *individual racism* discussed above, as well as the "geographical assumptions" that conventional international lawyers share with IR scholars, a "territorial trap" where the "territorial state unthinkingly serves as the container of society."[76] It also arises from the ongoing failure amongst critical scholars to "leverage the lenses" of Critical Race Theory and TWAIL; as Gathii points out, while the former seeks "to understand race in *domestic law*," the latter seeks "to understand imperialism in *international law*," without doing enough to "tie together and connect the domestic and the international."[77] This chapter seeks to address this by foregrounding the accounts of Third World states for whom "race" and racial domination was never a "domestic" matter; rather, as W.E.B. Du Bois put it in 1905, there was "but a local phase of a world problem."[78] Apartheid South Africa: Exception or Exemplar?

> This is a world problem, a problem for humanity.... If South African racism is not a domestic issue, then American racism also is not a domestic issue.
>
> —Malcolm X, "An Appeal to African Heads of State" (1964)

On September 27, 1966, the representative of Guinea rose to address the UN General Assembly, focusing his remarks on the "disgraceful and unexpected" recent judgment of the International Court of Justice in *Liberia & Ethiopia v. South Africa*, which had "immediately aroused indignation throughout the world" (singling out the duplicitous Australian Judge President who had engineered the Court's decision by fraud):[79]

> The underhand tactics of Sir Percy Spender... show clearly that this Judge, from a country where it is not so long since the aborigines were treated worse than the non-Whites of South Africa, has chosen to hold high the torch of anachronistic racism and colonialism.... It is indeed the alliance of colonial and racism forces with the illegitimate interests *of an obsolete world* that prevailed.

These remarks, like many others from delegates of the Third World and those of African states in particular, situated the problem of apartheid in South Africa and South West Africa within the broader struggle against Global White Supremacy, and the "obsolete ['white'] world." For example, the representative of Tanzania connected the struggle against "European racist brutality [in] South West Africa" to the African continent's long-running struggle against "racist domination, slavery and colonial exploitation."[80] For the representative of Mali, South West Africa was "but one link in the great international conspiracy seeking to keep southern African under the yoke... of the large economic interests of the Powers which... perpetuate racism, the most inhuman racial segregation and colonial oppression and domination," so that Western "capital interests ... [can] maintain the most outmoded forms of colonial slavery."[81] The representative of Ghana insisted that a "discussion of the sorry record of colonialism in southern Africa leads easily into a consideration of racialism, *which finds it most abhorrent expression in the policy of apartheid* of the Government of South Africa";[82] while that of Tanzania called on "all colonialists and their accomplices to listen to the cry for freedom of ... [those] still suffering under the inhuman yoke of colonial slavery."[83]

These were not isolated sentiments (although they were particularly sharply expressed in the 1966 General Assembly), rather they formed part of ongoing efforts by Third World states and scholars to push back against the West's attempts to *dis*-articulate apartheid from slavery and colonialism—historically and theoretically—and domesticate racial domination in the process. A little over a week before the ICJ's controversial decision was handed down, the representative of Tanzania in the Social Committee of the UN Economic and Social Council—Waldo Waldron-Ramsey (originally from Barbados)—"took the lead in advocating the link between slavery ... apartheid and, to a lesser extent, colonialism."[84] Specifically, Waldron-Ramsey led the efforts to "widen the actual definition of slavery" to include colonialism and apartheid as "related manifestations of it."[85] While the conjoining of colonialism and apartheid was commonplace (amongst Third World states, at least), the theoretical and historical *articulation* (i.e., connecting up) of slavery and colonialism was novel for international law (although it was a connection that had long been made in Black Radical Tradition).[86] The articulation of colonialism, apartheid, *and slavery* was (and remains) novel, in international law and beyond.[87]

Underpinning these now (mostly) forgotten efforts by representatives of the Third World was a radical account of "race" as a global structure of domination and super-exploitation, including of land and labor. It came at an important time. The *Convention on the Elimination of All Forms of Racial Discrimination*—adopted by the General Assembly one year beforehand—had signaled a move in the opposite direction, towards the domestication of race and dis-articulation of "exceptional" apartheid from the broader structures and articulations of Global White Supremacy, past and present. In 1965 the Belgium delegate to the Third Committee made this plain, noting that "it would be a gross error to stigmatize only the conventional western type of colonialism—whose evils were well known but whose historical value and significance were equally clear—and to ignore other forms of discrimination which were just as serious."[88] He then added with regard to certain strict enforcement measures being proposed (with a nod to 2020), that "his delegation saw little use for them in Western-type countries that already had effective bodies and institutions."[89]

This move towards the domestication of racial domination was not for lack of effort on the part of Third World states to draw these connections out during the drafting of CERD. For example, in response to the Canadian representative's claim that certain countries "were not yet ready for ... [or] did not share the traditional Western concept of human rights,"[90] the same Waldron-Ramsey (now) representing Tanzania told the General Assembly that "the Western world clearly had nothing to teach the developing countries in the matter of human rights; indeed, it was the Western world that had given birth to colonialism and slavery."[91] While the representative of Venezuela retorted that "Western countries had no reason to pride themselves... since it was in those countries that racial discrimination had originated and still existed."[92] Earlier on, the Sudanese representative had bluntly pointed out that "the colour bar was a phenomenon peculiar to European civilization."[93] Later on Waldron-Ramsey noted that colonialism "was based on the idea of national and racial superiority and it therefore *necessarily* entailed discrimination."[94] This latter formulation—namely that colonialism and "racial discrimination" were inextricable—was commonplace throughout the drafting of CERD (particularly amongst African states), as was the understanding that apartheid was (only) the "most abominable form" of racial domination.[95]

In the end, however, a literally and metaphorically domesticated account of racial domination emerged, and was consolidated in the decades that followed. The absurdity of Western states' de-politicized, de-historicized, and domesticated account was evident in the debate over a proposal led by African states to grant an automatic right of petition in CERD for inhabitants of colonial territories; on the understanding that not only was racial discrimination inevitable in such territories,[96] "colonialism was the most terrible form of racial discrimination, and it still existed."[97] In response, Western states argued that the proposal amounted to "racial discrimination" *against* colonial powers—rendering those with "colonial responsibilities," as the UK put it, a "sort of international second class"[98]—and "*in favour of* States which had no dependent territories" (as Italy explained).[99] The UK representative went further: arguing that as South Africa was (allegedly) *not* a colonial power,[100] such a provision would discriminate against *both* colonial powers and oppressed South Africa's in equal measure.[101] It's difficult to conceive of a more risible and cynical justification or comparison, let alone a more ahistorical and deracinated one.

The usefulness of deploying apartheid South Africa as a "sacrificial lamb" (both conceptually and as comparator) to deflect criticism and "preserve [White Supremacist] international order" was clear from the outset of the drafting of CERD. The United States delegate opened the debate in 1963 by directly comparing the two, arguing that despite his country's (racially) troubled past "it was advancing briskly and surely in the direction of equal rights for all," and claiming:

> People throughout the world recognized the difference between a country *which was having racial trouble because it was unwilling to make progress* [i.e., South Africa] and a country which was having such trouble precisely because it was making progress. Unlike those Governments which... imposed racial discrimination by means of legislative, administrative and other measures... [the US] used such measures to destroy racial discrimination.[102]

The comparison was historical too: while *in the past* Black people in America through "various regulations, customs and pretexts, both flagrant and covert ... had been barred from the mainstream of national life," the US representative claimed that "machinery of the [State] had *now* been mobilized to destroy racial discrimination in the United States society forever," "systematically breaking down the network of racial discrimination."[103] This set in the motion the progress narrative for those with unavoidable pasts and presents of colonialism, slavery, and segregation; unavoidable, in the case of the US, because it was going on outside the halls of the UN and affecting African diplomats.[104] In fact, a couple months beforehand, at its inaugural meeting, the Organisation of African Unity had condemned "racial discrimination in all its forms ... all over the world ... and particularly in the United States of America."[105] As pharmakon, however, apartheid South African was effectively deployed not only to redeem particular Western states but *the* (racial) state itself,[106] and *the* West. It also served to *re*-historicize race, as a universal evil that the West was the first to overcome, and place the US in the lead in "the fight against discrimination everywhere."[107]

This figuring of apartheid South Africa as an extreme (and isolated) form of institutionalized "racial discrimination" contributed to the *conceptual* depoliticization of race more generally: by containing (in multiple senses) the *structural* accounts of racial domination implicit in Third World states' symbolic and material concatenation of slavery, colonialism, apartheid, and racial capitalism. There were clearly different understandings of "race," racism, and racial domination amongst CERD's drafters, as there are today, "between racism as a complex of ideas, values, and attitudes and racism as an institutionalized politico-economic structure," as Mills describes them.[108] Broadly speaking, Western states preferred the former,[109] while those of the Third World hewed to the latter. Notably, this *structural* account of racial domination later informed the conceptualization of racial domination in the 1973 *International Convention on the Suppression and Publishment of the Crime of Apartheid*—led by African states—which defined apartheid as the "*domination* by one racial group of persons over any other racial group of persons," not only physically, but politically, socially, economically, and culturally.[110] This Convention was signed by over half the states in the world, but not a single state in the West. In recent times, however, a "liberal" reading down of apartheid as *discrimination*—rather than colonial domination—has (re-)emerged in respect of its implementation and expansion in Israel and occupied Palestine.[111]

Throughout the drafting of CERD in the 1960s, apartheid South Africa "spectacularly"[112] (over)represented these structural/systemic/institutionalized accounts of racial domination: as an unrepentant, vulgar, *de jure,* state-sponsored system of racial segregation and domination. What was left after these structural/systemic/institutional accounts were contained in and by "apartheid South Africa"—conceptually, and textually in article 3—was the deracinated account of race and racism as individual prejudice suggested in article 1 (acts of "distinction, exclusion, restriction or preference"). This account was subsequently narrowed down further through state practice to individual prejudice *with intent*.[113] While African states had insisted that these forms of racial "discrimination" and domination were connected, different by *degree* rather than kind,[114] formally "institutionalized white power" exemplified by apartheid would come to be seen as "a unique, localised, aberrant ... phenomenon" (to return to Robinson).[115] As the CERD Committee has noted, states came to understand article 3 "as directed exclusively to apartheid in South Africa and fail[ed] to examine whether forms of de facto racial segregation are occurring on their own territory."[116]

A decade before CERD was adopted, Fanon had predicted precisely the domestications that would ensue if racial domination was reduced to an individual "mental quirk ... [or] psychological flaw" (rather than a "characteristic whole," "a disposition fitting into a well-defined system" of exploitation):

> Racism is treated as a question of persons. "There are a few hopeless racists, but you must admit that on the whole the population likes ..."
>
> With time all this will disappear.
>
> There is the country where there is the least amount of *race prejudice* ...
>
> At the United Nations there is a commission to fight race prejudice.
>
> Films on race prejudice, poems on race prejudice, messages on race prejudice ...
>
> Spectacular and futile condemnation of race prejudice.[117]

"In reality," Fanon concluded, "a colonial country is a racist country," and "every colonialist group is racist."[118]

IV. CONCLUSION: A DIFFERENT 'WORLD PROBLEM'

> Our problem is your problem. Is it not a Negro problem, not an American problem. *This is a world problem.*
>
> —Malcolm X, "An Appeal to African Heads of State" (1964) (emphasis mine)

W.E.B. Du Bois and Malcolm X often referred to the Western states and the transnational "mighty organization of white folk" (the "same, vast remorseless machine in Berlin as in New York")[119] collectively as the "White World." They did so not only to reflect the *global* nature of White Supremacy, but also what Mills identifies as its "epistemological" dimension (or, perhaps, anti-epistemological).[120] They were not alone in this regard, as Lewis Gordon notes: "Race theorists, from Du Bois to Fanon to the present, have observed how people differentiated by race seem to live *in different worlds* even when in spatial proximity or under single national boundaries." As Mills puts it:

> To a significant extent . . . [whites] . . . live in an invented delusional world, a racial fantasyland . . . located in real space. There will be white mythologies, invented Orients, invented Africas, invented Americas, with a corresponding fabricated population, countries that never were, inhabited by people who never were—Calibans and Tontos, Man Fridays and Sambos—but who attain a virtual reality through their existence in travelers' tales, folk myth, popular and highbrow fiction, colonial reports, scholarly theory, Hollywood cinema, living in the white imagination and determinedly imposed on their alarmed real-life counterparts.[121]

In this sense, White Supremacy is a "world problem" of a different order.

International law is also a worldmaking project in both these senses: "a [global] juridical project at once grounded in both political commitment and acts of imagination."[122] A project of *white* worldmaking.[123] The task for Critical Race Theorists and international lawyers, then, is not only to hold together the structures and "ideologies of racial domination and racial injustices in a domestic, international, and transnational context,"[124] refusing their de-historization, de-politicization, and domestication (as well as the practices through which the "other science[s] of blackness . . . continue to be disavowed, excluded or re-forgotten in the Western academy's research agenda on race").[125] It is also to map the epistemological worlds that international law makes, and "determinedly impose[s],"[126] and those it makes impossible.[127]

NOTES

1. See John Dugard, "International Law and the 'Final' Constitution," *South African Journal on Human Rights* 11 (1995): 241; Erika De Wet, "Reception of International Law in the Jurisprudence of the South African Constitutional Court: Some Critical Remarks," *Fordham International Law Journal* 28 (2004–2005): 1532; and Neville Botha and Michele Olivier, "Ten Years of International Law in the South African Courts: Reviewing the Pasts and Assessing the Future," *South African Yearbook of International Law* (2005): 29.

2. Cedric J. Robinson, "On the Truth and Reconciliation Commission," in *Cedric J. Robinson: On the Racial Capitalism, Black Internationalism, and the Cultures of Resistance*, ed. HLT Quan (London: Pluto Press, 2019), 357.

3. I borrow this understanding of "domesticating" race from Debra Thompson. See Debra Thompson, "Through, Against and Beyond the Racial State: The Transnational Stratum of Race," *Cambridge Review of International Affairs* 26, no. 1 (2013): 133. See Darryl Li, "Genres of Universalism: Reading Race Into International Law, With Help From Sylvia Wynter," *UCLA Law Review* 67 (2021): 1686.

4. Collins Dictionary, accessed January 31, 2024, https://www.collinsdictionary.com/dictionary/english/domesticate. In 1985 the African National Congress's Oliver Tambo accused the Nationalist Government of seeking to "reform" apartheid "in order to tame the system of oppression and not to abolish it." "OR Tambo's forgotten speech at Chatham House," *Mail & Guardian*, July 9, 2020, https://mg.co.za/africa/2020-07-09-exclusive-or-tambo-chatham-house-speech/.

5. See Charles W. Mills, "White Supremacy a Sociopolitical System: A Philosophical Perspective," in *White Out: The Continuing Significance of Racism*, ed. Ashley W. Doane and Eduardo Bonilla-Silva (New York: Routledge, 2003): 35–48. As Mills notes: "Ironically, the most important political system of recent global history—the system of domination by which white people have historically ruled over and, in certain important ways, continue to rule over nonwhite people—is not seen as a political system at all." Charles W. Mills, *The Racial Contract* (Ithaca: Cornell University Press, 1997), 1–2.

6. Jacques Derrida, "Racism's Last Word," (1985) 12(1) *Critical Inquiry*: 293.

7. On the uses and usefulness of the terms "racism," "white racism," and "white supremacy," see Charles W. Mills, *Blackness Visible: Essays on Philosophy and Race* (Cornell University Press, 1998), 97–118. In order to avoid the evasions that arise from a depoliticized, de-historicized and domesticated accounts of "race," this study follows Mills's insistence on using the term "Global White Supremacy" (as opposed to "racism," or even "white racism"); to refer to the sociopolitical *system* that has brought about the "transnational, global, [and] historic domination of white Europe over nonwhite non-Europe and of white settlers over nonwhite slaves and indigenous peoples," (Mills, "White Supremacy," 37) and "left us with the racialized distributions of economic, political, and cultural power that we have today." Mills, *Blackness Visible*, 98.

8. Lewis Nkosi, "The Ideology of Reconciliation: Its Effects on South African Culture," in *Writing Home: Lewis Nkosi on South African Writing*, ed. Lindy Stiebel and Michael Chapman (Durban: UKZN Press, 2016), 149. See Joel M. Modiri, "The Jurisprudence of Steve Biko: A Study of Race, Law and Power in the 'Afterlife' of Colonial Apartheid" (PhD diss., University of Pretoria, 2017): 39–81.

9. As Glissant notes: "The West is not in the West. It is a project, not a place." Edouard Glissant, *Caribbean Discourse: Selected Essays* (Charlottesville: University Press of Virginia, 1989), 2.

10. "Open Letter to UN Human Rights Council to Convene a Special Session on Police Violence in the USA," June 9, 2020, accessed January 31, 2024, https://www.omct.org/en/resources/statements/open-letter-to-un-human-rights-council-to-convene-a-special-session-on-police-violence-in-the-usa-1. The Open Letter demanded that "endemic racism, hatred, fear and disparity finally be confronted," not only in the form of a Special Session, but also "an independent inquiry" which would report its findings to the Council and make "recommendations on how to ensure that the United States upholds its human rights obligations." See generally E. Tendayi Achiume, "Transnational Racial (In)Justice in Liberal Democratic Empire," *Harvard Law Review Forum* 134 (2021): 378.

11. Malcolm X, "An Appeal to African Heads of State," in *Malcolm X Speaks: Selected Speeches and Statements*, ed. George Breitman (London: Secker & Warburg, 1966), 75, 77. African member states responded with a Draft Resolution calling for "an independent international commission of inquiry . . . to establish the facts and circumstances relating to the systemic racism, alleged violations of international human rights law and abuses against Africans and peoples of African descent in the [US] . . . and other parts of the

world." The Draft Resolution specifically recalled "the historic resolution on racial discrimination in the [US]... adopted at the first ordinary session of the [OAU]... in Cairo from 17 to 24 July 1964," in response to Malcolm X's "humble plea." The Draft Resolution was "obliterated by a combination of geopolitical bullying and... liberal defusion." Achiume, "Transnational Racial (In)Justice," 387–88.

12. Malcolm X, "An Appeal," 75.

13. For example, the Netherlands insisted Member states "recognise that racism is a global issue, and that we are not here to talk about one country." UN Web TV, "Urgent debate on Racially Inspired Human Rights Violations - 40th Meeting, 43rd Regular Session Human Rights Council," June 17, 2020, video, https://webtv.un.org/en/asset/k1h/k1hyzi9vcl.

14. The European Union noted that racism "takes place in all regions of the world," while Denmark noted it "happens in all parts of the world." UN Web TV, "Urgent debate."

15. UN Web TV, "Urgent debate."

16. As the Netherlands put it, expressing "full confidence in the rule of law in the United States of America and its democratic institutions to effectively deal with these important issues." UN Web TV, "Urgent debate."

17. Australia expressed its "confidence in their transparent justice systems to address these issues appropriately." UN Web TV, "Urgent debate." For its part, Ukraine admired that "democratic traditions and equality ideas... deeply rooted within the American society." UN Web TV, "Urgent debate."

18. See Achiume, "Transnational Racial (In)Justice," 390.

19. Charles W. Mills, *Blackness Visible: Essays on Philosophy and Race* (Ithaca: Cornell University Press), 99–100.

20. UN Web TV, "Urgent debate."

21. UN Web TV, "Urgent debate."

22. See E. Tendayi Achiume and Gay McDougall, "Anti-racism at the United Nations," *AJIL Unbound* (2023): 83.

23. Malcolm X, "An Appeal," 76.

24. W.E.B. Du Bois, "Negro at Paris," *Chronicle (Rochester, N.Y)*, May 4, 1919.

25. Derrick Bell, *Faces at the Bottom of the Well: The Permanence of Racism* (New York: Basic Books, 1993).

26. See generally Christopher Gevers, "'Unwhitening the World:' Rethinking Race and International Law," *UCLA Law Review* 67 (2021): 1652. This is not to suggest that International Law was not system of racial domination before that time as well, but rather than as a racial regime it was re-invented along with International Law in the late nineteenth century. On this longer history see Siba N. Grovogui, *Sovereigns, Quasi Sovereigns, and Africans: Race and Self-Determination in International Law* (Minnesota: University of Minnesota, 1996) and Antony Anghie, *Imperialism, Sovereignty and the Making of International Law* (Cambridge: Cambridge University Press, 2005).

27. Mills, *Racial Contract*, 117.

28. Shilliam points out that "the master has never been the only scientist; the sufferers have always had their own sciences," which "continue to be disavowed, excluded or re-forgotten in the Western academy's research agenda on race." Robbie Shilliam, "Race and Research Agenda," *Cambridge Review of International Affairs* 26, no. 1 (2013): 154–55.

29. See Joel M. Modiri, "Global White Supremacy as/and Worldmaking: 'Race' in International Law and Development," in *The Oxford Handbook of International Law and Development*, ed. Ruth Buchanan et al. (Oxford: Oxford University Press, 2023), 546.

30. See Christopher Gevers, "'Land[s] beyond the White World:' (Re)imagining the International through Fiction," *Law & Literature* (2024).

31. See Mills, *Racial Contract*, 11.

32. Lassa Oppenheim, "Editor's Introduction," *Collected Papers of John Westlake*, ed. L. Oppenheim (Cambridge: Cambridge University Press, 1914), x.

33. John Westlake, *Chapters on the Principles of International Law* (London: CJ Clay & Sons, 1894), 143, 198.

34. John Westlake, *International Law* (Cambridge: Cambridge University Press, 1904), 208.

35. See Mills, *Racial Contract*, 63 (noting: "'White' people do not preexist but are brought into existence *as* 'whites' by the Racial Contract . . . The white race is *invented*, and one becomes 'white by law'").

36. Grovogui, *Sovereigns*, 9.

37. Frantz Fanon, *Black Skin, White Masks* (London: Pluto Press, 1986 [1952]), 2.

38. See Grovogui, *Sovereigns*, 9.

39. Eduardo Bonilla-Silva, "The Racial Grammar of Everyday Life in America," *Ethnic and Racial Studies* 32, no. 2 (2012): 174 (noting: "racial grammar provides the 'deep structure,' the 'logic' and 'rules' of proper composition of racial statements and, more importantly, of what can be seen, understood, and even felt about racial matters").

40. See Michel-Rolph Trouillot, *Silencing the Past: Power and the Production of History* (Boston: Beacon Press,1995), 76–77.

41. Stuart Hall, "Race, the Floating Signifier," in *Selected Writings on Race and Difference: Stuart Hall*, ed. Paul Gilroy and Ruth Wilson Gilmore (Durham: Duke University Press, 2021), 359.

42. Toni Morrison, *Playing in the Dark: Whiteness and the Literary Imagination* (New York: Vintage Books, 1993), 9. See further Mills, *Blackness Visible*, 41.

43. James Thuo Gathii, "Writing Race and Identity in a Global Context," *UCLA Law Review* 67 (2021): 1610.

44. James Thuo Gathii, "Studying Race in International Law Scholarship Using a Social Science Approach," *Chicago Journal of International Law* 22, no. 1 (2021): 77.

45. Gathii, "Studying Race," 91. On racial *aphasia*, see Thompson, "Beyond the Racial State," 45.

46. Mills, *Racial Contract*, 2 (noting, of philosophy, that "standard textbooks and courses have for the most part been written and designed by whites, who take their racial privilege so much for granted that they do not even see it as *political*, as a form of domination")

47. Morrison, *Playing in the Dark*, 9–10.

48. Shilliam, "Race," 153 (noting: it "enabled the master to sweep away his rubbish and redeem his humanity").

49. Patricia J. Williams, *The Alchemy of Race and Rights* (Cambridge: Harvard University Press, 1991), 49.

50. Morrison, *Playing in the Dark*, 46.

51. Mills, *Racial Contract*, 117.

52. Eduardo Bonilla-Silva, "Rethinking Racism: Towards a Structural Interpretation," *American Sociological Review* 62, no. 3 (1997): 467 (criticizing the prevailing theories of race and racism in social sciences that conceptualized racism "as a psychological phenomenon to be examined at the individual level").

53. Mills, *Blackness Visible*, 99–100.
54. Shilliam, "Race," 153.
55. Mills, *Blackness Visible*, 99–100.
56. Frantz Fanon, *Toward the African Revolution: Political Essays*, trans. Haakon Chevalier (Grove Press, 2008 [1952]), 38.
57. Shilliam, "Race," 153.
58. Michael Omi and Howard Winant, *Racial Formation in the United States* (New York: Routledge, 2015), 22.
59. Shilliam, "Race," 155.
60. Shilliam, "Race," 155, 153.
61. Shilliam, "Race," 155, 153.
62. Shilliam, "Race," 155 (noting: "[T]his research agenda is dominated by one story... What of the sufferers and their stories and politics? Are they merely fragments of raw data? Or do they have an epistemic part to play in the research agenda on race and racism?")
63. See Mills, "White Supremacy," 39–42.
64. See, for example, Special Issue of *Journal of International Economic Law* on "Racial Capitalism and International Economic Law."
65. See Stuart Hall, "Race, Articulation and Societies Structured in Dominance," in *Selected Writings on Race and Difference: Stuart Hall*, ed. Paul Gilroy and Ruth Wilson Gilmore (Durham: Duke University Press, 2021), 197.
66. Mills, *Blackness Visible*, 99. See further Charles W. Mills, "Materializing Race," in *Living Alterities: Phenomenology. Embodiment. Race*, ed. Emily S. Lee (Albany: SUNY Press, 2014), 19.
67. See Christopher Gevers, "Refiguring Slavery Through International Law: The 1926 Slavery Convention, the 'Native Labour Code' and Racial Capitalism," *Journal of International Economic Law* 25 (2022): 1.
68. W.E.B. Du Bois, "Of the Culture of White Folk," *Journal of Race Development* 7, no. 4 (1917): 439.
69. Frank Füredi, *The Silent War: Imperialism and the Changing Perception of Race* (New Brunswick: Rutgers University Press, 2010), 225–31 (emphasis mine).
70. Alfred Metraux, "UNESCO and the Racial Problem," *International Social Science Bulletin* 2, no. 3 (1950): 386.
71. See Thompson, "Beyond the Racial State," and Li, "Genres of Universalism."
72. Shilliam, "Race," 156.
73. Mills, *Racial Contract*, 20.
74. Charles W. Mills, "Global White Ignorance," in *Routledge International Handbook of Ignorance Studies*, ed. Matthias Gross and Linzey McGoey (New York: Routledge 2015), 223.
75. As Willoughby-Herard notes: "In the case of race, the racial in the domestic scene has so powerfully been positioned over the racial in the global scene that it has resulted in an often stilted research agenda that amasses and identifies cases of racial domination without a fully elaborated reason or purpose." Tiffany Willoughby-Herard, *Waste of a White Skin: The Carnegie Corporation and the Racial Logic of White Vulnerability* (Oakland: University of California Press, 2015), 168.
76. John Agnew, "'The Territorial Trap': The Geographical Assumptions of International Relations Theory," *Review of International Political Economy* 1, no. 1 (1994): 71.
77. Gathii, "CRT & TWAIL," 1614.

78. W.E.B. Du Bois, "Atlanta University" in *From Servitude to Service: Being the Old South Lectures on the History and Work of Southern Institutions for the Education of the Negro* (Boston: American Unitarian Association, 1905), 196–97.

79. U.N. GAOR, 21st Sess., 1414th plen. mtg., U.N. Doc A/21/PV.1414 (Sept. 23, 1966): 14–15. On Spender's role, see Victor Kattan, "Decolonizing the International Court of Justice," *Asian Journal of International Law* 5 (2015): 310–55.

80. U.N. GAOR, 21st Sess., 1417th plen. mtg., U.N. Doc A/21/PV.1417 (Sept. 26, 1966): 19.

81. U.N. GAOR, 21st Sess., 1433rd plen. mtg., U.N. Doc A/21/PV.1433 (Oct. 7, 1966): 6–7.

82. U.N. GAOR, 21st Sess., 1435th plen. mtg., U.N. Doc A/21/PV.1435 (Oct. 10, 1966): 10 (emphasis mine).

83. U.N. GAOR, 21st Sess., 1437th plen. mtg., U.N. Doc A/21/PV.1437 (Oct. 11, 1966): 5.

84. Jean Allain, *Slavery in International Law: Of Human Exploitation and Trafficking* (Leiden, Martinus Nijhoff, 2013), 149.

85. United Nations, Economic and Social Council, Social Committee, Summary Record of the 536th Meeting, July 7, 1966, U.N. Doc E/AC.7/SR.536 (December 14, 1966): 4–6.

86. See Gevers, "Refiguring Slavery."

87. Notably, in much of the historiography of CERD the slavery-colonialism-apartheid nexus is mentioned, but not explored. For example, Thornberry notes that "in the eyes of many delegates drafting the Convention, the most vivid international expression of racial discourse emerged from its employment in colonial expansion and in the justification of slavery," but this is not discussed in any detail. Patrick Thornberry, *The International Convention on the Elimination of All Forms of Racial Discrimination: A Commentary* (Oxford, Oxford University Press, 2016), 32.

88. U.N. GAOR, 20th Sess., Third Committee, 1349th mtg., U.N. Doc AC-3SR-1349 (Nov. 19, 1965): 345.

89. U.N. GAOR, 20th Sess., Third Committee, 1349th mtg., U.N. Doc AC-3SR-1349 (Nov. 19, 1965): 346.

90. U.N. GAOR, 20th Sess., Third Committee, 1345th mtg., U.N. Doc AC-3SR-1349 (Nov. 17, 1965): 325.

91. U.N. GAOR, 20th Sess., Third Committee, 1345th mtg., U.N. Doc AC-3SR-1349 (Nov. 17, 1965): 326–27. Waldron-Ramsey added that "discrimination" in newly independent African countries that aimed to "correct past injustices which had resulted in the degradation of the native Africans... achieve a more balance society [and] remedy the evils forced on them by the colonial powers" (i.e., "affirmative action"), should not be considered "violations of human rights."

92. U.N. GAOR, 20th Sess., Third Committee, 1345th mtg., U.N. Doc AC-3SR-1349 (Nov. 17, 1965): 326.

93. U.N. GAOR, 20th Sess., Third Committee, 1312th mtg., U.N. Doc AC-3SR-1312 (Oct. 20, 1965): 116–17.

94. U.N. GAOR, 20th Sess., Third Committee, 1364th mtg., U.N. Doc AC-3SR-1364 (Dec. 3, 1965): 441 (emphasis mine).

95. U.N. GAOR, 18th Sess., Third Committee, 1213rd mtg., U.N. Doc AC-3SR-1213 (Sep. 26, 1963): 9.

96. As Waldron-Ramsey put it: "Wherever there was a colonial territory there was racial discrimination against the colonial people." U.N. GAOR, 20th Sess., Third Committee, 1364th mtg., U.N. Doc AC-3SR-1364 (Dec. 3, 1965): 441.

97. U.N. GAOR, 20th Sess., Third Committee, 1364th mtg., U.N. Doc AC-3SR-1364 (Dec. 3, 1965): 439.

98. U.N. GAOR, 20th Sess., Third Committee, 1363rd mtg., U.N. Doc AC-3SR-1363 (Dec. 2, 1965): 434.

99. U.N. GAOR, 20th Sess., Third Committee, 1364th mtg., U.N. Doc AC-3SR-1364 (Dec. 3, 1965): 439 (emphasis mine). The Italian representative "wondered whether it was fair, after so clearly defining racial discrimination ... to discriminate in favour of States which has no dependent territories," noting that "[t]he important point was to have an instrument adopted which would strike at racial discrimination wherever it existed." As Egypt pointed out, this was not discrimination against colonial powers, it was ongoing colonialism that was discrimination. U.N. GAOR, 20th Sess., Third Committee, 1364th mtg., U.N. Doc AC-3SR-1364 (Dec. 3, 1965): 441.

100. Notably, domestic opponents of apartheid labelled it colonialism of a "special type" or "internal colonialism." See South African Communist Party, *The Road to South African Freedom* (London: Inkululeko Publications, 1962).

101. U.N. GAOR, 20th Sess., Third Committee, 1363rd mtg., U.N. Doc AC-3SR-1363 (Dec. 2, 1965): 434.

102. U.N. GAOR, 18th Sess., Third Committee, 1217th mtg., U.N. Doc AC-3SR-1217 (Oct. 1, 1963): 29–30 (emphasis mine).

103. U.N. GAOR, 18th Sess., Third Committee, 1217th mtg., U.N. Doc AC-3SR-1217 (Oct. 1, 1963): 29–30 (emphasis mine).

104. See Thomas Bostelmann, *The Cold War and the Color Line: American Race Relations in the Global Arena* (Cambridge: Harvard University Press, 2001), 1–2.

105. Adding its "appreciation for the efforts of the Federal Government ... to put an end to those intolerable malpractices which are likely to serious relations [with] ... African peoples and governments" and the US.

106. See David Theo Goldberg, "Racial States," in *Companion to Racial and Ethnic Studies,* ed. J. Solomos and D. T. Goldberg (Hoboken: Blackwell, 2001), 233.

107. U.N. GAOR, 18th Sess., Third Committee, 1217th mtg., U.N. Doc AC-3SR-1217 (Oct. 1, 1963): 29. For an account of the same "double move" in respect of combatting slavery, see Gevers, "Refiguring Slavery."

108. Mills, *Blackness Visible*, 100.

109. For example, New Zealand framed "racial intolerance ... [as] a dangerous sickness of the human personality," while Denmark referred to "certain attitudes and prejudices." U.N. GAOR, 18th Sess., Third Committee, 1216th mtg., U.N. Doc AC-3SR-1216 (Oct. 1, 1963): 27.

110. See Article II, *International Convention on the Suppression and Punishment of the Crime of Apartheid* (emphasis mine). See further Christopher Gevers, "Apartheid," in *The TWAIL Reader,* ed. Antony Anghie et al. (forthcoming).

111. Noura Erakat et al., "Race, Palestine, and International Law," *AJIL Unbound* 117 (2023): 77–78. See further Gevers, "Apartheid."

112. A distinct but related "spectacularization" of apartheid took place domestically, where (as Ramose argues) the "proliferation of 'anti-apartheid' organisations, especially in Western Europe ... had the infelicitous effect of misleading the gullible into the believe that apartheid ... was the fundamental problem ... [and] the question of freedom ... was reduced to the problem of the constitutional recognition of the 'civil rights' of the conquered people" rather than the restoration of "full, integral, comprehensive and unencumbered

sovereignty." M. B. Ramose, "In Memoriam: Sovereignty and the 'New' South Africa," *Griffith Law Review* 16 (2007): 319–20.

113. As Spain-Bradley argues, under article 1 of CERD "racial discrimination is linked to an act (distinction, exclusion, restriction or preference) that is connected to either a purpose or an effect," 21.

114. As Mills puts it, racist "ideas, value, and attitudes" were an "ideological accompaniment" to "an institutionalized politico-economic structure." Mills, "Theorizing," 99–100.

115. Robinson, "On the Truth and Reconciliation Commission," 357.

116. "Views of the Committee on the Elimination of Racial Discrimination on the Implementation of the International Convention on the Elimination of All Forms of Racial Discrimination and its Effectiveness," E/CN.4/WG.21/10, 17 September 2004, para. 9.

117. Frantz Fanon, "Racism and Culture (1956)," in *I Am Because We Are: Readings in Africana Philosophy*, ed. Fred Lee Hord et al. (Amherst: University of Massachusetts Press, 2016), 211–12 (emphasis mine).

118. Fanon, "Racism and Culture," 213.

119. W.E.B. Du Bois, *Dark Princess: A Romance* (Jackson: Banner Books, 1995 [1928]), 16.

120. Mills, *Racial Contract,* 18 (emphasis mine). Noting that "on matters related to race, the Racial Contract prescribes for its signatories an inverted epistemology, an epistemology of ignorance, a particular pattern of localized and global cognitive dysfunctions (which are psychologically and socially functional), producing the ironic outcome that whites will in general be unable to understand the world they themselves have made."

121. Mills, *Racial Contract,* 18–19.

122. Gerry Simpson, "Imagination," in *Concepts for International Law: Contributions to Disciplinary Thought*, ed. Jean d'Aspremont and Sahib Singh (Cheltenham: Edward Elgar, 2019), 421, 415. See generally Gevers, "Land[s] beyond the White World"; Joseph R. Slaughter, *Human Rights, Inc.: The World Novel, Narrative Form, and International Law* (New York: Fordham University Press, 2007).

123. Gevers, "Unwhitening the World."

124. Gathii, "CRT & TWAIL," 1610.

125. Shilliam, "Race," 155.

126. Mills, *Racial Contract,* 19.

127. See Modiri, "Global White Supremacy as/and Worldmaking," 562 (noting that "only the capacious work of epistemological transformation could be the master key to the unmaking of the white world").

CHAPTER FIVE

FROM METAPHOR TO MEMORY

Remembering Dantès Bellegarde and W.E.B. Du Bois in the Legal Definition of Slavery and Forced Labor at the League of Nations and the International Labor Organization

ADELLE BLACKETT[*]

INTRODUCTION

"I couldn't help saying to myself that *that* man would have brought $1500 at auction in New Orleans in 1860 for stud purposes."

John Avery McIlhenny, the oldest son of the Confederate whose enslaved Black workers invented Tabasco, was in U.S.-occupied Haiti in 1917 and was soon to become the most powerful U.S. civilian official. He looked up from his table in Port-au-Prince over to the table where another man was sitting and hurled those utterly objectifying words.

The man he was talking about was Maître Dantès Bellegarde, lawyer, diplomat, and soon-to-be member of the Permanent Court of Arbitration of the Hague. Bellegarde was later a recipient of a doctorate in law from several institutions, including Université Laval, and, most directly linked to the focus of this chapter, was a member of the League of Nations' 1924 and 1925 Temporary Slavery Commission. He would be considered one of the most "brilliant" and "eloquent" orators at the League of Nations, someone who could never give a boring speech.[1] Yet his grandson, Professor Patrick Bellegarde-Smith, opens his 2019 book, *In the Shadow of Powers*, with a foreword containing that jarring quote. Through it, he explains "discursive enslavement," that is, articulated encapsulation of the perceived impossibility of a Haitian Revolution that was conceptualized and led by enslaved Africans.[2] Any meaningful vision of full emancipation was silenced by the reduction of Black people to so-called "native labor."

It is through Bellegarde-Smith's oeuvre that I offer an unconventional foray through historical erasure. I trace the construction of the international law of slavery through the theme of resistance—albeit highly diplomatic resistance—of the twentieth-century Haitian descendants of enslaved Africans, embodying the determination of "[their] people never, never to be slaves again."[3] In doing do, I hope to honor a tradition of scholarship on slavery that centers Black leaders in its historical narratives, of which C.L.R. James in his definitive history on Haiti, *The Black Jacobins*, is the exemplar. I draw upon the language of "worldmaking," from political scientist Adom Getachew's lucid reminder in her pathbreaking recent account of decolonization, that the "*ideal* of a universal international society" is of "anti-imperial"—and specifically pan-African—"rather than European provenance."[4]

I argue that Bellegarde's valiant pursuit of that anti-imperial ideal under conditions of unequal inclusion (rather than traditional exclusion) was structurally limited; he could not single-handedly prevent the lessons of transatlantic slavery from slipping through the yawning gap that is the slavery–forced labor divide. But critical race theory is an act of memory.[5] Itself constantly in motion as both a framework and a movement, CRT insists on knowing a past that does not, cannot remain in the past.[6] It elucidates slavery's afterlives, challenging hardening processes of racialization. This challenge to legal liberalism can, indeed must, be extended to how we understand the presence of the past in international law, including the law of slavery.[7] By engaging with racial capitalism,[8] critical race theory offers a potent rejoinder to the metaphorical use of slavery in international law.[9]

Bellegarde sought a holistic vision of the law of slavery, one rooted in the understandings and lessons of the centuries-long transatlantic slave trade and its lessons and the centrality of workers' own resistances and aspirations.[10] I reveal little, therefore, by underscoring that Bellegarde's alternative vision was not ultimately the vision that won out in the 1926 Convention on Slavery—for that is not the point. Part of the worldmaking and a pivotal part of both Third World Approaches to International Law (TWAIL) and Critical Race Approaches to International Law (CRAIL), embodied notably by the path-setting work of Professors Henry Richardson III and Derrick Bell, is to look closely at and acknowledge the contributions of those who had the courage to offer alternative visions.[11] To see this work, to give it voice in law, can require us to look to international law's margins—a practice that unites critical scholarship in the field.[12] In some of my transnational labor law scholarship, this has meant mapping the transnational law-making of some of the most subaltern, historically marginalized workers, like domestic workers.[13] In this piece, it means following the somewhat sidelined involvements of an at once great yet invisible man.[14] It is a reminder to be deliberate about how the international law of slavery is itself enabled to evolve, and alive to the actors who should play a constitutive role in its reconstruction.[15]

CLAIMING THE NARRATIVE ON SLAVERY: SITUATING BELLEGARDE'S ROLE ON THE TEMPORARY SLAVERY COMMISSION

Bellegarde was all too alive to the persistence of slavery and its afterlives and brought his depth of insight to the work of the 1924 Temporary Slavery Commission at the League of Nations (Commission). As part of the Commission, he represented Haiti, one of only three independent Black states at the time.[16] The other two were Liberia (which by 1930 had faced an international Commission of Inquiry on slavery[17]) and Ethiopia, repeatedly referenced as Abyssinia (which became a League of Nations member in 1923 on the condition that it adhere to the Convention of St. Germain, and accept a special declaration to provide "any information required").[18] For Getachew, their unequal inclusion through a League of Nations–constituted racial hierarchy created the conditions that ensured their domination rather than sovereign protection.[19] The League's anti-slavery powers became the way this racial hierarchy was enforced.[20] It also conveniently deflected attention away from European powers' use of forced labor to maintain colonialism.[21]

Bellegarde could be frustrating to later pan-Africanists because of his strong attachment to French culture and pan-American society. Yet he participated in several of the historic pan-African Congresses, which ran from 1900–1945, and was highly respected by his contemporaries. Foremost was "scholar denied," leading African American sociologist, founder of the National Association for the Advancement of Colored People (NAACP), and leader of several of the pan-African Congresses, W.E.B. Du Bois.[22] Du Bois went so far as to refer to Bellegarde as the "international spokesman of the [Black People] of the World."[23] Bellegarde earned the reputation as fiercely independent-minded, someone who "never hesitated to speak out for what he considers just, whether it be women's rights or peasants' rights, anti-racism . . . pan-Americanism, or international cooperation."[24] He declared before the League of Nations that "[a] day will come when the League of Nations will have to concern itself with the race problem . . . a menace to universal peace."[25]

What becomes apparent in Bellegarde's engagements with the League of Nations mandate to study and report on the law of slavery "in all its forms"—the formulation in the St. Germain treaty of 1919 that he repeatedly referenced—was his commitment to an anti-colonial vision.[26] His engagements were thoughtful, measured, and forceful. He occupied the positionality central to CRT analysis— an insider-outsider, whose double consciousness, in Du Bois's terms, could enable him to translate and persuade with lucidity and finesse.[27] As a committee member,

Bellegarde held far more sway in the direction of that Commission's reports and recommendations than existing scholarly analyses suggest.

From a treaty-making perspective, the Temporary Slavery Commission's essential, but very careful, recommendation (by stating a preference) for the adoption of a League of Nations Slavery Convention can largely be attributed to Bellegarde's consistent interventions to that effect.[28] His substantive legal interventions translated into an understanding of the need to define and institutionalize measures to abolish, repair, and redress slavery in all its forms, which meant paying close attention to forced and compulsory labor, most importantly alongside the regulation of labor to ensure that it could take place in freedom. That capacious legal and institutional understanding of the Temporary Slavery Commission's legal mandate was far from shared.[29]

As historians have tended to remember it, Bellegarde's interlocutors on the Temporary Slavery Commission were essentially former colonial administrators. The Commission was chaired by the Director-General in the Ministry of the Colonies from Belgium, Albrecht Gohr. Several members, including Sir Frederick Lugard of Great Britain, the former governor of Nigeria; M. Van Rees of the Netherlands, the Former Vice-President of the Council of the Dutch East Indies; and Freire d'Andrade of Portugal, Former Minister of Foreign Affairs, were also members of the League of Nations' Permanent Mandates Commission. The rapporteur was none other than the Former Colonial Governor-General of France and Member of the French Colonial Academy, Maurice Delafosse.[30]

SLAVERY AS LABOR REGULATION

It should be underscored that the Commission's approach to addressing slavery as a political matter through the League of Nations was concerning to the ILO. For the ILO's first director general, Albert Thomas, the ILO had the constitutional competence to address slavery, with the term "slavery" designating "nothing other than conditions of work, over which the ILO had jurisdiction according to the preamble of Part XIII of the Treaty [of Versailles]."[31] Conditions of work needed to be understood broadly. He added that the ILO could most assuredly, under Article 421 of the Peace Treaty, foresee the application of decisions of the ILO to possessions and protectorates, with appropriate modifications.[32] Thomas instructed his staff to organize immediately, by confirming the ILO's willingness to collaborate with the mandates section on the question of slavery, and within the ILO to appoint "a man of the highest order" responsible for the study of slavery "in accordance with the mandates section of the League of Nations,"[33] the application of Article 421, the question of native labor, and "even" the conditions of work in China or in other countries.[34] Beyond the jurisdictional question, Thomas argued that the ILO, through its secretariat, possessed the technical skill to make this work possible. Thomas affirmed that to confide to the ILO a matter previously considered by the Assembly of the

League of Nations would demonstrate clearly that the two organizations form part of an integrated ensemble, which would yield public approbation.[35]

I confess that I would have loved to believe that an ILO charged with this mandate would have built a vision of labor that accorded more closely with a social justice approach. But little in the received historical accounts and in my own archival research gives me reason for hope. Shortly before Thomas's outreach on slavery, W.E.B. Du Bois had responded to entreaties from the ILO, having come through Geneva following the Second Pan-African Congress that met in London, Brussels, and Paris in late August and early September 1921.[36] In a petition addressed to the League of Nations, Du Bois called for the "conditions and needs of Native [Black] Labor especially in Africa and in the Islands of the Seas" to be understood and "properly settled."[37] For the Pan-African Congress, this would be impossible "so long as colored and especially [Black] labor is enslaved and neglected and that a first step toward the world emancipation of labor would be through investigation of Native Labor."[38] The second demand put self-government squarely on the table, and the third called on the League of Nations to use its good offices to redress the uncivilized treatment of persons of African descent and the extent of anti-Black racism throughout the world.[39] By working with Bellegarde, Du Bois wrote, it became increasingly possible to bring the status of Africa to the attention of the League, and the League published the petition as an official document.[40]

On October 10, 1921, ILO Director-General Albert Thomas responded to an internal minute sheet from a staff member and former U.S. Commissioner of Labor Statistics, Dr. Royal Meeker, regretting that he was not informed of Professor Du Bois's presence in Geneva and visit to the ILO (following the Second Pan-African Congress). Meeker had plainly asked Thomas whether he would "consider appointing a [Black] American to take charge" of the work regarding the "backward races" (as was proposed by the petition).[41] Thomas responded in terms that echoed the conclusions of the Pan-African Congress and Du Bois's own work, "je considère qu'il ne saurait y avoir de véritable protection du travail si nous ne nous préoccupons pas des conditions du travail noir."[42] He added that he had just visited the Mandates Commission with Edward Phelan—a future director-general of the ILO to give his opinion on slavery, forced labor, and the conditions of labor—and had met Professor Du Bois then. He specifically asked Meeker—since he said he knew Du Bois and appreciated his work—to help him "with all his power."[43] Meeker followed up with a letter to Du Bois asking for other suggestions, directing Du Bois to identify someone who has a knowledge of the peonage and forced labor systems in operation in the South-West, Mexico, and South America. On November 1, 1921, Du Bois responded to Meeker's letter with some suggestions, and in a handwritten postscript, gently mentioned his own interest in the position.[44]

As I have pursued my archival research, I have wondered—did Thomas actually see Du Bois's handwritten note offering his formidable services to the ILO? Was this just an unfortunate, missed historical moment? A minute sheet to the Director-General dated November 21, 1921, has forced me to recognize how invested I might have been in thinking that perhaps this was Meeker pumping the brakes, rather than the ILO's Director-General, Albert Thomas, himself. After all, in the same file, there is a memo about a leading Guadeloupean elected official based in metropolitan France—Gratien Candace,[45] who visited the ILO, and objected with force to Meeker assuming responsibility for negotiations on a native labor section, considering U.S. policies both in Liberia and in Haiti. Candace reportedly said that as a man of color representing pan-African organizations, he found it intolerable that via Meeker the U.S. should be controlling these dossiers. Meeker as the historical villain would have offered a convenient, but of course all too easy, archival conclusion.

And alas, a distinct internal minute sheet does in fact seem to direct Albert Thomas's attention to the letter. So far, I have found no reply to correspondence from Thomas on Du Bois's availability. But a reply was indeed sent to Du Bois by Meeker, in a terse letter dated December 2, 1921. Meeker said that the names were being placed on file and acknowledging the postscript recalled that the "funds are not now available for the setting up of the Section contemplated." Meeker added that if it were to become possible to take up this work, Meeker would communicate with Du Bois further. Rather than follow Du Bois's vision, moreover, the ILO entangled itself in a vision of "native" labor that was shaped by colonial administrators.[46]

Ultimately, the ILO was invited to communicate the name of one representative for the Temporary Slavery Commission, rather than take charge of the matter. The ILO appointee to the Temporary Slavery Commission, Harold Grimshaw,[47] came around by the second session in July 1925 to acknowledge that although "it might be held, in fact, that Part XIII of the Treaty of Peace of Versailles covered slavery. In his own view, however, so many political and social questions were involved in the abolition of slavery that it was well that the matter should be discussed by the League."[48] He sought instead to have a clear referral to the ILO by the Commission on the matter of forced labor, by acknowledging that the organization already had these powers under the Treaty of Versailles,[49] something that several commissioners were hesitant to do, but Grimshaw diplomatically forced their hand.[50]

THE LIMITS OF BELLEGARDE'S UNIVERSALIST STRATEGY

Bellegarde ultimately supported Grimshaw's view, but chiefly to the extent that he considered that "it did not seem to him to be absolutely correct to say that the Commission could not deal with the question of labor, because, as Mr. Grimshaw had justly shown, slavery was a form of labor." Bellegarde added:

> The object of enslaving a man was not to make an ornament of him but to make him work. For this reason, hundreds of thousands of African [Blacks] were transported to America during the period from the 15th to the 18th centuries.[51]

To Bellegarde's poignant claim, Commander Giovanni Roncagli from Italy, Secretary-General of the Italian Geographical Society, immediately replied "that M. Bellegarde, in quoting the example of the introduction of African[s] ... into America, was referring only to history."[52] Bellegarde went on record to affirm that "he did not accept the opinion according to which the question of native labor was unconnected with that of slavery."[53]

Yet transatlantic slavery was effectively treated as a thing of the past by most members of the Temporary Slavery Commission. The European colonial administrators showed little concern with their states' centuries-long entanglement with transatlantic slavery or their ongoing colonial role through the Mandate system of the League of Nations. What kept re-emerging beyond occasional forays into trans-African slavery[54] was the preoccupation with Liberia and "the very special case of Abyssinia."[55] This was not new. Even when the September 21, 1922, League of Nations Assembly resolution was adopted to address "the question of slavery," the text appeared as "Slavery in Africa" and suggested that the Assembly decided that only the question of the "recrudescence of slavery in Africa" was concerned. A rectification was required[56] to the Assembly's resolution, for presentation to the Council. But the context was unmistakable.

Much has been written on this unmistakable geopolitical dynamic. What is of particular interest for international lawyers is the extent to which race and racial discrimination were at once omnipresent and yet consistently erased. The term "native" labor is widely used, and every now and then it becomes palpably clear that the focus is on "colored labor" confined to employment by "white employers."[57] Moreover, it was explicitly stated that the language of "domestic slavery" was essentially and clearly about the natives, and more specifically, "native custom."[58] Attempts to capture some of the complexity of domestic slavery in certain African contexts—such as the ability of some "domestic slaves" to acquire and enjoy property and even assume certain positions were hotly contested and ultimately suppressed.[59] Bellegarde remained vigilant, resisting any suggestion that "a sudden act of emancipation must necessarily be prejudicial to the welfare of the natives."[60] He was clear about why: the formula "appeared to throw ... doubt on the complete success of the emancipation of the slaves in San Domingo, now Haiti."[61]

But his was ultimately a universalist strategy, which sought to privilege the inclusion of a broad range of forms of servitude within the scope of the Temporary Slavery Commission's report. That strategy was noble in its attempt to move the gaze away from a form of African exceptionalism that underscored the perceived impossibility of Black self-government. As anthropologist and international lawyer Darryl Li has recently argued through his reading of Sylvia Wynter's breathtaking work, "international law becomes a form of 'inscribing practice,' that is, 'an instrument for instituting subjects as particular kinds of humans—including in regimes of racialization.'"[62] For Du Bois, the color line must be understood as an "international phenomenon" with a "domestic iteration."[63] It allows the hierarchies and asymmetries that lie just behind the neutralizing veneer of a universalist text to persist under a coat of international protection.[64] Meanwhile, native labor remained devalued, exploitable, racialized, and ultimately excepted from the treaty.

One of Bellegarde's most pivotal interventions turned to the question of what sources could be relied upon, that is, who gets to claim the narrative of slavery. He urged fellow commissioners to "enquire closely into the spirit in which a report, even an official one, had been drawn up."[65] He had concerns about the way that Ethiopia and Liberia were singled out for condemnation. Bellegarde asserted that

> he belongs to a people which had emerged with violence from a most inhuman servitude and that he was therefore at least as much interested as his colleagues in shedding the utmost possible light on the question of slavery throughout the world.[66]

He continued,

> Had it really been prove[n] that slave-dealing existed in Liberia, as Mr. Grimshaw had stated, basing his statement on documents from the Foreign Office which emanated probably from British agents in that country? What would have been the situation of Liberia if, by good fortune, the General Rapporteur of the Commission had not been able to ascertain the exact position of the "Black Republic" and put forward personal information in opposition to these official documents?[67]

Bellegarde's caution and reference were clear: "It was evidently of value to the Commission to receive information from private sources, but in that respect, it should be especially cautious."[68] Bellegarde had on his mind an 1884 book considered the most insulting ever written about Haiti: *The Black Republic*, by former British Consul-General in Haiti, Sir Spencer St. John. Bellegarde quipped that "some authors, after spending a few hours in a country, considered themselves able to pass judgment on a people, its social life, its institutions, its morals."[69] He considered that "in writing 'The Black Republic,' [Sir Spencer St. John] had done a wrong to Haiti which had not yet been repaired."[70]

Sandwiched in between this detour to *The Black Republic* and his query about Liberia was a diplomatic yet unmistakable rebuke of the reliance on information from private sources in the report prepared by Grimshaw. Bellegarde took special issue with Grimshaw's suggestion that children were sold in Haiti.[71] Grimshaw was required to "explain exactly how he wished to modify" his text.[72]

Bellegarde's 1925 statements could not be divorced from his own entreaties. On December 12, 1924, Bellegarde asked the Director of the Mandates Section, Swiss diplomat, former professor, and founder of the Hayek and Friedman associated

Société du Mont-Pèlerin, William Rappard, to invite the NAACP, led by W.E.B. Du Bois, to respond to the questionnaire established by the Temporary Slavery Commission. He added that Dr. Du Bois's contribution to the inquiry would be "especially useful."[73] The response came from Commission Chairman Gohr, that he is not authorized to do so as the association was not designated by the government.[74]

A final consideration is Bellegarde's vision of free labor. Although it was Grimshaw who insisted that he would "concentrate above all on questions connected with the transition from slave to free labor,"[75] it was Bellegarde who expressed the concern to have native labor conditions benefit from "some kind of international labor charter."[76] He was immediately challenged by Delafosse, who thought it unlikely that France "would adhere to any international convention that included provisions relating to conditions of labor."[77] However, Bellegarde's intervention led Grimshaw not only to underscore how close some labor questions were to the question of slavery, but also to pledge ILO support for identifying solutions to address the question of forced labor. He indicated, moreover, that the ILO had already begun the study of the conditions of native labor, generally.[78] This was to lead, ultimately, to the ILO adoption of an ILO Forced Labour Convention, 1930 (No. 29).

It was when Bellegarde invited the Commission to distinguish between compulsory and forced labor that his attention to the kind of labor laws that would be necessary to enable free labor came into sharpest relief. Ever the diplomat, he argued that while the colonies, "which had known men of intelligence and generosity such as Sir. F. Lugard, M. Freire d'Andrade and M. Delafosse were fortunate[,] his colleagues would not deny that crying abuses did occur and that forced labor could be sometimes a means of re-establishing slavery, which had been abolished by law."[79] Reasoning from the Haitian experience of emigrants working in Cuba for a British company, Bellegarde argued that the consuls of Haiti in Cuba should be authorized to inspect the factories of the British company employing Haitian labor.[80] A proposal that might give native populations "a share in the economic life of the country" was essentially adjourned, though it came the closest to any positive labor vision that might have had a reparatory if not transformative thrust.[81]

Of course, so much of the work of this Temporary Slavery Commission and what ensued in the preparatory work for the Slavery Convention in 1926 was caught up in civilizational discourses that assumed "backward societies" whose "native social organization" was in "rapid disintegration" required "European administrations to assist the changes which were taking place by abolishing domestic slavery as a legal status."[82] It would be fair to read some of Bellegarde's interventions as espousing a somewhat similar view. What also emerges on closer scrutiny, however, is the way that Bellegarde seemed able to work within the established legal frameworks and colonial understandings, to then look, indeed move, past them. In responding to decided reticence about proposing a convention, Bellegarde noted that although "slavery was on the decrease," which he attributed to the "development of industry in native territories," he foresaw that the very development of industry "might lead also to the introduction of new forms of slavery."[83] How prescient he was.[84]

Bellegarde argued that it was the duty of the Commission to recommend measures to meet this danger.[85] He earned Grimshaw's support:

> he had come to the conclusion that the existing conventions on slavery, namely, the Brussels Act and the Treaty of St. Germain, were inadequate to meet the situation which had been revealed as a result of the enquiry of the Commission. They neither covered the whole ground, nor had they secured universal acceptance.[86]

Put to a vote, Delafosse and Lugard joined Bellegarde, Grimshaw, and the Chair.[87] As Bellegarde sought, a Convention was recommended.[88]

CONCLUSION: CRITICAL ACTS OF MEMORY

Bellegarde's contributions are another exemplification of the law-making and worldmaking undertaken by the descendants of enslaved Africans. As Professor Henry Richardson III has affirmed, people of African descent have long been "making demands to re-interpret and normatively change international law," with these claims made "in resistance to the constitutive process of slavery... demanding... the actual replacement of slavery with racial equity."[89] It is well known that there was not a straight path from the Temporary Slavery Commission's work to the 1926 Slavery Convention, and Viscount Cecil of Chelwood was closely interrogated in the House of Lords in 1925 over the license taken to ignore large swathes of the Temporary Slavery Commission, to the broad and permissive approach to forced labor in the draft of the Slavery Convention. Suffice it to state that Bellegarde was not a part of the subsequent work at the ILO on native/colored labor, nor was he part of the subsequent slavery or forced labor expert commissions. Bellegarde was called back to Haiti in 1933, and his distinguished international career continued, including in his formidable diplomatic role at the United Nations. In a moment when the notion of slavery is so repeatedly invoked for its heuristic power without engaging with the afterlives of slavery embodied in people of African descent, to recall Bellegarde's work is to continue to insist on the right to shape our own narrative. This work fundamentally destabilizes remnants of discursive slavery and keeps the focus on movement. Through critical acts of memory, this work reveals continuous movement through an intentional tradition that enables reconstruction.

NOTES

* An early version of this chapter was presented at the Canadian Council on International Law, October 20, 2021. I am grateful to the volume editors for encouraging me to participate in their pivotal volume, despite my inability to participate in the associated workshops due to my role chairing the federal Employment Equity Act Review Task Force in Canada. This research draws on archival work conducted at the ILO and the United Nations (League of Nations archives). I am grateful to the archivists in both institutions who supported my data acquisition visits and who facilitated my work during the pandemic. I also gratefully acknowledge the excellent, enthusiastic support of Labour Law and Development Research Laboratory research assistants, Fanta Ly and Husna Sarwar, McGill J.D. & B.C.L. candidates, as I researched and wrote this chapter and Mathilde Baril-Jannard and Priyanka Preet, McGill LL.M. candidates as I finalized this text for publication.

1. Will Mercer Cook, "Haiti's 'Youngest' Ambassador," *The Crisis Magazine*, April 1957, 215–18.

2. Brandon R. Byrd, "Foreword," in *In the Shadow of Powers: Dantès Bellegarde in Haitian Social Thought, Second Edition*, Patrick Bellegarde-Smith (Nashville: Vanderbilt University Press, 2019).

3. C.L.R. James, *The Black Jacobins* (New York: Random House, 1989), 198.

4. Adom Getachew, *Worldmaking After Empire: The Rise and Fall of Self-Determination* (New Jersey: Princeton University Press, 2019) (emphasis added). See also Justin Desautels-Stein, "A Prolegomenon to the Study of Racial Ideology in the Era of International Human Rights," *UCLA Law Review* 67 (2021): 1536 at 1540 (in explaining the ideological preconditions for such a "postracial" ideal, contends that "while it is certainly true that for more than a century international lawyers have wrestled with the problem of racial prejudice and the ability to craft international laws and institutions that might respond to and regulate that racism, what has been very rarely addressed is the way in which international legal thought is itself constituted by a structure of racial ideology.") See also Antony Anghie, *Imperialism, Sovereignty, and the Making of International Law* (Cambridge University Press, 2004).

5. There is a vast and rich tradition in Critical Race Theory centering the indeterminacy of racism and the eyes-wide-open approach to struggles for change, despite the odds. For an early and poignant contribution to this literature, see Derrick Bell, *Faces at the Bottom of the Well: The Permanence of Racism* (Basic Books, 1992). For a contemporary critique grounded in the memory of slavery, see Ariela J. Gross and Chantal Thomas, "The New Abolitionism, International Law, and the Memory of Slavery," *Law and History Review* 35 (2017): 99.

6. Kimberlé Crenshaw, "Twenty Years of Critical Race Theory: Looking Back to Move Forward," *Connecticut Law Review* 43 (2011): 1253.

7. Adelle Blackett, "On the Presence of the Past in the Future of International Labour Law," *Dalhousie Law Journal* 43 (2020): 955.

8. Powerful recent edited volumes focused on the relationship between racial capitalism, critical race theory, and Third World Approaches to International Law include: E. Tendayi Achiume and Aslı Bâli, "Race and Empire: Legal Theory Within, Through and Across National Borders," *UCLA Law Review* 67 (2021): 1386; James Gathii and Ntina Tzouvala, "Racial Capitalism and International Economic Law: Introduction," *Journal of International Economic Law* 25, no. 2 (2022): 199; Matiangai Sirleaf, ed., *Race and National Security* (Cambridge University Press, 2023).

9. Adelle Blackett, "Slavery Is Not a Metaphor: US Prison Labor and Racial Subordination Through the Lens of the ILO's Abolition of Forced Labor Convention," *UCLA Law Review 67* (2021): 1510.

10. Adelle Blackett, "Racial Capitalism and the Contemporary International Law on Slavery: (Re)membering Hacienda Brasil Verde," *Journal of International Economic Law* 25, no. 2 (2022): 344.

11. James Thuo Gathii, "Henry J. Richardson III: The Father of Black Traditions of International Law," *Temple International & Comparative Law Journal* 325, no. 31 (2017). There is a rich TWAIL and CRAIL scholarship, led by international legal scholar Henry Richardson III, that affirms and underscores, according to TWAIL scholar James Gathii, the commonality of Black experience in the foundational experience of slavery, and brings to light the "erasure" of those similarities and shared experiences.

12. Kimberlé Crenshaw Williams, "Unmasking Colorblindness in the Law: Lessons from the Formation of Critical Race Theory," in *Seeing Race Again: Countering Colorblindness across the Disciplines*, ed. Kimberlé Crenshaw Williams (University of California Press, 2019), 57 (conceptualizing critical race theory as a series of "dynamic engagements"). See also Arnulf Becker Lorca, "Eurocentrism in the History of International Law," in *The Oxford Handbook of the History of International Law*, ed. Bardo Fassbender and Anne Peters (Oxford University Press, 2012), 1503 (underscoring TWAIL's contribution to not only revisiting distorted historical narratives, but also to capturing the "trans-national" relationship between international law and "non-Western" people).

13. Adelle Blackett, "Emancipation in the Idea of Labour Law," in *The Idea of Labour Law*, ed. Guy Davidov and Brian Langille (London: Oxford, 2011), 420–36; Adelle Blackett and Anne Trebilcock, "Conceptualizing Transnational Labour Law," in *Research Handbook on Transnational Labour Law*, ed. Adelle Blackett and Anne Trebilcock (Cheltenham: Edward Elgar, 2015); Adelle Blackett, *Transnational Labour Law and Collective Autonomy for Marginalized Workers: Reflections on Decent Work for Domestic Workers* in *Research Handbook on Transnational Labour Law*, ed. Adelle Blackett and Anne Trebilcock (Edward Elgar, 2015), 230–44; Adelle Blackett, *Everyday Transgressions. Domestic Workers' Transnational Challenge to International Labor Law* (New York: Cornell University Press, April 2019).

14. Byrd, "Foreword," xiii; Ralph Ellison, *Invisible Man* (Random House, 1952).

15. Blackett, "Racial Capitalism and the Contemporary International Law on Slavery," 344.

16. Temporary Slavery Commission, *Minutes of the First Session*, League of Nations Doc A.18.1924. VI.

17. International Commission of Enquiry in Liberia—Communication by the Government of Liberia transmitting the Commission's Report (League of Nations Doc C.658.M.272, 1930); "The 1930 Enquiry Commission to Liberia," *Journal of the Royal African Society* 30, no. 120 (July 1931): 227–90. One member of the three-person committee of experts was Charles Spurgeon Johnson, an African American sociologist who was closely affiliated with Professor Robert Ezra Park from the University of Chicago and became the first Black president of Fisk University in 1946. See also Aldon Morris, *The Scholar Denied: W.E.B. Du Bois and the Birth of Modern Sociology* (University of California Press, 2017) (underscoring Du Bois's pivotal contributions to modern sociology and the disciplinary undermining that he faced by Robert E. Park and his affiliates).

18. Temporary Slavery Commission, *Minutes of the Second Session*, Eighth Meeting (Annex 2, Note on Conditions in Abyssinia), League of Nations Doc C.428.1557.1925.VI.

The survey of League of Nations members on the "question of slavery" prior to the Temporary Slavery Commission emanated from a September 6, 1922, draft resolution moved by Sir Arthur Steel Maitland, delegate for New Zealand. It referred specifically to "the recrudescence of slavery in Africa." The motion was subsequently discussed and ultimately the council adopted a resolution on September 26, 1922, that made the reporting on "the question of slavery" open to all League of Nations members. They were asked to supply the Council with any information that they see fit *(Proposition by Sir Arthur Steel Maitland that the Assembly Should Refer the Question of the Recrudescence of Slavery in Africa to an Appropriate Committee,* League of Nations Archives, Document 23252, R. 61.1922). This was hardly a success, as most states that responded denied the existence of slavery in their territories, and some such as the government of Finland expressly referenced the question of slavery in Africa to explain that they were barely interested ("n'a qu'un intérêt ideal") (*Letter from the Minister of Foreign Affairs of Finland to the Secretary General of the League of Nations,* League of Nations Files 25794). The survey led, however, to the establishment of the Temporary Slavery Commission, and specific follow-up on the African continent focused on "Abyssinia" and Liberia (*Dossier Concerning Co-operation between the International Labour Office and the Secretariat, in Dealing with the Question of Slavery,* League of Nations Archives 1/24088/23252). Giovanni Roncagli underscored the impossibility of "study[ing] slavery independently of the territories where it existed. The facts of slavery varied with the localities." Liberia and "Abyssinia" were the subject of very particular attention by the Commission and ultimately by the League, which is entirely consistent with a reading that the League of Nations preserved—indeed constituted—racial hierarchy, by "deploying the international structure of unequal integration" (Getachew, *Worldmaking After Empire,* 22).

19. Getachew, *Worldmaking After Empire,* 40. Lugard's memorandum on "Slavery in Abyssinia" was initially submitted to the League of Nations' Secretary General, Sir Eric Drummond, on November 10, 1922, and subsequently with corrections on February 5, 1923. Both were prior to Ethiopia's application for membership in the League. In detailed strategic notes, the League of Nations anticipated a system for the state that would be "little different in principle from the B class of Mandates" in which it would be "recognized as having reached a stage where "its existence as an independent nation can provisionally be recognised, subject to the rendering of administrative advice and assistance" *(The Mandates Question - IVth Assembly of the League of Nations, Geneva,* September 1923, League of Nations Archives R4/1/31426/161). This recalls the point made by E. Tendayi Achiume and Devon W. Carbado, "Critical Race Theory Meets Third World Approaches to International Law," *UCLA Law Review* 67 (2021): 1464 at 1471. Achiume and Carbado explain that "[acts of inclusion] are not fundamental reconfigurations of power but rather a particular technology through which to maintain, manage, and legitimize the prior hierarchal domestic and global racial orderings." They explain that "as the former colonies gained seats at the international law-making table, they had to contend with the hard reality that the former colonial powers had neocolonial aspirations. These aspirations manifested themselves in strategic mobilizations of international law and policy doctrines that were designed to maintain not only the subordinate status of the Third World Nations, but also the control First World nations had over the international legal system" ("Critical Race Theory Meets Third World Approaches to International Law," 1473).

20. Liberia and Ethiopia were not quite placed in a mandate as were former German colonies, but they were most assuredly "subjected to an international oversight that was

legitimized through their own consent" (Getachew, *Worldmaking After Empire,* 54). In particular, Getachew adds that the "League pointed to the absence of European rule to explain the persistence of slavery in the two African states" (*Worldmaking After Empire,* 55), as did the Anti-Slavery Society and an ILO memorandum from 1925 clarifying that Ethiopia and Liberia are the only two African states not under European control of some sort (59). Getachew underscores the role of pan-Africanist leaders in the English-speaking world, like leading sociologist and founder of the NAACP, Dr. W.E.B. Du Bois. Her work does not however take her to Dantès Bellegarde.

21. Getachew, *Worldmaking After Empire,* 53. She adds: "That the charge of slavery became the idiom through which black self-government would be undermined should strike us as deeply perverse not only because of Europe's central role in the transatlantic slave trade and slavery in the Americas but also because of the labor practices that characterized colonial Africa in the twentieth century" (Getachew, *Worldmaking After Empire,* 59).

22. It is beyond the scope of this chapter to engage with critiques of Pan-African. See e.g., Kehinde Andrews, "Beyond Pan-Africanism: Garveyism, Malcolm X and the end of the colonial nation state," *Third World Quarterly* 38 (2017): 2501–6. For Andrews, a fundamental limitation in Pan-Africanism was its acceptance of the colonial nation-state framework created by imperialism and a form of equality that aligned with classic liberal thought, rather than based on a politics of liberation.

23. *The Crisis Magazine*, 1926, cited in Byrd, "Foreword," xvi.

24. Cook, "Haiti's 'Youngest' Ambassador," 215.

25. Cook, "Haiti's 'Youngest' Ambassador," 216.

26. Temporary Slavery Commission, *Minutes of the Second Session*, Seventeenth Meeting held on July 22, 1925, League of Nations Doc C.426.M.157, 89: "Bellegarde recalled that he had also proposed in his report that the drawing-up of a general regulation in regard to slavery should be recommended. Article 11 of the Convention of St Germain was a notable step toward . . . since it concerned the suppression of slavery *in all its forms*."

27. Mari Matsuda, "When the First Quail Calls: Multiple Consciousness as Jurisprudential Method," talk presented at the Yale Law School Conference on Women of Color and the Law, April 16, 1988; Charles R. Lawrence III, "The Word and the River: Pedagogy as Scholarship as Struggle," *Southern California L. Rev.* 65 (1992): 2231.

28. Temporary Slavery Commission, *Minutes of the Second Session*, Seventeenth Meeting, July 1925, 89.

29. Temporary Slavery Commission, *Minutes of the Second Session*, First Meeting held on July 13, 1925, League of Nations Doc C.426. M.1571925.VI. For instance, Freire D'Andrade, vice-chairman of the Commission, "wished to remind the Commission, without prejudice for future discussion, that it had been suggested that the question of [forced labor] be referred to some other organization in more or less close relation with the ILO." Sir F. Lugard, in the same meeting in reply to Bellegarde, stated similarly that "a brief reference to forced is [only] desirable when we have concluded our discussion of slavery proper."

30. Temporary Slavery Commission, *Minutes of the First Session*, League of Nations Doc A. 18. 1924. VI.

31. *Archives of the ILO,* ILO Doc. L27/1/1 (1923). Adelle Blackett, "Theorizing Emancipatory Transnational Futures of International Labor Law," *AJIL Unbound* 113 (2019): 392.

32. Blackett, "On the Presence of the Past in the Future," 955. He also wrote to the first secretary general of the League of Nations, Sir Eric Drummond, to gently express that view, once an initial League of Nations consultative committee on slavery's report

was commissioned in 1922. September 26, 1922, by resolution of the Assembly; Letter of November 2, 1922, from the Secretary General of the League of Nations to the Director of the International Labour Office. The letter stated, "Je suis certain que l'aide que le Bureau international du Travail pourrait apporter à ces travaux serait particulièrement précieuse et que la documentation qu'il a déjà réunie à ce sujet servira très utilement à cette fin." Only some fifteen states replied to the Mandate Section's initial consultative letter, and the nature of the replies was considered to be "exceedingly unsatisfactory and the information given very meagre"—certainly an insufficient textual basis on which to move forward with a new convention (ILO Doc 27/1/1). For example, Canada responded, incidentally, by affirming that "slavery does not exist in this country and has long ceased to be a subject of any practical interest" (League of Nations Archives R61/1/24739/23251). Therefore, two options remained open to the international community. The first was to situate a temporary slavery commission within the pre-existing Mandates commission of the League of Nations. The other was to confide the matter to the ILO. But the matter was already in the League of Nations' hands, and it chose cooperation on its own terms. In its 4th Assembly, held in 1923, the Council of the League of Nations decided to form a Committee of Experts within the Permanent Mandates Commission, to again study the matter of slavery, with a view to elaborating a convention (League of Nations Doc, C. 385.1923). Those experts were to have expertise in colonial administration.

33. Author's translation.

34. It is noteworthy that Great Britain responded to the Temporary Slavery Commission's inquiry into slavery in part with a focus on the practice of employing young girls, "Mui-Tsai" in Hong Kong, through its colonial office. The memorandum focused on colonial legislation that was said to reduce abuse by emphasizing that the payment of money on adoption of the young girls conferred no rights, required registration, and could not be under ten years of age, adding that "over 10 years of age, the previous Mui Tsai became domestic servants and free agents, to be paid wages for their work." Memorandum, August 28, 1925, from Alexander Cadogan, London to the Secretary General (League of Nations Archives R62/1/25313/23252). It also provided a list of legislative texts on slavery relating to Egypt and the Sudan. As for the government of the Union of South Africa, which had also been conferred a League of Nations mandate for South-West Africa (now Namibia), it responded to the September 26, 1922, League of Nations Council resolution on the question of slavery, affirming that "it has no information to transmit to you in connection with this matter as happily slavery is not practiced within the confines of the Union or of the Mandated Territory of South West Africa" (League of Nations Archives R62/1/25147/23252). Likewise, Secretary Deane for the Commonwealth of Australia in a letter from Melbourne dated February 18, 1924, to the Secretary General of the League of Nations responded that "slavery has not been known to exist in any part of the territory administered by the Commonwealth Government" (League of Nations Archive R62/1/25802/23252).

35. Blackett, "On the Presence of the Past in the Future," 955.

36. Patrick Bellegarde-Smith, *In the Shadow of Powers: Dantès Bellegarde in Haitian Social Thought, Second Edition* (Vanderbilt University Press, 2019), 72.

37. *Mandates: Second Pan-African Congress August–September 1921* (League of Nations Doc A.148, 1921); W.E.B. Du Bois, "Manifesto to the League of Nations," *The Crisis* 23, no. 1 (1921): 18.

38. Du Bois, "Manifesto to the League of Nations," 18. Gil Gott describes W.E.B. Du Bois as a "radical race internationalist [. . .] who envisioned the type of political struggle

that would be necessary to challenge the epochal problem of 'capitalist imperialism,' a global system integrally linked to racial oppression" ("Critical Race Global?: Global Political Economy, and the Intersections of Race, Nation and Class" *U.C. Davis Law Review* 33, no. 4 (2000): 1513).

39. Du Bois, "Manifesto to the League of Nations," 18. The Congress anticipated the response that the League of Nations would have "little if any direct power" but it called upon the mandate of promoting peace and justice to urge it to take a "firm stand on the absolute equality of races" and create an international institute to study anti-Black racism and the protection of Black people.

40. W.E.B. Du Bois, in *History of the Pan-African Congress*, ed. George Padmore (Manchester: Hammersmith Bookshop, 1945), 21; a good survey of the development of Pan-Africanism is given in George Padmore, *Pan-Africanism or Communism* (New York: Doubleday Anchor, 1972), cited in Bellegarde-Smith, *In the Shadow of Powers*, 72; League of Nations Archive R60/1/21159/21159.

41. Archives of the ILO, 1921.

42. Archives of the ILO, 1921; Blackett, "On the Presence of the Past in the Future," 956.

43. Archives of the ILO, 1921.

44. Archives of the ILO, 1921.

45. Gratien Candace's apparent support for the Vichy government led to the end of his career following World War II. For a close critical assessment of Candace's role, see Dominique Chathuant, "Gratien Candace: une figure de la vie politique française: 2e partie: de Vichy à la Quatrième République (1940–1953)," *Bulletin de la Société d'Histoire de la Guadeloupe* 149 (January–April 2008): 3–131.

46. Blackett, "Theorizing Emancipatory Transnational Futures," 392. The ILO's jurisdictional space would come later, as the ILO took responsibility for the topic referred to as "native labor." The work on native labor at the ILO, despite other entreaties, followed the path of relying heavily on colonial administrators to elaborate what would become the native labor code (Blackett, "Slavery Is Not a Metaphor," 1512). A prominent African American social worker and first Executive Director of the National Urban League in the United States, George E. Haynes, received a comparable outreach to Meeker, who even suggested a methodology. When he wrote again to inform Meeker that he would be visiting Haiti and could write a brief report on Haitian peasant labor, Meeker replied to say that he was not sure that the ILO could publish it. Rather than a leading scholar representative of Black enfranchisement, Professor Joseph Chamberlain of Columbia Law School became the American member involved in preparing Convention No. 29 from 1927–1937, even though the United States only joined the ILO in 1934. It is worthy to note that the United States never joined the League, although it ratified the Slavery Convention, and it has yet to ratify Convention No. 29.

47. Letter dated June 26, 1924, from Director-General Albert Thomas to Secretary-General Sir Eric Drummond, confirming Grimshaw's nomination to the Temporary Slavery Commission. League of Nations Archives 1/24088/23252.

48. Temporary Slavery Commission, *Minutes of the Second Session*, Seventeenth Meeting, 85.

49. Temporary Slavery Commission, *Minutes of the Second Session*, Seventeenth Meeting, 86. The absence of a clear referral in the actual 1926 Slavery Convention was a source of disappointment for Albert Thomas, as he lamented in a letter to Sir Cecil of Chelwood in a letter dated September 17, 1926 (ILO Archives).

50. Temporary Slavery Commission, *Minutes of the Second Session*, Seventeenth Meeting, 87.

51. Temporary Slavery Commission, *Minutes of the Second Session*, Seventeenth Meeting, 86–87.

52. Temporary Slavery Commission, *Minutes of the Second Session*, Seventeenth Meeting, 87.

53. Temporary Slavery Commission, *Minutes of the Second Session*, Seventeenth Meeting, 88.

54. Temporary Slavery Commission, *Minutes of the Second Session*, Ninth Meeting held on July 17, 1925, League of Nations Doc C.426.M.157, 38.

55. Temporary Slavery Commission, *Minutes of the Second Session*, Fifth Meeting held on July 15, 1925, League of Nations Doc C.426.M.157, 26 (Delafosse). Sir F. Lugard tended to lead the charge. In agreeing with him, the Chair even suggested that "the Commission might consider slavery in its various forms without mentioning the countries where this traffic is said to take place, except in the case of States such as Abyssinia, which had recognised the existence of slavery within its territory." In his annex to the Temporary Slavery Commission's report, Lugard went so far as to express the view that "slave-trading and the organised slave trade can only be suppressed *by force*." The report appears to rely heavily on British and Italian sources. Interestingly in this annex, Lugard stresses that in Abyssinia the "slaves are not of the same race as their owners" (Temporary Slavery Commission, *Annex 2, Note on Conditions in Abyssinia*, League of Nations Doc C.428.1557.1925.VI).

56. Chairman of the Second Sub-Committee of the Sixth Committee (Mandates and Slavery) to the Honourable Sir Eric Drummond, Secretary General of the League of Nations, September 22, 1922. There is a reference to the mandate in SW Africa and the Bondelzwart Rebellion of 1922 in the files, but no reference is made to slavery. League of Nations Archives, 1922.

57. Temporary Slavery Commission, *Minutes of the Second Session*, First Meeting held on July 13, 1925, League of Nations Doc C.426.M.15, 9.

58. This view was reinforced in correspondence about whether to accept an offer by Polish Senator Stanislas Posner, apparently named by his government due to his connection with the Advisory Committee on Traffic in Women and Children, to provide information to the Temporary Slavery Commission, following a letter from Rappard suggesting that outreach by the League had been made to him as someone able to supply "useful and reliable information on the question of slavery" (*Letter from Rappard to Grimshaw, Geneva, 20 Nov. 1924*, League of Nations Archives 1/24088/23252). Posner himself affirmed that slavery had not existed in Poland since the thirteenth century. The President of the Temporary Slavery Commission also declined. The internal reasons suggested that while it could be useful to see whether some form of obligatory labor continued to exist in Poland that would limit an individual's liberty without reducing them to slaves, it was stated that "it seems to me that, since any compulsory work in a civilized people could probably exist only by force of law, I think that, in any case, any precise question concerning it should be addressed to the Polish government, the only responsible depositary and executor of the law" (*Letter from Stanislas Posner from Warsaw, 12 November 1924 to the Secretary General of the League of Nations; Correspondence from Roncagli to Rappard, Director of the Mandates Section, League of Nations, 9 December 1924; Letter from Grimshaw to Rappard, 16 December 1924*, League of Nations Archives, R.61, 1922, File 23252).

59. Temporary Slavery Commission, *Minutes of the Second Session*, Eighth Meeting held on July 16, 1925, League of Nations Doc C.426.M.15, 37.

60. Temporary Slavery Commission, *Minutes of the Second Session*, Tenth Meeting held on July 17, 1925, League of Nations Doc C.426.M.15, 47.

61. Temporary Slavery Commission, *Minutes of the Second Session*, Tenth Meeting, 47.

62. Darryl Li, "Genres of Universalism: Reading Race into International Law, With Help from Sylvia Wynter," *UCLA Law Review*, no. 67 (2021): 1706.

63. Getachew, *Worldmaking After Empire*, 20.

64. Blackett, "Racial Capitalism and the Contemporary International Law on Slavery," 354; Li, "Genres of Universalism," 1693.

65. Temporary Slavery Commission, *Minutes of the Second Session*, Fifth Meeting, 21–22.

66. Temporary Slavery Commission, *Minutes of the Second Session*, Fifth Meeting, 21.

67. Temporary Slavery Commission, *Minutes of the Second Session*, Fifth Meeting, 22.

68. Temporary Slavery Commission, *Minutes of the Second Session*, Fifth Meeting, 22.

69. Temporary Slavery Commission, *Minutes of the Second Session*, Fifth Meeting, 22.

70. Temporary Slavery Commission, *Minutes of the Second Session*, Fifth Meeting, 22.

71. Bellegarde states in Temporary Slavery Commission, *Minutes of the Second Session*, Fifth Meeting, 22, "In his interesting report, Mr. Grimshaw cited a passage from a book written about Haiti by Mr. Kuser, who mentioned that children were sold. Now in that country such transactions were not only unknown but impossible. The facts of the case were that peasants placed their children in families living in the towns. This was a means for them to obtain education for their children which it was not always easy to obtain in the country. The children thus 'placed' were employed on light domestic work adapted to their age. In accordance, however, with the law on obligatory education, they were sent to school and some of them had become lawyers, doctors, engineers, etc. No Haitian woman would ever agree to sell her child. It might be that Mr. Kuser, while travelling in the interior and not fully understanding the Haitian patois, had misunderstood the intention of some Haitian woman that he had seen coming towards his car. Why had he supposed that this woman wished to sell her child to him? The author of this information might have given it in good faith, but it might equally be supposed that he had had some interest, in the view of his family attachments [M. Kuser was the son-in-law of the American High Commissioner in Haiti], in justifying the political situation in Haiti. Hence arose the necessity, before taking account of his information, of making enquiries as to the author."

72. Temporary Slavery Commission, *Minutes of the Second Session*, Fifth Meeting, 24 (on Liberia) and 26 (discussion of the appropriate section for children sold to obtain food, as not being cases of "slave-dealing proper").

73. "nous serait fort utile"; Letter from Dantès Bellegarde, Association Haïtienne pour la Société des Nations, Port au Prince, to William Rappard, December 12, 1924. ILO Archives. For Du Bois's initially hopeful yet cautious and increasingly critical views on how to improve the conditions of Black labor, including in Liberia, see W.E.B. Du Bois, "Liberia and Rubber (1925)," in *W.E.B. Du Bois: International Thought*, ed. Adom Getachew and Jennifer Pitts (Cambridge University Press, 2022), 91; W.E.B. Du Bois, "Liberia," in *W.E.B. Du Bois on Africa*, ed. Eugene F Provenzo and Edmund Abaka (London: Routledge, 2019), 123; W.E.B. Du Bois, "Liberia, the League, and the United States (1933)," in *W.E.B. Du Bois: International Thought*, ed. Adom Getachew and Jennifer Pitts (United Kingdoms:

Cambridge University Press, 2022), 100; W.E.B. Du Bois, "Inter-Racial Implications of the Ethiopian Crisis—A Negro View," *Foreign Affairs* 14, no. 1 (1935): 82 at 85. See also Gregg Mitman, *Empire of Rubber: Firestone's Scramble for Land and Power in Liberia* (New York: The New Press, 2021).

74. Letter from Gohr to Bellegarde, January 16, 1925, ILO Archives. He added, however, that if the association itself addressed a communication to the Commission, there was a procedure with which to treat it.

75. Temporary Slavery Commission, *Minutes of the First Session*, Seventh Meeting held on July 12, 1924, League of Nations Doc A.18. 1924.VI, 31.

76. Temporary Slavery Commission, *Minutes of the Second Session*, Fourteenth Meeting held on July 20, 1925, League of Nations Doc C.426. M.157.1925.VI, 69. In this, he echoed Freire Andrade's statements to the League of Nations' Assembly.

77. Temporary Slavery Commission, *Minutes of the Second Session*, Fourteenth Meeting, 69.

78. Temporary Slavery Commission, *Minutes of the Second Session*, Fourteenth Meeting, 69–70.

79. Temporary Slavery Commission, *Minutes of the Second Session*, Fourteenth Meeting, 72.

80. Temporary Slavery Commission, *Minutes of the Second Session*, Sixteenth Meeting held on July 21, 1925, League of Nations Doc C.426. M.157.1925.VI, 79.

81. While this proposal on consular authority for factory labor inspection received some support, the proposal—in the form initially proposed by Sir F. Lugard—was presented without regard to its potential for developing the capabilities of native populations by giving them "a share in the economic life of the country." This was recognized by the French Governor to Togo, Bonnecarrère, in a 1923 address to the Mandates Commission, in which he explained that "natives shared proportionately with white population the profits of their work." For his anthropological approach to the classification of "native" races, see Ulrike Schürkens, "La pratique 'administrative-anthropologique' de la France au Togo: Les activités du gouverneur Bonnecarrère (1922–1931)," *Revue d'histoire Outre-Mers* 203 (1944): 55–70. Temporary Slavery Commission, *Minutes of the Second Session*, Seventeenth Meeting, 83.

82. Temporary Slavery Commission, *Minutes of the First Session*, Tenth Meeting, 49.

83. Temporary Slavery Commission, *Minutes of the Second Session*, Eighteenth Meeting, 91.

84. See e.g., Gregg Mitman, *Empire of Rubber: Firestone's Scramble for Land and Power in Liberia* (The New Press, 2021).

85. Temporary Slavery Commission, *Minutes of the Second Session*, Eighteenth Meeting held on July 25, 1925, League of Nations Doc C.426. M.157.1925.VI, 69.

86. Temporary Slavery Commission, *Minutes of the Second Session*, Eighteenth Meeting, 93.

87. The remaining three commissioners, Alfredo Freire d'Andrade, Roncagli, and Van Rees, let it be known that they would have voted in favor had there not been the suggestion included that an international convention is "a measure which seems to the Temporary Slavery Commission to be desirable" (Temporary Slavery Commission, *Minutes of the Second Session*, Eighteenth Meeting, 93). Interestingly, Lugard stresses in describing the nature of slavery in Abyssinia that the "slaves are not of the same

race as their owners" (Temporary Slavery Commission, Annex 2, *Note on Conditions in Abyssinia*).

88. Ultimately the special reports of the Commissioners were not annexed, but preserved in the archives of the secretariat, over Bellegarde's objection. And despite this, in subsequent deliberation, two of Sir F. Lugard's notes—on Abyssinia and on forced labor, were appended to the minutes.

89. Henry J. Richardson III, *The Origins of African-American Interests in International Law* (Durham: Carolina Academic Press, 2008), 80.

CHAPTER SIX

TRANSFORMING THE RACIALIZED INTERNATIONAL SYSTEM

Intellectual and Political Challenges

ROGERS M. SMITH

THE CHALLENGES OF AN IMPERIALLY AND RACIALLY STRUCTURED INTERNATIONAL SYSTEM

In a variety of disciplines, the last two decades display a new scholarly focus, with notable leadership from both radical international law scholars and scholars of Critical Race Theory. Not just in legal studies but in history, sociology, anthropology, international relations, a range of cultural studies disciplines, and virtually all the subfields of political science, a surge of outstanding works explore how the United States and other modern nations—including most of North, Central, and South America, Australia, New Zealand, and South Africa—originated as white settler colonies within a broader world system of self-proclaimed sovereign nation-states, hegemonically structured primarily by European and European-descended imperial powers. This scholarship has generated penetrating critiques of policies and institutions that continue to harm formerly colonized and Indigenous populations, often with special attention to national barriers blocking escapes from hardships via immigration. It has also sparked critical rethinking and reimagining of possibilities on a wide range of political, economic, and social issues.

Most scholars, to be sure, have known about white settler colonialism, global imperialism, and self-serving immigration restrictions all along. Writing as a highly traditional scholar in his last book, political scientist Samuel P. Huntington observed, "in its origins America was not a nation of immigrants, it was a society, or societies, of settlers . . . Its origins as an Anglo-Protestant settler society have, more than anything else, profoundly and lastingly shaped American culture, institutions, historical development, and identity."[1] Yet as Huntington acknowledged, he had previously not given much weight to that reality. Like all too many mainstream scholars, including many more liberal ones, Huntington had treated these aspects of America's origins as of, at best, marginal significance for understanding its political culture and historical development. By the early 2000s, Huntington felt compelled to revise his views, in part because he saw left-leaning political movements, often preceding and inspiring critical scholarship, gaining momentum in challenging many legacies of those origins. Huntington wished instead to preserve many historical features of America, in part through curbs on ethnoculturally diverse immigrants. But since Huntington's death in 2008, critical efforts intent on overcoming, not preserving, the legacies of colonialism have risen further, in scholarship and in politics around the world.

Precisely because my scholarship and political activities draw on and seek to aid these critical endeavors, here I wish to focus on the intellectual and political challenges they face, as well as several limitations in the ways some current critical scholarship addresses those challenges. To preview: the central intellectual challenge today is to imagine plausible alternatives to the structuring of the world primarily as a system of nation-states claiming absolute sovereignty, including plenary power to control migration on any grounds that a nation sees as in its self-interest. The central political challenge is that conservative, often authoritarian nationalisms are resurgent in many parts of the world, opposing all movements for constructive transformations in the prevailing nation-state system, including bans on racially biased immigration policies. The main limitation in some current critical scholarship is that, in the quest to expose an unjust status quo and to envision alternative, more equitable forms of political communities, critics sometimes oversimplify, presenting the histories, ideas, and practices of both colonizing and colonized peoples in too sharply a dichotomous fashion, instead of capturing the diversity and complexities that all communities display, as well as the ways the interactions of the colonized and colonizers have long shaped and reshaped them both. These tendencies work against the potential for progressive scholars to draw fully on what can be learned from the perspectives and histories of colonized peoples in order to imagine new political possibilities. They also risk sacrificing the potential of some of the ideas and values in colonizing nations to aid in the building of transformative political coalitions, a potential visible in American political development.

THE CURRENT CRITICAL SCHOLARLY CONSENSUS

Although historically scholars in many fields actually aided white settler colonialism and other forms of imperialism, James Thuo Gathii has argued persuasively that the rise of both Critical Race Theory (CRT) and Third World Approaches to

International Law (TWAIL) in major American law schools in the 1990s helped spur the far more critical attention to those topics that has since reshaped scholarship in many fields.[2] The Harvard Law School was a central incubator of both those developments (with Huntington residing nearby, perhaps anxiously, in Harvard's Center for International Affairs).[3] The core elements of the consensus that has since emerged among progressive scholars can be briefly stated, along with their implications for the politics of race, national borders, and immigration.

As political theorist Adom Getachew has written, the (partial) transformation of a world that was hegemonically ruled by openly racist European empires has produced a global system of highly unequal nation-states, one "incapable of realizing the ideals of a democratic, egalitarian, and anti-imperial future" free of domestic and international "domination" and "racial hierarchy."[4] Most critical scholars see it as well established that the immigration policies of wealthy nation-states, and many of the international laws invoked to justify them, have long worked on balance to preserve both domestic and international racial and economic inequalities.

In 2014, Alison Bashford could already observe that: "Immigration acts have long been analyzed as instrumental to the working of the modern nation-state," with "the history of settler-colonial race-based exclusions" especially "much studied."[5] Monika Batra Kashyap critiqued Trump policies in 2019 by building on the widely shared "premise that the United States is a present-day settler colonial society whose laws and policies function to support an ongoing structure of invasion called 'settler colonialism,' which operates through the processes of Indigenous elimination and the subordination of racialized outsiders."[6] In 2020, Hannah Gordon similarly contended that contemporary "U.S. immigration law and policy are designed to deny refuge to people Indigenous to the Americas in a way that echoes early jurisprudence denying citizenship to Native Americans" as "part of a settler-colonial project."[7] In the same vein, Justin Desautels-Stein has recently provided a rich historical analysis of how liberal international law thinking blended with racial ideologies from the outset, fostering a world of racialized boundaries that the linked emergence of human rights jurisprudence, antidiscrimination laws, and multiculturalism has not undone.[8] So long as efforts to preserve the borders of modern national peoples persist, he concludes, even the most apparently liberal reasons for "bounding the demos" will be arguments "for racial borders."[9]

Despite these agreements, there are important intellectual and political tensions in recent critical accounts of the global nation-state system and immigration policies. In 2021, historian Roxanne Dunbar-Ortiz published *Not "A Nation of Immigrants": Settler Colonialism, White Supremacy, and a History of Erasure and Exclusion*. Examining the original British colonial settlers in North America who created "a parallel empire to Great Britain, ultimately overcoming it," as well as how the U.S. then treated enslaved Africans, Mexicans, Irish refugees from

English colonial rule, southern and eastern Europeans, and Asians, Dunbar-Ortiz contended that "White nationalism was inscribed in the founding of the United States as a European settler-colonial expansionist entity, the economy of which was grounded in the violent theft of land and in racial slavery."[10] But she perceived some lessening in the racial bordering of the United States over time, while noting that this development threatened only to compound the burdens on those Indigenous peoples for whom *all* immigrants are encroaching settlers. In twenty-first century America, Dunbar-Ortiz maintained, "immigrants from Asia, Africa, Latin America, and the Caribbean are not pressured to become 'white,' as immigrants were in the past"; but "most remain indifferent or even negate the demands of Indigenous communities and the reality of settler colonialism," and so they become settlers by "default." She concluded, citing Mahmood Mamdani, that though the U.S. has to a limited degree been "deracialized" by a range of liberation movements, "America still remains a settler society and a settler state"—never, truly, a nation of immigrants.[11]

In addition to this political tension between the interests of Indigenous peoples and those of immigrants, the critical consensus on the origins and injustices of the existing nation-state system does not extend to full agreement on its driving forces and its mechanisms. Many scholars and activists refer to that system as resting on "racial capitalism," domestically and globally. Yet as many have noted, the term "racial capitalism" has a number of different, not wholly compatible meanings.[12] The term's current popularity probably arises in part because it provides an inspiring rallying cry for those opposed to both racist and capitalist injustices, while remaining ambiguous enough on the character and mechanisms of the linkages between them to permit it to be interpreted in different ways. It can be invoked by those who think it necessary to address racial inequalities prior to any radical transformation in capitalist economic inequalities; by those who feel instead that such a radical economic transformation must precede, and will generate, an end to racial inequalities; and by those who favor targeting both racial and economic inequalities at once, despite how difficult this is to do in practice.

Though the concept of "racial capitalism" has older roots, particularly in 1970s Marxist debates in South Africa, and this is not the place to explore them fully, many today trace the term to the late political scientist Cedric Robinson. He maintained in his 1983 book, *Black Marxism: The Making of the Black Radical Tradition*, that even European feudal systems of labor exploitation racialized their workers to justify their lowly statuses.[13] So Robinson saw capitalism as having emerged within already racialized nations, and as inherently racially exploitative. As he put it in *Black Marxism*, rather than arising from inequities originating with capitalism, "the social, psychological, and cultural origins of racism and nationalism both anticipated capitalism in time and formed a piece with those events that contributed directly to its organization of production and exchange."[14]

Many more recent analysts of racial capitalism do not follow Robinson's chronology or his account of racial and capitalist linkages. They portray modern racial ideologies as developing after feudalism in order to justify the violent expropriation of labor, land, and resources from populations subjected to European capitalist imperial expansion. Some racial capitalism analysts advance these views in amendment to or disagreement with Robinson. Some do not refer to his work at all. Nancy Leong, for example, has analyzed how today's "racial capitalist" systems use "nonwhite people" as valuable economic commodities by building on writings in Critical Race Theory, without citing Robinson.[15] Michael Javen Fortner has revised Robinson's conception of racial capitalism to stress how the "co-constitutive dynamics of racial capitalism" can foment "intra-racial fissures and cross-racial" class alliances, such as those between Black and white urban landlords, in ways that often work to bolster capitalism while deepening the hardships of the urban Black poor.[16] Though Fortner makes those consequences clear, questions remain about what he sees as propelling racial capitalist dynamics, and how.

Similarly, historian Jennifer L. Morgan argues that racism and capitalist profitability have been "co-constituted," without specifying the mechanisms of their linked emergence and persistence.[17] As Zachary Levenson and Marcel Paret have noted, most of the scholars and advocates who invoke "racial capitalism" simply do not seek to resolve whether there is "a preexisting racism that helps constitute capitalism, or whether racial differentiation is an effect of capitalism itself," or whether some other relationship is at work.[18] Nor do many clarify whether they believe that racism can survive without capitalism, or capitalism without racism. The ambiguities sometimes moderate but sometimes fuel conflicts over how political struggles against racism and capitalism should be conducted.

THE INTELLECTUAL CHALLENGE

Nonetheless, the greatest intellectual challenge for proponents of critical perspectives is not how to understand "racial capitalism." It is to imagine what sorts of political communities and economies, and what global structure of their relationships, should replace the existing system of predominantly capitalist nation-states. There are few blueprints delineating what a better, truly postcolonial world would look like, much less any consensus on one. There is only a widely shared aspirational sense of what progressives should seek, and an almost as widely shared strategy for where to look for ideas to construct a new global political imaginary. The aspiration is, again in Getachew's words, to achieve "an anti-imperial future" that sees the rise of "an egalitarian and domination-free world."[19] The most popular strategy among progressive scholars, especially younger ones, is to seek to build on the political visions of Indigenous, formerly colonized, and formerly enslaved peoples, rejecting or at least radically reimagining the elements of the European-rooted worldviews that generated and sustained imperialism.

Getachew herself pursues this strategy by analyzing the "worldmaking" envisioned by twentieth-century anticolonial nationalists, including Nnamdi Azikiwe, Michael Manley, Kwame Nkrumah, Julius Nyere, George Padmore, and Eric Williams.[20] And though she sees their specific ideas for international organizations, regional federations, and a "New International Economic Order" as having faltered, she believes that "intimations of a new language" for pursuing their goals "are afoot in the Movement for Black Lives, the Caribbean demand for reparations for slavery and genocide, and South African calls for a social and economic decolonization."[21] Getachew's turn to anticolonial thinkers as resources for imagining a more egalitarian world order echoes the extensive body of critical international law scholarship that seeks to advance fundamental rethinking of many precepts of European Enlightenment thought.[22] Along with Getachew, a number of other younger political theorists such as Shuk Ying Chan similarly urge turning to leading anticolonial intellectuals, rather than European or American thinkers.[23]

In the same spirit, but without a focus on Third World intellectuals, Adam Dahl has recently sought "to sever constitutional thought and practice" in America from its white settler "colonial foundations" in order to advance "more inclusive and egalitarian" political projects, "decolonizing democracy."[24] Like other critical scholars, Dahl interprets the American Revolution as an exercise in the construction of a European-derived, ethnoculturally restrictive society seeking to expand its own empire. He depicts the revolutionaries' cause as a quarrel between North American settlers and imperial authorities in London over whether the colonists and their communities should be equal to other English subjects and units within the British empire.[25] Dahl agrees with Dunbar-Ortiz that the refusal of the British to accept this status led only to the U.S. becoming a parallel empire to Great Britain.

Consequently, rather than seeking to draw on mainstream American figures, Dahl turns to the perspectives of North America's Indigenous tribes. He highlights the nineteenth-century Pequot activist William Apess, who aided the Mashpee tribe in its conflict with the Massachusetts state government by drawing up an "Indian Declaration of Independence."[26] The resolutions comprising it assert that "all men are born free and equal, says the Constitution of the country" (probably referring to Article 1 of the Massachusetts Constitution, though Dahl reads this as a reference to the U.S. Constitution, which does not contain that phrase). The first resolution contends that therefore, the tribe has "the right ... to rule ourselves."[27]

Though these resolutions' arguments might appear to echo the natural rights opening of the 1776 Declaration of Independence, Dahl interprets them as, at most, paralleling what he sees as the American revolutionaries' real claim, that their communities were entitled to equal self-governing rights within the British empire.[28] The denial of such self-governance to the Mashpees justified, in Dahl's reading of Apess, the "Indian Nullification" of their alleged conquest by Massachusetts and the United States.[29] He sees this nullification as crucial to how Apess "harnesses the authority of the Constitution and the Declaration" to clear space for an entirely distinct narrative of the injustice of American imperialism toward the continent's Indigenous peoples.[30] But Dahl rejects any contention that in so arguing, Apess used "liberal legal discourse" against the white settler state. Citing Michel Foucault, Dahl contends that liberal discourse, focused on social contract theories, "lacks the concept of 'conquest' in its theoretical repertoire"—an assertion made without discussing, for example, John Locke's chapter entitled "Of Conquest" in the *Second Treatise of Government*.[31] Dahl concludes that the Indigenous thought of figures like Apess provides more resources for "decolonizing democracy" than any other American political tradition.[32]

Previously in his 2010 book, *The Two Faces of American Freedom*, law professor and political scientist Aziz Rana similarly contended that "American experience is best understood as a constitutional and political experiment in . . . *settler empire*," a project that intertwined "expansion, immigration, race and class" in ways that "undermined the very promise" of the "uniquely American ideal of freedom."[33] Rana saw the American revolutionary generation as embracing a republican idea of freedom involving "continuous popular mobilization and direct control by insiders" over major economic and political decisions, but also "Indian dispossession and the coercive use of dependent groups, most prominently slaves."[34] He recognized that "at key periods" thereafter, "reformers and social movements" sought to reconceive American freedom "without either subordination or empire." But in Rana's eyes, these efforts "atrophied" in the twentieth century, placing "security at the center of political discourse" and entrenching "hierarchical forms of economic and political rule."[35]

Rana acknowledged that the American revolution had nonetheless given "birth to a liberating vision of collective possibility" that reformers later used to try to "create a new, universal, and nonimperial American polity," stripping "republican ideals of their oppressive roots" and making "free citizenship broadly accessible to all."[36] Yet while Rana has always credited what he calls America's "redemptive reform" movements with real accomplishments, he has over time judged them to be empirically and normatively insufficient. He believes they efface rather than redress the nation's settler colonial origins—roots that still sustain myriad inequalities, including the oppression of Indigenous peoples and denials of opportunities to many nonwhite Americans and immigrants.[37] These redemptive reform perspectives inevitably minimize the need for radical change through their presentations of American identity as centered on universalistic egalitarian commitments that require only fuller realization. In contrast, Rana has come to appeal to a "revolutionary reform" Black political tradition in America that he sees as having antecedents among radical African Americans during the Civil War, but as especially elaborated by the Black Panthers and others in the 1960s and '70s.[38]

Thus Rana has joined the rising tide of "decolonization" scholars who look to the perspectives of marginalized communities to find resources on which to build truly postcolonial forms of political life. He calls for an "anticolonial vision" that aims at "fundamental social transformation" of American racism, American power, and American political economy. In order to "imagine other alternatives," he counsels progressives to look especially to twentieth-century American Black radicals to discern "the structural economic and political changes that might in fact produce equal and effective freedom."[39]

In his 2023 book, Desautels-Stein similarly maintains that we "require tools for reenvisioning property and sovereignty, opening the door to structures of inclusion we have yet to discover," if we are to have political communities whose borders are not "inevitably racialized."[40] Like Rana and perhaps even more like Cedric Robinson, Desautels-Stein turns to W.E.B. Du Bois and other contributors to the "critical race tradition" to aid in discovering those tools. But while many critical scholars affirm the strategy of turning to the perspectives of the oppressed in order to reimagine the world's political communities and structures, so far progress toward a compelling new vision has been limited. Though Getachew has made a major contribution in highlighting the concerns of anticolonial nationalists to embed their new nations in a more egalitarian international system, she does not advocate for their specific proposals. In assessing whether the critical race tradition contains the necessary resources for the reimagining of sovereignty and property, Desautels-Stein concludes only, "Perhaps."[41] In politics as in scholarship, it is customary and understandable that critiques are often more powerful and persuasive than novel constructive proposals. At present the efforts to conceptualize new political and economic systems, international legal institutions, and immigration policies in ways that move beyond their current deep entanglements with systems of racial injustice remain largely in that condition.

I advance this judgment in sympathy, not rebuttal. Although my scholarship has primarily sought to explore ways that contemporary nation-states can become more egalitarian, inclusive, and democratic, it has not done so out of any desire to maintain a global system of sovereign nation-states now and forever. Instead, I have argued against sustaining traditional notions of state sovereignty, and for working to achieve a world in which people are recognized to legitimately have multiple, overlapping, in many cases loosely federated memberships in varied political communities, from local to global scales. I've argued that modern immigration controversies in particular cannot be resolved "by reasserting the allegedly unbridled sovereign prerogatives of national governments" and by dismissing the claims of all whom governments do not wish to recognize as belonging to them.[42] I have suggested that it would be far better for political communities to see themselves as "roughly equal and only 'semi-sovereign,'" as authoritative over some matters and not others, and as having obligations to engage in the cooperative development of policies "in which different governments perform different but complementary functions," and collectively enable all of their constituents to pursue lives in their multiple memberships as seamlessly, fluidly, and fully as possible, moving "freely among them."[43]

For those goals to be achieved in the United States, Indigenous communities would need to win recognition as having more "semi-sovereign" power than they now do, and the U.S. would have to embrace truly multilateral regional and global associations and policies in economic and security realms much more fully than it now does. It would also have an obligation to be more receptive to immigration, especially from those regions whose populations have been deeply shaped in their interests and identities by coercively enforced American policies. It is for me not only imaginable but desirable that the U.S. could eventually become part of regional, then global democratic political federations in which, over time, the U.S. and other nation-states would give way to the primacy of federated political communities very differently structured and denominated.

That vision appears to broadly resemble the world many contributors to the critical literature on white settler colonialism hope to see. As just noted, many believe that more specific guidance on what that world might look like can and probably must be drawn from the perspectives of the colonized. I agree that Indigenous thought and experiences, Black radical views, critical international law perspectives, and more are all resources that merit more serious consideration than they have received from mainstream scholars in virtually all disciplines.

As pertinent studies have multiplied in recent years, however, they have increasingly revealed the complexity and hybridity of Indigenous, radical, non-Western, and also long-predominant Western political views. In so doing, they have made less clear what it might mean to try to imagine a non-imperial world by turning from the thought of the colonizers to the colonized. Some of the colonized have previously been imperial peoples themselves. And because scholars are uncovering how deeply interwoven the worldviews of colonizers and the colonized have been over the past six centuries, it seems reasonable to seek to build a progressive politics on the best aspects of all these perspectives, instead of merely choosing sides and launching attacks. When we consider not just the profound intellectual challenges but also the enormous political obstacles facing efforts to move to a more egalitarian world of cooperative, semi-sovereign peoples, those considerations take on great weight.

THE POLITICAL CHALLENGE

The greatest political obstacle to transforming the current system of nation-states is the global resurgence of strongly nationalistic movements, most claiming to be populist, many overtly authoritarian, all insistent that their national sovereignty must be absolute and inviolate. From the British Right's successful Brexit advocacy to Viktor Orbán's "illiberal democracy" in Hungary to the Hindu nationalism of Narendra Modi and the heightened Chinese nationalism of Xi Jinping, the examples are legion. It is ironic that, as Dunbar-Ortiz notes at the outset of her book, the Trump administration agreed with the insistence of critical scholars like herself that the United States is not a nation of immigrants, but rather a settler society claiming sovereignty over conquered lands. Under Trump, the U.S. Citizenship and Immigration Services changed its mission statement, dropping the assertion that the agency "secures America's promise as a nation of immigrants" in favor of the goal of "safeguarding" the "integrity and promise" of "the nation's lawful immigration system," while "protecting Americans, securing the homeland, and honoring our values."[44] Those Trump immigration policies are why Huntington's latter-day endorsement of the view that American identity was "based upon an Anglo-American Protestant nationalism that was as much racial and religious as it was political," and his concern that immigration trends threatened this identity, led him to be called "a prophet for the Trump era."[45]

To assess how great a barrier to critical aspirations this nationalist trend poses, we must recognize that not only did Trump and his MAGA Republicans win historic victories in the 2024 U.S. elections, their brand of "national conservatism" also has many prominent adherents and advocates throughout the world. The most full-throated exponents are the so-called "NatCon" intellectuals, pundits, and political figures who have embraced the 2022 "National Conservatism Statement of Principles." It emerged from the National Conservatism Conferences begun in 2019, organized by the Edmund Burke Foundation and the Conservative Partnership Institute.[46] The Statement's signers are an impressive variety of older and newer conservative voices in America and many other countries. They include not only Yoram Hazony of the Edmund Burke Foundation, Mark Meadows, and former Senator and Heritage Foundation President Jim DeMint of the Conservative Partnership Institute, but also Charlie Kirk of Turning Point USA, Christopher Rufo of the Manhattan Institute, Carol Swain of the Texas Public Policy Foundation, and fellows of the Claremont Institute, the Hudson Institute, the Intercollegiate Studies Institute, the Hoover Institution, as well as leaders of Hillsdale College and the Center for Immigration Studies, among others. Among that broad range of supporters is the billionaire Peter Thiel, whose resources alone have provided the National Conservatism movement with a robust financial foundation.

Christopher DeMuth, Distinguished Fellow at the Hudson Institute, former president of the American Enterprise Institute, and chair of the National Conservatism Conference, has argued that a new, more aggressively nationalist conservatism is needed because "almost every progressive initiative subverts the American nation ... opening national borders ... transferring sovereignty to international bureaucracies ... elevating group identity above citizenship; fomenting racial, ethnic, and religious divisions ... defaming our national history as a story of unmitigated injustice."[47] Consequently, the NatCons' Statement of Principles opens: "we see a world of independent nations—each pursuing its own national interests and upholding national traditions that are its own—as the only genuine alternative to universalist ideologies now seeking to impose a homogenizing, locality-destroying imperium over the entire globe."[48]

"National Independence" is therefore the Statement's first principle, including a call for each nation to "maintain its own borders" and adopt "a policy of rearmament." It then rejects both imperialism and globalism, particularly opposing "transferring the authority of elected governments to transnational or supranational bodies." Though it calls for each nation to "chart its own course in accordance with its own particular constitutional, linguistic, and religious inheritance," its principles for structuring a "national government" simply paraphrase the preamble to the U.S. Constitution. It also endorses "the federalist principle," while cautioning that "in those states or subdivisions in which law and justice have been manifestly corrupted," the "national government must intervene energetically to restore order."[49]

The Statement's fourth principle makes clear that this conservative nationalism presents itself as religious nationalism: it states that where "a Christian majority exists, public life should be rooted in Christianity and its moral vision, which should be honored by the state and other institutions both public and private," though "Jews and other religious minorities are to be protected in the observance of their own traditions." The Statement goes on to urge public research to aid defense and manufacturing capabilities. But, incensed by the critical scholarly perspectives just reviewed, it condemns "most universities" as "partisan and globalist in orientation and vehemently opposed to nationalist and conservative ideas," so that they "do not deserve taxpayer support." The National Conservatives also urge "much more restrictive" immigration policies, even a moratorium, until countries "establish more balanced, productive, and assimilationist policies."[50]

With its appeal to all those with strong traditionalist senses of national and religious identities, and its accusations of how globalist progressives are harming much of the world's national populations, the national conservative movement has great potency. Now and for years to come, it will pose major barriers to efforts to try to move beyond self-proclaimed sovereign nation-states to a freer and more egalitarian world of semi-sovereign communities. The national conservatives are, after all, *correct* to say that their opponents reject national sovereignty and seek to transform the entire global nation-state system in radical ways. That makes it all the easier for the Right in many lands to stoke fears about the dangers of change.

THE INTELLECTUAL LIMITATIONS

It is consequently vital for progressive scholars and activists to strive to ensure that their endeavors are as defensible as possible. But because it is difficult to pursue progressive work without feeling passion for the cause, it is not surprising that sometimes the work is done in ways that give ammunition to conservative opponents. There are three types of errors or excesses into which some recent critical scholarship falls that especially risk doing just that. All represent forms of oversimplification that open the door to dismissive rejections.

The first is to treat all opponents of European imperialism as categorically anti-colonial and anti-imperialist, when forms of arguably unjust domination can be found in the histories of virtually all peoples. The second is to fail to recognize how extensively the interactions of Europeans and Indigenous peoples in North and South America, Africa, and Asia have shaped and reshaped the thinking of those expounding both European and non-European political traditions. The third, and perhaps most controversial, is the refusal to acknowledge that as a result, there are elements in European and American "mainstream" thought that have been and probably can be assets for progressive efforts to imagine and create a more equitable world order.

1. <u>The Complexities of the Colonized</u>. In a largely favorable review of Getachew's *Worldmaking after Empire*, Shuk Ying Chan has argued that while the anticolonial nationalists Getachew studied were compelling critics of European imperialism and champions of a reformed international system, they still exhibited many of the limitations of nationalism, arguably to a greater degree than Getachew acknowledges. They used their claims of nation self-determination "to deny their minorities equal rights to self-governance, and in some cases . . . to violently suppress them." They limited the powers of the transnational federations they professed to support, such as the African Union, in order to protect national governmental prerogatives; and they claimed full sovereignty over their natural resources.[51] Though Chan's own work seeks to find tools for reimagining a world shaped by imperialism through exploration of Third World intellectuals and leaders, she and other critical scholars pursuing this strategy are struggling with the gap between these figures' best ideals and many of their political practices.[52] Opponents of this turn have also stressed that many anticolonial leaders had Western educations, complicating any presentation of their thought or policies as straightforward opposition to all in Western traditions.

Similarly, Pekka Hämäläinen, the simultaneously acclaimed and assailed Finnish historian of North American tribes, has observed that in recent decades, "historians have conceived of entirely new ways of thinking about Native

Americans, Euro-Americans, and their tangled histories." North America's Indigenous peoples are now seen "as full-fledged historical actors" in "a dialectic process that created . . . new hybrid worlds that were neither wholly Indian nor European."[53] Hämäläinen is himself a seminal contributor to this development. He is controversial in part because in showing that the North American tribes displayed varied political, economic, and social arrangements and often adapted them over time as they interacted with Europeans and with each other, some tribes established forms of domination over other Indigenous peoples that Hämäläinen terms "imperial."

In *The Comanche Empire*, Hämäläinen argued that between 1750 and 1850 the Comanches became distinctive but long-successful imperialists, building an empire whose "borders were sites of mutualistic trade and cultural fusion" with white settlers, though "they were also sites of extortion, systematic violence, coerced exchange, political manipulation, and hardening racial attitudes" on all sides.[54] Hämäläinen told a related narrative of the Lakotan empire in his 2019 book, *Lakota America*.[55] Most recently, in *Indigenous Continent: The Epic Contest for North America*, Hämäläinen has sought to provide an overarching synthetic account, focused on Indigenous perspectives, of the "four-centuries-long war" of Native American peoples against "encroaching colonial powers." In his telling, this was a continental war in which many participants displayed courage and skill, but also harsh exercises of power, with some tribes as well as white settlers utilizing enslaved labor; though Hämäläinen judges that the European colonizers committed the "most atrocities."[56] To critics, Hämäläinen nonetheless appears to suggest a moral equivalence of empires that excuses white settler colonialism. He believes instead that he is capturing both accurate history and Native Americans' impressive historical agency.[57]

Whether or not he is correct in every particular, Hämäläinen shows in his works that while Native Americans and European settlers shaped each other, profound differences in their worldviews survived; that the Indigenous peoples of North America had a wide and evolving variety of political communities; and that even those that merit designation as slaveholding empires were conceived and operated in ways that were unlike European settler empires.[58] It is therefore reasonable to believe that, as Adam Dahl and others have suggested, much material for reimagining modern political communities can be found in the rich and complex array of Indigenous conceptions and practices, some of which have strong claims to having already been formative in American national identity. Yet given the evidence of Indigenous empires, it is impossible to view Indigenous thought as solely a wellspring for anti-imperialist democratic theorizing. The same is likely to be true of the perspectives of the colonized in many other parts of the world. The quest to draw upon them must recognize the complexities that recent scholarship has brought to light.

2. <u>The Hybridity of All Modern Peoples</u>. Despite Hämäläinen's stress on hybridity, one of his sharpest critics, the Shoshone historian Ned Blackhawk, has argued that he fails to grasp it fully. Reviewing Hämäläinen's most recent book, Blackhawk writes that in his "crude celebrations of Indigenous agency," Hämäläinen understates both how Native nations influenced the development of the American state, with for example the Cherokee, Chickasaw, and Choctaw nations all sending representatives to the Constitutional Convention, and how American governmental policies impacted the tribes, often brutally.[59] This critique only underlines, however, that even as it is beneficial to learn about the distinctive forms of political community among the North American Indigenous tribes and other non-European peoples around the world, it is also necessary to recognize the mutual reshaping that almost inevitably occurs when different communities interact, even under relations of unequal power.

Gathii has presented such hybridity as characteristic, indeed a strength, of TWAIL scholarship, noting that "Third World scholars have always been simultaneously critical of but clearly enamored by international law while offering how alternative or non-western ideals could introduce new meanings, standards, rules and norms of international law."[60] At times, however, scholars seeking to find alternative traditions to those of Western imperialism have resisted acknowledging this hybridity. Consider, for example, how Aziz Rana urges turning to Black radical traditions, particularly praising the vision of the Black Panthers in the 1960s. That vision was indeed radical, yet it was also undeniably hybrid. The Panthers' 1966 Ten-Point Platform and Program urged the courts to follow the Fourteenth Amendment. It culminated by quoting the opening paragraphs of the Declaration of Independence, contending that they justified a plebiscite, to be supervised by the United Nations, "to be held throughout the black colony . . . for the purpose of determining the will of black people as to their national destiny."[61] Yet Rana discusses the Panther Party Platform and Program without mentioning this pronounced reliance on the Declaration of Independence.[62]

David Graeber and David Wengrow's iconoclastic 2021 book, *The Dawn of Everything: A New History of Humanity,* advances a claim about hybridity that is particularly striking for debates over reliance on Western thought. Even as Graeber and Wengrow urge greater attention to the ideas of Indigenous thinkers, they contend that European Enlightenment ideas of freedom and equality actually originated with "the Indigenous critique" of Europe, the arguments of Native Americans like the Wendat statesman Kandiaronk that the elaborate hierarchical ranks and restrictions of European societies were degrading and immiserating.[63] They note that European intellectuals, raised in hereditary monarchical and aristocratic societies, did not readily conceive or accept premises of human freedom and equality. But while many Europeans sought to defend their rigidly inegalitarian political, social, and economic institutions against this Indigenous critique, Graeber and Wengrow maintain that major Enlightenment thinkers did so with increased respect for ideals of personal and communal liberty and equality that challenged the monarchical absolutism that had developed in concert with expanding European imperialism. Graeber and Wengrow's arguments suggest that at least some of the seeds of the popular republicanism and the broader appeals to human freedom and equality that would be used to justify the American revolution against Britain, as well as innumerable later political and social emancipatory movements, can be seen as Indigenous North American transplants to European thought, rather than as purely themes of Western colonizers.

Intellectual historians will surely debate the bold contentions of these revisionist authors, an anthropologist and archaeologist, for years to come. Yet along with the scholarship of Hämäläinen, Blackhawk, and other recent historians of Indigenous peoples, they provide reason to question a strategy of responding to white settler colonial legacies with wholesale rejection of the thoughts and practices of the European and American colonizers in favor of the perspectives of the colonized. It appears true that the thinking of both European colonizers and Indigenous peoples evolved through their encounters, incorporating aspects of the other's worldviews and ways of life. It is therefore not persuasive to dismiss all the thought of all historically prominent white Americans and Europeans as ineradicably committed to imperial domination.

It is also not politically wise to do so. To build broad, strong coalitions for change, it is most effective, whenever possible, to argue that those changes fulfill rather than assault some of the deeply held values and identities of those who might be brought to join in reform or even revolutionary causes. In pursuit of the daunting tasks of reimagining existing forms of political community, sovereignty, territory, and more, and then making real changes in the world, it makes sense to draw on all sources that have the potential to aid both in conceiving better societies and in winning support for those conceptions.

3. The Resources in Colonizing Communities. This political argument presumes, however, that there actually are valuable resources for progressives to be found even in the ideas of colonizing communities. Many critical scholars disagree, arguing with Audre Lorde that the master's tools will never dismantle the master's house. Yet when many Southern masters' homes were destroyed in the Civil War, it was with weapons and tools much like those whites had wielded against those they enslaved. And as Hämäläinen has maintained, although "Native Americans were for a long time stunted as historical agents, today it is the colonists and settlers who seem to be in danger of becoming caricatured, their motives and ambitions simplified, their complexity flattened. With the Indians commanding the center stage,

the whites often appear as a monolithic mass hell-bent on conquest." He calls for "taking the ideals, anxieties, and ambitions of the colonists seriously, tracing how they clashed and intertwined with Native ones, and how Lakota and European newcomers created lasting shared worlds even when they misunderstood, hated, and killed one another."[64]

Critical scholars render their works intellectually vulnerable when they fail to take the ideals of those they oppose as seriously as Hämäläinen recommends. I have noted how Rana's generally excellent book can be faulted for neglecting the Black Panthers' invocation and repurposing of the Constitution and especially the Declaration of Independence. Much of my argument here is driven by a vivid sense of how often the Declaration has served as a source of inspiration and an effective organizing tool for many liberation movements throughout history, and not only in America, though I focus on the U.S. here. I suspect a similar case can be made on behalf of at least some other prominent human rights documents, including ones in international law that critical scholars sometimes dismiss as irrevocably flawed products of racist, imperialist European thought.

It is striking, for example, that Dunbar-Ortiz, Kashyap, Gordon, and others considered here simply fail to discuss the Declaration of Independence and its historical political uses at all when they critique American political ideologies. Adam Dahl says only a bit more about the 1776 Declaration of Independence, merely noting the ways it did and did not anticipate Vermont's declaration of independence from New York and Vermont's 1777 Constitution, which asserted the constituent power of the people to create a new government.[65] He attends instead to the Declaration of Independence of the would-be State of Franklin, which sought unsuccessfully to secede from North Carolina. Dahl sees that declaration as more clearly expressing the core revolutionary goal of white Americans: asserting power to establish a separate, equal, and independent white settler community.[66]

Dahl goes on to interpret nineteenth-century American leaders, including Abraham Lincoln and Walt Whitman, as all white settler colonial thinkers.[67] He observes, for example, that Lincoln's free labor ideology depended on the government's acquisition of land for white Americans to work "on their own," and he stresses Lincoln's support for colonization of emancipated African Americans up through 1862.[68] But that is where Dahl's discussion of Lincoln stops. He does not mention that African American leaders persuaded Lincoln to abandon colonization, and that Lincoln came to endorse not only the Thirteenth Amendment, achieving emancipation nationwide without compensation for slaveholders, but also the franchise for many African Americans—the stance that spurred Lincoln's assassination. Nor does Dahl consider how Frederick Douglass, like Lincoln, interpreted the Constitution as an instrument for realizing the goals of the Declaration of Independence, which both men interpreted to require freedom for all.

Why do such omissions matter? Though they mar the accuracy of otherwise valuable critical scholarship, their greater significance, particularly now, is their political limitations. As many state legislatures in America and many governments throughout the world are seeking to place greater controls on what kinds of political history and analysis are taught and even read, it is a political liability for scholarship to be vulnerable to these kinds of criticisms. As nationalist conservatives seek to defund all public educational institutions that they see as propagating "woke" ideologies, it is self-defeating for progressive academics to produce patently partial accounts of major political figures and developments.

Still more seriously, progressive scholars and activists are likely to miss opportunities to build coalitions in favor of their positions if they seem to disdain political leaders, movements, and ideals that many potential recruits hold in high esteem. In order to show that it is reasonable to believe such opportunities exist, in the next section I try to demonstrate that such disdain has not characterized the most impactful progressive movements throughout U.S. history. The American record shows that the nation's most significant, though certainly not always successful, reform movements have consciously recognized that while the U.S. was indeed born out of white settler colonies, it was also born through a revolution that advanced ideals more potentially radical and transformative than the goals of most of the leading revolutionaries. Those revolutionary ideals, and not the restrictive elements emphasized by today's strange bedfellows of xenophobic nationalists and critical scholars, form the legacy of the nation's origins that should be recovered, revived, and extended today.

RECOGNIZING AMERICA AS A *REVOLUTIONARY* WHITE SETTLER PROTESTANT PATRIARCHAL COLONY

Even so, recent critical accounts of American identity and development help greatly to explain the powerful resistance many Americans have long shown toward receiving and naturalizing nonwhite immigrants, and toward granting full civic equality to current inhabitants and immigrants who do not share white Protestant origins, as well as much of the enduring hostility to tribal claims for more autonomous communal existences. The white settler colonial origins of the United States are the source of those ideological traditions I have previously labeled "ascriptive Americanism," and they clarify why this particular array of ascriptive identities has clustered together in American political thought.[69] They still fuel the often vicious forms of policing, border enforcement, and other policies and practices all too characteristic of both Republican and Democratic national administrations.

The problem with recent critical accounts is much less that they are wrong than that they are incomplete. Their depictions of America's origins too often ignore or minimize major political, economic, and ideological consequences of the revolution that were, if Graeber and Wengrow are right, in some ways the fruit of the Indigenous critique that had already shaped the thought of many Enlightenment authors influential in America. The case for the value of aspects of the nation's multiple ideological traditions for both "redemptive" and "revolutionary" reformers, to use Rana's terms, admittedly depends on how much significance should be attached to the Declaration of Independence's invocations of universal "inalienable rights," derived from "Nature and Nature's God," making all persons "created equal" in key respects. Critics often contend that the revolutionaries meant these words to refer only to propertied white Christian men, and surely some did. My claim is that their choice of language still has had major impacts, more than most revolutionary leaders expected, and in directions that some feared.

It is important to recognize that the use of natural rights phrasing was a much-debated choice in the revolutionary era. Leaders argued heatedly over the wisdom of employing such language in a range of documents. Some like John Rutledge of South Carolina, but also John Jay of New York, always feared the "subversive" potential of universalistic "rights talk" to undermine the hierarchies that characterized their white settler, Protestant, patriarchal societies. They preferred to cast the revolutionary cause solely in terms of the rights of Englishmen, the perspective that Dahl and others stress.[70]

The reality, however, is that at least when it came to revolutionary rhetoric, those conservative voices lost out in the crucible of the mid-1770s. To fire up support for the dangerous and uncertain cause of revolution, advocates found they had to ascend above the dry doctrines of the English common law and appeal to noble-sounding universal principles and aspirations. Innumerable historical episodes show that the choice to do so, even if largely rhetorical at the outset, gave those principles lasting though never-uncontested potency in American politics. It is revealing that today, even American NatCons who profess allegiance to 1776 are anxious about the disruptive implications of such "universalist ideologies."

Indeed, advocates of universal rights doctrines have always faced potent opposition in America. In the nation's founding era, events soon proved that conservatives like Rutledge did have reason to worry about natural rights discourses, and American political development soon became in large part a tale of often successful conservative resistance to pressures for change. Yet that history displays contests sometimes swinging one way, sometimes another, because leaders of the new "imagined community" of the United States frequently boasted of its commitments to equal rights for all. By doing so, they helped shape the values and identities of most Americans, enabling calls to live up to those principles to have just the kind of broad popular resonance that proponents of the nation's hierarchies have always dreaded.

To be sure, ideas of universal rights alone have never been able to win victories. Other powerful economic and political interests, as well as other ideas, have always contributed to the limited successes that reformers have achieved over the enduring interests entrenched by white settler colonialism. Still, the evidence is overwhelming that those seeking inclusive, egalitarian changes in American policies, as well as those opposing such changes, have regarded the ideological traditions set in train by, especially, the 1776 Declaration of Independence as formidable assets for reform efforts. As with the American revolutionaries, moreover, reformers' reliance on those traditions, even if chiefly for tactical purposes, has inescapably influenced the goals that they and their constituencies have pursued.

The examples begin in the revolutionary era itself. Massachusetts slaves unsuccessfully petitioned Massachusetts Governor Thomas Gage in 1774 to grant acknowledgment of their "naturel right to our freedoms."[71] Also in 1774, the African American poet Phillis Wheatley wrote to her friend Samson Occum, a Mohegan Indian who had become a Presbyterian minister, a letter soon published in the *Connecticut Gazette*. In it she echoed the arguments of John Locke's *Letter Concerning Religious Toleration* by approving Occum's call for "Negroes" to receive "their natural Rights" on the ground that "in every human Breast, God has implanted a Principle, which we call Love of Freedom; it is impatient of Oppression, and pants for Deliverance."[72]

In 1777, a Native American leader named Onitositah, sometimes called Corn Tassel by whites, resisted the demands of American revolutionary commissioners for Cherokee lands in Tennessee through arguments that also showed great familiarity with American discourses on "the law of nature," while expressing the kind of alternative Indigenous perspective Dahl rightly stresses. Maintaining that the Americans' own standards of "the law of nature and the law of nations" are "against you," Onitositah insisted that the facts showed the Cherokees remained an unconquered *"separate people"*; and he dismissed American complaints that Indians did not till the ground by asking, "Why the white people do not hunt and live as we do?"[73]

Though these advocates had limited immediate impact, the incorporation into the 1780 Massachusetts Constitution of the view that "all men are born free and equal, and have certain natural, essential, and unalienable rights" proved more consequential. In 1783, Chief Justice William Cushing stated in *Commonwealth v. Jennison* that "the people of America" had embraced sentiments "favorable to the natural rights of mankind, and to that innate desire of Liberty, with which Heaven (without regard to color, complexion, or shape of noses), has inspired all the human race." The embodiment of those views in Article I of the Massachusetts Constitution made "the idea of slavery ... inconsistent with our own conduct and Constitution."[74] This ruling was a key development in the "first emancipation," the gradual ending of slavery in the Northern states following the Revolutionary War.[75]

By ruling that enslavement was an unconstitutional violation of human freedom and equality, and through subsequent decisions treating resident African

Americans as citizens, if not fully equal citizens, the Massachusetts courts made the people of the new United States less thoroughly "white settlers" than they had been in the colonial era. And as the new nation became established, a wide variety of groups turned to the language of the now-venerated Declaration to articulate their grievances and aspirations. In 1829, the New York Working Man's Party promulgated "The Working Man's Declaration of Independence," championing the "natural and inalienable rights" of "one class of a community" against "other classes" who denied them a "station of equality."[76] In the first issue of *The Liberator* in 1831, William Lloyd Garrison thundered that the principle "maintained in the American Declaration of Independence, 'that all men are created equal, and endowed by their Creator with certain inalienable rights'" required "the immediate enfranchisement of our slave population."[77] In 1834, the Boston Trades' Union announced that "with the Fathers of our Country, we hold that all men are created free and equal, endowed by their Creator with certain unalienable rights," and that "laws which have a tendency to raise any peculiar class above their fellow citizens, by granting special privileges, are contrary and in defiance of those primary principles."[78] In 1848, the feminist Seneca Falls "Declaration of Sentiments" held it to be "self-evident" that "all men and women are created equal" and "endowed by their Creator with certain inalienable rights," which included the franchise for women.[79]

In the antebellum period, anti-slavery constitutionalists including Lysander Spooner and Frederick Douglass argued that the Constitution was an instrument to realize the principles of the Declaration of Independence, a view taken up in moderated form by Abraham Lincoln and the new Republican Party. Lincoln maintained that the purpose of America was to secure basic rights for "all people, of all colors, everywhere."[80] Though this view would probably have been rejected by many American revolutionaries, it gained elaboration and acceptance as the antebellum era proceeded. Notably for issues of America's identity as a white Protestant nation, Lincoln thought the Declaration's principles compelled opposition to the anti-immigrant Know Nothing movement of the 1850s, which attracted so many of his fellow Whigs. Lincoln believed those nativists falsely read the Declaration to hold "all men are created equal, except negroes and foreigners and Catholics."[81] Democrats like party pamphleteer Henry E. Riell similarly contended the Know Nothings were wrong because America was "destined, both politically and physically, to be the free asylum for the oppressed and distressed of the universal world," in keeping with the principles of the Declaration.[82] Opposed by these Declaration of Independence–based arguments as well as by political and economic interests favorable to European immigration, after some brief success in electing officeholders, the Know Nothings failed to achieve their restrictive goals.

Still more importantly, the Union's victory in the Civil War enabled Lincoln's Republicans, after his assassination, to ratify the Thirteenth, Fourteenth, and Fifteenth Amendments. They embedded the view that the Constitution aimed to secure for all the basic rights of the Declaration more firmly, though still not unequivocally, into that document. That development did not mean that the U.S. ceased to pursue white settler objectives. In 1879, Chief Joseph of the Nez Perce tribe, recently forced to resettle on reservations, wrote in the *North American Review* that whites and the tribes could become "one people" if Indians were granted "equal rights"—including rights to choose their teachers, to practice their religions, and to "think and act and talk" for themselves.[83] However, in the decades that followed, seizures of Native American lands only accelerated.[84]

Similarly, efforts to invoke the Declaration of Independence for more inclusive and egalitarian immigration and civil rights policies continued in the late nineteenth century, but often failed. Tennessee Republican William Moore opposed the Chinese Exclusion Act by contending that such a racist measure "by the United States, the recognized champion of human rights—the nation of all others in the world whose chief pride and glory it has been to truly boast of being known and recognized everywhere as the home of the free, the asylum of the oppressed, the land where all men, of all climes, all colors, all conditions, all nationalities, are welcome to come and go at will . . . is one that does so much violence to my own sense of justice that I cannot . . . consent to aid in establishing it."[85] Restrictionists derided his view as "utopian" and "absurd," and Chinese exclusion prevailed. Later, Massachusetts Senator George Hoar, an ardent anti-imperialist, defended the inhabitants of the territories acquired in the Spanish–American War by contending, "you will have to enlarge the doctrines of the Declaration of Independence . . . before you find your right to buy and sell that people like sheep."[86] He, too, saw his arguments rejected.

Those defeats are among the mountains of evidence that millions of Americans have never accepted compliance with the universalistic opening rhetoric of the Declaration of Independence as truly obligatory. Attention to the legacies of America's revolutionary origins is most important for grasping American struggles, not American successes. Nonetheless, those struggles show that the Declaration's principles have been widely understood to have dramatically transformative implications, and some successes have occurred. Famously, Martin Luther King, Jr. repeatedly turned to the "inalienable rights" proclaimed in the Declaration of Independence to justify his calls for national actions for racial equality, including in his March on Washington speech, which helped set the political stage for the 1964 Civil Rights Act and the 1965 Voting Rights Act.[87] Also in 1965, civil rights groups like the NAACP championed the repeal of the race-based national quota system for immigrants by contending, as President Lyndon Johnson put it, that those restrictions violated "the basic principles of American democracy," making them "un-American in the highest sense."[88]

Along with others, I have argued that Cold War pressures combined with civil rights protests to make those immigration reforms appear to be in the interests of many national elite actors. The new policies were not due to Declaration of Independence ideals alone. These changes came, moreover, accompanied by erroneous assurances that the demographics of the nation would not alter much, so that again, reforms achieved greater egalitarian inclusiveness, but without any full repudiation of America's white settler traditions.[89]

Yet there is no reason to dismiss the judgments of the advocates of these measures that the Declaration's language was invaluable for winning support, nor to assume that its invocation did not reflect any of their core commitments. The evidence is to the contrary. In the contestation that has always characterized American life, reliance on the universalistic rights principles of the Declaration has been a consistent practice used to combat white Christian patriarchal settler policies. As I have noted, even the Black Panthers' 1966 Ten-Point Platform and Program culminated in an invocation of the Declaration of Independence. Similarly, journalist Nikole Hannah-Jones, the chief architect of the *New York Times'* 1619 Project, is a leading target for conservative critics of what they see as radical maligning of America. Yet when Hannah-Jones went on to argue for a broad-ranging reparations agenda, she departed from much prevailing critical rhetoric by describing America as "a nation built on the espoused ideals of inalienable, universal rights," and she contended that "if we are to live up to the magnificent ideals upon which we were founded, we must do what is just."[90] To turn to African American thought, even radical Black thought, has therefore frequently included turning to the nation's revolutionary Declaration of Independence traditions, not away from them.

In sum, dismissing the value of invocations of the Declaration of Independence and the traditions of American identity that appeal to it violates the practices and professed ideals of even many of America's "revolutionary reformers." America was indeed born out of white Christian settler colonies of the British Empire, but their revolution against that empire, though limited, provided ammunition for assaults on imperial legacies that have since won vital victories, even if too few.

Yet it remains fair to ask: How truly transformative could a politics that embraced a sense of purpose grounded on the Declaration of Independence ever really be? Might not any substantial reliance on the manifesto of an eighteenth-century nationalist, not to mention imperialist, political project prove inadequate for any genuinely egalitarian reimagining and restructuring of the modern global system of nation-states? The answer is not clear. I think it *is* clear that from America's founding to the present, the revolutionaries' use of the Declaration to justify the creation of a new kind of political society has been a valuable precedent for arguments holding that in later times, further major political innovations will be needed if secure possession of the rights of life, liberty, and happiness for all humanity is really to be achieved. To paraphrase John Marshall, when it comes to the Declaration, we must never forget that it is a *revolution* we are expounding.

CONCLUSION

This documentation of the utility of the Declaration of Independence for progressive reform movements in America has not been meant to show that the Declaration and kindred Western documents provide the best foundation for imagining and pursuing a freer and more equal post-imperial world. The aim is not to discourage in the least the greater attention to Indigenous, Black radical, and formerly colonized thinkers and activists that many critical scholars are now pursuing. It is simply to encourage progressives to address the daunting intellectual and political challenges they now face, in America and around the world, by drawing on as many usable resources as possible. If we insist on stressing only the ways that the traditions of the various colonizing and colonized peoples differ, seeking to harden their opposition instead of exploring creative syntheses, we heighten the danger of defeat for all reform efforts. We risk handing the future over to those who read the lessons of the imperialist origins of many modern states not in the way most contemporary academics do, but in the grimly restrictive, exclusionary ways that Samuel P. Huntington came to embrace, and that Donald Trump and his NatCon counterparts are advocating fervently, and dangerously, today.

Yet while strident, pugnacious nationalists are in power in many countries now and are likely to win victories in many places in the years ahead, history suggests that it is far from futile to struggle against them, or to imagine new, more egalitarian forms of political community, and to seek to bring those new forms into existence. One of the boldest and most inspiring arguments that Graeber and Wengrow advance in *The Dawn of Everything* is that historically, human communities have not been rigidly determined by modes of production such as foraging, agriculture, or manufacturing, or by existing power coalitions. Instead, early human societies displayed "a carnival parade of political forms," from autocratic and hierarchical to far freer and more egalitarian ones.[91] The authors trace those enormous variations to human imagination and contingent political endeavors, rather than to any iron sociological, economic, or historical laws. History therefore gives us reason to believe that, although we humans remain the flawed beings who have committed so many follies and horrors throughout our existence, we are gifted with abilities to make our world anew, and to make it better, if we do not fear to change the many things that should never have been, and if we can summon the will and judgment to create the more just and free political communities that have not been yet, and yet must be.

NOTES

1. Samuel P. Huntington, *Who Are We? The Challenges to America's National Identity* (New York: Simon & Schuster, 2004), 39.
2. James Thuo Gathii, "TWAIL: A Brief History of Its Origins, Its Decentralized Network, and a Tentative Bibliography," *Trade Law and Development* 3, no. 1 (September 2011): 26–64; James Thuo Gathii, "The Promise of International Law: A Third World View," Grotius Lecture presented at the 2020 Virtual Annual Meeting of the American Society of International Law, June 25, 2020, available at SSRN: https://ssrn.com/abstract=3635509.
3. Gathii, "TWAIL: A Brief History," 28–29.
4. Adom Getachew, *Worldmaking after Empire: The Rise and Fall of Self-Determination* (Princeton: Princeton University Press, 2019), 2.
5. Alison Bashford, "Immigration Restriction: Rethinking Period and Place from Settler Colonies to Postcolonial Nations," *Journal of Global History* 9, no. 1 (2014): 27.
6. Monika Batra Kashyap, "Unsettling Immigration Laws: Settler Colonialism and the U.S. Immigration Legal System," *Fordham Urban Law Journal* 46, no. 3 (2019): 548.
7. Hannah Gordon, "Cowboys and Indians: Settler Colonialism and the Dog Whistle in U.S. Immigration Policy," *University of Miami Law Review* 74, no 3 (2020): 523–24.
8. Justin Desautels-Stein, *The Right to Exclude: A Critical Race Approach to Sovereignty, Border, and International Law* (New York: Oxford University Press, 2023).
9. Desautels-Stein, *Right to Exclude*, 317, 333.
10. Roxanne Dunbar-Ortiz, *Not "A Nation of Immigrants": Settler Colonialism, White Supremacy, and a History of Erasure and Exclusion* (Boston: Beacon Press, 2021), xx, xxii.
11. Dunbar-Ortiz, *Not "A Nation of Immigrants,"* xxvii, 270.
12. Ralph Michael and Maya Singhal, "Racial Capitalism," *Theory and Society* 48, no. 6 (2019): 851–81; Zachary Levenson and Marcel Paret, "The Three Dialectics of Racial Capitalism: From South Africa to the U.S. and Back Again," *Du Bois Review: Social Science Research on Race* 20, no. 2 (2022): 333–51, https://doi.org/10.1017/S1742058X22000212.
13. Cedric Robinson, *Black Marxism: The Making of the Black Radical Tradition*, 3rd ed. (Chapel Hill, NC: University of North Carolina Press, 2020, orig. 1983), 3; cf. Levenson and Paret, "The Three Dialectics," 2–3, 6–10. The 2020 edition of *Black Marxism* includes an illuminating foreword by Robin D. G. Kelley that, along with Kelley's earlier praise for it, has helped win new audiences for Robinson.
14. Robinson, *Black Marxism*, 9.
15. Nancy Leong, "Racial Capitalism," *Harvard Law Review* 126, no. 8 (2013): 2151–226.
16. Michael Javen Fortner, "Racial Capitalism and City Politics: Toward a Theoretical Synthesis," *Urban Affairs Review* 59, no. 2 (December 2021): 630–53.
17. Jennifer L. Morgan, *Reckoning with Slavery: Gender, Kinship, and Capitalism in the Early Black Atlantic* (Durham, NC: Duke University Press, 2021), 10.
18. Levenson and Paret, "The Three Dialectics," 13.
19. Getachew, *Worldmaking after Empire*, 182.
20. Getachew, *Worldmaking after Empire*, 2.
21. Getachew, *Worldmaking after Empire*, 182.
22. Gathii, "TWAIL: A Brief History"; Gathii, "The Promise of International Law."
23. Shuk Ying Chan, "Postcolonial Global Justice" (PhD diss., Princeton University, 2021), http://arks.princeton.edu/ark:/88435/dsp0137720g85k.

24. Adam Dahl, *Empire of the People: Settler Colonialism and the Foundations of Modern Democratic Thought* (Lawrence, KS: University Press of Kansas, 2018), 186–87.
25. Dahl, *Empire of the People*, 29–34.
26. Dahl, *Empire of the People*, 162.
27. Dahl, *Empire of the People*, 162.
28. Dahl, *Empire of the People*, 163.
29. Dahl, *Empire of the People*, 163–64.
30. Dahl, *Empire of the People*, 172, 176–83.
31. Dahl, *Empire of the People*, 158; John Locke, *Two Treatises of Government*, ed. Peter Laslett (New York: Cambridge University Press, 1963), 431–44.
32. Dahl, *Empire of the People*, 187.
33. Aziz Rana, *The Two Faces of American Freedom* (Cambridge, MA: Harvard University Press, 2010), 3.
34. Rana, *Two Faces*, 3.
35. Rana, *Two Faces*, 3–4.
36. Rana, *Two Faces*, 14.
37. Aziz Rana, "Colonialism and Constitutional Memory," *University of California Irvine Law Review* 5, no. 2 (2015): 268, 277.
38. Rana, "Colonialism," 271, 277–86.
39. Rana, "Colonialism," 288.
40. Desautels-Stein, *Right to Exclude*, 334–39.
41. Desautels-Stein, *Right to Exclude*, 339.
42. Rogers M. Smith, *Political Peoplehood: The Roles of Values, Interests, and Identities* (Chicago: University of Chicago Press, 2015), 246.
43. Smith, *Political Peoplehood*, 41, 199, 246.
44. Dunbar-Ortiz, *Not "A Nation of Immigrants,"* xi.
45. Huntington, *Who Are We?*, 49; Carlos Lozada, "Samuel Huntington, a Prophet for the Trump Era," *Washington Post*, July 18, 2017, https://www.washingtonpost.com/news/book-party/wp/2017/07/18/samuel-huntington-a-prophet-for-the-trump-era/.
46. Edmund Burke Foundation, "National Conservatism Statement of Principles," June 15, 2022, https://nationalconservatism.org/national-conservatism-a-statement-of-principles/.
47. Christopher DeMuth, "Why America Needs National Conservatism," *WSJ Opinion*, November 12, 2021.
48. Edmund Burke Foundation, "National Conservatism Statement of Principles."
49. Edmund Burke Foundation, "National Conservatism Statement of Principles."
50. Edmund Burke Foundation, "National Conservatism Statement of Principles."
51. Shuk Ying Chan, "Review: Worldmaking after Empire: The Rise and Fall of Self-Determination," *Ethics & International Affairs* 33, no. 3 (2019): 377.
52. Chan, "Postcolonial Global Justice."
53. Pekka Hämäläinen, *The Comanche Empire* (New Haven: Yale University Press, 2008), 6.
54. Hämäläinen, *The Comanche Empire*, 10.
55. Pekka Hämäläinen, *Lakota America: A New History of Indigenous Power* (New Haven: Yale University Press, 2019).
56. Pekka Hämäläinen, *Indigenous Continent: The Epic Contest for North America* (New York: W. W. Norton, 2022), xii–xiii.
57. Jennifer Schuessler, "Book Aims to Recast the Native Narrative," *New York Times*, September 22, 2022, C1.

58. Hämäläinen, *Comanche Empire*, 3–4, 14–15; Hämäläinen, *Lakota America*, 6.

59. Ned Blackhawk, "A New History of Indigenous America That Replicates Old Myths," *Washington Post*, October 4, 2022.

60. Gathii, "Promise of International Law," 23.

61. Judith Clavir Albert and Steward Edward Albert, eds., *The Sixties Papers: Documents of a Rebellious Decade* (New York: Praeger, 1984), 159–64.

62. Rana, "Colonialism and Constitutional Memory," 284.

63. David Graeber and David Wengrow, *The Dawn of Everything: A New History of Humanity* (New York: Farrar, Straus and Giroux, 2021), 27–62.

64. Hämäläinen, *Lakota America*, 7.

65. Dahl, *Empire of the People*, 51–54.

66. Dahl, *Empire of the People*, 61–63.

67. Dahl, *Empire of the People*, 135–53.

68. Dahl, *Empire of the People*, 135–39.

69. Rogers M. Smith, *Civic Ideals: Conflicting Visions of Citizenship in U.S. History* (New Haven: Yale University Press, 1997).

70. Daniel T. Rodgers, *Contested Truths: Keywords in American Politics since Independence* (New York: Basic Books, 1987), 46, 52–57; Richard R. Beeman, *Our Lives, Our Fortunes, and Our Sacred Honor: The Forging of American Independence, 1774–1776* (New York: Basic Books, 2013), 116–18, 139.

71. Anonymous Enslaved Persons, "Petition for Freedom to Massachusetts Governor Thomas Gage, His Majesty's Council, and the House of Representatives, 25 May 1774," *Massachusetts Historical Society*, MHS Collections Online, https://www.masshist.org/database/viewer.php?item_id=549#:~:text=In%20this%20document%20a%20group%20of%20enslaved%20people,natural%20right%20to%20be%20free%20with%20white%20citizens (masshist.org).

72. Phillis Wheatley, "Letter to Reverend Samuel Occum, February 11, 1774," *National Constitution Center*, https://constitutioncenter.org/the-constitution/historic-document-library/detail/phillis-wheatley-peters-letter-to-reverend-samuel-occum-february-11-1774; cf. John Locke, *A Letter Concerning Toleration*, ed. James Tully (Indianapolis, IN: Hackett Publishing Company, 1983), 52.

73. Onitositah, "Speech of Onitositah," in Samuel C. Williams, "Tatham's Characters Among the North American Indians," *Tennessee Historical Magazine* 7, no. 3 (October, 1971): 176–78, https://www.jstor.org/stable/44702575.

74. William Cushing, "Charge of the Chief Justice in *The Commonwealth v. Nathan Jennison*," *Proceedings of the Massachusetts Historical Society* 13 (1873–1875, Special Meeting April 1874), 294; Robert C. Winthrop, et al., "Special Meeting, April, 1874. Letter of Louis Agassiz; Description of the Washington Medals; The Commonwealth v. Nathaniel Jennison; Note by Chief Justice Gray; Massachusetts Declaration of Rights," *Proceedings of the Massachusetts Historical Society* 13 (1873): 282–304, https://www.jstor.org/stable/25079475.

75. Arthur Zilversmit, *The First Emancipation: The Abolition of Slavery in the North* (University of Chicago Press, 1967).

76. George Evans, "Working Man's Declaration of Independence," *Working Man's Advocate*, 1829, The Samuel Gompers Papers (umd.edu).

77. William Lloyd Garrison, "To the Public," *The Liberator* 1, no. 1 (January 1, 1831): 1, https://www.masshist.org/database/1698.

78. Trades' Union of Boston and Vicinity, "Declaration of Rights," *The Man* 2, no. 23 (June 12, 1834).

79. Elizabeth Cady Stanton and Mary M'Clintock, "Declaration of Sentiments," Convention at Seneca Falls, July 20, 1848, https://www.nps.gov/articles/declaration-of-sentiments.htm.

80. Abraham Lincoln, "Reply: Seventh Joint Debate, Alton, Illinois, October 15, 1858," in *The Lincoln-Douglas Debates*, ed. Robert W. Johannsen (New York: Oxford University Press, 1965), 304.

81. Abraham Lincoln, "Letter to Joshua Speed," August 24, 1855, https://www.abrahamlincolnonline.org/lincoln/speeches/speed.htm.

82. Henry E. Riell, "An Appeal to the Voluntary Citizens of the United States," *New York Evening Post*, 1840, https://babel.hathitrust.org/cgi/pt?id=hvd.hx2w4n&seq=5.

83. Chief Young Joseph, "An Indian's View of Indian Affairs," *North American Review* 128, no. 269 (April 1879): 432–33.

84. Paul Frymer, *Building an American Empire: The Era of Territorial and Political Expansion* (Princeton, NJ: Princeton University Press, 2017), 264–65.

85. William Moore, "Speech on the Chinese Exclusion Act," *Congressional Record* 13, Pt. 2, 47th Cong., 1st Sess., 2035, Congressional Record: Proceedings and Debates of the ... Congress - United States.

86. George F. Hoar, "Reply to Beveridge," *Congressional Record* 56, 1st Session, January 9, 1900: 712.

87. Martin Luther King, Jr., "I Have a Dream," in *From Many, One: Readings in American Political and Social Thought*, ed. Richard C. Sinopoli (Washington, D.C.: Georgetown University Press, 1997).

88. Lyndon B. Johnson, "Remarks on the Signing of the Immigration Bill," in *Public Papers of the President: Lyndon B. Johnson*, vol. 2 (Washington, D.C.: Government Printing Office, 1966), 1038.

89. Desmond S. King and Rogers M. Smith, *Still a House Divided: Race and Politics in Obama's America* (Princeton University Press, 2011), 238–40.

90. Nikole Hannah-Jones, "What Is Owed," *New York Times Magazine*, June 30, 2020, https://www.nytimes.com/interactive/2020/06/24/magazine/reparations-slavery.html?.

91. Graeber and Wengrow, *Dawn of Everything*, 4.

PART II
Peoples, Places, Perimeters, and Powers

CHAPTER SEVEN

HUMAN RIGHTS, COVID-19, AND GLOBAL CRITICAL RACE FEMINISM

Adrien K. Wing

I. INTRODUCTION

The COVID-19 pandemic affected millions and may be still affecting millions around the world. In each society, women faced a disproportionate burden on the front and back lines with respect to handling family matters, education, health, and employment. According to Phumzile Mlambo-Ngcuka, Executive Director of UN Women, "women are the real heroes of this crisis, even if they are not recognized as such. But curiously, there seems to be a lack of awareness that women are actually shouldering the response to this crisis. Even if they are saving lives, they remain unsung heroes."[1]

The author would like to dedicate this chapter to her extended family as over one hundred members were infected by COVID-19, some multiple times, and seven died prior to the development of the vaccine. Some women were infected while pregnant, and several infants were infected as well. No one knows the potentially enduring impact on these infants as we are still learning about long-term COVID-19 in adults.

The chapter uses a Global Critical Race Feminist (GCRF) theory approach to home in on a particular subgroup affected by COVID-19, women of color. Part II of the chapter provides an overview of COVID-19 and how it affected the globe, especially in its early stages, which is where most data still derive. Part III describes the GCRF approach that will be used to discuss legal solutions to COVID-19. Part IV elaborates on how the pandemic specifically affected women of color. Part V discusses intersectional praxis solutions based on international law. Part VI concludes with an eye towards the future, including pandemics.

II. COVID-19

This section provides a brief background on COVID-19. As of January 2024, there were over 774 million confirmed cases and 7 million deaths.[2] It remains unclear, however, how much we can believe concerning any statistic as some countries may not have had the ability to count properly. Additionally, the disease became highly politicized around the world, perhaps resulting in undercounting. The source of the virus has still not been confirmed, and the two main theories are the Wuhan, China live animal market,[3] or the nearby Wuhan Institute of Virology.[4] In early January 2020, Chinese authorities recognized a novel coronavirus as the cause of the pneumonia outbreak.[5] In that month, the World Health Organization (WHO) confirmed human-to-human spread,[6] and stated that the coronavirus outbreak was a Public Health Emergency of International Concern (PHEIC). On March 11, 2020, the WHO declared the novel coronavirus a pandemic.[7]

During the initial months of fear and uncertainty, United Nations member states began enacting emergency measures designed to stop or slow the spread of COVID-19.[8] These emergency measures included: "restricting travelers from countries with high infection rates; preventing inter- and intra-state movement; quarantines; surveillance using mobile telephone data; contact tracing digital apps; stay-at-home orders; limits on the number of people assembling in one place, and other restrictions on public gatherings."[9]

Our global understanding of the science behind the novel coronavirus has grown over time as the world dealt with quickly evolving variants, expedited vaccines, and booster shots. The virus affected countries differently, and various groups within nations in myriad ways. The least developed nations had limited access to vaccines.[10] As of January 2024, 70.6 percent of the global population had received at least one dose of the COVID-19 vaccine.[11] In the richest countries, 75 percent had been vaccinated, and 57 percent boosted. In the poorest nations, only 48 percent of people had been vaccinated, and 13 percent boosted.[12]

The pandemic severely disrupted the global economy.[13] Human rights scholars became very concerned about derogations of human rights.[14] Some fear that the effects of the pandemic will ultimately include affecting democracy itself, as autocratic regimes have used exaggerated or nonconsensual techniques against the pandemic.[15] Race, class, and environmental disparities became evident.[16]

The term "COVID Capitalism" was coined to "designate the ways capitalism and the novel coronavirus alter and amplify one another."[17] There was a prioritization in capitalist states "wherein profit-making takes priority over life-making endeavors like hospital funding and expansion, food distribution, and wage compensation from state funds."[18] According to Black feminist sociologist Whitney N. Laster Pirtle, "racial capitalism is a fundamental cause of the racial and socioeconomic inequities within COVID."[19] The social conditions affecting people of color shape the multiple diseases that interact with COVID-19, and include multiple risk factors such as housing segregation, homelessness, and medical bias.[20]

III. GLOBAL CRITICAL RACE FEMINISM OVERVIEW

This section provides a brief overview of GCRF. Professor Richard Delgado invented the term "Critical Race Feminism" (CRF) in his first reader on Critical Race Theory.[21] CRF emerged in the late 1980s and 1990s, when women of color who were Critical Race Theory (CRT) scholars focused on the unique lived experiences of women of color. They were dissatisfied with the implicit assumption in some CRT literature that women of color had experiences identical or similar to their male counterparts. Relatedly, these scholars noted that feminist jurisprudence seemed to presume that all the women were white, and failed to address the role of white supremacy throughout the feminist movement's history.[22] UCLA/Columbia Law Professor Kimberlé Crenshaw called for the law to "demarginalize" the status of women of color.[23] CRF could thus be viewed as a "feminist critique within CRT" and a "race critique within feminist discourse."[24]

Additionally, CRF draws inspiration from a variety of disciplines beyond the law, including, but not limited to, literature, sociology, history, anthropology, political science, education, and economics.[25] Those writing CRF articles were also attracted by the "womanist literature" done by Black women in other fields.[26] Womanism focuses on issues affecting Black women,[27] and promotes social justice and anti-oppression efforts broadly.[28]

Crucial CRF concepts to be used in this chapter include anti-essentialism, intersectionality, and praxis. We cannot design effective solutions to the problems of women of color unless we understand these concepts, and thus they are briefly discussed here. The concept of anti-essentialism connotes that we should not essentialize or stereotype the situation of all women and must reject assumptions that membership in a group dictates certain behaviors or outcomes.[29] Next, Crenshaw first coined the term "intersectionality" in her seminal article *Demarginalizing the Intersection of Race and Sex* where she described the double bind of simultaneous racial and gender prejudice.[30] Critical Race Feminists recognize that each person's various identities intersect to create a distinct human being with unique lived experiences.[31]

I have written about using intersectionality on an even broader basis. For example, the seventeen South African identities in its 1996 constitution are capable of being looked at on an intersectional basis: race, gender, sex, pregnancy, marital status, ethnic or social origin, color, sexual orientation, age, disability, religion, conscience, belief, culture, language, and birth.[32] Additional identities discussed include nationality, religion, language, culture, class, and political ideology.[33] I have also written about stature identity, i.e., how someone physically looks within the context of their group, with those considered most attractive achieving more educationally and economically in many instances.[34]

Praxis is the intersection of theory and practice. It takes legal theory beyond the classroom and ivory tower by using it in real life.[35] Praxis seeks to improve the lives of marginalized groups by engaging in action. Possibilities may be legal or nonlegal, ranging from handling cases to designing and executing relevant policies.

Although the original emphasis was American law, CRF has since expanded beyond. I have characterized this expansion as GCRF, which explores issues affecting women of color in the Global South and elsewhere.[36] Scholars have been producing publications and creating practical opportunities and initiatives to uplift women of color. Authors explore a wide array of topics including multiculturalism, immigration law, female genital surgeries, female infanticide, HIV/AIDS, and economic development.[37] GCRF explores the conflict between customs and Western constitutional norms and the tension between communitarianism and individualism.[38]

GCRF contributes to the development of international law, global feminism, and postcolonial theory by demarginalizing women of color in a theoretical and practical sense. "Women of color may be simultaneously dominated within the context of imperialism, neocolonialism, or occupation as well as local patriarchy, culture and customs."[39]

IV. WOMEN OF COLOR EXPERIENCED DISPROPORTIONATE HARM DUE TO COVID-19

The section next uses a GCRF analysis to see how COVID-19 has affected women of color. Statistics from the United States established that Black, Latino/a, and Native people disproportionately suffered from COVID-19, with rates of contraction, hospitalization, and death greater than their proportionate representation in the general population.[40] Concerning gender, on a global scale, COVID-19 fatalities were disproportionately men.[41] Some research suggested that compared to women, men's immune system responses are inferior at combating COVID-19.[42] However, in other contexts, COVID-19 has disparately harmed women. For example, women make up about three-quarters of all essential health care workers in America.[43] They had to stay home more to take care of the sick and educate children whose schools and activities were closed. First-choice N95 personal protection equipment (PPE) masks are designed in ways that successfully fit 95 percent of all men, but only 85 percent of all women.[44]

The COVID-19 pandemic triggered a "shadow pandemic" across the globe involving domestic violence. Women and girls were at greater risk of sexual abuse.[45] United Nations Secretary-General António Guterres acknowledged that "lockdowns and quarantines can trap women with abusive partners . . . urg[ing] all governments to make the prevention and redress of violence against women a key part of their national response plan to COVID-19."[46]

Domestic violence increased by upwards of 25 percent in some countries as a result of lockdowns. Victims faced limited access to protective services during periods of quarantine.[47] Various groups tried to address the problem.[48] For instance, CARE indicated that by August 2020, fifty-five countries were considering GBV (gender-based violence) response as part of their programs, compared to eight countries in mid-March. They were providing GBV services or referrals to 3.4 million people. Nineteen countries had specific advocacy agendas to fight GBV as part of their COVID-19 response. They were collecting sex-disaggregated data in sixty-one countries—compared to only twenty in March.[49]

To avoid essentialism, we need to look at what has happened to women in various regions of the world. Even in Europe, Deirdre Domingo, of Scottish Women's Rights Organisations, told the inquiry that the idea that the pandemic affected everyone equally should be "firmly dispelled." She said women, particularly from Black and minority ethnicities, were far more affected when compared to the wider population.[50]

Some African women went from a state of "acute poverty" to a state of "absolute poverty" as a result of the impact of coronavirus.[51] Council of Elders member Mrs. Graça Machel, a Mozambican former first lady and cabinet official as well as widow of the late South African President Nelson Mandela, noted the effect on African women.[52] They were hit particularly hard by economic downturn, which can lead to female children being forced into child marriages and early pregnancies.[53] As women are central to food production and produce the majority of food on the continent, COVID-19 disruptions to the supply chains threw the global food economy into disarray. Hunger and malnutrition contributed to high infant, child, and maternal mortality.[54] Curfews and lockdowns restricted women's access to support services. As stay-at-home orders expand to contain the spread of the virus, women with violent partners increasingly find themselves isolated from the people and resources that can help them.[55]

There were many problems in Asian countries as well.[56] COVID-19 had a major impact on the economies, and amplified vulnerabilities of women living in challenging economic backgrounds, difficult political situations, and security environments. Yet, there was a lack of gender-sensitive responses.[57] Research has been done on the impact of COVID-19 in three areas—gender-based violence, sexual and reproductive health and rights, and unpaid care work—in six countries: India, Indonesia, Malaysia, the Philippines, Thailand, and Vietnam. The report highlighted the interconnectedness of the challenges faced by women and called for a holistic gender-responsive approach based on a multi-sector analysis of the pandemic. The study outlined women's context-specific needs and provides recommendations to mitigate effects as well as to prepare for possible future crises.[58]

Another study in India[59] focused on economic violence, where it surged during periods of social distancing and lockdowns. This not only resulted in the reduction of safe spaces for women and girls, but also trapped them in a space where they were more easily economically exploited. COVID-19 lockdowns spawned a whole new class of economic abuse of women. Policies introduced by Pyongyang, North Korea, ostensibly to contain the spread of COVID-19, had grown ever more extensive and repressive, even as cases had waned.[60]

In Latin America, there have been similar problems relating to employment and income gaps,[61] as well as an educational catastrophe.[62] As in other regions, women were on the front lines in areas more heavily affected by the pandemic, and they may not have had jobs easily done at home. Plus, many women are self-employed and may have worked in the informal sector. As in all societies, the burden of housework, childcare, and caring for the ill fell on the women.[63]

To become even more precise in our analyses, we should look more in depth at particular countries, and also intersect with other identities, such as class, religion, minority status, etc. In other words, those intersections may lead to very different issues within each country. Due to space constraints, we will not discuss this level here.

V. COVID'S UNEQUAL IMPACT HIGHLIGHTS THE NEED FOR INTERSECTIONAL PRAXIS SOLUTIONS BASED ON INTERNATIONAL LAW

In this section, we need to determine what praxis might be helpful in the design of solutions for the long term. While the first tools considered will always be national law, the chapter now emphasizes international law. As usual, the solutions must be intersectional, both within international law options as well as with domestic/comparative law options. Additionally, law alone is not the solution, so intersectionality would include solutions dealing with physical and mental health, employment, education, criminal justice, social work, and family life, among other areas. The section mainly focuses on international treaties, but also includes regional documents as well.

First, women of color could have and maybe still can resort to relief from one of the relevant international treaties if their state is a party to that treaty. The International Justice Resource Center collected the various guidance from supranational bodies regarding COVID-19.[64] They could claim that the state did not properly seek to derogate from the treaty provisions or did so in an unnecessary way. They would apply to the relevant committee for that treaty, assuming the committee has competence to examine individual complaints, either through ratification or accession to an Optional Protocol[65] or by making a declaration to that effect under a specific article of the Convention.[66] Complaints may also be brought by third parties, i.e. organizations, on behalf of individuals, provided the individuals have given their written consent.[67]

The Chairpersons of the ten United Nations Treaty Bodies[68] urged leaders to ensure that human rights are respected in government measures to tackle the public health threat posed by the COVID-19 pandemic.[69] "Only by including all people in COVID-19 strategies can the pandemic be combatted," said Hilary Gbedemah, who was Chair of the CEDAW Committee and head of the group that brings together the respective committee chairs.[70] The ten experts called on States to adopt measures to protect the rights to life and health, and to ensure access to health care to all who need it, without discrimination. They urged governments to take extra care of those particularly vulnerable to the effects of COVID-19, including older people, people with disabilities, minorities, indigenous peoples, refugees, asylum seekers and migrants, people deprived of their liberty, homeless people, and those living in poverty. They also stressed that women are at a disproportionately high risk, because in many societies they are the main caregivers for sick family members.[71]

This section next discusses the following treaties: International Covenant on Civil and Political Rights (ICCPR);[72] International Covenant on Economic, Social, and Cultural Rights (ICESCR);[73] Convention on the Elimination of Racial Discrimination (CERD);[74] Convention for the Elimination of Discrimination against Women (CEDAW);[75] Convention on the Rights of the Child (CRC);[76] Convention on Rights of Persons with Disabilities (CRPD,);[77] International Health Regulations (IHR);[78] and InterAmerican Commission on Human Rights (IACHR) resolutions.[79] Emphasis is put on ICCPR, ICESCR, and CEDAW.

ICCPR

Restrictions regarding COVID-19 have been found in six broad areas relevant to ICCPR: (1) restrictions on speech and assembly, including right to access public spaces;[80] (2) intrusions on privacy; (3) modifications to or delays in electoral processes; (4) denials of justice and fair trial;[81] (5) the right to life; and (6) antidiscrimination. Regarding the antidiscrimination principle, the United Nations Human Rights Committee (HRC) has indicated that it is of "crucial importance both for individuals and for society as a whole" and "constitutes a fundamental right, the effective protection of which is the prerequisite for the enjoyment of all other human rights."[82] The HRC also noted that "the duty to protect life... implies that States parties should take appropriate measures to address the general conditions in society that may give rise to direct threats to life." Those include: "the prevalence of life-threatening diseases."[83] Gender-based violence may implicate the right to life and freedom of movement, mandatory quarantining making matters worse.[84]

Most countries declared states of emergency under ICCPR article 4.[85] This article requests that states notify the UN Secretary-General if they intend to derogate from their international human rights obligations because of a crisis.[86] It is an "escape mechanism" that allows states to restrict their citizens' rights that are preserved in the text of the ICCPR, while still being in compliance.[87] Article 4 establishes crucial safeguards to prevent emergency measures from permanently eroding protections for human rights.[88] The HRC issued guidance recognizing that in response to COVID-19, states may need to derogate from or limit some obligations, but must do so in accordance with relevant international legal rules, including the concepts of necessity, proportionality, and nondiscrimination.[89] It may be necessary, for example, to restrict large gatherings or to require people to wear masks around others.

Six months into the pandemic, only 21 countries of the 173 parties had issued notices of intent to derogate their international human rights obligations under their measures to combat COVID-19.[90]

By 2021, this number had only increased to 30 out of 173.[91]

ICESCR

Apart from civil and political rights, several States also derogated from economic, social, and cultural rights.[92] Under ICESCR, there are numerous potential violations affecting women of color, including: right to health care; right to food; right to education; right to work; and right to participate in public cultural life. While most of the emergency decrees do not specifically refer to ESC rights, they constitute de facto derogation to some of these rights. States have positive obligations to protect the rights to life and health.[93] The steps to be taken by State Parties include those necessary for "the prevention, treatment and control of epidemic, endemic, occupational and other diseases."[94]

There are additional norms that apply in cases of emergencies, including epidemics. General Comment No. 14 of the Committee on Economic, Social, and Cultural Rights (CESCR) elaborates on specific obligations that, at a minimum, offer persuasive legal arguments on the scope of State's obligations.[95] Various paragraphs[96] are of great relevance to global health emergencies as they set the specific legal obligations of States concerning the right to health, reflecting treaty and customary international law obligations. Moreover, there have been numerous secondary effects on physical health, including suspension of vaccination campaigns and impacts on maternal health.[97]

Equality is a core component of the right to health that must be enjoyed by everyone "without discrimination of any kind."[98] Moreover, other aspects of human rights are "prerequisites" for the right to health, such as "rights to science."[99] The CESCR reminded states in 2020 that they "have a duty to make available and accessible to all persons, without discrimination, especially to the most vulnerable, all the best available applications of scientific progress necessary to enjoy the highest attainable standard of health."[100] There have been governments' encroachment upon categories of rights long targeted, such as Polish government action against sexual and reproductive rights.[101]

ICESCR Article 11 recognized "the fundamental right of everyone to be free from hunger." Despite the world's declarations of a fundamental right to food and commitments to protect this right, food insecurity and malnutrition continue to plague the world. The COVID-19 pandemic exacerbated and magnified these inequalities in food security. The United Nations has identified availability, accessibility, and adequacy as key elements to securing the right to food.[102] States are responsible for protecting their people's right to food even during times of emergencies and disasters.[103] In recent decades, agriculture has been neglected as arable land has been converted into residential, commercial, and industrial areas, and developing nations moved away from subsistence farming to more profitable cash crops, thus becoming more dependent on imported food.[104] As the COVID-19 pandemic has proven, a nation's domestic food security cannot rely on the international market during a crisis.[105]

In late 2023, there was an attempt to draft a pandemic treaty. It failed to enshrine the right to health and the right to benefit from scientific progress,[106] perhaps indicating a failure to learn from the COVID-19 pandemic.

CEDAW

CEDAW has overlapped with other treaties and includes such issues as equal access to health care services.[107] Many states have deemed sexual and reproductive health services as elective and thus nonessential due to shifts in resources, thus preventing individuals from being able to access such services.[108]

While the text of CEDAW does not address violence against women, two General Recommendations by the CEDAW Committee (General Recommendation No. 19 in 1992 and an updated General Recommendation No. 35 in 2017) expressly refer to violence against women as falling under the obligations of the treaty.[109] The updated General Recommendation No. 35 on gender-based violence against women further establishes the binding obligation of states to prohibit gender-based violence, holding that such prohibition has now developed into customary international law.[110] Thus, all states are now bound by this prohibition. The CEDAW Committee requires States to repeal or modify all gender-neutral laws that perpetuate existing inequalities.[111]

In its "Guidance Note on CEDAW and COVID-19," the CEDAW Committee developed ideas for countries to consider for the problems faced by women.[112] It called on States parties to:

1. Address the disproportionate impact of the pandemic on women's health.
2. Provide sexual and reproductive health as essential services.
3. Protect women and girls from gender-based violence.
4. Ensure equal participation of women in decision-making.
5. Ensure continuous education.
6. Provide socioeconomic support to women.
7. Adopt targeted measures for disadvantaged groups of women and girls, including minorities and indigenous women, older women, women with disabilities, migrants, refugees, LGBTQ, and women in poverty.
8. Protect women and girls in humanitarian settings and continue implementing the women, peace, and security agenda.
9. Strengthen institutional response, dissemination of information, and data collection.[113]

OTHER INTERNATIONAL TREATIES

CERD, CRC, and CRPD are among the treaties that intersect with each other in the context of the pandemic. CERD prohibits discrimination on basis of race, color, and without distinction as to equality before the law in terms of economic, social, and cultural rights such as the right to public health and medical care.[114] CRC acknowledges special obligations owed to girls for appropriate health care services during and shortly after pregnancy.[115] Many girls dropped out of school during the pandemic due to an increasing need for them to assume domestic and caring responsibilities.[116] CRPD notes that States Parties recognize that women and girls with disabilities are subject to multiple discriminations, and in this regard shall take measures to ensure the full and equal enjoyment by them of all human rights and fundamental freedoms.[117]

IHR

When the WHO Director-General declared COVID-19 a PHEIC,[118] the power to do so was derived from IHR article 12. IHR is a multilateral treaty designed to regulate State behavior in the face of a disease outbreak.[119] While the IHR was most recently revised in 2005, the framework stems back to the International Sanitary Conferences of the 1800s.[120] IHR's purpose is to "prevent, protect against, control and provide a public health response to the international spread of disease in ways that are commensurate with and restricted to public health risks, and which avoid unnecessary interference with international traffic."[121] There have always been problems with compliance, and COVID-19 was no different.[122] Celestina Rodogno has argued that the IHR is legally insufficient to tackle PHEICs. It has consequently been turned into a tool for soft power diplomacy, which can undermine the IHR's objective.[123] IHR clearly needs to be reimagined.

IACHR RESOLUTIONS

In addition to international treaties and documents, there are relevant regional documents. Latin America has been the most active.[124] The IACHR approved two resolutions: "Pandemic and Human Rights in the Americas, Human Rights of Persons with COVID-19" (Resolution 1/2020)[125] and "COVID-19 Vaccines and Inter-American Human Rights Obligations" (Resolution 4/2020).[126] The first one, approved in April 2020, introduces a general framework of human rights standards and obligations and recommends member States to take all urgent measures that may be necessary to protect the rights to life, health, and personal safety of individuals within a jurisdiction.

It also urges States to adopt an intersectional human rights approach in their strategies, policies, and measures to deal with the COVID-19 pandemic and its consequences.[127]

It includes specific sections on State obligations. It notes that policies and measures should use a human rights approach that includes "gender . . . diversity, and intersectionality."[128] Any decisions or measures taken "must take gender, intersectional, linguistic and intercultural perspectives particularly into account."[129] All government responses on gender, based on intersectionality, should look at "the different contexts and conditions that could increase the vulnerability to which women are exposed, such as, inter alia, economic difficulties, age, status as a migrant or displaced person, disability, incarceration, ethnic or racial origin, sexual orientation, and gender identity and/or expression."[130] Women must be involved in decision-making.[131] Services must be enhanced to combat gender-based violence.[132] Female health care professionals on the front lines must have "means of reducing their double workload as professionals and as homemakers."[133]

The intersectionality discussed in the second resolution specifically mentions people of African and tribal descent and the need to disaggregate "data concerning ethnic or racial origin, gender, age and disability."[134] It is quite comprehensive.

In order to overcome the social stigma associated with COVID-19 and potentially discriminatory behavior toward persons perceived to have been in contact with the virus, measures must be adopted immediately that include gender equality and intersectional perspectives, as well as differential approaches, in order to highlight the added risks of violating the human rights of persons, groups, and collectivities in the region that are especially vulnerable or who have historically suffered exclusion, such as persons living in poverty or on the street, older adults, persons deprived of liberty, indigenous peoples, tribal communities, Afrodescendants, persons with disabilities, migrants, refugees, and displaced persons in other human mobility contexts, LGBTI persons, children and adolescents, and women, particularly pregnant women and victims of gender-based violence.[135]

VI. CONCLUSION

Using a GCRF approach, this chapter has illustrated how women of color have borne disproportionate burdens due to COVID-19. It provided some intersectional praxis solutions based on international law, noting how existing mechanisms such as treaties have been inadequate. The conclusion lists possible ways forward. First, we must be prepared not only for the sequelae from COVID-19, but for future pandemics. As a world, we have not seemed to learn all that we should have from COVID-19, especially as it impacted women of color.

Second, as Machel has stated: "We have been presented the opportunity to reimagine and redesign our society into a vibrant and equitable one. We must place women and women's leadership at the core of the response and beyond."[136] Without women centrally involved, their realities may be ignored or underplayed.

Third, we should not essentialize women. Women of color must be part of designing international, national, and local, legal and nonlegal solutions for the future. All areas of emphasis, including employment, domestic abuse, and other criminal justice matters, as well as medical fields must be examined carefully. Generic solutions may inadvertently exclude women of color, perpetuating or expanding their marginality.

Fourth, all solutions should be intersectional in nature, which will help people all over the world. The IACHR documents are the best for listing the various identities involved.

Fifth, we cannot afford for solutions to be merely theoretical. Praxis must exist on all levels. Ivory scientific and legal towers must connect with international, national, and local grassroots communities. Resources have to be found, and cannot only be guided by capitalist principles.

Sixth, we must learn from COVID-19, and create an effective intersectional pandemic treaty that would work. This may be the hardest to achieve since so many international treaties do not function effectively, even in the richest countries.

Seventh, to deal with potential short-term issues, governments should develop national stockpiles of essential staple goods and commodities and work towards becoming as self-sufficient as possible, particularly for key food items.[137] Governments need to reprioritize the need for agriculture. While they are revitalizing their agricultural sector, governments need to build up essential food reserves, which can alleviate the damage of crop failures and protect against trade and market disruptions.[138]

Eighth, as the Elders have said: "Allocation of response resources should be targeted towards the immediate needs of managing the virus as well as future-looking to simultaneously dismantle the structural, systemic barriers which reinforce inequality and disenfranchisement."[139] Women must be assisted by government economic policies in the business and farming sectors, with equal pay for equal work. Barriers to female inheritance must be corrected in many parts of the world. Online learning may assist females to achieve proper education. Needless to say, health care systems must be strengthened.[140] Criminal justice systems must enhance protection against gender-based violence.[141]

Ninth, an Asian report highlights the interconnectedness of the challenges faced by women and calls for a holistic gender-responsive approach based on a multi-sector analysis of the pandemic. The study outlines women's context-specific needs and provides recommendations to mitigate effects as well as to prepare for possible future crises.[142] Hence, human rights bodies and mechanisms must reinforce their role not only as curbing actively abusive behavior by states, but also as spurring negligent states to act appropriately.[143] Accordingly, state policies can eliminate gender bias in resource allocation and fund diversion, and call for collective action to defeat gender inequality.[144]

Last, but not least, providing for human dignity when combating a pandemic is important.[145] While dignity is not recognized as a human right in the United States, some other countries have led the way. The constitution of South Africa has concretized this notion: "Everyone has inherent dignity and the right to have their dignity respected and protected."[146] Hakeem Yusuf calls for a paradigm shift for ESCR rights to an international cooperation model that upholds and advances human dignity.[147]

NOTES

1. Laetitia Kaci, "Women Are the Unsung Heroes of This Crisis," *The UNESCO Courier*, June 16, 2020, https://en.unesco.org/courier/2020-3/women-are-unsung-heroes-crisis#:~:text=Women%20are%20the%20real%20heroes,that%20this%20perception%20will%20change.

2. World Health Organization, "COVID-19 Epidemiological Update," January 19, 2024, https://www.who.int/publications/m/item/covid-19-epidemiological-update.

3. Jen Christensen, "New Studies Agree that Animals Sold at Wuhan Market are Most Likely What Started Covid-19 Pandemic," *CNN*, July 27, 2022, https://www.cnn.com/2022/07/26/health/wuhan-market-covid-19/index.html.

4. Lawrence O. Gostin and Gigi K. Gronvall, "The Origins of Covid-19—Why It Matters (and Why It Doesn't)," *New England Journal of Medicine* 388, no. 25 (June 22, 2023): 2305–8, https://www.nejm.org/doi/full/10.1056/NEJMp2305081.

5. CDC Museum, "COVID-19 Timeline," January 5, 2022, https://www.cdc.gov/museum/timeline/covid19.html.

6. CDC Museum, "COVID-19 Timeline."

7. Mayo Clinic Staff, "Coronavirus Disease 2019 (COVID-19)," April 1, 2022, https://www.mayoclinic.org/diseases-conditions/coronavirus/symptoms-causes/syc-20479963#:~:text=In%20March%202020%2C%20the,19%20outbreak%20a%20pandemic.

8. Eric Richardson and Colleen Devine, "Emergencies End Eventually: How to Better Analyze Human Rights Restrictions Sparked by the COVID-19 Pandemic under the International Covenant on Civil and Political Rights," *Michigan Journal of International Law* 42 (2020): 105.

9. Richardson and Devine, "Emergencies End Eventually."

10. Ruchita Jain, "A Trip to Inequity: How the TRIPS Agreement Hinders Access to Needed COVID-19 Therapeutics," *Boston College Intellectual Property & Technology Forum*, June 1, 2023, https://sites.bc.edu/iptf/.

11. Our World in Data, "Coronavirus (COVID-19) Vaccination," accessed January 5, 2024, https://ourworldindata.org/covid-vaccinations.

12. United Nations Department of Economic and Social Affairs, "Least Developed Countries (LDCs)," accessed February 5, 2024, https://www.un.org/development/desa/dpad/least-developed-country-category.html.

13. Oleg Yaroshenko et al., "COVID-19, the Global Financial Crisis, and the Regulation of Labor Migration," *International Journal of Legal Information* 50, no. 3 (2022), https://doi.org/10.25115/eea.v39i9.5692.

14. Richardson and Devine, "Emergencies End Eventually."

15. Ricardo De la Pena, "The Political Repercussions of a Pandemic," *ISA Investigaciones Sociales Aplicadas*, Mexico, July 2022, https://www.v-dem.net/media/publications/Users_Working_Paper_45.pdf.

16. Samantha Newman, "What a Waste! An Evaluation of Federal and State Medical and Biohazard Waste Regulations during the COVID-19 Pandemic and Their Impact on Environmental Justice," *Villanova Environmental Law Journal* 34, no. 1 (2023), https://digitalcommons.law.villanova.edu/elj/vol34/iss1/3.

17. Charisa Smith, "When COVID Capitalism Silences Children," *Kansas Law Review* 71, no. 4 (2023): 553–94.

18. Smith, "When COVID," 555.

19. Whitney N. Laster Pirtle, "Racial Capitalism: A Fundamental Cause of Novel Coronavirus (COVID-19) Pandemic Inequities in the United States," *Health Education & Behavior* 47 (2020): 504, https://journals.sagepub.com/doi/pdf/10.1177/1090198120922942.

20. Pirtle, "Racial Capitalism," 504.

21. See Richard Delgado, ed., *Critical Race Theory: The Cutting Edge* (Philadelphia: Temple University Press, 1995).

22. Adrien Katherine Wing, "Critical Race Feminism and Human Rights," in *Human Rights*, ed. Christien van den Anker and Rhona Smith (London: Oxford University Press, 2005), 74–76.

23. See Kimberlé Crenshaw, "Demarginalizing the Intersection of Race and Sex: A Black Feminist Critique of Antidiscrimination Doctrine, Feminist Theory and Antiracist Politics," *University of Chicago Legal Forum* 1, no. 1 (1989), http://chicagounbound.uchicago.edu/uclf/vol1989/iss1/8.

24. Adrien Katherine Wing, ed., *Critical Race Feminism*, 2nd ed. (New York University Press, 2003).

25. Wing, *Global Critical Race Feminism*.

26. The Womanist Movement, 2018, https://library.law.howard.edu/civilrightshistory/womanist.

27. The Womanist Movement.

28. Patricia Hill Collins, "What's in a Name: Womanism, Black Feminism, and Beyond," *The Black Scholar* 26, no. 10 (Winter/Spring 1996): 9–17. https://www.jstor.org/stable/41068619.

29. Angela P. Harris, "Race and Essentialism in Feminist Legal Theory," in *Critical Race Feminism: A Reader*, 2nd ed., ed. Adrien Katherine Wing (New York University Press, 2003), 34–41.

30. Kimberlé Crenshaw, "Demarginalizing the Intersection of Race and Sex: A Black Feminist Critique of Antidiscrimination Doctrine, Feminist Theory and Antiracist Politics," *University of Chicago Legal Forum* 1, no. 1 (1989). http://chicagounbound.uchicago.edu/uclf/vol1989/iss1/8.

31. Harris, "Race and Essentialism."

32. South African Constitution, Art. 9 (3) (1996).

33. Wing, "Critical Race Feminism and Human Rights," 76.

34. Wing, *Global Critical Race Feminism*.

35. See Robert Williams, "Vampires Anonymous and Critical Race Practice," *Michigan Law Review* 95 (1997): 741–65.

36. Wing, "Critical Race Feminism and Human Rights," 75–76.

37. Wing, "Critical Race Feminism and Human Rights," 76.

38. Wing, "Critical Race Feminism and Human Rights," 76.

39. Wing, "Critical Race Feminism and Human Rights," 76.

40. Berta Esperanza Hernández-Truyol, "Awakening the Law: A LatCritical Perspective," *Seattle Journal of Social Justice* 20, no. 4 (2022): 927–64; Centers for Disease Control, "Health Equity Considerations and Racial and Ethnic Minority Group," 2019, https://www.cdc.gov/coronavirus/2019-ncov/community/health-equity/race-ethnicity.html#fii2. https://perma.cc/SRD9-MRWF; Daniel Wood, "As Pandemic Deaths Add Up, Racial Disparities Persist—And in Some Cases Worsen," *NPR*, September 23, 2020, https://www.npr.org/sections/health-shots/2020/09/23/914427907/as-pandemic-deathsadd-up-racial-disparities-persist-and-in-some-cases-worsen [https://perma.cc/2QXKWR3E].

41. Rick Harrison, "Sex Differences in COVID-19 Immune Responses Affect Patient Outcomes," *Women's Health Research at Yale*, August 26, 2020, https://medicine.yale.edu/whr/news-article/sex-differences-in-covid-19-immuneresponses-affect-patient-outcomes/ [https://perma.cc/LEV7-G4S7].

42. Harrison, "Sex Differences."

43. Danielle D'Annibale et al., "Viewing the COVID-19 Pandemic Through a Sex and Gender Lens," *Journal of Women's Health* 30, November 20, 2021, https://doi.org/10.1089/jwh.2020.8847.

44. D'Annibale, "Viewing."

45. Rasna Warah, "The Invisible Pandemic: COVID-19's Toll on African Women & Girls," July 2021, https://www.one.org/africa/blog/invisible-pandemic-gender-based-violence.

46. Scott Neuman, "Global Lockdowns Resulting in 'Horrifying Surge' in Domestic Violence, U.N. Warns," *NPR*, April 6, 2020, https://www.npr.org/sections/coronavirus-live-updates/2020/04/06/827908402/global-lockdowns-resulting-in-horrifying-surge-in-domestic-violence-u-n-warns.

47. "COVID-19 and the Impact on African Women: All Responses Must Respect the Gendered Impacts of the Pandemic," *The Elders.Org*, June 18, 2020, https://theelders.org/news/covid-19-and-impact-african-women-all-responses-must-respect-gendered-impacts-pandemic.

48. Emily Janoch, "6 Months of Transforming COVID Responses," *CARE*, September 10, 2020, https://www.care.org/news-and-stories/news/6-months-of-transforming-covid-responses/?gclid=9bc2dcd9bf7a166b2361bfe95f650eba&gclsrc=3p.ds&&utm_medium=cpc&utm_source=bing&utm_campaign=Paid+Search_Bing+Grant_Evergreen_Intent_Dynamic&utm_term=DYNAMIC+SEARCH+ADS&msclkid=9bc2dcd9bf7a166b2361bfe95f650eba.

49. Janoch, "6 Months."

50. Judith Duffy, "Scottish Inquiry Hears Women and Children Were Worst Affected by COVID Pandemic," *The National (Scotland)*, October 26, 2023, https://www.pressreader.com/uk/the-national-scotland/20231026/281505050904933.

51. Antonio Cascais, "COVID-19 Places Extra Burden on African Women," *DW*, June 13, 2020, https://www.dw.com/en/covid-19-places-extra-burden-on-african-women/a-53795533.

52. The Elders, "COVID-19."

53. The Elders, "COVID-19."

54. The Elders, "COVID-19."

55. Warah, "The Invisible Pandemic."

56. Peny Rahmadhani et al., "COVID-19 Crisis and Women in Asia Economic Impacts and Policy Responses," 2021, https://library.fes.de/pdf-files/bueros/nepal/18152.pdf.

57. Rahmadhani, "Covid-19."

58. Ana Marie Antonio et al., "COVID-19 Crisis and Women in Asia, Gender-based Violence, Sexual and Reproductive Health and Care Work," 2021, https://library.fes.de/pdf-files/bueros/nepal/18375.pdf.

59. Punita Chowbey, "India: How COVID Enabled New Forms of Economic Abuse of Women," *The Conversation*, November 30, 2023, https://theconversation.com/india-how-covid-enabled-new-forms-of-economic-abuse-of-women-212822.

60. Amanda E. Newman, "North Koreans Under 'Reign of Fear,' Starved and Forced to Work, U.N. Hears," *New York Times*, August 17, 2023, https://www.nytimes.com/2023/08/17/world/asia/un-north-korea-human-rights.html.

61. Victor Idrogo, "COVID-19: The Costly Setback in Latin American Women's Progress," *World Bank*. March 4, 2021, https://www.worldbank.org/en/news/feature/2021/03/04/la-covid19-costoso-retroceso-en-los-avances-de-la-mujer-latinoamericana.

62. UNICEF, "Two Years After: Saving a Generation," June 2022, https://www.unicef.org/lac/en/reports/two-years-after-saving-a-generation.

63. Idrogo, "Covid-19."

64. International Justice Resource Center, "Covid-19 Guidance from Supranational Human Rights Bodies," *IJRC*, October 27, 2021, https://ijrcenter.org/covid-19-guidance-from-supranational-human-rights-bodies/#States_of_emergency_and_exception.

65. The relevant treaties are ICCPR, CEDAW, CRPD, ICESCR, and CRC.

66. The relevant treaties are CERD, CAT, CED, and CMW.

67. United Nations Human Rights Office of the High Commissioner, "Complaints about Treaty Body Violations," accessed February 6, 2024, https://www.ohchr.org/en/treaty-bodies/complaints-about-human-rights-violations.

68. The ten treaty bodies, or Committees, are the UN Human Rights Committee; the Committee on Economic, Social, and Cultural Rights; the Committee on the Elimination of Racial Discrimination; the Committee on the Rights of Persons with Disabilities; the Committee on the Rights of the Child; the Committee on the Elimination of Discrimination against Women; the Committee against Torture and its Subcommittee on Prevention of Torture; the Committee on Enforced Disappearances; and the Committee on Migrant Workers.

69. United Nations Human Rights Office of the High Commissioner, "UN Human Rights Treaty Bodies Call for Human Rights Approach in Fighting COVID-19," March 24, 2020, https://www.ohchr.org/en/press-releases/2020/03/un-human-rights-treaty-bodies-call-human-rights-approach-fighting-covid-19?LangID=E&NewsID=25742.

70. United Nations Human Rights Office of the High Commissioner, "UN Human Rights."

71. United Nations Human Rights Office of the High Commissioner, "UN Human Rights."

72. International Covenant on Civil and Political Rights, Art. 4, December 16, 1966, 993 U.N.T.S. 171.

73. International Covenant on Economic, Social and Cultural Rights, Art. 11, para. 2, December 16, 1966, 993 U.N.T.S. 3.

74. Convention on the Elimination of Race Discrimination, December 21, 1965, 660 U.N.T.S. 195.

75. Convention on the Elimination of All Forms of Discrimination Against Women, December 18, 1979, 1249 U.N.T.S. 13.

76. Convention on the Rights of the Child, November 20, 1989, 1577 U.N.T.S. 3, Art. 24(2)(d).

77. Convention on Rights of Persons with Disabilities, March 30, 2007, 2515 U.N.T.S. 3.

78. World Health Organization: Revision of the International Health Regulations, Art. 12, May 23, 2005, 44 I.L.M. 1013 [hereinafter IHR].

79. InterAmerican Commission on Human Rights.

80. Karima Bennoune, "'Lest We Should Sleep:' COVID-19 and Human Rights," *American Journal of International Law* 114, no. 4 (2020): 666–76, https:// doi:10.1017/ajil.2020.68.

81. Oona Hathaway et al., "COVID-19 and International Law Series: Human Rights Law—Civil and Political Rights," *Just Security*, November 24, 2020, https://www.justsecurity.org/73520/covid-19-and-international-law-series-human-rights-law-civil-and-political-rights/; Bennoune, "Lest We Should Sleep," 669.

82. UN Human Rights Committee, General Comment No. 36, para. 2, UN Doc. CCPR/C/GC/36 (September 3, 2019); Bennoune, "Lest We Should Sleep."

83. UN Human Rights Committee, General Comment No. 36.

84. United Nations Secretary-General, "Policy Brief: The Impact of COVID-19 on Women," April 9, 2020, https://www.un.org/sites/un2.un.org/files/policy_brief_on_covid_impact_on_women_9_apr_2020_updated.pdf.

85. ICCPR; Center for Civil and Political Rights, "States of Emergencies in Response to the COVID-19 Pandemic," accessed August 5, 2023, https://datastudio.google.com/u/0/reporting/1sHT8quopdfavCvSDk7tzvqKISoLjiuo/page/dHMKB.

86. Richardson and Devine, "Emergencies End Eventually," 106.

87. Richardson and Devine, "Emergencies End Eventually," 106.

88. Richardson and Devine, "Emergencies End Eventually," 106.

89. Human Rights Committee, Statement on Derogations from the Covenant in Connection with the COVID-19 Pandemic, UN Doc. CCPR/C/128/2, April 24, 2020.

90. Richardson and Devine, "Emergencies End Eventually," 106.

91. "Human Rights Abuses Have Increased Since COVID," December 5, 2022, https://internationalviews.org/2022/12/covid-and-human-rights-torture-and-extrajudicial-killings-have-increased-since-2020/.

92. Roman Girma Teshome, "Derogations to Human Rights During a Global Pandemic: Unpacking Normative and Practical Challenges," *American University International Law Review* 33, 37, no. 2 (2022), https://digitalcommons.wcl.american.edu/auilr/vol37/iss2/6.

93. See U.N. Human Rights Committee, CCPR General Comment No. 36 on Article 6 of the International Covenant on Civil and Political Rights, on the right to life, para. 26, U.N. Doc. CCPR/C/GC/35 (Sept. 3, 2019).

94. U.N. Committee on Economic, Social, and Cultural Rights, CESCR General Comment No. 14: The Right to the Highest Attainable Standard of Health (Art. 12), para.16, 44(b)–(c), U.N. Doc. E/C.12/2000/4, Aug. 11, 2000.

95. CESCR General Comment No. 14.

96. ICESCR, para. 34, 28 35, 29 36, 30, and 37.

97. See Doctors Without Borders, "Keeping Essential Medical Services Running During the COVID-19 Pandemic," May 22, 2020, https://www.doctorswithoutborders.org/what-we-do/news-stories/story/keeping-essentialmedical-services-running-during-covid-19-pandemic.

98. ICESCR, Art. 2(2).

99. United Nations Special Rapporteur in the Field of Cultural Rights, Report, UN Doc. A/HRC/20/26, May 14, 2012.

100. CESCR, General Comment No. 25 (2020) on Science and Economic, Social and Cultural Rights, UN Doc. E/C.12/GC/25, at para. 70 (Apr. 30, 2020).

101. OHCHR Press Release, "Poland Urged Not to Criminalise Sex Education or Tighten Access to Abortion," April 16, 2020, https://www.ohchr.org/EN/NewsEvents/Pages/DisplayNews.aspx?NewsID¼25796&LangID¼E.

102. Ying Chen, "Protecting the Right to Food in the Era of COVID-19 and Beyond," *Georgia Journal of International & Comparative Law* 49, no. 1 (2021): 1–44.

103. Chen, "Protecting," 25.

104. Chen, "Protecting," 30.

105. Chen, "Protecting," 31.

106. Human Rights Watch, "Draft Pandemic Treaty Fails to Protect Rights," November 7, 2023, https://www.hrw.org/news/2023/11/07/draft-pandemic-treaty-fails-protect-rights.

107. CEDAW, art 12(1).

108. Fatemah Albader, "Discrimination against Women: Under the Magnifying Glass of COVID," *Georgetown Journal of Gender & Law* 23, no. 3 (2022): 433–48.

109. Marsha A. Freeman, "Addressing Gender-Based Violence: CEDAW and Political Will," *Gender Policy Report*, November 28, 2018; CEDAW General Recommendation No. 19: Violence against women, U.N. Doc. CEDAW/GEC/3731 (1992), para.1; CEDAW General Recommendation No. 35 on gender-based violence against women, updating general recommendation No. 19, U.N. Doc. CEDAW/C/GC/35 (2017).

110. CEDAW General Recommendation No. 35, para. 2.

111. CEDAW General Recommendation No. 35, para. 32.

112. Committee on the Elimination of Discrimination Against Women, "Guidance Note on CEDAW and COVID-19," UN OHCHR, accessed October 13, 2021, https://view.officeapps.live.com/op/view.aspx?src=https%3A%2F%2Fwww.ohchr.org%2Fsites%2Fdefault%2Ffiles%2FDocuments%2FHRBodies%2FCEDAW%2FStatements%2FCEDAW_statement_COVID-19_final.doc&wdOrigin.

113. Committee on the Elimination of Discrimination Against Women, "Guidance Note on CEDAW and COVID-19," April 2020, https://cambodia.ohchr.org/sites/default/files/InfoNotes/CEDAW_Guidance_note_COVID-19%2022%20April%202020.pdf.

114. CERD, art 5(e) (iv).

115. CEDAW, Art. 12(2); ICESCR, Art. 10(2).

116. Stefania Giannini, "Covid-19 School Closures around the World will Hit Girls Hardest," *UNESCO*, March 31, 2020, https://www.unesco.org/en/articles/covid-19-school-closures-around-world-will-hit-girls-hardest.,

117. CPRD, art 6.

118. World Health Organization, "Statement on the Second Meeting of the International Health Regulations," (2005) Emergency Committee Regarding the Outbreak of Novel Coronavirus (2019-nCoV), January 30, 2020, https://www.who.int/news/item/30-01-2020-statement-on-the-second-meeting-ofthe-international-health-regulations-(2005)-emergency-committee-regarding-the-outbreak-of-novelcoronavirus-(2019-ncov) [https://perma.cc/JQY9-8HN5].

119. IHR.

120. Norman Howard-Jones and the World Health Organization, "The Scientific Background of the International Sanitary Conferences 1851–1938," *History International Public Health* 1 (1975), https://iris.who.int/handle/10665/62873.

121. IHR, Art. 2.

122. Celestina Radogno, "Reconceptualizing the International Health Regulations in the Wake of COVID-19: An Analysis of Formal Dispute Mechanisms and Global Health Diplomacy," *Yale Journal of Health Policy, Law & Ethics* 21 (2022): 90–151.

123. Radogno, "Reconceptualizing," 94.

124. See also Jonatan Echebarria Fernández, "The European Union's Four Freedoms of Movement and the COVID-19 Pandemic: Lessons Learned and a Critical Analysis," *Columbia Journal of European Law* 28: 239 (2020); https://doi.org.:10.15166/2499-8249/437.

125. IACHR, https://www.oas.org/en/iachr/decisions/pdf/Resolution-1-20-en.pdf.

126. IACHR, https://www.oas.org/en/iachr/decisions/pdf/Resolution-4-20-en.pdf.

127. Antonia Urrejola Noguera and Soledad Garcia Munoz, "The IACHR's Comprehensive Response to the COVID-19 Pandemic and Its Intersectional Impacts on Human Rights," *University of Miami International & Comparative Law Review* 29, no. 2 (2022), https://repository.law.miami.edu/umiclr/vol29/iss2/8/.

128. IACHR, para. 3e of 1/2020.

129. IACHR, para. 27 of 1/2020.

130. IACHR, para. 49 of 1/2020

131. IACHR, para. 50 of 1/2020.

132. IACHR, para. 51 of 1/2020

133. IACHR, para. 52 of 1/2020.

134. IACHR, Human Rights of Persons with Covid-19, Res. 4/2020 (July 27, 2020, at para. 72–75).
135. IACHR, para. 24 of 4/2020.
136. The Elders, "COVID-19."
137. Chen, "Protecting," 28.
138. Chen, "Protecting," 31.
139. The Elders, "COVID-19."
140. The Elders, "COVID-19."
141. The Elders, "COVID-19;" Caroline Bettinger-Lopez et al., "The Duty to Protect Survivors of Gender-Based Violence in the Age of COVID-19: An Expanded Human Rights Framework," *University of Miami International & Comparative Law Review* 29, no. 2 (2022): 235–66.
142. Shebana Alqaseer et al., "COVID-19 Crisis and Women in Asia, Gender-based Violence, Sexual and Reproductive Health and Care Work" (Friedrich Ebert Siftung, 2021), https://library.fes.de/pdf-files/bueros/nepal/18375.pdf.
143. Bennoune, "Lest," 670.
144. Albader, "Discrimination," 445.
145. See, e.g., Berta Esperanza Hernández-Truyol, "Hope, Dignity, and the Limits of Democracy," *Ne. University Law Review* 10: (2018): 654–90. http://dx.doi.org/10.2139/ssrn.3303316.
146. South Africa Constitution, Art. 10 (1996).
147. Hakeem Yusuf and Philip Oamen, "Realising Economic and Social Rights Beyond COVID-19: The Imperative of International Cooperation," *Indiana International & Comparative Law Review* 32, no. 1 (2022): 43–68.

CHAPTER EIGHT

LAW AND EPIDEMIOLOGY IN THE MAKING OF GUANTANAMO

Aziza Ahmed

INTRODUCTION

On December 6, 1990, Haiti elected a new president: Reverend Jean-Bertrand Aristide. His election unseated Jean-Claude Duvalier, who came to power in 1971. Jean-Claude and his father, who had presided over Haiti before him, were known for their violent rule.[1] Less than one year after Aristide's election, a military coup resulted in Duvalier stepping back into power. Haitians fled the political upheaval. Many boarded boats to the United States.[2]

Another crisis was also in motion: the human immunodeficiency virus (HIV) was circulating quickly among populations. While basic scientific knowledge about the virus was growing, much was unknown. HIV tests were not widely available around the world (they would not be until nearly two decades later) and who would be most at risk for contracting HIV was an unsettled question.[3]

These two events intersected when the United States began to intercept Haitians at sea and transported some of the detained to Guantanamo Bay, Cuba. Individuals were taken to the U.S. Naval Base on Guantanamo Bay, where their asylum claims were processed.[4] While some of the migrants held at Guantanamo Bay were able to enter the United States,[5] those who tested HIV positive were forced to remain in the U.S. military–owned compound and detention center.

The detention of people living with HIV in Guantanamo has received much activist and scholarly attention at the time and still today.[6] This essay, in a volume on critical race theory (CRT) and Third World Approaches to International Law (TWAIL), relies on this scholarship to consider how CRT and TWAIL are necessary to understand the legal and political realities that produced this moment of detention. CRT focuses our attention on the implicit and explicit invocations of race and otherness embedded in the understanding of Haitians and HIV, creating the possibility for detention. TWAIL, in turn, unsettles the idea that the we can think about moments of Haitian migration into the United States as discrete or singular. Rather, TWAIL turns our attention to a longer history that allows us to see the management of Haitians entering the United States in continuity with a longer colonial past.[7]

THE RACIAL CONSTRUCTION OF AIDS

A core insight of critical race theory is the formation of race by institutions including law and science.[8] The AIDS crisis underscores how together, the powerful discourses of epidemiology—the science of public health—and law can construct a racial narrative that, in turn, shapes the legal and scientific response to an epidemic.[9]

The early days of the AIDS epidemic were filled with what sociologist Ulrich Beck has described as expert-generated non-knowing. Without a test, epidemiologists pieced together symptoms that seemed to constitute a new illness circulating in the population and resulting in the untimely deaths of many.[10]

Before the disease had a name, epidemiologists identified four groups as high risk for HIV. In the vernacular of the time, these groups were Haitians, heroin users, homosexuals, and hemophiliacs (4-H).[11] A list of symptoms was slowly found to be indicative of this new condition. As the only group identified by nationality rather than risk behavior, Haitians stood out.[12]

The listing of Haitians as a 4-H group dates back to a 1982 Centers for Disease Control (CDC) report. The CDC regularly issues Maternal Mortality and Morbidity reports. These reports allow the CDC to convey scientific updates on public health information. The 1982 report focused on a cluster of illnesses that had only otherwise been identified in patterns among men who have sex with men and drug users.[13] This illness would later be named AIDS based on a set of symptoms and, eventually, a blood test that would measure CD4 counts.

The majority of men who appeared in this CDC study, however, did not identify as having had sex with men or as having used drugs. It left an open question at a time when little was known about HIV, and heterosexual sex was not considered a major driver: why were these men showing the symptoms of this perplexing new illness? With little else to rely on, being Haitian itself became seen as a suspect category for carrying a new disease that was claiming the lives of many. The epidemiological assertions in this early period of AIDS began to reinscribe Haitians as a unique source of contagion. As leading scholar on migration, detention, and race A. Naomi Paik shows in her detailed accounts of this period, that this chapter draws from, nationality was conflated with disease.[14]

Black migrants from Haiti became the face of a new external threat to public health in the United States.

HAITIAN MIGRATION

Political instability in Haiti during the 1980s and 1990s would push tens of thousands of migrants out of the country and into open waters headed to the United States. The political turbulence in Haiti that resulted in this migration was not born of the moment: colonialism and the rebellions that followed produced both instability and possibility. The extraction of wealth from Haiti to France and the debt burdens on the country undermined the country's ability to rise out of poverty.[15]

When the coup occurred in 1991,[16] the U.S. government and Haiti had an existing agreement that allowed the U.S. to intercept boats in international waters and do assessments of possible asylum claims on boats.[17] Under the terms of this agreement, those with asylum claims were taken to the United States while those who were determined not to have plausible claims were taken back to Port-au-Prince. With the influx of migrants in 1991, Haitians interdicted at sea were taken to Guantanamo Bay, Cuba, and remained there while their asylum claims were assessed by U.S. officials.[18]

By all accounts, the conditions in Guantanamo were terrible. Migrants slept in tents. Standing portable toilets resulted in sanitation problems. Among those held were pregnant women and children.

The convergence of the AIDS epidemic and the arrival of refugees resulted in one of the most alarming moments of the early AIDS response. As Haitians were being sorted by U.S. government officials based on the possibility of attaining asylum in the United States, the U.S. government also began to attempt to ascertain HIV status. HIV-positive Haitians were taken to a separate camp, Camp Bulkeley. Family members of those diagnosed with HIV were also taken to the camp. The poor conditions for HIV-positive migrants mirrored those in the camp generally with the added issues of receiving adequate medical care. As this was ongoing, in February 1992, the Immigration and Naturalization Service (INS) general counsel produced a new policy stating that people who were positive for HIV must have a second interview establishing the individual's refugee status.[19]

The separate and ongoing detention of Haitians detected with HIV dovetailed with the social stigmatization of the disease that continued in the United States. Gay men and drug users bore the brunt of moralizing about HIV.[20] With the war on drugs picking up steam, and a racist discourse about welfare and disability deployed by the Reagan administration, race, too, became a central feature of understanding public health crises. AIDS was no exception. Early on epidemiologists began to theorize that the virus that caused AIDS had traveled from Africa, the product of crossover from animal to human, and then to Haiti and into the United States.[21] Various versions of this theory circulated, but most pointed to Haitian migration as a possible source of HIV's origination in the United States. As described by Africana Studies Professor Georges Fouron, the theory trafficked in the idea that the arrival of Haitian migrants was bringing "disease" and "disarray" into the United States.[22] Conflated with Black Haitian migrants, contagion became associated with AIDS, and who was to blame for the circulation of the virus to begin with.[23] This, coupled with existing border policies that were the product of a long history of exclusion in the United States, produced the background legal conditions that would allow for the detention of Haitians intercepted by the United States coast guard.[24]

THE LEGAL AND ACTIVIST RESPONSE

The terrible conditions of the camp led to protest.[25] Inside the camp, Haitians began a hunger strike in protest of their conditions. Several fell unconscious.[26] As word of the terrible conditions spread, activists and advocates began to organize. The activist group ACT UP, in partnership with Black AIDS Mobilization and others, took on the issue of Haitians in Guantanamo, holding protests in New York City at the Immigration and Naturalization Service's detention center. Protest flyers called for marches and candlelight vigils to protest the "270 women, men, and children [who] have been subjected to systematic brutality and inhumane conditions."[27] ACT UP advocates demanded the release of Haitians detained on Guantanamo. Other organizations also protested. TransAfrica and the NAACP held actions in front of the White House calling for the release of all Haitians. *New York Times* coverage of the protest, which brought together advocates for international and domestic racial justice, documented that many African Americans in the United States felt the policy of Haitian detention was "inherently racist." In planning for the protest of "immoral" actions, TransAfrica and the NAACP sent a circular to potential volunteers to prepare to be detained.[28] Black movement leaders including Jesse Jackson visited the camp, bringing additional visibility to the problem and putting pressure on political leaders.

Eventually, Haitian Services Center and the Center for Constitutional Rights began to litigate on behalf of the people living with HIV in Guantanamo. As described by Michael Ratner, co-counsel for the detained, the case built on the ongoing political mobilization by activist groups and was fueled by hope that the Clinton administration would eventually dissolve the policy against Haitians.

In his reflection on the litigation, Ratner describes the political atmosphere shifting.

> Two of us went to the camp at the end of January 1993, the height of the hunger strike. The situation was desperate. The Haitians had lost a lot of weight, and many had been hospitalized. Our clients were adamant. They said we could do what we believed was legally necessary, and that they would not oppose us. However, we had not gotten them out, and now they would decide how to act. In many ways, the hunger strike was the strategic turning point. It brought the press, well-known personalities, and politicians to Guantanamo. It made the HIV camp a public issue. It also made us, the lawyers, pay a lot more attention to our clients. From the strike forward, we were a continuous presence in the camp. Whether we liked it or not, our clients had set the course for an outside agitational strategy.[29]

In solidarity with the detained individuals, civil rights activist Jesse Jackson also went on a fast, sustaining national attention to the issue.[30]

The case reached the federal courts in 1993. Judge Sterling Johnson of the Eastern District of New York described the "inadequate" services for Haitians living with HIV, especially those who had become severely ill. Military physicians had complained about the inability to adequately care for people with HIV and requested the evaluation of HIV-positive individuals. The requests were denied repeatedly by the INS.[31] In fact, he notes, rather than explain or defend the medical facilities in Guantanamo, the government admitted that the facilities were inadequate during the trial. Judge Johnson concluded that the detention facilities represented

> nothing more than an HIV prison camp presenting potential public health risks to the Haitians held there. There is no dispute that because HIV+ individuals are immuno-suppressed, they are more susceptible to a variety of infections, many of which can be transmitted from one person to the next. No major outbreak of infectious disease has occurred yet, but by segregating HIV+ individuals, the Government places the Haitian detainees at greater risk of contracting infections, including tuberculosis, measles and other life threatening diseases, than if they were permitted to live in the general population.[32]

The opinion was in line with concerns raised by public health officials from the Assistant Secretary of Health and the Centers for Disease Control, who each warned of a public health crisis.[33]

While the election of Bill Clinton failed to produce the desired result of release,[34] following the decision, New York City agreed to resettle the Haitian immigrants. One hundred of the Haitians landed in New York.[35] By June of 1993, the remainder of the Haitian detainees had entered the United States.[36]

CRT AND TWAIL

Rather than view the story of the detention of HIV-positive Haitians as a legal response to a set of time bound rational concerns by the United States government in the face of a growing public health crisis, CRT and TWAIL points us to the co-productive dimensions of law and epidemiology in the context of Haitian migration and allows us to read this moment as situated within a longer history of race and world-making.[37]

Critical race theorists have long pointed to the role of biological race and scientific claims in the project of racialization.[38] Scholars of the AIDS crisis have shown how race and nationality became intertwined with both disease and outsider status.[39] The race and outsider status of Haitians set in motion the legal process that resulted in their detention. This legal infrastructure was bolstered by the epidemiological facts set into motion by the Centers for Disease Control, a key signaling institution, as described by Cathy Cohen and Gerald Oppenheimer, as to how we should understand the disease.[40] The discourse of epidemiological experts facilitated the idea that, as Paula Treichler describes, "disease is a knowable biological phenomenon whose strange and seemingly contradictory aspects are ultimately illusory: decoded by experts, its mysteries will one by one become controllable material realities."[41]

In writing of the representations of disease in the AIDS epidemic, Treichler notes that the disease was racialized and rested on from prior epidemics: "Discourse about AIDS in the Third World shares but exaggerates this premise, first equating the Third World (especially Africa, 'the dark continent') with the savage, the alien, or the incomprehensible, then asserting the importance and achievability and control."[42] Noted physician and medical anthropologist Paul Farmer writes in *AIDS and Accusation* that the willingness to blame is based on a deep-seated and historical racism that had long shaped the relationship between the United States and Haiti.[43]

Race, to borrow a framing from Chantal Thomas, became a technology of governance, this time in the context of public health.[44] Viewing race as such recalls a broader history of the role of immigration law in the story of Haitian migration and the management of disease in the United States. Laws governing Chinese exclusion are paradigmatic. Chinese immigrants were not only seen as disruptive to American cultural values and labor, but were also often blamed for carrying disease. Legal scholar Kerry Abrams notes that Chinese women were often seen as "harbingers of disease." They were specifically targeted for exclusion in the Page Act of 1875, for example, which banned Chinese "prostitutes" from entering the United States.[45]

And, too, TWAIL mandates a consideration of the broader colonial histories that produce these racialized, contemporary legal and public health crises.[46] Here the work of A. Naomi Paik is instructive. In interrogating the role of prison camps, she writes of the Haitian detention in Guantanamo that "histories of racism and refugee exclusion do not stand alone but are intimately bound to the (neo) imperial relations the United States has established in the Caribbean." The country's long history of colonization and slavery, and the revolutions that followed, laid the groundwork for the interventions of new global powers, including the United States, that would shape the political futures and possibilities of the country and the people within it.[47] These factors together would drive Haitian people to board boats to the United States in what TWAIL scholar Tendayi Achiume has described as transnational life: an existence that takes people beyond their sovereign borders but keeping within the neocolonial frames that governs the possibilities of their existence.[48]

CONCLUSION

Designated as a high-risk group for HIV by the CDC, Haitian migrants in the United States were racialized and categorized as diseased outsiders who threatened to worsen an existing public health crisis. As Paik argues, a conflation of race, nation, and disease facilitated the legal frameworks that made the detention of Haitians living with HIV in Guantanamo possible. Critical race theory and TWAIL allows us to see this moment as more than a singular instance of injustice remedied through the courts. Instead, the detention of Haitians living with HIV shows how outsider status is continually made in relationship to race and disease, and how it is legitimated by law and epidemiology.

NOTES

1. Carlos Ortiz Miranda, "Haiti and the United States during the 1980s and 1990s: Refugees, Immigration, and Foreign Policy," *San Diego Law Review* 32 (1995): 673.

2. For a longer description of this political moment see A. Naomi Paik, *Rightlessness: Testimony and Redress in US Prison Camps Since World War II* (UNC Press Books, 2016), 85–103.

3. There is a longer discussion of the law, politics, and science of AIDS in Aziza Ahmed, *Risk and Resistance: How Feminists Transformed the Law and Science of AIDS* (Cambridge University Press, forthcoming).

4. "Haitian Asylum Seekers USA," Amnesty, February 2, 1993, https://www.amnesty.org/en/wp-content/uploads/2021/06/amr510051993en.pdf.

5. "Executive Order 12779 Prohibiting Certain Transactions with Respect to Haiti," The American Presidency Project, October 28, 1991, https://www.presidency.ucsb.edu/documents/executive-order-12779-prohibiting-certain-transactions-with-respect-haiti. Many people died en route to the United States. Kenneth Freed, "Hundreds Dead in Sinking of Overloaded Haiti Ferry: Disaster: Only 285 Survivors are Found from 2,000 Believed Aboard the Boat When it Capsized in a Storm," *LA Times*, February 19, 1993, https://www.latimes.com/archives/la-xpm-1993-02-19-mn-284-story.html.

6. Many scholars have detailed this moment. This chapter draws on the descriptions of the historical moment from the work of Paul Farmer, *AIDS and Accusation: Haiti and the Geography of Blame, Updated with a New Preface* (University of California Press, 2006); Michael Ratner, "How We Closed the Guantanamo HIV Camp: The Intersection of Politics and Litigation," *Harvard Human Rights Journal* 11 (1998): 187; Karma R. Chávez, *The Borders of AIDS: Race, Quarantine, and Resistance* (University of Washington Press, 2021), 3–16; A. Naomi Paik, "Carceral Quarantine at Guantánamo: Legacies of US Imprisonment of Haitian Refugees, 1991–1994," *Radical History Review* 2013, no. 115 (2013): 142–68; A. Naomi Paik, "Testifying to Rightlessness: Haitian Refugees Speaking from Guantánamo," *Social Text* 28.3 (2010): 39–65l; Paik, *Rightlessness*.

7. Describing race as a technology of governance, see, Chantal Thomas, "Race as a Technology of Global Economic Governance," *UCLA Law Review* 67 (2020): 1860.Achiume, "Migration as Decolonization."

8. On the connection between law, science, and race, see Khiara M. Bridges, "The Dangerous Law of Biological Race," *Fordham Law Review* 82 (2013): 21; Dorothy Roberts, *Fatal Invention: How Science, Politics, and Big Business Re-create Race in the Twenty-first Century* (New Press/ORIM, 2011); Devon W. Carbado and Daria Roithmayr, "Critical Race Theory Meets Social Science," *Annual Review of Law and Social Science* 10 (2014): 149–67.

9. Ahmed, *Risk and Resistance*; Larry Rohter, "Long Exodus Nears for H.I.V.-Infected Refugees from Haiti," *New York Times*, June 13, 1993, https://www.nytimes.com/1993/06/13/us/long-exodus-nears-end-for-hiv-infected-refugees-from-haiti.html.

10. Ulrich Beck and Peter Wehling, "The Politics of Non-Knowing," in *The Politics of Knowledge*, ed. Patrick Baert and Fernando Dominguez Rubio (Routledge, 2011).

11. Linda G. Marc et al., "HIV among Haitian-born Persons in the United States, 1985–2007," *Aids* 24, no. 13 (2010): 2089–97. Institut Pasteur, "40 Years of HIV Discovery: The First Cases of a Mysterious Disease in the Early 1980s," May 5, 2023, https://www.pasteur.fr/en/research-journal/news/40-years-hiv-discovery-first-cases-mysterious-disease-early-1980s#:~:text=1982%20-%20"4H%20disease",only%20concern%20"these%20populations; Andrew R. Moss et al., "Aids in the 'Gay' Areas of San Francisco," *The Lancet* 321, no. 8330 (April 21, 1983): 923–4. https://doi.org/10.1016/s0140-6736(83)91346-6.

12. Describing the 4-H categorization in relationship to Haitian identity see Paik, *Rightlessness*, 100. For an overview of the early politics on AIDS see Ahmed, *Risk and Resistance*.

13. "The occurrence of severe opportunistic infections among 32 Haitians recently entering the United States is a new phenomenon. The in vitro immunologic findings and the high mortality rate (nearly 50%) for these patients are similar to the pattern recently described among homosexual males and IV drug abusers." "Opportunistic Infections and Kaposi's Sarcoma among Haitians in the United States," CDC, July 9, 1982, https://www.cdc.gov/mmwr/preview/mmwrhtml/00001123.htm#:~:text=of%20e%2Dmail.-,Opportunistic%20Infections%20and%20Kaposi%27s%20Sarcoma%20among%20Haitians%20in%20the%20United,have%20been%20reported%20to%20date.

14. Paik, "Carceral Quarantine at Guantánamo," 142–68; Paik, "Testifying to Rightlessness," 39–65l; Paik, *Rightlessness*.

15. Liliana Obregón, "Empire, Racial Capitalism and International Law: The Case of Manumitted Haiti and the Recognition Debt," *Leiden Journal of International Law* 31.3 (2018): 597-615; E. Tendayi Achiume, "Migration as Decolonization," *Stanford Law Review* 71 (2019): 1509.

16. "U.S. Processing of Haitian Asylum Seekers," United States General Accounting Office, April 9, 1992, https://www.gao.gov/assets/t-nsiad-92-25.pdf.

17. Haitian Centers Council, Inc. v. Sale, 823 F. Supp. 1028, 1034-1038 (E.D.N.Y. 1993).

18. Haitian Centers Council, Inc. v. Sale, 823 F. Supp. 1028, 1034-1038 (E.D.N.Y. 1993).

19. Haitian Centers Council, Inc. v. Sale, 823 F. Supp. 1028, 1034-1038 (E.D.N.Y. 1993).

20. Paul Farmer, *AIDS and Accusation*; Paula A. Treichler, *How to Have Theory in an Epidemic: Cultural Chronicles of AIDS* (Duke University Press, 2020).

21. Treichler, *How to Have Theory in an Epidemic*; Charles W. Hunt, "Racism and AIDS: African Origin Theories of HIV-1," *Explorations in Ethnic Studies* 17, no. 2 (1994): 155–75; Merrill Singer; "The Politics of AIDS: Introduction," *Social Science & Medicine* 38, no. 10 (1994): 1321–4.

22. Georges E. Fouron, "Race, Blood, Disease and Citizenship: The Making of the Haitian-Americans and the Haitian Immigrants into 'the Others' during the 1980s–1990s AIDS Crisis," in *Transnational Citizenship Across the Americas* (Routledge, 2015), 57–71.

23. Paik, "Carceral Quarantine at Guantánamo"; Fouron, "Race, Blood, Disease and Citizenship."

24. On migration as a product of colonialism see Achiume, "Migration as Decolonization."

25. Fouron, "Race, Blood, Disease and Citizenship." Paik describes protest in the camp in Paik, *Rightlessness*, 114-150.

26. "Hunger Strike at Haitian Camps," Guantanamo Public Memory Project, https://gitmomemory.org/timeline/resisting-and-protesting-guantanamo/hunger-strike-at-haitian-camps/.

27. ACT-UP Protest Flyer, *Shut Down the Guantanamo Prison Camp! HIV Is Not A Crime* (on file with author).

28. Barbara Crossette, "2 Groups Plan Protest Against Haitian Policy," *New York Times*, August 23, 1992, https://www.nytimes.com/1992/08/23/world/2-groups-plan-protest-against-haitian-policy.html.

29. Ratner, "How We Closed the Guantanamo HIV Camp."

30. Ratner, "How We Closed the Guantanamo HIV Camp"; Philip J. Hilts, "7 Haitians Held at Guantanamo Unconscious in a Hunger Strike," *New York Times*, February 15, 1993, https://www.nytimes.com/1993/02/15/world/7-haitians-held-at-guantanamo-unconscious-in-a-hunger-strike.html.

31. Haitian Centers Council, Inc. v. Sale, 823 F. Supp. 1028, 1038 (E.D.N.Y. 1993).

32. Haitian Centers Council, Inc. v. Sale, 823 F. Supp. 1028, 1038–39 (E.D.N.Y. 1993).

33. Haitian Centers Council, Inc. v. Sale, 823 F. Supp. 1028, 1038–39 (E.D.N.Y. 1993).

34. Ratner, "How We Closed the Guantanamo HIV Camp." For an account of activism around Haiti see Karma R. Chávez, "ACT UP, Haitian Migrants, and Alternative Memories of HIV/AIDs," *Quarterly Journal of Speech* 98, no. 1 (2012): 63–8.

35. Maggie Schreiner, "Haitian Refugees, ACT UP New York, and the Transnational Dimensions of Local Organizing for AIDS Housing," The Gotham Center for New York City History, April 5, 2023, https://www.gothamcenter.org/blog/haitian-refugees-and-act-up-ny.

36. As A. Naomi Paik notes, the camp was later reopened once again holding Haitians and then Cuban refugees.

37. James Thuo Gathii, "Writing Race and Identity in a Global Context: What CRT and TWAIL Can Learn from Each Other," *UCLA Law Review* 67 (2020): 1610.

38. Roberts, *Fatal Invention*; Bridges, "The Dangerous Law of Biological Race," 21.

39. Paik describes the conflation of race, nation, and disease. Fouron, "Race, Blood, Disease and Citizenship."

40. Cathy Cohen, The Boundaries of Blackness: AIDS and the Breakdown of Black Politics (University of Chicago Press, 1999), 123; Gerald Oppenheimer, "Causes, Cases, and Cohorts: The Role of Epidemiology in the Historical Construction of AIDS," in *AIDS: The Making of a Chronic Disease*, eds. Elizabeth Fee and Daniel Fox (University of California Press, 1992): 49-83.

41. Treichler, *How to Have Theory in an Epidemic*, 379.

42. Treichler, *How to Have Theory in an Epidemic*, 100–1.

43. Detailed in Hunt, "Racism and AIDS: African African Origin Theories of HIV-1"; Farmer, *AIDS and Accusation*.

44. Thomas, "Race as a Technology of Global Economic Governance."

45. Kerry Abrams, "Polygamy, Prostitution, and the Federalization of Immigration Law," *Columbia Law Review* 105 (2005): 641.

46. Matiangai Sirleaf, "White Health and International Law," in *Race, Racism, and International Law*, ed. Devon W. Carbado et al. (Stanford University Press, forthcoming 2025).

47. Paik, "Carceral Quarantine at Guantánamo."

48. Achiume, "Migration as Decolonization."

CHAPTER NINE

WHITE HEALTH AND INTERNATIONAL LAW

Matiangai Sirleaf*

INTRODUCTION

Global health law has reified the subaltern positions of many Black, Indigenous, and other subordinated peoples who lack(ed) law-making power nationally, regionally, or internationally, and were not able to translate their health priorities into law. Despite its ambitions, global health law as a field does not escape the structural limitations and racial hierarchies imposed by the larger field of international law. Traditionally, international law provides that only States can make binding law. They can do so either through treaty or through custom—treaties through contracts between States, and custom through the general behavior of states out of a sense of legal obligation to behave or not behave in a certain way. Both primary sources of law-making internationally are ones that subaltern peoples under colonial rule and/or foreign occupation did not generally have access to create. A small club of States dictated the terms of entry for other peoples to statehood. People of the Global Majority, those deemed outside of the family of purported "civilized nations," did not have their sovereignty or systems of governance and ways of being recognized. Indeed, around the United Nations and the World Health Organization's (WHO) founding, 750 million people, about a third of the world's population, were subject to colonial domination and rule. Since the WHO's inception, the issue of whether it can make a clear enough break from the coloniality of global health law has been a central issue shaping its work. Anibal Quijano conceptualizes "coloniality" of power as the vestiges and legacies of colonialism, which captures the racial, political-economic, social, and other hierarchies that European colonialism imposed that have lingered after formal decolonization and continue to oppress historically subordinated peoples.[1]

This chapter traces the construction of race[2] and racism[3] in the development of global public health. It explores the connections, legacies, and important disjunctions between tropical medicine[4] and global public health. It considers the primacy given to White health as one of the animating purposes behind the emergence of the global public health regime. White health as a concept reflects the "racialization of diseases," which attaches racial meaning to illnesses based on the racial groups that tend to be socially associated with a given disease.[5] It provides a perspective for conceptualizing the prioritization of the health concerns of those racialized as White, not because these concerns are unique biologically, but to draw attention to the signifying role of racism and the political, economic, legal, and social privileging and salience given to ailments thought to touch and concern White peoples and the needs of capital.[6] This chapter considers the role of international law in facilitating this prioritization. The central question this chapter interrogates is to what extent White health and White interests then and now continue to inform the global health agenda.

This chapter begins with an exploration of the creation of racialized states. It then discusses how these states' burgeoning public health efforts were racialized and introduces the framework of health justice as a productive lens for probing the role of laws, policies, and institutions in creating and sustaining health inequities. Subsequently, it traces the path from tropical/colonial medicine to global health to illustrate the fundamental role of racism and classism in the development of the field. The piece then addresses whose health is prioritized internationally by considering how the vestiges of colonial medicine in global health remain with current efforts to contain infectious diseases. Doing so reveals the nexus between White health and global health and is crucial for rendering structural racism and classism visible, and for understanding how global health inequalities continue to be constructed around zones of sacrifice. Next, the chapter considers how current reform efforts are not clearly pointing towards decolonial futures that eliminate health inequalities stemming from structural racism, colonialism, class exploitation, and other forms of subordination. The chapter concludes that global health law as a field tends to look exclusively at what the powerful were(are) able to create in terms of legal architecture, which produces a highly constrained and shallow vision of our past and limits our ability to envision more emancipatory futures.

RACIALIZED STATES & PUBLIC HEALTH

The global health law regime emerged coterminously with the creation of the nation-state and the erection of racialized borders. E. Tendayi Achiume has argued that contemporary national borders of the international order are inherently racial.[7] In other words, they enforce exclusion and inclusion in racially disparate ways.[8] Achiume uses the term "racial borders" to refer to territorial and political border regimes that disparately curtail movement, mobility, and political incorporation membership based on race, and sustain international migration and mobility as racial privileges.[9] Her analysis importantly frames race as both a political and territorial boundary, positioning it alongside other forms of border infrastructure, ranging from physical walls to the institution of citizenship.[10] While her analysis is centrally aimed at international migration law, it has a number of implications for global public health law.

As I have argued elsewhere, "the foundation of the nation state itself was influenced by the racialization process."[11] This process involved "the extension of racial meaning to a previously racially unclassified relationship, social practice or group."[12] Thus, as Europeans subjugated different societies and peoples, they socially constructed race as a natural occurrence and came up with a racial categorization system for the human species.[13] Racialized social systems constructed by White Europeans allocated different economic, political, social, and other rewards to groups along racial lines.[14] Significantly, the racialized construction of the nation-state was legitimated by scientific racism. Scientific racism refers to the scientific and biomedical endeavor to support and explain variance between human groups as innate and involving a qualitative racial hierarchy.[15] This racial hierarchy then created and reified categories such as "Indians" and "Negroes." Scientific racism was used to justify, propose, and project scientific findings and theories, which facilitated and reinforced the enactment of racist social policies.[16] Scientific racism was intrinsically intertwined with the "civilizing mission" of European imperial expansion and helped to facilitate the subjugation of Black, Indigenous, and other historically subordinated groups.[17] Racialized social systems then created vested interests in keeping or transforming the society's racial structure[18] nationally and transnationally. In this way, the formation of nation-states was the result of drawing borders internally and externally for "we" vs. "them," "insider" vs. "outsider," and "foreigner" vs. "alien" at all levels of racialized societies.[19]

In the same way that racialized borders structurally benefit some nations and racial groups at the expense of others in terms of disparate international mobility, similar racial privileging is seen in the realm of health. In previous work, I analyze how the "racial valuation of diseases" elucidates "how norms—based on status, stereotype, and bias about the ill-health of peoples of color—have crystallized, ossified, [and] spread globally."[20] The "construction of racial valuation was shaped by the project of scientific racism, which imbued race with 'objective,' 'scientific' significance that legitimized beliefs of White racial superiority."[21] For instance, efforts to improve the health of subordinated populations in internal or external colonies were explicitly tied to racial capitalism,[22] wherein being usable and being a thing of importance is a functional relationship between dominant and subordinated groups.[23] Racial capitalism is an especially useful construct for tracing the historical development of geographically localized systems of racial stratification and hierarchies. Huey Long, a Louisiana Senator, clearly articulated this privileging when he declared, "Whites have decided nigras have got to have public health care. Got to give 'em clinics and hospitals. Got to keep 'em healthy. That's fair and it's good sense ... you wouldn't want a colored woman ... watching over your children if she had pyorrhea, would you?"[24] Long's statement invokes a highly racialized perspective that the health of Black peoples was not regarded as valuable in and of itself, but only in relationship to how our ill health might impact the health of White peoples. The privileging of White health in and between states manifested in a way that public health systems created to improve the ill health of Black, Indigenous, and other peoples were only developed as scientific knowledge expanded to confirm that germs know no color line.[25]

Because disease-carrying microorganisms do not differentiate amongst their victims, those concerned for the health of peoples racialized as White could not afford to ignore the health of peoples racialized as Black. Jim Crow laws in the United States could not prevent germs from measles, tuberculosis, pneumonia, or typhoid from spreading, which necessitated action that included historically subordinated groups in public health interventions.[26] Similarly, in South Africa, concern for the health and wellness of Black peoples was driven primarily by their proximity to the White population and the potential negative impact that this might have on White interests.[27] For example, because leprosy was perceived to be a "Black disease," harsh measures were enacted that allowed for compulsory segregation of all lepers due to fears that the disease was spreading and affecting White peoples.[28] While many Black lepers were detained on Robben Island, White lepers were allowed to remain quarantined at home.[29] Interest convergence[30] necessitated the inclusion of Black, Indigenous, and other peoples in public health efforts. This was also evident in Cuba. For example, William Crawford Gorgas and the Yellow Fever Commission successfully eradicated yellow fever in Havana, Cuba, "through the imposition of legal sanctions, forced home fumigation, and strict surveillance. Such extremities were taken not for the benefit of local Cuban nationals, [who] were largely immune to the disease, but rather for the 'threat to newcomers, especially to the invading American military troops, most of whom were susceptible to the disease.'"[31] The resulting health inequalities created by systems of medical apartheid and their persistent legacies tend to be naturalized, backgrounded, and treated as inevitable in public health.

Helpfully, Lindsay Wiley, Ruqaiijah Yearby, and other health law scholars have clarified a model for unearthing "the role of laws, policies, and institutions in creating, perpetuating, and (potentially) dismantling subordination within health care, public health, and beyond—which it names as the root cause of health inequities."[32] Health justice is a generative perspective domestically, but it also aids in revealing how removed global health is from a "distinctively *social*, communitarian ethic of care."[33] Health justice is not simply a theoretical framework. It is praxis. Health justice also captures the movement for community "power building and transformational change to eliminate health inequities and secure distinctively collective interests in access to health care and healthy living conditions."[34] With this grounding, the section below turns to surfacing the influence of classism, racism, and other forms of subordination in the emergence, design, and implementation of the global health regime.

TROPICAL & COLONIAL MEDICINE

Tropical and colonial medicine was a key mechanism for the translation of imperial priorities into policy.[35] The field assisted with the construction of the idea of the "tropics" as a particularly unhealthy geography, one marked with difference and disease. Furthermore, the very conceptualization of "tropical diseases" is a misnomer—because malaria, cholera, leprosy, and dengue, for example, all used to be endemic in the Global North. Their disappearance in Europe and North America are in large part due to addressing underlying determinants of health in these areas, as opposed to the inherent pathology of the tropical climate or environment. The WHO itself has acknowledged that inequality in health is informed by social determinants of health, which "is the product of the conditions in which people are born, grow, live, work, and age, and their access to power, resources and decision-making."[36] Colonialism and its persisting legacies of exploitation are key social determinants of health that continue to shape the distribution of power and resources in the world and influence people's lived realities. Analyses that elide the operation of colonialism, structural racism, and class hierarchies, miss crucial ways that the global health regime developed.

Tropical medicine emerged to render the region more hospitable to Europeans and their colonies and was a crucial aspect of colonial subjugation and expansion. For example, French colonial authorities in Senegal used the bubonic plague to further segregationist ends by closely linking the Black population to the disease, since they conceived of Black peoples as a "barbaric collective that threatened the order and health conditions in the 'European' city."[37] Consequently, even though the infection rate amongst Black Africans was not higher than that of any other racial group, French authorities imposed harsh measures in Senegal, which included "burnings of huts, along with the formation of quarantine camps."[38] They also imposed a *cordon sanitaire* that would function as a dividing line well after the 1914 outbreak of the plague in Dakar.[39] Similarly, for the British colonial authorities in Sierra Leone, the preferred method of fighting malaria was residential segregation.[40] Several analyses have demonstrated how sanitation concerns were used as a pretext for furthering segregationist ends.[41] Colonial medicine was perceived as a necessary part of the transformation of otherwise "backward" regions.

Tropical medicine took place in colonial settings and often depended on the coercive power of the colonial administrative state to implement its interventions.[42]

Certainly, the power structure of colonialism both relied on and perpetuated "ideas of racial differences and superiority as tools for economic exploitation and cultural sovereignty—infantilizing colonized populations and situating them as incapable of self-governance—using evolutionary and essentialist rationalizations."[43] Under colonialism, colonized peoples were perceived as "incapable of improving their own health," and "the existence of local medical knowledge and existing public health infrastructures in colonized lands were subverted and colonial health services were designed primarily to protect the health of European and American personnel who were essential to upholding the colonial economy."[44] For instance, in 1905, the British Indian Plague Commission ran experiments wherein "epidemiologists released rats and guinea pigs into houses suspected of harboring" the plague and "returned days later to retrieve them," but only "if such animals proved to be infected did officials then remove the human inhabitants."[45] Likewise, during the midst of the smallpox epidemic and the influenza pandemic, British colonial authorities in Sierra Leone neglected the health needs of the population.[46] Tropical medicine was generative for colonialism because as advances took place in the field, it furthered imperialist ends by enabling troops to better cope with unfamiliar diseases to be healthy enough to fight Indigenous populations resisting colonial domination and subjugation.[47] Unsurprisingly then, tropical medicine grew to specifically focus on vector-borne diseases and infectious disease control,[48] since these diseases had the most implications for the expansion of colonial empires.

COLONIAL MEDICINE TO GLOBAL HEALTH

The continued privileging of communicable diseases in global health, which touch and concern White majoritarian interests, is a clear legacy of colonial and tropical medicine. European imperial expansion meant that public health concerns became globalized and required cooperation with other imperial powers for the treatment and prevention of diseases. International law served as a vehicle for empires to perfect racial hierarchy and class subordination and global health was no exception. Standard accounts on how global health law emerged misinform us significantly about the development of the field. In the first part of the twentieth century there were about thirteen international agreements concerning collaboration on health control measures.[49] Negotiations to build the nascent global health regime even predated[50] the 1884 Berlin Conference wherein European imperial powers partitioned the African continent into territorial spheres of influence. Colonial powers prioritized global public health because they wanted to coordinate sufficiently restrictive quarantine regulations that would facilitate the unimpeded expansion of their imperial trades without exposing their populations in the mother country to diseases from colonial territories.[51] European colonizers prioritized defensive measures against contagion from racialized and "diseased" territories when formulating the global health regime. For instance, Adrien Proust, one of the leading French voices during the International Sanitary Conferences, authored several works on "the defense of Europe" against exotic diseases.[52] The 1892 Convention solely concerns cholera and sanitation measures for westward shipping to European countries due to concerns that the Suez Canal could be a conduit for the introduction of cholera from India to Europe.[53] Consequently, the 1893 Convention required state parties to inform each other without delay if any outbreaks of cholera occurred within their territories.[54]

Additionally, European powers feared that Muslim pilgrims returning to Europe posed a serious threat,[55] following a cholera epidemic in Mecca, which claimed the lives of 30,336 people.[56] The Sanitary Convention of 1894 is thus singularly dedicated to the pilgrimage to Mecca and the preventive measures mandated at ports of departure, the sanitary surveillance of pilgrims traversing the Red Sea, and the sanitary controls for shipping in the Persian Gulf.[57] Similarly, following a serious epidemic of the plague in India,[58] some Europeans were anxious that their other colonial territories might be affected.[59] Subsequently, the International Sanitary Convention of 1897 added the plague as a disease warranting international prioritization and notification.[60]

These treaties exemplify how colonial powers shaped not only the emergence of the global health regime but also what diseases deserved international attention and prioritization, to the extent they impacted the needs of capital and imperial trade. This was also reflected in the 1926 Convention, which modified the 1912 Convention and required international notification for the first confirmed cases of cholera, plague, and yellow fever, as well as small pox, and typhus.[61] Notably, there were millions of cases of typhus in Poland and the Soviet Union following World War I.[62] The expansion of the list of diseases that deserved international recognition under the 1926 Convention coincided with the increasing importance of these diseases in the Global North.

During the 1930s, the *Aedes aegypti* mosquito was endemic in parts of southern Europe, and several outbreaks of dengue arose as a result.[63] Subsequently, thirteen European countries agreed to prioritize the prevention of the spread of dengue under the International Convention for Mutual Protection against Dengue Fever.[64] This again exemplifies how the relevance or irrelevance of diseases depended on whether they converged with White interests and the needs of capital. It was not as if diseases prioritized for international law-making were the only diseases afflicting populations globally. Indeed, communicable diseases like hookworm and malaria[65] were also prevalent, but these were not the focus of the early global health treaties.

Negotiations on controlling and preventing the spread of diseases also involved discussions on the establishment of an international body. As early as 1874, a convention to establish a permanent International Commission on Epidemics was negotiated but never adopted.[66] Additionally, in 1881, a convention to establish a permanent International Sanitary Agency of Notification was discussed but similarly not implemented.[67] More progress was made at the regional level in the Americas, when the countries in this region established the International (later renamed the Pan American) Sanitary Bureau in 1902.[68] Notably, the 1903 Sanitary Convention provides that the French Government proposed the establishment of an "international health office at Paris."[69] These efforts laid the groundwork for the establishment of the Office International d'Hygiène Publique (OHIP) in 1907. The main aim of this office was to disseminate facts and documents of public health interest. In practice, this meant prioritizing infectious diseases of concern to White majoritarian interests like cholera and the plague.[70] In addition, the International Sanitary Convention of 1926 required States Parties to notify the OHIP of the "existence of an epidemic of typhus or of smallpox."[71] The OHIP operated until 1950 and primarily focused on the adoption of the International Sanitary Conventions.[72]

Members of the new League of Nations also endeavored to "take steps in matters of international concern for the prevention and control of disease."[73] Under the covenant, all existing international agencies were to be placed under the direction of the League.[74] However, since the United States was not a member of the League,[75] two separate institutions existed to address infectious diseases—the preexisting OHIP discussed above, and the newly created Health Organization of the League of Nations. This organization was "created to provide epidemiological analysis, develop technical standards and support countries."[76] Under the League, White interests continued to drive the global health agenda. This led some commentators to conclude that "as compared with what it has done for other parts of the world . . . the Health Committee of the League of Nations itself has done remarkably little for the African continent."[77]

It was not until the 1944 modification of the International Sanitary Convention that the global public health regime began requiring States to send epidemiological information for diseases not preordained as significant by the Global North.[78] Under the 1944 Convention, states parties, so far as it was possible, were to send at regular intervals notifications of communicable diseases discovered in their countries to the Health Division of the United Nations Relief and Rehabilitation Administration,[79] which temporarily administered the Sanitary Conventions.[80] Against this background, it is crucial to understand global health as a field that emerged from, ratified, and exacerbated extant hierarchies along racial, class, and other lines of subordination.

WHOSE HEALTH

Unlike predecessor institutions, the World Health Organization was to be global not just in name but in substance. Its constitution drafted in 1946 states that "the enjoyment of the highest attainable standard of health is one of the fundamental rights of every human being without distinction of race, religion, political belief, economic or social condition."[81] The WHO's Constitution acknowledges a broad understanding of the right to health.[82] It reflects the nascent commitment to international health expressed in the United Nations Charter.[83] States founded the WHO based on the premise that "the health of all peoples is fundamental to the attainment of peace and security and is dependent upon the fullest cooperation of individuals and states."[84]

The WHO's basic principles indicate that the privileging of White interests and the needs of imperial trade would presumably be less central. The Constitution defines health as "a state of complete physical, mental and social well-being and not merely the absence of disease or infirmity."[85] Yet, this robust conceptualization of health has not been implemented in practice. Instead, the WHO has continued an inordinate focus on specific communicable diseases. In 1969, the World Health Organization's Health Assembly revised, consolidated, and renamed the International Sanitary Regulations as the International Health Regulations (IHRs).[86] The multiple overlapping obligations from earlier sanitary regulations had led to a complex situation where some states were parties to some instruments and not others.[87] The 1969 Regulations still only related to cholera, the plague, and yellow fever—diseases that had previously been designated as most disruptive to imperial trade. There was still not much space or consideration given to human rights like equality,[88] or an extensive conception of the right to health.[89] The underlying premise of the system remained the same—notification requirements for three infectious diseases marked as significant, which would then trigger an international response that imposed travel and trade restrictions to contain the spread of these three predetermined diseases.

Moreover, while the WHO's secretariat is supposed to be responsive to all member states, it leans and gravitates towards the ministries of health in the Global North's expressed priorities. Their competing interests tend to dictate the direction or indirection of global health law and policymaking. The law and political economy of global health is such that powerful states and commercial interests can exert influence and constrain the WHO's autonomy and range of action. Global North States provide the primary sources of funding to the organization, so these donors can set the budgetary priorities and policy parameters of the WHO. Global North States are also more likely to have nationals who are WHO experts and personnel and inform decision-making.[90] Thus, the WHO's perpetuation of racialization continues through the de facto domination of the institution by Global North countries.

Juxtaposing the WHO's formative principles against the priorities and demands from the Global South is instructive. Following a period of heightened decolonization, newly independent countries who had fought for their liberation sought to reshape the world in equitable ways. The Non-Aligned Movement of

States founded in 1961, brought together countries from Asia, Africa, the Americas, and the Middle East to advance their interests and priorities through a Declaration on the Establishment of a New International Economic Order (NIEO) in May 1974. One of the Declaration's provisions pertains to giving "developing countries access to the achievements of modern science and technology and the creation of indigenous technology for the benefit of the developing countries."[91] Notably, one of WHO's elemental principles is the belief that "the extension to all peoples of the benefits of medical, psychological, and related knowledge is essential to the fullest attainment of health."[92] Notwithstanding this, WHO has not substantially shaped its health policies towards redistributive ends to give effect to this principle. Additionally, the basic documents of the World Health Organization to date make no mention of reparations.[93] In contrast, the NIEO proclaims "the right of all States, territories and peoples under foreign occupation, colonial domination or apartheid to restitution and full compensation for the exploitation and depletion of, and damages to, the natural resources and all other resources of those States, territories and peoples."[94] Moreover, the constitutive instruments of the WHO do not provide for substantial or minimal affirmative action or special measures to address or even ameliorate global health inequities.[95] Instead, the primary sources of the World Health Organization are conspicuously silent on repairing and redressing historical and ongoing injustices in health.[96] In short, the global public health regime was not created to further health justice. If it were, as I argue elsewhere, it would prioritize "fixing the systemic and structural barriers embedded in law and policy especially as it relates to anti-subordination efforts."[97]

Instead, the WHO's emphasis remains on the kinds of contagious diseases that were centered in "tropical" colonial medicine, even when the ambit of the organization and its treaty are supposed to be broader. The 2005 International Health Regulations exhibit this. They are currently the main international modality for regulating communicable diseases.[98] It includes some important advances: instead of preordaining three diseases requiring notification, the IHRs employ an "all hazards" approach, which includes all public health events. In addition, the IHRs envision a more reactive system that uses real-time evidence and information to make decisions based on surveillance. Under the IHRs, the WHO can make wide-ranging recommendations concerning travel advice, restrictions on travel in certain regions, quarantines, customs restrictions, vaccination protocols, as well as measures relating to food safety.[99] Yet, the WHO's recommendations are merely non-binding forms of advice given to States.[100] The IHRs ostensibly provided a framework that is supposed to deprioritize simply controlling things at the border, and is instead aimed at detecting and containing diseases at the source.

Even so, the 2005 Regulations still background the extant structural conditions in the international system that give rise to and limit the ability of states to develop core capacities for surveillance and response to diseases. The Regulations assign primary responsibility for implementing health measures to combat infectious diseases to national authorities and component parts.[101] Under the Regulations, states parties have a legal obligation to develop better functioning health systems to detect disease, surveil, report, verify, notify, respond and collaborate.[102] All states parties are also legally obligated to cooperate to help build health capacities.[103] Yet, the 2005 Regulations do not specify how this should be operationalized. Accordingly, global health inequality and vulnerability is minimized in the Regulations, with incapacity to address infectious diseases treated primarily as a matter of individual state responsibility and failure. While the targeted communicable diseases changed incrementally over the years,[104] the racialization of diseases, the prioritization of White interests, as well as the needs of capital influencing the regime's actions and inactions, have remained constant. Below, I turn to how the WHO's ineffectual response to the COVID-19 pandemic is a reflection of how its past continues to inform the present.

BACK TO THE FUTURE

The COVID-19 pandemic created an opening to name and remedy the privileging of White interests in global public health and potentially shape more emancipatory futures. The COVID-19 pandemic exposed the deficiencies in global health's governing logics in myriad ways. The regime's marginalization of the significance of countries' varying capacities to effectively respond to disease outbreaks meant that many health systems were ill-equipped and overwhelmed.

Moreover, the lack of a robust monitoring and accountability mechanisms for evaluating behavior allows considerable room for States to implement policies not based on any public health rationale.[105] Under the 2005 Regulations, "States Parties and the Director-General" need only report to "the Health Assembly on the implementation of these Regulations as decided by the Health Assembly."[106] This lax regulatory framework enables structural racism and provides States with substantial opportunity to make choices shaped by implicit and/or explicit racism. Notwithstanding the provision that health measures be "applied in a transparent and non-discriminatory manner,"[107] throughout the COVID-19 pandemic, States made decisions informed by "outdated but persistent settler-colonial conventions that have mapped illness and disease on to racialized peoples and certain geographic regions."[108]

The WHO declared COVID-19 a public health emergency of international concern on January 30, 2020.[109] The IHRs define a Public Health Emergency of International Concern (PHEIC) broadly as "an extraordinary event, which is determined . . . (i) to constitute a public health risk to other States through the international spread of disease and (ii) to potentially require a coordinated international response."[110] The WHO consistently "advised against the application of travel or trade restrictions to countries experiencing COVID-19 outbreaks."[111] However, by February 27, 2020, thirty-eight countries had already reported measures "that significantly interfere with international traffic in relation to travel to and from China or other countries, ranging from denial of entry of passengers, visa restrictions, or quarantine for returning travelers."[112] Revealingly, a newspaper in France carried the headline "Yellow Alert" on its front page.[113]

Early reactions were not merely efforts at disease containment. In the United States, the understanding of COVID-19 as racialized and "foreign" constrained the space initially for consideration of community transmission.[114] The overreliance on blanket travel bans as a magical solution to stop the spread of a highly infectious novel disease concomitant with the lackadaisical approach to implementing screening measures at airports in the United States and elsewhere indicates how the racializing of COVID-19 led to problematic public health law and policy decisions. Both the policies of the Trump administration with the overt signaling to racializing diseases as "Kung Flu," and the covert signaling to this racialization under the Biden administration with testing requirements for COVID-19 at one point limited solely to travelers coming from China evidence this. States seemingly assumed that the virus is engaged in racialized border control efforts, checking documents and nationalities to determine who to infect next.[115] These racial and colonial logics influencing COVID-19 law and policymaking are evident in innumerable ways.[116]

Another example is the swift decision by countries in the Global North to cut off southern African countries following South Africa's genomic sequencing of the Omicron variant.[117] Instead of being rewarded for tracing and alerting the world to a variant that was already circulating in Europe,[118] the United Kingdom, the United States,[119] the European Union, and others were hasty to make decisions informed by "Afrophobia," as the President of Malawi aptly termed it.[120] One newspaper published a literal depiction of the racialization of diseases—replete with brown viruses with stereotypical phenotypical Black features traveling on a boat with the South African flag towards European shores.[121] The Ebola epidemic had also "resuscitated historical images of Black African bodies as uncontainable and disease-ridden and sparked racialized fears."[122] This fear of the racialized other and their diseases reminds us quite powerfully how the history of diseases and responses to diseases are linked to politics of racial exclusion and racial subordination.

The global health regime was mostly relegated to the sidelines for some of the most consequential questions and was markedly underutilized for settling key disputes arising from the COVID-19 pandemic. For example, the 2005 IHRs provide for dispute resolution via: negotiation between state parties, referral of disputes to the Director General of the WHO, arbitration, and utilizing the dispute settlement mechanisms of other organizations. The Regulations also stipulate "in the event of a dispute between WHO and one or more States Parties concerning the interpretation or application of these Regulations, the matter shall be submitted to the Health Assembly."[123] India and South Africa chose to bring one of the most contentious disputes concerning the need for unhindered global sharing of technology and know-how for diagnostics and therapeutics for COVID-19 before the World Trade Organization (WTO) and not the World Health Organization.[124] The WTO's final decision resulted in a "pyrrhic victory," which I argue elsewhere, did not significantly advance health equity and was woefully inadequate given the scale of the needs.[125] In light of the devastating consequences of the COVID-19 pandemic, the necessity of an equitable and health justice oriented global public health regime could not be more glaringly urgent or apparent.

THE MORE THINGS CHANGE, THE MORE THEY STAY THE SAME

In May 2022, the World Health Assembly formally initiated a revision process under the auspices of an Intergovernmental Working Group on Amendments to the 2005 International Health Regulations.[126] States from the Global North and South proposed amendments to the Regulations.[127] The World Health Assembly passed amendments to the IHRs in June 2024. Like past efforts, the Regulations aim to "prevent, prepare for, protect against, control and provide a public health response to the international spread of disease in ways that are commensurate with and restricted to public health risk and which avoid unnecessary interference with international traffic and trade."[128] The system of state surveillance and notification persists with some modifications.[129] Significantly, the IHRs now empower the Director General of the WHO Secretariat to determine both whether there is a public health emergency of international concern and a pandemic emergency. The amended Regulations also clarify that a pandemic emergency is "a public health emergency of international concern that is caused by a communicable disease and: (i) has, or is at high risk of having, wide geographical spread to and within multiple States; and (ii) is exceeding, or is at high risk of exceeding, the capacity of health systems to respond in those States; and (iii) is causing, or is at high risk of causing, substantial social and/or economic disruption, including disruption to international traffic and trade; and (iv) requires rapid, equitable and enhanced coordinated international action, with whole-of-government and whole-of-society approaches."[130] The revised Regulations still orient the regime towards privileging diseases that are perceived as touching and concerning the center because of their disruption to the interests and the needs of capital.

Moreover, the IHRs, including recent amendments, do not reference historic or ongoing structural discrimination in public health, medicine, or global public health.[131] The numerous genocides against Indigenous peoples, the Transatlantic trade in enslaved Africans, the dispossession, colonialism, and host of unfreedoms imposed on subaltern peoples that structure the international order are seemingly erased. For example, the United Kingdom's involvement in the Transatlantic trade in enslaved persons alone is estimated to have resulted in harms totaling $24 trillion, not including the substantial nonmonetary and dignitary harms. Yet, the formative instruments of WHO do not even acknowledge nor mention slavery, genocide, nor colonialism.[132] This is representative of how global health tends to render subordination invisible.

Similarly, the role of neocolonialism (the ways in which former colonial powers retain their influence and power following formal decolonization, such that the nominally independent States retain their dependency) is seemingly irrelevant in global health. Researchers have found that between 1960 and 2018, the Global North through unequal exchange drained (relying on exchange-rate differentials) "from the South totaled $62 trillion (constant 2011 dollars), or $152 trillion when accounting for lost growth."[133] In 2015 alone, "the North net appropriated from the South 12 billion tons of embodied raw material equivalents, 822 million hectares of embodied land, 21 exajoules of embodied energy, and 188 million person-years of embodied labor, worth $10.8 trillion in Northern prices—enough to end extreme poverty 70 times over."[134] The continuing subordination that has rendered some states especially vulnerable to precarity and immiseration is seemingly forcibly forgotten despite the devastating impact and effect that this has on health systems, health infrastructure, the health outcomes of peoples, and the quality of life and well-being of individuals around the globe.

Concomitantly, institutions like the World Bank and the International Monetary Fund proliferate neoliberal policies like structural adjustment reforms, which means that many nations in the Global South undertake austerity measures to "right-size" their budgets. These measures prioritize servicing debt to external creditors and balancing budgets and deficit spending, which limits health spending and investment in social welfare and the public sectors of countries in the Global South. The inordinate focus on implementing neoliberal reforms in the Global South undercuts efforts to build capacities of health systems and generates substantial challenges for redressing global health inequalities.

The reforms to the IHRs must be contextualized considering this geopolitical law and economy. While the 2024 Regulations for the first time include promoting equity and solidarity as foundational principles,[135] tellingly, solidarity is never mentioned again in the Regulations.[136] Although the WHO is founded in part based on the presumption that extending scientific knowledge to all is critical for attaining the highest levels of health,[137] to the extent the global health regime has embraced this principle, it has done so based on an aid-based model. But, as the South African representative forcefully argued during remarks requesting temporary intellectual property waivers to effectively respond to the COVID-19 pandemic, "The problem with philanthropy is that it cannot buy equality."[138]

The revised Regulations are not poised to further substantive equality. They create a coordinating financial mechanism which will rely on charitable giving.[139] Yet, dependency on voluntary contributions already reflects the status quo in global health. For instance, COVAX is the main initiative WHO uses to provide COVID-19 vaccinations to people in the Global South and it is funded through elective gifts.[140] Nevertheless, a philanthropic model that relies primarily on the munificence of others for resources is a fundamentally flawed approach to building health systems and health infrastructure. It has not worked to address health needs.[141] It also does not advance health, nor justice. The Regulations continue the problematic legacy of requiring States to create capacity by fiat. With no clear nor consistent funding commitments, it is difficult to undertake the prevention surveillance, reporting, notification, verification, preparedness, response, and collaboration activities required. Significantly, studies have found that negligible amounts of the gross national income (a mere 0.1%) of sixty-six high-income economies is all that would be needed to meet the core obligations of the right to health.[142] Considering this, the loose obligations in the revised IHRs for States to "to collaborate with each other, to the extent possible, in developing, strengthening and maintaining core capacities" rings especially hollow.[143] What is needed are concrete and specific obligations for actors in the Global North to provide dedicated financial resources to those in the Global South for advancing health justice.

The Regulations do not evidence a commitment to health justice since they do not demonstrate "the importance of distinctively collective, *public* interests in universal access to affordable, high quality healthcare"[144] and relevant health products. Instead, all five references to equitable access to relevant health products to respond to public health emergencies of international concern are merely process related.[145] The substance of what has changed in the Regulations is negligible. The obligations that States are under are so filled with claw-back clauses and largely discretionary duties that States basic commitments have not materially changed. For instance, article 13(9) stipulates that "States Parties shall undertake, subject to *applicable law* and *available resources*, to collaborate with, and assist each other and to support WHO." (emphasis mine). States are also under article 13(9)(c), "to make available, *as appropriate*, relevant terms of their research and development agreements for health products related to promoting equitable access." (emphasis mine). Even more incredulously, article 13(9)(b) stipulates that States should "engage with and encourage relevant stakeholders operating in their respective jurisdictions to facilitate equitable access" to health products. The Regulations pretend as if the larger incentive-structure towards profit maximization in pharmaceuticals, which is protected by monopoly rents and underwritten by the international intellectual property regime,[146] can be meaningfully distributed through meetings to cajole manufacturers and other actors to engage in philanthropy. As with prior IHRs, the 2024 amendments do not tangibly challenge entrenched commercial interests. The amended IHRs do not require redistribution of relevant health products such that Global North actors are obligated to equitably share them. Yet, distributive justice requires consideration of not just allocation procedures, but also how the total amount of benefits and burdens are to be distributed, as well as the pattern of distribution that results.

The revised Regulations refer to work WHO already engages in. Article 13(8) illustrates this point when it provides that, "WHO shall facilitate, and work to remove barriers to, timely and equitable access by States Parties to relevant health products." However, WHO has ongoing efforts like COVAX for COVID-19 vaccine distribution, which was created prior to the amended IHRs to do just this. Further, article 13(8)(c) provides that if relevant international law allows (like the intellectual property regime), WHO can support States (where requested) to scale up and geographically diversify the production of relevant health products (as appropriate). Also, article 13(8)(e) stipulates that WHO can support States (where requested and as appropriate) to promote research and development and strengthen local production of quality, safe and effective relevant health products. But, WHO ostensibly does this already through public private partnerships like GAVI, the Vaccine Alliance.[147] Given this, the celebration of the reforms to the IHRs appears overblown and premature.

The IHRs are aimed more towards creating the illusion of a better tomorrow through building more legal processes and mechanisms, as opposed to effectuating material change in peoples' lived realities. For instance, the revised Regulations include verbiage, which sounds meaningful, but on closer inspection is not. For instance, article 13(8)(a) says that the Director General can author reports on the accessibility, availability, and affordability of relevant health products, publish them, and consider these assessments when giving recommendations. The problem, however, is *not* a lack of information on the unaffordability, unavailability, or inaccessibility of essential medicines, therapeutics, and diagnostics. Furthermore, even if such reports were influential to the Director General's thinking in formulating prospective recommendations, any such recommendations are merely non-binding guidance to actors, which makes this provision inconsequential. Additionally, article 13(8)(b) stipulates that the Director General, with several caveats: can make use of WHO's own mechanisms, facilitate (in consultation with states), establish (as needed), coordinate (as appropriate) with other distribution mechanisms for relevant health products based on public health needs. This language is included in the treaty, as if WHO is not already regularly conducting such activity through mechanisms like the Pandemic Influenza Preparedness Framework.[148]

The amended Regulations preserve the status quo in myriad ways. Several aspects of the revised IHRs appear to give, but simultaneously take power from WHO within the same breath. Case in point, article 13(8)(d) provides that where manufacturers consent, WHO can share with States, upon their request, the product dossier related to a specific relevant health product for the purpose of facilitating regulatory evaluation and authorization by the State. This provision allowing WHO to share information with states, if allowed by pharmaceutical companies, makes the redundant nature of the amended Regulations plain. The amended IHRs are noticeably silent on what happens if a drug manufacturer does not consent. The WHO's inability to impose sanctions or countermeasures on States or other actors for non-compliance or undermining its recommendations remains a live issue.[149]

The amended IHRs are still incredibly dependent on self-monitoring, self-reporting, and peer accountability. The revised Regulations create a State Parties Committee,[150] to be "facilitative and consultative in nature only, and function in a non-adversarial, non-punitive, assistive and transparent manner."[151] The unamended Regulations already provide for several review procedures. The creation of more legal architecture is mere ceremony. It is yet another indicator that the revised IHRs are not fit for purpose in meeting health needs nor furthering health justice.

The reforms are also not likely to change the obfuscation of racialized hierarchies of care and concern. It is essential to foreground the rampant racial devaluation of Palestinian lives that serves as a backdrop to global public health negotiations. States amended the IHRs amidst the lethal combination of hunger and disease and the entirely preventable public health emergency in Palestine that stretches beyond the direct harm from violence and includes indirect health ramifications and consequences including the reintroduction of polio in Gaza. A UN Development Program official remarked that Israel's actions have resulted in devastation not seen since 1945 and has wiped out "[a]ll investments in human development . . . for the last 40 years in Gaza."[152] The omission of any provisions to concretely address these and other structural determinants is illuminating.[153] The amended Regulations are glaringly silent on reparative justice and redressing historical and continuing injustices in health. The genocide in Palestine clarifies how zones of sacrifice persist. Usha Natarajan helped clarify the concept of zones of sacrifice for me—wherein the bodies, lives, health, wellbeing of the vulnerable, of those on the periphery, those marginalized in society, who are treated as waste, as if they are disposable.

The revised Regulations continue a forced forgetting. From 1892 when the first sanitary convention was enacted, to the present moment, the field of global health law has continually expanded, even where its provisions have not worked to significantly improve the health and well-being of the People of the Global Majority and has prioritized the needs of imperial trade. At a minimum, a health justice framework requires that health measures and societal efforts "as a whole must prohibit, amend, or repeal laws adversely affecting health, and end discrimination and racial bias."[154] Yet, WHO's regulatory framework has generally failed to account for the fact that a significantly higher level of health and well-being for all people is attainable through a fuller and more effective use of the world's resources, and that the current maldistribution in health and wellbeing is not inevitable or natural.

PERSISTENCE OF COLONIALITY

To date, the most prominent attempt at the decolonization of global health law and furthering health justice occurred at the WHO and UN Children Fund's 1978 International Conference on Primary Health Care held in Alma-Ata, in the Soviet Union. Influenced by advocacy from the Global South, States asserted a new vision for health through a legally non-binding declaration. The 1978 Declaration of Alma-Alta affirms the 1948 WHO Constitution and goes further, providing that "governments have a responsibility for the health of their peoples which can be fulfilled only by the provision of adequate health and social measures."[155] The Declaration represents a call for WHO to return to first principles, and to eschew the vertical disease-specific programs that predominated during colonial and tropical medicine, and continued with WHO's subsequent policy making.

The Declaration proclaims:

> that the attainment of the highest possible level of health is a most important world-wide social goal whose realization requires the action of many other social and economic sectors in addition to the health sector.[156]

It goes on to stress that "the existing gross inequality in the health status of the people particularly between developed and developing countries, as well as within countries, is politically, socially and economically unacceptable and is, therefore, of common concern to all countries."[157] Additionally, the Declaration insists that economic "and social development, based on a New International Economic Order, is of basic importance to the fullest attainment of health for all and to the reduction of the gap between the health status of the developing and developed countries."[158]

Due to resistance from States in the Global North, the Declaration of Alma-Ata did not substantially reorient WHO's health policies. A common criticism from the North was that the slogan "Health for All by 2000" was not feasible or realistic. Instead, within a year, the Rockefeller Foundation organized a conference in 1979 to identify the most cost-effective health strategies on Health and Population in Development. Donor States narrowed their contributions to the WHO in favor of initiatives like "selective" primary health care. WHO's policies were thus diametrically opposed to advancing primary healthcare and instead continued the practice of focusing on select communicable diseases as detailed above.

Given the exclusive and oppressive process of international law-making historically, what does not get included as law is as important as what is incorporated into law, and for what reasons. If implemented, the Declaration of Alma-Ata would have required far-ranging policy reforms and transformation in global public health that would have inevitably challenged entrenched commercial interests. Tellingly, the Declaration was never enacted into law. It is frequently cited[159] and represents the road not taken.

Instead, the coloniality of global health persists.[160] The structuring of many interventions continue to assume the necessity of White saviorism,[161] which in turn reflects the "White Man's Burden"[162] to save supposedly uncivilized, ignorant, and diseased natives from themselves. Global health, like colonial medicine, still continues to displace and supplant local systems of knowledge production[163] and focus on biomedical one-off solutions. These methods prioritize quick fixes[164] as opposed to structural approaches that would require adopting a health justice approach and addressing the underlying social determinants of health. The current tendency to emphasize individual responsibility in global health also harkens back to colonial discourse and rhetoric that blamed "natives"[165] for their ailments as opposed to inequitable resource distribution. Such ahistorical accounts surfaced during the Ebola epidemic and tended to blame marginalized populations for being noncompliant and facilitating the spread of disease,[166] including narratives that obscured geopolitical and structural factors that facilitated disease transmission.[167]

Additionally, contemporary global health interventions continue to reflect the top-down dynamics of colonial approaches to tropical medicine, with little to no consultation with local communities.[168] Further, global health partnerships frequently involve relationships between countries and researchers in the Global North and South wherein former colonial powers and people living within these countries exercise significant influence, power, privilege, and control over resources.[169] This dynamic has created a global health regime where powerful men, often older and White, "sit in boardrooms in established colonial institutions in the Global North and are responsible for setting the health agendas for countries miles away, with little to no significant involvement of local leaders."[170] Moreover, such partnerships are often skewed in how the distribution of benefits is allocated.[171] These partnerships do not reflect the framework of health justice as they are generally not developed through "collective action grounded in community engagement, empowerment, and participatory parity."[172]

Further, "colonial mentality"[173] continues to influence people's behavior in global health. For example, Renee Bach, a twenty-year-old high school graduate from Virginia with no medical training, took it upon herself to establish and run a center for severely malnourished children in Uganda, wherein 105 of the 940 children under the center's care died.[174] Her decision to found the center came from a volunteer missionary trip, where she had "a very, very profound feeling and experience," and felt "there was something that I was supposed to do."[175] The audaciousness and exceptional nature of her actions, which resulted in the deaths of already vulnerable children, is intrinsically linked to long histories of drop-in missionary trips and White saviorism in colonial medicine. Her actions also reflect an unspoken assumption in global health: that whatever one's qualifications, they must be more than those of the Indigenous population. Moreover, Bach's ruse was able to continue for five years in part because of the long-standing practice of short-term medical mission trips and aid organizations that routinely parachute doctors in and out of countries in the Global South.[176] The legacy of inequity in global health is such that "even if you have never worked in global health, the color of your skin and the accent of your voice may unduly confer upon you a level of authority" in communities that have internalized coloniality such that foreignness connotes expertise, "that you likely do not deserve and should not have."[177] The continued persistence of coloniality in multifaceted forms has devastating consequences in global health.

TOWARD TRANSFORMATION?

Global health cannot and should not be divorced, decontextualized, nor depoliticized from its historical roots and governing logics. Global health law through both omission and commission furthers inequalities, hierarchies, and subordination. Zones of sacrifice marked by profound inequality persist and remain unremarked upon, as if global health exists in a vacuum. Global health law in theory and practice can either work to address the devastating consequences of colonialism, class hierarchies, structural racism, and other forms of subordination in health, ratify, or exacerbate them. Instead, when the global health regime engages with inequality, it tends to do so shallowly: as a function of income-disparities between States, using monikers like low and middle-income or labels such as developed and developing countries. This practice diverts attention away from historicizing or contextualizing how structural inequity was created and is sustained.

Global health law can protect, under protect, overprotect, or fail to protect. It is not and cannot be neutral. Global health law reflects the choices and practices of States and other actors, which includes both action and inaction. Enforced silences and failures to rectify on the part of global health law is a choice that ratifies the status quo. This chapter demonstrates how the global health regime's legacy and praxis has not created nor supported conditions that sustain health or justice in meaningful ways. More recent initiatives ostensibly aimed at reshaping the field have not sufficiently disturbed coloniality and subordination, nor do they seem primed to do so.

Member States of the United Nations in 2015 agreed to an urgent call for action which recognized "that ending poverty and other deprivations must go hand-in-hand with strategies that improve health and education, reduce inequality," amongst others.[178] All 191 UN Member States agreed to seventeen Sustainable Development Goals (SDG) by the year 2030. SDG 3 concerns ensuring "healthy lives and promoting well-being for all at all ages," underpinned by thirteen targets that cover a wide spectrum of health.[179] Ensuring healthy lives includes seeking to "achieve universal health coverage, including financial risk protection, access to quality essential health-care services and access to safe, effective, quality and affordable essential medicines and vaccines for all," as well as ensuring "universal access to sexual and reproductive health-care services, including for family planning, information and education, and the integration of reproductive health into national strategies and programmes."[180]

The non-transformational nature of the project is evident in how none of the Sustainable Development Goals specifically integrate elimination of inequalities due to colonialism, racism, and structural discrimination into its framework of targets and indicators, including the targets and indicators under SDG 3,[181] as well as SDG 10, which is dedicated to "reducing inequality within and among countries."[182] There is a powerful need to "acknowledge the central role of racism in the national" and international discourses "on racial inequities in health, and paradigmatic shifts are needed to inform equity-driven policy and practice innovations that would tackle the roots of the problem of racism and dismantle health inequities."[183] Yet, countries were not even asked to evaluate whether they have materially ameliorated racial inequality nor health inequalities specifically as part of the SDGs. This glaring omission reflects the continued unknowing. This chapter surfaces the role of global health through omission and commission in structuring and reifying racialized hierarchies of care and concern.

As the world approaches 2030, States and other actors are assessing and evaluating their progress on the different goals and targets of the SDGs. The scale and pace of change has not been fast enough nor deep enough for most targets, including the health-related ones to be met. The United Nations Secretary General released a dire report in April 2023.[184] He warned, "Halfway to the deadline for the 2030 Agenda, we are leaving more than half the world behind. We have stalled or gone into reverse on more than 30 percent of the SDGs."[185] He urged, "Unless we act now, the 2030 Agenda will become an epitaph for a world that might have been."[186] The UN continues to urge collective action to "mobilize the resources and investment needed for developing countries to achieve the SDGs."[187] Yet, as indicated earlier, the problem is not one of scarcity. Indeed, the current maldistribution of resources has resulted in just twenty-six people having the same wealth as half of the world's population and record levels of inequality.[188]

The chasm between the Global South and the Global North on addressing obscene levels of global health inequality are currently stalling initiatives to draft an international treaty for "pandemic preparedness and response to build a more robust global health architecture"[189] These efforts to enact a Pandemic Prevention, Preparedness, and Response treaty reached an impasse in 2024. The World Health Assembly has extended the negotiation deadline to conclude a Pandemic Agreement until May 2025.

The ever-shifting negotiating text for the treaty provides substantial cause for concern about how transformational a final treaty text will be, if one is concluded. One indication that the treaty negotiation process is not furthering health justice is how it has failed to incorporate distributive justice principles like the Common But Differentiated Responsibility (CBDR) principle. CBDR reflects the effort to achieve equity between richer countries in the Global North and poorer states in the Global South. Under it, richer countries agree to take on higher obligations to combat things like environmental concerns to reflect consumption and production patterns, as well as the unequal distributions of risks that result in more devastating environmental consequences for poorer countries.[190] For example, CBDR is reflected in many aspects of the Paris Agreement, including the differentiation between developing and developed countries in the Annex that stresses the importance of financing and technology transfer for developing nations.[191]

CBDR is based in part on the principle of solidarity.[192] It reflects the role of the Global South in shaping international law by demanding more equitable rules aimed at promoting substantive equality, rather than mere formal equality. CBDR has two main elements: (1) common responsibility describes the shared obligations of two or more states towards the protection of a particular resource;[193] and (2) a range of different burden-sharing arrangements that consider each nation's particular circumstances, especially its ability to prevent, reduce, and control the problem.[194] Some actors in the Global North have balked at CBDR, criticizing it as divisive and have opposed shouldering higher obligations. Others have expressed caution about transposing a principle primarily associated with international environmental law and applying it in global public health law.

Notwithstanding these concerns, CBDR remains a viable principle for adoption in global public health. In earlier work, I argue for the expansion of the common but differentiated responsibilities principle to include the challenges posed by infectious diseases.[195] The principle "provides an equitable and effective method for addressing mutual risks posed by a pandemic through differentiated and common obligations in ways that account for structural realities."[196] The principle has received less and less prominence with each subsequent negotiating text. For example, WHO's conceptual zero draft released in February 2023 embraces the principle of common but differentiated responsibilities and capabilities in pandemic prevention, preparedness, response, and recovery of health systems.[197] At the time of writing, the May 2024 draft is the latest publicly available negotiating text.

It does not mention the common but differentiated principle by name. However, the preambular language states:

> that differences in the levels of development of Parties engender different capacities and capabilities in pandemic prevention, preparedness and response and acknowledging that unequal development in different countries in the promotion of health and control of disease, especially communicable disease, is a common danger that requires support through international cooperation, including the support of countries with greater capacities and resources, as well as predictable, sustainable and sufficient financial, human, logistical, technological, technical and digital health resources.[198]

The operative provisions of the draft pandemic agreement envisions a coordinating financial mechanism to "leverage voluntary monetary contributions for organizations and other entities"[199] Like the recent revisions to the International Health Regulations, the proposed treaty does not oblige countries in the Global North to provide sustainable financial resources. The proposed treaty text does not reflect a disaggregation of burden sharing of obligations nor does it designate specific percentages for financial commitments.

Moreover, the sources for financing in the potential accord are already being substantially reduced. For instance, language concerning securing contributions from "pandemic-related product manufacturers," which appeared in the June 2023 text, is omitted in the May 2024 text.[200] Further, the option to address the harmful effects of structural adjustment programs by converting "debt repayment into pandemic prevention, preparedness, response and recovery investments in health, to be attained under individually negotiated 'debt swap' agreements," that was included in the June 2023 draft has disappeared from the May 2024 draft.[201]

Considering the global health inequalities exposed and worsened by the COVID-19 pandemic, the latest draft pandemic agreement does not contain stringent enough provisions related to the geographically diversified production and distribution of health products, the transfer of technology, and a mechanism for pathogen access and benefit-sharing that would sufficiently differentiate burdens, benefits, and obligations between the Global North and South actors to further health justice. Current provisions impose only minimal obligations, that are primarily process-related that asks States to support, facilitate, and encourage specific objectives.[202] Further, many of the provisions concerning implementation are framed vaguely and are contingent on each individual States' assessment of feasibility and/or appropriateness.[203] Thus, like the 2024 Revisions to the International Health Regulations, the negotiations for the pandemic treaty seem positioned to reinforce the status quo. It remains to be seen if this trajectory of limiting the potential for real transformation will be reversed if a final treaty text is concluded.

More significantly, it is urgent to disturb the tendency in global health to view the generation of more law as an end goal, in and of itself.

It is imperative that the field engage explicitly with people of the Global Majority to consider how their relative positions have informed their health priorities and claim-making if the field is to make a substantial break from the coloniality of the past. Otherwise, global health law risks reinscribing the functioning of imperial power and reifying the subaltern positions of those who lack(ed) law-making power. Indeed, the demands in the NIEO and the emancipatory visions articulated in the Declaration of Alma Ata for global health seem like a distant memory. Yet, the Declaration exists. It is a constant reminder that health for all is attainable, and that budgets are statements of our values. It powerfully asserts that:

> through a fuller and better use of the world's resources, a considerable part of which is now spent on armaments and military conflicts. A genuine policy of independence, peace, détente, and disarmament could and should release additional resources that could well be devoted to peaceful aims and in particular to the acceleration of social and economic development of which primary health care, as an essential part, should be allotted its proper share.[204]

The Declaration marks one of the few moments in global health's history where any accounting of this maldistribution of resources is acknowledged. This provision is especially crucial to reflect on in the present moment with some States' seemingly limitless devotion to dedicating resources to military-industrial complexes and endless wars. This is evidenced most recently by States' continued flow of armaments sustaining the slaughter in Palestine and the evisceration of civilian infrastructure including health facilities. There is an urgent need to fundamentally reject and disrupt this praxis, which includes demanding that the misallocation of resources that fuel war machines and de-prioritizes communities' and individuals' health and wellbeing end. Returning to these articulated visions of decolonization, anti-subordination, reparative and health justice, and building on this radical imagination and praxis, is essential for transformation in global health and any potential emancipatory futures.

NOTES

* This chapter draws heavily from my work on race and global health, especially the following pieces: Matiangai Sirleaf, "White Health as Global Health," *AJIL Unbound* 117 (2023): 88–93, https://doi.org/10.1017/aju.2023.12; Matiangai Sirleaf, "Disposable Lives: COVID-19, Vaccines, and the Uprising," *Columbia Law Review Forum* 121, no. 5 (2021): 71–94; Matiangai Sirleaf, "Entry Denied: COVID-19, Race, Migration and Global Health," *Frontiers in Human Dynamics* 2 (2020): article no. 599157, https://doi.org/10.3389/fhumd.2020.599157. I am especially appreciative of the research assistance provided by Zainab Ansari, Mary Atta-Dakwa, Matthew Byanyima, Alexis Lovings, Tamia Morris, and Karah Palmer as well as the editorial assistance of Susan McCarty.

1. For further discussion, see generally Anibal Quijano, "Coloniality of Power, Eurocentrism, and Latin America," *Nepantla: Views from South* 1, no. 3 (2000): 533–80.

2. This chapter understands race as the socially constructed and contingent system of meaning that societies attach to morphology, ancestry, and other characteristics. See Ian Haney López, *White by Law: The Legal Construction of Race*, 10th anniversary ed. (New York: NYU Press, 2006), xxi, 10; see also Michael Omi and Howard Winant, *Racial Formation in the United States*, 3rd ed. (New York: Routledge, 2015), 111 (defining race).

3. This chapter conceptualizes racism as a "societal system in which actors are divided into 'races,' with power unevenly distributed (or produced) based on these racial classifications." Yin C. Paradies, "Defining, Conceptualizing and Characterizing Racism in Health Research," *Critical Public Health* 16, no. 2 (2006): 143–57, 145. See also Errol A. Henderson, "Hidden in Plain Sight: Racism in International Relations Theory," *Cambridge Review of International Affairs* 26, no. 1 (2013): 71–92, 72 ("Racism is the belief in, practice, and policy of domination based on the specious concept of race. It is not simply bigotry or prejudice, but beliefs, practices and policies reflective of and supported by institutional power, primarily state power. For more than a century, social scientists, in general, have maintained that race and racism are among the most important factors in world politics"); Matiangai V. S. Sirleaf and Tendayi Achiume, "Reflecting on Race, Racism, and Transitional Justice," *International Journal of Transitional Justice*, 18, no. 1 (2024): 1–17, 3 https://doi.org/10.1093/ijtj/ijae007 (defining racism as "the material expression of the exclusionary practices and subordinate inclusionary practices that flow from specific forms of racialization, which necessarily takes different shapes and forms in various times and spaces.").

4. Tropical medicine became a recognized field during the height of Western colonization. Frank Snowden, "Tropical Medicine as a Discipline," Yale University, n.d., https://oyc.yale.edu/history/hist-234/lecture-15.

5. Matiangai Sirleaf, "Racial Valuation of Diseases," *UCLA Law Review* 67, no. 6 (2021): 1820–59, 1822. See also Carl Abbott, "The 'Chinese Flu' Is Part of a Long History of Racializing Disease," *Bloomberg: CityLab*, March 17, 2020, https://www.bloomberg.com/news/articles/2020-03-17/when-racism-and-disease-spread-together (noting that "Disease outbreaks are often racialized and made vehicles for nativist beliefs and ethnic hatreds").

6. See, e.g., W. C. Gorgas, "The Conquest of the Tropics for the White Race," *Journal of the American Medical Association* 52, no. 25 (1909): 1967–9 (president's address discussing the need for malaria control in the Canal Zone to render the Panamá Canal suitable for further colonial exploitation).

7. See generally E. Tendayi Achiume, "Racial Borders," *Georgetown Law Journal* 110, no. 3 (2022): 445–508.

8. Achiume, "Racial Borders," 448.

9. Achiume, "Racial Borders," 448.

10. Achiume, "Racial Borders," 450.

11. Sirleaf, "Entry Denied," 4.

12. Omi and Winant, *Racial Formation in the United States*, 13.

13. See, e.g., Matthew Clair and Jeffrey S. Denis, "Sociology of Racism," in *International Encyclopedia of the Social & Behavioral Sciences*, 2nd ed. (Amsterdam: Elsevier, 2015), 857–63, https://doi.org/10.1016/B978-0-08-097086-8.32122-5.

14. Eduardo Bonilla-Silva, "Rethinking Racism: Toward a Structural Interpretation," *American Sociological Review* 62, no. 3 (1997): 465–80, 474.

15. See generally Elazar Barkan, *The Retreat of Scientific Racism: Changing Concepts of Race in Britain and the United States between the World Wars* (New York: Cambridge University Press, 1992); Saul Dubow, *Scientific Racism in Modern South Africa* (Cambridge: Cambridge University Press, 1995).

16. See Rutledge M. Dennis, "Darwinism, Scientific Racism, and the Metaphysics of Race," *Journal of Negro Education* 64, no. 3 (1995): 243–52.

17. Sirleaf, "Entry Denied," 4.

18. See Bonilla-Silva, "Rethinking Racism," 471.

19. Sirleaf, "Entry Denied," 4. See also Harsha Walia, *Border and Rule: Global Migration, Capitalism, and the Rise of Racist Nationalism* (Chicago: Haymarket, 2021), 3 (arguing that "the US–Mexico border must be understood not only as a racist weapon to exclude migrants and refugees, but as foundational organized through, and hence inseparable from, imperialist expansion, Indigenous elimination, and anti-Black enslavement").

20. Sirleaf, "Racial Valuation of Diseases," 1841.

21. Sirleaf, "Racial Valuation of Diseases," 1841.

22. "Racial capitalism" is a term coined by Cedric Robinson that refers to the centrality of race in structuring social and labor hierarchies in capitalist economies. See generally Cedric J. Robinson, "Racial Capitalism: The Nonobjective Character of Capitalist Development," in *Black Marxism: The Making of the Black Radical Tradition*, 3rd ed. (Chapel Hill, NC: University of North Carolina Press 2020), 9.

23. Achille Mbembe, *On the Postcolony*, trans. A. M. Berrett et al. (Berkeley: University of California Press, 2001), 187.

24. See Roy Wilkins, "Huey Long Says—An Interview with Louisiana's Kingfish," *The Crisis*, February 1935, at 41, 52.

25. See Andrea Patterson, "Germs and Jim Crow: The Impact of Microbiology on Public Health Policies in Progressive Era American South," *Journal of the History of Biology* 42, no. 3 (2009): 529–59, 536.

26. Patterson, "Germs and Jim Crow," 537.

27. Dubow, *Scientific Racism in Modern South Africa*, 170.

28. Harriet Deacon, "Racism and Medical Science in South Africa's Cape Colony in the Mid- to Late Nineteenth Century," *Osiris* 15 (2000): 190–206, 204.

29. Deacon, "Racism and Medical Science," 204.

30. See generally Derrick A. Bell, Jr., "*Brown v. Board of Education* and the Interest-Convergence Dilemma," *Harvard Law Review* 93, no. 3 (1980): 518–33 (discussing interest convergence).

31. Randall M. Packard, *A History of Global Health: Interventions into the Lives of Other Peoples* (Baltimore: Johns Hopkins University Press, 2016), 20.

32. Lindsay Wiley et al., "Introduction: What is Health Justice?" *Journal of Law, Medicine & Ethics* 50 (2022): 636–40.

33. Wiley et al., "Introduction," 636.

34. Wiley et al., "Introduction," 636.

35. Jin Un Kim et al., "A Time for New North–South Relationships in Global Health," *International Journal of General Medicine* 10 (2017): 401–8, 402, https://doi.org/10.2147%2FIJGM.S146475.

36. World Health Organization, "Health Equity and its Determinants, World Health Day 2021: It's Time to Build a Fairer, Healthier World for Everyone, Everywhere," April 6, 2021, https://www.who.int/publications/m/item/health-equity-and-its-determinants.

37. Liora Bigon, "A History of Urban Planning and Infectious Diseases: Colonial Senegal in the Early Twentieth Century," *Urban Studies Research* (2012), art. no. 589758, 2, https://doi.org/10.1155/2012/589758.

38. Bigon, "A History of Urban Planning and Infectious Diseases," 9.

39. Bigon, "A History of Urban Planning and Infectious Diseases," 7–8.

40. See generally Stephen Frenkel and John Western, "Pretext or Prophylaxis? Racial Segregation and Malarial Mosquitos in a British Tropical Colony: Sierra Leone," *Annals of the Association of American Geographers* 78, no. 2 (1988): 211–28.

41. See, e.g., Richard C. Keller, "Geographies of Power, Legacies of Mistrust: Colonial Medicine in the Global Present," *Historical Geography* 34 (2006): 26–48.

42. Packard, *History of Global Health*, 14, 20 (noting that "results such as were obtained in Havana in the suppression of yellow fever during the American occupation cannot be obtained elsewhere, where the disease is widely spread, without the undisputed authority and the means that were the command of the Government of Intervention in Cuba. These powers in reality amounted to martial law").

43. Zeinabou Niamé Daffé et al., "Anti-Racism and Anti-Colonialism Praxis in Global Health—Reflection and Action for Practitioners in US Academic Medical Centers," *American Journal of Tropical Medicine and Hygiene* 105, no. 3 (2021): 557–60, https://doi.org/10.4269/ajtmh.21-0187.

44. Daffé et al., "Anti-Racism and Anti-Colonialism Praxis," 557–8.

45. Keller, "Geographies of Power," 38. See also A. M. Branfoot et al., "Reports and Papers on Bubonic Plague; Plague Research Commission, Reports on Plague Investigations of India," *Journal of Hygiene* 6, no. 4 (1906): 467–82.

46. For further discussion, see generally Festus Cole, "Sanitation, Disease and Public Health in Sierra Leone, West Africa, 1895–1922: Case Failure of British Colonial Health Policy," *Journal of Imperial & Commonwealth History* 43, no. 2 (2015): 238–66, https://doi.org/10.1080/03086534.2014.974901.

47. For further discussion, see Margaret Lock and Vinh-Kim Nguyen, *An Anthropology of Biomedicine* (Malden, MA: Wiley-Blackwell, 2010) (discussing how the field of tropical medicine is a discipline intrinsically linked to European colonialism in tropical places and the high mortality rate sustained by imperialists).

48. For further discussion, see Ryan Johnson, "Colonial Mission and Imperial Tropical Medicine: Livingstone College, London, 1893–1914," *Social History of Medicine* 23, no. 3 (2010): 549–66, https://doi.org/10.1093/shm/hkq044 (discussing how the medicine practiced was imbued with colonial ambition).

49. WHO, Proceedings of the Special Committee and of the Fourth World Health Assembly on WHO Regulations No. 2 (1952), 1 (discussing the background to the International Sanitary Conferences and any resulting treaties from 1851 to 1938).

50. See David P. Fidler, "International Law and Global Public Health," *University of Kansas Law Review* 48, no. 1 (1999): 1–58, 17 (table noting the Convention and Regulations on maritime traffic and the control of plague, cholera, and yellow fever negotiated in 1851 but never adopted; the Convention simplifying the proposed 1851 Convention and Regulations negotiated in 1859 but never adopted; and the Convention on quarantine negotiated by three South American states in 1873, but never ratified by any party).

51. Norman Howard-Jones, *The Scientific Background of the International Sanitary Conferences 1851–1938* (Geneva: World Health Organization, 1975), 11.

52. Howard-Jones, *Scientific Background*, 82.

53. See International Sanitary Convention of 1892, art. 4 (January 9, 1892) (noting measures to prevent cholera). See also Howard-Jones, *Scientific Background*, 65.

54. International Sanitary Convention of 1893, Title I (April 15, 1893).

55. See Howard-Jones, *Scientific Background*, 73.

56. Howard-Jones, *Scientific Background*, 73.

57. International Sanitary Convention of 1894 (April 3, 1894).

58. See Howard-Jones, *Scientific Background*, 78.

59. See Howard-Jones, *Scientific Background*, 78.

60. International Sanitary Convention of 1897, chapters I–IV (March 19, 1897).

61. International Sanitary Convention of 1926, art. 1 (June 21, 1926).

62. Howard-Jones, *Scientific Background*, 93.

63. Francis Schaffner and Alexander Mathis, "Dengue and Dengue Vectors in the WHO European Region: Past, Present, and Scenarios for the Future," *Lancet Infectious Diseases* 14, no. 12 (2014): 1271–80, 1271, https://doi.org/10.1016/s1473-3099(14)70834-5.

64. International Convention for Mutual Protection against Dengue Fever (July 25, 1934).

65. Pratik Chakrabarti, *Medicine & Empire: 1600–1960* (Basingstoke: Palgrave Macmillan, 2014), 202 (discussing some of the early work of the Rockefeller Foundation on these diseases, which provides some indication of the other communicable diseases that global health actors were focusing on around that time).

66. See Jones, *Scientific Background*, 39–40.

67. Jones, *Scientific Background*, 45.

68. Elizabeth Fee and Theodore M. Brown, "100 Years of the Pan American Health Organization," *American Journal of Public Health*, 92, no. 12 (2002): 1888–9, https://doi.org/10.2105/AJPH.92.12.1888 ("By 1902, when the United States was seeking trade expansion overseas, it regarded Latin America as belonging to its sphere of influence, a rich resource for raw materials, and a potentially vast market for manufactured goods. Interfering with the expansion of commerce, however, was a complicated mosaic of differing quarantine, inspection, and exclusion regulations that impeded the movement of goods. The International Union of American States thus called for the creation of a sanitary bureau to draft uniform sanitary laws and regulations").

69. International Sanitary Convention of 1903, art. 18(1).

70. Jones, *Scientific Background*, 86.

71. International Sanitary Convention of 1926, art. 1(3).

72. Lawrence O. Gostin et al., "The WHO's 75th Anniversary: WHO at a Pivotal Moment in History," *BMJ Global Health* 8, no. 4 (2023): e012344, https://doi.org/10.1136/bmjgh-2023-012344.

73. Covenant of the League of Nations, art. XXIII (1920).

74. Covenant of the League of Nations, art. XXIV.

75. Clarence A. Berdahl, "United States and the League of Nations," *Michigan Law Review* 27, no. 6 (1929): 607–36, 607.

76. Gostin et al., "The WHO's 75th Anniversary," 2.

77. E. Thornton and A. J. Orenstein, "Co-ordination of Health Work in Africa," in *Report of the Pan-African Health Conference Held at Johannesburg, November 20th to 30th, 1935* (Geneva: League of Nations, 1936), 208–9.

78. Compare International Sanitary Convention of 1944, art. 5A, with art. 5B.

79. See International Sanitary Convention of 1944, art. 5B.

80. International Sanitary Convention of 1944, art. I.

81. See WHO Constitution preamble, July 22, 1946, 14 U.N.T.S. 185 (entered into force April 7, 1948).

82. Compare International Covenant on Economic, Social and Cultural Rights (ICESCR) art. 12(1), Dec. 16, 1966, 993 U.N.T.S. 3 (recognizing the right to health in an international treaty in 1966), with WHO Constitution, preamble (recognizing the right to health in the preamble of the treaty in 1946).

83. See, e.g., UN Charter, art. 13(1)(b) (noting that the General Assembly shall initiate studies and make recommendations promoting international cooperation in health amongst others); art. 55(b) (noting that the UN shall promote solutions to international health, and other problems); and art. 60 (creating an Economic and Social Council).

84. WHO Constitution, preamble.

85. WHO Constitution, preamble.

86. WHO, *International Health Regulations (1969)* (Geneva: WHO, 1969).

87. P. G. Stock, "The International Sanitary Convention of 1944," *Proceedings of the Royal Society of Medicine* 38, no. 7 (1944): 309–16, 311 (noting that the Convention did not contain a proposal to include influenza among the diseases covered).

88. International Convention on the Elimination of All Forms of Racial Discrimination (CERD) art. 5, Dec. 21, 1965, 660 U.N.T.S. 195 (parties "undertake to prohibit and to eliminate racial discrimination in all its forms and to guarantee the right of everyone, without distinction as to race, color, or national or ethnic origin, to equality before the law"); see also ICESCR art. 2(2), December 16, 1966, 993 U.N.T.S. 3 ("States Parties to the present Covenant undertake to guarantee that the rights enunciated in the present Covenant will be exercised without discrimination of any kind as to race, colour, sex, language, religion, political or other opinion, national or social origin, property, birth or other status").

89. Compare ICESCR, art. 12(2) (full realization of right to health includes: "provision for the reduction of the stillbirth-rate and of infant mortality and for the healthy development of the child; (b) The improvement of all aspects of environmental and industrial hygiene; (c) The prevention, treatment and control of epidemic, endemic, occupational and other diseases; (d) The creation of conditions which would assure to all medical service and medical attention in the event of sickness.").

90. J. Benton Heath, "Global Emergency Power in the Age of Ebola," *Harvard International Law Journal* 57, no. 1 (2016): 1–48, 11 ("The relative autonomy of international bureaucracies may create inequality among states (or among other relevant actors), insofar as some states have greater capacity to influence experts").

91. New International Economic Order (NIEO), G.A. Res. 3201 (S-VI), p, U.N. Doc. A/3201 (May 1, 1974).

92. WHO Constitution, preamble.

93. See generally WHO, Basic Documents, forty-ninth edition (2020) [hereinafter Basic Documents].

94. NIEO, f.

95. Compare WHO, Basic Documents (absence of affirmative action or special measures) with CERD, art. 1 (noting that "Special measures taken for the sole purpose of securing adequate advancement of certain racial or ethnic groups or individuals requiring such protection as may be necessary in order to ensure such groups or individuals equal enjoyment or exercise of human rights and fundamental freedoms shall not be deemed racial discrimination").

96. See generally WHO, Basic Documents (absence of these concepts).

97. Matiangai Sirleaf, "We Charge Vaccine Apartheid?" *Journal of Law, Medicine & Ethics* 50 (2022): 726–37, 727.

98. See generally WHO, International Health Regulations (2005), third edition (Geneva: WHO, 2016).

99. WHO, International Health Regulations (2005), arts. 15, 18(1).

100. WHO, International Health Regulations (2005), art. 1 (referring to temporary and standing recommendations as "non-binding advice issued by the WHO").

101. WHO, International Health Regulations (2005), art. 4.

102. WHO, International Health Regulations (2005), Annex I.A (detailing the core capacity requirements for surveillance and response).

103. WHO, International Health Regulations (2005), Annex I.A(3) ("State parties and WHO shall support assessments, planning and implementation processes...").

104. See WHO, Resolution WHA26.55 209 Official Records, 29 (1973) (amending the IHR's provisions relating to cholera). See also WHO, Resolution WHA34.13, 217 Official Records, 21, 71, and 81 (1974) (amending the IHRs to exclude smallpox as a named disease following its eradication).

105. Compare Wendy Rhymer and Rick Speare, "Countries' Response to WHO's Travel Recommendations During the 2013–2016 Ebola Outbreak," *Bulletin of the World Health Organization* 95, no. 1 (2017): 10–17, https://www.ncbi.nlm.nih.gov/pmc/articles/PMC5180350/pdf/BLT.16.171579.pdf.

106. See generally WHO, International Health Regulations (2005), art. 54.

107. WHO, International Health Regulations (2005), art. 42. This provision was unaltered in the 2024 amendments.

108. Sirleaf, "Entry Denied," 1.

109. WHO, Statement on the Second Meeting of the International Health Regulations (2005) Emergency Committee Regarding the Outbreak of Novel Coronavirus (2019-nCoV), January 30, 2020, https://www.who.int/news/item/30-01-2020-statement-on-the-second-meeting-of-the-international-health-regulations-(2005)-emergency-committee-regarding-the-outbreak-of-novel-coronavirus-(2019-ncov).

110. WHO, International Health Regulations (2005), art. 1.

111. WHO, Updated WHO Recommendations for International Traffic in Relation to COVID-19 Outbreak, February 29, 2020, https://www.who.int/news-room/articles-detail/updated-who-recommendations-for-international-traffic-in-relation-to-covid-19-outbreak.

112. WHO, Updated WHO Recommendations.

113. Motoko Rich, "As Coronavirus Spreads, So Does Anti-Chinese Sentiment," *New York Times*, February 3, 2020, https://www.nytimes.com/2020/01/30/world/asia/coronavirus-chinese-racism.html.

114. Sirleaf, "Entry Denied," 6.

115. Ibid., 7.

116. For instance, both the Trump and Biden administrations weaponized the Title 42 clause of the Public Health Services Law to restrict the entry of Haitian and Latin American asylum seekers at the Mexico border. See "Q&A: US Title 42 Policy to Expel Migrants at the Border," Human Rights Watch, April 8, 2021, https://www.hrw.org/news/2021/04/08/qa-us-title-42-policy-expel-migrants-border; "What Does the End of Title 42 Mean for U.S. Migration Policy?" *Carnegie Reporter*, June 5, 2023, https://www.carnegie.org/our-work/article/what-does-end-title-42-mean-us-migration-policy/.

117. Joe Hernandez, "African Leaders Condemn Travel Restrictions as Omicron Variant Spreads Globally," *NPR: Goats and Soda*, November 30, 2021, https://www.npr.org/sections/goatsandsoda/2021/11/30/1059780197/african-leaders-condemn-travel-restrictions-as-omicron-variant-spreads-globally.

118. "Omicron COVID Variant Was in Europe before South African Scientists Detected and Flagged It to the World," *CBS News*, November 30, 2021, https://www.cbsnews.com/news/omicron-variant-covid-in-europe-netherlands-before-alert-raised/.

119. President Biden (@POTUS), Twitter (Nov. 29, 2021).

120. African (@ali_naka), Twitter (Nov. 28, 2021).

121. "The Newspaper La Tribuna de Albacete and Its Cartoonist Apologise for a Cartoon," *JR Mora*, November 24, 2021, https://jrmora.com/en/the-newspaper-la-tribuna-de-albacete-cartoonist-apologise-cartoon/.

122. Sirleaf, "Racial Valuation of Diseases," 1849. See also Meenadchi Mohanachandran, "The Othering of the Black Community in News Media Reports During the 2014 Ebola Epidemic," *Nexus: The Canadian Student Journal of Anthropology* 25 (2017): 44–51, 44–45 (discussing how "public reaction in North America was disproportionate to the reality of the disease on this continent. Although Ebola was highly unlikely to spread beyond the few people who contracted it, the media promoted panic and hysteria surrounding a potential North American epidemic. This was accomplished largely by racializing the disease and attributing it to the Black body, which had a detrimental impact on Black North Americans as it further oppressed an already marginalized population. This is similar to trends that occurred during the 2003 SARS outbreak in Toronto").

123. WHO, International Health Regulations (2005), art. 56.

124. See generally Communication from India and South Africa, Waiver from Certain Provisions of the TRIPS Agreement for the Prevention, Containment and Treatment of COVID-19, IP/C/W/669 (October 2, 2020), https://docs.wto.org/dol2fe/Pages/SS/directdoc.aspx?filename=q:/IP/C/W669.pdf&Open=True; World Trade Organization, Ministerial Decision on the TRIPS Agreement, Ministerial Conference Twelfth Session WT/MIN(22)/30 WT/L/1141, June 22, 2022.

125. See generally Sirleaf, "We Charge Vaccine Apartheid?" 726–37.

126. World Health Organization. Report of the Review Committee Regarding Amendments to the International Health Regulations (2005), Geneva; 2023, https://apps.who.int/gb/wgihr/pdf_files/wgihr2/A_WGIHR2_5-en.pdf.

127. See, e.g., WHO, Strengthening WHO Preparedness for and Response to Health Emergencies: Proposal for Amendments to the International Health Regulations (2005), Seventy-Fifth World Health Assembly Provisional Agenda Item 16.2, WHO A75/18 (Apr. 12, 2022) (proposing substantial amendments to article 5 which deals with surveillance, article 6 which concerns notification, article 9 concerning reporting, article 10 concerning verification, and article 11 relating to providing information to the WHO, amongst others). See also WHO, Report of the sixth meeting of the Working Group on Amendments to the International Health Regulations (2005), para 7, A/WGIHR/6/3 (Jan. 8, 2024) (including proposals for amendments that relate broadly to equity, capacity-building, and financing to support capacity-building and the implementation of the International Health Regulations).

128. WHO, International Health Regulations (2005), art. 2 (amended).

129. WHO, International Health Regulations (2005), arts. 5–6 (amended).

130. WHO, International Health Regulations (2005), art. 1 (amended).

131. Compare WHO, International Health Regulations (2005), (amended) (Geneva: WHO, 2024) (note the absence of race or racism), with WHO, International Health Regulations (2005), third edition (Geneva: WHO, 2016) (note the absence of the reference to race and racism).

132. See WHO, Basic Documents (note the absence of these and related terms); see also WHO, International Health Regulations (2005) (amended).

133. Jason Hickel, Dylan Sullivan, and Huzaifa Zoomkawala, "Plunder in the Post-Colonial Era: Quantifying the Drain from the Global South Through Unequal Exchange," *New Political Economy* 26, no. 6 (2021): 1030–47.

134. Jason Hickel, Christian Dorninger, Hanspeter Wieland, and Intan Suwundi, "Imperialist Appropriation in the World Economy: Drain from the Global South through Unequal Exchange, 1990-2015," *Global Environmental Change* 73 (2022), no. 102467.

135. WHO, International Health Regulations (2005), art. 3 (amended).

136. See generally WHO, International Health Regulations (2005) (amended).

137. WHO Constitution, preamble.

138. World Trade Organization, Council for Trade-Related Aspects of Intellectual Property Rights, Minutes of Meeting, Apr. 7, 2021, 5, IP/C/M/97/Add.1 (noting South Africa's representative's remarks).

139. WHO, International Health Regulations (2005), art. 44bis (amended).

140. COVAX: Working for Global Equitable Access to COVID-19 Vaccines, WHO, https://www.who.int/initiatives/act-accelerator/covax.

141. See, e.g., Anna Rouw, Jennifer Kates, Josh Michaud & Adam Wexler, "COVAX and the United States," *Kaiser Family Foundation* (Feb. 18, 2021), https://www.kff.org/coronaviruscovid-19/issue-brief/covax-and-the-united-states (discussing how COVAX has an overall funding target (2020–2021) of $11.1 billion but faces a $7.2 billion funding gap).

142. See e.g., G. Ooms & R. Hammonds, "Taking Up Daniels' Challenge: The Case for Global Health Justice," *Health and Human Rights Journal* 12 (2010) no. 1: 29, 37.

143. WHO, International Health Regulations (2005), Annex 1(4) (amended).

144. Wiley et al., "Introduction," 637.

145. WHO, International Health Regulations (2005), art. 13 (amended).

146. For further discussion see Sirleaf, "Disposable Lives," 88–93.

147. WHO is one of the founding members of GAVI, the Vaccine Alliance. See GAVI, https://www.gavi.org/operating-model/gavis-partnership-model/who (describing how WHO "supports and facilitates research and development, sets standards and regulates vaccine quality and develops evidence-based policy options to guide vaccine use and maximise country access.").

148. The World Health Assembly created this initiative in May 2011. See Pandemic Influenza Preparedness Framework, https://www.who.int/initiatives/pandemic-influenza-preparedness-framework (the framework brings "together Member States, industry, other stakeholders and WHO to implement a global approach to pandemic influenza preparedness and response. Its key goals include: to improve and strengthen the sharing of influenza viruses with human pandemic potential; and to increase the access of developing countries to vaccines and other pandemic related supplies.").

149. See generally WHO, International Health Regulations (2005) (the Regulations do not include any enforcement mechanism for state parties that fail to comply with its provisions).

150. WHO, International Health Regulations (2005), art. 54bis (amended).

151. WHO, International Health Regulations (2005), art. 54bis (amended).

152. "Gaza will need largest post-war reconstruction effort since 1945 UN says." *Al Jazeera*, May 2, 2024, https://www.aljazeera.com/news/2024/5/2/gaza-will-need-largest-post-war-reconstruction-effort-since-1945-un-says.

153. WHO, International Health Regulations (2005), Annex 2 (contains a decision matrix that has non-binding guidance on whether a public health event is serious. The instrument includes a list where " armed conflicts" is named as a concomitant factor that may hinder or delay the public health response, which can contribute to an event having a high health impact.). The IHRs do not have provisions aimed at addressing the relationship between armed conflict and communicable diseases. See generally WHO, International Health Regulations (2005),

154. Emily Benfer, "Health Justice: A Framework (and Call to Action) for the Elimination of Health Inequity and Social Injustice," *American University Law Review* 65 (2015): 275–351.

155. WHO Constitution, pmbl.

156. Declaration of Alma Alta, art. 1 (1978), https://cdn.who.int/media/docs/default-source/documents/almaata-declaration-en.pdf?sfvrsn=7b3c2167_2.

157. Declaration of Alma Alta, art. 2.

158. Declaration of Alma Alta, art. 3.

159. For example, another international conference on Primary Health Care took place in Astana, Kazakhstan in October 2018. It resulted in another non-binding declaration, which references the Declaration of Alma-Ata. See Declaration of Astana, pmbl., art.1, October 26, 2018, https://www.who.int/publications/i/item/WHO-HIS-SDS-2018.61.

160. Eugene T. Richardson, "On the Coloniality of Global Public Health," *Medicine Anthropology Theory* 6, no. 4 (2019): 101–18, 103, https://doi.org/10.17157/mat.6.4.761 (defining coloniality as "the matrix of power relations that persistently manifests transnationally and intersubjectively despite a former colony's achievement of nationhood.").

161. Colleen Murphy, "What Is White Savior Complex, and Why Is It Harmful? Here's What Experts Say," *Health*, September 20, 2021, updated August 17, 2023, https://www.health.com/mind-body/health-diversity-inclusion/white-savior-complex (defining what the White Savior Complex is, as an ideology that is acted upon when a White person, "from a position of superiority," attempts to help or "rescue a BIPOC ... community or person." This is done consciously or unconsciously. People with this complex "have the underlying belief that they know best or that they have skills that BIPOC people do not have." This "centuries-old concept that dates back to when many White Westerners believed they had the knowledge, ingenuity, and skills to solve the other people's problems worldwide").

162. Rudyard Kipling, *The White Man's Burden* (1899), http://www.kiplingsociety.co.uk/poems_burden.htm (poem calling for imperialism and colonialism). In the poem, Kipling urges the United States to take up the "burden" of empire, as had Britain and other European nations. Compare H. T. Johnson, "The Black Man's Burden," *Voice of Missions*, VII (1899), 1, reprinted in Willard B. Gatewood, Jr., *Black Americans and the White Man's Burden, 1898–1903*, at 183–4 (Urbana, IL: University of Illinois Press, 1975) (responding to Kipling and asserting that Black and brown peoples have been exploited and are the ones burdened by colonialism and imperialism). For further discussion, see generally Bill Easterly, *The White Man's Burden: How the West's Efforts to Aid the Rest Have Done So Much Ill and So Little Good* (New York: Penguin Press, 2006).

163. Ali Arazeem Abdullahi, "Trends and Challenges of Traditional Medicine in Africa," *African Journal of Traditional, Complementary and Alternative Medicines* 8, no.

5 supplement (2011): 115–23, http://doi.org/10.4314/ajtcam.v8i5S.5 (discussing how "In some extreme cases, TM (traditional medicine) was outrightly banned. For instance, the South African Medical Association outlawed traditional medical system in South Africa in 1953. In addition, the Witchcraft Suppression Act of 1957 and the Witchcraft Suppression Amendment Act of 1970 also declared TM unconstitutional thereby disallowing the practitioners from doing their business in South Africa. The ban of TM was partially based on the belief that the conception of disease and illness in Africa was historically embedded in 'witchcraft' where, in Western knowledge, witchcraft reinforces 'backwardness,' 'superstition' and 'dark continent'"). See also Daffé et al., "Anti-Racism and Anti-Colonialism Praxis," 557–8 (noting that "The emergence of schools of tropical medicine and hygiene in that epoch ensured that knowledge production in colonial settings was incorporated into the field of international health. Over time, these ideas and practices became the basis of expertise about health problems in the 'developing world.' As a result, even in post- and non-colonial settings, international health experts continued to perpetuate colonial ideas that became 'naturalized as global health science'").

164. See Anna Nonaka and Ava Arshadi, "Do Healthcare Mission Trips Cause More Harm than Good?" *Synapse*, May 10, 2016, https://synapse.ucsf.edu/articles/2016/05/10/do-healthcare-mission-trips-cause-more-harm-good (describing how some volunteer health activities are duplicative, in competition with local healthcare providers, cause damage to local health systems or encourage reliance on outside help, and short-term "band-aid" efforts neglect underlying disease and leave the local community without assistance when the "volunteers" leave).

165. See Goncalves, "Readings of the Coloniality of Power," 2 (discussing how the "emergence of COVID-19 was undeniably accompanied by the international responsibility narrative, according to which health professionals across the globe sought to attribute the emergency of the SARS mutation which led to the resulting global pandemics to specific behaviors. What initially seemed to be a preventive scientific measure, nonetheless, soon became an attempt to blame predetermined cultures, nations, or ethnicities. The most notably affected nation was the People's Republic of China, following Donald Trump, Jair Bolsonaro and other far-right leaders' 'China Virus' narrative, according to which not only Chinese eating habits would have initiated human-to-human viral transmission, but the country's government was named responsible for its spreading, amidst several other . . . theories").

166. Peter O'Dowd, "Global Public Health, Colonialism, and Why So Many People Die of Preventable Diseases," WBUR, March 9, 2021, https://www.wbur.org/hereandnow/2021/03/09/colonialism-global-public-health (interviewing and quoting Eugene T. Richardson) (discussing the response by some to Ebola "to say that people are responsible for the outbreaks because of their ignorance and calling them super spreaders, instead of calling the mining companies that steal the diamonds super spreaders, is to me just a perspective choice. And so the intervention is not MSF. It's actually reparations for these colonial legacies"). See also Kevin J. A. Thomas, "Fighting Coronavirus Fear with Empathy: Lessons Learned from How Africans Got Blamed for Ebola," *The Conversation*, February 6, 2020, https://theconversation.com/fighting-coronavirus-fear-with-empathy-lessons-learned-from-how-africans-got-blamed-for-ebola-130997 (noting how during "the Ebola crisis, negative responses from Americans who used caricatures of immigrants' ethnicity to stigmatize them as carriers of disease only worsened immigrants' stress and fear. For example, many heard racist tropes about Africans' presumed penchant for kissing corpses and their habit of consuming exotic beasts").

167. Richardson, "On the Coloniality of Global Public Health."

168. Madelon L. Finkel et al., "What Do Global Health Practitioners Think About Decolonizing Global Health?" *Annals of Global Health* 88, no. 1 (2020): article no. 61, 1, https://doi.org/10.5334/aogh.3714 (discussing how, "as part of a paradigm shift, attention needs to be paid to creating a more equal and equitable representation of researchers in LMICs in decision-making, leadership roles, authorship, and funding allocations. There needs to be agreement in defining basic principles of best practices for global partnership").

169. For example, The Global Health 50/50 report found that 85 percent of global organizations active in the healthcare field have headquarters in Europe and North America, with two-thirds in just three countries: Switzerland, the United Kingdom, and the United States. Global Health 50/50, *The Global Health 50/50 Report 2020: Power, Privilege and Priorities* (London: Global Health 50/50, 2020), 16, https://globalhealth5050.org/wp-content/uploads/2020/03/Power-Privilege-and-Priorities-2020-Global-Health-5050-Report.pdf. Further, countries in the Global South receive significant aid from global health organizations such as the UN, WHO, philanthropists like the Bill and Melinda Gates Foundation, and Wellcome Trust who, through their funding, hold the power to set global health agendas. Global Health 50/50, *The Global Health 50/50 Report 2020*. The report also found that more than 70 percent of the leaders in a sample of two hundred global health organizations are men, and that more than 80 percent are nationals from the Global North and more than 90 percent were educated in countries in the Global North. Global Health 50/50, *The Global Health 50/50 Report 2020*.

170. Kurchi Mitra, "Global Health's Colonial Roots and Lessons to Learn from the Global South," Students for Global Health, December 22, 2022, https://studentsforglobalhealth.org/2020/12/22/global-healths-colonial-roots-lessons-to-learn-from-the-global-south//.

171. For further discussion, see Quentin G. Eichbaum et al., "Global Health Education: Rethinking Institutional Partnerships and Approaches," *Academic Medicine* 96, no. 3 (2021): 329–35, https://doi.org/10.1097/acm.0000000000003473. See also John Kulesa and Nana Aqua Brantuo, "Barriers to Decolonising Educational Partnerships in Global Health," *BMJ Global Health* 6, no. 11 (2021): e006964, https://doi.org/10.1136/bmjgh-2021-006964 (describing how global health educational partnerships can perpetuate colonial legacies that limit access to health care and contribute to poor health outcomes; noting how barriers arise when attempting to decolonize global health and that global health partners may struggle to ensure inclusion of all social and cultural groups affected by global health work).

172. Wiley et al., "Introduction," 636.

173. A term coined by the late Fela Kuti, Afrobeats pioneer and human rights activist, which refers to the process by which formerly colonized peoples internalize the underlying assumptions of colonialism such that it guides their behavior. See Keziah Jones Fela Kuti, Colonial Mentality, Lyrics.com https://www.lyrics.com/lyric/964438/Fela+Kuti/COLONIAL+MENTALITY ("Colo-mentality

If you say you be colonial man

You don be slave man before

Them don release you now

But you never release yourself"). See also Maysoon Hussain, Mitra Sadigh, Majid Sadigh, Asghar Rastegar, and Nelson Sewankambo, "Colonization and decolonization of global health: which way forward?" *Global Health Action* 16, no. 1 (2023) https://doi.org/10.1080/16549716.2023.2186575 (discussing how "colonial mentalities" were evident during the COVID-19 pandemic).

174. Nurith Aizeman and Malaka Gharib, "American with No Medical Training Ran Center for Malnourished Ugandan Kids. 105 Died," *NPR*, August 9, 2019, https://www.npr.org/sections/goatsandsoda/2019/08/09/749005287/american-with-no-medical-training-ran-center-for-malnourished-ugandan-kids-105-d.

175. Aizeman and Gharib, "American with No Medical Training."

176. See Irmgard Bauer, "More Harm than Good? The Questionable Ethics of Medical Volunteering and International Student Placements," *Tropical Diseases, Travel Medicine, and Vaccines* 3 (2017): article no. 5, 4, https://doi.org/10.1186%2Fs40794-017-0048-y ("Hence, short-term medical missions are, at best, a quick fix solution; at worst, they are perpetuating and supporting the factors that lead to poor health. Missions [surgical or otherwise] do not address health care problems, such as poverty and overstretched health care infrastructure. 'Fistula tourism' does not change a broken system; without addressing a broken system, any 'help' can only be a short-term fix which may benefit individual patients but does not improve long-term access to quality health care. Many governments rely and depend on international volunteers, often with little to no regulation or coordination. This dependence, and also the usually free volunteer services, may remove any incentive for a government to invest in health care or in preventative programs").

177. Abraar Karan, "It's Time to End the Colonial Mindset in Global Health," Opinion, *NPR*, December 30, 2019, https://www.npr.org/sections/goatsandsoda/2019/12/30/784392315/opinion-its-time-to-end-the-colonial-mindset-in-global-health.

178. United Nations Sustainable Development, The 17 Goals, https://sdgs.un.org/goals.

179. United Nations Sustainable Development, Goal 3: Targets and Indicators, https://sdgs.un.org/goals/goal3#targets_and_indicators.

180. United Nations Sustainable Development, Goal 3: Targets and Indicators.

181. United Nations Sustainable Development, Goal 3, https://sdgs.un.org/goals/goal3.

182. United Nations Sustainable Development, Goal 10: Targets and Indicators, https://sdgs.un.org/goals/goal10#targets_and_indicators.

183. Ruth Enid Zambrana and David R. Williams, "The Intellectual Roots of Current Knowledge on Racism and Health: Relevance to Policy and the National Equity Disclosure," *Health Affairs* 41, no. 2 (2022): 163–70, http://doi.org/10.1377/hlthaff.2021.01439.

184. Progress towards the Sustainable Development Goals: Towards a Rescue Plan for People and Planet: Report of the Secretary-General (United Nations, 2023), https://digitallibrary.un.org/record/4014344?v=pdf.

185. United Nations, "UN Chief Calls for Fundamental Shift to Put the World Back on Track to Achieving the Sustainable Development Goals," press release, April 26, 2023, https://www.un.org/sustainabledevelopment/blog/2023/04/press-release-un-chief-calls-for-fundamental-shift-to-put-world-back-on-track-to-achieving-the-sustainable-development-goals/.

186. United Nations, "UN Chief Calls for Fundamental Shift."

187. United Nations, "UN Chief Calls for Fundamental Shift."

188. United Nations, "UN Chief Calls for Fundamental Shift."

189. WHO, "Global Leaders Unite in Urgent Call for International Pandemic Treaty," press release, March 30, 2021, https://www.who.int/news/item/30-03-2021-global-leaders-unite-in-urgent-call-for-international-pandemic-treaty.

190. See, e.g., Paris Agreement to the United Nations Framework Convention on Climate Change, December 13, 2015, in Report of the Conference of the Parties on the Twenty-First Session, U.N. Doc. FCCC/CP/2015/10/Add.1, Annex (2016) ("This Agreement

will be implemented to reflect equity and the principle of common but differentiated responsibilities and respective capabilities, in the light of different national circumstances"); United Nations Framework Convention on Climate Change art. 3, May 9, 1992, S Treaty Doc. No. 102–38, 1771 U.N.T.S. 107 (enumerating the principles of common but differentiated responsibilities by which treaty signers are expected to abide).

191. Paris Agreement, arts. 4, 9–10.

192. UN Conference on the Human Environment, Stockholm Declaration on the Human Environment, UN Doc. A/CONF.48/14/Rev.1 (June 1972) (explaining in Principle 24 that states are obliged in the spirit of solidarity to cooperate in preventing transboundary pollution).

193. See, e.g., Convention on Biological Diversity preamble, June 5, 1992, 1760 U.N.T.S. 79 (noting that conserving "biological diversity is a common concern of humankind"); Convention for the Protection of Cultural Property in the Event of Armed Conflict with Regulations for the Execution of the Convention 1954, preamble, May 14, 1954, 249 U.N.T.S. 240, http://unesdoc.unesco.org/images/0018/001875/187580e.pdf [https://perma.cc/P749-JMWK] ("Being convinced that damage to cultural property belonging to any people whatsoever means damage to the cultural heritage of all mankind, since each people makes its contribution to the culture of the world"); International Convention for the High Seas Fisheries of the North Pacific Ocean preamble, May 9, 1952, 4 U.S.T. 380, 205 U.N.T.S. 65 (categorizing conservation efforts towards tuna as serving the common interest of mankind).

194. See, e.g., International Treaty on Plant Genetic Resources for Food and Agriculture, art. 7.2(a), Nov. 3, 2001, T.I.A.S. No. 17-313, 2400 U.N.T.S. 303 (entered into force June 29, 2004) (directing international cooperation to establish and strengthen the capabilities of developing countries and economies in transition); International Treaty on Plant Genetic Resources for Food and Agriculture, art. 8 (requiring parties to promote the provision of technical assistance to developing countries and economies in transition).

195. See generally Matiangai Sirleaf, "Responsibility for Epidemics," *Texas Law Review* 97, no. 2 (2018): 285–354.

196. Alexandra Phelan and Matiangai Sirleaf, "Decolonization of Global Health Law: Lessons from International Environmental Law," *Journal of Law, Medicine & Ethics* 51 (2023): 450–3.

197. WHO, Conceptual Zero Draft for the Consideration of the Intergovernmental Negotiating Body at its Fourth Meeting, art. 4(8), WHO A/INB/4/3 (Feb. 2023) [hereinafter Zero Draft].

198. WHO, Intergovernmental Negotiating Body to draft and negotiate a WHO convention, agreement or other international instrument on pandemic prevention, preparedness and response, WHO A77/10 (May. 2024) (Appendix Proposal for the WHO Pandemic Agreement) [hereinafter May 2024 Draft].

199. May 2024 Draft art. 20.

200. Compare WHO's Bureau text of the WHO convention, agreement or other international instrument on pandemic prevention, preparedness and response, art. 19(3)(a)(ii), WHO A/INB/5/6 (June 2023) [hereinafter June 2023 Draft] with May 2024 Draft.

201. Compare June 2023 Draft, art. 19(6) Option 19A (6)(a) with May 2024 Draft.

202. See generally May 2024 Draft.

203. See generally May 2024 Draft.

204. Declaration of Alma Alta, art. 10.

CHAPTER TEN

RACE AND POLITICS IN INTERNATIONAL CRIMINAL LAW
Case Studies from the Arab World

WADIE E. SAID

The images are indelible and searing. Former Iraqi President Saddam Hussein, looking disheveled and disoriented, being captured by American forces in late 2003, only to be executed three years later as representatives of the Iraqi state look on as he is hanged.[1] The chaotic scenes of destruction in Beirut, in the aftermath of the February 2005 bombing of former Prime Minister Rafik al-Hariri's motorcade, which killed him and several others.[2] The reports and pictures of destroyed villages in Darfur in the early 2000s, the result of Sudanese state forces and affiliated militias attacking local rebels in a struggle over control of the land.[3] All three of these scenarios, however disparate, produced criminal prosecutions of a transnational/political nature, geared at holding accountable the architects of the violence noted above.

However, attempting to actually hold accountable perpetrators of politically motivated atrocities for their crimes is a difficult enough proposition in the abstract. When the accused are leaders or high officials of sovereign states, usually only extraordinary circumstances justify or allow for the prosecution of such individuals, as the prospect of head of state immunity or immunity for official acts looms as a significant barrier to accountability. In the modern Arab world, this proposition remains true even if the *victim* of a political assassination is a former high-ranking government official. This chapter explores the three recent examples from the Arab world of efforts to prosecute individuals for their roles in large-scale politically motivated crimes, using principles of international criminal law or human rights law as a basis for liability. The examples discussed here are the Special

Iraqi Criminal Tribunal (SICT), designed to prosecute the former leaders of Iraq, chief among them the deposed president Saddam Hussein;[4] the Special Tribunal for Lebanon (STL), which was established in contentious circumstances to try those responsible for the killing of al-Hariri in February 2005;[5] and the arrest warrant and indictment of former Sudanese President Omar al-Bashir issued by the International Criminal Court in 2009, based on suspected crimes committed by Sudanese forces in the region of Darfur.[6]

The common thread between these disparate attempts at securing some form of justice for the victims is their locus in the Arab world, and the corresponding Arab identity of the suspects. Most directly, in the first half of the twentieth century, several American federal courts considered the question of whether people from the Middle East were, in fact, legally "white," so as to qualify for naturalization in the United States. In the words of John Tehranian, the result was that they were "generally deemed white by law—but just barely," adding that despite this legal categorization, "their racial status remained open to contestation."[7] While the phenomenon of racializing Arabs as unthinking and inveterate terrorists in the modern era has long been understood,[8] more recently Arab identity has been subsumed into a larger construct of Muslim as terrorist, or what Sahar Aziz calls "the racial Muslim."[9] Drawing on Mahmood Mamdani's construct of "good Muslim, bad Muslim," Aziz reasons that the more a Muslim is associated with Western or American interests, the less likely they are to be racialized as terrorists, and vice versa.[10] In light of these dynamics concerning the fluidity of Arab racial status, and the fact that impartiality is impossible in such circumstances, the efforts discussed here to force criminal prosecution as a solution in the face of deep-seated problems have persevered precisely because they serve American interests in the region. When viewed in light of the racially ambiguous construct of Arab identity, however, as well as the impossibility of proper accountability in a politically fractious and contested region, these legal efforts were always bound to fail.

The result is one in which an outside power, rather than the local populations, dictates the role that legal accountability plays, not in the service of rebuilding societies and bringing bad actors to justice, but for larger geopolitical objectives. Promoting those objectives is furthered by the presence of local actors willing to align themselves with American interests, using the formal mechanisms of law and accountability, thereby imbuing the process with an unfounded sense of legitimacy. Additionally, this result is masked by the message that because Arabs are somehow incapable of holding themselves accountable, they need outside help, even if that help takes the form of prosecutions that leave a legacy that is negative in almost every way. Throughout the varied tribunals, the three prosecutorial efforts examined here represent efforts to force through a kind of victor's justice, unrelated to any larger political project of reconciliation or turning the page, and unmoored from the standard procedural protections the accused in a criminal prosecution should enjoy. This chapter reviews and reflects on each of the three examples noted above in turn.

The charges in the first trial of the SICT stemmed from a 1982 incident in the Iraqi city of Dujail, where a failed assassination attempt on Hussein's life prompted a massive backlash by state forces.[11] Hundreds of the town's residents were detained and tortured, and ultimately close to 160 of them were extrajudicially killed at the hands of the regime in what can only be described as a reprisal.[12] Without wishing to minimize the horrible nature of the detentions, torture, and killings in the wake of this incident, it can hardly be characterized as among the worst, or most notorious, of the Hussein government's crimes against its own people, or for that matter, the peoples of the region. The focus on the Dujail incident denies the possibility of a full accounting of the Hussein regime's excesses, which cover the use of chemical weapons in the 1980–88 Iran–Iraq War, the 1988 gassing of Iraqi Kurds during what became known as the Anfal campaign, and finally the 1990–91 invasion and occupation of Kuwait.[13] Conveniently, in the case of the first two examples, Iraq received large amounts of military hardware and political support during the 1980s from the United States, which accordingly reaped the benefit of not having its own role examined in a criminal tribunal it helped design, one which avoided accounting for the Hussein regime's many crimes over the nearly two and a half decades of its rule.[14] After all, the genesis of the SICT was an earlier adjudicative body called the Iraqi Special Tribunal (IST), which was created by a decree of the Coalition Provisional Authority (CPA)—the entity created by the American-led occupying powers to rule over Iraq after the 2003 invasion—in December 2003, just prior to the capture of Saddam Hussein.[15] The CPA had conceived of a special Iraqi criminal court, as opposed to an international or hybrid tribunal, to serve as the ostensible empowering embodiment of a sovereign state exercising its right to pursue accountability for crimes of international dimension on its soil.[16] Thus, accountability for any crimes Iraqi forces committed in Iran or Kuwait were presumably covered by IST's terms, in theory at least.[17] While the SICT replaced the IST in August 2005, primarily because of the latter's questionable legitimacy as the brainchild of the occupying authorities, it retained almost all the IST's features, so the link to the American military could never truly be erased.[18] In actuality, the American government prioritized Hussein's prosecution to the point where it spent hundreds of millions of dollars to make it a reality.[19] In an effort to eschew an international or alternate site tribunal, U.S. officials helped draft the statutes that ensured his trial on charges of genocide, war crimes, and crimes against humanity, crimes that did not previously exist in Iraqi law.[20]

The critical link to the American occupation forces was borne out by the fact that the prosecution proceeded in the shadow of a contentious policy of "de-Baathification," that is, the removal of members of Hussein's ruling Baath Party from positions of influence and governance, with the goal of denying the party the opportunity to return to power.[21] De-Baathification was so central to the CPA's work that the first two orders the ruling authority issued in May 2003 laid out its broad parameters, the implementation of which would be controversial, difficult to implement, and convoluted. Even these first two orders were followed by a host of others, as well as the establishment of an Iraqi commission on the implementation of de-Baathification.[22] It was particularly relevant to the prosecution of Saddam Hussein and his fellow defendants, as being trained as a judge in Iraq during the long years of Baath Party rule required membership in the party.[23] The specter of de-Baathification would loom large throughout the SICT's proceedings during the Dujail trial; in July 2005, several of its administrative staff were dismissed on that basis.[24] More critically, the Iraqi de-Baathification commission replaced presiding judge Said Al-Hammashi in January 2006, due to his perceived independence and insistence on a fair legal process. Al-Hammashi had only just replaced the previous presiding judge, Rizgar Mohammed Amin, who had resigned as a result of public criticism that he exhibited leniency toward Hussein.[25] Finally, a last-minute October 2006 shuffle in the composition of the tribunal's judges initiated by the de-Baathification committee just prior to the issuance of the verdict in the Dujail prosecution ensured that Hussein would receive the death penalty.[26]

The tribunal was marked by other improprieties, such as lack of defense access to key documentation and witness statements, the absence of the right to consult with counsel, and the inability to properly confront prosecution witnesses on the stand.[27] The shadow of U.S. occupation loomed large in practical terms as well, as the prosecution took place in an Iraq effectively ruled by the American military, which also exercised custody over the Iraqi defendants.[28] The SICT itself had depended on American advisers and financing to keep functioning properly, due to a dearth of qualified staff to run such an institution.[29] Accordingly, the SICT's legitimacy and ability to deliver impartial justice were deeply affected. Perhaps most chilling of all were the repeated attacks on defense counsel, with at least three lawyers—including one of Hussein's own lawyers—killed by armed Iraqi elements, thereby raising the very apt question of whether the trials should have even been held in Iraq under such conditions.[30]

With a guilty verdict and death sentence issued in the Dujail prosecution on November 5, 2006, Saddam Hussein was executed on December 30 that same year in a televised spectacle that featured his domestic Iraqi political opponents jeering him before his hanging.[31] Less than two months had elapsed between the sentence and its imposition, an impossibly short time if one is looking for certainty and clarity in what is the most irreversible of criminal penalties, especially as the right to appeal a criminal conviction and sentence militates against such haste. Numerous leading Iraqi political figures had all but guaranteed his execution, with several calling for it without the need for any type of trial or judicial process.[32] His prosecution had resolved very little, other than to spare the blushes of those foreign powers—the United States, Germany, the Gulf countries—that may have been implicated in Iraqi chemical warfare and aggression against Iran and Iraq's own Kurdish population. Otherwise, it helped send Iraq down the lane of civil war and sectarian conflict. Presently, Iraq remains riven by political dysfunction and divided between several armed groupings, rendering the security and well-being of its citizens illusory. The rule of law does not exist, especially in criminal cases with a political bent, as the death penalty is meted out liberally and with minimal due process.[33]

While Saddam Hussein and his regime's leading figures were hardly sympathetic characters, consider what his prosecution signifies based on its details. The world's preeminent power took complete control of a sovereign nation's legislative and judicial processes to deliver a show trial of the paradigmatic figure of the Arab dictator, a kind of stereotypical precursor to Mamdani's "bad Muslim." To do so, it imported high concepts of international law—geared to protect the most vulnerable among us from the depredations of violent regimes—into domestic law, yet it did not want any international actors outside its control becoming involved with trying former Iraqi political figures. As representatives of the quintessential Arab dictatorial regime, Hussein and his fellow defendants did not really engender much sympathy on a symbolic level, and the evidence and nature of their crimes put paid to any notion of their actual innocence. But in the wake of the now-discredited 2003 American invasion of Iraq, such a manipulated and vengeful prosecution could only have been allowed to happen in this prominent member state of the Arab world, whose natural resources are of key interest to outside powers, even if its people's rights are not.

The STL faced a similar series of circumstances, in that it was set up to establish responsibility for al-Hariri's killing in a divided and geostrategically important region, where American interests were well-known. But from the outset, establishing a tribunal to try the perpetrators of the bombing was a fraught exercise. As an initial matter, Syria had maintained military control of much of Lebanon from 1976 on and, as a political opponent of al-Hariri, was the initial suspect behind his death. Indeed, the killing was a prime catalyst in Syria's eventual withdrawal from Lebanon shortly thereafter. The UN Security Council immediately condemned the killing and called it a terrorist act. But the initial UN-commissioned report into the killing was marred by procedural irregularities and took a clear position that Syria was responsible, which suggested political bias more than access to actionable evidence. When, in 2006, the UN Security Council passed a resolution establishing an international tribunal for Lebanon, a court whose goal was to try only those responsible for the attack on al-Hariri, it was in response to a request by the Lebanese prime minister, an ally of the United States. As Lebanon was divided politically, its ratification of what eventually became the STL occurred in dubious circumstances that probably violated its own constitution: the prime minister favored the STL, whereas the president and speaker of Parliament—more closely aligned with Syria—did not.[34]

While the Lebanese authorities had initially detained four generals viewed as close to the Syrian regime in August 2005 in connection with the investigation of the killing, those generals were ultimately cleared of involvement and released in 2009.[35] In 2011, the STL indicted the only suspects it would ever formally charge for killing al-Hariri: five individuals identified as members of the Lebanese political and military organization Hezbollah.[36] Syria and its high officials were no longer suspected. The only problem was that the STL was created as a hybrid court—it had a mix of international and Lebanese judges, who were to apply Lebanese law—that was located in the Netherlands, thereby complicating compliance with its directives in Lebanon itself.[37] Indeed, Hezbollah—possibly the most powerful Lebanese political group and certainly the country's most effective military force—refused to make any of the accused available to the court. Eventually, the STL decided to try them in absentia, a questionable decision to say the least.[38]

In the meantime, the STL broke new legal ground, albeit in a controversial manner. In February 2011, shortly after the first indictments were issued, the Appeals Chamber of the STL issued an interlocutory decision declaring that there existed a customary crime of international terrorism, and that the tribunal could apply it against the defendants via domestic Lebanese criminal law dealing with terrorism offenses.[39] As it is well-known that there is no internationally agreed upon definition of terrorism, this ruling could have been the fortuitous result of the main proponent of the notion that there is such a customary law being the president of the STL Appeals Chamber, the late Italian jurist Antonio Cassese.[40] In a trenchant critique of the opinion, Ben Saul lays out its problematic reasoning and effect.[41] As an initial matter, he notes that *"there simply is no crime of transnational terrorism in customary international law."*[42] Further, he writes that the Appeals Chamber's opinion

> is not an instance of the ordinary kind of incremental judicial activism that necessarily tailors the law to novel circumstances. Rather, it is an example of a judiciary transforming itself into a global legislature, creating entirely new law and exceeding the accepted bounds of the judicial function. In a fit of disguised legislative activism, it invented a new and *post facto* international criminal liability for terrorism, resulting in the radical expansion of liability under Lebanese criminal law as it was understood in 2005.[43]

While Saul's critique is both accurate and to the point, the Appeals Chamber's opinion had a sense of inevitability about it. The STL bills itself as "the first tribunal of international character to prosecute terrorist crimes" and needed the requisite juridical framework to make that claim, regardless of how weak and far-reaching its underlying legal reasoning.[44] The key question of why this particular crime—the killing of al-Hariri, a critical Lebanese ally of the United States, France, and Saudi Arabia—was prosecuted in this way, out of all others in Lebanon, a country that has seen a disproportionate number of politically motivated killings over the past fifty years, with hardly anyone of note being held accountable, remains unanswered.[45] Put another way, of what benefit is it to Lebanon, which is still suffering from the unresolved tensions of the civil war period (1975–90), all the while lurching from one extreme political and economic crisis to another, to have such a tribunal purporting to settle customary international law on terrorism?

There is also the matter of terrorism and its association in the public consciousness with Arabs and Muslims, a phenomenon most pronounced in the United States, but one that has spread to the realm of the UN as well. Having the STL declare a customary international law prohibition on terrorism, which it then defines for the first time ever in an international or hybrid tribunal, allows it to deploy the law against one of the paradigmatic terrorist organizations in the eyes of the United States and most of Europe: Hezbollah. That the STL initially proceeded on a theory that the Syrian government was responsible for the al-Hariri killing and then changed course to point the finger at operatives of Hezbollah may be a mere coincidence, but consider the facts from a geopolitical perspective. Blaming Syria for the killing helped accomplish a major policy goal of the United States and its Lebanese allies when it led to Syrian withdrawal from Lebanon. With Syrian forces gone, there was no further political need to prosecute any Syrian government operatives, who were unlikely to ever be handed over for trial in any event. Shifting the focus to Hezbollah reifies the notion of the Arab and Muslim group as the model terrorist, even in the eyes of local Middle Eastern actors and a quasi-international tribunal, which has given its imprimatur to this branding. The organization had long been deemed terrorist by the United States—it was on the first list of designated Foreign Terrorist Organizations in 1997 and has remained there ever since—and many of its European allies.[46] Further, that the STL—rooted in an Arab country with a large Muslim population—would tackle the issue of terrorism as a criminal matter is also curious when judged in the light of recent international criminal prosecutorial efforts. For example, the founding statute of the International Criminal Court does not mention a crime of terrorism, nor do the statutes of the International Criminal Tribunal for the Former Yugoslavia or the International Criminal Tribunal for Rwanda.[47] The closest analogue occurs in the statute of the Special Court for Sierra Leone, which mentions "acts of terror" as a criminal offense, without much further definition, but does not reference "terrorism" as a crime under international law.[48] This is of course not to suggest that international criminal law serves as an unassailable standard, but rather to show how the application of a supposed international crime of terrorism in the Arab/Muslim context helps feed the construct that associates those populations with terrorism more generally.

In an era of Islamophobia and deep political tensions in the Middle East, this state of affairs does not inspire confidence in the impartiality or viability of the STL. It also sends a similar message to that of the SICT: Arab defendants, whether dictators or terrorist organizations, need to be punished, with due process and impartiality rendered secondary concerns. The crimes tried in both tribunals occurred in the Arab world and featured Arab victims, admittedly. The concerns in the Dujail prosecution were not so much those of guilt or innocence, but of a rushed and sloppy process riddled with legal errors and outside interference that was designed to avoid a fuller accounting of political crimes in the wake of an illegal American occupation. In the STL context, the issue of guilt or innocence was far more controversial as a matter of evidence, but limiting the prosecution to one incident with a prominent victim as the only one worth pursuing in a country with legions of victims of politically motivated violence over its recent history strikes a strange chord. In December 2020, at the end of the trial in absentia of the four remaining defendants on charges related to the al-Hariri killing, the STL found one guilty and three not guilty.[49] In March 2022, two of the defendants acquitted at the trial phase had the judgments against them reversed and were convicted on all counts by the Appeals Chamber.[50] All three were given multiple life sentences. Again, the result aligned with American interests in bringing the prosecution, even as procedural particularities ultimately led to the guilty verdicts. As it is unlikely the convicted defendants will ever be surrendered to the court, the business of the STL is effectively over, with only a symbolic judgment of guilt based on the presentations of the prosecution in a trial in absentia.[51] Even then, that two of three defendants who were ultimately found guilty were acquitted at the trial phase raises serious questions about the nature of the evidence against them. Regardless, as far as making the point about who and what represents terrorists and terrorist groups, Arab Muslims were deployed in the key roles, which follow a depressingly familiar script.

The final example of efforts to interpolate international criminal prosecution in the context of an Arab country involves the issuance of an arrest warrant in 2009 by the ICC for Sudanese President Omar al-Bashir based on alleged crimes he committed in the Darfur region of the country.[52] The charges ultimately included war crimes, crimes against humanity, and genocide against several groups resident in Darfur—the Fur, Masalit, and Zaghawa—and constituted the first instance of the ICC indicting a sitting head of state.[53] Efforts to apprehend al-Bashir over the years were hampered by the fact that when he was president, other countries in the African Union and the Arab world to which he traveled refused to arrest him and send him to the Hague, at least in part because they feared a similar fate for their leaders were they to be indicted by the ICC. After he was deposed from the presidency in 2019, the various subsequent incarnations of the Sudanese government have pledged to send him to the Hague for trial, although that has yet to occur. The current civil conflict in Sudan only makes his fate that much more murky.

Al-Bashir, who was indicted along with a small number of other officials believed responsible for the violence in the region, represents three overlapping phenomena when it comes to the issue of international law and race. The first is the framing of the conflict in Darfur as between "Arab," represented by both the Sudanese government and local residents and their affiliated militias, and "African," represented primarily by the Fur, Masalit, and Zaghawa, with the Arab as tormentor of the African.[54] The second involves the larger dynamic of the ICC's previously exclusive practice of only indicting and prosecuting individuals from the African continent.[55] Synthesizing much of the recent criticism of the ICC's prosecutorial practices, Rachel López argues that "the near exclusive focus on Black defendants is the result of rules that systematically heighten Black guilt, while minimizing White guilt."[56] In other words, as Kamari Clarke notes, visual representation matters in efforts at accountability: "if the 'victim' looks like a Holocaust survivor, then 'victims' of colonial violence cannot be recognized as they are; if the 'perpetrator' looks like a black African man implicated in mass rape or torture, then particular North American or European heads of state may not look like perpetrators from their desks."[57] The ICC pursues defendants like al-Bashir, while rarely considering the responsibility of white actors for crimes of an international nature, with the arrest warrant issued by the ICC against Russian President Vladimir Putin and Russia's commissioner for children's rights in 2023 and the more recent arrest warrants against Israeli Prime Minister Benjamin Netanyahu and former Defense Minister Yoav Gallant in 2024 exceptions to this rule.[58] Al-Bashir thus occupies a role as both African and Arab; as an African, he is part of the nearly exclusive class of individuals who have been formally charged by the ICC, and as an Arab, he was the leader of a violent effort to repress and dispossess Africans. He is simultaneously the worst of Arab and African combined, even as the Darfur criminal allegations proclaim that those two identities are at war with each other. Finally, involving the ICC distinguishes the al-Bashir prosecution from the SICT and STL in that local actors—Iraqi and Lebanese, respectively—played a large role in those tribunals. ICC prosecution marginalizes the role of the Sudanese population in holding accountable their former leader, whereas the two earlier efforts relied heavily on the presence of local actors as judges and lawyers to run their course. The symbolism is fraught; where the local, non-African Arab is allowed to play a central role in the prosecution in Iraq and Lebanon, the same cannot be said of the Arab located in Africa, who can only serve as a witness in a prosecution where none of the officials are from Sudan and which is located in Europe. African-ness is therefore a kind of hindrance to local efforts at accountability in a way that Arab identity in the Middle East is not. In each example, however, the result demonstrates the contrived and opportunistic role outside actors play in utilizing principles of criminal law accountability for their own interests. In the Iraqi and Lebanese contexts, the creation of special tribunals reflects the strategic calculations of foreign powers such as the United States and France, among others. In the Sudanese context, the interests of foreign powers are less direct and—in combination with the court's near-exclusive focus on African defendants—ICC prosecution seems even more clear in its message about what process an African defendant is due.

The framing of Darfur as Arab vs. African distorts the nature of the conflict in the region and assumes clear racial or ethnic differences that do not necessarily exist.[59] Rather than a racially driven confrontation between the bad Arab (as aggressor) and innocent African (as victim), a more accurate description may be that of a contest over scarce natural resources between settled farmers and nomadic herders in a region rapidly undergoing desertification.[60] Elsadig Elsheikh posits further that the heavy hand of the Sudanese elite, itself relying on racialized stratifications imposed on the country by British colonialism, makes use of the artificial Arab vs. African construct to pursue its own interests in resource control and cementing power.[61] He further notes that the ICC prosecution was hardly what Sudan would want or require to emerge from decades of military dictatorship, internal repression, and civil war, remarking that it is a solution imposed by external actors without regard to what would benefit the Sudanese people as a whole.[62] Whatever the case may be, the Arab represents the villain in the conflict, much like the Arab-as-terrorist trope from the STL, and the Arab-as-dictator from the SICT. Al-Bashir, like Saddam Hussein in the Iraqi context, does not have clean hands and is certainly not a sympathetic actor. However, his crimes and excesses have not been limited to Darfur, and were probably continuous in the thirty years he held power after overthrowing the elected Sudanese government in 1989. Choosing the Darfur allegations as the sole basis to prosecute him raises questions as to the politicized nature of his prosecution and the Darfur situation more generally, in an echo of the dynamics surrounding the Dujail prosecution. In particular, Mahmoud Mamdani has pointed out that the Ugandan government of President Yoweri Museveni has engaged in large-scale ethnic cleansing in northern Uganda similar to the actions of the Sudanese government in Darfur, but only the leaders of its antagonist—the Lord's Resistance Army—have been indicted by the ICC due to the Ugandan government's being allied with the United States.[63]

It is on this last note that the examples from the Arab world discussed here converge into a more cohesive theme: that of the nonwhite bad Arab whose extraordinary treatment at the hands of the law serves great power interests. The result is politicized justice at its most cynical, with three different tribunals—one a domestic court internalizing international law principles, the second a hybrid extraterritorial court with both Lebanese and foreign judges practicing domestic and international law, and the third the leading global criminal tribunal—producing results that go beyond mere victor's justice to serve as organs for projecting American foreign policy goals. The message of the Arab as dictator/terrorist/racial genocidaire is delivered via flawed legal processes to justify the occupation of Iraq, respond to an attack on its local ally in Lebanon, and punish a leader who has been hostile to the United States. Those are not the only reasons for the respective legal actions, as in at least two of the examples the individuals prosecuted or charged had blood on their hands, but by insisting on politicized justice, we end up with doubt and resentment. Rather than heal Iraq's divisions, the Saddam Hussein verdict and execution fanned the flames of a violent civil war. The STL has done nothing to bring al-Hariri's killers to justice but was certainly viewed as aligned with one side in Lebanon's long-divided society. It remains to be seen what will happen with al-Bashir, but his prosecution will likely not impact Sudan greatly, as it is far more concerned with the troubled transition to civilian rule in the wake of a military determined to hang on to power. Regrettably, the lasting impression of all these prosecutorial efforts is that of the Arab as an unsympathetic figure who gets the justice he (all of those charged are male) deserves.

NOTES

1. Neil MacFarquhar, "Saddam Hussein, Defiant Dictator Who Ruled Iraq with Violence and Fear," *New York Times*, December 30, 2006; Ewan MacAskill and Michael Howard, "How Saddam Died on the Gallows," *The Guardian*, December 31, 2006, https://www.theguardian.com/world/2007/jan/01/iraq.iraqtimeline.

2. "Rafik al-Hariri, Ex-Premier of Lebanon, Dies at 60," *New York Times*, February 15, 2005.

3. Lydia Polgreen, "Army Accused of Razing Darfur Town," *New York Times*, October 9, 2007.

4. Human Rights Watch, "The Former Iraqi Government on Trial," October 16, 2005, https://www.hrw.org/legacy/backgrounder/mena/iraq1005/iraq1005.pdf.

5. "The Special Tribunal for Lebanon website," accessed February 6, 2023, https://www.stl-tsl.org/en.

6. "Al Bashir Case," *International Criminal Court*, accessed February 6, 2023, https://www.icc-cpi.int/darfur/albashir.

7. John Tehranian, *Whitewashed: America's Invisible Middle Eastern Minority* (New York: NYU Press, 2009), 63. The conclusion that peoples from the Middle East are white for legal purposes contrasts with Supreme Court decisions—also from the first half of the twentieth century—holding that the Japanese and people from the Indian subcontinent are not white, and thus not eligible to naturalize, thereby signifying the illogical and socially constructed nature of race as a legal category. Devon Carbado, "Yellow by Law: The Story of Ozawa v. United States," in *Race Law Stories*, ed. Rachel F. Moran and Devon Wayne Carbado (Los Angeles: Foundation Press, 2008), 224–35.

8. Edward W. Said, "The Essential Terrorist," review of *Terrorism: How the West Can Win*, ed. Benjamin Netanyahu, *The Nation*, June 14, 1986, https://www.thenation.com/article/archive/essential-terrorist/; Susan M. Akram and Kevin R. Johnson, "Race and Civil Rights Pre-September 11, 2001: The Targeting of Arabs and Muslims," in *Civil Rights in Peril: The Targeting of Arabs and Muslims*, ed. Elaine C. Hagopian (London: Pluto

Press, 2004), 18; Leti Volpp, "The Citizen and the Terrorist," *University of California, Los Angeles, Law Review* 49, no. 5 (June 2002): 1575–76.

9. Sahar F. Aziz, *The Racial Muslim: When Racism Quashes Religious Freedom* (California: University of California Press, 2021), 17.

10. Aziz, *The Racial Muslim*, 6 (citing Mahmood Mamdani, *Good Muslim, Bad Muslim: America, the Cold War, and the Roots of Terror* [New York: Harmony Books, 2004]).

11. Human Rights Watch, "The Former Iraqi Government on Trial," 6.

12. John F. Burns, "A Town That Bled Under Hussein Hails His Trial," *New York Times*, July 3, 2005.

13. Arshin Adib-Moghaddam, "The Whole Range of Saddam's War Crimes," *Middle East Research and Information Project*, Summer 2006, https://merip.org/2006/06/the-whole-range-of-saddam-husseins-war-crimes/.

14. Adib-Moghaddam, "The Whole Range of Saddam's War Crimes."

15. Human Rights Watch, "The Former Iraqi Government on Trial," 3.

16. Human Rights Watch, "Memorandum to the Iraqi Governing Council on 'The Statute of the Special Iraqi Tribunal,'" December 2003, https://www.hrw.org/legacy/backgrounder/mena/iraq121703.htm.

17. Human Rights Watch, "Memorandum to the Iraqi Governing Council."

18. Human Rights Watch, "The Former Iraqi Government on Trial," 4, 17–18.

19. Ellen Knickmeyer, "Hussein Halts Trial Again, Setting Off Wave of Criticism," *Washington Post*, January 25, 2006.

20. Daoud Khairallah, "The Hariri and Saddam Tribunals: Two Expressions of Tortured Justice," *Contemporary Arab Affairs* 1, no. 4 (2008): 602–3.

21. Miranda Sissons and Abdulrazzaq al-Saiedi, *A Bitter Legacy: Lessons of De-Baathification in Iraq* (New York: International Center for Transitional Justice, March 2013), 9, https://www.ictj.org/sites/default/files/ICTJ-Report-Iraq-De-Baathification-2013-ENG.pdf.

22. Sissons and al-Saiedi, *A Bitter Legacy*, 9–14.

23. Sissons and al-Saiedi, *A Bitter Legacy*, 16–17.

24. Sissons and al-Saiedi, *A Bitter Legacy*, 16–17.

25. Sissons and al-Saiedi, *A Bitter Legacy*, 16–17.

26. Sissons and al-Saiedi, *A Bitter Legacy*, 16–17.

27. United Nations Office of the High Commissioner for Human Rights, "Tragic Mistakes in the Trial and Execution of Saddam Hussein Must Not Be Repeated," January 3, 2007, https://www.ohchr.org/en/statements/2009/10/tragic-mistakes-made-trial-and-execution-saddam-hussein-must-not-be-repeated.

28. Knickmeyer, "Hussein Halts Trial Again, Setting Off Wave of Criticism."

29. Knickmeyer, "Hussein Halts Trial Again, Setting Off Wave of Criticism."

30. John F. Burns and Christine Hauser, "Third Lawyer in Hussein Trial Is Killed," *New York Times*, June 21, 2006.

31. MacAskill and Howard, "How Saddam Died on the Gallows."

32. United Nations Office of the High Commissioner for Human Rights, "Tragic Mistakes in the Trial and Execution of Saddam Hussein Must Not Be Repeated."

33. Amnesty International, "Mass Execution of 21 Individuals Is an Outrage," news release, November 17, 2020, https://www.amnesty.org/en/latest/press-release/2020/11/iraq-mass-execution-of-21-individuals-is-an-outrage/.

34. The statements in this paragraph are derived from Khairallah, "The Hariri and Saddam Tribunals: Two Expressions of Tortured Justice," 590–93.

35. Ian Black, "Lebanese Generals Held Over Rafiq al-Hariri Killing to Be Released," *The Guardian*, April 29, 2009, https://www.theguardian.com/world/2009/apr/29/rafiq-hariri-suspects-release.

36. Anne Barnard and Sewell Chan, "Mustafa Badreddine, Hezbollah Military Commander, Is Killed in Syria," *New York Times*, May 13, 2016.

37. Special Tribunal for Lebanon, "About the STL," accessed February 6, 2023, https://www.stl-tsl.org/en/about-the-stl.

38. Special Tribunal for Lebanon, "The Cases," accessed February 6, 2023, https://www.stl-tsl.org/en/the-cases/stl-11-01/accused.

39. UN Special Tribunal for Lebanon (Appeals Chamber), "Conspiracy, Homicide, Perpetration, Cumulative Charging, STL-11-01/I," February 16, 2011, Interlocutory Decision on the Applicable Law: Terrorism.

40. Ben Saul, "Legislating from a Radical Hague: The United Nations Special Tribunal for Lebanon Invents an International Crime of Transnational Terrorism," *Leiden Journal of International Law* 24, no. 3 (2011): 678 ("The majority of states and scholars do not recognize a customary crime of terrorism, with the prominent exception of one eminent jurist, Antonio Cassese, who happened to be President of the Appeals Chamber").

41. Saul, "Legislating from a Radical Hague," 678.

42. Saul, "Legislating from a Radical Hague," 678 (emphasis in original).

43. Saul, "Legislating from a Radical Hague," 678.

44. Special Tribunal for Lebanon, archived at https://exhibits.stanford.edu/virtual-tribunals/catalog/nb441sq7196; for more about Stanford's acquisition of the STL collection, see https://library.stanford.edu/news/virtual-tribunals-debuts-special-tribunal-lebanon-collection.

45. For example, the perpetrators of some of the greatest atrocities of the Lebanese civil war, such as the 1982 Sabra and Shatila massacres of Palestinian refugees by members of the Phalange militia, are well-known and at large, yet have never faced any type of accountability for their crimes. Nadim Houry, "Lebanon's Silence Over Sabra and Shatila Is Shameful," Human Rights Watch, September 18, 2015, https://www.hrw.org/news/2015/09/18/lebanons-silence-over-sabra-and-shatila-shameful (noting that the end of the civil war brought with it a general amnesty to all participants in the hostilities).

46. United States Department of State, "Foreign Terrorist Organizations," accessed February 6, 2023, https://www.state.gov/foreign-terrorist-organizations; Kali Robinson, "What is Hezbollah?," *Council on Foreign Relations*, May 25, 2022, https://www.cfr.org/backgrounder/what-hezbollah.

47. International Criminal Court, "Rome Statute of the International Criminal Court," July 17, 1998, https://www.icc-cpi.int/sites/default/files/RS-Eng.pdf; United Nations, "Updated Statute of the International Criminal Tribunal for the Former Yugoslavia," May 2009, https://www.icty.org/x/file/Legal%20Library/Statute/statute_sept09_en.pdf; United Nations, "Updated Statute of the International Criminal Tribunal for the Prosecution of Persons Responsible for Genocide and Other Serious Violations of International Humanitarian Law Committed in the Territory of Rwanda and Rwandan Citizens Responsible for Genocide and Other Such Violations Committed in the Territory of Neighbouring States, between 1 January 1994 and 31 December 1994,"

Security Council Resolution 955, https://www.ohchr.org/en/instruments-mechanisms/instruments/statute-international-criminal-tribunal-prosecution-persons.

48. Residual Special Court for Sierra Leone, "Statute of the Special Court of Sierra Leone," accessed February 6, 2023, http://www.rscsl.org/Documents/scsl-statute.pdf.

49. Special Tribunal for Lebanon, "Key Developments (Case Timeline)," accessed February 6, 2023, https://www.stl-tsl.org/en/the-cases/stl-11-01/key-developments.

50. Special Tribunal for Lebanon, "Key Developments (Case Timeline)."

51. Special Tribunal for Lebanon, "Key Developments (Case Timeline)." The STL also attempted to sanction two Lebanese newspapers for publishing information about witnesses covered by the tribunal's order of confidentiality; while one action was dismissed, *al-Akhbar* newspaper and its editor-in-chief Ibrahim al-Amin were assessed fines for violating the court's rules of disclosure. These secondary actions constituted an unusual attempt by an extraterritorial hybrid court to impose penalties on Lebanese newspapers operating locally for publishing information that, though subject to the STL's confidentiality order, was clearly in the public interest. Additionally, there is the question of whether accountability for al-Hariri's killing was really the STL's main, or only, goal. In an article from October 2024, written as the Israeli invasion of Lebanon was in its initial phases, criminal justice expert and legal scholar Omar Nashabe, who served as a consultant to the STL's defense bar, wrote an article detailing how the discovery process in the STL worked. He noted that in the investigatory phase that lasted from 2008 to 2012, the shift from Syrian to Hezbollah suspects allowed the prosecutor's office to gather exhaustive amounts of information on the structure of Hezbollah and the identity of many of its members, which he says was then passed via American channels to the Israeli authorities, who exploited that information in armed hostilities with Hezbollah. Omar Nashabe, "What Does the International Court Have to do With the Assassination of Hezbollah Leaders?," *The Public Source*, October 8, 2024, https://thepublicsource.org/blog/lebanon-front/assassination-hezbollah-leaders.

52. "Al Bashir Case."

53. "Al Bashir Case."

54. Scott Anderson, "How Did Darfur Happen?," *New York Times*, October 17, 2004.

55. Adjoa Assan, "The ICC and Africa," *Australian Institute of International Affairs*, July 2, 2021, https://www.internationalaffairs.org.au/resource/the-icc-and-africa/.

56. Rachel López, "Black Guilt, White Guilt at the International Criminal Court," *Race and National Security* (October 6, 2022): 13, https://papers.ssrn.com/sol3/papers.cfm?abstract_id=4237581.

57. Kamari Maxine Clarke, *Affective Justice: The International Criminal Court and the Pan-Africanist Pushback* (North Carolina: Duke University Press, 2019), 26.

58. Peter Beaumont, "What Does the ICC Arrest Warrant for Vladimir Putin Mean in Reality?," *The Guardian*, March 17, 2023, https://www.theguardian.com/world/2023/mar/17/icc-arrest-warrant-vladimir-putin-explainer; Tim Lister, "Netanyahu Arrest Warrant Tests Western Commitment to International Law," *CNN*, Dec. 4, 2024, https://www.cnn.com/2024/12/04/middleeast/icc-arrest-warrants-putin-netanyahu-analysis-intl/index.html (noting the fact that several Western countries, chief among them the United States, have refused to honor the arrest warrants were Netanyahu or Gallant to visit their territories).

59. Alex de Waal, "Who are the Darfurians? Arab and African Identities, Violence and External Engagement," *African Affairs* 104, no. 415 (2005): 181.

60. Mahmood Mamdani, "The Politics of Naming: Genocide, Civil War, Insurgency," *London Review of Books*, March 8, 2007, https://www.lrb.co.uk/the-paper/v29/n05/mahmood-mamdani/the-politics-of-naming-genocide-civil-war-insurgency.

61. Elsadig Elsheikh, "Sudan and the International Criminal Court Revisited: The Dilemma of Retributive Justice and the Question of 'Responsibility to Protect,'" *Othering and Belonging Institute*, August 18, 2015, https://belonging.berkeley.edu/sudan-and-international-criminal-court-revisited-dilemma-retributive-justice-and-question.

62. Elsheikh, "Sudan and the International Criminal Court Revisited."

63. Howard W. French, "The Darfur the West Isn't Recognizing as it Moralizes About the Region," *New York Times*, March 29, 2009.

CHAPTER ELEVEN

UKRAINIAN RACIAL CONTRACTING AND THE GEOPOLITICS OF WELCOME IN INTERNATIONAL REFUGEE LAW

Marissa Jackson Sow[*]

As coverage of Ukraine's defensive efforts against Russia's 2022 invasion overtook mass and social media, two disturbing phenomena quickly became apparent. The first was the overt premising of support for Ukraine and its people upon Ukrainian Whiteness.[1] The second emerged as video footage of Ukrainians violently stopping non-White residents of Ukraine from boarding trains out of Ukraine.[2] As Ukrainians tried to flee for their lives, seeking safety from Russian missiles in neighboring Eastern European countries, Ukrainian officials used race as a method for sorting who was eligible for escape and who was not: video footage displayed Ukrainian officials using brutal physical force to exclude people of African, Caribbean, Arab, and other people of color from trains out of the country—claiming that the convoys were only meant for White women and children.[3] These phenomena spoke volumes—and in overtly racial terms—concerning who was entitled to welcome, and who was not.

The United Nations promotes the idea that all people have equal human rights[4] and that all nations have an equal right to self-determination under international law.[5] Yet, as the Ukrainian example shows, not all people, and not all states, are treated equally within the international law regime. At the time of the initial development of the contemporary international law, European settler colonialism was an actuality, and White supremacist ideology—which characterized Black, Asian, and Indigenous peoples as uncivilized barbarians in need of European tutelage—fueled colonial order and postcolonial law.[6]

Unfortunately, colonialism still exists;[7] moreover, the racialized vision of the world promulgated by Enlightenment-era and Early Modern European philosophers for the world remains reflected in every aspect of the development of the contemporary global legal and institutional orders.[8] Tellingly, a colonial-era Trusteeship Council Chamber was quite literally constructed into the United Nations' headquarters and remains in existence under the same name.[9] Because the system of settler colonialism depended upon racial formations for its survival, the United Nations' investments in colonialism (the formal control and exploitation of Global Southern nations and territories by European and North American nations) and neocolonialism (the continued exercise of political, legal, economic, and other pressures on formerly colonized nations by former colonial powers and emerging geopolitical powers) are inherently racialized, as are the terms of the social contract justifying the UN's very existence.

In the decades since the UN's establishment, White-led Western state parties to the United Nations have systematically resisted efforts at decolonization of colonized territories,[10] substantive racial justice programs,[11] and decolonial structural economic transformation.[12] This perspective on such resistance by Western states relies upon claims that the colonial powers are simply invested in maintaining an extant geopolitical hegemony, which positions the United States, Canada, and European allied states like Ukraine—known within the United Nations system as the Western European and Others Group (WEOG)—in a position of permanent economic, military, and political dominance over the rest of the world[13]—and for the world's good. However, a closer look at the geopolitical solidarity between Western states reveals that race, and not geography, is what binds them and their interests together.[14] Their consistent opposition to efforts to restructure the international law and order by neocolonial powers and their allies in the face of the much larger coalition of Black, Brown, and Indigenous postcolonial states seeking transformations is microcosmic of just how central race and racialization are to the WEOG bloc's maintenance of geopolitical order, and the role that the international legal regime plays in supporting the racial contract for which the powers have bargained. Colonialism is dependent upon racialization,[15] and fidelity to a colonial—and thus, inherently racist—legal and geopolitical order remains foundational to the substance and practice of international law.[16]

This chapter focuses on the Ukrainian humanitarian crisis as a microcosmic example of the centrality of race and neocoloniality to the interpretation of international norms—and the application of laws—governing refuge and migration. Ukraine's bold use of race as leverage for global support of its defense against the 2022 Russian invasion, and as arbiter of who is deserving of humanitarian protection, has been particularly stunning, and illustrates the lasting influence of colonialism on international law. The willingness of the West to offer refuge to Ukrainians while refusing protection to equally legitimate Black and Brown protection-seekers from the Global South is also impossible to ignore.[17] Western support for Ukraine's defensive war against Russia, and its eagerness to offer welcome—both to Ukrainian refugees and to Ukraine as a fuller member of the European bloc—offers a contemporary example of how, even in the service of ostensibly noble causes, public international law and refugee law in particular ensure that, throughout the global institutional order, Whiteness remains supreme. The disparate treatment of Ukrainian refugees and non-White protection-seekers is only shocking if not considered within the larger context of the racialization of movement facilitated by colonial formations.

The refugee law regime stands as evidence of international law's commitment to a neocolonial order that privileges racial hegemony over justice for protection-seekers.[18] And yet, the insistence upon structuring and manipulating international law to protect people raced as White while excluding from those same protections people raced as non-White may appear to be the manifestation of public international law's commitment to order over a justice-focused application and enforcement of laws,[19] but this also reveals that the binary between justice and order is a false one. Within the international refugee law regime, White supremacist order *is* the standard for justice. Racial contract theory—and specifically, the Whiteness as Contract framework, which identifies Whiteness as a system that guarantees power, privilege, and rights for people raced as White necessarily at the expense of people raced as non-White[20]—makes space for reframing.

This chapter makes a bold claim: that racism and White supremacy in refugee and humanitarian law persist with the support of international law, and not despite it. The chapter describes the stunning disparities between the Western world's reception of Ukraine into the European project, and of Ukrainian refugees, and its indifference and hostility to humanitarian crises in the Global South. It identifies Whiteness as the standard for a right of welcome and non-Whiteness as a state of perpetual exclusion from the protections of international law—including the rights to refugee and free movement.

The chapter identifies racial contracting as a system of laws, institutions, and agreements that, while usually veiled by procedure, structure, and legal substance, has been boldly employed to offer up the right of welcome to Ukraine and Ukrainians because of their Whiteness while simultaneously hardening borders vis-à-vis equally legitimate Black and Brown protection-seekers. Premising legal protection for Ukraine and Ukrainians upon White identity reveals that race is a tacitly understood standard for who is granted the power to govern, the freedom to move, the right of welcome, and access to protection under international law. It also reveals, with equal clarity, who is relegated to the blunt force of exclusion from decision-making authority regarding the laws of refuge, and from refuge itself.

I. UKRAINE AND THE WHITE RIGHT TO PROTECTION

Ukraine's physical exclusion of non-White people from humanitarian protections, along with its contrasting pleas for global empathy and aid because of most Ukrainians' status as White people, were meant to formally establish Ukraine as a White state. As Ukrainian security forces and border guards used physical force to keep African residents from fleeing the Russian invasion in 2022,[21] Ukraine was making clear, race-based assertions about who Ukrainians are and cannot be, with the twin goals of achieving support for its war against Russia and obtaining greater access to the privileges of European identity. Ukrainian officials were employing a twisted iteration of Derrick Bell's interest convergence theory to negotiate Ukraine's Whiteness:[22] in ostensible exchange for their bravery in fighting Russia (and their provision of justification for the United States and its allies to join in that fight), Ukraine expected greater stakeholdership in the White European project, achieving membership in the European Union months after the Russian invasion.[23]

A. NEGOTIATING UKRAINE'S WHITENESS CONTRACT

Pro-Ukraine rhetoric has emphasized Ukrainian Whiteness as unequivocal, and it has revealed a desire by Ukraine and Western powers to fully incorporate Ukraine into the European project. Whiteness was the prerequisite, and pundits offered up Ukrainian Whiteness as justification for their accession to the racial contract and the Racial Superstate. In a televised interview, Ukraine's Deputy Chief Prosecutor stated that "it's very emotional for me because I see European people with blue eyes and blonde hair being killed"[24] despite Ukrainians' significant ethnic and phenotypic diversity.[25] Even more striking was the distinction between them and the people the pundits considered less deserving of protection: as Christians, as White people, as Europeans, they were nothing like Syrians, or Muslims, or Arabs, for whom perpetual misery was to be expected, and somehow, merited.[26] NBC News correspondent Kelly Cobiella summarized Western urgency concerning Ukraine contrasted with hesitancy to assist Middle Eastern victims of global humanitarian crises plainly: "Just to put it bluntly, these are not refugees from Syria. These are refugees from neighboring Ukraine . . . That, quite frankly, is part of it. These are Christians. They're White."[27]

Ukraine's exclusion of Black and Brown people from trains and buses taking Ukrainians to safety outside of Ukraine manifests another racialized Ukrainian expectation: because Ukraine had allowed non-White people to study, work, and live in Ukraine during peacetime, those non-White people should stay in harm's way, or at least wait behind White people in the queue to safety during the war. Black people who arranged their own transportation out of Ukraine reported being physically stalled and even physically assaulted by Ukrainians who did not believe that they should be able to leave Ukraine or enter neighboring European countries.[28] Ironically, Ukrainian forces also actively sought to recruit young African men residing in Africa to fight on behalf of Ukraine during this time, angering African governments and adding insult to the injury to the Afrodescendant people that border officials had deemed unworthy of safety.[29] Of the claims that Ukrainian officials were discriminating against non-White people at the Ukrainian borders, the Ukrainian Ambassador to the United Kingdom made the telling suggestion, "Maybe we will put all foreigners in some other place so they won't be visible . . . And (then) there won't be conflict with Ukrainians trying to flee in the same direction."[30]

Sometimes safety is secured through flight; at other times, it is achieved by staying in place. The disparate experiences of White Ukrainian refugees and non-White people fleeing Ukraine reveal that no matter the path to safety, Whiteness remains safety's price. Having successfully bargained for Whiteness, in exchange for a defensive battle against an antagonizer of the Western global powers, Ukrainians received a universal right of Whiteness: the right of Welcome—and with it, a right to go, come, and stay.[31] Designation as White people guarantees that Ukrainians are legitimately present wherever they find or take themselves—whether as colonizing settlers, as policymakers, as migrants, or as asylum-seekers.

B. BLACK, BROWN, AND PERPETUALLY FOREIGN

The support and welcome that Ukrainians have enjoyed since the Russian invasion has been decidedly selective; other protection-seekers have struggled and failed to obtain refuge or similar levels of popular and rhetorical support if, unlike Ukrainians, they are non-White. The enthusiastic welcome of Ukrainian refugees by states such as the United Kingdom and the United States in 2022 was particularly striking because of both states' policies of refusing admission to, and even deporting, refuge seekers of noticeably darker skin tones, from Global Southern states.[32] Despite public international law's formal embrace of non-discrimination, it systematically constructs Black, Brown, and Indigenous people as barbaric[33] and, therefore, outside of law, as perpetual strangers, and worse, as criminals, or even as human contraband.[34] This is a legacy of the coloniality upon which international law was established. According to Tendayi Achiume, "even though international human rights principles sustain a more cosmopolitan approach to borders, international law as a whole still most faithfully reflects the political theory of liberal nationalists, who defend the sovereign right to exclude as existential."[35] Who is to be excluded, unfortunately, has everything to do with the centrality of race to nation-states' ongoing nation-building projects.

While the United Kingdom was preparing to welcome, and settle, Ukrainian refugees, it contracted with Rwanda, in a deal worth over 140 million British pounds, to remove undesired asylum-seekers (hailing from Africa and Asia) from the United Kingdom to Rwanda.[36] At the same time, the United States' disparate treatment of Haitian and other Caribbean protection-seekers contrasted with that given to Ukrainian protection-seekers was reaching the pinnacle of starkness: Ukrainians attempting to enter the United States via the U.S.–Mexico border in 2022 were granted entry as the Biden administration kept Black and Brown migrants out as per the Trump-era Title 42 public health restrictions, which used the COVID-19 health crisis as justification to avoid granting entry to migrants from certain Central American and Caribbean nations.[37] Immigration and asylum lawyers described the disparate treatment as "mind-blowing."[38] Meanwhile, in the United Kingdom, where the government was extending a warm welcome to Ukrainians,[39] reports emerged that resettled Ukrainians were complaining about being resettled near too many Muslim[40] people and people of color.[41]

The American response to protection-seekers—with Haitians as a notable example—reflects a confluence of somewhat obvious racism and geopolitical machinations.[42] The United States has long been significantly less inclined to recognize political persecution in Haiti and maintains a tradition of disregarding Haitian claims for asylum.[43] As Haitian citizens began fleeing the brutal Duvalier regime in 1972, refugees seeking entry to the United States were systematically arrested, jailed, and expelled. The Carter administration then created an immigration category of "entrants" for Haitian and Cuban refugees, to treat the two groups of protection-seekers more similarly.[44]

The Reagan regime, however, changed the Carter policy, and jailed Haitian refugees who landed in the United States.[45] Moreover, it relied on the Coast Guard to intercept boats of refugees to keep them from reaching American soil in the first instance.[46] Subsequent administrations systematically welcomed Cubans to the United States while diverting HIV-positive Haitian protection-seekers and people related to them[47] to Guantanamo Bay and detaining them there, outside of American legal jurisdiction.[48] On Guantanamo Bay, many refugees slept on the floor and endured other human rights violations—the United States federal government served them rotten food and denied them medical care, for example, and failed to screen the refugees for potential asylum eligibility—opting to simply return them to Haiti once it began to close the Guantanamo Bay camps.[49]

Using public health concerns to veil race and nationality-based discrimination against refugees is an old strategy that, as detailed by Matiangai Sirleaf, is part of colonialism's legacy.[50] Sirleaf contends that concerns about public health are fundamentally concerns about *White* health: "Colonial powers prioritized global health because they wanted to coordinate sufficiently restrictive quarantine regulations that would facilitate the unimpeded expansion of imperial trade without exposing their populations in the mother country to diseases from colonial territories."[51] Long before the blanket travel bans of the COVID-19 era, the Centers for Disease Control labeled Haitians as high risk for HIV infection based on their nationality, and a federal judge[52] had to order the Clinton administration to either treat the refugees or send them to a place where they could receive treatment, deploring the Guantanamo Bay camp as an "HIV prison camp" and "squalid," and ultimately ordering that the Haitian refugees be removed from the camp.[53] Throughout this time period, the US government regularly categorized Haitian refugees as migrants and categorized Cubans as refugees to justify its patterns of welcome and exclusion.[54] Decades later, the summary categorization by Western nations of Black and Brown protection-seekers as undesirable migrants, and not as genuine refugees, persists, as do the developments of legal rules and procedures to exclude them from Western territories.

II. THE REFUGEE LAW REGIME'S RACIAL CONTRACT

Who, then, is the law of refugees meant to serve? Whose human rights are meant to be protected under public international law? The grants of movement and entry to White refugees and denials to Black and Brown refugees replicate the terms of the colonial order—free movement for White people, including movement that involved colonization and territorial theft, and systematic containment of Black and Brown people, who must remain in place so that they can be effectively and efficiently ruled by their colonial masters. Not only do Western states apply refugee law disparately between Ukrainians and refugees from Black and Brown nations, but they have exempted Ukrainians from immigration law restrictions while categorically refusing to apply refugee law to Black and Brown protection-seekers at all.[55]

International refugee law is often criticized for replicating neocolonialism;[56] in the first instance, postcolonial nations were still ruled by European powers at the time that the United Nations was established[57] and the Refugee Convention drafted.[58] Even since formal decolonization, however, former colonial powers have been able to guarantee for themselves an inexorably disproportionate share of decision-making capital throughout the global institutional order,[59] including concerning who should qualify for and receive asylum in Western nations. These states dominate the public international law regime, using tribunals, councils, and committees to serve their national political interests in maintaining global dominance and White supremacy. They also contribute to ongoing destabilization of the Global South, and accordingly, contribute to the factors that push people to seek humanitarian assistance and asylum in other nations.[60]

Achiume has written at length about the United Nations' role as a neocolonial institution invested in maintaining a White supremacist geopolitical order,[61] and she has argued that its refugee law regime has always sought to exclude non-White people from protection. But there is more: freedom of movement is a term of Whiteness that was fundamental to settler-colonialism, and it remains a benefit of Whiteness under the neocolonial geopolitical order,[62] codified very cleverly through the global refugee law regime.

As she explains, "the regime excluded Third World, non-white refugees. The confluence of First World nation-state interest meant that the UN Refugee Convention definition of a refugee, which restricted status to those fleeing events in Europe, by design and effect racialized the very first international legal definition of a refugee."[63] Similarly, other scholars have described "the construction of 'the refugee' as a 'forced' 'non-Western' object without will or socio-cultural history, to be rescued by the benevolent West"[64] as "the central point of overlap between racialization and refuge in the contemporary context of refugee reception."[65]

For his part, James Hathaway has also called into question the popular assumption that international refugee law is meant to "institutionaliz[e] societal concern for the well-being of those forced to flee their countries, grounded in the concept of humanitarianism and in basic principles of human rights."[66] Rather, he says, it "increasingly affords a basis for rationalizing the decisions of states to refuse protection"[67]—a position supported by the U.S. government's "default 'no asylum policy' for Central Americans"[68] and its "longstanding history of excluding immigrants into the country based on race or national or ethnic origin."[69]

Conversations concerning whether international law is justice-oriented or order-oriented are not novel, but the reaction of the Global North to the war in and for Ukraine is a reminder of the debate's perennial relevance. It is, perhaps, exactly because of the tension between prevailing practical constructions of refugees and other protection-seekers as undesirable people undeserving of refuge until proven otherwise, and the need for Western powers to create a picture of Ukrainian protection-seekers as not only deserving, but desirable, that the policymakers and pundits emphasized the Whiteness of Ukrainian refugees so strongly. Underneath the exclamations regarding Ukrainian love for modern technology was a reassuring whisper: *these people will not disturb the preferred imbalance of power; no, they will make a fantastic addition to the global White body politic—they will reinforce, not threaten, the racial contract.*

Where Whiteness and racial contracting are concerned, the rule of law is not at odds with a racist geopolitical order; the two are, instead, one and the same. If, indeed, the difference between who is a refugee deserving the remedies provided under international law and who is a migrant seeking to abuse a foreign nation's immigration processes boils down to whether one is from Ukraine or Haiti, and thus, White versus Black, then is Whiteness itself not the law? If Whiteness is not only skin color, but the very incarnation of lawfulness, it then follows, per Whiteness as

Contract, that Whiteness might also be Order, and Justice—which, in the case of humanitarian law, includes a right of Welcome—a benefit of Whiteness.

The Ukrainian case study highlights the relationship between Whiteness and law, in both national and international contexts. It is because the West wished to welcome Ukraine into the global body politic that Ukraine was elevated from conditional to fuller Whiteness,[70] and the enhanced stakeholdership in international law inherent thereto. As the war against Russia has progressed, with seemingly boundless material support from its European and American allies, Ukraine has made good on its negotiated Whiteness wherever opportunity has allowed;[71] it successfully applied for European Union membership, continues to lobby for NATO membership, and has joined the Western colonial powers in their opposition to the United Nations' legislative decolonization efforts.

III. WHITENESS AS CONTRACT—AND WELCOME— IN INTERNATIONAL LAW

Racial contract theory, and especially as it applies to race as a global system of oppression,[72] is particularly helpful in unveiling the role of race with respect to public international law broadly, and specifically relating to the West's enthusiastic, race-based support of Ukraine after the Russian invasion. The concept of the racial contract was Charles Mills's critical response to the failures of his predecessors and peers to account for racialized peoples and nations as equals, or at all, in their considerations of the social contract.[73] Extrapolated to the Racial Superstate,[74] racial contract theory serves as a useful contemporary challenge of the pervasive, sustained, and worldwide exclusions of non-White people from legal personhood.[75]

The theory of Whiteness as Contract builds upon this work by clarifying that Whiteness is not only a matter of skin or eye color. Whiteness is instead a system of sorting privileges of power originating with slavery, settler colonialism, and other racializing projects. Categorizing Ukrainians as White does not change the fact that many Ukrainians are not in possession of White skin; it does, however, give Ukraine and its citizenry a level of sovereignty and power from which Black and Brown nations and people are systemically excluded. Whiteness is valuable capital that is bargained for by people who are, and who aspire to be, raced as White.[76] Whiteness guarantees: full legal personhood; public citizenship and the benefits attached thereto; and a recognized right to both commercial contract and proprietorship and socio-political negotiating power and proprietorship.[77]

Whiteness permits Ukrainian protection-seekers the use of legal mechanisms designed to help them secure safety through freedom of movement across national borders. Those excluded from Whiteness, and especially those people raced as Black and Indigenous, are, conversely, excluded from the body politic (or public personhood); subordinated to partial or contingent legal personhood, if granted any at all; and deprived of commercial and political contracting authority and proprietorship per the personal whims, or political and economic needs, of the Racial State. According to Chantal Thomas, "the migrant as outsider is both excluded from and necessary to the nation-state. The existence of foreigners, being nonmembers, validates and gives value to the modern concept of a membership society: the social contract."[78] To be non-White is to be both necessary to give meaning to the body politic from which one is excluded, and a permanent stranger to the body politic, to be permanently rejected and reviled.[79]

Western philosophers were explicit in their exclusion of those they considered to be savages from their conceptions of a civilized body politic that developed and would maintain liberal democracy. This exclusion was based on their beliefs that some people were not capable of public, political life, and could (and should), on that basis, be bereft of legal personhood and, instead, conquered and ruled by free, sovereign states.[80] John Stuart Mill wrote that "the only purpose for which power can be rightfully exercised over any member of a civilized community, against his will, is to prevent harm to others."[81] From this thesis, he excepted certain peoples, setting forth that "this doctrine is meant to apply only to human beings in the maturity of their faculties.... [W]e may leave out of consideration those backward states of society in which the race itself may be considered in its nonage."[82] Per Mill, "despotism is a legitimate mode of government in dealing with barbarians, provided the end be their improvement, and the means justified by actually effecting that end."[83] This political philosophy lent weight to justifications of the transatlantic slave trade and colonial expansion—a system of global conquest and governance in which Mill was personally and directly implicated as chief examiner for the British East India Company.[84]

European philosophers made clear that their visions for free society did not include the people we now identify as people of color; rather, they envisioned a world in which full and evolved personhood was to be attributed to people of European descent, and with that personhood, personal liberties and collective sovereignty.[85] Not so for the postcolonial world, for which despotism, enslavement, and colonial subjugation under enlightened, sovereign states were, in their view, the only possible options. Colonial subjugation required the containment of the colonized; accordingly, restrictions on the movements of the colonized, especially in cases of emergency,[86] have remained built into the structure of international law, and in the selective interpretation and enforcement of its laws relating to asylum and protection-seeking today.[87]

By relegating Black and Indigenous people to classification as barbarians in their work, classical theorists removed them from the protections and power of law while making explicit provisions for their oppression and subjugation thereunder.[88] These philosophers envisioned a world in which people whom they judged capable of reason were imbued with legal rights and duties that could be optimized and managed via the creation of the nation-state bound together by the citizens' common investment therein. Theorists such as Mill, Locke, and Rousseau thus articulated a social contract that benefits only men whom they raced as civilized, or White.

Mills's racial contract theory unveils the privileging of Whiteness over non-Whiteness by classical philosophers and thus, their contemplation of a Racial State.[89] He also contemplated a Racial Superstate, which, too, was negotiated by a global White body politic.[90] The Racial Superstate is comprised of predominantly White and White-led states that bargain amongst themselves, based on Whiteness, for maximum legal protection, wealth, and might. Excluded from the global body politic and its bargaining are the Black and Indigenous states that were colonized by, and which remain subordinated under, the Racial States. Within the international law regime, the contracting States—the former and neocolonial powers—negotiate and renegotiate international law, and the interpretation and enforcement thereof, to maximize legal protection, political power, and liberty for themselves at the expense of Black and Indigenous States, which the Racial States subject to extraction, surveillance, punishment, and constraint.

The negotiation of a neocolonial social contract by European and American powers has left Global Southern peoples tacitly excluded from international law per colonial philosophy concerning the subpersonhood of Global Southerners and formally subordinated within it—formal participation in global affairs by the postcolonial nations and their citizens notwithstanding.[91] The racialized nature of this neocolonial exclusion—after all, it was colonization and the development of contemporary racism that made some people Europeans and White, others Asian, some Indigenous, and still others Africans and therefore Black—is merely a matter of fact. Moreover, colonial rule, repression, and extraction have long contributed to migration flows motivated by economic opportunities, as well as the flights of refuge-seekers fleeing conflicts catalyzed and instigated by colonial and neocolonial machinations.[92] This deceptive arrangement—*de jure* equality of freedoms and sovereignty per law and *de facto* neocolonial oppression and destabilization—forms a White supremacist Superstate and a geopolitical order in which Whiteness is the price for power, access, and legal protections.

Western states maintain their geopolitical leverage—leverage acquired through their resource extraction from their colonies[93]—over postcolonial states through negotiations for financial assistance packages. Financial assistance from Western states is, of course, made possible through the accumulation of wealth extracted from the postcolonial states during the colonial era. States that would be inclined to challenge Western states must do so at the risk of losing their access to capital. Indeed, the European Union has, in reaction to African disapproval of economic sanctions on Russia levied in support of Ukraine—sanctions that African leaders believe to have exacerbate a global food crisis that has left African people starving—begun to weigh the possibility of threatening unenthusiastic African countries with financial disinvestment.[94] Western states rely upon colonial notions of sovereignty and manifest destiny to justify the waging of wars, including defensive wars such as the Ukraine's defense efforts, with full knowledge that their interventions result in mass human movements. Whether or not these states are prepared to welcome the moving humans has much to do with the races and nationalities of the humans doing the moving.

The role of race in the interpretation and enforcement of international law is often minimized, and where it cannot be ignored, it demands excuse based on claims that the perpetrators of racial injustice do more good than harm so long as they ascribe to liberalism.[95] To keep the global racial contract out of sight, and thus relatively immune from critique or, still worse, rescission, the sovereignty and authority of Black and Brown states is not curtailed within the global institutional order based on explicitly racial lines, but rather, according to geopolitical, and largely colonial, frontiers. By associating Whiteness with legality and non-Whiteness with relentless illegality, global racial contracting is justified as inevitable and necessary. By limiting the right of welcome to White Europeans and making freedom of movement a guaranteed benefit of White identity—and by, conversely, limiting all movement by non-European and non-White peoples to that specifically desired and required by the Western powers for their own economic benefit—White governorship of a Racial Superstate may proceed undisturbed. Whiteness does not only control international law, then, but becomes the law itself.

Euro-American support of Ukraine's defensive war stands out because the usual euphemisms and strained justifications for Western machinations have been eschewed in favor of bold, racist terms. Similarly, the terms of global racial contracting have also become bolder, and balder; instead of trying to convince nations full of starving people that their starving serves a greater good, the European Union is now opting for a straightforward, quid pro quo, transactional approach to aid packages for their former colonies—aid for you if you support Ukraine, none if you do not.[96] As postcolonial states and people of color within the Western powers have become more vocal, and more organized, in agitating against racism and neocolonialism and lobbying for a new antiracist global social contract, the signatories to the existing racial contract are also becoming more strident in their support therefor, begging the question of whether international law intends, at all, to provide equal justice under human rights and humanitarian law for aggrieved persons of all races, or if its primary goal is ensuring that the laws of Whiteness remain supreme.

IV. TOWARD A NEW INTERNATIONAL LAW REGIME

Defining Black, Brown, and Indigenous protection-seekers as ineligible for asylum *per se* removes them from the realm of law and permanently relegates them to a state of nature[97]—where they are subject to law as potential violators thereof, and never contractors therein or beneficiaries thereof. It preserves a colonial order, by containing Global Southerners based on racist stereotypes concerning their criminality, corruption, dishonesty, economic desperation, indiscipline, propensity for disease, and even their reproductive capacity. Their freedom of movement would be a breach of the neocolonial racial contract undergirded by the refugee law regime and is thus intolerable to the neocolonial overlords.[98] John Adams famously described the republic as a government of laws, not of men.[99] The international law regime is indeed a system of laws, but it is also fundamentally a system of men—*legal* men. Understanding that one's Whiteness, or lack thereof, is the arbiter of one's legal personhood offers a sobering reminder that the public international law regime still systematically excludes people raced as non-White from legal protection because they are also altogether excluded from law, remaining relegated to Nature according to the terms of the racial contract.

Whiteness is zero-sum: those who are not granted the privileges of Whiteness are subject to its violence. They do not receive the protections of international law, but they are held to account thereby. International law—the texts of which say that all are to be treated equal,[100] while the systems and structures declare some more equal than others—exists to keep them *in* order. The settler colonialism that reverberates worldwide today in the form of poverty, wars over resources and ethnic conflicts, and even the impacts of climate change also empowered Western states to become White, and based on that Whiteness, to become wealthy nuclear powers. These states choose to grant and deny refuge according to the terms of their racial contracts, and in so doing they sustain a public international law regime and a racial superstate thoroughly devoted to White supremacy.

The construction of Whiteness resembles a bit the game of chicken-and-egg: it is unclear whether contracting authority and proprietorship—understood in the international affairs context as geopolitical and economic power—facilitates one's membership into the fraternity of global Whiteness, or rather, if one's membership in the fraternity of global Whiteness facilitates a nation's access to, and control of, contracting authority and proprietorship. It is clear, however, that even partial exclusion from Whiteness and its benefits has concrete, costly, and even deadly consequences for those excluded therefrom.

As in racial states, the question of who "we the people"[101] are demands a response at the international level. At no state of the development of the international law, human rights, or international economic regimes was the Global South considered as an equal negotiating power, or at all. The international law regime has the potential to provide equal protections under law to the world's citizenry; however, this potential only exists if the regime makes the choice to rescind its racial contract and its corresponding complicity with a global institutional order that creates misery for many to afford prosperity for some, and which uses racialization as a tool to justify selective protection and rule of law for some and neglect and sacrifice of others.

In *The Social Contract*, Rousseau expresses his confidence that social contracts can be rescinded. He says: "I am here assuming what I think I have shown; that there is in the State no fundamental law that cannot be revoked, not excluding the social compact itself; for if all the citizens assembled of one accord to break the compact, it is impossible to doubt that it would be very legitimately broken."[102] Social contracts are regularly renegotiated, reformed, and rescinded; in theory, at least, racial contracts, too, can be revoked.[103] However, White supremacy is so fundamental to our legal regimes, and so essential to their perpetuation, that it can be difficult to imagine new legal, political, and social realities. Indeed, practically every attempt of the Global South to disrupt the racial contract is interrupted or otherwise undermined by White states using legal machinery that has long served their racialized geopolitical interests.

CONCLUSION

The international law regime can only provide equal justice under law if it renounces the longstanding practice of providing protection to those raced as White while refusing to offer protection to those raced as non-White. For this renunciation to occur, the regime must reject the colonial assumptions of White superiority and African, Arab, Asian, Middle Eastern, and Indigenous inferiority that have informed and infected the structures, policies, and procedures of international law and governance. The regime must part ways with the idea that some states are more sovereign than others, and that some people are more deserving of human rights protection and humanitarian assistance than others. Within the United Nations specifically, the tiering of state sovereignty and accession to the system of White exceptionalism must come to an immediate end.

Only by ceasing the practice of offering welcome to some and excluding others will international law become a system of justice instead of remaining, in its present form, a technology of barbarism and racist violence. There is no path forward for international law as a tool for justice for all unless the contracts of the existing regime are discarded and a new, truly postcolonial and radically anti-racist regime is renegotiated. The obsession of Western states with White power remains a formidable obstacle to the possibility of a regime overhaul. However, if ever there is a will, this will be the way.

NOTES

* This chapter benefited from extremely generative and generous feedback from Eddie Bruce-Jones, Hank Chambers, Erin Collins, Rebecca Crootof, Justin Desautels-Stein, Martha Ertman, Jim Gibson, Ben Heath, Riley Keenan, Corinna Lain, Jaya Ramji-Nogales, Matiangai Sirleaf, Allison Tait, Kevin Woodson, the faculty of the Washington and

Lee School of Law during the Washington and Lee-Richmond Junior Faculty Exchange, the encouragement of the very dear, ever-inspiring Lutie A. Lytle sisters, and the brilliant research assistance of Alexis Hills and Courtney Mason. The chapter was inspired by the courageous leadership and devoted mentorship of the late Honorable Sterling Johnson, Jr., who boldly insisted upon justice for Haitian refugees and taught each of his law clerks the importance of legal and moral courage.

1. See Alan MacLeod (@AlanRMacLeod), "[Thread] The most racist Ukraine coverage on TV News. 1. The BBC - 'It's very emotional for me because I see European people with blue eyes and blonde hair being killed' - Ukraine's Deputy Chief Prosecutor, David Sakvarelidze," X, Feb. 27, 2002, 11:37 a.m., https://twitter.com/AlanRMacLeod/status/1497974245737050120.

2. See Monika Pronczuk and Ruth MacLean, "Africans Say Ukrainian Authorities Hindered Them from Fleeing," *New York Times*, March 1, 2022, https://www.nytimes.com/2022/03/01/world/europe/ukraine-refugee-discrimination.html. For reporting on the United Nations complaint filed on behalf of African protection-seekers who faced discrimination while attempting to flee Ukraine, see Curtis Bunn, "Global Group of Black Attorneys File U.N. Complaint for African Refugees," *New York Times* online, March 4, 2022, https://www.nbcnews.com/news/nbcblk/ben-crump-civil-rights-attorneys-file-un-complaint-african-refugees-rcna18529.

3. See Pronczuk and MacLean, "Africans Say Ukrainian Authorities Hindered Them from Fleeing"; Bunn, "Global Group of Black Attorneys File U.N. Complaint for African Refugees."

4. See, for example, Universal Declaration of Human Rights, Art. 6, which states that "Everyone has the right to recognition everywhere as a person before the law," and Art. 7, which states that "All are equal before the law and are entitled without any discrimination to equal protection of the law. All are entitled to equal protection against any discrimination in violation of this Declaration and against any incitement to such discrimination." United Nations General Assembly, *The Universal Declaration of Human Rights*, December 10, 1948, 217 A (III).

5. The United Nations Charter sets forth that among the purposes of the United Nations are development of "friendly relations among nations based on respect for the principle of equal rights and self-determination of peoples." United Nations, *Charter of the United Nations*, October 24, 1945, 1 UNTS XVI.

6. For a discussion of how the concept of sovereignty developed in the 1800s was based on the belief that legal sovereignty was for European, or "civilized" states—a belief that excluded non-European states from the international body politic, see Antony Anghie, *Imperialism, Sovereignty and the Making of International Law* (Cambridge: Cambridge University Press, 2004), 11.

7. The United Nations recognizes the existence of seventeen non-self-governing territories today. This number does not include Puerto Rico, the Northern Mariana Islands, or other contested or non-independent territories around the world. See United Nations, "Non-Self-Governing-Territories," https://www.un.org/dppa/decolonization/en/nsgt.

8. Christopher Busey and Tianna Dowie-Chin have written that "antiblackness has been and continues to be central to the making of Western empire and modernity as we know it. However . . . the social education discipline has yet to fundamentally advance a critical analytic that captures the specificity of global antiblackness and the invention of

Black as non-human and non-citizen." Christopher L. Busey and Tianna Dowie-Chin, "The Making of Global Black Anti-citizen/citizenship: Situating BlackCrit in Global Citizenship Research and Theory," *Theory & Research in Social Education* 49, no. 2 (2021): 153.

9. See United Nations Gifts, Trusteeship Council Chamber, *United Nations*, https://www.un.org/ungifts/trusteeship-council-chamber.

10. The United States explained its vote opposing United Nations' efforts in 2021 at decolonization of American colonies in a letter from the Deputy Ambassador to the United Nations addressed to the United Nations' General Assembly. See United States Mission to the United Nations, "Explanation of Vote on Agenda Items 59–63: Decolonization," November 9, 2021, https://usun.usmission.gov/explanation-of-vote-on-agenda-items-59-63-decolonization/ (asserting that the UN placed "too much weight on independence as a one-size-fits-all option for a territory's people in pursuit of their right of self-determination").

11. See United Nations, *A/HRC/51/L.28/Rev.1 Vote Item 9 - 44th Meeting, 51st Regular Session Human Rights Council*, United Nations WebTV, October 7, 2022, https://media.un.org/en/asset/k1u/k1umbr5x6x; Chiamaka Okafor, "Ukraine, US, UK, Others Vote Against Concrete Action Against Racism," *Premium Times Nigeria*, October 9, 2022, https://www.premiumtimesng.com/news/top-news/558806-ukraine-us-uk-others-vote-against-concrete-action-against-racism.html?tztc=1.

12. See Ben Norton, "West Opposes Rest of World in UN Votes for Fairer Economic System, Equality, Sustainable Development," *Geopolitical Economy Report*, December 22, 2022, https://geopoliticaleconomy.com/2022/12/22/west-un-vote-economic-system-equality/#:~:text=On%20December%2014%2C%202022%2C%20123,the%20UN's%20193%20member%20states. For detailed information on the General Assembly's attempts at global structural economic transformation and Western opposition thereto, see Meetings Coverage and Press Releases, "General Assembly Takes Up Second Committee Reports, Adopting 38 Resolutions, 2 Decisions," United Nations, December 14, 2022, https://press.un.org/en/2022/ga12482.doc.htm.

13. Thomas Pogge has described the global economic order as "determined by a tiny minority of its participants whose oligarchic control of the rules ultimately also rests on a huge preponderance of military power." Thomas Pogge, *World Poverty and Human Rights: Cosmopolitan Responsibilities and Reforms* (Cambridge: Polity Press, 2002), 96.

14. See E. Tendayi Achiume, "Transnational Racial (In)Justice in Liberal Democratic Empire," *Harvard Law Review Forum* 134 (2021): 388, noting in footnote 38 that the WEOG group is the only group bound together based upon geopolitics rather than geography. The only WEOG states who could be said to not be White-led or majority-White are Israel and Turkey, but these states are generally accorded some level of White or White-adjacent identity and privilege.

15. For a discussion of how settler colonialism used race and racialization to sustain itself in the United States, see Natsu Taylor Saito, *Settler Colonialism, Race, and the Law: Why Structural Racism Persists* (New York: New York University Press, 2020).

16. According to E. Tendayi Achiume, "Today, international law repudiates colonialism, but colonialism remains essential to sustaining the political and economic dominance of the First World." E. Tendayi Achiume, "Migration as Decolonization," *Stanford Law Review* 71 (2019): 1543. Consider also the United Kingdom's explanation of its 2022 vote against a United Nations anti-racism resolution, in which its representative noted that the UK did "not agree with claims made in this resolution that states are required to make

reparations for the slave trade and colonialism, which caused great suffering to many but were not, at that time, violations of international law." Rita French, "UN Human Rights Council 51: UK Explanation of Vote on Racism Resolution (Speech)," October 7, 2022, https://www.gov.uk/government/speeches/un-human-rights-council-51-uk-explanation-of-vote-on-racism-resolution. The United States has also repeatedly voted against the resolution and, in 2021, also cited the obligation of former colonial powers to pay reparations among the reasons for its vote. See United States Mission to the United Nations, "Explanation of Vote for the A Global Call for Concrete Action for the Elimination of Racism, Racial Discrimination, Xenophobia and Related Intolerance," November 15, 2021, https://usun.usmission.gov/explanation-of-vote-for-the-a-global-call-for-concrete-action-for-the-elimination-of-racism-racial-discrimination-xenophobia-and-related-intolerance/.

17. For example, Palestinian protection-seekers generally cannot resettle in the United States. Though the United Nations reports that there are nearly six million Palestinian refugees worldwide, within the last twenty years only two thousand of these refugees have resettled in the United States because the American refugee admission process renders them ineligible and because the United Nations agency tasked with handling Palestinian refugees does not offer resettlement services. By contrast, the US government has resettled 100,000 Ukrainian refugees within the United States since 2022. See Catherine E. Shoichet, "Will Palestinian Refugees Come to the U.S.?" *CNN* online, October 30, 2023, https://www.cnn.com/2023/10/30/us/palestinian-refugees-gaza-war-cec/index.html.

18. See Marissa Jackson Sow, "Ukrainian Refugees, Race, and International Law's Choice Between Order and Justice," *American Journal of International Law* 116, no. 4 (2022): 698–709.

19. Jackson Sow, "Ukrainian Refugees, Race, and International Law's Choice Between Order and Justice."

20. See Marissa Jackson Sow, "Whiteness as Contract," *Washington & Lee Law Review* 78, no. 5 (2022): 1810–1.

21. See Rashawn Ray, "Commentary: The Russian Invasion of Ukraine Shows Racism Has No Boundaries," Brookings, March 3, 2022. https://www.brookings.edu/articles/the-russian-invasion-of-ukraine-shows-racism-has-no-boundaries/.

22. Derrick A. Bell claimed that the Black people in the United States only experience civil rights progress when their interests are aligned with the interests of White people, in a theory he called interest convergence. See Derrick A. Bell, "Brown v. Board of Education and the Interest-Convergence Dilemma," *Harvard Law Review* 93 (1980): 518–33. In the case of Ukraine, the war with Russia has allowed Ukraine to achieve greater European identity and capital—and greater association with Whiteness—by providing the United States and Western Europe with opportunity and justification to fight Russia.

23. By contrast, Ukraine continues to seek membership in NATO, and has used its war efforts to bolster its application but has thus far remained unsuccessful. See David L. Stern et al., "Ukraine Wants and Expects an Invitation to Join NATO. Allies Are Not Sure," *Washington Post*, July 7, 2023, https://www.washingtonpost.com/world/2023/07/07/ukraine-nato-vilnius-summit-leaders/.

24. See Philip S. S. Howard et al., "Ukraine Refugee Crisis Exposes Racism and Contradictions in the Definition of Human," *The Conversation*, March 21, 2022, https://theconversation.com/ukraine-refugee-crisis-exposes-racism-and-contradictions-in-the-definition-of-human-179150.

25. Per the 2001 Census—the only Census ever taken in Ukraine—over 75 percent of Ukrainians identify as ethnically Ukrainian, which is an Eastern Slavic ethnic group. Minority groups include Russians, Belarusians, Moldovans, Jews, Crimean Tatars, Romanians, Roma, and Polish, and small populations of non-European people. See Sergiu Constantin, "Ethnic and Linguistic Identity in Ukraine? It's Complicated," *Eurac Research*, March 21, 2022, https://www.eurac.edu/en/blogs/mobile-people-and-diverse-societies/ethnic-and-linguistic-identity-in-ukraine-it-s-complicated.

26. See Josephine Harvey, "CBS Journalist Apologizes for Saying Ukraine More 'Civilized' Than Iraq, Afghanistan," *HuffPost*, February 27, 2022, https://www.huffpost.com/entry/media-racism-ukraine-conflict-coverage_n_621c08ffe4b0d1388f16a3dc.

27. Ruchir Sharma (@ruchirsharma_1), Twitter (now X), February 26, 2022, accessed July 22, 2023, https://twitter.com/ruchirsharma_1/status/1497655099979714563?ref_src=twsrc%5Etfw%7Ctwcamp%5Etweetembed%7Ctwterm%5E1498029803089416195%7Ctwgr%5E68b7fdfc278042815de0d7c9f6674027b1befbda%7Ctwcon%5Es3_&ref_url=https%3A%2F%2Fnewsone.com%2F4296556%2Fafrican-students-flee-ukraine-spotlights-racial-bias-refugee-crisis%2F (discussing Polish welcome of Ukrainian refugees versus Polish reluctance to accept Syrian refugees in 2015).

28. See Shannon Dawson, "Black Women Raise $60,000 To Help African Students Flee Ukraine Amid Russian Invasion," *NewsOne*, March 2, 2022, https://newsone.com/4297955/black-women-raise-funds-to-help-african-students-flee-ukraine/.

29. See Chrispin Mwakideu, "Ukraine Bid to Enlist African Fighters Slammed," *DW*, March 8, 2022, https://www.dw.com/en/ukraines-bid-to-recruit-fighters-from-africa-sparks-uproar/a-61049323. Russia has also sought to hire Africans to fight as mercenaries in Ukraine. See Dasha Litvinova, *AP*, March 26, 2023, https://apnews.com/article/russia-ukraine-war-mobilization-recruits-military-draft-9339329bba5a5dc6956fe588bab98961. Russia has also recruited African men to fight against Ukraine. See Giulia Paravicini et al., "The Africans Fighting on Russia's Front Line in Ukraine," *Reuters*, June 22, 2023, https://www.reuters.com/investigates/special-report/ukraine-crisis-russia-wagner-africa/.

30. Howard et al., "Ukraine Refugee Crisis Exposes Racism."

31. According to Achiume, "freedom of movement is, in effect, politically determined and racially differentiated." Achiume, "Migration as Decolonization," 1530.

32. Philip Marcelo reported that "the U.S. prepares to welcome tens of thousands of Ukrainians fleeing war [as] the country continues to deport scores of African and Caribbean refugees back to unstable and violent homelands where they've faced rape, torture, arbitrary arrest and other abuses." Philip Marcelo, "In U.S.'s Welcome to Ukrainians, African Refugees See Racial Bias," *PBS NewsHour* online, https://www.pbs.org/newshour/politics/in-u-s-s-welcome-to-ukrainians-african-refugees-see-racial-bias.

33. The word *barbarian* comes from the Greek word *barbaros*, used by the early Greeks to describe all foreigners. Encyclopedia Britannica online, s.v. "barbarian," last updated November 23, 2023, https://www.britannica.com/topic/barbarian. Many thanks to Martha Ertman for sharing this insight.

34. Saito discusses the perpetual foreignness of non-White Americans and the consequences, from the internment of Japanese Americans during World War II to the deportations of American citizens and assumptions that non-White Americans speak English as a non-native language. See Saito, *Settler Colonialism, Race and the Law*.

35. Achiume, "Migration as Decolonization," 1516.

36. See "One-way Ticket to Rwanda for Some UK Asylum Seekers," *BBC* online, April 14, 2022, https://www.bbc.com/news/uk-politics-61097114.

37. See Laura E. Alexander et al., "Race and Religion Have Always Played a Role in Who Gets Refuge in the U.S.," *Yes Solutions Journalism*, May 13, 2022, https://www.yesmagazine.org/social-justice/2022/05/13/race-and-religion-refuge.

38. Catherine E. Shoichet, "As the US Rolls Out the Welcome Mat for Ukrainian Refugees, Some See a Double Standard at the Border," *CNN* online, March 29, 2022, https://www.cnn.com/2022/03/29/us/ukrainians-us-mexico-border-cec/index.html.

39. See, e.g., Lee Edwards, "Britain's Post-humanitarian Response to Ukraine: Preserving a Racist Migration Regime," *Media@LSE* (blog), March 10, 2022, https://blogs.lse.ac.uk/medialse/2022/03/10/britains-post-humanitarian-response-to-ukraine-preserving-a-racist-migration-regime/.

40. Sahar Aziz has written of "Muslims... being treated as a race, and more specifically, a suspect race, rather than as a religious minority to be protected from persecution." Sahar Aziz, *The Racial Muslim: When Racism Quashes Religious Freedom* (Oakland: University of California Press, 2022), 3.

41. See Channel4News (@Channel4News), "'Too many Muslims, too many people with different skin colours.' Andrea, a host for the Homes for Ukraine scheme, tells @darshnasoni how 'shocked' she was at how difficult a Ukrainian refugee found adjusting to ethnic diversity and cultural values in the UK," X, January 26, 2023, https://x.com/Channel4News/status/1618625171769761792?s=20.

42. See Jasmine Aguilera, "Where Migrants Suffered Matters at the U.S.-Mexico Border," *TIME* online, April 13, 2022, https://time.com/6166535/ukrainians-mexico-border-title-42/.

43. Aguilera, "Where Migrants Suffered Matters."

44. See Congressional Research Service, "U.S. Immigration Policy on Haitian Migrants," May 17, 2011, https://crsreports.congress.gov/product/pdf/RS/RS21349/19.

45. See Sale v. Haitian Centers Council, 509 U.S. 155 (1993).

46. See Sale v. Haitian Centers Council, 160.

47. See Sale v. Haitian Centers Council, 160.

48. See Sale v. Haitian Centers Council, 160.

49. See Sale v. Haitian Centers Council, 160.

50. See Matiangai Sirleaf, "White Health as Global Health," *American Journal of International Law* 117 (2023): 88–93.

51. Sirleaf, "White Health as Global Health," 89.

52. Mike Clary, "Judge Orders All Haitians Free from U.S. Camp," *Los Angeles Times* online, June 9, 1993, https://www.latimes.com/archives/la-xpm-1993-06-09-mn-1228-story.html.

53. Clary, "Judge Orders All Haitians Free."

54. Achiume rightly notes that "whereas international refugee law and international human rights law impose restrictions on states' right to exclude nonnationals whose lives are endangered by the risk of certain forms of persecution in their countries of origin, no similar protections exist for economic migrants." Achiume, "Migration as Decolonization," 1509.

55. Ian Kysel has noted that "preventing people from making a claim for asylum at all, which Title 42 does, goes against international law," deploring disparate treatment of refugees based on race and nationality as "the continued rejection of refugee law." Aguilera, "Where Migrants Suffered Matters."

56. See James Thuo Gathii, "Writing Race and Identity in a Global Context: What CRT and TWAIL Can Learn From Each Other," *UCLA Law Review* 67 (2021): 1623.

57. Per the United Nations website, "When the United Nations was established in 1945, 750 million people—almost a third of the world's population then—lived in Territories that were non-self-governing, dependent on colonial Powers." Those non-self-governing territories would not have been able to participate in the negotiations relating to the establishment of the UN. "The United Nations and Decolonization," United Nations, https://www.un.org/dppa/decolonization/en/about.

58. The Convention Relating to the Status of Refugees was adopted by the UN General Assembly on July 28, 1951. See UN General Assembly, Convention Relating to the Status of Refugees, July 28, 1951, United Nations Treaty Series, vol. 189, p. 137.

59. See Achiume, "Migration as Decolonization," 1518–19.

60. B. S. Chimni has linked the failures of the neoliberalism espoused by Western states to the creation of refugee crises. See B. S. Chimni, "The Geopolitics of Refugee Studies: A View from the Global South," *Journal of Refugee Studies* 11, no. 4 (1998): 360–63.

61. See Achiume, "Transnational Racial (In)Justice in Liberal Democratic Empire," 380.

62. Achiume has noted that "because of the persisting racial demographics that distinguish the First World from the Third—demographics that are, in significant part, a product of passports, national borders, and other successful institutions that partially originated as technologies of racialized exclusion— most whites enjoy dramatically greater rights to freedom of international movement (by which I mean travel across borders) than most nonwhites." Achiume, "Migration as Decolonization," 1530–31.

63. E. Tendayi Achiume, "Race, Refugees, and International Law," in *The Oxford Handbook of International Refugee Law* (Oxford: Oxford University Press, 2021), 56.

64. Christopher Kyriakides et al., "Introduction: The Racialized Refugee Regime," *Refuge* 35, no. 1 (2019): 5.

65. Kyriakides et al., "Introduction," 5.

66. James Hathaway, "A Reconsideration of the Underlying Premise of Refugee Law," *Harvard International Law Journal* 31, no. 1(1990): 130.

67. Hathaway, "A Reconsideration," 130.

68. Kaila C. Randolph, "Executive Order 13769 and America's Long-standing Practice of Institutionalized Racial Discrimination Towards Refugees and Asylum Seekers," *Stetson Law Review* 47, no. 1 (2017): 21.

69. Randolph, "Executive Order 13769," 28.

70. See Marissa Jackson Sow, "Fighting for Whiteness in Ukraine," *Creighton Law Review* 56, no. 2 (2023): 129–42.

71. Jackson Sow, "Fighting for Whiteness in Ukraine," 129–42.

72. See Charles W. Mills, *Blackness Visible: Essays on Philosophy and Race* (Ithaca: Cornell University Press, 1998), 126.

73. See Charles W. Mills, *The Racial Contract* (Ithaca: Cornell University Press, 1997), 1.

74. See Mills, *The Racial Contract*, 33–39.

75. Mills, *The Racial Contract*, 1–2.

76. See Jackson Sow, "Whiteness as Contract," 1828–31.

77. Jackson Sow, "Whiteness as Contract," 1828–31.

78. Chantal Thomas, "Transnational Migration, Globalization, and Governance: Theorizing a Crisis," in *The Oxford Handbook of The Theory of International Law* (Oxford: Oxford University Press, 2016), 916.

79. Thomas, "Transnational Migration, Globalization, and Governance," 916.

80. James Thuo Gathii has commented on contemporary reverberations of this philosophy of race in international law, critiquing "assumptions that international legal knowledge is exclusively produced in the West for consumption and governance of the Third World." See James Thuo Gathii, "The Promise of International Law: A Third World View," *American University International Law Review* 36, no. 3 (2021): 379.

81. John Stuart Mill, *On Liberty* (New York: Dover Publications, 2002), 2.

82. Mill, *On Liberty*, 23.

83. Mill, *On Liberty*, 23. See also Mills, *The Racial Contract*, 57 (quoting John Adams as saying, "Negroes, Indians, and [Kaffirs] cannot bear democracy") and James Thuo Gathii, who has noted that "just as slavery dehumanized Blacks as degenerate and outside the boundaries of humanity in the construction of the United States as a White racial state, European/White international law was constructed to relegate non-European peoples who were considered to live outside the bounds of humanity and therefore outside of sovereignty." Gathii, "Writing Race and Identity in a Global Context," 1613.

84. Mill, *On Liberty*, iii.

85. Mill, *On Liberty*, 22–23. Also consider Sir Henry Maine's description of contract as an equalizer in a world in which, prior to the emergence of contract, people were defined by—and relegated to—status. Maine's liberal vision for contract as a technology for equality is exactly the type of philosophy critiqued by Charles Mills, as Maine's philosophy cannot account for the stickiness of racial status, which cannot so easily be contracted away. See Henry Sumner Maine, *Ancient Law: Its Connection with the Early History of Society, and its Relation to Modern Ideas* (London: John Murray, 1861).

86. See Sirleaf, "White Health as Global Health," 89–93.

87. Critical scholars of international law recognize that colonialism is "not an event" but a social formation and a "structure" that allows colonizing powers "not only to profit from but also occupy permanently the territories they colonize"—formal decolonization notwithstanding. Ntina Tzouvala, "Review Essay: Settler Colonialism, Race, and the Law: Why Structural Racism Persists by Natsu Taylor Saito," *Melbourne Journal of International Law* 21, (2020): 9 (reviewing Natsu Taylor Saito, *Settler Colonialism, Race, and the Law: Why Structural Racism Persists* [New York: New York University Press, 2020]).

88. See Mills, *The Racial Contract*, 53.

89. See Mills, *The Racial Contract*, 83.

90. Mills, *The Racial Contract*, 37.

91. Achiume, "Migration as Decolonization," 1539–46.

92. Global Southerners have long referred to the process of "colonizin' in reverse," a phrase made famous by Jamaican poet Louise Bennett-Coverley to describe the process of migrating to the colonial metropolis in search of safety or economic opportunity. See Louise Bennett-Coverley, "Colonization in Reverse" (1966), https://www.poetrybyheart.org.uk/poems/colonization-in-reverse. This process of reverse colonization was also studied by the ethnographer Dominic Pasura, who documented the reasons for the "illegal" migrations offered by Zimbabweans who had migrated to the United Kingdom. Dominic Pasura, "Competing Meanings of the Diaspora: The Case of Zimbabweans in Britain," *Journal of Ethnic & Migration Studies* 36, (2010): 1445, 1448–52.

93. See Achiume, "Migration as Decolonization," 1518.

94. See Vince Chadwick, "Exclusive: Internal Report Shows EU Fears Losing Africa over Ukraine," *Devex*, July 22, 2022, https://www.devex.com/news/exclusive-internal-report-shows-eu-fears-losing-africa-over-ukraine-103694.

95. Achiume connects the defensiveness of liberal states against accountability for race-based human rights violations vis-à-vis postcolonial states to the reality that "the liberal project is an imperial project." Achiume, "Transnational Racial (In)Justice," 396.

96. For a discussion of the "bullying" that postcolonial states faced from WEOG member states over the resolution negotiations, including threats from the United States to cut international aid if they insisted upon the commission of inquiry, see Achiume, "Transnational Racial (In)Justice," 389 (citing Sejal Parmar, "The Internationalisation of Black Lives Matter at the Human Rights Council," *EJIL: TALK!* June 26, 2020, https://www.ejiltalk.org/the-internationalisation-of-black-lives-matter-at-the-human-rights-council).

97. See Mills, *The Racial Contract*, 12.

98. See Achiume, "Migration as Decolonization," 1518n29 (noting "the role that race has played in determining whose international mobility is worthy of protection, and whose international immobility is prioritized and ultimately achieved through containment to the regions of their birth").

99. Part the First, Article XXX, Massachusetts Constitution of 1780.

100. See, e.g., United Nations General Assembly, "Universal Declaration of Human Rights, art. 1," New York: United Nations General Assembly, 1948.

101. Thomas Jefferson et al., *Declaration of Independence*, July 4, 1776 (United States).

102. Jean-Jacques Rousseau, *The Social Contract* (United States: G.D.H. Cole, 1920), 69.

103. Consider Sir Henry Maine's famous observation that the "movement of the progressive societies has hitherto been a movement from Status to Contract." Maine, *Ancient Law*, 170. Maine's observation is complicated by a consideration of race, and in this chapter, I have written about the use of contract to negotiate, and reify, hegemonic racial status. The geopolitical shift away from European colonialism in the mid-twentieth century gave postcolonial nations the formal ability to contract at the international level; however, the de facto reality is that, in terms of economic, political, and military might, their geopolitical power, and thus, their statuses, have not improved—and neither have the statuses of their citizens vis-à-vis a Euro-American dominated refugee regime. A change in their statuses can only result from an abandonment of the extant global racial contract.

CHAPTER TWELVE

UNSETTLING THE BORDER

Sherally Munshi*

> A colony is a ravaged home.... [T]here is no going home from a colony.[1]
>
> —ANN LAURA STOLER

INTRODUCTION

When lawmakers, philosophers, or citizens ask who should be allowed to cross borders, under what circumstances, and on what grounds, they often leave unexamined the historical formation of the border itself. National borders are taken for granted as the backdrop against which normative debates unfold. Liberals and conservatives offer very different arguments for maintaining or loosening border restrictions, but the colonial processes that have given rise to national borders seldom enter the frame of normative debate.[2] This essay seeks to bring the border itself into the frame of normative consideration by exploring not only the colonial dimension of national borders, but also the ways in which national borders themselves circumscribe and constrain the liberal imaginary. Unsettling the framework within which we conventionally address questions of migration is a first step toward cultivating an expanded political imaginary, one that leads us beyond the deadening impasse of border imperialism.

For decades, the U.S. immigration system has been described by liberals and conservatives as "broken," but attempts to fix it have been stymied by the failure to achieve compromise. But as a candidate for president, Donald Trump almost single-handedly reframed the immigration debate, recasting immigrant exclusion in unabashed terms of white nationalism. Upon taking office, Trump and his administration implemented a series of viciously anti-immigrant policies, testing the norms of polite discourse and legal constraint, often leaving his critics bewildered at the apparent weakness of our public norms and the inability of our institutions to constrain the president, particularly in his campaign to exclude or expel racialized immigrants. The Muslim ban, the separation of parents from children, proposals to end birthright citizenship—all of these were met with demonstrations of liberal outrage. That outrage, however genuinely felt, has failed to give rise to either a sustained critique of white nationalism or racial capitalism; nor has it enabled us to imagine meaningful alternatives to our contemporary border regime.

Critics of our contemporary border regime—especially those who advocate a more thoroughgoing analysis of its origins and effects—are often asked, "So are you in favor of open borders?" The question is often a gesture of dismissal rather than a genuine form of engagement. And it is almost always premature. Most of us who live in the United States do not have a very deep understanding of what our immigration policies are, what they do, how they came to be. Before we can meaningfully address the question of open borders, we need to unsettle borders—to defamiliarize, disenchant, and recontextualize borders by critically examining the historical processes, legal developments, and intellectual and discursive formations that naturalize and legitimate them.

I focus on the southern border of the United States because it has become a particularly dense site of contestation and meaning-making. But to be clear, with the term *border*, I am referring not only to what Nicholas De Genova describes as the spectacle of encounter that naturalizes both the law of nations and "illegality" of migrants, but to an epistemic regime, one that governs and constrains our political, disciplinary, and ethical framing of contemporary questions about migration, coexistence, and survival.[3] Immigration is not simply about turning up at the border; the spectacle of the border tends to obscure the histories of colonialism and conquest that have shaped contemporary border regimes, the extractions and displacements of capital that have set people in motion, the racial economies managed by shifting technologies of recruitment and criminalization, the political rationalities and embodied sensibilities produced by imperial practices of keeping peoples in place.[4] Drawing on the work of decolonial critics like Anibal Quijano, Walter Mignolo, and Macarena Gómez-Barris, the critical approach to immigration discourse taken in this essay is one that attempts to loosen itself from colonial modernity, conventional frames of knowledge, and disciplinary habits of seeing like a state, and to rehearse ways of knowing otherwise, apprehending the complexity within which we live by engaging submerged histories and reclaiming relations cleaved by the border.[5]

I use the term *unsettling*, first, to invoke the growing body of scholarship devoted to exploring the still unfolding history of colonial capitalism and the settler nation in the Americas, including the work of legal scholars exploring the ways in which settler colonialism has shaped the development of U.S. law.[6] And second, I use this term to suggest that we cannot adequately address, critique, or contest the violence of the U.S. border regime without directly confronting the ways in which settler colonialism, as a social formation, has given shape not only to contemporary racial geographies and legal institutions, but the epistemological frames, disciplinary conventions, and political and ethical imaginaries that obscure their ongoing violence. Lawyers in particular often refer to questions as settled when those questions were answered so deep in the past—or have been buried under the weight of so much authority—that they cannot be reexamined without risking some social or epistemic upheaval. But that is precisely the kind of reexamination for which I advocate here. Questions whose answers are well settled have not necessarily been answered correctly or put to rest. They are often the questions that continue to haunt our present.

A colony is not a home, Ann Stoler writes, but a "ravaged home . . . rendered unhomely for those on whom it is imposed, as well as for those to whom it is offered as a stolen gift. There is no being 'at home,' only unsettled waiting for something else, for release from those unfulfilled promises and that anxious unfilled labor."[7] No border wall will make America great again, but neither will any proposed bipartisan compromise resolve our immigration crisis once and for all. To imagine our way beyond current crises and impasse, we need not only to confront our colonial past, but also to proliferate alternative sources of political agency and authority, which in turn might lay the groundwork for addressing old questions anew. We might begin to imagine our way beyond the colony, Stoler suggests, by pursuing "new comparisons and convergences" across lines of division drawn by the settler colonial nation.[8] I conclude by bringing into focus recent expressions of identification and solidarity between Indigenous and immigrant communities who recognize in their shared experience both a common grievance against settler colonialism and the potential to reimagine the terms of coexistence.

I. BEYOND BORDER NATIONALISM

In January of 2017, as one of his first acts as U.S. President, Donald Trump signed an executive order authorizing the construction of a wall along the southern border of the United States. The planned wall would cut across the ancestral lands of the O'odham peoples, bisecting the Tohono O'odham reservation, which now straddles the U.S.–Mexico border.

The O'odham had lived in the Sonoran Desert for thousands of years before European settlers arrived. After the Mexican–American War in 1848, when the United States seized two-thirds of Mexico, the international boundary line was drawn at the Gila River, north of O'odham lands. A few years later, the United States purchased additional lands from Mexico, shifting the international boundary line south of the Gila River, dividing O'odham land and people.[9] O'odham living north of the border would be considered U.S. citizens; those living south of the border would not. The O'odham themselves were never consulted about the division.[10] The purchase had little immediate effect on the lives of the O'odham, who continued to move freely across their ancestral lands. But in the mid-twentieth century, the O'odham lost territory on both sides of the colonial border to settlement, mining, railroad construction, national parks, and a U.S. bombing range.[11]

More recently, O'odham land has become the site of intensified border enforcement. In 1994, the Clinton administration heightened border enforcement in places like Tijuana–San Diego and Juárez–El Paso, forcing migrants from border towns and into the scorching desert, where they are likely to die of thirst or exhaustion. Indigenous critics underscore the cynicism with which the enforcement policy, called "prevention through deterrence," weaponizes sacred Indigenous lands while exploiting human vulnerability.[12] Increased border enforcement has resulted in an increase in unauthorized migration and drug trafficking over the O'odham reservation and neighboring towns, bringing intensified policing to tribal land.[13] Tribal members themselves are routinely stopped by U.S. Customs and Border Patrol, and those without American citizenship may be deported to Mexico.[14]

Since the 1990s, gated barriers have divided O'odham land. These gates are opened for family reunions and tribal celebrations, but they stand in the way of exercising a prior freedom—to migrate across ancestral lands, to visit family, to collect water.[15] For millennia, migration had been an essential strategy for O'odham survival in an arid desert, allowing for trade with adjacent tribes and flexibility in the face of political displacement and climatological disruption.[16] Now, O'odham lands are the site of constant surveillance. In 2014, the U.S. government awarded an Israeli company a $145 million contract to build a network of fifty-three towers, integrating various drones, mobile sensors, cameras, and radars to track and record any movement across a stretch of the southern border, including O'odham land. Tribal members cannot leave or return to their land without passing through a checkpoint.[17] They carry identification to avoid detention or deportation.[18]

President Trump never built his promised wall, but during his final weeks in office, construction crews began blasting through a stretch of Organ Pipe Cactus National Monument, destroying sacred O'odham sites and causing irreversible environmental damage. Among other things, the border wall, which would replace an existing vehicle barrier, would prevent wild animals—deer, horses, coyotes, and jackrabbits, among other animals the O'odham regard as their relatives—from moving freely and accessing the Quitobaquito Springs, an oasis in the desert, the only source of water for miles.[19] In September of 2020, O'odham activists succeeded in temporarily blocking construction crews that were approaching a sacred spring. During the standoff, a protestor appealed to the construction workers:

> Quit your job. Your job is temporary, and your damage is forever . . . We're crying for our water, for our people, for our future generations . . . O'odham will be here forever, regardless, on both sides of the border. We exist on both sides of . . . this imaginary line. We covered this whole area, our people. Indigenous tribes all along the border, we're not scared of you . . . and we'll be here cleaning up your mess.[20]

With such few words, the protestor wrenches us from the usual framework within which contemporary immigration debates are staged, and invites us, along with the construction workers she addresses, into a vastly expanded time-space. She explodes what we might refer to as national time or settler time—the linear history or progress narrative of settler national development—to open and unfurl another time frame, a time of extinction and survival, a time before and after the United States. "This wall will fall, just like you. We'll still be here cleaning up your mess."[21] For more than 150 years, the O'odham have survived the cleaving of their land, the separation of their community, and the rupture of their community's relationship to the land. Trump's border wall is not an exceptional violence. Instead, it represents only the most recent violation in a long, unbroken history of colonial invasion.

The election of Donald Trump stunned many white Americans, but others were far less surprised, recognizing his victory to be continuous with forms of patriarchal white supremacy that remain foundational to the settler nation.[22] Nell Painter, for instance, observed that, for many Americans, the election of Trump "seemed to come from some place other than America," as if its "meanness of spirit" had been blown in from "some hateful foreign country."[23] But white nationalism is no foreign contagion. The white nationalism that reveals itself with periodic violence has its roots in the ground itself, in the very construction and composition of the United States, a country founded in conquest, shaped by histories of territorial expansion, Indigenous removal, and immigration policies that have tended to promote white settlement while frustrating racialized migration.[24] The white nationalism that now overwhelms immigration discourse is not merely a corruption of immigration discourse. Instead, immigration policy has played a critical role in creating and maintaining a racial state, which is itself the source of white nationalist ideology. White nationalism, in other words, is bound up with the border itself.

The term "white nationalism" is generally reserved to denounce the expressive racism now resurgent on the far right. But the same term might also be used to identify a more muted, less scrutinized set of assumptions and attitudes shared by a wider, respectable majority of white liberals who have become complacent with our contemporary border regime. Within the liberal imaginary, formal racism was effectively vanquished in the 1960s, when antiracist movements brought an end to white supremacy at home and colonial rule in other parts of the world. These movements brought an end to formal racism and old imperial hierarchies, but established in their place new, more discreet forms of spatial division. Etienne Balibar has described the resurgence of nationalism in the postcolonial era as a form of "neo-racism."[25] This neo-racism "does not postulate the superiority of certain groups or peoples in relation to others but 'only' the harmfulness of abolishing frontiers."[26] Racism, instead, disappears into the naturalized horizon of national borders.

This sort of nationalism, what we might call *border nationalism*, distinguishes itself from the white nationalism of the far right in that it disavows the expressive racism of white supremacists. But it leaves wholly unexamined a global racial order shaped by centuries of colonialism and empire. Even those who strenuously disavow the expressive white nationalism of Donald Trump take for granted the contemporary division of the world—white spaces of relative affluence and security enclosed and walled off from nonwhite spaces of relative impoverishment and instability.

Within the United States, border nationalism takes for granted the whiteness of the contemporary nation space. Benedict Anderson has taught us to recognize flags and monuments, those grandiose symbols punctuating the landscape with deliberate meaning, as self-conscious sites of national identification; critical Indigenous scholars have begun to turn our attention to the landscape itself—the naturalized space of the nation—shaped by histories of white settlement, Native elimination, racial subordination, exclusion, and the strenuous avoidance of those same histories.[27] When most Americans think of California, for instance, they may conjure images of tech and celebrity but seldom Chinese rail workers, Mexican farm workers, or Indigenous Tongva. If white nationalism is the term we reserve for the kind of identification represented by Confederate flags, border nationalism is the political unconscious, the deep structures of feeling or common sense cultivated by social landscapes, legal institutions, and political discourse that tend to naturalize a contemporary racial geography. The proposed wall appears to most Americans as an obscene monument to white nationalism, but those same Americans often take for granted the social landscapes and racial geographies cut by the border itself.

The O'odham remind us that there is nothing natural or inevitable about the United States' contemporary borders. Nor is there anything natural or inevitable about the United States' assertion of a unilateral right to restrict the movement of others. Their survivance reminds us not only of their community's prior and persistent claim to lands now situated within the United States, but of their prior claim to move freely across those same lands. That freedom of movement, though formally recognized by the United States, is one that predates the United States and the nation-state system—and is exercised independently of it.

Indigenous persistence confronts us with both the "ongoing life" of settler colonialism and its "failure," as Audra Simpson has argued.[28] Settler colonialism is not simply the regrettable prehistory to the founding of our liberal democracy. Instead, it a violence that ramifies, giving rise to a complex set of legal institutions, social arrangements, political rationalities, and cultural narratives that maintain themselves, in part, by obscuring their origins and naturalizing their effects. And yet settler colonialism remains a "failure," in Simpson's account, because it remains incomplete. "It takes a great deal of work," Aileen Moreton-Robinson notes, "to maintain Canada, the United States, Hawai'I ... as white possessions."[29] It takes a great deal of work—ideological work, but also routine violence—to maintain the essential whiteness of a nation on a continent of nonwhite people.

In her *Mohawk Interruptus*, Simpson recognizes Indigenous assertions of presence and priority as acts of political resistance, disruptive of the imagined unity between the settler nation and Indigenous land. She focuses her analysis, in part, on the very acts of resistance practiced by the Iroquois (Haudenosaunee), whose confederacy spans the U.S.–Canadian border.[30] Many Iroquois refuse to display their Canadian passports at the Canadian border. They insist on crossing the border with passports issued by the Haudenosaunee Confederacy, invoking rights to Iroquois movement guaranteed by the Jay Treaty of 1794, signed by the United States and Great Britain.[31] By refusing to display their Canadian passports, Iroquois endure the irritation and hardship of political nonrecognition, risking immigrant detention, but they also refuse the national identity imposed on them by colonial governments.

Simpson reads such acts of defiance as part of a broader "politics of refusal," which she offers as an alternative to a politics of "recognition," so widely embraced within liberal societies as a meaningful corrective to historical violence. Recognition of Indigenous difference has itself been a primary technique of colonial governance.[32] Claiming for themselves a freedom of movement that is prior to, outside of, and independent of state dispensation, these Indigenous activists invoke alternative forms of sovereignty, sources of self-determination.

How might an acknowledgment of Indigenous priority—a prior relation to both land and movement—unsettle the nation-state frame through which questions about immigration are often raised? What do settlers and recent immigrants owe to the Indigenous peoples from whom this land was stolen? What do we owe to Indigenous peoples who moved freely across an undivided continent? And how might questions like these help us to reframe contemporary immigration debates and to imagine our way beyond the impasse that has defined immigration debates, the dead ends of settler nationalism, and colonial capitalism?

These are questions that cannot be answered without acknowledging indigeneity as an ethical and epistemic starting point. Like Simpson, I use the term indigeneity not to refer to a particular ethnographic subject, but to recognize a form of political agency that exceeds the liberal democratic nation-state frame.[33] Indigeneity, in this sense, is not a circumscribed identity, but a political practice—the work of preserving and proliferating relationships between peoples and land that are not reducible to, remain outside of, and continuously challenge colonial modernity.[34] It is a politics of persistence that exposes the colonial roots of the modern state and the essential restlessness of colonial capitalism that continuously uproots people, turning homelands into zones of extraction while forcing displaced peoples to labor in the service of a global economy that reproduces and intensifies racialized inequality and instability.[35]

II. REMAPPING THE CRISIS

In *The Undercommons*, social theorists Stefano Harney and Fred Moten open their chapter on settler colonialism and its "surrounds" with a classic Hollywood image, one of a rugged frontiersman defending his encampment against the Indians who surround him. Hollywood, they write, had an "upside down" way of representing settler colonialism, "inverting... the role of aggressor so that colonialism is made to look like self-defense."[36] The image itself, Harney and Moten point out, is not a false image: The settlers are, as a matter of fact, surrounded by Natives. The image represents a certain truth. What is false, or unreal, is the settler's understanding or construction of his relationship to the Natives who surround him. It is the settler who threatens the Native—not the other way around. It is the settler who introduces danger to the scene, who invades. And it is his own act of invasion that occasions his terror, which he then uses to justify the catastrophic violence that he inflicts on others in the name of self-defense.

For the past decade, unauthorized migration has been described as a "crisis." But for whom and in what sense is it a crisis? The language of crisis is sometimes used to acknowledge the extreme vulnerability of migrants forced to flee their circumstances. More often, it is used to refer to the threat that unauthorized migrants pose to the existing global order. What is often presented to us as a crisis of unruly people is really a crisis of state power—a crisis of authority, legitimacy, and control. Unauthorized migration confronts us with the essential instability of our contemporary world order. It confronts us with the essential failure of the international system of nation-states, which took shape after the decline of formal empire mainly to preserve imperial asymmetries and to keep people in place. Within the western hemisphere, unauthorized migration confronts us with the catastrophic ramifications of settling a white nation in an Indigenous continent.

BORDERING AN EMPIRE

In his book *How to Hide an Empire*, historian Daniel Immerwahr refers to the familiar representation of the United States—the outline of the contiguous forty-eight states—as the "logo map."[37] Maps often lie, as geographers acknowledge, but Immerwahr's quarrel with the logo map is that it bears almost no resemblance to the country's legal borders. Most maps of the United States now include Hawai'i and Alaska, floating in the peripheries and seldom drawn to scale, but they almost never include Puerto Rico, though Puerto Rico is home to 3.5 million American citizens. Nor do they include the United States' other inhabited territories—American Samoa, Guam, the U.S. Virgin Islands, and the Northern Mariana Islands—or the hundreds of uninhabited (or depopulated) islands that the United States has annexed over the past half century.[38] Immerwahr argues that, in fact, it is almost impossible to visualize the current contours of the American empire, in his words, a "[p]ointillist [e]mpire," now encompassing roughly a thousand military bases across the globe.[39] The problem with the logo map, in his account, is that it allows Americans to imagine themselves an ordinary nation while disavowing the nation's colonial history and imperial dimensions.

There are other ways in which the conventional map obscures the settler imperial character of the United States. First, the logo map, bordered by oceans east and west, tends to naturalize the United States' current dimensions, rendering its continental sweep as inevitable as the land mass stretching "from sea to shining sea." Of course, there is nothing natural or inevitable about the United States' coastal borders. Instead, they represent the culmination of long-contested processes of territorial expansion, Indigenous displacement, racial enslavement, and white settlement.[40] In the first half of the nineteenth century, the United States doubled, then tripled in size, purchasing vast territories from France, annexing the Republic of Texas, and seizing half of Mexico. Indigenous peoples, among the other hundreds of thousands crossed by the border—European settlers, free and enslaved Africans, Mexicans and mestizos—were seldom consulted by the empires that traded their lands. By the second half of the nineteenth century, the United States no longer recognized tribal sovereignty at all, asserting instead unilateral sovereign power—"plenary power"—over Indigenous peoples and lands. The plenary power doctrine, a doctrine with its origins in colonial conquest, was given its current sweeping articulation in the late nineteenth century—a paradoxical high moment of both imperial expansion and exclusionary nationalism—through the experience of accelerated Indian removal, overseas expansion, and Asian exclusion.[41]

If, within the national imaginary, the west coast has come to represent the boundlessness of settler ambition—manifest destiny—the southern border represents its racial limit. For the United States, territorial expansion, legal historians have observed, has been constrained primarily by its attachment to whiteness.[42] For instance, at the end of the Mexican–American War in 1848, when Congress was faced with the opportunity to acquire large swaths of Mexico, it resolved to take as much land as possible with as few people as possible, reluctant to incorporate into the national body a mass of racialized others. Abraham Lincoln, at the time a representative from Illinois, recommended that the United States should take "the unsettled half" of Mexico, into which the United States could "introduce an American population." Of the populated half, he worried, "we could derive little benefit from it," since "it was not proposed to kill the Mexican population to drive them out, to confiscate their lands and property, or to make them slaves."[43] Another test of the nation's willingness to incorporate nonwhite others came after the end of the Spanish–American War in 1898, when the United States claimed possession of several overseas territories. Then, in the *Insular Cases* of 1901, the Supreme Court innovated a framework for claiming possession of territories while denying constitutional rights to the inhabitants of those territories, implementing a differentiated rule of law predicated on racial difference.

Just as the image of the bordered nation tends to naturalize a violently constructed nation-space, it also tends to naturalize a brutally engineered identity between people and place throughout North America. For centuries, European imperialism oversaw the mass transfer of millions—free as well as forced migrants—always for the benefit of empire states and their settler counterparts. European imperialism set the world in motion, but within Europe and its settler counterparts today, immigration debates seem to conjure a far more static image of the world, structured around the imagined identity between people and place. Contemporary immigration debates seem to take for granted, as Akhil Gupta and James Ferguson have written, an image of the world as it appears on the world map, an "inherently fragmented space, divided by different colors into diverse national societies, each 'rooted' in its proper place."[44] The solidity of the U.S. inkblot on the world map gives the impression of a fixed identity between a territory and its inhabitants, suppressing not only the considerable heterogeneity among those living in the United States, but also the multiplicity of migrations—again, free and forced—that have brought involuntary relation to different peoples into geographic proximity.

In much of postcolonial Asia and Africa, the nation-state form is widely recognized to be an ill-fitting imposition, reflecting the monoculturalist preoccupations of imperial Europe rather than the varied experience or political longings of the formerly colonized.[45] The United States, unlike former colonies in Asia, Africa, and South America, is not a postcolonial nation. It has never been decolonized. It remains a settler colony. Its declaration of national independence ended one form of imperial relation only to inaugurate another. Freeing itself of the limits imposed by the British government, the United States would enlarge itself with new intensity, relying, as it had as a colony, on the exploitation of enslaved Africans and the expropriation of Indians. Within this landscape of racial diversity, Natsu Taylor Saito shrewdly observes, whiteness emerges as a peculiar form of national identity, "constructed and defended as a rigidly exclusive category precisely because it is not a descriptor of national origin but a marker of entitlement to colonial power, privilege and property."[46]

Critical histories of immigration law tend to focus our attention on the role that racialized exclusion—the racial bar and ethnic quotas—has played in preserving white nationalism since the late nineteenth century, often overlooking the role the practices of racial *inclusion*—recruitment and incorporation—have played in shaping both racial geography and national identity. Through the nineteenth century, European immigrants were encouraged to participate in the project of colonial settlement by federal, state, and local governments, which offered varieties of material and ideological inducements to new Americans.[47] These settlers were lured across oceans and a vast continent with promises of cheap land, voting rights, and citizenship. By contrast, their Asian counterparts were recruited (or conned) to labor but denied the same privileges of political membership. They were denied the right to own land and were frustrated in their attempts to establish families.[48]

And while histories of immigration law tend to focus on acts of legislative exclusion, they tend to overlook legal and extra-legal acts of *forced expulsion*—periodic campaigns to remove racialized others have also played an important role in maintaining the United States' racial character. It is no coincidence that the euphemism now used to refer to the deportation of immigrants—"removal"—is the same euphemism once used to refer to the expulsion of Indigenous peoples, just as it is no accident that the word "rendition" was once used to refer to the capture and return of fugitive slaves.[49] In the United States, the history of removal is one that has repeated itself continuously, not only as a strategy for eliminating Indigenous peoples—from the continent as well as overseas territories—but periodically purging Black, Asian, and Latin Americans from their homes.

THE POST/COLONIAL BORDER

Colonial borders never merely represent an existing divide. Instead, as Achille Mbembe suggests, colonial borders produce the difference that they govern, "writing on the ground a new set of social and spatial relations."[50] The U.S.–Mexico border, as it was drawn and redrawn, did not merely mark an existing division between national territories or people. Instead, the border played a critical role in dividing national territories and distinctly racialized national communities, yielding, as María Josefina Saldaña-Portillo put it, "the United States as nonindigenous space atop Mexico as indigenous space."[51] Beyond linguistic and cultural differences, the essentialized difference maintained by the southern border, particularly within the American imaginary, is the difference between white and nonwhite, civilized and barbarian, settler and Indian.

After the Mexican–American War, a war of conquest, the United States seized the northern third of Mexico. Even in the "unsettled half" of Mexico, as Lincoln anticipated, American conceptions of national identity would clash violently with the existing racial heterogeneity that had come to define northern

Mexico, a borderland that had become home to especially diverse multiracial and multiethnic communities.[52] While the United States largely conceived of itself as a white nation, by the mid-nineteenth century, the Mexican government had begun to promote a very different sort of racial ideology, *mestizaje*, a postcolonial national unity rooted in practices of racial admixture and assimilation.[53] The racial diversity that had come to define northern Mexico at the time of annexation was both a reflection of Mexico's national ideology and the result of land policies intended to promote settlement along its northern frontier.

Long before Mexico declared its independence from Spain, its northern territory, though sparsely populated, had been home to diverse Indian communities, including Tohono O'odham, Yaqui, Mayo, Pima, and Opata.[54] In the early nineteenth century, as the new Mexican government sought to establish supremacy in the region, it was forced to contend with powerful raiding tribes, the Apache and Comanche who exercised considerable control over the region.[55] The tribes themselves had turned to raiding Spanish settlements in northern Mexico as part of a larger strategy for survival after they had been removed by the United States from the northern plains.[56] Soon after it declared its independence, the Mexican government enacted a law to encourage migration to and settlement on the northern frontier to serve as a buffer against raiding Indians. The settlement law drew a diverse population of newcomers, including Indians who had been displaced from parts of Florida and Texas, as well as African Americans who had escaped southern slavery. These new settlers were lured by promises of land, freedom, and membership within a national community that they recognized to be more inclusive of racial and ethnic difference than that of the United States.[57]

After the war, in the Treaty of Guadalupe Hidalgo, signed in 1848, the United States promised that Mexicans living in the annexed territory would be allowed to enjoy the rights and privileges of citizenship—though citizenship at the time was restricted to "free white person[s]."[58] According to the Treaty, Mexicans in the annexed territory could choose to stay or "to remove" to Mexico, to retain their Mexican citizenship, or become Americans. Either way, their property rights would be "inviolably respected."[59] In practice, however, citizenship and property rights were enjoyed only by an elite white minority. The diverse majority living in the region who, until then, had enjoyed a certain equality within Mexican society, was less easily absorbed into the U.S. national body.[60]

Nonwhite people living in the annexed territories were particularly vulnerable to being deprived of land and citizenship; the territories themselves became part of the United States only after white Americans established control of them. After annexation, mestizos and afromestizos living in the annexed territories were routinely adjudged racially ineligible for citizenship; afromestizos suddenly found themselves governed by a repressive Black code; Indians were categorically denied citizenship and lost control of lands promised to them by the Spanish Crown and recognized by Mexico.[61] Long after the United States formally annexed roughly two-thirds of Mexico's territory, as Gloria Anzaldúa recalls, poor, nonwhite communities on both sides of the border were cheated or frightened out of their lands by armed vigilantes, agricultural businesses, and often even neighbors.[62] "Gringos in the U.S. Southwest consider the inhabitants of the borderlands transgressors, aliens—whether they possess documents or not, whether they're Chicanos, Indians or Blacks."[63] Those who did not belong were violated with impunity, "raped, maimed, strangled, gassed, shot."[64]

Anticipating that Mexicans living in the annexed territories would be consigned to second-class citizenship, Mexican treaty negotiators sought assurances that annexed territories would be quickly "incorporated into the Union of the United States."[65] California, with its vast territory, relatively few Mexicans and Indians, and many recent white settlers, was granted statehood almost immediately after the war. But incorporation of the remaining territory, with its diverse population, would remain stalled for decades.[66] As Senator Henry Clay later explained, New Mexico Territory, with its "variety of races ... pure and mixed," was "not now, [nor] for a long time to come ... prepared for State government."[67] The Territory was gradually carved into separate states and incorporated as they gained white majorities—Colorado in 1876, Utah in 1896—but for decades, the remaining territory would remain suspended in what Kevin Bruyneel has described as a colonial "third space."[68] It was not until 1912, after a flood of white settlers doubled the population, that New Mexico and Arizona were granted full statehood—last among the contiguous forty-eight.[69]

The international boundary line that now divides the United States from Mexico thus obscures another set of international relations—between Indigenous nations and settler colonial nations.[70] Saldaña-Portillo demonstrates that over the course of the nineteenth century, as the United States and Mexico recast themselves as postcolonial nations, each adopted divergent constructions of national identity—the United States "broadly exclusionary" and Mexico "broadly incorporative."[71] But neither construction, she insists, can claim independence from the Indigenous worlds they displaced. The United States' exclusionary national form has been entirely shaped by Indigenous dispossession and displacement. Mexico's incorporative national form, *mestizaje*, relies on the simultaneous appropriation and erasure of Indigenous claims to territorial belonging, as well as the erasure of Indigenous difference through assimilation and miscegenation.

Notwithstanding their differences, Saldaña-Portillo observes, the United States and Mexico were united in the view that the elimination of "savage" Indians was essential to the establishment of the nation-state system within the western hemisphere.[72] In an often overlooked provision of the Treaty of Guadalupe Hidalgo, the United States promised to defend Mexico against the threat posed by "savage" Indians, "in the same way, and with equal diligence and energy, as if the same incursions were mediated or committed within its own territory, against its own citizens."[73] What is striking about the provision, Saldaña-Portillo notes, is its articulation of an equality and "solemn" bond between the United States and Mexico—until then, warring enemies—forged in their common defense of the emerging nation-state system within the hemisphere against the threat of savage uprising.[74]

THE BORDER IS NOT A LINE

The United States has never been contained by its own borders. The United States was founded in resistance to the imposition of a border, namely the Proclamation Line of 1763, drawn by the British Crown to constrain settler expansion and protect Indians from settler encroachment.[75] Immerwahr observes that the logo map, outlining the contiguous forty-eight states, represents the territorial limits of the country as they were for only three years. It was only three years after the Gadsden Purchase was ratified, filling out the logo map and dividing the Tohono O'odham tribe, that the United States began to annex small islands across the Caribbean and Pacific, entering a new phase of overseas imperialism.[76]

Territorial occupation is only one form of imperialism. Since the late nineteenth century, the United States has innovated various forms of neo-imperialism, including the manipulation of other states through the assertion of military power and the imposition of capitalist arrangements.[77] The southern border, materially and symbolically, is particularly bound up with the United States' neo-imperial relation to its neighbors in Latin America. The border is not a line, Ann Stoler reminds us, but a regime of "managed mobilities, mobilizing and immobilizing populations, dislocating and relocating peoples according to a set of changing rules and hierarchies."[78] Laws governing migration from Latin America for the past century have been largely governed by the whims of the United States economy, pulling and pushing migrants across the border in periodic cycles of absorption and expulsion. The border has become a technology for producing expropriable persons: the criminalization of migration renders unauthorized immigrants vulnerable to hyper-exploitation as workers; as potential prisoners, they have become a source of income- and political capital–generation as the United States partners with for-profit prisons for immigrant detention.[79]

Migration itself has been compelled not only by labor demands in the United States but also by mass displacements caused by U.S. policies, including the imposition of free trade agreements, introduction of foreign aid, geopolitical organization of the war on drugs, and the effects of climate change.[80] Harsha Walia offers the enormously useful term "border imperialism" to refer to the ways in which the United States' assertion of economic and military power stimulates and provokes the very migrations it seeks to prevent—particularly within the hemispheric context.[81] In his 2012 documentary *Harvest of Empire*, based on a book with the same title, Juan Gonzalez traces major migrations from the Caribbean and Central America—Puerto Rico, Cuba, Dominican Republic, El Salvador, Mexico, Guatemala, Nicaragua—to a continuous history of U.S. economic policy and military intervention.[82] In some instances, he traces the roots of migration to a history of formal occupation or domination, as from Puerto Rico and Cuba. Others—the mass exodus of women and children from El Salvador, the migration of Indigenous Guatemalans, for instance—he traces to decades of informal and covert U.S. intervention in Central America. Gonzalez's documentary plods through atrocities in one country after another—and though the bloody particulars vary from country to country, the expansion of U.S. power remains constant. Over the course of the film, the grid of nation-states that organizes the film begins to give way to another picture: one of a centuries-long hemispheric invasion.

WAYWARD MOVEMENTS

In the days leading up to the 2018 midterm elections, President Trump sought to drum up support for conservative candidates by promising to defend the nation against an immigrant "invasion."[83] As a caravan of migrants, most of them Guatemalans and Hondurans seeking asylum, made its way up the continent, the president sent five thousand armed guards to the southern border and threatened that they might be ordered to shoot.[84] He referred to the caravan—which included women, children, and people in wheelchairs—as an "onslaught," suggesting that it harbored "criminals," "unknown Middle Easterners" (terrorists, presumably), and "diseases." On one occasion, he said, "These aren't people. These are animals."[85] Trump's Democratic opponents had relatively little to say in response, apparently heeding the advice of strategists who convinced them that they had nothing to gain by challenging his characterization of events or his assertion of state power.[86]

But the arrival of the caravan, like any encounter with another, confronts us with an ethical challenge. Emmanuel Levinas famously seized upon the face-to-face encounter as a foundational scene of ethics.[87] The physical encounter with another confronts us with our mutual vulnerability—each is exposed to the threat of violence from the other—and in turn, our inescapable relation and responsibility to one another. Postcolonial critics have cast doubt on Levinas's model, arguing that the scene of supposed mutuality staged in his face-to-face encounter tends to efface the real inequality that has historically conditioned the philosopher's encounter with the Other.[88] But at the very least, the physical presence of the Other has the potential to disrupt phantasmic constructions of the Other—as terrorist, invader, or other faceless abstraction.

In this vein, Guillermo Torres has urged white Americans to "give these migrants/immigrants a lingering look. A respectful look. See the face of Native

America."[89] He suggests that white Americans who boast of their Indian ancestry, real or imagined, ought to welcome these migrants, as they would welcome their distant relatives. "Indian bloodlines do not stop at the present-day U.S.-Mexico border," he reminds us, and "there is little difference between a Navajo or Aztec, or Mayan and Opòn . . . Inka or Cherokee." These migrants, Torres wants us to recognize, "are not the comfortable, rich European settlers with fair skin and blue and green eyes, the ones who have raped Mexico and Latin America for riches and resources."[90] They are overwhelmingly Indigenous peoples whose ancestors lived on this continent before it was divided.

After the Trump administration adopted its zero-tolerance policy in April 2018, seven children have died in U.S. custody.[91] If we were to give them a respectful look, we would recognize that all but one of them were Indigenous—not simply Guatemalan, as is often reported. At least five of these children were Maya.[92] "We are the majority in Guatemala," Juanita Cabrera Lopez explains, "yet we are the most abandoned and neglected by the state."[93] Cabrera Lopez, Executive Director of the International Mayan League and advocate for Indigenous migrants, insists that when we remember the children whose lives were "stolen," we not only say their names but recognize their Indigenous nations: Claudia Patricia Gómez González, Maya Mam, twenty years old, from San Juan Ostuncalco, Quetzaltenango, died May 23, 2018; Jakelin Caal Maquín, Maya Q'eqchi', seven years old, from San Antonio Secortez, of Raxruhá in Alta Verapaz, died December 7, 2018; Felipe Gómez Alonzo, Maya Chuj, eight years old, from Nentón, Huehuetenango, died December 24, 2018; Juan de León Gutiérrez, Maya Ch'orti', sixteen years old, from Caserio Tizamarte in the village El Tesoro, Camotán, Chiquimula, died April 30, 2019; Wilmer Josué Ramírez Vásquez, whose Indigenous nation has not yet been identified, two years old, from Chiquimula, of Ch'orti' Maya territory, died May 14, 2019; Carlos Gregorio Hernández Vásquez, Maya Achi, sixteen years old, from San José el Rodeo, Cubulco Baja Verapaz, died May 20, 2019.[94]

The caravan is not an invasion but a movement for survival, undertaken not exclusively but overwhelmingly by Indigenous Americans who have been uprooted, most recently, by genocide, land dispossession, and environmental disruption—forms of violence in which the United States has had a direct hand.[95] Since 2018, the number of children and families fleeing Guatemala for the U.S. border has doubled; in the first half of 2019, U.S. authorities apprehended more children from Guatemala than from Honduras and El Salvador combined.[96] Most of these children come from the western highlands of Guatemala, where Indigenous communities have struggled to hold on to their land for more than a century.[97]

Though they have been made foreigners, these Indigenous migrants are not strangers to the United States. A long history of political adventurism, economic exploitation, and resource extraction has made them intimate relations. Almost as soon as Guatemala, Honduras, and El Salvador gained their independence from

Spain in 1821, American entrepreneurs took advantage of political and economic insecurity in the region to secure their own interests, often with direct support from the U.S. government. It was only a few years later that the United States, with its articulation of the Monroe Doctrine, claimed supreme authority over the western hemisphere.

Jakelin Caal Maquín was born in Alta Verapaz, where Maya Q'eqchi' have struggled to remain since the arrival of Spanish settlers.[98] Since the mid-nineteenth century, Maya Q'eqchi' have been displaced by waves of land speculators, *ladino* coffee planters, and German and American entrepreneurs.[99] Q'eqchi' who resisted were routinely killed or exiled.[100] Local governments sided with the owners of the emerging plantation economy, facilitating the judicial and extrajudicial transfer of land from peasants to planters while establishing bureaucratic and punitive regimes designed to ensure planters a cheap and captive supply of peasant laborers. In 1888, ninety-seven Alta Verapaz Maya farmers owned farms comparable in size to plantations; by 1949, none did.[101]

The Q'eqchi', alongside other Indigenous communities resisting exploitation and repression, stood to benefit from ambitious land reform projects initiated by President Jacobo Árbenz in 1952. But within two years, the democratically elected president was ousted by a military coup orchestrated by the CIA. The United Fruit Company, the U.S. multinational whose vast interests in Guatemala would have been affected by the proposed land reform, lobbied Congress to intervene. Rebellion followed, then further repression. The conflict took a dark turn after 1965, with the arrival of U.S. security advisor John P. Longan who, before coming to Guatemala, had earned a reputation for extreme violence as a U.S. Border Patrol agent. In Guatemala, Longan trained an elite death squad that, with three months, had kidnapped, tortured, and assassinated at least thirty people, unleashing a terrifying brutality in the region.[102]

The litany of offenses committed by the United States in Guatemala—and throughout Central America—is by now familiar, but it is worth emphasizing that what the United States often refers to as a civil war was primarily a U.S.-orchestrated war against Indigenous peoples resisting dispossession, exploitation, and political repression. Grandin, a historian of the war, writes that rural villagers "fought to establish land rights, end forced labor, and assure the ability simply to survive."[103] Before the end of the conflict, the U.S.-backed military in Guatemala had murdered an estimated 200,000 people.[104] During the most brutal final years of the conflict, over 100,000 Mayas were killed with unfathomable cruelty. A 1996 peace agreement brought an end to the extreme violence but did nothing to redistribute lands, as had been promised, or to prevent further Indigenous dispossession. Instead, at the urging of the United States and international development groups, the Guatemalan government opened large swaths of the country to foreign investments in mining and damming projects, the production of African palm oil, and hardwood timbering—forms of extractive capitalism that further threaten Indigenous survival.[105]

Indigenous communities, in turn, have resisted their imposition. In Huehuetenango, where Felipe Gómez Alonzo lived, local people resisted the building of the Northern Transversal Highway, a project initiated before the war to open northern Guatemala to resource extraction. They resisted the project not because they have no need for roads, but because the Israeli company contracted to build it threated to destroy a protected forest adjacent to the community's only supply of fresh drinking water.[106] A few miles away, Indigenous activists have been imprisoned and murdered for defending lands against extractive industries. In 2018, Guatemala experienced the sharpest rise yet in the number of environmental activists murdered, making it the deadliest country for environmental activists per capita.[107] Most of those killed were leaders of the Campesino Development Committee (CODECA), an Indigenous-led social movement advocating for land redistribution, energy nationalization, and a plurinational state.[108] Within a day of the worst killings, Felipe and his father concluded their two-thousand-mile journey to the United States border to request asylum. He died in U.S. custody six days later.[109]

The arrival of the migrant unsettles the very mapping of reality on which our border regime is premised, challenging the colonial divisions that have distanced the United States from those affected by its interventions. The border obscures both relation and responsibility. Our task is to remap and rename the crisis. It is also to recognize and receive the migrant Other, not as an object of sympathy, but as a fully realized political subject, one who carries in her movement the capacity to renew our democratic vision and to redefine the conditions of our shared existence. Immigration restrictionists, not surprisingly, recognize the political subjectivity of border crossers only in terms of criminality; their unauthorized movement renders them "illegal." But those who favor a more open border policy also participate in the epistemic erasure of migrant agency. Economistic approaches to relaxing border restrictions regard migrants as inert objects, moved by the push and pull of invisible hands, and value them as units of human capital.[110] Humanitarian approaches readily identify the crying child, the caged body, the muted corpse as the object of sympathy and human rights, but not the self-authorized freedom seeker.[111] Liberal arguments sounding in the language of fundamental rights tend to reinscribe not just the universalist pretensions of political liberalism, but also its individualist assumptions, the very constructions of independence and sovereignty that underwrite colonial capitalism.

The migrant caravan, a political movement with plainly performative dimensions, resists this conventional effacing. Judith Butler observes that mass demonstrations have the power to call into question the character of our democratic orders.[112] As embodied actions, mass demonstrations call out the inadequacy of democratic discourse and deliberation, the language and arena within which political battles are thought to be fairly waged. As collective actions, mass demonstrations call into question the representativeness of our democratic institutions, confronting them with an alternative expression of popular will and the prospect for real self-determination. In this sense, the arrival of the migrant caravan challenges American democracy by confronting it with its constitutive exclusion, calling into question how an American people defines itself. Jacques Rancière has described democratic practice as precisely this—as "the inscription of the part of those who have no part."[113] The Q'eqchi' farmer may never hold the status of citizen, she may be denied fundamental rights and formal recognition, but with her arrival, she challenges these circumscriptions to insist that she is a part of our political community all the same.

The movement began on October 12, 2018, the 526th anniversary of Christopher Columbus's arrival in the Americas, when roughly a thousand men, women, and children convened at the bus terminal of San Pedro Sula, Honduras, one of the most violent cities in the world, in one of the poorest countries on the continent.[114] Because they refuse to live under the threat of gang violence, Roberto Saviano has called the migrant caravan "the biggest anti-mafia march the world has ever seen."[115] Recognizing that border controls allow the state to regulate and maintain wage differentials—often consigning migrants to labor for U.S. employers and consumers for lower wages and with fewer protections—Massimiliano Tomba affirms the unauthorized movement of migrant laborers as a form of insurgency.[116] Unauthorized labor migration, he recognizes as a form of "workers' resistance to control and ... of self-determination of the wage against capital."[117]

The caravan, like unauthorized migration generally, in this view, represents not just a flight from repression but a movement against it, a refusal to be confined by borders, especially when those borders consign people to conditions of violence and poverty that render life unlivable. By traveling together, the migrants of the caravan shield one another from rape and robbery, and free themselves from dependence on coyotes.[118] Engaged in collective acts of way-making, the migrants of the caravan rehearse a form of citizenship that is not reducible to legal status or entitlement.[119]

While the caravan announces itself as public performance and concerted action, those who make the journey in stealth and solitude are also part of a larger political movement. Affirming the political character and collectivity of Black Southerners who refused to submit to the humiliations of Jim Crow, W.E.B. Du Bois recast the Great Migration as a political action, a "general strike." Drawing on Du Bois's reconceptualization, Saidiya Hartman gathers the movement of Black women and girls who made their way to Northern cities only to find themselves ensnared by regulations that rendered them criminals, delinquents, "wayward" subjects of discipline and reform.[120] Hartman recuperates the revolutionary character of these wayward girls: "Waywardness," she writes, is

> the avid longing for a world not ruled by a master, man or the police. The errant path taken by the leaderless swarm, in search of a place better than here.... The unregulated movement of drifting and wandering... ambulatory possibility, interminable migrations... the everyday struggle to live free. The attempt to elude capture by never settling... Waywardness is a practice of possibility at a time when all roads, except the ones created by *smashing out*, are foreclosed.[121]

To recognize such movements as revolutionary movements is not to romanticize the migration of those forced to flee their homes—to be clear, the recognition of an ante-colonial freedom of movement necessarily includes the freedom to stay. Instead, it is to affirm the political subjectivity of those who resist regulation and enclosure and to reclaim a shared capacity to imagine our way beyond the enclosures of the present.

An Indigenous uprising that was also a transnational movement, the caravan is a gesture toward a political community that extends beyond the nation-state, a gesture made by those who have never adequately been represented by the nation-state. It is, at once, an act of rebellion—an autonomous movement, made independently and in open defiance of nation-state bordering practices—and an insistence on relationality and reciprocity.

CONCLUSION

In this essay, an attempt to underscore the relation between settler colonialism and the border, I have preferred to use the term "unsettling" to "decolonizing" because, as Yarimar Bonilla puts it, "there is no precolonial status to return."[122] The work of unsettling requires more than an unwinding of history or rewriting of imperial maps. Instead, it calls on us to desert, to "destitute," and to "delink" from the colonial episteme and, in turn, to recover and reaffirm ways of being that have been devalued and disavowed by the settler modernity.[123] Recognizing that settler colonialism continuously produces divisions among those it governs, the work of imagining alternatives to our contemporary regime requires that we draw new lines of continuity, comparison, and convergence among peoples and histories variously affected by settler colonialism.

In this sense, the critical response to family separation and detention policies issued by Indigenous activists and thinkers is instructive, offering an important corrective to Trump exceptionalism by resituating his administration's policies within a widened framework of settler nationalism. For instance, in July of 2019, after the government announced plans to open a child detention center at Fort Sill, a military base in Oklahoma, Indigenous peoples led a protest to block access at the site.[124] Recalling histories of Indigenous confinement and displacement, one critic explained, "We, as Indigenous peoples, know the pain and generational trauma that comes from Fort Sill and camps just like it."[125] Fort Sill was opened as a military base in 1869 to house U.S. soldiers during the so-called Indian Wars, wars of U.S expansion.[126] In 1894, it was used to imprison nearly 400 Apache men, women, and children, including the Apache leader, Geronimo, who died there in 1909.[127] During World War II, the base was used to intern about 350 Japanese Americans. Survivors of internment joined in protesting the reopening of Fort Sill, identifying it as a site of continuous violence used to contain and suppress perceived threats to settler nationalism. A seventy-five-year-old activist and filmmaker, Satsuki Ina, holding an enlarged photograph of herself as a child at the camp, explained, "We are here today to protest the repetition of history."[128]

Actions like these confront the settler nation with repressed histories of violence while shoring up common grievances across lines of difference. In 2017, for instance, Indigenous leaders and undocumented immigrants convened a daylong meeting devoted to "cross-cultural remembrance and solidarity."[129] Indigenous leaders expressed solidarity with undocumented youth by recalling their own history of being denied citizenship and travel without documentation. Organizers of the meeting identified the work of remembrance and exchange as both an essential corrective to nationalist narratives and critical to imagining a "collective beginning."[130]

Creating the conditions for imagining a collective alternative requires an unsettling of the framework of liberal inclusion to which advocates for immigration often appeal. This framework tends to reinscribe the sovereignty of the white settler nation while minoritizing others. The differences between liberal and Indigenous protests against the Muslim ban are illustrative. After President Trump issued an executive order banning travel from several Muslim-majority countries, Indigenous activists joined hundreds of others in protest, but they also used the occasion to reassert their priority and to challenge settler constructions of national belonging. As protestors at the Los Angeles airport sang the national anthem and renditions of "This Land Is Your Land"—songs intended to sound the protestors' challenge to the Muslim ban in notes of patriotism and inclusivity—the Tongva, the original inhabitants of what is now Los Angeles, played drums as they performed a traditional welcome ceremony.[131]

Nick Estes and Melanie Yazzie, Indigenous activists and scholars, marched behind the Tongva, holding placards that read "No Ban on Stolen Land" and "Refugees Welcome on Native Land," at once inviting identification and solidarity among the nation's outsiders and reasserting sovereignty over land and questions of migration.[132] The gesture is not uncomplicated, but it expands our framework of understanding by denying the United States its claim to determine, as Estes writes, "who belongs or who doesn't to a settler nation," while rejecting the settler nation's criteria for inclusion.[133] The authority to welcome is articulated not strictly in terms of temporal priority—who was here first—but in terms of a capacity to rehabilitate the conditions of our shared coexistence. Estes concluded his essay by describing a scene of welcome:

> The Tongva drummers surrounded a Muslim family, singing them an honor song. The singers welcomed them to their homelands. Tears streamed down a young girl's face. She wore a hijab. Moments earlier she appeared frightened. Now at peace. This is what it means to go back to where you came from. Nothing about the complex human condition of shared grief, love, and solidarity is alien to that place of freedom. Call it home.[134]

NOTES

* This essay is adapted from an article published in the *UCLA Law Review* in 2021.

1. Ann Laura Stoler, "Colony," in *Political Concepts: A Critical Lexicon*, ed. Adi Ophir and Ann Laura Stoler (New York: Fordham University Press, 2018), 45, 56.

2. See Joseph H. Carens, *The Ethics of Immigration* (Oxford: Oxford University Press, 2013); Michael Walzer, *Spheres of Justice: A Defense of Pluralism and Equality* (New York: Basic Books, 1983); Arash Abizadeh, "Democratic Theory and Border Coercion: No Right to Unilaterally Control Your Own Borders," *Political Theory* 36, no. 1 (Feb. 2008): 37–65.

3. See Nicholas De Genova, "Spectacles of Migrant 'Illegality': The Scene of Exclusion, the Obscene of Inclusion," *Ethnic and Racial Studies* 36, no. 7 (May 2013): 1180–98.

4. See Nicholas Mezzadra and Brett Neilson, *Border as Method, or The Multiplication of Labor* (Durham: Duke University Press, 2013); Etienne Balibar, "What is a Border," in *Politics and the Other Scene* (New York: Verso, 2002): 75–86.

5. See Anibal Quijano and Michael Ennis, "Coloniality of Power, Ethnocentrism, and Latin America," *Nepantla: Views From the South* 1, no. 3 (2000): 533–80; Walter Mignolo, "Geopolitics of Sensing and Knowing: On (De)coloniality, Border Thinking, and Epistemic Disobedience," *Confero* 1, no. 1 (2001): 129–50; Macarena Gómez-Barris, *The Extractive Zone: Social Ecologies and Decolonial Perspectives* (Durham: Duke University Press, 2017).

6. See, e.g., the work of Alexander Aleinikoff, Stuard Banner, Bethany Berger, Jennifer Chacón, Seth Davis, Christina Duffy Burnett, Paul Frymer, Laura Gómez, Kelly Lytle Hernández, Leila Kanwar, Carrie Rosenbaum, and Natsu Taylor Saito.

7. Stoler, "Colony," 56.

8. Stoler, "Colony," 56.

9. See Greg Grandin, *The End of the Myth: From the Frontier to the Border Wall in the Mind of America* (New York: Metropolitan Books, 2019), 149–53; Daniel Immerwahr, *How to Hide an Empire: A History of the Greater United States* (New York: Farrar, Straus and Giroux, 2019), 77–78; Rachel St. John, *Line in the Sand: A History of the Western U.S.–Mexico Border* (Princeton: Princeton University Press, 2011), 48–50, 63–70, 75.

10. See "History & Culture," Tohono O'odham Nation, accessed March 23, 2020, [https://perma.cc/WSM6-FFLE].

11. Nellie Jo David, "MTW2020 Webinar - Day 3 - O'Odham," posted May 27, 2020, Migrant Trail Walk, YouTube video, [https://perma.cc/CTC5-9477]; see also Ryan Deveraux, "'We Are Still Here': Native Activists in Arizona Resist Trump's Border Wall," *Intercept*, posted November 24, 2019, [https://perma.cc/9N7S-F8R7].

12. Nellie Jo David et al., "Tear Down the Walls w/ the O'odham Anti-Border Collective," September 21, 2020, *Red Nation Podcast*, interview by Melanie Yazzie and Nick Estes, SoundCloud audio, [https://perma.cc/29FN-SWC9]; Nellie Jo David, "Fighting Trump's Border Wall w/ Nellie Jo David," January 13, 2020, *Red Nation Podcast*, interview by Nick Estes, SoundCloud audio, [https://perma.cc/L7HF-S6G9]; Nellie Jo David, "O'odham Land Defenders Lead Indigenous Resistance to Trump's Border Wall Amid Militarized Crackdown," interview by Amy Goodman, *Democracy Now!*, October 12, 2020, Video, 42:19. https://www.democracynow.org/2020/10/12/organ_pipe_national_monument_border_wall.

13. Randal C. Archibold, "Border Fence Must Skirt Objections from Arizona Tribe," *New York Times*, September 20, 2006, [https://perma.cc/Z7CT-FZSB].

14. Archibold, "Border Fence"; David Kelly, "A Tribe Caught in Middle," *L.A. Times*, March 21, 2004, 12:00 a.m., [https://perma.cc/BW6N-9QY4].

15. "History & Culture," Tohono O'odham Nation.

16. Blake Gentry et al., "Indigenous Survival and Settler Colonial Dispossession on the Mexican Frontier: The Case of Cedagi Wahia and Wo'oson O'odham Indigenous Communities," *Journal of Latin American Geography* 18, no. 1 (2019): 65, 66.

17. See Oscar León, "The Government Can and Will Just Waive Any Rights That We Have Today," *The Real News Network*, October 1, 2019, video, [https://perma.cc/4XX6-L5GD]; see "What We Do," Elbit Systems, [https://perma.cc/7DRG-Y3YA].

18. León, "The Government Can and Will"; Tay Wiles, "A Closed Border Gate Has Cut Off Three Tohono O'odham Villages from Their Closest Food Supply," *Pacific Standard*, February 7, 2019, [https://perma.cc/3D2S-ET8V].

19. Oscar León, "Tohono O'odham Nation: 'All These Areas Can Collapse,'" *The Real News Network*, September 15, 2019, video, [https://perma.cc/DHF6-TRHK].

20. O'odham Anti Border Collective, "Before Borders and Barriers Existed O'odham Were Inclusive of All Life and People. As O'odham We Exist Beyond the Lines, We Exist in Circles, We Exist Because," Facebook, video, September 22, 2020, 11:26 p.m., [https://perma.cc/6DAZ-QCKY]; see also Raphael Romero Ruiz, "Protest at Border Wall Site on Hia-Ced O'odham Territory Ends in Standoff, Scuffle," *AZCentral*, September 21, 2020, [https://perma.cc/3NWG-ALD7].

21. O'odham Anti Border Collective, "Before Borders."

22. See Jonathan Rosa and Yarimar Bonilla, "Deprovincializing Trump, Decolonizing Diversity, and Unsettling Anthropology," *American Ethnologist* 44, no. 2 (2017): 201, 201–2.

23. Nell Irvin Painter, "In 'Stony the Road,' in Henry Louis Gates Jr. Captures the History and Images of the Fraught Years After the Civil War," review of "Stony the Road: Reconstruction, White Supremacy, and the Rise of Jim Crow," by Henry Louis Gates Jr., *New York Times*, April 18, 2019, [https://perma.cc/JT9M-N7NB].

24. Radhika Viyas Mongia, "Race, Nationality, Mobility: A History of the Passport," *Public Culture* 11, no. 3 (1999): 527, 528–29. Viyas Mongia uses the term "raced-migration" to refer to the voluntary migration of nonwhite peoples to white metropoles at the turn

of the twentieth century, the problem that gives rise to modern formulations of the nation-state and migration control.

25. Etienne Balibar, "Is There a 'Neo-Racism'?," in *Race, Nation, Class: Ambiguous Identities*, ed. Etienne Balibar and Immanuel Wallerstein, trans. Chris Turner (New York: Verso, 1991), 17.

26. Balibar, 21; see also Justin Desautels-Stein, "International Law's Race Problem," *UCLA Law Review* 67 (2020).

27. Benedict Anderson, *Imagined Communities: Reflections on the Origin and Spread of Nationalism*, revised ed. (New York: Verso, 1991). See generally Jean M. O'Brien, *Firsting and Lasting: Writing Indians Out of Existence in New England* (Minneapolis: University of Minnesota Press, 2010); Mark Rifkin, *Settler Common Sense: Queerness and Everyday Colonialism in the American Renaissance* (Minneapolis: University of Minnesota Press, 2014).

28. Audra Simpson, *Mohawk Interruptus: Political Life Across the Borders of Settler States* (Durham: Duke University Press, 2014), 33.

29. Aileen Moreton-Robinson, *The White Possessive: Property, Power, and Indigenous Sovereignty*, (Minneapolis: University of Minnesota Press, 2015), xi.

30. See Moreton-Robinson, 117–29.

31. Moreton-Robinson, 1–2, 7.

32. Moreton-Robinson, 11–12. See generally Glen Sean Coulthard, *Red Skin, White Masks: Rejecting the Colonial Politics of Recognition* (Minneapolis: University of Minnesota Press, 2014).

33. See, e.g., The Red Nation, *The Red Deal: Indigenous Action to Save Our Earth* (New York: Common Notions, 2021), 2 (identifying indigeneity as "a political condition that challenges the existence and domination of colonial nation-states").

34. See, e.g., Gómez-Barris, *The Extractive Zone*, 2–5; Audra Simpson, "On Ethnographic Refusal: Indigeneity, 'Voice' and Colonial Citizenship," *Junctures* 9, no. 67 (2007).

35. See Simpson, Mohawk Interruptus, at 1–35; J. Kēhaulani Kauanui, "'A Structure, Not an Event': Settler Colonialism and Enduring Indigeneity," *Lateral*, no. 5.1 (2016), [https://perma.cc/9NMX-6AST].

36. Stefano Harney and Fred Moten, *The Undercommons: Fugitive Planning & Black Study* (Minor Compositions, 2013), 17 (quoting Michael Parenti); see also Antony Anghie, *Imperialism, Sovereignty and the Making of International Law* (New York: Cambridge University Press, 2004), 292.

37. Immerwahr, *How to Hide an Empire*, 8–13.

38. See Tom C. W. Lin, "Americans, Almost and Forgotten," *California Law Review* 107, no. 4, (2019): 1249; David Vine, *Island of Shame: The Secret History of the U.S. Military Base on Diego Garcia* (Princeton: Princeton University Press, 2009).

39. Immerwahr, *How to Hide an Empire,* 213; see David Vine, "Where in the World Is the U.S. Military?," *Politico*, July/August 2015, [https://perma.cc/JA6W-V9WP].

40. See generally Paul Frymer, *Building an American Empire: The Era of Territorial and Political Expansion* (Princeton: Princeton University Press, 2017).

41. Sherally Munshi, "'The Courts of the Conqueror': Constitutionalism, Colonialism, and the Time of Redemption," in *Law's Infamy: Understanding the Canon of Bad Law*, ed. Austin Sarat et al. (New York: New York University, 2021), 50–95; T. Alexander Aleinikoff, *Semblages of Sovereignty: The Constitution, the State, and American Citizenship* (Cambridge: Harvard University Press, 2002), 11–38; Kanstroom, 64–67; Natsu Taylor

Saito, "Race and Decolonization: Whiteness as Property in the American Settler Colonial Project," *Harvard Journal on Racial & Ethnic Justice* 31 (2015): 31–67.

42. See Frymer, *Building an American Empire*, 11–17; Immerwahr, *How to Hide an Empire*, 80–82.

43. Immerwahr, *How to Hide an Empire*, 196.

44. Akhil Gupta and James Ferguson, "Beyond 'Culture': Space, Identity, and the Politics of Difference," *Cultural Anthropology* 7, no. 1 (February 1992): 6.

45. See generally Frantz Fanon, *The Wretched of the Earth*, trans. Constance Farrington (New York: Grove Press, 1963); Rabindranath Tagore, *Nationalism* (San Francisco: Book Club of California, 1917).

46. Saito, "Race and Decolonization," 62.

47. See Aziz Rana, "Colonialism and Constitutional Memory," *U.C. Irvine Law Review* 5, no. 2 (2015): 263–88.

48. See generally Kerry Abrams, "Polygamy, Prostitution, and the Federalization of Immigration Law," *Columbia Law Review* 105, no. 3 (2005): 641–82; Rose Cuison Villazor, "Rediscovering Oyama v. California: At the Intersection of Property, Race, and Citizenship," *Washington University Law Review* 87, no. 4 (2010): 979–1016.

49. E.g., Illegal Immigration Reform and Immigrant Responsibility Act of 1996 (IIRIRA), Pub. L. No. 104–208, 110 Stat. 3009.

50. Achille Mbembe, *Necropolitics* (Durham: Duke University Press, 2019), 79.

51. María Josefina Saldaña-Portillo, *Indian Given: Racial Geographies Across Mexico and the United States* (Durham: Duke University Press, 2016), 3–6.

52. Frymer, *Building an American Empire*, 196.

53. While the inclusionary ideology of *mestizaje* embraced by the Mexican government extended freedoms and opportunities to Indigenous, mestizo, and afromestizo peoples that were unavailable in the United States, *mestizaje* was and is not without its own failings. Critics have argued that colonial hierarchies of race and caste were often preserved even within a formal discourse of antiracism and hybridity. Jared Sexton has argued that dreams of transcending racial difference through amalgamation are often dreams of eliminating any trace of Indigenous or Black difference. Writing specifically of José Vasconcelos's vision of la raza cosmica, Sexton writes that its "eugenicist impulses and implications are unavoidable," rendering the nationalist utopia of *mestizaje* not so unlike "the 'ethnic absolutism' of Anglo-Saxon white supremacy." Jared Sexton, *Amalgamation Schemes: Antiblackness and the Critique of Multiracialism* (Minneapolis: University of Minnesota Press, 2008), 201 (footnote omitted); Saldaña-Portillo, *Indian Given*, 26–27. Saldaña-Portillo emphasizes the way in which *mestizaje* roots indigenize the postcolonial nation by incorporating the figure of the Indian, on the one hand, while deracinating Indigenous peoples through assimilationist policies, on the other.

54. St. John, *Line in the Sand*, 45.

55. See generally Brian DeLay, *War of a Thousand Deserts: Indian Raids and the U.S.–Mexican War* (New Haven: Yale University Press, 2008); Pekka Hämäläinen, *The Comanche Empire* (New Haven: Yale University Press, 2008).

56. See generally Brian DeLay, "Independent Indians and the U.S.–Mexican War," *The American Historical Review* 112, no. 1 (February 2007): 35.

57. See Saldaña-Portillo, *Indian Given*, 26–27, 115–16.

58. Act of Apr. 14, 1802, ch. 28, 2 Stat. 153 (repealed 1940).

59. Treaty of Peace, Friendship, Limits, and Settlement, Mex.–U.S., art. VIII, Feb. 2, 1848, 9 Stat. 922 [hereinafter Treaty of Guadalupe Hidalgo].

60. Laura E. Gómez, *Manifest Destinies: The Making of the Mexican American Race* (New York, NYU Press, 2018), 62.

61. Saldaña-Portillo, *Indian Given,* 140–41; see also Morrison v. California, 291 U.S. 82, 95n5 (1934) ("Indians not born in the United States ... are ineligible for citizenship.... Whether persons of [Mexican] ... descent may be naturalized in the United States is still an unsettled question"); Gómez, *Manifest Destinies,* 83–87, 103.

62. Gloria Anzaldúa, *Borderlands/La Frontera: The New Mestiza,* 4th ed. (San Francisco: Aunt Lute Books, 2012), 29.

63. Anzaldúa, *Borderlands/La Frontera,* 25.

64. Anzaldúa, *Borderlands/La Frontera,* 25.

65. Treaty of Guadalupe Hidalgo, art. IX. Laura Gómez notes that the original draft of the treaty provided that the annexed territory would be incorporated as one or more states "as soon as possible." Gómez, *Manifest Destinies,* 44. The U.S. Senate voted to revise the language to assure that states would be incorporated "at the proper time (to be judged of by the Congress of the United States)." Gómez, *Manifest Destinies,* 44 (emphasis omitted).

66. Gómez, *Manifest Destinies,* 47.

67. Gómez, *Manifest Destinies,* 47.

68. Kevin Bruyneel, *The Third Space of Sovereignty* (Minneapolis: University of Minnesota Press, 2007), 3–21; see also Downes v. Bidwell, 182 U.S. 244 (1901) (plurality opinion) (describing Puerto Rico's status within the United States); Cherokee Nation v. Georgia, 30 U.S. (5 Pet.) 1, 17 (1831) (referring to Indian tribes as "domestic dependent[s]").

69. See Frymer, *Building an American Empire,* 204–5; "New Mexico and Arizona Statehood Anniversary (1912–2012)," National Archives, accessed Aug. 17, 2016, [https://perma.cc/WXH3-EP76].

70. As Indigenous scholars remind us, notwithstanding the United States' assertion of sovereignty over Indian tribes, all "Indian affairs" remain matters of international relations.

71. Saldaña-Portillo, *Indian Given,* 138.

72. Saldaña-Portillo, *Indian Given,* 137–38.

73. Treaty of Guadalupe Hidalgo, art. XI.

74. Treaty of Guadalupe Hidalgo, art. XI.

75. Grandin, *The End of the Myth,* 17–21.

76. Immerwahr, *How to Hide an Empire,* 47.

77. See generally David Harvey, *The New Imperialism* (New York: Oxford University Press, 2003); Alyosha Goldstein, "Toward a Genealogy of the U.S. Colonial Present," in *Formations of United States Colonialism,* ed. Alyosha Goldstein (Durham: Duke University Press, 2014), 1; Paul A. Kramer, "The Geopolitics of Mobility: Immigration Policy and American Global Power in the Long Twentieth Century," *American Historical Review* 123, no. 2 (April 2018): 393.

78. Stoler, "Colony," 52; Ann Laura Stoler, "Interior Frontiers," *Political Concepts,* May 29, 2018, [https://perma.cc/XHR9-4S5D].

79. Jason L. Morín et al., "Cosponsoring and Cashing In: US House Members' Support for Punitive Immigration Policy and Financial Payoffs from the Private Prison Industry," *Business and Politics* 23, no. 4 (December 2021): 492–509.

80. See generally Peter Andreas, *Border Games: Policing the U.S.–Mexico Divide*, 2nd ed. (Ithaca: Cornell University Press, 2009); Douglas Massey, *Beyond Smoke and Mirrors: Mexican Immigration in an Era of Economic Integration* (New York: Russell Sage Foundation, 2003); Ronald L. Mize and Alicia C. S. Swords, *Consuming Mexican Labor: From the Bracero Program to NAFTA* (Ontario, University of Toronto Press, 2011).

81. Walia writes that "border imperialism" consists of: "Four overlapping and concurrent structurings: first, the mass displacement of impoverished and colonized communities resulting from asymmetrical relations of global power, and the simultaneous securitization of the border against those migrants whom capitalism and empire have displaced; second, the criminalization of migration ... third, the entrenchment of a racialized hierarchy of citizenship by arbitrating who legitimately constitutes the nation-state; and fourth, the state-mediated exploitation of migrant labor." Harsha Walia, *Undoing Border Imperialism* (Oakland: AK Press, 2013), 4.

82. Eduardo Lopez and Wendy Thompson-Marquez, dir., *Harvest of Empire: The Untold Story of Latinos in America* (Onyx Films, 2012).

83. Tanvi Misra, "On Weaponizing Migration," *Bloomberg*, November 2, 2018, [https://perma.cc/UF6E-EKH4].

84. Misra, "On Weaponizing Migration"; see also "Trump: US Troops Will Consider Rocks Thrown at Them at Border as 'Firearms,'" *Guardian*, video, November 1, 2018, accessed Sept. 6, 2020, [https://perma.cc/S2PX-9LEN].

85. See "Donald Trump and the 'Onslaught' From Central America," *Economist*, October 27, 2018, [https://perma.cc/T32N-A8TK]; Todd J. Gillman, "Trump Insists in State of the Union That Dangerous 'Onslaught' of Migrants Justifies Border Wall," *Dallas Morning News*, February 6, 2019, 10:50 p.m., [https://perma.cc/CFC8-K9NN]; Josh Hafner, "On Politics Today: Trump Calls Undocumented People 'Animals,' Rhetoric With a Dark Past," *USA Today*, May 16, 2018, 11:04 p.m., [https://perma.cc/YMX3-W35G].

86. See Roberto Suro, "Democrats Are AWOL on Immigration. They Need to Speak Up," Opinion, *Washington Post*, November 1, 2018, 12:37 p.m., [https://perma.cc/5LQN-FEBC].

87. Emmanuel Lévinas, *Totality and Infinity: An Essay on Exteriority*, trans. Alphonso Lingis (Dordrecht: Kluwer Academic Publishers, 1991).

88. See Simone Drichel, "Face to Face with the Other Other: Levinas Versus the Postcolonial," *Levinas Studies* 7, no. 21 (2013); Shu-mei Shih et al., "Introduction," in *The Creolization of Theory*, ed. Françoise Lionnet and Shu-mei Shih (Durham: Duke University Press, 2011), 1, 14.

89. Guillermo Torres, "If You Respect Native American Culture Then Help Actual Native Americans Trying to Cross Our Border," Opinion, *Dallas Morning News*, January 12, 2018, 5:00 p.m.; see also James Giago Davies, "Hispanic Immigrants Are Mostly Indians," *Native Sun News Today*, July 10, 2019, [https://perma.cc/WYL8-B3V7].

90. Torres, "If You Respect."

91. See Nicole Acevedo, "Why Are Migrant Children Dying in U.S. Custody?," *NBC News*, May 29, 2019, 1:44 p.m., [https://perma.cc/5EH6-RB5R].

92. International Mayan League/USA, "Statement by Juanita Cabrera Lopez, Maya Mam Nation, Executive Director of the International Mayan League, At the Faith Vigil for Children Dying at the Border," Facebook, May 23, 2019, [https://perma.cc/R3EM-SEY7].

93. International Mayan League/USA, "Statement by Juanita Cabrerea Lopez."

94. International Mayan League/USA, "Statement by Juanita Cabrerea Lopez."

95. International Mayan League/USA, "Statement by Juanita Cabrerea Lopez."
96. See Jonathan Blitzer, "How Climate Change Is Fueling the U.S. Border Crisis," *New Yorker,* April 3, 2019, [https://perma.cc/DT6W-DCC4]; see also Rachel Nolan, "A Translation Crisis at the Border," *New Yorker,* December 30, 2019, [https://perma.cc/C97R-U6YR].
97. See Blitzer, "U.S. Border Crisis."
98. See Greg Grandin and Elizabeth Oglesby, "Who Killed Jakelin Caal Maquín at the US Border?," *The Nation,* December 17, 2018, [https://perma.cc/LG8L-MELH].
99. See Greg Grandin, *The Last Colonial Massacre: Latin America in the Cold War,* updated ed. (Chicago: University of Chicago Press, 2011), 24, 140.
100. Grandin and Oglesby, "Who Killed Jakelin."
101. See Grandin, *Last Colonial Massacre,* 26.
102. Greg Grandin and Elizabeth Oglesby, "Washington Trained Guatemala's Killers for Decades," *The Nation,* January 25, 2019, [https://perma.cc/PT2F-DY46].
103. Grandin, *Last Colonial Massacre,* 139.
104. Grandin, *Last Colonial Massacre,* 74.
105. See Grandin and Oglesby, "Who Killed Jakelin"; John Vidal, "How Guatemala Is Sliding into Chaos in the Fight for Land and Water," *The Guardian,* August 19, 2018, 4:00 a.m., [https://perma.cc/6BBS-4B24].
106. Grandin and Oglesby, "Who Killed Jakelin."
107. Global Witness, *Enemies of the State? How Governments and Business Silence Land and Environmental Defenders* (Global Witness, July 2019), 23; Sandra Cuffe, "Land, Environmental Activist Killings Surge in Guatemala," *Al Jazeera,* July 29, 2019, [https://perma.cc/K3VA-HNML].
108. See Cuffe, "Killings Surge in Guatemala"; Vidal, "Fight for Land and Water."
109. See Grandin and Oglesby, "Washington Trained Guatemala's Killers."
110. See, e.g., Bryan Kaplan and Zach Weinersmith, *Open Borders: The Science and Ethics of Immigration* (New York: First Second, 2019), 27–54.
111. For critiques of humanitarian discourse, see generally Didier Fassin, *Humanitarian Reason: A Moral History of the Present,* trans. Rachel Gomme (Berkeley: University of California Press, 2012); Miriam Ticktin, *Casualties of Care: Immigration and the Politics of Humanitarianism in France* (Berkeley: University of California Press, 2011).
112. Judith Butler, *Notes Toward a Performative Theory of Assembly* (Cambridge: Harvard University Press, 2015), 2.
113. Jacques Rancière, *Dissensus: On Politics and Aesthetics,* trans. and ed. Steven Corcoran (London: Continuum International Publishing Group, 2010), 66.
114. Roberto Saviano, "The Migrant Caravan: Made in USA," *New York Review,* March 7, 2019, [https://perma.cc/DWT2-NRZ8]; see also Kate Linthicum, "Homicides Have Fallen Dramatically in Honduras. So Why Are People Still Fleeing?," *L.A. Times,* December 14, 2018, 3:00 a.m., [https://perma.cc/NUJ9-ENU8].
115. Saviano, "Migrant Caravan." Saviano, an Italian journalist, is best known for endangering his own life by exposing the inner workings of the Camorra, an organized crime syndicate that has long terrorized the people of Naples.
116. Massimiliano Tomba, "Differentials of Surplus-Value in the Contemporary Forms of Exploitation," *The Commoner,* no. 12 (2007): 23, 25, 35.
117. Tomba, "Differentials of Surplus-Value," 35.
118. Tomba, "Differentials of Surplus-Value," 35.

119. See, e.g., "Evidencing Violence and Care Along the Central American Trail Through Mexico," *Social Service Review* 92, no. 3 (September 2018): 432.

120. Saidiya Hartman, *Wayward Lives, Beautiful Experiments* (New York: W. W. Norton & Company, 2019), 227–28.

121. Hartman, *Wayward Lives,* 227–28.

122. Yarimar Bonilla, "Unsettling Sovereignty," *Cultural Anthropology* 32, no. 3 (2017): 330–9.

123. Walter D. Mignolo, "Delinking: The Rhetoric of Modernity, the Logic of Coloniality and the Grammar of De-Coloniality," *Cultural Studies* 21, nos. 2–3 (March/May2007): 449, 453; Jack Halberstam, "Strategy of Wildness," *Critique & Praxis 13/13*, February 25, 2019, [https://perma.cc/99CC-YB4B]; see Corey Snelgrove et al., "Unsettling Settler Colonialism: The Discourse and Politics of Settlers, and Solidarity with Indigenous Nations," *Decolonization: Indigeneity, Education & Society* 3, no. 2 (2014): 1, 2, 17–25.

124. Indigenous Environmental Network, "Indigenous Peoples Led Shutdown at Ft. Sill Immigration Detention Center," accessed June 5, 2020, [https://perma.cc/ZFU9-X4K2].

125. Indigenous Environmental Network, "Indigenous Peoples Led Shutdown."

126. Gillian Brockell, "Geronimo and the Japanese Were Imprisoned There. Now Fort Sill Will Hold Migrant Children Again, Sparking Protests," *Washington Post*, June 23, 2019, 7:40 a.m., [https://perma.cc/G7ML-8QBJ].

127. Brockell, "Geronimo and the Japanese."

128. Brockell, "Geronimo and the Japanese."

129. Isha Aran, "How Native Americans and Immigrants Are Coming Together to Define the Future of Resistance," *Splinter*, September 20, 2017, 2:32 p.m., [https://perma.cc/9SSD-4K25].

130. National Congress of American Indians and Define American, "In Historic Meeting Native Nation and Immigrant Leaders Forge New Alliances," press release, September 18, 2017, [https://perma.cc/UBN7-GUE5]. For recent essays exploring the relationship between colonialism and legal memory, see Seth Davis, "American Colonialism and Constitutional Redemption," *California Law Review* 105, no. 6 (2017): 1751–806; Munshi, "The Courts of the Conqueror"; Rana, *Colonialism and Constitutional Memory*, 13.

131. Nick Estes (@nick_w_estes), "At the LAX Muslim Ban protest in 2017, several white women screamed at us, 'Go back to where you came from!' The march was led by Native and Tongva people who," Twitter (now X), July 14, 2019, 12:53 p.m., [https://perma.cc/QX4A-GLLS].

132. Elizabeth Ellis, "The Border(s) Crossed Us Too: The Intersections of Native American and Immigrant Fights for Justice," *Emisférica* 14, no. 1 (2018), [https://perma.cc/6DX3-XFLA].

133. Nick Estes, "Go Back to Where You Came From," *Open Space*, November 4, 2019.

134. Estes, "Go Back."

CHAPTER THIRTEEN

RACE AS A TECHNOLOGY OF GLOBAL POLITICAL ECONOMY

C̲ʜ̲ᴀ̲ɴ̲ᴛ̲ᴀ̲ʟ̲ ̲T̲ʜ̲ᴏ̲ᴍ̲ᴀ̲s̲

In the international law context, what is the connection between law's co-constitution of racialization and global economic inequality, both in historical formations and in contemporary manifestations? This chapter offers a structural and historical account of the role of race in global political economy—in particular, how to understand racialization as part of the process by which institutions of economic hierarchy not only were created but continue to be legitimated. It offers the conception of race as a technology: the product of racialized forms of knowing that serve the practical goal of maintaining and legitimating hierarchy.[1]

In drawing out these aspects from a critical race perspective, one could demonstrate these phenomena through a range of critical methods. First, external critique highlights the actual harm that legal rules and institutions reflecting racial hierarchies generate in creating and perpetuating economic inequality. Second, internal critique demonstrates that such outcomes are not the inevitable result of the applicable rules and institutions, but rather reflect a choice to adopt a particular set of applications in the context of a range of possible approaches. Third, ideological critique argues that the external harm and internal indeterminacy of the status quo is obscured and justified by reference to prevailing political commitments to putatively liberal legality (legitimate-ideological critique). Fourth and finally, an additional mode of ideological critique argues that this legitimation and mediation occurs not only via justificatory practices arising from liberal legality, but also arises in the context of historical commitments to white supremacy that, though no longer generally avowed, nevertheless operate to suggest that racial hierarchies result from innate superiorities and inferiorities, rather than as a result of ongoing law, policy, and practice (illegitimate-ideological critique).[2]

I. AN ANALYSIS OF KEY SECTORS OF GLOBAL POLITICAL ECONOMY

The next part considers the global economic order in two of its dimensions linked closely with slavery and colonialism: the production of commodities, and the procurement of labor. Labor is discussed here as an element of economic production, even though a social justice perspective would deny a commodified view of labor,[3] because understanding the political economy logics at play is a crucial aspect of understanding the injustice that has resulted in treating labor as a commodity.

These subparts look at the international legal norms, instruments, and organizations that shape global economic governance in these realms. They then identify the critiques of international law with respect to their reinforcement of inequality. They end with a consideration of the critical perspectives discussed above to illuminate the dynamic of racialization in global political economy. The contours of this analysis are necessarily presented in broad strokes, and should be understood as a call to further research and study.

A. COMMODITY PRODUCTION

The international law governing commodity production arises primarily from the treaty regimes established at the end of World War II, reflecting a general commitment within leading states in the international community to the importance both of coordination and of liberalization of economic activity across borders. With respect to international trade, the General Agreement on Tariffs and Trade (GATT) established a set of basic principles and practices in 1948, and formed the basis for the creation in 1995 of the World Trade Organization (WTO), the overarching body for multilateral trade law. The International Monetary Fund and the World Bank also played a role in determining trade policy, particularly in their role as advisors to countries seeking financial assistance, by in some cases conditioning that assistance on borrower countries' willingness to adopt liberalizing reforms.

The self-conception of the international trade regime is that its central objective is to maximize market openness: Hence, both the GATT and WTO Preamble set out as purposes "the substantial reduction of tariffs and other barriers to trade and ... the elimination of discriminatory treatment in international commerce."[4] GATT/WTO law establishes several legal mechanisms towards these ends. For example, all member states must make commitments to nondiscriminatory treatment of other members. Additionally, the treaties provide for members to negotiate reciprocal trade barrier reductions. The prevailing narrative of contemporary international economic law is that it has been largely successful in achieving market liberalization—so much so that the same successes have provoked a backlash against globalization in recent years.

This narrative was key to the triumphalism that prevailed in the 1990s and 2000s with the fall of the Soviet bloc and the end of the Cold War. The narrative featured two key aspects: one about the nature of markets and the other about the nature of the laws and institutions that facilitated their expansion. Markets, so the narrative went, could only function if supported by good institutions: the rule of law was key to sustaining economic growth. Such conventional wisdom was reflected in the tenets of development policy as articulated in international economic institutions: The reason for the success of the West, and the stagnation of developing countries, lay in a twin failure of markets and institutions. Markets were not sufficiently open, and not sufficiently supported by the rule of law.

In some ways, this narrative fit what was happening in international economic law. The establishment of an enhanced multilateral trade regime (the World Trade Organization), the rise of strong regional trade regimes (NAFTA, the EU), and the proliferation of international investment treaties and the institutions that supported them: all these spoke to a strong political commitment to the promotion and growth of market economies and the need for laws and institutions to do so.[5]

Yet at the same time, the prevailing narrative covered over glaring flaws and contradictions that threw its viability into deep question. With respect to the narratives surrounding the economic impact of "the rule of law," the premise that good governance or the rule of law promoted economic growth was never satisfactorily proven, and instead operated as a stunning example of ideology.[6] From a TWAIL/CRT perspective, this ideology reproduced and echoed earlier narratives of the civilization standard. Instead of civilization, it was now governance and rule of law, but the clear implication or subtext was that an innate difference in culture, as marked by ethnic and racial difference, had yielded more corrupt, less effective institutions and thereby generated lower levels of economic growth.

The premise that economic growth depended on market openness was perhaps even more crucial than the questionable premise that economic growth depended on good governance. Again, this notion spoke to an underlying ideology of liberal legality that configured freedom not only in political but also in economic relations—freedom of contract, freedom in markets—as a marker of evolution. This in turn, from a TWAIL/CRT perspective, played on a subtext of racial and cultural difference that explained and legitimated the unequal economic relationship between the Global North and South.

The critique of the normative emphasis on market openness, as implemented through international economic law, encompasses a range of arguments from the postcolonial perspective. First, there is the argument that formal legal equality perpetuates structural inequality. In this case, a principle establishing formal equality among states, in respect of their economic regulations, would only serve to perpetuate dominance of the more powerful states over others. Accordingly, during the period of decolonization, a primary focus of newly independent states was to procure international recognition of the importance of special and differential treatment of weaker economies in order to allow them to benefit from policies designed to correct for substantive inequality between themselves and stronger economies.[7]

Second is the argument that the focus on market openness in international economic law ignores the historical reality that industrialized states achieved development not by engaging in free trade but rather by engaging in highly strategic and protective trade. When rich countries were developing, they benefited from policies which provided their growth industries with substantial protection, and sought liberalization only when their economies had strengthened to the point that they could be more competitive. The economist Ha-Joon Chang has called this "kicking away the ladder": The economically powerful states, in insisting on global norms of market openness, were seeking to prevent economically weaker states from employing the same policies that they themselves had used to achieve growth.[8] And in contemporary economic times, the developing states that have most successfully industrialized, for example in East Asia, have done so while maintaining significantly protective domestic trade policies.

Third is the argument that, not only was market openness not the norm at the time when developed countries were industrializing, but also it has not been the norm in the current trade regime with respect to the sectors that are of greatest economic importance for developing countries. For most of the post–World War II trade regime, the international trade rules on agriculture and textiles were blatantly in violation of the GATT rules. Developed states maintained domestic trade policies that openly contravened GATT law. For example, GATT Article XI prohibits the general use of quantitative restrictions, such as import quotas, to protect domestic industries.[9] While there were some limited exceptions, developed countries maintained broad quota systems for textiles and agricultural products that were not permitted by those exceptions, in order to protect their domestic industries. Additionally, while GATT/WTO law disallows subsidies favoring a particular industry, developed countries have maintained generous subsidies, for example, for their domestic farmers.

This occurred even though the same states, in the context of establishing the GATT, pledged fealty to the principle of free trade under which developed countries should have ceded market share in these types of products to developing country producers that could produce them more cheaply. Not only did developed countries maintain these domestic market protections, but they also established and maintained international agreements in textiles[10] and in a range of agricultural commodities.[11] Only with the advent of the WTO in 1995 did developed countries agree to dismantle these protections;[12] however, in many instances that process has not occurred satisfactorily.

In sum, the ideal of market openness that flowed from liberal legality as expressed in international economic law operated to perpetuate the dominance of developed countries over developing countries. In its implementation through commitments to formal nondiscrimination, it allowed for more powerful economic actors to dominate less powerful actors. In its historical and contemporary non-implementation, it reflected a clear bias towards more powerful economic actors.

Although the critique of international economic law from a developing country perspective has been well established, the additional analysis of this set of arrangements in respect of racial justice has not explicitly ever really been addressed. But a consideration of the critical legal theory and economic history literatures referenced above can surface such considerations in both historical and contemporary respects.

It is no historical accident that agricultural production was located in the Global South and in countries that were formally colonies of the Global North. The use of these territories for the production of raw materials needed to fuel industrialization was an explicit and overridingly vital purpose of colonialism. Cotton, sugar, cocoa, bananas, oil, tin, rubber, tea, coffee, minerals, and so many other commodities made the colonial world a source of vast wealth accumulation for developed economies and the industrialists within them. These economies were organized in order to explicitly incorporate them into chains of wealth production that would benefit those in the developed world. They were not intended to produce any level of self-sufficiency nor local profitability, but were designed to be dependent on and peripheral to the Global North. When these territories won recognition as independent states—as equal sovereigns—the rules and practices shaping international economic relations did not facilitate substantive economic independence or equality.

The biases of international economic law against developing countries lend themselves, in consideration of the critical methods discussed above, to external critique in that they lead to the perpetuation of economic inequality. They also reflect particular and contingent applications of the underlying norms—for example, a substantive rather than formal interpretation of the normative imperative to eliminate discriminatory treatment would have yielded much different rule arrangements in respect of developing countries. These predispositions support a legitimate-ideological critique because the presentation of the system as committed to liberal legal objectives of market openness disguises the ways in which the system contravenes those objectives and how those objectives, in and of themselves, also perpetuate inequality. And they support illegitimate-ideological critique in that white supremacy—whether avowed or operating at an unconscious or implicit level—allows for a hierarchy in which it seems natural and reasonable for peoples of color remain stratified in the bottom.

B. LABOR MIGRATION

The international law of sovereignty entails the right to exclude noncitizens. It is this fundamental tenet of international law that shapes the framework of labor migration in today's economy. Because states maintain their territorial prerogative over immigration, workers who wish to travel across borders must submit to the border controls and police controls of the destination country. While these systems themselves are products of domestic law, the right of states to maintain such law is recognized under international law.

From at least a couple of perspectives, the presumptive exclusion of nonnationals appears uncontroversial. To begin with, if one thinks about labor as a commodity, the presumptive exclusion of workers would be no different than the presumptive exclusion of goods—neither sea vessels bearing shipment containers (carriers of goods) nor airplanes (carriers of people) may cross a territorial border without permission of the destination state.

But people are not goods. Under liberal legality, humans are endowed with rights through which they exercise individual agency. International law, in endorsing this conception, has struggled with the tension it induces between law as articulating the will of states exercised over people, and law as articulating the will of individuals exercised against states. With respect to the movement of people across borders, that dichotomy itself represents a conceptual border that has shifted over time. In earlier eras, states were more concerned with preventing people from leaving their territories (for reasons of national security and monetary policy, among others) than with preventing their entry.[13] Thus, international lawyers in the nineteenth century advocated for the human right to freedom of movement as centering around the right to leave any given territory as a reform of then-prevailing state practice. This normative battle was ultimately successful: The right to "leave any country" is now enshrined in international human rights law.[14]

This is not so, of course, for the right of entry. The right of territorial entry is tied to citizenship status.[15] Thus, the same instruments of international human rights law that protect individual rights of territorial exit also deny individual rights of territorial entry. From the currently conventional point of view in international human rights law, then, the right to authorize territorial entry and so to exclude people also appears uncontroversial. Yet, because that premise contradicts the core commitments to equality and autonomy of the human rights corpus, it is increasingly contested.

If sovereign borders generate moral harm through their contravention of tenets of liberalism, they also carry economic significance that reflects and reproduces global inequality. Cross-border labor migration is a powerful tool for poverty reduction. For many developing countries, the volume of remittances received by their nationals working abroad exceeds the funding received through development aid from international organizations or other governments.[16] For this reason, many economists and international lawyers have stated that nothing would better contribute to global poverty reduction and a fairer global distribution of income than to establish broad-based labor mobility.

Moreover, the logic of market openness would criticize national borders as restraints on trade.[17] Many trade experts have argued that migration flows should be directly incorporated into the globalization project.[18] If the justifications for trade liberalization are valid, this point of view goes, then they should apply to trade provided by workers in addition to other forms of commerce. Applying an economic perspective to national boundaries, one can see them as operationalizing a form of protectionism. The wealth of rich country economies is policed and enforced through borders and exclusion.

Yet international law reflects virtually the opposite: There is a striking absence of generally sanctioned work authorization, even in this era of concerted globalization. Even as, over the past few decades, international economic law has greatly (though not consistently) expanded governmental commitments to open domestic markets, as discussed in the preceding subpart, the prevailing regime has very much reflected an "open markets but closed borders" dynamic, establishing freedom of movement for goods and capital, but not people. This dynamic arises out of a politics of territorial exclusion that is deeply underwritten by international law, which enforces a conception of sovereignty that entails the right to exclude.

The argument here is not that a pro-market perspective should be more pervasively adopted. Rather, it is that careful attention should be directed to how and when market controls—such as borders—are imposed, and what their effects are. Immigration controls do not deter migration in a world that is both highly unequal and highly interconnected. Rather, those controls make it more likely that some people's movements across borders will be unauthorized, and that those people will then be vulnerable to exploitation. Immigration controls constitute the single most significant legal determinant of "modern-day slavery"—that is to say, highly precarious and oppressive exploitation that is primarily borne today by migrants with nontraditional documentary status.[19]

In the previous subpart on commodity production, the postcolonial critique noted the ways in which formal equality can perpetuate substantive inequality. In that subpart, the focus was the set of rules that establish free trade under international economic law discussed. Similarly, with respect to labor migration discussed in this subpart, we see the operation of a formally neutral rule in a way that reinforces global inequality. Rather than establishing a norm of openness, however, in this case the principle in question is one of closure—the right of territorial exclusion of nonnationals. Because this presumptive exclusion occurs against a backdrop of economic hierarchy across nations, it protects and reinforces it.

A postcolonial critique of international law on migration, then, would note that the economic effects of the current arrangement in international law is to perpetuate inequality and hierarchy between rich and poor countries, and among their citizens. It would also emphasize that the status quo differs significantly from the international law that prevailed at the very beginning of the modern era—the period of conquest—in which jurists proclaimed a natural law that recognized rights of travel and hospitality, establishing presumptive admissibility rather than exclusion.[20] From this perspective, the pursuit of movement across borders by peoples of the Global South towards the Global North represents an equitable claim in addition to an economically redistributive one. This historical critique acts as a mirror image to that of the changes in international trade law over time.

Subpart A, above, looked at the substantive inequality arising from formal equality; the historical contingency of the currently prevailing norm; and the ways in which the currently prevailing norm is often contradicted by actual practices. One can see something of this same unevenness, too, with respect to labor migration. Although noncitizens are presumptively excluded, the reality is that citizens of richer countries enjoy far greater effective mobility than citizens of poorer countries.

If the postcolonial critique of migration law and policy demonstrates how the status quo perpetuates inequality, the question then becomes how this analysis relates to the racial justice perspective. Much of the critical theory discussed above in part I noted the mutual constitutiveness of "race" and "nation." Racial formations, as many of these thinkers demonstrated, have played an important role in structuring global economic inequality. It follows then, that these racial formations also shape the landscape of citizenship and migration in global political economy. Birthright citizenship in affluent society, as Ayelet Shachar observes, should be thought of as a form of property inheritance, as a valuable entitlement transmitted by law.[21] This argument forms a striking parallel to Cheryl Harris's work on racial privilege as a form of property.[22]

Racial privilege and national citizenship are deeply interlinked: Conceptions of statehood have been deeply tied to ethnonational identity.[23] This analysis requires a consideration of the effects, in political economy, of the legal framing of citizenship as a mechanism for exclusion. Categories of slavery and citizenship are integrally connected to political economy and economic inequality, both historically and contemporaneously. From this perspective, it is hardly coincidental that forms of precarious and exploitative work that were done historically by individuals marked by the legal status (accompanied often by a racial designation) of slave or servant have been taken up today by those marked by the legal status of noncitizen.

Returning to the four methods set forth above, external critique applies to the principle of sovereign territorial exclusion because of its perpetuation of inequality. Internal critique applies because the status quo is historically contingent, and only one of many possible arrangements even under its own principles. Legitimate-ideological critique applies because references to norms of sovereign equality as well as to certain conceptions of citizenship obscure the harmful global impact and internal contingency of the status quo. And illegitimate-ideological critique applies because of the essential work that white supremacy in its xenophobic manifestations does to neutralize or justify the pervasive cruelty and severity of the current framework.

C. CONCLUSIONS ON INTERNATIONAL LAW AND POLITICAL ECONOMY

International law maintains presumptive norms establishing "open markets but closed borders." That arrangement reinforces global inequities. It not only contradicts both actual practices today, in many cases, but it also departs from the presumptions of earlier eras, further revealing its normative contingency. Today's international law reflects "open markets but closed borders," but earlier international law reflected "closed markets, open borders." Each juxtaposition has mirrored the interests of powerful over less powerful global actors.

The contours of the international law and policy that effectuate these outcomes take varying forms. At times, the prevailing norm rejects formal differentiation, and embraces formal equality, and yet does so in a way that reproduces substantive inequality. In this category, one can place the ideal of liberalization and nondiscrimination of international economic law, and its effects on economic production; and the ideal of sovereign prerogative over the territorial entry of noncitizens in international human rights law, and its effects on labor migration.

Moreover, in many instances, the discourse of such international norms acknowledges differentiation in ways that are nonracial, but that nevertheless carry a subtext that reflects and reinforces racialized power.

II. RACE AS A TECHNOLOGY OF GLOBAL ECONOMIC GOVERNANCE

Based on the discussions of the previous parts, a race critical perspective would argue that racial formations both justified early practices setting up the cognizable modern economy, and continue to perpetuate and legitimate practices of exclusion to this day. These contemporary effects are significantly mediated by laws and institutions.

The puzzle for the current project is to articulate how that analysis plays out in the global context. In what ways has race served as more than a mere correlative variable alongside other determinative metrics of hierarchy? How has the function of racialization structured economic relations both in historical background and in modern-day practice? In thinking about these practices of material subordination and ideological legitimation, the concept of race, more precisely of racialization, as a technology proves useful.

The term technology as used here goes beyond the concrete artifact.[24] It extends to the set of knowledge practices involved in the construction, legitimation, and enforcement of social categories—in this case, identity categories. The term is meant to bring attention to both the social construction of knowledge, and the active, practical application of that constructed knowledge, drawing insights from science and technology studies[25] as well as discourse theory.[26] The term highlights the active dimension of social construction,[27] by analytically incorporating a role of strategic decision-making, expertise, and knowledge. In that sense, the term highlights somewhat different considerations than the term social construct: A social construct might be something we all live within, built at some point in the past; a technology emphasizes the practice of continual use and application.

In considering race as a technology, we can think about the interlocking dimensions of racialization necessary to service the larger objectives of economic governance as the following: empirics (how the categories were themselves constructed, and how knowledge was used to substantiate those categories); legal rule (the role of law and lawmaking in helping to construct and police these categories); and economic allocation and production (the specific ways that racialization was then deployed in the service of global political economy), itself dependent on the first two forms of racialization (empirics and legal rule). These first two have received extensive attention in numerous literatures familiar to the legal academy; the last, on economic allocation and production, is the subject of renewed attention within literatures on racial capitalism. I will take each of these illustratively in turn. Before proceeding, I note again that this discussion is necessarily abbreviated, and should most properly be read as outlining an agenda for further research.

A. RACE AS A TECHNOLOGY OF EMPIRICS

As applied to the concept of race, the phrase "technology of empirics" highlights how knowledge that purported to be about the natural world was deeply constructed.[28] Information presented as empirical was in fact imbued by racialized ideology, so as to render racial hierarchy seemingly natural, in accord with incontrovertible realities, and therefore inevitable. With respect to race, one begins, of course, with racial ideology presented as the science of biology. The conception of biological race experienced a heyday in the pseudoscience of the nineteenth century, which endorsed the sociopolitical categories that had by then arisen.[29] This was subsequently debunked: Scientists have demonstrated that there is more biological and genetic variation within racial categories than across them, exposing as spurious the notion that a single marker such as skin color could stand in for or reliably reference a larger set of traits.[30] Nevertheless, the concept of race as a biological or genetic feature continues to play a foundational role in shaping how people see the contemporary world—and crucially, how they understand race as an immutable, physiological phenomenon, as opposed to a social phenomenon.

Such notions supported the development of the one-drop and similar concepts of race.[31] More formally, the one-drop rule is a rule of hypodescent: "Anyone with a known Black ancestor is considered Black."[32] When considered afresh, the oddness of such a rule becomes immediately apparent, not only because it relies on the concept of race, but also because, for this rule to apply, there must be no such rule for any other racial group since, in the early U.S. paradigm, multiraciality was not permitted.[33] In this paradigm, Blackness was a marker transmitted through the blood that was both supremely potent[34] and fundamentally degrading. This hematological conception reflected scientific understanding of the time. As is well understood—and as enforced by the law discussed in the next subpart—this was a supposedly biological designation that consigned its members to a subservient caste.

The "master discourse of racial difference" took on varying incarnations in various localities.[35] In the United States, the racial division in its early formulation was essentially binary; in other societies, the spectrum featured additional gradations. Many other societies with a significant African-descended population and strong racial classifications, like Brazil and South Africa, nevertheless differed from the United States in recognizing multiracial categories and situating them in the racial hierarchy.[36] Societies elsewhere in the settler colonial world without significant African-descended populations focused on language, caste, or other ethnic markers to differentiate groups. The result, as Tayyab Mahmud writes,

> was a contextual construction of race, remarkable for its contingency, plasticity, and malleability. The structure of this construction involved: (i) slippage of classificatory categories, whereby "race," "caste," "tribe," "stock," and "nation," were used interchangeably; (ii) racialization of the constructs, whereby all these categories were posited as being essentially biological and hereditary, questions of blood and descent; (iii) a two-tier scheme of racial hierarchy, under which ... all natives were deemed racially inferior to the colonizers' race.[37]

The one-drop rule, marking all those in the United States with any African heritage as Black, worked alongside and reinforced the ancient Roman law of determining the status of children who were the issue of free men and enslaved women.[38] That rule, in the ancient Roman law, was that the status of the child followed the status of the mother (in contrast to other legal systems, such as Islamic law, in which a child borne of a slave mother would follow the status of the father and could be freed).[39] In the United States, the ancient Roman precept reemerged, supported by a hematological concept of race, and in particular, Blackness,[40] as a supremely powerful and potent marker transmitted through the blood.

Beyond biomedical constructs, numerous other sources of knowledge arose to reinforce the precepts of white supremacy. It was "in the context of Europe's colonial expansion that modern disciplines of geography, anthropology, history, and literature developed to make the expanding world intelligible and manageable."[41]

B. RACE AS A TECHNOLOGY OF LEGAL RULE

The reinforcement of racialized difference historically depended on multiple tools of governance. In the antebellum United States, the constitutional law permitting chattel slavery and the state laws permitting recovery of fugitive slaves constituted only the most broadly applicable forms of racialized governance. Forcible and racialized difference was everywhere: in the criminalization of reading and writing by enslaved persons; in the evidentiary rules discounting their testimony; in the amnesty granted for the murder of enslaved persons who were declared runaways or who were undergoing punishment at the time of their death; and in countless other local and state laws.[42] Post Reconstruction, the "Black codes" of the Jim Crow South transposed these aims into the elaborate regulatory infrastructure of racial segregation.[43] Discourses of Eurosupremacy in the U.S. settler colonial context shaped the legalized subordination not only of African descended peoples but also of other non-European peoples, from Indigenous societies to Chinese and other non-European migrant workers.[44]

The administrative projects of colonialism elsewhere were no less complex. Colonial administrations in the Americas and Asia depended on the insistence of cultural/racial difference, and the cultural/racial difference in part grew out of the legal apparatus established by colonial administrations. In colonial India, for example, "vagrancy laws called for the deportation of whites whose deviant behavior undermined the mystique of their race; Cantonments Acts designed urban spaces to ensure segregation; Contagious Diseases Acts contained interracial sexual relations; and judicial procedures prohibited natives to sit in judgment over the colonizers."[45] In colonial Mexico, the development of *"generos de gente"* (*españoles, indios, negros, mulatos, meztizos*, etc.) involved the entrenchment of ethnogeographic, ethnoreligious, and socioeconomic stereotypes into legal discourse, generating systems of institutionalized discrimination.[46] In colonial Brazil, categories of racialization bore the imprint of the imperial Portuguese "regulations for Purity of Blood (*Estatutos de Pureza de Sangue*)" aimed at identifying Europeans of non-Christian heritage as well as Indigenous, African, and mixed categorizations.[47] Across vastly disparate colonial encounters, these master narratives and discourses of difference performed the same magic: to insist that social categories in any given context, so different from the next, nevertheless reflected an inherent and immutable reality of natural and inevitable hierarchy, understood in racial terms.

C. RACE AS A TECHNOLOGY OF ECONOMIC PRODUCTION

The racial caste system was profoundly related to structuring the means of economic production. Racialization constituted one technology of rule, of domination—not only by those actors with the formal authority to rule, such as governments, but also those with the capacity to exercise control—in this case, all those committed to particular modes of production. This is because its application was a means of denoting the boundaries of physical property—those who were subject to the laws of forced labor. As such, it also entailed access to preferable terms of labor that would profit capitalists in the slavery economy. Planters, traders, and investors—all who benefited from the slavery economy—had a stake in maintaining a racialized system of economic production in which racial caste enabled forced labor. As the abolitionist movement grew in the nineteenth century, capitalists invested in the commodity economy looked on askance. The *American Cotton Planter* declared in 1853: "The slave-labor of the United States, has hitherto conferred and is still conferring inappreciable blessings on mankind. If these blessings continue, slave-labor must also continue, for it is idle to talk of producing Cotton for the world's supply with free labor. It has never yet been successfully grown by voluntary labor."[48]

Racial differentiation served as a device for demarcating differential roles in production and consumption: forced labor versus indentured servitude, raw materials production versus industrial production, and so on. It served as a marker for sorting various individuals and groups into various roles in the global economy. In the era of formal slavery and colonialism, the production of commodities and the movement of labor formed two sides of the Triangular Trade: Enslaved Africans were shipped to the Americas; there, their coerced labor harvested the commodities of cotton, sugar, bananas, and so on; and these raw materials were then transported to industrial centers for manufacturing. Peoples of color from other parts of the world were designated particular economic roles as well. In colonial India, for example, the placement of Indians in indentured labor and movement of them to the Americas, where they often occupied "tertiary sectors of the economy," served as an essential building block in the "global hierarchy of races."[49] The practices of racial hierarchization in economic production, here as well, have survived their formal recognition.

The technology of race, of racialization, in global economic governance included the application of expertise and knowledge, as well as of mechanisms of enforcement and control, to harness the appearance of natural and inevitable hierarchy to legitimate profoundly unequal and exploitative systems of production. All three dimensions of racialization summarized here—the presentation of racialization as empirical and natural fact, the enforcement of racial caste through legal rule, and the organization of economic production according to racial caste—worked together and reinforced each other.

CONCLUSION

The conception offered in this chapter, of race as a technology of global economic governance, highlights multiple connections between racialization, law, and global political economy: race as a technology of empirics, in which racial categories purported to be based on empirical knowledge; race as a technology of legal rule, in which laws and institutions helped to shape, as well as enforce, the identity constructs purportedly rooted in empirical knowledge; and race as a technology of economic allocation and production, itself dependent on the knowledge and practice of the technologies of empirics and legal rule, in which one's racial identity has directly influenced one's place in global chains of production and consumption.

Racialization in political economy has constituted a social phenomenon of enormous historical and contemporary significance. Technologies of empirics, of legal rule, and of economic production served to establish and entrench racial hierarchies that are reflected to this day. They have informed, at various levels of explicitness, the principles and practices that shape global economic governance. The project of uncovering and articulating these dynamics has been shared across a range of scholarly disciplines. This chapter has endeavored to contribute to the formation of an analytical framework for this vast, and urgent, project. So much more remains to be done.

NOTES

1. A common definition of technology is "the practical application of knowledge especially in a particular area." Merriam-Webster Dictionary, https://www.merriam-webster.com/dictionary/technology [https://perma.cc/Z99D-AEYK]. A premise of the argument put forward here is that the "knowledge" in question reflects and serves an overall paradigm of racial hierarchy.

2. For an early version of this framework, see Chantal Thomas, "Critical Race Theory and Postcolonial Development Theory: Observations on Methodology," *Villanova Law Review* 45 (2000): 1195.

3. See, e.g., Int'l Lab. Org. [ILO], *International Labour Conference: Declaration Concerning the Aims and Purposes of the International Labour Organisation*, at 4 (May 10, 1944) https://www.ilo.org/wcmsp5/groups/public/---dgreports/---dcomm/documents/normativeinstrument/wcms_698995.pdf [https://perma.cc/3KVM-NMNR].

4. General Agreement on Tariffs and Trade, Oct. 30, 1947, 61 Stat. A-11, 55 U.N.T.S. 194 [hereinafter GATT]; Marrakesh Agreement Establishing the World Trade Organization, Apr. 15, 1994, 1867 U.N.T.S. 154.

5. See Quinn Slobodian, *Globalists: The End of Empire and the Birth of Neoliberalism* (Harvard University Press, 2018) (arguing that neoliberalism can best be understood as a project not to abolish economic regulation, but to reconstitute it in the service of particular market practices and ideals).

6. Chantal Thomas, "Law and Neoclassical Economic Development in Theory and Practice: Toward an Institutionalist Critique of Institutionalism," *Cornell Law Review* 96 (2011): 967.

7. See Kevin Kennedy, "Special and Differential Treatment of Developing Countries," in *The World Trade Organization: Legal, Economic and Political Analysis*, ed. Patrick F. J. Macrory et al. (New York: Springer, 2005). The principle of special and differential treatment encompassed policies of both developed and developing countries. For developing countries, it meant special entitlements to maintain higher trade barriers than would otherwise be permitted (see, e.g., the special rule for developing countries on quantitative restrictions [GATT, at art. XVIII]). For developed countries, it meant committing to providing developing countries with especially favorable market access in certain categories. See Decision, *Differential and More Favourable Treatment, Reciprocity and Fuller Participation of Developing Countries*, para. 2(a), n.3, L/4903 (Nov. 28, 1979), GATT B.I.S.D. (26th Supp.), at 203 (1980).

8. Ha-Joon Chang, *Kicking Away the Ladder: Development Strategy in Historical Perspective* (Anthem Press, 2003).

9. GATT, art. XI, Oct. 30, 1947, 61 Stat. A-11, 55 U.N.T.S. 194

10. Agreement Regarding International Trade in Textiles, Dec. 20, 1973, GATT B.I.S.D. (21st Supp.), at 3 (1975).

11. International Sugar Agreement, Mar. 20, 1992, 1703 U.N.T.S. 203; Second International Tin Agreement, Sept. 1, 1960, 403 U.N.T.S. 3.

12. Agreement on Textiles and Clothing, Apr. 15, 1994, Marrakesh Agreement Establishing the World Trade Organization, Annex 1A, 1868 U.N.T.S. 14; Agreement on Agriculture, Apr. 15, 1994, Marrakesh Agreement Establishing the World Trade Organization, Annex 1A, 1867 U.N.T.S. 410.

13. Martin Lloyd, *The Passport: The History of Man's Most Travelled Document* (Sutton Publishing, 2003).

14. See, e.g., International Covenant on Civil and Political Rights art. 12(2), Dec. 16, 1966, 999 U.N.T.S. 171 [hereinafter ICCPR] ("Everyone shall be free to leave any country, including his own").

15. See, e.g., ICCPR, at art. 12(4). ("No one shall be arbitrarily deprived of the right to enter his own country").

16. OECD, "Remittances to Developing Countries Far Exceed Official Development Assistance (ODA)," in *Perspectives on Global Development 2017: International Migration in a Shifting World* (Paris: OECD Publishing, 2016), https://doi.org/10.1787/persp_glob_dev-2017-graph60-en.

17. The common law principle against restraint of trade has been expressed as follows: "The public have an interest in every person's carrying on his trade freely: so has the individual. All interference with individual liberty of action in trading, and all restraints of trade of themselves, if there is nothing more, are contrary to public policy, and therefore void." Nordenfelt v. Maxim Nordenfelt Guns & Ammunition Co. Ltd. [1894] AC 535 (HL) 565 (appeal taken from Eng.).

18. Howard F. Chang, "Migration as International Trade: The Economic Gains from the Liberalized Movement of Labor," *UCLA Journal of International Law and Foreign Affairs* 3 (1998): 371–414; Sungjoon Cho, "Development by Moving People: Unearthing the Development Potential of a GATS Visa," in *Developing Countries in the WTO Legal System*, ed., Joel P. Trachtman and Chantal Thomas (New York: Oxford University Press,

2009), 457–74; Joel P. Trachtman, *The International Law of Economic Migration: Toward the Fourth Freedom* (UPJohn Press, 2009).

19. Chantal Thomas, "Immigration Controls and 'Modern-Day Slavery,'" in *Revisiting the Law and Governance of Trafficking, Forced Labor and Modern Slavery*, ed. Prabha Kotiswaran (Cambridge University Press, 2017): 212.

20. Chantal Thomas, "What Does the Emerging International Law of Migration Mean for Sovereignty?," *Melbourne Journal of International Law* 14 (2013): 392.

21. Ayelet Shachar, *The Birthright Lottery: Citizenship and Global Inequality* (Harvard University Press, 2009).

22. See Cheryl I. Harris, "Whiteness as Property," *Harvard Law Review* 106 (1993): 1707.

23. See, e.g., Devon W. Carbado, "Racial Naturalization," *American Quarterly* 57 (2005): 633.

24. This concept as used here arguably features a broader scope than the way the term is deployed, for example, in Radhika Mongia's brilliant work on the passport as a technology for regulating migration. Radhika Viyas Mongia, "Race, Nationality, Mobility: A History of the Passport," *Public Culture* 11 (1999): 527; Radhika Mongia, *Indian Migration and Empire: A Colonial Genealogy of the Modern State* (Duke University Press, 2018). Mongia's use of the term evokes the style of James Scott's *Seeing Like a State* in the discussion of statehood as significantly arising from a set of administrative practices. James C. Scott, *Seeing Like a State: How Certain Schemes to Improve the Human Condition Have Failed* (Cambridge University Press, 1998). The important insight of such works is that the enforcement of foundational concepts such as sovereign rule depended on the existence of a wide range of technologies and capacities. The development and enforcement of border control, for example, in the subject of Mongia's study, depended on the existence of mechanisms of governance that can detect valid and invalid entries and can mobilize resources of coercion and legitimation to effectuate exclusionary policy. See Mongia, "Race, Nationality, Mobility," 528. As the Trump administration's focus on expanding the U.S.'s southern border wall demonstrated, even powerful and technologically advanced countries have only partially achieved physical control of their borders. Borders, even of powerful countries bent on deterrence and exclusion of unauthorized entry, remain porous. The porosity of borders has in turn engendered a phalanx of ancillary and extraterritorial techniques of border control designed to prevent the physical arrival at the border of persons unauthorized for entry. But all of these practices must be politically and ethically justified—it is here that the scripts of nation, and the partially subtextual scripts of race and ethnicity, do their work. The passport in Mongia's analysis is "one concrete technology that harnesses this strategy to produce the 'nationalized' migrant body." Mongia, *Indian Migration and Empire*, 113. The term technology as I use it in the present analysis extends out of the concrete artifact of, for example, the passport, to refer to this larger "strategy," in Mongia's terms. Mongia, *Indian Migration and Empire*, 113.

25. The field of science and technology studies (STS) highlights how knowledge about the natural world is inescapably shaped by structures of social interaction and by the cultural and political formations that influence human understanding. A foundational work in this field is Thomas S. Kuhn, *The Structure of Scientific Revolutions,* 3rd ed. (University of Chicago Press, 1996).

26. The notion of technology I use here is influenced by the tradition of discourse analysis and in particular by the notion of the "*dispositif*" as a mode of structuring knowledge.

Though often translated as device or apparatus, translating *dispositif* as "technology" emphasizes the continual need for the inscription and reinscription, for the practice of knowledge in addition to its reification. The concept of the *dispositif* was given illuminating discussion in an interview with Michel Foucault:

> What I want to place under the rubric of the term *dispositif* is a heterogenous combination of discourses, institutions, ... regulations, laws, administrative measures, scientific formulations, and precepts of philosophy, morality, philanthropy ... in short, what is said as well as unsaid: these are the elements of the *dispositif*. The *dispositif* itself is the network, the interlinkage, that is established across these elements. [It is also] the nature of the linkage among these heterogenous elements. As such, it can appear both as an institutional program, and also on the contrary as an element that obscures a practice that itself remains invisible, or that functions as a reinterpretation of that practice ... [Finally, the *dispositif*] takes on a particular formation at a given historical moment and functions in response to the exigencies of that moment. The *dispositif* as such functions strategically. It for example was able to focus on the reabsorption of a free-floating population that an essentially mercantilist society would find burdensome: there, we see the strategic imperative, unfolding within the matrix established by the *dispositif*, becoming gradually a mechanism for the control and subjection of madness, mental illness, and neurosis.

D. Colas et al., "Le jeu de Michel Foucault, " *Ornicar? Bulletin Periodique du Champ Freudien,* July 1977, 62 (translation my own), http://1libertaire.free.fr/MFoucault158 .html [https://perma.cc/4UEM-PRBW]. For further discussion of knowledge production through discourses and *dispositifs* as "flows of knowledge throughout time and space," see Siegfried Jäger and Florentine Maier, "Analysing Discourses and Dispositives: A Foucauldian Approach to Theory and Methodology," in *Methods of Critical Discourse Studies,* 3rd ed., ed. Ruth Wodak and Michael Meyer (Sage, 2016), 109, 111.

27. Thanks to Seth Davis for raising this question.

28. Tayyab Mahmud, "Colonialism and Modern Construction of Race: A Preliminary Inquiry," University of Miami Law Review 53 (1999): 1226 ("'Scientific racism,' which dominated European thought, saw itself as based on 'science,' the body of knowledge rationally derived from empirical observation, then supported the proposition that race was one of the principal determinants of attitudes, endowments, capabilities and inherent tendencies among human beings"); Alexander D. Barder, "Scientific Racism, Race War and the Global Racial Imaginary," *Third World Quarterly* 40 (2019): 209 ("[A] global racial imaginary construed the world as profoundly hierarchical; it posited that races were intrinsically incommensurable.... These ideas about hierarchy ... emerged out of the widespread acceptance of scientific racism and social Darwinism as the 'scientific' background of politics more generally").

29. See generally Thomas F. Gossett, *Race: The History of an Idea in America,* 2nd ed. (Oxford University Press, 1997), 54–83 (providing an account of how nineteenth-century medicine, natural history, ethnology, anthropology, and other disciplines developed assertions of racial superiority and inferiority); John P. Jackson, Jr. and Nadine M. Weidman, *Race, Racism, and Science: Social Impact and Interaction* (Rutgers University Press, 2004), 29–128 (describing the rise of scientific racism in the nineteenth century and its prevalence into the first half of the twentieth century).

30. See R. C. Lewontin, "The Apportionment of Human Diversity," in *Evolutionary Biology,* ed. Theodosius Dobzhansky et al. (Springer, 1972), 381, 396, 397. Over the years the

racial view of genetics has resurfaced periodically, see, for example, Armand Marie Leroi, "A Family Tree in Every Gene," Opinion, *New York Times*, March 14, 2005, https://www.nytimes.com/2005/03/14/opinion/a-family-tree-in-every-gene.html [https://perma.cc/ZL8A-3ZM7]. For further discussion and affirmation of Lewontin's essential conclusions in light of contemporary genetic science and technology, see John Dupré, "What Genes Are and Why There Are No Genes for Race," in *Revisiting Race in a Genomic Age*, ed. Barbara A. Koenig et al. (Rutgers University Press, 2008), 39. For a discussion of the complexities and continued significance of racial and ethnic categories in scientific research, see Pamela Sankar et al., "Race and Ethnicity in Genetic Research," *American Journal of Medical Genetics* 143A, no. 9 (2007): 961. For discussions targeted to more popular audiences, see Heather L. Norton et al., "Human Races Are Not Like Dog Breeds: Refuting a Racist Analogy," *Evolution: Education and Outreach* 12, no. 17 (2019); Megan Gannon, "Race Is a Social Construct, Scientists Argue: Racial Categories Are Weak Proxies for Genetic Diversity and Need to Be Phased Out," *Scientific American*, February 5, 2016, https://www.scientificamerican.com/article/race-is-a-social-construct-scientists-argue [https://perma.cc/RTV9-X5QU].

31. See Christine B. Hickman, "The Devil and the One Drop Rule: Racial Categories, African Americans, and the U.S. Census," *Michigan Law Review* 95 (1997): 1161.

32. Hickman, "The Devil and the One Drop Rule," 1163.

33. Hickman, "The Devil and the One Drop Rule," 1163.

34. Judith Surkis has powerfully argued in another context how crucial the assertion of difference that was inherent and immutable was necessary component for the mediation of a social world that purported to be based on principles of universal equality, and yet maintained clear hierarchies and exerted domination and rule. Judith Surkis, *Sex, Law, and Sovereignty in French Algeria, 1830–1930* (Cornell University Press, 2019).

35. Mahmud, "Colonialism and Modern Construction of Race," 1228.

36. Anthony W. Marx, *Making Race and Nation: A Comparison of the United States, South Africa, and Brazil* (Cambridge University Press, 1998).

37. Mahmud, "Colonialism and Modern Construction of Race," 1228.

38. See Paul Finkelman, "Slavery in the United States: Persons or Property?," in *The Legal Understanding of Slavery: From the Historical to the Contemporary*, ed. Jean Allain (Oxford University Press, 2012), 105, 110–11.

39. For a discussion of the ancient Roman law, see Youval Rotman, *Byzantine Slavery and the Mediterranean World*, trans. Jane Marie Todd (Harvard University Press, 2009), 25–81. For a discussion of this rule in Islamic law, see Jonathan A. C. Brown, *Slavery & Islam* (Simon & Schuster, 2019).

40. For work on the ontologies of Blackness, see Roger William Reeves, "Black Western Thought: Toward a Theory of the Black Citizen-Object" (PhD diss., University of Texas at Austin, 2012) (on file with the University of Texas at Austin Library), 1–62.

41. Mahmud, "Colonialism and Modern Construction of Race," 1226.

42. See Eric Foner, *Reconstruction: America's Unfinished Revolution 1863–1877* (Cambridge University Press, 1988).

43. See Douglas A. Blackmon, *Slavery by Another Name: The Re-enslavement of Black Americans From the Civil War to World War II* (Icon Books, 2012).

44. See Natsu Taylor Saito, *Settler Colonialism, Race, and the Law: Why Structural Racism Persists* (NYU Press, 2020), 79–153 (examining how narratives of racial superiority have shaped U.S. law across these groups).

45. Mahmud, "Colonialism and Modern Construction of Race," 1225.

46. Robert C. Schwaller, *Géneros de Gente in Early Colonial Mexico: Defining Racial Difference* (Duke University Press, 2016), 48–49. Schwaller emphasizes that in their earliest formations in the sixteenth century, these categories reflected "incipient racial attitudes" rather than modern conceptions of race, in part because they had not yet incorporated the pseudoscientific conceptions of racial biology that arose in the eighteenth century. Schwaller, *Géneros de Gente,* 49.

47. Hebe Mattos, "'Pretos' and 'Pardos' between the Cross and the Sword: Racial Categories in Seventeenth Century Brazil," *European Review of Latin American and Caribbean Studies* 80 (2006): 43.

48. Sven Beckert, *Empire of Cotton* (Harvard University Press, 2015), 119.

49. Mahmud, "Colonialism and Modern Construction of Race," 1240.

CHAPTER FOURTEEN

BARBARIANS AT THE GATE

The NIEO and the Stakes of Racial Capitalism

Vasuki Nesiah[*]

> The spirit of the barbarians, which the Western peoples thought they had tamed by centuries of struggle, is abroad again and threatens to destroy the civilizing work of all these centuries.
> —Wilhelm Röpke, *Against the Tide*[1]

> The barbarians, when they come, will legislate.
> —C. P. Cavafy, "Waiting for the Barbarians"[2]

For the United Nations General Assembly (UNGA), 1974 was a banner year of legislative achievement, and the passage of the New International Economic Order (NIEO) declaration was its crowning glory.[3] Its advocates saw the NIEO as laying the foundation for economic self-determination that would ensure that political self-determination was not just a formalist achievement but a substantive realization that finally turned the chapter on a Eurocentric economic architecture. The UNGA legislative ambitions gave expression to an approach to decolonization as not the event of national emancipation but an ongoing process of world-making after colonialism.[4] It spoke to a political horizon that went beyond formal legal equality and the rules of the game that were inherited from colonialism. It also epitomized the paradoxical subject position of post-colonial sovereignty, seeking inclusion in a world order that they wanted to transform.

THE POST-COLONIAL GENERAL ASSEMBLY

The rules of inclusion within the United Nations reflected the fact that the world order was forged by colonialism and slavery. For the formerly colonized, political independence was soon followed by an "and we are not saved" experience of those entrenched racial and economic inheritances. New member states at the United Nations had to confront and strategize around the international landscape that the UN navigated and helped reproduce, from its capital flows to its civilizational imaginaries, from center to periphery. It is in this context that the countries of the Global South approached their evolving numbers at the General Assembly as offering a new kind of opportunity to undertake the unfinished work of decolonization through collective action. In the early decades of the UN, post-colonial states may have been largely united in the emancipatory euphoria of having defeated European colonialism, but these states were not characterized by a corresponding ideological unity on their future economic path and whether they defined their economic horizon within the terms of global capitalism, or through resistance to those terms. Given this diversity, the passage of the NIEO declaration in the GA was a remarkable achievement and reflected a strategic vision of how the General Assembly could function.[5]

The NIEO was only one of a series of remarkable GA resolutions in 1974. The 1974 GA Resolution 3292 requesting that the International Court of Justice (ICJ) give an advisory opinion on the decolonization of the Western Sahara was particularly significant.[6] The judgment on the Western Sahara presented the first international judicial ruling challenging the coherence and legitimacy, legal or otherwise, of the notion of *terra nullius* that had been mobilized in the material dispossession of Indigenous people across the globe, from the Americas to Australia.

That same year, the GA passed Resolution 3236, which affirmed the inalienable rights of the Palestinian people to self-determination, national independence, and sovereignty, and the right of Palestinians to return to their homes and property. Most significantly, it was followed that same day by Resolution 3237, which gave the PLO observer status. South Africa was also suspended from the GA in 1974 for the system of apartheid it had established in South Africa and Namibia (then South West Africa). Indeed, that year, South Africa was nearly ousted from the United Nations altogether when the GA forwarded a resolution asking the Security Council to review South Africa's membership, and it was only the triple veto of the US, UK, and France that ensured the apartheid state was not expelled. We could read the twin 1974 actions of including the PLO and suspending South Africa as having a connective tissue reflecting the commitment to decolonization that the GA had expressed over a decade earlier in the 1960 decolonization resolution, GA 1514.[7] The implication of that connection is that apartheid is not just a system of racist governance, but a system of racist colonial governance. On this reading the GA emerges as already ahead of today's conversation about the nexus between settler colonialism and apartheid in the occupied territories.

The steady path of the GA towards the NIEO could be said to have been launched with the 1960 resolution calling for the Granting of Independence to Colonial Countries and Peoples. That year, 1960, was also the year the GA launched the first development decade that then opened the door to a whole range of other resolutions on matters that became critical to the NIEO.[8] It reflected the conviction of that generation of third world leaders that (in Kwame Nkrumah's words) "the struggle against colonialism does not end with the attainment of national independence"; the struggle for economic independence from the Global North was the new front of struggle once independence was achieved.[9] One can see a steady drumbeat of increasingly vocal action by members of the GA from the Global South that sought to restructure the world order on both fronts. The year 1960 also saw seventeen African countries gain independence, the largest in a single year to date. Yet, unsatisfied with the pace of decolonization, the following year, the GA passed a resolution calling for all member states and the United Nations to take more concerted steps advancing the implementation of GA 1514.

Partha Chatterjee has argued that the real significance of the 1955 Bandung Conference was its representation of an alternative ethos of collective political agency and cooperation to un-make imperial governance. For Chatterjee, the formal equality of nations at the GA, colonial and post-colonial alike, is the institutional embodiment of this Bandungian ethos of democratic governance of international affairs.[10] The NIEO is a poster child for this project of "un-making" a world made by colonialism through a faith in post-colonial multilateralism. Twenty-nine governments were represented at Bandung in 1955. Twenty years later, when the NIEO declaration was passed, there were 139 governments represented in the GA—the majority of which were newly independent nations. This decisive and determined trajectory was anticipated in 1955—emboldening to the formerly colonized, and threatening to the formerly colonizing.

In 1961, the Global South also began caucusing outside of the halls of the UN by creating the Non-Aligned Movement (NAM), which had its first meeting in Belgrade in 1961. This turned out be a pivotal platform for transnational solidarity and strategic interventions navigating the terrain of the Cold War to advance the interests of the Global South. Yet using the institutional resources of the United Nations was equally critical, and in 1964 the GA passed a resolution creating the United Nations Conference on Trade and Development (UNCTAD) that played a vital role in the NIEO process. In 1965, the General Assembly passed Resolution 2106 and opened the International Convention on the Elimination of All Forms of Racial Discrimination (CERD) for signatures.[11] While the US had previously been allergic to any initiative that drew attention to its own =damning record of racial oppression, activists were able to take advantage of the confluence of decolonization processes across the world, the global anti-apartheid movement, and social movements within the West to press for passage of CERD. In the same period, the GA also passed resolutions on technology transfer and development financing.

It was followed in the next years with a series of resolutions on the independence of countries like Namibia and the Western Sahara. Thus the GA continued to move forward on multiple interrelated fronts of political, legal, and economic dimensions of the world order. The NIEO itself gave voice to these interconnected dimensions when it gave a prominent place to the "full permanent sovereignty of every State over its natural resources and all economic activities."[12] From apartheid to settler colonialism, the GA of that period was abuzz with reformist projects taking on the unfinished work of decolonization processes in multiple arenas. This was the milieu from which the NIEO declaration emerged in 1974.

THE DARKER NATIONS OF BANDUNG

The NIEO is often written about in terms of the alternative economic visions at stake, including its provoking of a disciplinary and professional backlash in influential sectors of "Global North"–based economists that led to their abandoning the received wisdom of Keynesianism to embrace neoliberalism. Indeed, neoliberalism's new dawn in the 1970s is partly tied to this economic debate and opposition to the NIEO's alternative economic analysis and prescriptions. But a focus on the economic domain does not tell the whole story. The neoliberal economic vision was intricately intertwined with a vision of the social order of international society, a vision that was grounded in a racial and civilizational vision of governance and expertise. The opposition to the NIEO's economic policy vision is inextricably tied to this social vision and the post-imperial dynamics of global governance that the 1974 GA represented. The NIEO resolution trumpeted that the "colored peoples" of the world were seizing the reins of power.[13]

At the 1955 Bandung conference, President Sukarno's welcoming speech noted that the conference was the largest gathering of "colored peoples" from across the world. The conference described itself as focused on "colonialism and racialism." This gathering of "darker nations" was all about the conjoined struggles against colonial and racial oppression—what Richard Wright's report of the Bandung conference, *The Color Curtain,* described as "a conglomeration of the world's underdogs."[14] The conference communiqué made particular mention of apartheid South Africa to denounce its policies and applaud resistance from people of African and Asian descent. However, its driving mission was not a focus on the enduring colonial injustices in particular countries; rather, it was a project of collectively imagining an alternative anti-colonial future for a world order made by colonialism. This involved both an agenda for transnational solidarity in anti-racist struggle, and an analysis of empire as structural "racialism" on a global scale.

Racialism was both an old-fashioned way of denoting racism and a future-oriented way of connoting race-making and racial taxonomies as fundamentally colonial projects.[15] Richard Wright's account poignantly conveys how attendees spoke of the racism they experienced and denounced, as well as their ambivalence about foregrounding, even in critique, a colonial episteme of race. This ambivalence was not the "post-racist" lens familiar to us today from the American right, but the quintessential "post" colonial challenge of un-making colonial legacies when it was no longer possible to return to the pre-colonial status quo. Thus even figures like Jawaharlal Nehru and Carlos Romulo were grappling with contradictory impulses of decrying racialism's structural crippling of post-colonial futures while not allowing that struggle to overdetermine the future.[16] These ambivalences and contradictions were not symptoms of prevarication, but instead signs of the utopic ambitions of that moment—or what Frantz Fanon described as the "lasting tension of his freedom."[17] The Bandung final communiqué's denouncing of "racialism" as a form of "cultural suppression" speaks to this fraught, paradoxical positionality: it is not only protesting the suppression of the particular cultures of Brown and Black people (although that too), but it is also denouncing the culture of race and race-making as a structural dimension of imperialism. In this spirit, the communiqué calls for "Asian and African cultural co-operation" as a form of anti-essentialist un-making of "colonialism and racialism" that stood intertwined with the communiqué's demands for economic cooperation to un-make the economic architecture of the world order. The gathering of the colored people in 1955 was in itself an effort to render a new world order thinkable. Arguably, the tricontinental apogee of these intertwined projects was the NIEO.

THE COLOR OF BACKLASH

The German economist Wilhelm Röpke, a key figure in what was to become the Geneva school of neoliberalism, shared Chatterjee's reading about the significance of sovereign equality. But for him, this was threat, not promise. Like the elder statesmen of Bandung—Sukarno, Nehru, Nasser—Röpke didn't live to see the 1974 GA in action. However, if the NIEO was the crowning achievement of Bandung, the neoliberal counteroffensive to Bandung was the crowning achievement of Röpke and his Mont Pelerin Society cohorts. In 1955, the same year as the Bandung conference, Röpke marked the threat of the tidal wave of new sovereigns and urged that "one of the urgent needs of our time" was precisely "to diminish national sovereignty" so that countries without the "moral infrastructure" for the global marketplace did not control the direction of global society.[18] For Röpke, holding off the barbarians at the gate by diminishing national sovereignty was not a project of shifting authority to a contender for global sovereign power like the GA but of creating the infrastructure for a neoliberal economic order. The GA was drowning out Europe's voice, the tyranny of the majority trumping civilizational expertise. For Röpke, champion of apartheid South Africa, the 1974 GA would have been exhibit A—the same GA that passed the NIEO created a seat at the table for Palestine, while showing South Africa the door.

The subsequent unfolding of the South Africa story at the General Assembly offers a telling window into the significance of intertwined fronts of colonialism, racism, and economic policy. Throughout the 1960s and 1970s, the General Assembly passed a series of resolutions denouncing apartheid and calling for boycotts and other kinds of pressure against South Africa. This was not only a call to other member states but also a call to UN agencies, including the World Bank and the IMF, the two institutions most identified with neoliberal policies in the Global South. By the early '80s, the General Assembly rebuked these agencies for not complying with its sanctions regime and continuing to invest in and support the apartheid government.[19] It is significant that the leadership and composition of these two agencies remain fundamentally undemocratic, with voting rules in the Bank and the IMF weighted overwhelmingly towards wealthy countries, and with leadership resting exclusively with American and European appointments.

The racial composition of these different agencies and claims about the nexus between racial composition and ideas about civilization, expertise, and ideology emerged again and again as a nodal point of debate in ways that were themselves revelatory about the racial politics of those making these connections. Röpke was not alone in his fears about the newly empowered third world and that they might exercise their "moral infrastructure" (to use his terms) in ways that challenged the white supremacist vision he held on to. Protesters against the PLO resolutions at the gates of the UN in 1974 complained about the new composition of the GA and its threat to world order.[20] Achille Mbembe characterizes this period as one of "anti-third world Eurocentrism" that emerged into the global public sphere in the 1950s but "reached its apogee in the 1970s in the critique of dependence and unequal development theories and the attempts to establish a more just international economic order."[21] In Mbembe's historical taxonomy it is a period that follows "primitive Eurocentrism" of the imperial age, and one that precedes the "late-Eurocentrism" that came with the consolidation of neoliberalism. Indeed, one can see the late 1970s after the defeat of the NIEO as a kind of interregnum where the bloom of decolonization was in decay and "things fell apart."[22]

THE ALLURE OF THE RACE BLIND MARKET

For Röpke, Friedrich Hayek, and others in their cohort, decolonization was what was bringing about the dissolution of the center, and it is a world governed by these new sovereigns that was a threat to civilization and the old world order. The global market on the other hand could be a buffer zone, mediating the collective force of these new sovereigns that now threatened to dominate the world—or, in Quinn Slobodian's words, the neoliberal notion of the market represented a "militant globalism" that was "based on institutions of multitiered governance that are insulated from democratic decision making."[23] Democracy had two references here. Firstly, it referred to the masses of these new nation states and their effort to hold their leaders accountable; they had been rendered indigent by colonialism and exerted pressure on their political leaders to enact policies that would facilitate greater redistribution. It also referred to democracy on a world scale in institutions of global governance such as the GA. In contrast to a non-representative Security Council, the GA opened the door to newly independent states representing the vast majority of the world's peoples. The 1974 resolutions were a testament to the fact that the "colored peoples" of the world, having entered the gates, had forged solidarities that mobilized their GA majority to legislate towards alternative futures. Racialized fears of this collective force played a constitutive role in neoliberal economic analysis. Neoliberalism was not just a set of economic policies that majority white countries advanced; rather, neoliberalism was itself an expression of white supremacy; the neoliberal marketplace was the final defense against the movement of "colored peoples . . . towards Bethlehem" in greater and greater numbers.

The pivotal contrasts between the dependency-theory-inflected NIEO economic vision ("a new deal for the world") and the neoliberal one was evident in the different agendas for the distributive consequences, racial and otherwise, of these alternative programs for world order. Crucially, there were also differences in the disciplinary knowledges and policy expertise that framed and analyzed strategic choices and trade-offs. Thus each of the divergences in particular policy orientations (for instance, the advisability of sovereigns enacting tariff controls and establishing subsidies for local industries) can be situated in contrasting analytic orientations in the study of the political economy of development. For instance, the overarching economic vision of the NIEO leaned towards sovereigns being empowered to enact such policy measures in choosing partial and strategic engagement with the global market while aiming for the telos of economic self-sufficiency as a framing goal in development planning. The people of the third world were seeking to change the rules of global governance, and the new rules proposed by the NIEO emerged from an alternative analysis of global markets and how they functioned. The NIEO's framework was informed by the work of third world economists such as the Argentinian Raúl Prebisch, who was the first Executive Secretary of the UN Economic Commission for Latin America (CEPAL); CEPAL emerged as a central incubator for the ideas that informed the NIEO by analyzing how global markets engendered dependency, and how dependency was a mechanism for neocolonial exploitation.[24] Prebisch himself would then go on to become the first Secretary General of the United Nations Conference on Trade and Development (UNCTAD), which expanded beyond Latin America to play a pivotal role as a central think tank for what became the NIEO. The Sri Lankan economist and diplomat Dr. Gamani Corea created the Group of 77 at the first UNCTAD meeting in 1964 to help secure a collective "third world" presence in the global public sphere; Corea became the third Secretary General of UNCTAD in 1974 when the NIEO declaration was passed. CEPAL and UNCTAD were institutional avenues to decolonizing the politics of knowledge in the field of political economy and development; the "third-worldist" economic policy networks that they drew on and mobilized prioritized the interests of the Global South in the analysis of world systems. This vibrant heterodoxy in economic thought can itself be situated in a larger milieu of postcolonial theorizing in the 1970s, with critical interventions such as Walter Rodney's *How Europe Underdeveloped Africa* and Edward Said's *Orientalism* emerging in this same period.[25]

The political promise and intellectual insights of the NIEO did not represent an isolationist and atavistic nationalism; Indeed, arguably, many postcolonial sovereigns had their finest hour in venues such as the general assembly and the NAM. As already noted, this was a period when these bodies constituted an international habitus where third world polities could thrive through collective action facilitating emancipatory national planning alongside transnational solidarities that were not limited by the horizon of the nation-state. Internally, some of the most powerful third world states had become repressive in crushing dissent because of internal authoritarianism (consider the state of emergency called by Indira Gandhi in the mid-70s) and deathly collusions with Cold War alliances (such as the anti-communist massacres in Indonesia in the mid to late '60s). However, on a global plane, anti-colonial nationalisms channeled into a progressive vision of transnational solidarities and future-oriented collective action that was aimed at transforming the institutional arrangements of world order. Indeed, this fundamentally optimistic tricontinental internationalism is a striking feature of the GA resolutions of 1974.

The neoliberals may also be called internationalists, but their globalism stood in opposition to the third-world economists' emphasis on national economic planning and their reading of the pernicious dynamics of neocolonial dependency. The central directive of the neoliberal vision was of market-driven interdependence—or, in Slobodian's language, "encasement of the market in a spirit of militant globalism."[26] Moreover, this globalism was one where racism was baked into the universal only to emerge again in notions of economic expertise, good governance, and failed states, with the alternative internationalism of the "colored peoples" of the world rendered inaudible.

DECONSTRUCTING POST-RACIAL TECHNOCRACY

Today, some analysts of right-wing politics and policies argue that there is an internal tension between neoliberalism and white supremacy; they posit a dichotomy of the universalist rationalities of the market versus the particularist rationalities of racism. Accordingly, a familiar framing of this landscape describes neoliberalism as race-neutral and technocratic in vision (even if not in consequence); in contrast, white supremacy is described as fundamentally anti-technocracy, and hostile to social scientific knowledge. The history and circumstance of the GA resolution in support of the NIEO in 1974 allows us to better understand how this framing of the political and intellectual landscape does not fully capture the racial-capitalist grammar that is internal to both neoliberalism and white supremacy. The economic ordering of the world and the racial ordering of the world cannot be so easily disentangled. As captured so pithily by Ruthie Gilmore, "capitalism requires inequality, and racism enshrines it";[27] the NIEO was an effort to contest that inequality, and the distribution of resources and meanings that enshrined it on a global scale. It represented a radical material redistribution of economic resources but also of the racialized and race-making social capital that was part of the infrastructure of global governance.

It is significant that the social capital at stake included not only the racial composition of who sits in the GA in 1974, but also the intellectual traditions of economic knowledge and development policy networks that informed the agendas of those around the table. These traditions and networks tell a complex story, including about the difficulty of disentangling whose voices are privileged and the content of the knowledge produced. Advocates of the NIEO recognized that the continuities from colonial to post-colonial world orders included the racial hierarchies and distinctions that shaped economic thought and macro-economic planning. A monopoly on these domains (on what constituted "expertise" and what defined economic "knowledge") were part of the "wages of whiteness"[28] that had been delivered by centuries of slavery and colonialism that had made up the old economic order—or in Röpke's words, the "civilizing work of all these centuries."[29] The alchemy of CRT and TWAIL cuts through these disciplinary conceits and canonical knowledge systems in ways that connect the dots between authoritative knowledge and the ideas and ideologies that have helped reproduce the racial and colonial privileges that characterize the world as we know it. Consider the reflections of CRT scholars Richard Delgado and Jean Stefancic on American jurisprudence, where they observe that the very language of law carries with it a canonical interpretation predicated on silencing questions of race and power: "The law does have a canon. It consists of terms like 'just,' 'fair,' 'equal,' 'equal opportunity,' 'unfair to innocent whites,' 'nice,' 'deserving,' and 'meritorious,' all with canonical meanings that reflect our sense of how things ought to be, namely much as they are."[30] In similar spirit TWAIL has deconstructed terms in international law and policy such as "development," "free trade," "progress," "good governance," and "human rights" to analyze the work they do in obfuscating questions of race and power, colonial legacies and contemporary world ordering. When critical interventions draw on intellectual traditions that have resisted the racial hierarchies and distinctions that shape economic thought and macro-economic planning, they are also contesting epistemic hierarchies that are built into the disciplinary and professional grammar of fields like international economic law.[31]

The wages of resistance include the inheritance of traditions that inform and inspire radical political imagining of alternative world orders. For instance, one might connect the dots from the spirit of tricontinental internationalism that infused the NIEO with the World Social Forum that emerged from Porto Alegre (and elsewhere) at the beginning of the new millennium.[32] In similar vein, one can hear echoes of the NIEO's commitment to economic self-determination in the networks of cooperative economics and mutual aid networks that are proliferating in different parts of the world, from City Plaza and other migrant squats in Southern Greece,[33] to Dalia and initiatives for food sovereignty in the West Bank,[34] to the "cooperative commonwealth" in Jackson, Mississippi.[35] Relatedly, one could track continuities between the NIEO and contemporary calls for reparations for the slave trade and colonialism that resist and unsettle the regime of trade and aid that shape economic precarity and climate injustice today.[36] These boldly visionary initiatives may resonate with the insurgent and decolonial spirit of the NIEO but they are not nostalgia projects limited by the statist horizon that was the hallmark of the 1970s General Assembly. Rather, they speak to the historical conjuncture of the current moment and the political imagination that has been shaped by a chastened vision of the state, and an emboldened vision of how we might profit from institutional experimentation. In this the scholarly analogs may include not only CRT and TWAIL, but also Indigenous studies and feminist social reproduction theory in remapping how we connect the dots between production and reproduction, law and community, knowledge and practice. The strengths of these new initiatives in practice and theory include the fact that they are responsive to local priorities, learn from social movements, and are animated by transnational solidarities. Whether they can also be the path to a new international economic order is the challenge that lies ahead.

NOTES

* An earlier, shorter version of this piece was published in *Progressive International*, January 5, 2023, https://progressive.international/blueprint/30202c48-1324-4831-81e5-829f588d9492-nesiah-the-nieo-against-racial-capitalism/en.

1. Wilhelm Röpke, *Against the Tide*, ed. Elizabeth Henderson (Regnery Publishing, 1969), 93. I was led to read *Against the Tide* after first encountering Röpke's worries about an imperiled western civilization in Jessica Whyte's brilliant history of the twinned lives of neoliberalism and human rights in *The Morals of the Market: Human Rights and the Rise of Neoliberalism* (Verso, 2019). In *Against the Tide*'s essays of warning, admonition, and lamentation, Röpke is as worried about the threats from within Europe as he is about the threats from without. Writing in the aftermath of the war, he seeks to raise the alarm not just about the socialist threat from the East or the rising tide of dissent from the Global South, but also the Keynesianism that had become the hegemonic wisdom in the finance ministries of post-war Western Europe.

2. *Cavafy: Poems*, ed. and trans. Daniel Mendelsohn (Everyman's Library, 2014).

3. GA Resolution 3201 (S-VI), *Declaration on the Establishment of a New International Economic Order*. The passage of the NIEO resolution was followed by a series of implementing resolutions: "Recalling its resolutions 3201 (S-VI) and 3202 (S-VI) of 1 May 1974 containing the Declaration and the Programme of Action on the Establishment of a New International Economic Order, 3281 (XXIX) of 12 December 1974 containing the Charter of Economic Rights and Duties of States and 3362 (S-VII) of 16 September 1975 on development and international economic co-operation." https://www.refworld.org/docid/3b00f2324.html.

4. Adom Getachew, *Worldmaking After Empire: The Rise and Fall of Self-Determination* (Princeton, 2019).

5. Umut Özsu, "'In the Interests of Mankind as a Whole': Mohammed Bedjaoui's New International Economic Order," *Humanity* 6, no. 1 (2015): 129, 131. https://muse.jhu.edu/article/576930/pdf.

6. Western Sahara, Advisory Opinion 1975 I.C.J. 12 (Oct. 16). http://www.worldcourts.com/icj/eng/decisions/1975.10.16_western_sahara.htm.

7. Declaration on the Granting of Independence to Colonial Countries and Peoples, General Assembly resolution 1514 (XV); see https://www.un.org/dppa/decolonization/en/about#:~:text=1960,a%20right%20to%20self%2Ddetermination.

8. Resolutions adopted on the reports of the Second Committee; see https://documents-dds-ny.un.org/doc/RESOLUTION/GEN/NR0/167/63/PDF/NR016763.pdf?OpenElement.

9. The speech was given at the inauguration of the OAU in 1963; see "Dr. Kwame Nkrumah Speaks in Addis Ababa in 1963," *CENCSA*, 1963, https://consciencism.wordpress.com/history/dr-kwame-nkrumah-speaks-in-addis-ababa-in-1963/#:~:text=Speaking%20in%20Addis%20Ababa%20on,of%20African%20Unity%20(OAU). Significantly, this appreciation of a new front of struggle was about the struggle on a global plane addressing the world system; independence also brought new fronts of internal struggle in many nations (by minorities for instance) and these same third world leaders were much less appreciative of these struggles. In some contexts, these struggles led to war (Biafra most famously perhaps) and even the creation of new states such as Bangladesh and Eritrea.

10. Partha Chatterjee, "The Legacy of Bandung," in *Bandung, Global History and International Law: Critical Pasts and Pending Futures*, ed. Luis Eslava et al. (Cambridge University Press, 2017).

11. Resolutions adopted on the reports of the Third Committee; see https://documents-dds-ny.un.org/doc/RESOLUTION/GEN/NR0/218/69/PDF/NR021869.pdf?OpenElement.

12. Principle 4.(e) of GA Resolution 3201.

13. The phrase "colored peoples" is a direct reference to Sukarno's opening speech at Bandung, April 18, 1955. "Opening address given by Sukarno (Badung, 18 April 1955), CVCE, accessed December 18, 2024, https://www.cvce.eu/en/obj/opening_address_given_by_sukarno_bandung_18_april_1955-en-88d3f71c-c9f9-415a-b397-b27b8581a4f5.html.

14. Richard Wright, *The Color Curtain: A Report on the Bandung Conference* (The World Publishing Company, 1956), 135.Wright, who had been working in Paris with Aimé Cesaire and others on pan-African projects such as the literary review *Présence Africaine*, heard about the conference, and felt an immediate connection between the negritude movement and the aspirations of the conference and traveled to Indonesia so that he could attend it.

15. For an analysis of "race-making" in the American context see, the classic by the Fields sisters, Karen Fields and Barbara Fields, *Racecraft: The Soul of Inequality in American Life* (Verso, 2014).

16. It was certainly a form of utopian thinking that seems out of reach today. Yet, perhaps this was permissible ambition in the historical conjuncture of that moment. Having defeated their colonial rulers, the freedom fighters of that era were emboldened to do the impossible in reimagining the world that might have been if not for "colonialism and racialism"—this was their "tryst with history." Thus from the time of its entry into the United Nations, India made the struggle against what Nehru describes as the "Nazi doctrine of racialism" a foreign policy priority, and challenging the insistence of South Africa and her allies that racism was a domestic issue, Nehru argued that this struggle was "a world cause in which all people who believe in freedom are interested." In Nehru's words: "The struggle in South Africa is ... not merely an Indian issue. It concerns all Asians whose honour and rights are threatened, and all the people in Asia should, therefore, support it. It concerns ultimately the Africans who have suffered so much by racial discrimination and suppression. It is a struggle for equality of opportunity for all races and against the Nazi doctrine of racialism. ... Our cause thus becomes a world cause in which all people who believe in freedom are interested." Quoted in A. E. Davis and V. Thakur, "'An Act of Faith' or a New 'Brown Empire'?: The Dismissal of India's Transnational Anti-Racism, 1945–1961," *Commonwealth and Comparative Politics* 56, no. 1 (2018): 22–39. doi:10.1080/14662043.2018.1411230.

17. Frantz Fanon, *Black Skins, White Masks* (Pluto, 1986), 231.

18. Quoted by Quinn Slobodian, *Globalists: The End of Empire and the Birth of Neoliberalism* (Harvard University Press, 2019), 11, 149; see also Wilhelm Röpke, *International Order and Economic Integration* (D. Reidel Publishing Company, 1959), 250.

19. For instance, see Resolution 172 D. (8–10) that specifically call out the Bank and the IMF. https://documents-dds-ny.un.org/doc/RESOLUTION/GEN/NR0/407/98/PDF/NR040798.pdf?OpenElement.

20. Peter Khiss, "100,000 Rally at the U.N. Against Palestinian Voice," *New York Times,* November 5, 1974, //www.nytimes.com/1974/11/05/archives/100000-rally-at-the-un-against-palestinian-voice-100000-rally-at-un.html. Abba Eban, Israel's former Foreign Minister, is quoted declaring bitterly: "The United Nations, in its present composition and mood, would refuse to support the Ten Commandments because they came out of Israel."

21. Achille Mbembe, "Notes on Late Eurocentrism," trans. Carolyn Shread, *Critical Inquiry,* July 1, 2021, https://critinq.wordpress.com/2021/07/01/notes-on-late-eurocentrism/.

22. In his poem, *The Second Coming,* W. B. Yeats's original formulation was "Things fall apart; the centre cannot hold: mere anarchy is loosed upon the world, the blood-dimmed tide is loosed, and everywhere, the Ceremony of innocence is drowned." Chinua Achebe saw this as an apt account of the drowning of postcolonialism's innocence and borrowed from it for the title of his novelistic account of that historical record, *Things Fall Apart* (Penguin, 1994).

23. Slobodian, *Globalists,* 12, 15.

24. For a riveting account of how CEPAL came to play that pivotal historical role, see Margarita Fajardo, *The World That Latin America Created: The United Nations Economic Commission for Latin America in the Development Era* (Harvard University Press, 2022).

25. Walter Rodney, *How Europe Underdeveloped Africa* (Bogle-L'Ouverture, 1972); Edward Said, *Orientalism* (Pantheon, 1978).

26. Slobodian, *Globalists,* 16.

27. "Geographies of Racial Capitalism with Ruth Wilson Gilmore," Mapping Capital, accessed December 19, 2024, https://mapping.capital/wp-content/uploads/2022/04/geographies_of_racial_capitalism_with_ruth_wilson_gilmore.pdf.

28. I refer here to W.E.B. Du Bois's analysis in *Black Reconstruction* (Harcourt, Brace and Company, 1935), of how the wage of whiteness was not only the material profit from racialized systems of exploitation and dispossession, but also the psychological wage that may help empower white people because of the *relative* advantage it conferred in terms of their sense of self and self-regard; Du Bois was trying to explain why white workers may hold on to anti-Black racism even if they were materially disadvantaged by not having cross-racial solidarity with the Black workers. I draw on Du Bois's terminology to underscore that the profit of white privilege in this context was not only material; in this context there was also the profit from having a privileged voice in the discipline and profession of economics.

29. The alternative expertise that the NIEO can be taken to represent includes a diverse range of scholars from the Global South such as Andre Gunder Frank, *Capitalism and Underdevelopment in Latin America: Historical Studies of Chile and Brazil* (Monthly Review Press, 1969); Eric Williams, *Capitalism and Slavery* (University of North Carolina Press, 1994); Walter Rodney, *How Europe Under Developed Africa* (Bogle-L'Ouverture, 1972); Fernando Henrique Cardoso and Enzo Faletto, *Dependency and Development in Latin America* (University of California Press, 1970); and Raúl Prebisch, *The Economic Development of Latin America and its Principal Problems* (UN Department of Economic Affairs, 1950).

30. Richard Delgado and Jean Stefancic, "Hateful Speech, Loving Communities: Why Our Notion of a Just Balance Changes So Slowly," *California Law Review* 82 (1994): 851, 862. https://doi.org/10.2307/3480934.

31. A project of reparative history has to include resisting historical amnesia about lessons learned from expressions of dissent amongst oppressed peoples of the Global South and elsewhere. Priyamvada Gopal, *Insurgent Empire: Anticolonial Resistance and British Dissent* (Verso, 2019).

32. This is an echo of the connection that Michael Hardt draws between the spirit of Bandung and Porto Alegre in "Port Alegre: Today's Bandung," *New Left Review* 14 (March/April 2002): 112. https://newleftreview.org/issues/ii14/articles/michael-hardt-porto-alegre-today-s-bandung.

33. *Refugee Hosts* (blog), "A Successful Alternative to Refugee Camps: A Greek Squat Shames the EU and NGOs," January 26, 2018, https://refugeehosts.org/2018/01/26/a-successful-alternative-to-refugee-camps-a-greek-squat-shames-the-eu-and-ngos/.

34. For more on the Dalia Association's food sovereignty initiative, see: https://www.dalia.ps/community-programs/food-sovereignty; see also, Abdalaziz Al-Salehi, *Palestinian National Food Sovereignty in Light of the Colonial Context* (Dalia Association, 2021).

35. For more on Cooperation Jackson, see https://cooperationjackson.org/.

36. See Vasuki Nesiah, "A Double Take on Debt: Reparations Claims and Regimes of Visibility in a Politics of Refusal," *Osgoode Hall Law Journal* 59, no. 1 (2022): 153, 178, 183. doi: https://doi.org/10.60082/2817-5069.3740. For reparations proposals by the Caribbean Community (CARICOM), see https://caricom.org/caricom-ten-point-plan-for-reparatory-justice/; for the proposal for a tricontinental alliance to protect rainforests with Brazil, Indonesia, and the DRC taking the lead, see Patrick Greenfield, "Brazil, Indonesia and DRC in talks to form 'Opec of rainforests,'" *The Guardian*, November 5, 2022, https://www.theguardian.com/environment/2022/nov/05/brazil-indonesia-drc-cop27-conservation-opec-rainforests-aoe.

CHAPTER FIFTEEN

RACE CONSCIOUSNESS AND CONTEMPORARY INTERNATIONAL LAW SCHOLARSHIP
The Political Economy of a Blind Spot

Akbar Rasulov[*]

INTRODUCTION

The argument that I want to explore in this chapter has two starting points. The first comes from a conversation I had some years ago with a colleague. We were both at the start of our careers, still unmoored institutionally, anxious and ambivalent about the whole publish-or-perish culture. My colleague, as it so happens, grew up in the Middle East and came from an Arab background. As it also so happens, one of the hottest topics in international law at the time was the Arab Spring. Predictably, I asked him if he considered writing about it. His answer has stuck with me ever since: "No, because I don't want to become a professional Arab."

There are many interesting aspects to this statement, to be sure. But the point that I wish to make is that, first, it offers a great window into the subject that I am about to raise; and, second, how long it takes you to work out what he might have meant by "becoming a professional Arab" will probably say a lot more about where in the politics of our discipline you belong than you might suspect.

My second starting point comes from what appears to be a "theoretical question." Why is so little interest, relatively speaking, being shown in contemporary *international law scholarship* (ILS) in questions of race and racism? That is to say, why are discussions of race and racism—or what one might call more generally a culture of *race consciousness*—not more widespread in the broader intellectual landscape of our discipline?

There exists a school of thought that holds that in contemporary ILS the concept of race, having been "transmuted into the more comprehensive notion of civilization,"[1] now receives attention every time international lawyers talk about topics like colonialism, the civilizing mission, or the Empire. Seen from this perspective, race consciousness forms part and parcel of the so-called Third World Approaches to International Law (TWAIL) tradition, which would make it a rather prominent presence in the intellectual landscape of contemporary ILS. I do not agree with this view. Pursuing a theoretical orientation that focuses on subjects like colonialism, Eurocentricity, and imperial exploitation is not quite the same thing as expressing an interest specifically in questions of race and racism. One can, certainly, find a degree of overlap between the two lines of inquiry, and often they can be brought together with great results.[2] But there is little gain to be had from lumping them together for theoretical purposes.

At its root, the argument that I present in these pages is an exercise in *Marxian ideology critique*. The story it tells is a story about the implicit rationalization and normalization of a certain form of social life via the reproduction at the level of the corresponding discursive formation of a certain regime of theoretical blind spots and sanctioned ignorance. The general disinclination on the part of contemporary academic international lawyers to explore questions of race and racism, I would like to suggest, in other words, is not just a random state of affairs but the product of a pervasive ideological dynamic. The ideological regime in question, however, is not something that exists in the "external plane," but solely in the internal social space of ILS itself. Put differently, what we are looking at is not a grand world-historic ideology like neoliberalism or socialism, but a much more "local," field-specific ideology that structures and shapes the discipline of international law as a field of social relations. For reasons that will be made clear later, the name I propose to give to this ideology is *academic libertarianism*.

Stated in more concrete terms, the argument that I want to present in this chapter is an attempt to understand the workings of contemporary ILS as *a knowledge economy* and the role that the relative suppression of race consciousness from the surface of the ILS discourse plays in the political stabilization of this economy. In its main contours, it goes something like this: It is not at all surprising that race consciousness does not enjoy a more prominent place in contemporary ILS. The structure of every intellectual landscape, ultimately, is a reflection of the lived social realities of the respective community, and the lived social reality of contemporary ILS is characterized, among other things, by an enormous amount of racialized exclusion and marginalization. If the discipline were to admit a greater measure of critical race awareness into its thinking about the world, it would increase the likelihood that the same kind of critical awareness would also be extended to its thinking about itself. The problem with that sort of shift in its patterns of self-consciousness is that it would almost certainly undermine the political stability of the discipline's established economy of knowledge.

The statement that the lived reality of contemporary ILS is permeated with a certain degree of racism is not one that can be left without a further clarification. Race, as I understand for the purposes of the present argument, is a social construct, and the concept of racism does not just describe a creed or a program that is explicitly declared or embraced. Nor is it reducible only to deliberate and manifest expressions of bigotry or attempts to derive a "political science" from "biology." What one should understand by it, rather, is a certain kind of *social regime* that is grounded in, and oriented towards the reproduction of, practices leading to the constitution and distribution of economic and political power that is skewed along the lines and continua expressive and constitutive of what are commonly recognizable as racialized hierarchies and categories.[3]

The story that I want to tell in these pages is not a story about international law and Critical Race Theory (CRT), by which term I understand a historically specific cross-disciplinary formation that first began to take shape in the 1980s, in the United States, and that has as one of its defining traits a commitment to exploring the complex role of race and racism in the American society. The story that I want to tell here is a story about international law and *race consciousness*: a way of thinking about the world that also proceeds from the assumption that questions of race and racism are important, and that paying attention to them should inform our engagement with the world and our understanding of our place in it, but that is not necessarily identical or reducible to CRT.[4] No doubt, there exists a certain genealogic connection between the two. But the exact shape of this connection is not always clear, and a reader whose main interests lie in learning more about CRT and international law perhaps would be best advised turning elsewhere.[5]

Defined in these terms, the concept of race consciousness, one might say, conveys the idea of a certain kind of *worldview* or *theoretical orientation*. To "have" it is to show attentiveness to how different norms, practices, and processes may fit or challenge the social structure of race relations and to recognize the consistent centrality of that to the broader politico-economic fabric. To *have* race consciousness, however, does not necessarily mean to *be* race conscious—at least not in the sense in which this concept is sometimes understood in the US: feeling a sense of obligation towards one's race or wanting to act on its behalf.[6] Having race consciousness also does not mean being exclusively "race-centric" and ignoring questions of class politics, postcolonial justice, and gender-based politics, or rejecting the idea of the universal human dignity.

THE DISCIPLINE AS AN ECONOMY OF KNOWLEDGE PRODUCTION

The first part of my argument centers around the idea of looking at legal scholarship as an economic system.[7] It suggests, in a nutshell, that the best way to make sense of the internal logic of ILS as a field of production is to approach it through the lens of concepts like "appropriation," "extraction," and "added value." It proceeds generally from two observations. The first observation is that there has emerged in recent years a certain *hierarchy of genres of legal scholarship* or *modes of scholarly inquiry* in contemporary ILS that ranges roughly from traditional positivist and doctrinal scholarship, to policy analysis, to comparative international legal studies, international legal history, and various forms of critical ILS. The second observation says that if we look more closely at this hierarchy of genres, what we are going to find behind it is an *economy of knowledge production*. What separates the different genres of ILS from one another, in other words, is the different types of knowledge products they generate, different knowledge-productive technologies they deploy, and different places they occupy in the discipline's broader process of *value creation*.

Fundamentally, all productive processes revolve around the same general formula. A certain group of people takes up a certain set of raw materials to which they apply a certain set of technologies in order to generate a certain product.[8] In the process of doing so, they not only transform the raw materials in question into the intended product but also create a certain modicum of new value that is added to these materials that would not otherwise have existed. What the concept of *added value* represents in this context, thus, can be seen as both a measure of that which separates, economically, the raw materials from the finished product and a measure of the actual labor contribution made by the producers.[9] A different way of putting this is to say that whenever one acquires the final product, alongside the value of its material components, one also acquires the fruit of its maker's labor.

Why does this last detail need to be noted? Because it tells us something important about the actual economics of production. Schematically, every form of production follows one of two basic scenarios. Under the first scenario, the raw materials in question are taken from what more or less accurately can be characterized as the "natural reservoir." Think, for instance, of how brickmakers use clay to produce bricks or how steelworkers use iron ore to produce sheet metal. Under the second scenario, by contrast, the raw materials are drawn from what in effect are products produced by other people. Think of how the bricks made by the brickmakers are taken up as building materials by the construction industry, or how sheet metal is taken up by carmakers. What in one line of production represents the end result, in another becomes a part of the *initial material inputs*. Under both scenarios, the creation of added value proceeds apace. But while in the first scenario the added value is added to the respective chunk of "natural resources," in the second scenario it is added on top of a previously created chunk of added value, which makes it possible to describe the resulting product, in relative terms, as a *higher-added-value* (HAV) product.

And so, to go back to our earlier point about the hierarchy of genres, what the idea of looking at ILS as a system of knowledge production allows us to recognize is that as we move through the different levels of this hierarchy—from state practice–focused positivist ILS to discourse-centric history-of-ideas ILS, to ideology- and narratology-centric critical ILS—what we are essentially working through is the progression from the relatively primitive scenario of knowledge production that is built around light-touch processing of the "natural resources" supplied by the external legal reality to scenarios that are more or less explicitly premised on the *appropriation* and *extraction* of the added value created by other acts of legal scholarship. And that, inevitably, brings us to the question of the *intra-disciplinary division of labor* and the underlying ideology that legitimizes and sustains it.

To adjust slightly the phrasing proposed by the Cambridge economist Piero Sraffa, what the second scenario described above essentially illustrates is how much of our modern economy revolves around the *production of products via the subsumption (within them) of other products*,[10] or, in other words, how much of our wealth as a society consists, in practice, in the accumulation of greater and greater chunks of added value compiled on top of one another. The greater the proportionate share of HAV production, the greater the overall presence of added value within the overall structure of the economy. As every next article absorbs within itself the added value created by the producers of those articles that were subsumed as part of its material inputs, the relative share occupied by added value—that is to say, by the fruit of (other) people's labor—continually increases, meaning that the longer the chain of value creation extends the more the aggregate value stock that surrounds us becomes, in economic terms, just a shape-shifting embodiment of the variously subsumed acts of labor.[11]

Note, however, one important point about subsumption. It is not at all self-evident how and under what conditions the process of subsumption actually ought to take place. Nothing in Sraffa's formulation, for instance, tells us how much recognition and compensation we ought to give to those producers whose products we subsume within our own process of production. Nor does it tell us how we ought to construct the relationship between the subsumer and the subsumee. What if without those products which the subsumee provides, the subsumer could not even start operating? Imagine running a bakery if you don't have a steady supply of flour. Should we regard this kind of relationship as a species of dependence or exploitation? If the subsumed products can be put to a number of different uses, should we make the subsumer ask for the subsumee's permission before they can convert them for use in their own production? How much control should the subsumee have over the subsumer's decisions? How much credit should they be able to claim for the latter's success? What about risk and liability?

The reason why it is important to recognize all these indeterminacies is because they reveal something very crucial about how real-world economies work in practice, and it is that no real-world economy can, in fact, operate without an underpinning *economic ideology*. To get anything off the ground, you need, in other words, an effective collective consensus—a shared set of beliefs and a tradition of implementing them in practice—about how economic relations between people can be best organized that would help you fill in all of those blanks that we have just listed.

None of the questions flagged up above lends itself to a simple technical resolution. There is no logical reason, for instance, for requiring or not requiring the subsumer to ask for the subsumee's permission; both answers are equally plausible. A different way of putting this is to say that each of these matters is essentially a matter of *political choice*. And the choices we make about these matters as a society—what we decide should be the correct way for the producers of HAV products to absorb the products produced by other producers—determines, in the end, not only the overall volume of our economy—how much added value there is going to be created in total—but also its actual structure—which particular types of HAV products are going to be produced and in what proportion.

It should not be difficult to see what relevance all of this has for our thinking about ILS. Before we turn to that point, however, let me add one more detail: what has been described so far in Sraffian terms as subsumption can also be characterized, in Marxian terms, as *appropriation*. To subsume as part of our material inputs somebody else's product does not just mean absorbing it in some metaphorical sense. It also means appropriating it, that is to say, asserting our economic power over it, making it our own.

The reason why it is beneficial to make this switch in vocabulary at this point is because, firstly, it helps attract our attention to the fact that each of the questions mentioned above, in addition to being a political question, is also, at its root, a question about the distribution of property rights. This means that in thinking about the political economy of contemporary ILS it pays dividends not only to look into what sort of political vision permeates this economy but also to review what *regime of property rights* has de facto developed within it—both in the sense of what types of property relations can take place within ILS between different groups of scholars and in the sense of what types of property relations can take place in respect to what types of knowledge products.

In the second instance, the shift from the vocabulary of subsumption to that of appropriation also teaches us to recognize that when we subsume somebody else's product within our own production, what we do, in effect, is proceed to make our own not only those immediate materials out of which this product is composed but also the added value inserted into it by its producer. And when it is the acquisition specifically of that added value that serves as the principal motivation for our decision to subsume the product, the property-focused orientation of the concept of appropriation allows us to recognize that the relationship between the subsumer and the subsumee in this case, rather being simply that of appropriation, is, in fact, that of *extraction*.

How should one understand this last point? If the producer of an HAV product sets out to make use of somebody else's product mainly because of what added value the latter inserted into it through their labor, then it is not just true that it is *that act of labor* that they primarily seek to benefit from. What is also happening here, in economic terms, is that by targeting specifically that part of the subsumed product that corresponds to this act of labor, the subsumer, in effect, also tries to isolate it from the rest of its economic structure, or, in other words, to extract the one from the other just like one might extract a kernel of gold from a chunk of ore or a microchip from a washing machine.[12]

The most common modes of appropriation used in modern capitalism include acts such as buying, licensing, leasing, stealing, expropriating, seizing without permission, making use of publicly available resources, etc. Some of these acts involve a relatively high degree of compensation and a measure of reciprocal influence between the subsumer and the subsumee. Others bring to mind the popular idea of anarchy—a free-for-all where all those who can do whatever they want and all those who can't put up with the outcome—or what in private law terms one might also describe using the term *damnum absque injuria*.[13]

The relevant thing to bear in mind here in any event is twofold. First, that the ensemble of rules and principles that regulate the conditions and forms of appropriative transactions constitutes what is otherwise known as the general regime of appropriation, and the main element that connects this regime to the rest of the economy is that operative economic ideology mentioned earlier. Second, the main principle that sits at the heart of the general regime of appropriation in contemporary ILS is the *principle of academic freedom*, and the background economic ideology that entrenches and justifies it is essentially a species of economic libertarianism.

A different way of approaching this point would be to say that when it comes to what the discipline of international law accepts today as the more or less natural state of affairs in matters of knowledge economy, it is all just one endless field of *damnum absque injuria*. Everyone is basically free to subsume whatever scholarly products they want, and the specter of extractivism is ineradicable and ever present. Why? Because what the principle of academic freedom means above all, from an economic point of view, is the freedom to appropriate without being limited as to the mode or consequences.

One way to understand what I am about to say now is to think of it as a reflection on the implicit ambivalence of knowledge. There exists a fundamental discontinuity between knowledge as the subjective quest for the truth and the process of self-discovery and knowledge as an "industrial complex." In the former perspective, the idea of academic freedom describes what is basically a deeply utopian regime of self-care or, to use a Foucauldian term, the cultivation of the self.[14] In the latter perspective, it describes an approach to organizing the underlying systems for the society-wide production, dissemination, and consumption of insights, arguments, and ideas. And what the principle of academic freedom has come to stand for in ILS in that context—what *economically significant regulatory implications* it has come to acquire in the knowledge economy of the contemporary international law academia—is essentially the agreement that, subject to the general prohibition of plagiarism, every international law scholar is free to use in their own work the works of other scholars (i.e., to appropriate the added value created by them) without needing to obtain their permission or provide them with any greater compensation than a duly placed citation and acknowledgment.

One can guess where the argument goes next. Through its embracement of what in effect can be called the ideology of *academic libertarianism*, contemporary ILS has come to not only accept but also defend and legitimize a culture of extractivism, exploitation, and "economic parasitism."[15] Not everyone who benefits from this state of affairs, of course, sees it that way. But the tricky part here is also that not everyone within the discipline's invisible college can actually benefit from this state of affairs, which brings us, inevitably, to the next question. What can we glean about the general intra-disciplinary profile that is characteristic of those international law scholars who are best placed today to take advantage of the economic privileges granted by academic libertarianism? And what does all of that have to do with race and racism?

RACE, EXCLUSION, AND MARGINALIZATION IN THE DISCIPLINE'S GLOBAL DIVISION OF LABOR

The second part of my argument has a slightly different complexion. In its most basic contours, it can be summarized thusly. Over the last thirty years the patterns of knowledge production in academic international law have developed in a way that in structural terms seems strongly reminiscent of what used to be called the "development of underdevelopment."[16] That is to say, when it comes to the production of different genres of international legal scholarship, the international structure for the division of labor that has emerged within the discipline appears to follow *a clearly detectable core-periphery logic* in that the ability to engage in more theoretically complex forms of legal scholarship is not distributed equally between the discipline's Western and non-Western institutional circuits. This inequality, on closer look, has *a consistently racialized dimension* that has both economic (exploitation) and political (exclusion and marginalization) components. To be sure, the racism in question here is not the brute racism of apartheid, and it does not operate by dividing the discipline's invisible college into whites and non-whites. But a "racism without races" is still racism, and even if it takes a more complex process to uncover its footprints, it deserves to be called out as such.[17]

Note the framing of the argument: there are two separate patterns here—a core-periphery separation and the racialization of the inequalities that result from it—and the causal dynamics behind them is not attributed to any abstract essences or totalities, be it the West, Eurocentricity, or neoliberalism. The story we are looking at is still a story about the intra-disciplinary economy of knowledge. The main emphasis this time, however, falls on the question of distribution. How are the knowledge-productive technologies involved in the production of different types of ILS distributed across the discipline's internal geography? What sort of insights can we surmise from that about ILS-related international division of labor? And what sort of politics can be said to arise from all this?

The starting point of the story, in its broadest outlines, will be familiar to most readers.[18] Starting from sometime around the mid-1990s, a gradually deepening division began to form within the discipline's internal theoretical landscape. On the one hand, a steadily growing proportion of Western-based international law scholars seemed to have started to rate less and less highly what one might call the traditional modes of ILS inquiry, in particular, positivism and doctrinal analysis. On the other hand, positivism and doctrinal analysis continued to remain the principal modes of scholarly knowledge practiced in the non-Western segment of the discipline. Furthermore, just as the discipline's invisible college started to become more and more globalized, the actual social base of its intellectual leadership still seemed to be comprised almost exclusively of scholars who either worked or completed their professional training at the same handful of leading Western universities.

As the discipline saw out the second decade of the new century, both trends seemed to continue. In the Western-based segment, the fortunes of positivism and doctrinal analysis never recovered, and when it came to the production of scholarship that went beyond the traditional canons of positivist and doctrinal writing, the relative presence of non-Western-trained scholars did not seem to increase either. Meanwhile, the vast majority of the discipline's theoretical trend-setters continued to be concentrated around the same relatively small institutional circuit spread across Europe, North America, and Australia.

What sense can we make of this dynamic? Going back to some of the observations made in the previous section suggests a number of potential avenues of inquiry. In the first place, recalling that both positivism and doctrinal analysis are essentially knowledge-productive protocols, the apparent mystery of their geographically uneven decline and persistence can be quickly reframed as a story about innovation, technical progress, and the politics of technology transfers. What has been the general availability of the kind of disciplinary know-how that might enable a given group of legal scholars to adopt a particular set of knowledge-productive technologies? If a particular set of technologies has stopped being used as actively in one locale but continues to be used in another locale, does it have anything to do with the lack of training opportunities required for a successful technological upgrade in the latter?

In the second place, going back to the idea that the taxonomy of scholarly genres is essentially a reflection of the different modes of disciplinary value creation, could the unevenness of ILS's theoretical geography be a projection of some kind of Ricardian specialization and trade dynamics? Do international law scholars in some locales have a relative comparative advantage when it comes to the production of certain forms of scholarship? Or should we push the analysis further and try to make sense of this pattern in a way that is more reminiscent of the kind of arguments typically advanced by the *Global Value Chain* (GVC) tradition?[19] It may be helpful to recall that in added value terms positivism and doctrinal analysis represent far more basic forms of knowledge production than, say, critical international law or the history of ideas. At the same time, both of the latter genres also often depend on the continuous supply of positivist and doctrinal knowledge products. Can this relationship of dependence hold the key to ILS's uneven theoretical geography?

It does not take much critical insight to conclude that it might. All one really needs to do is to connect the idea of disciplinary GVCs to the earlier noted fact that in contemporary international law the established regime of appropriation not only tolerates but, in fact, legitimizes the practices of value extraction, and a whole series of interpretative possibilities immediately suggest themselves.

First possibility: the noted geographic discrepancies in theoretical and methodological trends are essentially a reflection of the inequality in accessing (i) *subject-specific methodological training*; and (ii) requisite *socialization opportunities* needed to convert the acquired training into *practice-ready scholarly know-how*.

Labor skills do not develop in a vacuum. To write international legal history competently, one has to learn not only the "abstract theory" part—what different historical methodologies exist and how each of them works—but also the "applied mechanics" side of the business—how to defend and deflect different kinds of historically oriented criticisms, how to frame a historical argument depending on which audience one is writing for, etc. Where the former aspect can in principle be mastered via textual sources, the latter for the most part cannot. To develop a satisfactory grasp of the practical know-how, one needs active and prolonged embedding in a network of mentors, informal advisers, and peers. While many law schools around the world can provide their students with these kinds of opportunities when it comes to positivism and doctrinal scholarship, not many can do the same for the kind of theory-heavy genres that have gained popularity in the discipline over the last thirty years.

Seen in these terms, the unevenness of ILS's theoretical geography can essentially be explained as the result of the spatially expressed institutional discrepancies between different universities. The sources of this discrepancy are multiple: an unequal distribution of financial resources, institutional reputation, capacity to attract and retain training staff, etc. But one of them seems to stand out: the rapid expansion of what one might call the *standard disciplinary toolbox* that began in the early to mid-1990s at places like Harvard, Toronto, Helsinki, and the LSE.[20]

Second possibility: the same argument as above, with the additional twist that the most important part in this expansion process was the fact that, in a way, it has never ended. As the rest of the discipline began to play catch-up vis-à-vis the first-mover institutions, it became increasingly clear that not everyone, ultimately, would be able to keep up. Some universities would have to drop out of the chase due to the general lack of resources, others because of the lack of incentives. In the end, most Western-based institutions that would be traditionally regarded within the discipline as centers of educational excellence stayed in the race. The vast majority of the non-Western-based institutions did not.

Again, the basic story, in its broadest outline, should be familiar to most readers. For most of the post–World War II era, what had been required in terms of general methodological competence for an international law scholar to be able to rise to a position of relative intra-disciplinary prominence was to know how to work with black-letter law and to master the standard protocols of positivist reasoning and doctrinal analysis, that is, the kind of scholarly skillset that one could be trained in as well at Lagos and Tehran as in London or New York. From the mid-1990s onwards, however, things began to change. The basic toolbox, of which one's mastery was regarded as evidence of professional competence, started to expand. First were added some elements from the traditional Critical Legal Studies (CLS) repertoire—structuralism, feminism, literary theory, the liberal international relations tradition, and managerial science. Then came transnational network theory, Carl Schmitt, Foucauldian biopolitics, postcolonial theory, and neo-Marxism. Then it was the turn for empiricism, the Cambridge School of historiography, more discourse analysis, more Marxism and Foucault, and even a dash of behavioral economics. Unless you were based at an institution where these new trends were being set, the bar, it seemed, just kept constantly being raised each time you came close to reaching it. It was not enough anymore to know your Foucault, your Derrida, and your apology-to-utopia. If you wanted to stay in the mix, there was a further list of new frameworks to master. If you could not keep up, no problem, but SDT and GSP logics could only go so far, and the rest of the field would not be waiting for you—meet the business side of academic freedom.[21] The tipping point, whenever it may have taken place, seems now far behind us. The idea that everyone in the field would be able to catch up is obvious fiction. If the latest patterns in "theory fad" are anything to go by, it seems one also needs now to add to the toolbox various elements of data science, Latour, and critical post-humanism.

There may be several hundred universities in the world that offer training in international law. But outside top-tier schools in Europe, North America, and Australia, how many of them can be realistically expected to provide the kind of training and socialization opportunities that would allow their students to master a disciplinary toolbox of that scale? And what would happen to those students who do not get their training from these top-tier schools? What sort of second-class status will they be compelled to accept?

It should not be hard to see where the racialized exclusion element comes from. Correlations do not have to be absolute. It is true that not everyone who completes their training at those top-tier universities is white and not everyone who does not is a person of color. It is also true that we can find a great deal of exclusion and stratification within the legal-educational sectors in Europe, America, and Australia too. It is certainly true, furthermore, that the post-1990 methods expansion was not brought about so as to marginalize and penalize people of color. But it is *also* true that in the discipline's global institutional context it is people of color who bear a disproportionately higher burden of this epistemic development—both because of the institutional locales at which they typically tend to complete their training and because of what kind of social and cultural capital is normally required to gain admission to those top-tier schools. And it is true also that in a world where racism has morphed into postmodern xenophobia, the racialized other is not really going to fare any better just because their otherness is no longer constructed in terms of their skin color but "culture" and general "foreignness."

Third possibility: the same argument as above but avoiding any hint of the unintended consequences narrative. The persistent unevenness in the discipline's theoretical geography is neither a fluke nor a flaw, but a feature. It's what the discipline "actually wants." The unevenness of ILS's internal theoretical landscape is both a consequence and a condition of its *internal division of labor*. One group of international law scholars has to stay in low-added-value production lines so that another group can engage in method-heavy scholarship.

The argument can be approached in two different ways. From a neoclassical economics point of view, what we are looking at here is basically a combination of *outsourcing* and *rent-seeking*. From a Marxist perspective, it is a classic case of *neocolonial exploitation*.

The economic rewards attached to the production of positivist and doctrinal scholarship are no longer considered sufficiently appealing among Western-based international law scholars essentially for the exact same reason why shipbuilding no longer seems profitable in the advanced industrial economies. Whatever may have been the original reason for it, the steady increase in method-heavy scholarship in Western international law academia over the last thirty years has created a distinct form of pressure in the respective academic job markets. As appointments and promotions committees began to reward those scholars whose work in the light of the newly redefined conception of disciplinary competence qualified as "original" and "theoretically ambitious," the relative attractiveness of positivism and doctrinal analysis among Western-based international law scholars precipitously declined.

In the discipline's global academic periphery, the dynamics of job competition by contrast developed along markedly different lines. The fact that outside a relatively narrow circle of leading Western universities the kind of training that was required to produce "methodologically advanced" ILS was not as easily attainable has meant that, on the whole, neither did the practice of engaging in non-positivist and non-doctrinal inquiries become as familiar and widespread in non-Western academic locales, nor did the employers in those locales become "conditioned" to look down on positivist and doctrinal writings.

Though the details did not always turn out the same in every "national market," this combination of differentiated job dynamics and access to advanced methods training gives us a good starting point for understanding how and why, as modes of scholarly inquiry, positivism and doctrinal analysis were able to retain a higher degree of popularity within the discipline's global academic periphery than within its core. To explain how and why that possibility has turned into reality requires us to add one more detail to the picture: the idea that the discipline's demand for the kind of knowledge products the generation of which is associated with positivist and doctrinal scholarship continues to remain sufficiently high in aggregate terms.

Recall once more the implications of Sraffa's argument. A large part of what qualifies as method-heavy scholarship, by its very design, tends to be unavoidably subsumptionist. To be sure, not every piece of history-of-ideas scholarship or critical discourse analysis *requires* as part of its material inputs the use of work produced by other international law scholars. Significant clusters of critically and historically oriented ILS build on materials "taken" from state practice or the discourse of international institutions. And yet the general tendency is certainly there. The higher the coefficient of added value within a given category of ILS products, the higher, generally, the likelihood that in order for this type of product to be produced efficiently a considerable amount of positivist and doctrinally oriented scholarship will have to have been subsumed and appropriated by its producers—even if only in the sense of the general reasoning and rhetorical trajectories of the final argument needing to be developed in reference to (i.e., with reliance on) the reasoning and rhetorical trajectories supplied by such scholarship.

Given this pattern of economic organization, the global-division-of-labor implications seem to be relatively self-evident. In order for scholars working in the discipline's top-tier locales to be able to engage in the production of method-heavy scholarship, a considerable proportion of their colleagues working in the discipline's academic periphery should engage in producing the kind of knowledge products that this scholarship needs as part of its material inputs.[22] The only question is how to ensure that they continue doing exactly that.

A quick glance at the general patterns of neocolonial governance provides two ready answers: *development traps* and *tariff escalation*. The first concept describes essentially the proliferation of policies that tends to result in self-perpetuating institutional and cultural loops that lead to stagnating productivity and minimize the likelihood of radical structural change in the given locale. A good example would be the encouragement of brain drain from third-world countries through the institution of highly skilled migrant programs in Europe and North America. The second concept describes the practice of imposing higher barriers to entry for downstream products (processed and semi-processed goods) so as to incentivize the exporters to concentrate on the supply of upstream products (less-processed goods and primary commodities). A good example would be the imposition of no tariffs on the imports of raw cotton but a positive tariff on the imports of cotton textile. Moving from tariffs to non-tariff measures, a less immediately recognizable but equally effective "solution" would be the enactment of considerably less stringent technical standards for the less processed form of the commodity or the enactment of standards that are so patently unlikely to be met by producers in the global periphery that they rationally end up gravitating towards those lines of production whose standards they can meet.

And this, at last, is where we return to the question of the "professional Arab."

There are today essentially only two roles which the majority of non-Western-trained scholars find are left for them in ILS's political economy. The first is that of the *specialist local informer*: a provider of data about their national legal regimes, current political developments, and various other pieces of information that their colleagues based outside the region might not otherwise have the opportunity or the incentive to find out for themselves. Since the main function of such scholarship is to supply the material inputs for other scholars' work, the only quality assurance requirements and standards it will generally have to meet are that the information provided remains accurate and the textual execution of its delivery is minimally competent.

Even if they may otherwise seem totally unsophisticated in their broader theoretical thinking, even if they can hardly tell the critical genealogy of a discourse from its posthuman materialities, the field will happily forgive the specialist local informants their shortcomings. Because that is not what the role it assigns to this class of scholars requires of them. Even if their writing is full of errors and their style is not at all elegant, it will be looked on favorably. But only so long as they stick to the script. The moment they try to venture into global policy advocacy or ambitious theoretical interventions, the gloves will immediately come off. Some of the tariffs just do not apply here the same way.

The second career path, if one does not like the idea of becoming a local informant, is to become *the token Other*. An authentic postcolonial, a utopian third-worlder, an unreconstructed pan-Arabist, a soft-focused "Asian values" enthusiast—every discipline needs a certain group of human metonyms representing whatever abstract identitarian categories need to be evidenced to exist so as to be studied, acknowledged, denounced, cautioned against, and so on. Where the local informant scholar basically operates as ILS's equivalent of a tin miner or a coffee farmer, the token Other is meant to provide the living embodiment of a Theme. The idea is to turn oneself into a fetishized symbol, a footnotable figure whose primary function is to bring greater texture to whatever claims about the internal diversity, richness, and inclusivity of the discipline are being made by other scholars in their work.

Stick to these roles, keep to these boundaries, and it will not matter how smooth your writing style is, or how nuanced your decolonial reflexivity and regression analysis skills might be. The rest of the field will look on your scholarship benevolently and you will have every chance to export it outside your "national market." And what does it matter, after all, that what they will subsume and extract from that will not be just the fruit of your labor but your very identity and personality? What does it matter that the rest of the field will only listen to you because of the "African" or the "Asian" in you, not the "international lawyer"? What does it matter if everyone knows that in this discipline one can be a "professional Arab" and a "professional Brazilian" but not a "professional Briton" or a "professional German"? At least you are getting the chance to join the discipline's global scene and not get stuck in whatever parochial morass passes for your national international law society.

And, sure, sometimes all this will feel humiliating, and even when it does not, the sense of alienation that comes with it will be impossible to suppress. It is hard not to start feeling dubious about yourself as a legal scholar when the rest of the field keeps letting you know, however tactfully, that your greatest value, as far as they are concerned, lies in you being an expert in something that is really just a part of who you are or where you come from, not what you know or have done. Even more so, perhaps, when that place or that identity are not, in fact, a part of how you otherwise think of yourself.[23]

And, sure, sometimes you will feel incredulous that you are actually meant to show gratitude for all that (which you probably do, since the field could as easily have picked someone else to take your part). And sometimes no one is even going to pretend that you are not there only to help make up the numbers ("you'll be on the third panel, just after lunch, with all the other non-white names"). But rather than getting worked up about all of this, consider instead the next possibility.

Fourth possibility: broadly the same as the third possibility, but a much stronger accent has to be placed on the idea that whatever rewards the Western-based segment of the discipline can draw from this division of labor are essentially a species of *rent* traditionally so defined.[24]

The evolution of the discipline's epistemic conventions and *quality assurance protocols* (QAP) over the last thirty years has resulted, among other things, in two curious trends. Firstly, it has produced a model of scholarly know-how that turned the ability to demonstrate *a certain kind of mastery* of the non-traditional legal methodologies—be it Foucauldian genealogy or quantitative analysis—into a de facto sorting device for separating the discipline's invisible college along a quasi-economic continuum of "intellectual elites" and "intellectual underclasses." What has to be demonstrated often has only a very indirect relation to the actual theoretical tradition in question. The point is not whether you "really understand" Foucault or data science but whether you know how to convey the idea that you do in a certain prescribed way.

Secondly, in combination with the discipline's embracement of academic libertarianism, it has also helped create a system of intra-disciplinary politics that successfully obscures the discipline's tendency to exclude the members of its intellectual underclasses from *full disciplinary citizenship* in the sense that as "low-skilled workers" they may still partake in the discipline's formal institutions—by, for example, serving on editorial boards and heading learned societies—but they have much less of a say in shaping its course of theoretical and cultural development as an economy. Whatever political capital the members of these underclasses may accumulate—and some of them accumulate a lot of it—tends to be of a more formal and more conservative variety than the political capital of the methods-capable "intellectual elites," which naturally opens the space for the more pragmatically minded elements of the latter to enter into a strategic union with the less dogmatic elements of the former to establish what in the broader politico-economic setting acts as the discipline's *ruling elite*. Not all the members of the discipline's ruling elite defined in these terms are also members of its *appropriator class* in the Marxo-Sraffian sense of the term. But there is a significant degree of correlation between them.

Note the framing of the argument: the kind of intra-disciplinary politics we are talking about is not one that derives so much from the ability to control the discipline's formal processes and institutions but also—and mainly—from the power to define its QAP. The reason why it is important to recognize this fact is because, firstly, it tells us that the source of the ruling elite's power over the discipline is fundamentally "economic" in that it is rooted in its ability to determine what counts as value in ILS.

Secondly, it also suggests that what makes this system of politics so effective is the fact that neither in its self-presentation nor in terms of how it is experienced by those who are caught up in it does it appear to be "political." There is a great deal of denial swishing around and, because of the "excuse" provided by the emergence of new methods and theories in ILS, most of it is extremely plausible. Yes, one may admit it is true that the troop of disciplinary gatekeepers entrusted to enact and enforce these QAP in performing their functions end up determining the conditions of access to, and thus also the relative productivity of, all the different genres of ILS and, through that, influence their relative attractiveness in career-economic terms and realize in practice the above-noted system of tariff escalation. But, no, one can still insist they do so only in the name of preserving standards and promoting excellence, and the fact that these standards have now become more complex to trace means that it is not always possible to verify how neutrally they are being applied. But that is why we have peer review, and neither empowering one's peers nor preserving standards and promoting excellence, of course, has anything "political" about it.[25]

Fifth possibility: there was nothing immediately exclusionary or anti-democratic about the post-1990 explosion of new theories and methods in ILS. It is the fact that this explosion happened in a field committed to academic libertarianism and possessed of a political momentum that made it inclined towards the marriage of institutional and intellectual elites that ultimately caused the entire cascade of issues detailed above: economic stratification, intra-disciplinary marginalization, core-periphery dynamics, exploitation, etc. And one of the central elements that often gets overlooked in that process is the cultivation of *extreme individualism* as the default self-image of an ILS practitioner.

Like playing sports, the production of scholarship is basically a form of learned behavior. Repeatedly practicing a given set of activities molds the accompanying consciousness. The practices of *enacting authorship*—asserting and attributing responsibility for scholarly work, directing and answering criticism, writing rejoinders, citing, referencing, and commissioning publications—determine not only the basic social parameters of how ILS production is carried out; they also shape the basic political phenomenology of the producers in question. That phenomenology today is structured around an *utterly individualistic consciousness*. Not that there is anything surprising about this. For people whose business lies in the production of work judged for its "originality" (new contribution to the literature) and "authenticity" (not plagiarized or derivative), to have an exaggerated sense of their own individuality seems an entirely predictable outcome. How could it be otherwise? Even in the most self-consciously postmodernist segment of CLS, as Pierre Schlag notes, the figure of the monolithic authorial persona had never seriously come up for deconstruction.[26]

There is a direct line that goes from the structure of phenomenology to the patterns of social organization. One does not have to acknowledge it as ideology to recognize that how we experience ourselves at the individual level can have enormous implications for how the discipline organizes itself vis-à-vis its less historically prominent demographics. The more we buy into radically individualized conceptions of scholarly work, the more natural we find the libertarian model of knowledge. The more we embrace the libertarian model of knowledge, the more readily we assume that whatever gains we reap as ILS producers come to us solely because we have earned them through our own talent and effort, rather than, say, access to the right mentor-mentee networks. The more inclined we are to view our economic achievements as solely the fruit of our own effort, the less open we become to questioning why others around us are not reaping the same gains. The less open we are to questioning that, the more predisposed we are to acquiesce in the established status quo.

Note the framing again: the argument I am making here does not say that the expansion of the discipline's basic methodological toolbox has produced the same effects within the discipline's official structures of internal organization that, say, literacy and property-ownership requirements did under Jim Crow. The argument, rather, is that (a) the expansion of this toolbox amidst ILS's continuing love affair with academic libertarianism provided an opportunity for the emergence of a new set of exclusionary QAP; and (b) this together with individualism-induced blindness to questions of labor then had a broadly comparable impact, though not on our discipline's formal institutions as such but, to use a line from Philip Allott, on "the conversation that we are"[27]—the discipline conceived not so much as a network of institutional apparatuses but as an imagined community constituted by a common project and animated by a shared sense of theoretical agenda.

One of the most significant moments in the discipline's journey towards critical self-awareness in recent decades has been its growing acceptance of the fact that the traditional narrative, which says that ILS exists primarily to supply some external community of international practitioners with knowledge products that are useful to, and valued by, them, is ultimately nothing but a myth. The knowledge circuits of the discipline are by and large, and have been for a long time, autonomous from the needs and demands of any identifiable class of "practitioner-beings," and for the most part it seems safe to say large segments of the discipline today recognize this fact.[28]

But not every coming-to-consciousness process reaches its logical conclusion. The moment we began to walk away from the mythology of export-oriented knowledge production, in principle, should have also become the moment we recognized that the various QAP by which the discipline judges and evaluates the different kinds of scholarship produced within it do not, in the end, have any more objective base than *our own beliefs, tastes, and preconceptions*. We are, as it were, all that there is to what we ask of ourselves, and it is entirely up to us whether we should go on asking the same thing, make the demands even stricter, or perhaps cut ourselves some slack.

And yet, for some reason or another, for all its obvious logicality, somehow, this second-step recognition never came.

There is a whole tangle of "big ideas" that our argument risks falling into at this point: Nietzsche's theory of *ressentiment* and the "ascetic ideal," Feuerbach's concept of alienation, Fromm's critique of the fear of freedom, Sartre's idea of bad faith, and Sloterdijk's updating of it.[29] But rather than going into all of that, let me restate again that last point. That set of QAP and purportedly objective and neutral standards of academic excellence in reference to which all ILS work is evaluated has for its basis nothing more than the collective consensus of its invisible college. Whatever politics the operation of these QAP and standards might enable, the responsibility for that falls squarely on our shoulders and nobody else's.[30]

THE POLITICAL ECONOMY OF A BLIND SPOT

There remains one final point that needs now to be addressed. What is so special about race consciousness in ILS? In this Cambrian explosion of new theories and methodologies that the discipline's appropriator class and ruling elite has encouraged, why has there been so little uptake for this particular theoretical orientation?

The answer I propose to give to this question is twofold. Firstly, like with any theoretical orientation, bringing race consciousness into scholarly writing is not a skill the mastery of which can emerge spontaneously. The same problem of spatially actualized inequalities in know-how that was noted earlier applies here too. The relatively low levels of race consciousness–structured ILS output in non-Western institutional locales, I think, can be essentially understood in these terms. It is not the case that non-Western-trained international lawyers do not have any race consciousness more generally or cannot recognize the importance of race and racism to international law. But to be able to convert this awareness into the kind of scholarly discourse that would meet the kind of standards of argument presentation that the discipline has *chosen* to adopt in relation to HAV legal scholarship requires a degree of training and know-how that is not easily available for someone in the global academic periphery.

Note the thrust of the argument. This is not just an argument about access to training. This is an argument about what happens when you combine a regime of tariff escalation for HAV products and what Barbara Flagg calls the *white transparency phenomenon*[31]—the tendency of the white culture not to acknowledge itself as a culture—within the confines of a knowledge economy profoundly committed to denying the idea that academic libertarianism is a political program. The refusal to recognize the fundamental contingency and cultural relativity of the discipline's existing system of QAP may not be exactly equivalent to the endemic failure of white people to recognize whiteness as a reality that is neither culturally nor politically weightless. But the two phenomena are not too far apart. The embracement of the white transparency position, writes Flagg, "often [serves as] the mechanism through which white decisionmakers who disavow white supremacy" immediately go on to "impose white norms on blacks" and "require black assimilation even when pluralism is the articulated goal."[32] One does not need to be a veteran of many editorial battles to recognize that a similar dynamic is also present in ILS.

The second part of the answer speaks to a slightly different set of factors. Its starting point is the idea that a large part of why race consciousness has been absent from ILS can be understood in terms of an intra-disciplinary class politics, where the discipline's appropriator class deploys a Freudian-style defense mechanism in order to stabilize the ideological environment conducive to its interests.

The discipline of international law may not have nearly as many redeeming features as it likes to assume. But even the most jaded among its practitioners tend to approach their jobs with a certain sense of integrity. As Terry Eagleton puts it:

> There is [always] the case of [someone] who commits himself to the ruling social order on entirely cynical grounds [but] most people feel uncomfortable at the thought of belonging to a seriously unjust form of life. [When they do end up endorsing it, then e]ither . . . they must believe that these injustices are *en route* to being amended, or that they are counterbalanced by greater benefits, or that they are inevitable, *or that they are not really injustices at all*. It is part of the function of a dominant ideology to inculcate such beliefs.[33]

A large part of what makes academic libertarianism as an ideology so powerful is the sheer elegance with which, when needed, it can explain away any given blind spot or pattern of theoretical biases in ILS. Once you start with the assumption that the market is always already free, every distributive outcome achieved in it automatically becomes not only natural—in the sense of it not being the product of somebody's willful intervention—but also democratically legitimate—in the sense of it being the product of exactly what the community itself had chosen. There is nothing wrong or problematic from an academic libertarianism point of view about the relative lack of race consciousness in contemporary ILS. If the discipline really wanted to have more race and racism-centered discussions, it could easily have that. Nothing stops it from pursuing that goal. The fact that so little race-focused discourse is taking place in ILS today only goes to show how little need the discipline actually has for it. There are no blind spots here, only a well-functioning market. Supply responds to demand. That which is and has been is exactly what has to be.

One of the main functions of ideologies, notes Eagleton, is to help forge coherence within those groups that purport to hold them.[34] A classic way in which this goal is often achieved is by removing the scope for any form of self-questioning that could lead the group's members to doubt the justice of their group's cause or its day-to-day lived realities. What we have with contemporary ILS and the question of the relative absence of race consciousness is a classic example of *Freudian repression*: a mechanism of defense driven by essentially political considerations, the central aim of which is to stabilize and protect the existing system for the division of labor within the discipline that favors the interests of its appropriator class, without subjecting the members of that class to any unnecessary unpleasantness that may come from feelings of shame or embarrassment. Or as Anna Freud would put it, it is a typical case of a *reaction formation* triggered by a form of *superego anxiety*.[35]

The point to recognize here is that the underdevelopment of race consciousness in ILS is not just a passive by-product of the appropriator class not really being bothered to pay enough attention to questions of race and racism in global politics. It is an active strategy, though not one of a Sartrean bad-faith nature. The latter, as Duncan Kennedy points out, is a process that never stops. With repression the idea is to remove "the repressed" element once and for all so one would even be able to recognize it if one saw it again. With bad faith, by contrast, one is always going to know what one is hiding and why, which means constantly engaging in some form of denial and lying-to-oneself every time the problematic issue resurfaces.[36] There is (as yet) no indication that the suppression of race consciousness in contemporary ILS has reached that stage of phenomenological duality.

As a socio-economic unity, the discipline's appropriator class shapes the discipline's political economy and its ideology. But within this unity there exist different elements competing for dominance. Some of them work on making their segment of the invisible college more conscious of its role. Some work on strengthening their grip over the ILS economy via the co-optation of its disciplinary gatekeeper troop—often through thinly coded appeals to "rigor" and "neutrality" or the need to keep the discipline "relevant" and "responsive."

Not everyone, however, follows the same track. The work started by David Kennedy at the Brown International Advanced Research Institutes and continued at the Institute of Global Law and Policy (IGLP) is a case in point. In part an attempt at effecting an extensive knowledge-technology transfer, but mostly an endeavor to build a network that would provide scholars from the global academic periphery with access to social embedding opportunities otherwise only available in the discipline's core locales, the IGLP quite possibly has been the single most successful attempt at pushing back against the discipline's ruling elite within living memory.[37]

To be sure, every redistribution project has its limitations. The IGLP and its Global Scholars Academy are hardly an exception.[38] But lighting a candle almost certainly does more good than cursing the darkness.

CONCLUSION

Changes in knowledge protocols, argues Emile Durkheim, rarely act as causes of social disintegration but often as its consequences.[39] The bonds of solidarity within a community do not weaken because some of its members develop different ways of practicing knowledge. Quite the contrary: they develop such ways *because* the weakening of those bonds has already long commenced.

The expansion of the discipline's theoretical toolbox and the enthusiastic embracement of new methods and writing styles by international law academics trained at elite Western universities did not usher in the turn to class stratification and racialized exclusion and marginalization within the invisible college detailed above. But they provide us with a window into how these processes unfolded.

Over the course of the last thirty years, the idea of what should be recognized as disciplinarily valuable knowledge in ILS has undergone radical transformation. An important part of this transformation followed the basic lines of the Sraffian model in that a notably greater share of knowledge production in the *global circuits* of ILS occurs today through a process of subsumption than ever before. One of the direct corollaries of this evolution has been the deepening of the global division of labor within the discipline's invisible college, a peculiarly obscure political regime that—so long as one intended to take part in the global ILS conversation, rather than, say, remain within the national ILS scene—quickly came to structure the field of intellectual and ideological possibility in contemporary ILS.

A central element that ensured this process was the formation of a new set of discipline-specific QAPs and standards of argument presentation. Ostensibly objective and neutral in character, the emergence of these new standards and protocols was neither spontaneous nor purely functional. What underpinned it, rather, was an entirely political and, more specifically, class-political dynamic. A product of highly questionable economic imperatives, it has greatly benefited from being able to connect itself to the continuously changing expectations of disciplinary competence that were brought on by the ongoing expansion of the discipline's basic methodological toolbox. Taking advantage of the apparently unceasing character of this expansion, this new system of standards and protocols over the course of the last two decades gradually came to perform a number of functions that went far beyond the mere preservation of rigor and academic excellence. Two of them, in particular, have had a strongly pronounced political dimension: (i) the *gatekeeping function* by means of which the new QAP helped give form to new class-stratificational dynamics within the ILS community; and (ii) the kind of *universalizing assimilationist function* that Flagg describes under the heading of "white transparency" by means of which the new QAP helped cover up and obscure the consistently racialized exclusion and marginalization patterns that accompanied this class-stratification dynamic.

The fact that these standards and protocols have also helped operationalize, implement, and obscure the practices of tariff escalation within the discipline's global economy of knowledge presentation and publication provides a further telling insight into the uniquely important role that the repression of race consciousness in contemporary ILS—a process ensured not least by the continuing dominance of academic libertarianism and a decidedly individualist phenomenology of scholarly labor—performs today in the discipline's internal political stabilization.

A lazy way of reacting to the argument presented in these pages would be to view it as the revival of the old "elitism critique" once directed against CLS.[40] For what it is worth, let me just note that in my eyes it is most certainly not that. Nor is it really a complaint about the excessive spread of discourse analysis or any other "crit methodology."[41] A large part of my own work makes active use of these methodologies, and it would be insincere for me not to acknowledge how much my own career has benefited from the post-1990 methods-expansion in ILS.

But it is not, of course, the "rise of critique" that is the real issue here. Nor is it the idea of academic freedom per se, nor the fact that some scholars may simply like positivist scholarship a lot less than they do critical narratology. There is nothing wrong or intellectually uncomplimentary about being good at non-doctrinal work and not at all at doctrinal analysis, or about wanting to experience one's unique individuality, or about celebrating intellectual diversity and thinking that the legal academia is all the richer for it. To read the argument presented in these pages as a narrative that centers on *this* dimension of academic freedom would be to miss its most important point: there exists a large world of difference between knowledge as the personal pursuit of truth and self-discovery and knowledge as an industrial complex. What holds true in one context does not always do so in the other.

The gift that was given to modern ILS by the critical tradition was not perfect. But many parts of it were brilliant and inspiring, and much of it promised to help us reclaim our dignity as thinkers, scholars, and colleagues. Instead of using this gift to make ILS into something more inclusive and egalitarian, we have managed to let it get co-opted in the service of a newly strengthened system of value extraction, exclusion, and marginalization, installing an academic division of labor that denies to most of us the benefits not only of intellectual dignity but also of full disciplinary citizenship.

Hiding its neocolonial realities behind its libertarian hypocrisies, the knowledge economy of ILS increasingly finds itself today in a state of mounting internal contradiction. Torn between forces and trends it can neither dismiss, nor acknowledge, nor fully suppress, it is tumbling towards a breaking point. If one were a fan of Hegelian metaphors, one might say it is high time for Minerva's bird to make its appearance. Until then, the options we are left with, it seems, are either to rage or to cringe.

NOTES

*I am grateful to Duncan Kennedy for helping me sharpen my argument in ways I didn't even know it needed and for the remarkable generosity of his feedback. My thinking about the issues discussed in these pages has also benefited from conversations with Arnulf Becker Lorca, Justin Desautels-Stein, James Devaney, Michael Fakhri, Gail Lythgoe, Charlie Peevers, Ikboljon Qoraboyev, Mavluda Sattorova, Christine Schwöbel-Patel, Mohammad Shahabuddin, Thomas Skouteris, Christian Tams, and Dina Waked. I am particularly thankful to James and Christine for their generous feedback on an earlier draft. This chapter is based on a paper delivered at the Critical Race and International Law workshop held at the Sciences Po Ecole de Droit, in June 2023.

1. Antony Anghie, "Civilization and Commerce: The Concept of Governance in Historical Perspective," *Villanova Law Review* 45, no. 5 (2000): 887.

2. See, e.g., Christopher Gevers, "'Unwhitening the World': Rethinking Race and International Law," *UCLA Law Review* 67, no. 6 (2012): 1652.

3. For further discussion, see Etienne Balibar, "Is There a 'Neo-Racism'?," in *Race, Nation, Class: Ambiguous Identities*, Etienne Balibar and Immanuel Wallerstein, trans. Chris Turner (London: Verso, 1991), 17; Frantz Fanon, "Racism and Culture," in *Toward the African Revolution*, trans. Haakon Chevalier (New York: Monthly Review Press, 1967), 29.

4. For other (and dissimilar) usages of the term, see Kimberlé Crenshaw, "Race, Reform, and Retrenchment," *Harvard Law Review* 101, no.7 (1988): 1331, at 1369–81; Gary Peller, "Race Consciousness," *Duke Law Journal* 1990, no. 4 (1990): 758.

5. One could do much worse on this front than start with Chantal Thomas, "Critical Race Theory and Postcolonial Development Theory: Observations on Methodology," *Villanova Law Review* 45, no. 5 (2000): 1195.

6. See James Pitts, "The Study of Race Consciousness: Comments on New Directions," *American Journal of Sociology* 80, no.3 (1974): 665, at 667–68.

7. I develop this aspect of the argument in more detail in Akbar Rasulov, "The Discipline as a Field of Struggle: The Politics and the Economy of Knowledge Production in International Law," in *International Law's Invisible Frames*, ed. Andrea Bianchi and Moshe Hirsch (Oxford: Oxford University Press, 2021), 180.

8. See Louis Althusser, *Philosophy for Non-Philosophers*, trans. G. M. Goshgarian (London: Bloomsbury Academic, 2017), 85–90.

9. The concept of added value is not a Marxian concept. In its most common articulation, it is usually associated with taxation and national accounting. For further discussion, see Mariana Mazzucato, *The Value of Everything* (London, Allen Lane, 2018), 77–90; Paul Krugman and Robin Wells, *Economics*, 4th ed. (New York: Worth Publishers, 2015), 634–35. Since it places an excessive focus on the idea of sales prices, however, that is not the sense in which this concept is used here. The closest Marxian alternative would have been "surplus value." The reason why I chose not to go with it here is because of its idiosyncratic complexity, grounded mostly in the attempt to connect the question of value creation to the social reproduction of the given labor force. While I am not opposed to this way of framing the broader issue of value creation, it did not seem to me helpful in the present case. For an example of a Marxian discussion of surplus value, see, e.g., David Harvey, *The Limits to Capital* (rev. edn.; London: Verso, 2006), 20–24, 61–68.

10. See Piero Sraffa, *Production of Commodities by Means of Commodities* (Cambridge: Cambridge University Press, 1960).

11. The classical Marxian line, of course, is that all commodities are really just "congealed masses" of human labor by which they were produced. See Karl Marx, *Capital: Volume I*, trans. Ben Fowkes (London: Penguin, 1990), 130–31, 142. For further discussion, see Diane Elson, ed., *Value: The Representation of Labour in Capitalism* (London: Verso, 2015), 68–69, 94–98, 130–39.

12. This is not the traditional or canonical definition of value extraction. Compare Mazzucato, *Value of Everything*, 1–8.

13. See John R. Commons, *Legal Foundations of Capitalism* (New York: Macmillan, 1924), 97–99.

14. See Michel Foucault, *The Care of the Self*, trans. Robert Hurley (New York: Pantheon Books, 1986), 43–68.

15. It is worth recalling that characterizing positivists and doctrinal scholars as part of the "exploited class" does not imply that they are the least well-paid members of the international law academia. Many of them, in fact, are financially quite well-off, and many practitioners of the more extractive modalities of ILS are not. The tendency to reduce class positions to levels of income is common but analytically counterproductive. What place one occupies in the discipline's knowledge economy has little to do with how much remuneration one receives from one's employers.

16. See Andre Gunder Frank, "The Development of Underdevelopment," *Monthly Review* 18, no. 4 (1966): 17.

17. See Balibar, *Neo-Racism*.

18. I am told that this story may not look so familiar to readers embedded predominantly in the US ILS scene or, for that matter, the German and French ILS scenes. This would not be surprising. In thought-production terms, the national ILS scenes in the US, France, and Germany have become significantly more parochial and internationally detached over the last two decades or so. The advantages of this include a certain measure of autonomy from the global trends as well as a form of economic divergence that in a certain sense enables the participant scholars to inhabit a parallel professional reality. A different way of going about it would be to say that the story I present here is the story of the *global (or globalized) ILS scene*, which, if the general Marxist claim about capitalism is correct, (a) represents today, causally, the most important economic scene in ILS; and (b) in terms of its internal laws of development, exists "in its own right" and quite separately from all the national ILS scenes. The question of how exactly one can draw a boundary between the global and the national in this context is, of course, a difficult one and certainly deserves separate treatment. For what it is worth, however, let me note that a large part of what fuels the separation between the global and the national ILS scenes, especially for those scholars who come from outside the global North, follows easily identifiable linguistic lines: the global ILS is virtually exclusively Anglophone (even if it is not, for all that, necessarily UK- or US-centric).

19. See Peter Gibbon et al., "Governing Global Value Chains: An Introduction," *Economy & Society* 37, no. 3 (2008): 315.

20. For further background, see Akbar Rasulov, "What is Critique? Towards a Sociology of Disciplinary Heterodoxy in Contemporary International Law," in *International Law as a Profession*, ed. Jean d'Aspremont et al. (Cambridge: Cambridge University Press, 2017), 189, at 207–18.

21. The principle of *special and differential treatment* (SDT) and the *generalized system of preferences* (GSP) are the two main doctrines through which the discipline, historically,

has tended to process the idea that actors who have been put into economically disadvantageous positions by the kinds of international politics that the discipline at the time had no issues with may nevertheless deserve to be cut some slack in what they can be expected to contribute to the global economy.

22. Due to limitations of space, in this argument I only consider the disciplinary equivalent of an autarky. The pressure to maintain certain levels of positivist and doctrinal production may be driven not only by the discipline's own internal production needs but also by its commerce with the outside world.

23. Everyone can get turned into a token or a metonym. There is nothing unusual about that. In a sense, that is the basic nature of law as a discipline. But some tokens and metonyms are more disempowering and alienating than others. For further discussion of metonymization in legal academia, see Pierre Schlag, "My Dinner at Langdell's," *Buffalo Law Review* 52, no. 3 (2004): 851.

24. "Within mainstream economics, rent is defined [as] the profit attainable specifically due to dearth of market competition [or] a payment not justified by the requirements of an efficient economy." Brett Christophers, *Rentier Capitalism* (London: Verso, 2020), xxiii.

25. One does not have to be a card-carrying Foucauldian to see the opening for a critique of the power/knowledge regime here. It is worth recalling, however, that the payoff for the disciplinary gatekeepers is not only politico-economic but also psycho-social. See Duncan Kennedy, "A Cultural Pluralist Case for Affirmative Action in Legal Academia," *Duke Law Journal* 1990, no. 4 (1990): 705, at 720.

26. See Pierre Schlag, "'Le Hors de Texte, C'Est Moi': The Politics of Form and the Domestication of Deconstruction," 11 *Cardozo Law Review* 11, no. 5–6 (1990): 1631, at 1638–44.

27. See Philip Allott, *The Health of Nations* (Cambridge: Cambridge University Press, 2002), 263.

28. It is not easy to pinpoint exactly when this particular penny started to drop. But one landmark text that immediately comes to mind is David Kennedy, "When Renewal Repeats: Thinking against the Box," *New York University Journal of International Law and Politics* 32, no. 2 (2000): 335.

29. See Friedrich Nietzsche, *On the Genealogy of Morality*, trans. Carol Diethe (Cambridge: Cambridge University Press, 1994), 72–128; Ludwig Feuerbach, *The Essence of Christianity*, trans. George Eliot (New York: Prometheus Books, 1989), 12–32; Erich Fromm, *The Fear of Freedom* (London: Routledge, 2003); Jean-Paul Sartre, *Being and Nothingness*, trans. Hazel Barnes (London: Routledge, 2003), 70–94; Peter Sloterdijk, *Critique of Cynical Reason*, trans. Michael Eldred (Minneapolis: University of Minnesota Press, 1987). See also Pierre Schlag, *The Enchantment of Reason* (Durham, NC: Duke University Press, 1998), 104–6.

30. The point that remains unclear is what might be the role of the rest of the discipline in this. Should we be speaking here of "silent complicity" or "beneficial complicity"? Cf. Andrew Clapham and Scott Jerbi, "Categories of Corporate Complicity in Human Rights Abuses," *Hastings International and Comparative Law Review* 24, no. 3 (2001): 339.

31. See Barbara Flagg, "'Was Blind, but Now I See': White Race Consciousness and the Requirement of Discriminatory Intent," *Michigan Law Review* 91, no. 5 (1993): 953, at 957.

32. Flagg, "'Was Blind, but Now I See.'"

33. Terry Eagleton, *Ideology: An Introduction* (London: Verso, 1991), 27 (emphasis added).

34. Eagleton, *Ideology*, 45.

35. For further background, see Anna Freud, *The Ego and the Mechanisms of Defense*, rev. ed. (New York: International Universities Press, 1966), at 8–10, 49–50, 54–56.

36. See Duncan Kennedy, *A Critique of Adjudication* (Cambridge, MA: Harvard University Press, 1997), 199–200.

37. For further background, see https://watson.brown.edu/biari/institutes/brown/2009 and https://iglp.law.harvard.edu.

38. For further background, see https://iglp.law.harvard.edu/events/.

39. Emile Durkheim, *Suicide: A Study in Sociology*, trans. John Spaulding and George Simpson (London: Routledge, 2002), 123–24.

40. For a summary, see Mari Matsuda, "Looking to the Bottom: Critical Legal Studies and Reparations," *Harvard Civil Rights-Civil Liberties Law Review* 22, no. 2 (1987): 323, at 342–45.

41. Nor is it a version of the great replacement theory-style claims made on behalf of positivism and doctrinal studies in some ILS circles. The story of these claims—and the politics they channel—will have to wait, however, for another occasion.

CHAPTER SIXTEEN

AN UNRELIABLE FRIEND?

*Human Rights and the Struggle
Against Racial Capitalism*

NTINA TZOUVALA[*]

INTRODUCTION

This paper is part of a broader effort to think about race/ism in international law. Along with others[1] I am attempting to do so neither in the liberal register of formal equality nor in the post-modern terrain of identity and difference. Rather, it is my intention to think about race/ism as a form of domination and exploitation that is uniquely modern in its origins and its formation has been determined by imperialism and the global spread of capitalist relations of production.[2] If we accept this premise, then international economic law becomes an obvious place to focus on as a field where race/ism becomes articulated within international law.[3] This is a tricky endeavor. As a rule, international economic lawyers have not shown a sustained interest in race/ism and/or think that their field offers a rational ordering of the global economy that has nothing to do with the supposedly irrational prejudices that animate racism.[4] Similarly, those concerned about issues of racial inequality in international law do not tend to specialize in international economic law, but they rather focus their energies on fields such as human rights or, in circumstances of extreme violence and repression, international criminal law and transitional justice.[5] At times, the latter group turns their attention to international economic law, but they do so through the prism of human rights law, hoping that racial inequality may be named and addressed within global economic governance in the vernacular of human rights. There are, of course, exceptions to this division of labor and overall orientation.[6] However, it is accurate to say that international economic law has been insulated from concerns about racial (in)justice and that to the extent that the two encounter each other this meeting takes places in the terrain of human rights. In this brief chapter, I interrogate whether international human rights law is, indeed, the appropriate vehicle for incorporating concerns about racial justice into international economic law. I do so by revising two substantially very similar cases, *von Pezold* and *Campbell*, that were decided at the intersection between the two legal fields by different tribunals. By highlighting the problematic assumptions and outcomes of these cases, I call for de-exceptionalizing human rights within anti-racist legal theory and practice.

INTERNATIONAL INVESTMENT LAW AND HUMAN RIGHTS: BEYOND FRAGMENTATION

Another way of putting the above is that to think about race and political economy in international law requires that we think through and against the fragmentation of the discipline. After all, debates about human rights and international economic law never go away. They only ever die down for a brief period of time (if that) only to resurface, perhaps framed slightly differently but following the same patterns of argument and incorporating the same basic assumptions. The late 1990s and early 2000s witnessed extensive debates about the potential conflict and convergence between international trade law and the law of international financial institutions on the one hand and human rights on the other.[7] These debates took place in the shadow of broader disciplinary conversations about the professionalization and specialization of international law as drivers of its fragmentation.[8] As it has been often the case in the past thirty years, the parameters of the fragmentation debate were heavily determined by the scholarly work and practice of Martti Koskenniemi.[9] Influenced by the work of Niklas Luhmann on systems theory,[10] Koskenniemi posited that international law has fragmented into different subfields that incorporate different values and priorities, rely on different legal rules and protocols, and even attract and create different types of lawyers. These fields have, he posited, become incommensurable with each other, and serious work is required in order to make them legible to each other. Summarizing this predicament, Koskenniemi famously proclaimed that once we know which institution is going to decide a topic, we can make an educated guess about how the topic is to be disposed of.[11]

Philip Alston also articulated this presumed divergence between human rights and international trade law in his (in)famous debate with Ernst-Ulrich Petersmann. In Alston's eyes, Petersmann was performing an illegitimate move of "merger and acquisition" when trying to mobilize the language of human rights in defense of the WTO.[12] For Alston, this was an objectionable move insofar as human rights center human dignity, while international economic law only deals with individuals for instrumental purposes in service of the global market.[13] More recent work, such as the empirical legal scholarship of Dafina Atanasova on conflict clauses, does not always articulate this position explicitly, but relies on the very idea that there are quantitatively extensive and qualitatively significant enough conflicts between investment law and human rights/environmental law that an organized, state-controlled approach to them is desirable.[14] To borrow the language of Samuel Moyn from a slightly different—yet adjacent—debate, the human rights/business and human rights communities have generally conceptualized human rights as "powerless companions"[15] to the rise of international economic law, nevertheless insisting that this powerlessness is not necessary but contingent and, therefore, can be overcome.[16] This view finds apparent support in the fact that numerous arbitral tribunals have refused to consider or give due weight to arguments relying on international human rights law. Arbitrators often do so by invoking their limited competence as defined in the relevant investment treaties.[17] In this telling, incorporation of human rights in both investment treaties and arbitral practice will enable a better balancing of the rights of investors and home states and will allow the latter to pursue legitimate domestic policies, including rectifying patterns of racial injustice.

The assumption that investment law is from Mars and human rights are from Venus does not fare well when brought in contact with reality. Take for example, Alston's reaction to Petersmann's arguments about the mutually reinforcing agendas of human rights and the WTO with accusations of intellectual dishonesty, especially in regards to the content and overall outlook of human rights law.[18] Even though many aspects of Alston's critique are difficult to refute, his wholesale rejection of Petersmann's approach ignores both conceptual and historical synergies between human rights and neoliberal economic governance. Conceptually, the prioritization of individualism, skepticism toward majoritarian politics, and a preference for legalized and judicial solutions to social conflict bring the two closer together than generally assumed by human rights activists and scholars.[19] In terms of history, the work of critical scholars, notably Jessica Whyte, has revealed that far from simply having an economistic vision, neoliberal thinkers defended the free market as a moral order and as a necessary precondition for (some) human flourishing.[20] Even though it is open to debate to what extent this thinking has shaped contemporary human rights law, the idea that neoliberal invocations of human rights were necessarily opportunistic or obviously without merit collapses under the weight of the evidence marshaled by Whyte. In regards to race/ism in particular, post-colonial scholars have long documented the racialized underpinnings of much human rights scholarship and practice, especially insofar as notions of innocent victimhood, savagery, and spectacular violence and suffering came to be firmly associated with racialized people and authorized practices of foreign intervention and administration throughout the 1990s and early 2000s.[21]

In addition, scholars such as Whyte, Quinn Slobodian, and Arun Kundnani have documented the complicated and largely symbiotic relationship between neoliberal thinking and racism.[22] Both Whyte and Kundnani have emphasized that for neoliberals such as Friedrich Hayek the free market was the distinct civilizational achievement of European peoples and their descendants. As a result, facially illiberal measures, such as migration controls, were justified by neoliberals as necessary for the maintenance of the "civilizational" preconditions of the free, competitive market. More so, Whyte has documented how challenges to (neo)liberal capitalism were conceptualized by neoliberals not simply as economically misguided but as primitive assaults against a more advanced civilization.[23] In this context, economic heterodoxy becomes both moralized and racialized: to question property rights and competitive markets is to revolt against (white) civilization itself and to show oneself to be trapped in tribal communalist fantasies. As I have argued elsewhere, this entanglement between race/ism, capitalism, and civilization is central to international law as a whole,[24] and as I will argue shortly, it also permeated the judgments in both the *Campbell* and the *von Pezold* cases.

THE *VON PEZOLD* CASE: RACE AND PROPERTY AFTER (?) SETTLER COLONIALISM

Besides conceptual analysis and intellectual history, there are also empirical reasons to doubt the assumption that the values and priorities of human rights and investment law are fundamentally different, with the former offering a markedly more progressive vision of the international legal order than the latter. In her indispensable work, Silvia Steininger has documented how human rights are regularly invoked by claimants in front of investment tribunals and, more so, that tribunals have often (although not invariably) been responsive to these invocations.[25] In particular, the right to property, especially as elaborated by the European Court of Human Rights, and the right to fair trial/due process are often seen by both scholars and practitioners as compatible with and complimentary of protections offered by investment treaties.[26]

Taking stock of these quantitative approaches, my own work "zooms in" and offers a close reading of one particular case, the *von Pezold* award against Zimbabwe.[27] This is a particularly apposite arbitration for a number of reasons: First, even though international investment law often invokes racialized tropes and has co-created a racially stratified world, *von Pezold* is one of very few cases where questions of race not only were discussed openly but also formed the backbone of some of the most central findings of the tribunal. Secondly, the events that formed the background of the case were similar to those of the *Campbell* case, which was decided on grounds of international human rights law.[28] Even though the Southern African Development Community Tribunal (SADC Tribunal hereafter) was not specifically a human rights court, this parallel application of international investment law and international human rights law to the same set of facts allows us to examine the assumption that the latter would lead to different, more racially just outcomes than the former.

A detailed history of the land question in Zimbabwe surpasses the purposes of this short note. It suffices to say that as in other Anglo settler colonies,[29] land became a major focus of the white, settler political economy early on, as well as a driver of racialization and racial subordination.[30] Law, domestic as well as international, was a major force that effectuated and legitimized this process, especially after the Privy Council's pronouncement that the laws of the concerned Indigenous peoples were too low in the "civilizational" scale to be recognized by the common law.[31] As a result, the property rights and interests of Indigenous peoples were erased with a stroke of the (judicial) pen. The period of explicit white-minority rule under Ian Smith (1965–1980) represented an organized effort to entrench and deepen white supremacy in Rhodesia, especially in light of the acceleration of decolonization across the continent. Rhodesia not only became a symbol of defiant white supremacy across the world,[32] but on a practical level it represented an overall successful effort to legally entrench white control over the economy, and especially over land, at a time when racialized peoples across the globe were demanding a more equitable share of wealth and resources.[33]

The military standstill between the white-minority government and the national liberation movement meant that the transition to black-majority rule was managed internationally, and it largely entrenched the patterns of unequal land distribution into law.[34] A combination of legal impediments and the willingness of Zimbabwe's government (especially during the 1990s) to appear investor-friendly meant that until the early 2000s very little progress had been made in regards to land redistribution and resettlement. The same period was marked by the rise of urban-based opposition against Robert Mugabe's rule that posed a credible threat against ZANU-PF's continuing domination over Zimbabwean politics.[35] Therefore, when rural protests broke out in the early 2000s demanding comprehensive land redistribution, ZANU-PF used this as opportunity not only to partially solve the land question but also to reconsolidate support by its predominantly rural constituency. In the midst of escalating violence, the government passed a series of constitutional amendments and new laws providing for the scheduling of large tracts of land without compensation (save for improvements) and without legal remedy.[36] The legislation did not make reference to race, but the vast majority of properties scheduled for expropriation belonged to white farmers. That said, a small number of farms owned by black supporters of the opposition were also scheduled for expropriation.[37] Despite Western far-right rhetoric about "white genocide," the primary victims of physical violence during the process were black agricultural workers, who were killed at a rate of at least 8 to 1 compared to white farmers.[38] In fact, left-wing critics of Mugabe have argued that the biggest losers of the reform were not white farmers but black agricultural workers, who became displaced from their jobs without clear alternatives.[39] These final few points are important, insofar as they raise questions about the SADC and investment tribunals' findings of anti-white racial discrimination.

The *Campbell* case was decided first (2008), and it was marred by controversy from the very beginning. This was because the jurisdiction of the SADC Tribunal to decide on matters of international human rights law was disputed. The Tribunal relied on a brief reference to "human rights, democracy, and the rule of law" in Article 4 of the SADC Treaty to establish its subject-matter jurisdiction over the claim that the white farmers had been racially discriminated against in contravention to international human rights law.[40] Given that the language of the relevant amendment was at its face racially neutral, the focus of the SADC Tribunal's analysis was indirect racial discrimination.[41] The Tribunal found for the claimants based on the following reasoning: Even though the expropriation amendment was facially racially neutral, it impacted exclusively white farmers. The Tribunal appeared to deduce this exclusivity of impact at least partly from the fact that all the claimants in this case were white.[42] In addition, the Tribunal stressed the beneficiaries of the process were not those in most need, but political allies of the government.[43] Accordingly to the majority of the judges, a socially just and politically neutral choice of beneficiaries would (combined with compensation and a non-arbitrary process of selection of the land to be expropriated) would have led to a different finding on the matter.[44] Nevertheless, the majority showed little interest in the respondent's argument that given the country's colonial history, a process of land redistribution would be likely to disproportionately affect white landowners, who historically owned the bulk of fertile land.[45] The tribunal's finding was not unanimous. In a brief dissenting opinion Justice Tshosa from Botswana remarked that during the proceedings Zimbabwe noted that some black farmers had also had their lands expropriated, and that the applicants did not contest this claim.[46] As a result, he argued, this was not a racially discriminatory process.[47]

The Tribunal's ruling was extremely controversial, both amongst supporters of Zimbabwe's actions and beyond. E. Tendayi Achiume, for example, has repeatedly criticized the Tribunal's unwillingness to address the potential permissibility of facially discriminatory measures in order to address structural inequalities as formulated in Art. 2(2) of the Convention on the Elimination of Racial Discrimination (CERD hereafter).[48] In addition, Admark Moyo has observed that the Tribunal did not at all entertain the possibility that the axis of discrimination in this instance was not race, but rather political opinion.[49] Perhaps more accurately, the Tribunal did take note of the partisan nature of the redistribution process but only to buttress its finding of racial discrimination. As Moyo notes, this is a doctrinally dubious argument, since the legitimacy of the governmental ends does not automatically preclude the possibility of discriminatory means.[50]

My point here is not, however, a doctrinal one. Still, these doctrinal inconsistencies reveal important aspects of the Tribunal's reasoning, which adopted both a "color-blind" and a hyper-racialized approach at the same time: First, the historical interconnectedness of land ownership and race in Zimbabwe was elided in ways that potentially rendered all measures with a racially differential impact legally indefensible. This elision combined with the Tribunal's lack of engagement with Article 2(2) of the CERD casts a shadow of international unlawfulness upon all measures that seek to rectify racial injustices, even if they were to be adopted under less chaotic and politically dubious circumstances than those prevailing in Zimbabwe around 2000. Simultaneously, the Tribunal appears hyperaware of questions of race to the detriment of other divisions that were very much alive within Zimbabwe at the time. In that respect, the Tribunal appears to take at face value Mugabe's rhetoric and disregards the instrumentalization of the land question by the government. This combination of color-blindness and hyperawareness of race creates an argumentative cascade that legitimizes current patterns of wealth distribution however unequal and tied to violence they may be.

A very similar argumentative move is present in the investment tribunal's reasoning in the *von Pezold* case. Even though the tribunal did not cite the findings of *Campbell*, it was institutionally (and certainly informally) aware of it, since it was invoked by the claimants.[51] As I have argued elsewhere, the arbitrators performed three simultaneous moves that allowed them to find for the claimants: they temporarily confined racism in the past; they associated racism and the domestic (and not the international); and they conceptualized racism as a political and irrational (as opposed to political economic) phenomenon.[52] In so doing, the tribunal concluded that the expropriation process had been racially discriminatory against white farmers and rejected Zimbabwe's argument about the colonial legacies of land distribution as a driver of differential treatment.[53] Much like the SADC Tribunal, the investment tribunal showed acute awareness of the political tensions of the time, but not in a way that cast doubt on its racially hyperaware stance. For instance, the tribunal rejected Zimbabwe's defense of emergency, arguing that what was at stake at the time was not the survival of the state/nation but that of the ZANU-PF government.[54] In addition, the tribunal also drew attention to the fact that government allies disproportionately benefited from the process of redistribution, but much like in *Campbell*, this finding did not raise any questions as to whether race was the only/most relevant axis of discrimination in this instance, or whether political opinion needed to be considered too.

All in all, both decisions share an apparent contradiction (color-blindness and hyper-focus on race), which, however, can be harmonized through its effects: the invisibilization of race/ism as a structure of dominance and dispossession recasts all conflicts with a racial dimension as uniquely irrational and fixated on race as phenotype ("skin color") in ways that transcend other political divisions and conflicts.[55] By taking race/ism out of history and political economy, both tribunals exceptionalized the situation in Zimbabwe and refused to read it as part of broader political clashes and transformations within the Zimbabwean society. This is not a unique argumentative move. As critical race theorists have argued in the context of the US and as James Gathii has shown in the context of international economic law in particular, color-blindness has become a crucial mechanism for the perpetuation of racial subordination in (neo)liberal legal systems.[56] Even though this is true across the board, the centrality of human rights law in both decisions is worth taking seriously. This is because, as others have noted, the language of human rights is ideally placed to perform these decontextualizing moves in the context of economic decision-making.[57]

Human rights scholars have criticized the tribunal's refusal to allow a human rights NGO and a group of Indigenous peoples to make submissions as *amici curiae*. The tribunal argued that it did not have jurisdiction to hear arguments based on international human rights law and that, regardless of whether it was true or not, there was an appearance of partisanship in favor of the respondents by the two groups.[58] What has been relatively neglected in the existing human rights scholarship is that despite this procedural order, the tribunal was otherwise willing to engage with human rights law in the merits stage of the case. The first instance, of course, was the tribunal's engagement with the CERD when determining the issue of discrimination against the investors. Secondly, the tribunal made a brief—but important—reference to the jurisprudence of the Inter-American Court of Human Rights, when discussing the issue of moral damages.[59] This was because the arbitrators took the unusual (yet not unprecedented) step of awarding both physical and corporate persons with moral damages for the violence suffered in the process of the land occupations and expropriations.[60] In fact, the arbitrations reached this decision despite the fact that they admitted that their jurisdiction over natural persons was at the very least doubtful and despite the fact that many of these incidents of violence concerned (black) farm employees, who were not claimants in this case.[61] Nevertheless, the tribunal concluded that there was a need to unequivocally condemn the acts of Zimbabwe, which (somehow) established its jurisdiction over such claims.[62] Despite not mobilizing explicitly the language of human rights, the tone adopted by the tribunal in these paragraphs is one of moral indignation and condemnation that is rarely found in investment law jurisprudence. Relatedly, the Inter-American Court case cited concerned not foreign investors but the forced disappearance by the Peruvian Police of a student accused of being a Shining Path member, rendering human rights an authoritative source of law.

My point here is that the tribunal was internally inconsistent in determining whether human rights fell within its subject-matter jurisdiction and, more broadly, on whether they constituted useful authorities in the crafting of its judgment. Indigenous rights were held to be clearly beyond its ambit, despite the relevant BIT's reference to "public international law," while the CERD and the Inter-American Court were considered relevant authorities. This differential recourse to human rights is not beyond rational explanation. There are two ways of so doing. First, following the analysis of Tomer Broude and Caroline Henckels, we could read the selective engagement with human rights in the *von Pezold* arbitration as an example of how investor rights, and in particular property rights, are conceptualized differently from the rights of local communities impacted by foreign investment.[63] The former are conceptualized as presently protected, clear in their scope, and certain (if unexplained) in their foundation, while the latter are seen as aspirational, speculative, and vague.[64] Using cognitive psychology, Broude and Henckels argue that these divergent understandings explain the preferential treatment of investors' rights by arbitrators who seek to avoid a loss (the supposedly tangible investors' right) rather than achieve a gain (the protection of local communities' rights).[65] One need not subscribe to this particular explanatory framework to recognize that there are two distinct conceptualizations of rights at play with immediate impact upon the way that disputes are settled that at the same time lack adequate justification.

The above-mentioned scheme explains the use of human rights in many arbitral awards, including in *von Pezold*. However, one cannot ignore the particularities of this specific case as one that deals explicitly with race. Throughout the award the arbitrators constructed blackness and whiteness in fundamentally opposing terms and blended selectively race and political economy: the existence of (white) investment in the country was treated as self-evidently beneficial; the white claimants were afforded unlimited deference by the arbitrators who relied entirely on their testimony on a number of issues even in the absence of corroborating evidence; their suffering was centered and concretely monetized through the awarding of compensation for moral damages. On the other hand, both the respondent but also black Zimbabweans as a whole were treated with suspicion and mistrust: their arguments were summarily dismissed or not even allowed to be heard in the case of the aspiring *amici curiae*; they were portrayed as inherently violent and anarchic; and their suffering was either ignored or monetized for the benefit of their white employers. In other words, the arbitrators used human rights alongside investment law to protect "whiteness as property."[66] The image of the subject to be protected is one of a self-possessed and possessive white investor who is economically industrious and productive and is being unfairly persecuted by the irrational, violent, and incompetent post-colonial state (and its citizens). Despite the emphasis of both tribunals on "skin color," what is protected is not whiteness as a series of haphazardly assembled phenotypical characteristics, but as "ownership of the Earth."[67]

This brings me back to my initial observations about the existence of multiple visions of human rights and, in particular, the entanglement between capitalist economic order, race, and civilization in liberal and neoliberal thought. What becomes clear from the above analysis is that these entanglements cannot only be the concern of intellectual historians, indispensable as their work may be.[68] Rather, a close engagement with the jurisprudence of difference tribunals shows the widespread influence of these ideas. In fact, read together *Campbell* and *von Pezold* reveal that there is nothing inherent in one or the other international legal field that will automatically prevent such a bringing together of race, property, and economic activity in ways that entrench the racially and economically unequal status quo. Parenthetically, the important differences between the geographic and racial make-up of the two tribunals also reveal the limitation of a politics of judicial representation and diversity and/or of making a supposedly pre-ideological "lived experience" the anchor of conceptual analysis. The stark parallels between the jurisprudence of two tribunals with markedly different membership indicate that the reach of such a conservative reading of human rights may not be homogeneous across different groups, but it is certainly not directly explained by judicial identity either.

CONCLUSION

The temptation to conclude with a nevertheless redemptive note is a great one. Ben Golder has noted that even the greatest critics of human rights cannot refrain from the temptation of rehabilitation.[69] On the terrain of race in particular, the split between Critical Race Theory and Critical Legal Studies is often attributed in part to the objections of the former group against the rights-skepticism of the latter.[70] I am afraid, though, that I have no redemptive note to offer, but this may not be such a bad thing. For my position is not one of accepting or rejecting human rights claims as a whole,[71] but rather one of treating human rights as an ordinary legal field in the struggle against racism: a field that can offer valuable tools, create dangerous traps, or be useless at times. In any case, it is an ordinary legal field that needs to be won through argumentative and, more importantly, through material struggle, but it does not constitute a natural or obvious ally for anti-racists any more than international investment law does. The flip side of this is, of course, assuming that engagement with international investment law is even possible and desirable for those engaged in anti-racist struggle, there is no reason to believe that arguments from without the field will be more persuasive and effective than arguments from within. In the case of *von Pezold* a more honest engagement with Zimbabwe's past and present racialization of land ownership would have compelled the tribunal to reject the racial discrimination claim, which in turn would have had tangible, important implications for Zimbabwe's effort to invoke the necessity as a circumstance precluding wrongfulness or for the viability of restitution as the appropriate remedy in this instance. This would not be a panacea, especially in the context of a legal field that has been designed to protect foreign investors from the challenges of decolonization, democracy, and redistribution. However, the realization that human rights law is not necessarily the only way of achieving more racially just arguments in international law could pave the way for understanding that arguments in international economic law can be critiqued (if not defeated) in their own terms, without the assistance of unreliable friends.

NOTES

* I wish to thank the volume's editors as well as Jessica Whyte and Colm O'Cinneide for their insightful comments. Errors and omissions remain my own.

1. My work is particularly influenced by the writings of Robert Knox and Brenna Bhandar, who write on race, law, and capitalism from a Marxist perspective: Robert Knox, "Valuing Race? Stretched Marxism and the Logic of Imperialism," *London Review of International Law* 4, no. 1 (2016): 81; Robert Knox, "Haiti at the League of Nations: Racialisation, Accumulation and Representation," *Melbourne Journal of International Law* 21, no. 2 (2020): 245; Brenna Bhandar, *Colonial Lives of Property: Law, Land, and Racial Regimes of Ownership* (Durham NC: Duke University Press, 2018).

2. This approach builds on the extensive work of black and Indigenous Marxists. Amongst many: Eric Williams, *Capitalism and Slavery* (Chapel Hill, NC: University of North Carolina Press, 2004 [1944]); C.L.R. James, *Black Jacobins: Toussaint L'Ouverture and the San Domingo Revolution* (New York: Vintage Books, 1989 [1938]); Franz Fanon, *The Wretched of the Earth,* trans. Constance Farrington (New York: Grove Press, 1963); Glen Sean Coulthard, *Red Skin, White Masks: Rejecting the Colonial Politics of Recognition* (Minneapolis, MN: University of Minnesota Press, 2014).

3. In 2022, the *Journal of International Economic Law* published its first ever special issue on racial capitalism and international economic law. See: James T. Gathii and Ntina Tzouvala, "Racial Capitalism and International Economic Law: Introduction," *Journal of International Economic Law* 25, no. 2 (2022): 199.

4. For a fuller articulation of this argument see: Ntina Tzouvala, "Invested in Whiteness: Zimbabwe, the von Pezold Arbitration, and the Question of Race in International Law," *Journal of Law and Political Economy* 2, no. 2 (2022): 226.

5. The literature is vast. For some examples, see: Anna Spain Bradley, "Human Rights Racism," *Harvard Human Rights Journal* 32 (2019): 1; Erika George, "Racism as a Human Rights Risk: Reconsidering the Corporate 'Responsibility to Respect 'Rights," *Business and Human Rights Journal* 6, no. 3 (2021): 576; Carola Lingaas, *The Concept of Race in International Criminal Law* (Abingdon, Oxfordshire: Routledge, 2020).

6. This includes the work of James T. Gathii and Chantal Thomas. See: Chantal Thomas, "Critical Race Theory and Postcolonial Development Theory," *Villanova Law Review* 45, no. 5 (2000): 1195; Chantal Thomas, "Race as a Technology of Global Economic Governance," *UCLA Law Review* 67, no. 6 (2021): 1860; James T. Gathii, "Representations of Africa in Good Governance Discourse: Policing and Containing Dissidence to Neo-Liberalism," *Third World Legal Studies* 18 (1998–1999): 65; James Thuo Gathii, "The Promise of International Law: A Third World View," *American University International Law Review* 36, no. 3 (2021): 377.

7. Once again, the literature can only be indicative: Gabrielle Marceau, "WTO Dispute Settlement and Human Rights," *European Journal of International Law* 13, no. 4 (2002): 753; Joost Pauwelyn, *Conflict of Norms in Public International Law: How WTO Law Relates to other Rules of International Law* (Cambridge: Cambridge University Press, 2003); Andrew T. F. Lang, "Reflecting on 'Linkage': Cognitive and Institutional Change in the International Trading System," *Modern Law Review* 70, no. 4 (2007): 523; Daniel B. Bradlow, "The World Bank, the IMF, and Human Rights," *Transnational Law and Contemporary Problems* 6 (1996): 47; Korinna Horta, "Rhetoric and Reality: Human Rights and the World Bank," *Harvard Human Rights Journal* 15 (2002): 227; Galit A. Sarfaty, *Values in Translation: Human Rights and the Culture of the World Bank* (Stanford: Stanford University Press, 2012).

8. For some examples see: Martti Koskenniemi and Paivi Leino, "Fragmentation of International Law? Postmodern Anxieties," *Leiden Journal of International Law* 15, no. 3 (2002): 553; Anne-Charlotte Martineau, "The Rhetoric of Fragmentation: Fear and Faith in International Law," *Leiden Journal of International Law* 22, no. 1 (2009): 1; Tomer Broude, "Keep Calm and Carry on: Martti Koskenniemi and the Fragmentation of International Law," *Temple International and Comparative Law Journal* 27 (2013): 279.

9. See: Koskenniemi and Leino, "Fragmentation"; Martti Koskenniemi, "Fragmentation of International Law: Difficulties Arising from the Diversification and Expansion of International Law" (Geneva: International Law Commission, August 2006).

10. Luhmann's work is cited twice, once directly and once indirectly in Koskenniemi's ILC report: "Fragmentation of International Law," 24, 33.

11. Martti Koskenniemi, "The Politics of International Law-20 Years Later," *European Journal of International Law* 20 no. 1 (2009): 7, 10.

12. Philip Alston, "Resisting the Merger and Acquisition of Human Rights by Trade Law: A Reply to Petersmann," *European Journal of International Law* 13, no. 4 (2002): 815.

13. Alston, "Resisting the Merger," 826.

14. Dafina Atanasova, "Non-economic Disciplines Still Take the Back Seat: The Tale of Conflict Clauses in Investment Treaties," *Leiden Journal of International Law* 34, no. 1 (2021): 155.

15. Samuel Moyn, "A Powerless Companion: Human Rights in the Age of Neoliberalism," *Law and Contemporary Problems* 77, no. 4 (2015): 147.

16. See for example: Brunno Simma and Theodore Kill, "Harmonizing Investment Protection and International Human Rights: First Steps toward a Methodology," in *International Investment Law for the 21st Century: Essays in Honour of Christoph Schreuer*, ed. Christina Bider et al. (Oxford: Oxford University Press, 2009); Yannick Radi, "Realizing Human Rights in Investment Treaty Arbitration: A Perspective from within the International Investment Law Toolbox," *North Carolina Journal of International Law* 37, no. 4 (2011): 1107; Atanasova, "Non-economic Disciplines." For two opposing views, which nevertheless accept the normative divergence between international economic and international human rights law see: Johannes Hendrik Fahner and Matthew Happold, "The Human Rights Defence in International Investment Arbitration: Exploring the Limits of Systemic Integration," *International and Comparative Law Review* 68, no. 3 (2018): 741; Jason Beckett, "Fragmentation, Openness and Hegemony: Adjudication and the WTO," in *International Law and National Autonomy*, ed. Meredith Kolsky Lewis and Susy Frankel (Cambridge: Cambridge University Press, 2011).

17. For a comprehensive overview of the relevant jurisprudence see: Silvia Steininger, "What's Human Rights Got to Do With It? An Empirical Analysis of Human Rights

References in Investment Arbitration," *Leiden Journal of International Law* 31, no. 1 (2017): 33; Silvia Steininger, "Investment and Human Rights in the Shadow of the Pandemic: Recent Developments in 2020," *Yearbook of International Investment Law & Policy* (2022): 1.

18. This is evident in Alston's loaded language. He accuses Petersmann of "misappropriation," of "historical revisionism," of citing sources that do not, in fact, support his arguments, and of insufficient engagement with the literature. Alston, "Resisting the Merger," 815, 827, 819, 839.

19. See: Wendy Brown, "'The Most We Can Hope for'? Human Rights and the Politics of Fatalism," *South Atlantic Quarterly* 103, nos. 2–3 (2004): 451; Anne Orford, "Beyond Harmonization: Trade, Human Rights and the Economy of Sacrifice," *Leiden Journal of International Law* 18, no. 2(2005): 179.

20. Jessica Whyte, *The Morals of the Market: Human Rights and the Rise of Neoliberalism* (London, New York: Verso, 2019).

21. Makau Mutua, *Human Rights: A Political and Cultural Critique* (Philadelphia: University of Pennsylvania Press, 2002); Anne Orford, *Reading Humanitarian Intervention: Human Rights and the Use of Force in International Law* (Cambridge: Cambridge University Press, 2003).

22. See especially: "The Central Values of Civilization are in Danger," in Whyte, *The Morals*; Quinn Slobodian, "A World of Races," in *Globalists: The End of Empire and the Birth of Neoliberalism* (Cambridge, MA: Harvard University Press, 2018); Arun Kundnani, "The Racial Constitution of Neoliberalism," *Race & Class* 61, no. 1 (2021): 51.

23. Whyte notes that Hayek's last book, *The Fatal Conceit,* was initially planned to be titled *The Taming of the Savage*. Whyte, *The Morals*, 90.

24. Ntina Tzouvala, *Capitalism as Civilisation: A History of International Law* (Cambridge: Cambridge University Press, 2020), 67–73.

25. Silvia Steininger, "What's Human Rights Got to Do," 43–45.

26. José E. Alvarez, "The Human Right of Property," *University of Miami Law Review* 72, no. 3 (2018): 580; Pierre-Marie Dupuy, "Unification Rather than Fragmentation of International Law? The Case of International Investment Law and Human Rights Law," in *Human Rights in International Investment Law and Arbitration,* ed. Pierre-Marie Dupuy et al. (Oxford: Oxford University Press, 2009).

27. von Pezold v. Zimbabwe (Award) (ICSID Arbitral Tribunal, Case No ARB/10/15, July 28, 2015) ("von Pezold").

28. Mike Campbell v. Zimbabwe SADC (T) Case 02/2008, November 28, 2008 ("Campbell").

29. See: Natsu Taylor Saito, *Settler Colonialism, Race, and the Law: Why Structural Racism Persists* (New York: New York University Press, 2020); Bhandar, *Colonial Lives*.

30. Henry Moyana, *The Political Economy of Land in Zimbabwe* (Gweru: Mambo Press, 1984); Robin Palmer, *Land and Racial Domination in Rhodesia* (London: Heinemann, 1977); A. S. Mlambo, "'This is Our Land': The Racialization of Land in the Context of the Current Zimbabwe Crisis," *Journal of Developing Societies* 26, no. 1 (2010): 39.

31. "Some tribes are so low in the scale of social organization that their usages and conceptions of rights and duties are not to be reconciled with the institutions and legal ideas of civilized society. Such a gulf cannot be bridged . . . Between the two there is a wide tract of much ethnological interest, but the position of the natives in Southern Rhodesia within it is very uncertain; clearly they approximate to the lower than to the higher limit." Lord Sumner *In Re Southern Rhodesia* [1919] AC 21, at 233–34.

32. Rhodesia was particularly appealing to supporters of segregation in the United States. See: Stephanie R. Rolph, "The Citizens' Council and Africa: White Supremacy in Global Perspective," *Journal of Southern History* 83, no. 3 (2016): 617. The white-minority government and its local supporters intentionally cultivated these transnational links. See: Josia Brownell, "Out of Time: Global Settlerism, Nostalgia, and the Selling of the Rhodesian Rebellion Overseas," *Journal of Southern African Studies* 43, no. 4 (2017): 805. Rhodesia still resonates with white supremacists. The Charleston shooter, Dylan Roof, owned and wore Rhodesian symbols.

33. Adom Getachew, *Worldmaking after Empire: The Rise and Fall of Self-Determination* (Princeton, NJ: Princeton University Press, 2019).

34. The transition was brokered by Britain, and it involved the constitutionalization of the agreement that the government would not expropriate any land for ten years after independence. See: Alois S. Mlambo, "'Land Grab' or 'Taking Back Stolen Land': The Fast Track Land Reform Process in Zimbabwe in Historical Perspective," *History Compass* 3, no. 1 (2005): 1, 8–10.

35. See: Brian Raftopoulos, "The Labour Movement and the Emergence of Opposition Politics in Zimbabwe," *Labour, Capital and Society* 33, no. 2 (2000): 256.

36. For a concise analysis see: Lionel Cliff et al., "An Overview of Fast Track Land Reform in Zimbabwe: Editorial Introduction," *Journal of Peasant Studies* 38, no. 5 (2011): 907.

37. *von Pezold*, para. 501.

38. See: Wendy Willems, "Remnants of Empire? British Media Reporting on Zimbabwe," *Westminster Papers in Communication and Culture* (2005): 91.

39. See generally: Amanda Hammar et al., eds., *Zimbabwe's Unfinished Business: Rethinking land, state and nation in the context of crisis* (Harare: Weaver Press, 2003).

40. For some insightful analyses of the case see: Admark Moyo, "Defending Human Rights and the Rule of Law by the SADC Tribunal: Campbell and Beyond," *African Human Rights Law Journal* 9, no. 2 (2009): 590; Dunia Zongwe, "The Contribution of Campbell v. Zimbabwe to the Foreign Investment Law on Expropriations," *Comparative Research in Law & Political Economy* Research Paper No. 50/2009; E. Tendayi Achiume, "The SADC Tribunal: Socio-Political Dissonance and the Authority of International Courts," in *International Court Authority*, ed. Karen J. Alter et al. (Oxford: Oxford University Press, 2017); E. Tendayi Achiume, "Transformative Vision in Liberal Rights Jurisprudence on Racial Equality: A Lesson from Justice Moseneke," in *A Warrior for Justice: Essays in Honor of Dikgang Moseneke,* ed. Penelope Andrews et al. (Claremont: Juta Press, 2018).

41. *Campbell*, 53.

42. *Campbell*, 51–52.

43. *Campbell*, 53.

44. *Campbell*, 54.

45. "The Respondent, for its part, refuted the allegations by the Applicants that the land reform programme is targeted at white farmers only. It argued instead that the programme is for the benefit of people who were disadvantaged under colonialism and it is within this context that the Applicants' farms were identified for acquisition by the Respondent. The farms acquired are suitable for agricultural purposes and happen to be largely owned by the white Zimbabweans." *Campbell*, 44.

46. Mike Campbell (Pvt) Ltd. & 78 Others v. Zimbabwe (Dissenting Opinion - Onkemetse B. Tshosa), 1.

47. *Dissenting Opinion*, 2.
48. Achiume, "The SADC Tribunal"; Achiume, "Transformative Vision."
49. Moyo, "Defending Human Rights," 605–6.
50. Moyo, "Defending Human Rights," 606.
51. *von Pezold*, paras 16, 456, 486.
52. Tzouvala, "Invested in Whiteness."
53. *von Pezold*, paras 656–57.
54. *von Pezold*, paras 631–32.
55. Both decisions contained repeated references to race as "skin color." See: *von Pezold*, paras. 465, 501, 657; *Campbell*, 52.
56. Kimberlé Williams Crenshaw et al., *Seeing Race Again: Countering Colorblindness across the Disciplines* (Berkeley, CA: University of California Press, 2019); James T. Gathii, "Beyond Color-Blind International Economic Law," *AJIL Unbound* 117: 61.
57. Dimitri Van Den Meerssche, "A Legal Black Hole in the Cosmos of Virtue—The Politics of Human Rights Critique Against the World Bank," *Human Rights Law Review* 21, no. 1 (2021): 80.
58. Lucas Bastin, "Amici Curiae in Investor-State Arbitrations: Two Recent Decisions," *Australian International Law Journal* 20 (2013): 95, 100–4.
59. Castillo-Paez v. Peru (IACHR) (Reparation and Costs), November 27, 1998, CLEX-180 cited in *von Pezold*, 274n95.
60. *von Pezold*, para. 917.
61. *von Pezold*, para. 915.
62. *von Pezold*, para. 915–16.
63. Tomer Broude and Caroline Henckels, "Not All Rights Are Created Equal: A Loss–Gain Frame of Investor Rights and Human Rights," *Leiden Journal of International Law* 34, no. 1 (2021): 93.
64. Broude and Henckels, "Not All Rights," 101–2.
65. Broude and Henckels, "Not All Rights," 104–7.
66. Cheryl I. Harris, "White as Property," *Harvard Law Review* 106, no. 8 (1993): 1707.
67. W.E.B. Du Bois, *Darkwater: Voices from Within the Veil* (New York, London: Verso Books, 2016), 18.
68. Whyte, "The Morals"; Tyler Stovall, *White Freedom: The Racial History of an Idea* (Princeton, NJ: Princeton University Press, 2021).
69. Ben Golder, "Beyond Redemption? Problematising the Critique of Human Rights in Contemporary International Legal Thought," *London Review of International Law* 2, no. 1 (2014): 77.
70. See: Mari J. Matsuda, "Looking to the Bottom: Critical Legal Studies and Reparations," *Harvard Civil Rights-Civil Liberties Law Review* 22 (1987): 323. Matsuda's piece was part of a symposium that solidified the split between CRT and CLS.
71. In this respect, I am in agreement with Van Den Meerssche: "The invocation of this legal register, I argued, should be strategically evaluated and cannot be defended on either doctrinal or axiological grounds. In making this intervention, my pragmatic aim is not to undermine the values or aspirations underlying the human rights project (vis-à-vis the Bank) but to enhance awareness of the potentially pathological performative effects of translating political concerns in the dual register of universal reason and legal expertise." Van Den Meerssche, "A Legal Black Hole," 106.

PART III
Critical Race Theory and International Law

CHAPTER SEVENTEEN

POSTRACIAL XENOPHOBIA

An Abbreviated History of Racial Ideology in International Legal Thought

JUSTIN DESAUTELS-STEIN

The past several years bore witness to a welcome development in legal thought, namely, a resurgence of interest in racism as a configuring problematic for international law. What has marked this as a resurgence, as such, is a keen grasp on the past. Indeed, what most of the participants seem to understand is that a critical race approach to international law isn't new, exactly—the last century boasted many precedents, or at least precursors. But by the second decade of the twenty-first century, that family of precedents and precursors was all but forgotten. For all of the many approaches to international law, from Third World approaches to Feminist approaches to Cosmopolitan, Pluralist, Transnational, Economic, and so many others, an approach informed by critical race theory is missing. Why?

I believe that the strange silence surrounding "racism and international law" has little to do with a lack of interest or a lack of effort—the discipline is chockfull of both. Nor is it the result of a secret, racist cabal (or if it is, it's news to me). It is rather an historical effect, and more specifically, the effect of a centuries-spanning historical narrative about international law's campaign to eliminate racial prejudice. In this chapter, I begin with a rehearsal of this traditional narrative—a narrative that ultimately suggests the fortuitous irrelevance of a racial approach to international law. I will then contrast this historical portrait with a critical race approach to international law. From this perspective, which emphasizes the role of racial ideology in international legal thought, I identify three structures: classic racial ideology, modern racial ideology, and contemporary racial ideology, or what

I also term "postracial xenophobia."[1] My argument is that racism's failure to make international law's intellectual agenda is not mere happenstance, but rather that it is the work of ideological mystification. As ideologies tend to do, the trouble with postracial xenophobia is that it deters its own diagnosis.[2]

With respect to the traditional historical narrative, it might begin with the discovery of the New World by the Spanish, it might begin with Westphalia, it might begin with the Congress of Vienna. It doesn't really matter, so long as the story begins in a vulgar moment of hatred and bigotry, a moment in which international law serves the interests of domination and exploitation. The story begins here, so as to beat a hasty retreat, showing signs that for however unsavory were international law's beginnings, things eventually got better. And indeed, after we make it past the ugliness of the Franco-Prussian War, and beyond the avarice of the Berlin Conference of 1885, the signs of a coming change were signaled with the Japanese defeat of the Russians, and then the collapse of the German, Ottoman, Hapsburg, and Russian empires after World War I. With the arrival of the League of Nations, the imperial victors collected the debris and instituted a new approach to the formerly colonized world. This approach, known as the Mandate System, was riddled with difficulties and inconsistencies, but the consensus was that this was surely more "civilized." While not everyone was destined for independence, many of these peoples were already on their way, and for those that weren't, the hope was that they would be, soon. Or if not soon, someday.

Things got better after another world war came and went, and the Mandate System became the Trusteeship System. Even better, those imperial holdings that survived the arrival of the League of Nations were funneled into the new apparatus and dubbed Non-Self-Governing Territories under the United Nations Charter. Into the 1950s and up through the 1970s, things got better still as international law decolonized and the vast majority of the former colonies gained independence. At the same time, international law's old race problem was improving with respect to its gaining commitment to an antidiscrimination principle. In the context of the League, the former colonizers had instituted a new Minority Rights Treaty System, intended to provide degrees of autonomy and respect for ethnic, cultural, national, and linguistic minorities. Yes, the minority rights system was an advance over nineteenth-century imperialism, and yes, it was troubled in its own right. But things got better after World War II and the Minority Rights system eventually transformed into the International Human Rights system. On the foundation of international treaties like the International Convention on the Elimination of Racial Discrimination and the International Covenant on Civil and Political Rights, a general norm prohibiting states from discriminating on the basis of race (among other things) emerged as the best practice for conceptualizing international law's antiracism. Indeed, by the end of the twentieth century, for many international lawyers it had become unclear why anything other than the antidiscrimination principle was needed in the effort to fight racism. Since its vulgar beginnings, international law had surely come a very long way.

Another development evolving in the last decades of the twentieth century and up into the twenty-first helped to shore up the idea that everything had been moving in the right direction. As sociologists became more sophisticated in their analyses of racism as an empirical phenomenon, a consensus emerged that it was an error of overgeneralization to talk about "racism." In fact, there were *racisms*. To suggest a general theory of racism—a form of domination and exploitation that crossed cultural borders willy-nilly—was to inadvertently flatten out the real diversity of lived experience. Racism meant different things to different peoples at different times, and the role of the analyst was to take this particularity, this specificity, this hyper-locality, as seriously as possible. General or global theories of racism necessarily overlooked these particularities, and as a result, mischaracterized the true nature of the racisms that populated the world over. All in all, this sociological directive toward the local and away from the global—or to theorize the global *through* the local—went hand in glove with the antidiscrimination directive monopolizing international legal thought. The effort would focus on the persistence of individual acts of discriminatory behavior, and certainly from the perspective of international law, on the elimination of individual acts on the part of the state. Racism was not gone—not yet. But with time, and with more effort to make international law more effective, the antidiscrimination principle would drive human rights law as far as it could go in the effort to rid the world of bigotry. Of course, at the end of the day, the persistence of racism is a problem of the mind and the heart, and tools beyond the ken of international law would be required to get *there*.

And it is here that this traditional historical narrative delivers us: there is no critical race approach to international law because international law has already done everything it can do. A racial approach to international law is—thankfully—unnecessary. Moreover, a global approach that went beyond the antidiscrimination principle would make the mistake of ignoring the particularities of cultural experience, masquerading a single culture's experiences with race as the real nature of racism for everyone, everywhere. The upshot is that if we nevertheless suspect that racial structures exist beyond the reaches of human rights law, and that a global approach might be warranted, we need to look beyond the confines of the traditional historical narrative.

One way to do so is to emphasize an idea that has been crucial to critical race theory for decades, and that is the idea that racism functions beyond the "surface" level of irrational and individual acts of discrimination, and performs as a "deeper" structure of racial ideology.[3] Without a doubt, scholars use the term "structure" in many, many ways. In my work,[4] I use the phrase "structure of racial ideology" by blending two disciplinary perspectives.[5] On the one side is the tradition known as structuralism, indebted to thinkers like Ferdinand de Saussure, Claude Levi-Strauss, Roland Barthes, Hayden White, Duncan Kennedy, and Roberto Unger. On the other is the tradition of racial ideology, and I have been particularly influenced here by Denise Ferreira da Silva, Saidiya Hartman, Nahum Demetri Chandler, Cedric Robinson, Stuart Hall, Kimberle Crenshaw, and Cheryl Harris. Very briefly, this methodological orientation suggests something like the following.

In the wake of Saussurean semiotics, literary theorists, anthropologists, and other social scientists of the mid-twentieth century conceptualized bodies of text and bodies of social life as language-systems, and these language-systems were composed as structures.[6] In the context of law (as a body of text, as a body of social life), law as a language-system could be organized around three levels: grammar and syntax, lexicon, and argumentative style. As I have argued elsewhere, there is very likely a wide plurality of legal languages, but the one that I have focused on is the language of liberal legal thought.[7] This is a philosophy of law gleaned from liberal political theory, and repackaged as a semiotic structure. At the level of grammar and syntax, liberal legal thought is constituted by three basic rules. The first rule espouses the primacy of individual rights and freedoms in a competitive marketplace. The second stresses social interdependence, social welfare, and the necessity of the police power. The third is what many might call "the rule of law" and that I call "naturalizing juridical science." It is a rule demanding a harmonizing reconciliation, through legal means, of the unavoidable conflicts and tensions between applications of the first two rules. At the level of the structure's lexicon there are "bodies of rules," the indeterminate vocabulary of the legal system. At the level of style there are those patterns of argument and techniques of legal reasoning that move out from the grammar, gain content in the lexicon, and finish with productions of legal utterance. At least in the context of liberal legal thought, unlike the open-ended texture of the lexicon, the terrain of style is relatively fixed. There are formalistic patterns, functionalist patterns, and pragmatist patterns.

"Ideology" functions at every level of the language-system.[8] What interests me here, as we return to the question of how to interrogate the possibility of "racial structure" in international legal thought, is the ideological function of argumentative style, and what I mean is the following. The traditional historical narrative counsels a perspective that envisions racism as a local and diverse and prevalent phenomenon, and an antidiscrimination principle that works best when it adapts to particular cultural circumstance. From the structuralist perspective, however, we can look for racism as it functions in the language of law itself, both producing and maintaining systems of privilege hiding in the blind spots of the antidiscrimination framework.[9] In the context of liberal legalism, the core set of rules constituting the "body of international law," international law as a "field," are those rules that set the terms for what is known as the "domestic analogy."[10] The domestic analogy is a helpful place to begin our structuralist activity, since this is the generative material for all conceptions of community in liberal legal thought, both in the register of domestic and international orderings. (Note that liberal legalism has no vocabulary for community as "group rights.") And what in particular is it about the domestic analogy, and its particular way of conceptualizing the "sovereign," that appears most relevant to the delineation of insiders and outsiders? It is a central piece of the lexicon, the sovereign's "right to exclude."

We tend to be more familiar with the property owner's right to exclude the world from her property, and so when I refer to the sovereign's right to exclude, I introduce a terminology for specifying the right of the sovereign, as opposed to that enjoyed by the individual property owner. There are two dimensions to the sovereign's right to exclude, what I call a right of *imperium* and a right of *dominium*.[11] The right of *imperium* is the sovereign's right to mark the line between international society and the world of outlaws, the line between the rights-bearing members of the international legal order and the rights-less. The right of *imperium* is, in other words, the sovereign's right to exclude the world from membership in a global *demos* of sovereigns. And while it is certainly mistaken to suggest that in liberal legal thought there is provision for a global democracy, it is nevertheless accurate to say that the domestic analogy positions sovereigns in the self-referential posture of both citizens and rulers of a global order. They are "citizens" because they are subjected to a law they are meant to obey. They are "rulers" because all law (on this positivist gloss) is derived from the consent of the sovereign to be bound. The right of *imperium* is consequently a right to not only identify the rules of the international legal order, but it is also a right to determine its scope. The sovereign's right of *dominium*, in contrast, is territorial. It unpacks as the right of a sovereign to say to all other sovereigns "keep out," as well as a right to fashion its legal, political, economic, and social arrangements in any way that it wishes. The former aspect of the right of *dominium* is often characterized as a right of nonintervention, while the latter is called the sovereign's right of self-determination.

The structure of racial ideology with which I'm presently concerned is the one that *racializes* the sovereign's right to exclude. Racial ideology, in this sense, is an argumentative practice. In legal thought, it is a mode of naturalizing juridical science in which patterns of argument moving through the indeterminacy of a conceptual lexicon produce relations of racial subjection, exclusion, and discrimination.[12] In this case, the space of the conceptual lexicon I'm interested in is the sovereign's right to exclude, and the ways in which the structure constructs that right through racial discourse. In the remainder of this chapter, I will summarize a history of three structures in which the right to exclude is fashioned in the argumentative practices of racial ideology. Before doing so, a further word on what I mean here by "racialization" and "deracialization," since I have a very specific use in mind. When I refer to the "racialization" of the right of *imperium*, for example, I mean that jurists begin to use arguments about racial identity as a way of justifying and legitimizing the idea that the sovereign has the right to determine the particular borderlines of the international world. When I say that this right "deracializes," I mean that the form of justification has shifted away from the mode of racial ideology that had been previously in place. Thus, when I explain below that the right of *imperium* will deracialize in the morph from the classic to the modern structure, or that the right of *dominium* deracializes in the morph from the modern to the contemporary, my aim is to chart a progression from one form of legal argument and into another. It is not, in contrast, a way of saying that anything about national politics or international affairs has, in the actual world, become any less racist. Nevertheless, I use the prefix "de-" in order to denote the juridical experience that racial discourse has left off, leaked out, or just stopped. I return to this point below when I discuss the relation between deracialization and postracialism.

The classical problem for international lawyers of the seventeenth and eighteenth centuries was a problem of provenance. Where did international law come from, how did it bind, how did natural law and positive law interact, etc. After the end of the Napoleonic Wars, a new set of questions gained urgency in the minds of nineteenth-century international thinkers, and these were largely about how to justifiably delimit the international legal order. And the problem really was one of justification—as the "Great Powers" of Europe surveyed the new order, it became increasingly difficult to explain why *these* peoples and not *those* peoples enjoyed the full rights of sovereignty, on the basis of religion, or military power, or geography. As the century wore on, international lawyers developed solutions for international law's boundary problem, and an increasingly common one was a model in which the Great Powers existed at the center. One step out was "the Family of Nations," another step out was the realm of semi-civilized peoples, and further out still was the outlaw world of the uncivilized. But here was the problem: how to legitimately justify these lines and markers?

Racial ideology fit the bill. For more than a century ethnologists, anthropologists, and biologists had been working to forge a new view of humanity. This new view recast the human species as a racial species, the human being as a racial being, and racial identity as the skeleton key for revealing what humans truly were, and what they ought to be. These racial classification schemes were presented as empirical statements about the natural world, and at the same time, as hierarchies of development and competence. It was but a short step for international lawyers of the nineteenth century to borrow these racial typologies from their university colleagues, and craft racial justifications for categorizing the rights and duties of legal persons in the international legal order. When the racial ideology of phrenology, of blood and bone, of white-over-Black, moved into place as an argumentative strategy for characterizing and qualifying the borders of international society, this marked the racialization of the sovereign's right of *imperium*. This encounter between a racial mode of legal argument and *imperium* is the first step in identifying the structure of "classic racial ideology" in international legal thought.

What, however, of the right of *dominium*? A characteristic facet of sovereign rule had, up until this time, included the right of sovereigns to exclude other sovereigns from their respective territories. Much murkier, however, was the idea that the sovereign enjoyed discretion to bar individual migrants from their national communities. Indeed, at least as early a writer as Francisco Vitoria had claimed that rulers were obliged to hospitably receive foreigners. The current belief in the sovereign's plenary power to determine its own immigration controls has its origins in the racialization of the sovereign's territorial right to exclude—the right of *dominium*—and this was developing in the last decades of the twentieth century.

When the right of *dominium* racialized, we can identify a morphing between the classic and the modern structure of racial ideology. That is, in classic racial ideology, the right of *imperium* has racialized, but the right of *dominium* has not—territorial exclusion remains a matter of negotiating the boundaries between sovereigns, and the racial overtones of the discourse operate in the space of *imperium*. However, when territorial exclusion gains justification through racial ideology, the structure of argument shifts into the mode of modern racial ideology. Furthermore, in modern racial ideology, while the right of *dominium* is racializing, the right of *imperium* is beginning a process of *de*racialization. Let me explain.

As discussed above in the "traditional narrative," it is true that at the turn of the twentieth century international lawyers were beginning to shift away from formalistic racial ideology as a means for explaining the boundaries of the international legal order, and toward a more functionalist understanding of legal personality, rights, and duties. In a herky-jerky tumble of plans and decisions, racial ideology was becoming less persuasive, giving way to newer modes of economic ideology. To be sure, it wasn't that the right of *imperium* was becoming more egalitarian—it was rather that one way of justifying hierarchy was replacing another, as schedules of racial development slowly gave way to schedules of economic development. And all of this is a part of the traditional narrative's notion of progress, that racism was exiting the international legal system as the new League of Nations and its architectures were erected. The trouble is that a simple focus on how racial ideology was losing explanatory power in the context of the League is tremendously misleading. The sovereign's right to exclude was not being cleansed of racial ideology, not even remotely. It was changing its shape.

At roughly the same time that racial arguments about international law's boundary problem were losing steam, national politicians and regulators were facing a dynamic similar to that which had dogged international lawyers since the Congress of Vienna. Here was the problem more familiar to democratic theory: terrified of massive inflows of migrants from Asia and Southern Europe, how to justifiably seal off the integrity of the nation, to protect the borders of national communities? Once again, racial ideology fit the bill, only this time the race science of the mid-nineteenth century was replaced by the race science of the twentieth, in the form of eugenics. This was the context for the first border control regimes, the beginnings of immigration law, and the stillbirth of what might have been an international migration law. Thus, it was hardly the case that racial ideology was evacuating the sovereign's right to exclude—it had moved to another part of town, shifting its vulgar stance from the boundaries of international society to the borders of national communities.

To restate before moving forward, we can say that in classic racial ideology, the sovereign's right of *imperium* is racialized, while the right of *dominium* is not. In modern racial ideology, the right of *imperium* begins a process of deracialization, while the right of *dominium* drinks down a heavy dose of racial discourse. However, the relationship between *dominium* and racial ideology is more complex than this, for while the territorial right of exclusion was indeed pressed into the service of racial hierarchy here in the context of migration, the right of *dominium* would very soon experience a different sort of racialization in the context of decolonization. Between the 1950s and the 1970s, the sovereign's right of *dominium* was regularly characterized as the key to dismantling what was explicitly conceived to be a racial global order. If the formerly colonized peoples could gain "mastery over their house," to enjoy the rights of nonintervention and self-determination, to say for themselves what ought to be the destinies of their communities and their resources—this would be the way to undo an international hierarchy that was as racist as it was colonialist.

The result is that, over the course of the twentieth century, the use of racial ideology in the register of the right of *dominium* was increasingly complex. From one angle, it appeared contradictory. As it emerged in the interwar years, racial ideology was deeply racist. It cast the right of *dominium* as the means for excluding the "inferior races" on the basis of eugenicist beliefs about racial heredity, and shored up the world's first immigration laws along models that looked eerily like the "Family of Nations" models used by international lawyers a generation earlier. Later in the century, in contrast, the racialization of *dominium* developed as a means for counteracting a global racial hierarchy. From another angle, however, this apparent sense of contradiction dissolves. Among other things, what unites the discourse of racial ideology in the modern register of *dominium* (in contexts of both migration and decolonization) is a shared sense about the essentially *natural* primacy of the sovereign's right to determine the contours of the national community. Indeed, what had been an entirely up-for-grabs set of questions about the viability of an international migration law at the beginning of the twentieth century had morphed by the century's middle decades into a point of consensus about the "plenary power."

Traditional historical accounts of the relationship between international law and racism tend to misunderstand and underestimate the ways in which racial ideology continued to function throughout the twentieth century. As I have suggested, it is a mistake to focus on the transition from the heyday of imperialism into the League and UN systems and conclude that international law's race problem was largely solved. Indeed, that traditional account is entirely blind to the ways in which a vulgar racial ideology of hierarchy and domination duplicated itself, morphing from one type of borderland (the boundaries of international society) to another (the boundaries of national political communities). What's more, the whole idea that boundaries possessed racial content, or more to the point, that border regimes could function as sites for experimenting with and potentially undoing larger structures of racial subjugation—passed right out of sight.

And it is here that I mark the point of passage between modern racial ideology and contemporary racial ideology: once it has become entirely unclear how or why the rights of *imperium* and *dominium* might have any meaningful relation with racial justice (this is what I mean by "deracialization"), we have entered the lands of the contemporary, aka "postracial xenophobia." How does this transition take place? Simply put, the apparent sense that racial discourse has uncoupled from justifications for the right of *dominium* is due to the rise of the antidiscrimination principle in international human rights law. That principle did its work in each of the two contexts mentioned above. On the side of immigration, and by the middle decades of the twentieth century, it became increasingly problematic to rely upon racial criteria for shaping immigration laws. With the advent of the civil rights paradigm, the idea that states could discriminate on the basis of race, nationality, or ethnicity was falling out of favor. On the side of decolonization, the antidiscrimination principle was slowly displacing the right of *dominium* as the best practice for conceptualizing antiracist strategy in international law. Certainly by the century's end, and after the end of apartheid, the view that the sovereign's rights of nonintervention and self-determination might be related to racism had largely if not entirely been eclipsed by human rights law as really the only game in town.

International law's contemporary racial ideology depends on precisely this idea—*that there is no* contemporary racial ideology in the machinery of international law. Or, to put it differently, contemporary racial ideology holds racism as a social problem always lurking on the outsides, a strange and irrational type of prejudice that is largely a matter of social psychology. To the extent that international law has a role to play, that role is carried out in the context of international human rights law. The problem here is a problem of effectiveness, of enforcement—not a problem internal to international law itself. This, at any rate, is the message of contemporary racial ideology.

Classic Racial Ideology	Modern Racial Ideology	Contemporary Racial Ideology
• Right of Imperium (Racialized) • Right of Dominium (Not Racialized)	• Right of Imperium (Deracialized) • Right of Dominium (Complex Racialization)	• Right of Imperium (Deracialized) • Right of Dominium (Deracialized)

FIGURE 17.1 *The Evolution of Racial Ideologies*

But what *is* contemporary racial ideology? If we continue to look to the sovereign's right to exclude as an exemplary site, we should recall that in classic racial ideology, the right of *imperium* has racialized, but the right of *dominium* has not. In modern racial ideology, the right of *imperium* has deracialized, and the right of *dominium* has undergone a form of complex racialization. In contemporary racial ideology, the rights of *imperium* and *dominium* have each deracialized, yielding the apparent conclusion that racial ideology and racial discourse are no longer relevant in the space of the border regime (either at the level of international society, or at the level of national political community). As a result, the key for understanding contemporary racial ideology is the term "deracialization."

As I mentioned earlier, I have used the term "deracialization" to mark an ideological effect—and that effect is the sense that racial discourse has removed itself from the discourse. And that is the point: by the time racial ideology has morphed into international law's contemporary phase, the connection between the sovereign's right to exclude and racial hierarchy has become entirely unclear. My argument, however, is that contemporary racial ideology is much more than a way of describing a generalized state of confusion. It is that contemporary racial ideology *works*. And it works *hard*. It works to mystify, mask, and repackage forms of racial hierarchy, which works to deter any diagnosis that might dislodge it. Its work depends on the assumption that fundamental concepts like the sovereign's right to exclude have *deracialized*.

In the remainder of this chapter I would like to summarize my critique of deracialization, and more particularly, the way in which contemporary racial ideology cloaks the sovereign's right to exclude with what I call "postracial xenophobia." The CRT premise is that in the history of international law's use of racial ideology, the separate moments in which the sovereign's right to exclude have deracialized, along with contemporaneous bursts of victory in which the project of racial justice has ostensibly moved forward, have left fundamental commitments to racial ordering unaddressed. In the global context of the international legal order, the function of postracial xenophobia is to make this all the more difficult to understand.

Let's begin with the deracialization of the sovereign's right of *dominium*, and its two separate effects. First, the ascendance of the sovereign's unilateral right to fashion its border regime killed off the possibility of a fulsome international migration law, and replaced it with an antidiscrimination approach to refugee and asylum law, as well as an antidiscrimination approach to a domestically oriented immigration law in orbit around the sovereign's "plenary power." Second, the sovereign's right of self-determination was ultimately uncoupled from the project of racial justice and retooled as a vehicle for the protection of international human rights. This was the case for both the nascent indigenous rights movement that would take off at the century's end, as well as in the works of many scholars affiliated with the more international side of LatCrit studies and in certain streams of thought associated with TWAIL. In neither context—that of migration nor the critique of settler colonialism—was there an effort to grapple with the means by which the right of *dominium*—as a system for separating communities of human beings on the basis of collective identity, on the basis of an available *xenos*—functions to produce and maintain a field of racial hierarchy.[13]

A similar story was at work in the context of *imperium*. Racial justifications for the sovereign's imperial right to exclude seemed to begin a long process of disappearance with the advent of the League era. And certainly by the time of decolonization, the idea that racial ideology might supply a means for explaining the limits of the international legal order was almost out of sight. But in what sense? If the distribution of wealth and resources had been organized along the lines of a once-prevalent racial logic, in what way had international society transcended racism if those lines remained in place—even if justified by other means? There is no shortage of excellent work on today's false promise of "sovereign equality." But very little of it frames the problem as having much to do with racial ideology, and in particular, the way in which the sovereign's right of *imperium* constitutes the figure of the outsider. Once again, deracialization did not mean an end to racism— it ended one way of talking about racism and paved the way for another.

It is to this problem—the background relation between the right to exclude and what I call the racial *xenos*—that the ideology of postracial xenophobia so effectively redirects our attention. To be sure, this process of redirection, mystification, and obfuscation functions differently in the registers of *imperium* and *dominium*, but what unites the ideological effect is its postracialism. In my usage, postracialism is a mode of naturalizing juridical science in which patterns of argument moving through the indeterminacy of a conceptual lexicon produce relations of racial subjection, exclusion, and discrimination. Among other things, what distinguishes the postracial mode from the modern and classic modes of racial xenophobia is the way in which its argumentative patterns rely upon two separate developments that had matured by the end of the twentieth century: the transformation of racial identity in the context of physical anthropology, and the transformation of colorblindness in the context of legal thought.

With respect to the first transformation, recent advances in genetics helped open the door to the idea that we have moved beyond race as a meaningful way of scientifically classifying the human being.[14] Indeed, there has long been consensus among physical anthropologists that the older idea of a range of racial development, in which the white race functions as the original standard, is completely erroneous. In fact, what we know now is that the first modern human bodies are traced to Ethiopia, and it was from this originary source in Africa that the rest of the human population that migrated around the planet had first descended.[15] We also know that these modern humans were polytypic, meaning that local populations of the human species came to differ in the expression of physical characteristics. Of course, there was tremendous diversity *within* these local populations as well. In older modes of racial xenophobia, the concept of race referred to geographically patterned variation in physical features within the human species. The concept of racial xenophobia, or biological determinism, included hierarchies built into these patterns. Today, physical anthropologists and biologists focus on human DNA—that is, on the genotypes rather than the phenotypes—and study patterns of allele frequency. True, there is evidence that clusters of genes exist in discrete populations—populations that track the major geographical regions of the world: Africa, East Asia, Melanesia, the Americas, and Eurasia. And if allele frequencies correlate with populations of human beings in geographical patterns, is this support for the biological existence of race, after all? Not really. The bottom line is the oft-quoted conclusion that gene variations occur with far more frequency *within* subpopulations than *between* them. As Robert Jurmain and colleagues explain:

> [Racial] typologies are inherently misleading because any grouping always includes many individuals who don't conform to all aspects of a particular type. In any so-called racial group, there are individuals who fall into the normal range of variation for another group based on one or several characteristics. For example, two people of different ancestry might differ in skin color, but they could share any number of other traits, including height, head shape, hair color, eye color, and ABO blood type. In fact, they could easily share more similarities with each other than they do with many members of their own populations. To blur this picture further, the characteristics that have been traditionally used to define races are polygenic; that is, they're influenced by more than one gene and therefore exhibit a continuous range of expression. So it's difficult, if not

impossible, to draw distinct boundaries between populations with regard to many traits.[16]

If your game is about isolating genotypes in the effort to prove the existence of "the human races," the classification will necessarily be global. Which, of course, would unwind any connection between the so-called race and some geographical location. To be sure, sexual selection (non-arbitrary choice of mates) among individuals can and does result in higher frequencies of certain genes among members of local populations. But the long-standing and recurring mistake is the question-begging effort to conflate the frequency of those genes with something called "race," or any other genetic phenomena. The bottom line for contemporary physical anthropology is that while genetic variation in the human species is certainly real, these variations cut across every traditional form of racial typology: there is more genetic diversity within the so-called "human races" than there is between them.

Current developments in genetics were only one reason—but a pretty strong one—among many for the general trend toward reframing racial identity as a social construction, rather than understanding race in the genes. A related development was that with the collapse of race and racial ideology, many scholars gravitated to the view that the better way to address social hierarchy was through the prism of culture. As Anthony Appiah argued thirty years ago, "Talk of 'race' is particularly distressing for those of us who take culture seriously. For, where race works ... it works as an attempt at metonym for culture, and it does so only at the price of biologizing what *is* culture, ideology."[17] We know today that there aren't races in the world, but rather "communities of meaning, shading variously into each other in the rich structure of the social world."[18] Walter Benn Michaels put the point more colorfully: "Treating race as a social fact amounts to nothing more than acknowledging that we were mistaken to think of it as a biological fact and then insisting that we ought to keep making that mistake. Maybe we ought to stop making the mistake."[19] "There is no need for a distinct (critical) theory of 'race,'" Antonio Darder and Rodolfo Torres representatively suggest. As they argued in their influential *After Race*, "It is high time we disrupt the continued use of a dubious concept that cannot help but render our theorizing ambiguous and problematic. In its simplest terms, this ambiguity is most visible in the inconsistency with which the term 'race' is applied—sometimes meaning ethnicity, at other times referring to culture or ethnicity."[20] Among the most prominent alternative sites for the interrogation of power and domination has been that of culture. Illustrative concepts like "cultural citizenship," they argue, "attempt to engage difficult and often conflicting questions of citizenship with respect to culture, identity, and political participation.... Key to the concept is a critical universalism that fundamentally respects the particularities of populations while working to dismantle structures of inequality that interfere with the exercise of human rights."[21]

The scientific disavowal of race and the concomitant turn to culture as the "real" battleground for social justice is the first ideological hallmark of postracial xenophobia. The second is the transformation of colorblindness. Critical race theorists have argued that after the 1960s a new racism replaced Jim Crow, a racism that was "colorblind."[22] At the same time, political theorists have similarly suggested that the last third of the twentieth century came under the spell of "neoliberalism."[23] As I have argued elsewhere, the concepts of colorblindness and neoliberalism are mutually reinforcing.[24] Eduardo Bonilla-Silva has explained that colorblindness is a form of racial ideology that "explains contemporary racial inequality as the outcome of nonracial dynamics."[25] From a colorblind perspective, there is no reason to treat people differently on the basis of race, including reasons grounded in ameliorating prior histories of racial subordination. The key to prohibiting racial discrimination, on this view, is prohibiting racial discrimination, plain and simple. To the extent racial groups face varying challenges in their life circumstances, colorblindness points to ineffective performance in a competitive marketplace, due either to individual weakness or cultural difference. As for neoliberalism, this is an ideology of the market in which persons and states came to be analogized as both members of firms and as themselves firms, "and in both cases as appropriately conducted by the governance practices appropriate to firms."[26] As Wendy Brown says, in neoliberalism "both persons and states are expected to comport themselves in ways that maximize their capital value in the present and enhance their future value, and both persons and states do so through practices of entrepreneurialism, self-investment, and/or attracting investors."[27] Neoliberalism in its racial register yields the ideology of neoliberal colorblindness: a view of race and racism as anomalous effects of persons, firms, and sovereigns competing and exchanging in a world ripped from its historical and political contexts. The warrant for this relentlessly colorblind decontextualization of race and racism is that there is no value added in judging anything on the basis of race.

Neoliberal colorblindness yielded a culture of racelessness that only came into effect once the antiracist racialization associated with modern racial ideology had run its course. The deracialized character of postracial ideology, David Theo Goldberg observed, "marks the moment that a society is accepted into (or even as a momentary moral leader of) the world. It marks, in a word, the moment of globalization's relative (and repeated) triumph. To be of the world, in the world, in worldly society, racism nominally has been rejected. Now the category of race must be erased. But we are being asked to give up on race before and without addressing the legacy, the roots, the scars of racisms' histories, the weights of race."[28] Neoliberalism helped push a view of antiracialism—not because of a commitment to white supremacy—but instead because there wasn't any longer a point to arguing about racial supremacy at all. Goldberg put his finger on it when he argued that it was only in the waning hours of what I have been calling modern racial ideology—those moments in which human rights minimalism, neoliberalism, and postmodernism were coming to the surface—that the broad effort to get past race, to get beyond it, to get after it, to go *postracial*, was really coming into its own. An ethos of anti*racism* was replaced with an ethos of anti*racialism*, where what was more important than identifying global structures of racial domination, subjection, and exclusion was being against race itself. Goldberg wrote:

> I am suggesting that in the wake of whatever nominal success, antiracist struggle gave way in each instance to antiracial commitments at the expense of antiracist effects and ongoing struggle. . . . Antiracism requires historical memory, recalling the conditions of racial degradation and relating contemporary to historical and local to global conditions. If antiracist commitment requires remembering and recalling, antiracialism suggests forgetting, getting over, moving on, wiping away the terms of reference, at best (or worst) a commercial memorializing rather than a recounting and redressing of the terms of humiliation and devaluation. Indeed, antiracialism seeks to wipe out the terms of reference, to wipe away the every vocabulary necessary to recall and recollect, to make a case, to make a claim.[29]

What Goldberg was here calling antiracialism in 2008, he later dubbed the postracial in 2015. In my view, the clinching difference between colorblindness and postracialism is the introduction of pragmatism. What, however, makes this postracial attitude necessarily pragmatic? In the context of legal thought, it is the transformation of neoliberalism that offers the key. By the first decades of the twenty-first century, neoliberalism morphed into "pragmatic liberalism" as it settled into an "everyday" practically oriented sensibility that was entirely hospitable toward the hodgepodge of techniques that had preceded it. Pragmatic liberalism was, as a structure of legal thought, pastiche. To borrow from Fredric Jameson, we can think of pragmatic liberalism as the "imitation of dead styles, speech through all the masks and voices stored up in the imaginary museum of a now global culture," a style of legal argument "which randomly and without principle but with gusto cannibalizes . . . styles of the past and combines them in overstimulating ensembles."[30]

Indeed, by the 2010s the main faith traditions that had kept the candle burning for either formalism or functionalism as "truly" believable techniques for the production of legally necessitated outcomes had largely petered out.[31] What remained as the mainstream view was not, however, a wholesale effort to replace these modes of naturalizing juridical science with a completely new legal style. Rather, the dominant ethos became a status quo complacency, content with the use of small-scale trial-and-error serial borrowing. Use a bit of functionalism here, some formalism there, whatever might work in the effort to solve this problem, here and now. Anything grander, anything more totalizing, anything more objective, anything more *structural* was a fool's errand. At the same time, what counted as a problem, what counted as a benchmark, what counted as good governance—everything that counted at all—was measured in terms of return on investment, in terms of a market lexicon for effective outcomes.

This, at any rate, is a glimpse of the type of pragmatism that displaced neoliberalism as a mode of naturalizing juridical science. This pragmatist style is notable for its ideological emphasis on doing "what works" with the available resources, and in the context of liberal legalism, this suggests an open attitude toward various manifestations and combinations of formalist and functionalist arguments alike. It is a legal pastiche that, in the context of raciality, explains what in 2011 Kimberle Crenshaw had already labeled postracial pragmatism.[32] In its nebulous and ever-oscillating character, postracial pragmatism, Crenshaw explained,

> jettisons the liberal ambivalence about race consciousness to embrace a colorblind stance even as it foregrounds and celebrates the achievement of particular racial outcomes. In the new post-racial moment, the pragmatist may be agnostic about the conservative erasure of race as a contemporary phenomenon but may still march under the same premise that significant progress can be made without race consciousness. This realignment brings liberals and some civil rights activists on board so that a variety of individuals and groups who may have been staunch opponents of colorblindness can be loosely allied in post-racialism.[33]

———

These two elements of postracialism—(1) the genetic critique of "racial identity" coupled with the turn to cultural integrity as the real goal for social justice, and (2) the pragmatic reorientation of neoliberal colorblindness—unite as an ideological manifold. The way from here to what I have been calling "postracial xenophobia" leads us to the encounter between postracial ideology and the lexical properties of the sovereign's right to exclude. The patterns of argument are certainly distinguishable in the distinctive registers of *dominium* and *imperium*: in the discourse of the former, there is a pragmatic oscillation between multiculturalism and nationalism about the appropriate way to justify the boundaries of the relevant cultural units (regardless of whether these units are subnational or national); in the discourse of the latter, pragmatism orients the discourse away from the project of global democracy. Indeed, the problems associated with bounding subnational, national, and postnational collectives are certainly distinguishable, but what ultimately grounds the ideology of postracial *xenophobia* (as opposed to postracialism unmodified) is the postracial technique for racializing the *xenos*.

Inherent to the sovereign's right to exclude is an insider/outsider dynamic, or what Patrick Wolfe called a "xenology," a means for distinguishing between human collectivities.[34] That is, the right to exclude demands borders. And in this demand for borders, for insiders and outsiders, there is the supplemental demand that such insiders and outsiders *exist*—and if they don't, then the right to exclude must produce them.[35] In this light, the right to exclude is unavoidably coercive. It draws lines and interpellates subjects,[36] and it is precisely through the bounding of subjection that the right to exclude is definitively committed to the production of foreignness, to the *xenos* and, relatedly, xenophobia. What is foreign is what is excludable, and this much inheres in the sovereign's right to exclude. This line of reasoning suggests that if the right to exclude constitutes the liberal conception of sovereignty, then sovereignty requires the production of a *xenos*, a foreigner, an outsider. It is in this sense that I argue for a structural linkage between sovereignty and xenophobia, a generalized alertness to, if not anxiety about, the perennial outsider, the foreign mass, the barbarian horde.

It is commonplace in political theory to assume that in order for democracy to be viable, it must be attached to a discrete community. Democracy depends, that is, on insiders and outsiders—in order for there to be a "we," there must also be a "them." As Arash Abizadeh has argued, however, liberal defenses of nationalism and multiculturalism, of the sort offered by David Miller and Will Kymlicka, tend to ultimately collapse into demands for ethnic cores. At the end of the day, these theories delineate a "we" and a "them" as *ethnoi*, and as critical race theory has long engaged, what often lies beneath the façade of the *ethnos* is race.[37] What must be excavated is the question of whether the so-called necessity of bounding the *demos* simply turns out to be a subliminal argument for racial borders. It isn't that nationalism or multiculturalism or liberal democracy are intrinsically committed to the constitution of a racial *xenos*. It is rather that, in this liberal register, the act of *boundary-making* is racial.[38]

If the imposition of racial borders appears unavoidable, it is only because of our deep dependencies on the apparatus of naturalizing juridical science in liberal legal thought—and our sense that for however unfortunate these boundaries might be, they are *realistic*. Postracial xenophobia's production of an unavoidable realism, as well as its domestication of global antiracist strategy, is a victory over a great many things, and a great many people, including the formerly colonized, migrants, national minorities, indigenous communities, and every other type of racial *xenos* leveraged in the ideological fulcrum.

NOTES

1. This chapter draws heavily on Justin Desautels-Stein, *The Right to Exclude: A Critical Race Approach to Sovereignty, Borders, and International Law* (New York: Oxford University Press, 2023).

2. Thanks to Larry Helfer for helpful conversation around this point.

3. See, e.g., Saidiya Hartman, *Scenes of Subjection: Terror, Slavery, and Self-Making in Nineteenth-Century America* (New York: Oxford University Press, 1993); Nahum Demetri

Chandler, *X: The Problem of the Negro as a Problem for Thought* (New York: Fordham University Press, 2014); Stuart Hall, *Essential Essays*, vol. 1 (Durham: Duke University Press, 2019).

4. Justin Desautels-Stein, *The Jurisprudence of Style: A Structuralist History of American Pragmatism and Liberal Legal Thought* (New York: Cambridge University Press, 2018).

5. Desautels-Stein, *Right to Exclude*, 62–102.

6. See, e.g., Richard Macksey and Eugenio Donato, eds., *The Structuralist Controversy: The Languages of Criticism & the Sciences of Man* (Baltimore: Johns Hopkins University Press, 2007).

7. Desautels-Stein, *Jurisprudence*, 172–96.

8. Justin Desautels-Stein and Akbar Rasulov, "Deep Cuts: Four Critiques of Legal Ideology," *Yale Journal of Law & the Humanities* 31, no. 2 (2021): 435.

9. Kimberle Crenshaw, "Race, Reform, and Retrenchment: Transformation and Legitimation in Antidiscrimination Law," *Harvard Law Review* 101, no. 7 (1988): 1331; Kimberle Crenshaw, "Mapping the Margins: Intersectionality, Identity Politics, and Violence against Women of Color," *Stanford Law Review* 43, no. 6 (1991): 1241.

10. Martti Koskenniemi, *From Apology to Utopia: The Structure of International Legal Argument* (New York: Cambridge University Press, 2005).

11. Desautels-Stein, *Right to Exclude*, 43–61.

12. Desautels-Stein, *Jurisprudence*, 123–71; Desautels-Stein, *Right to Exclude*, 97–103.

13. Patrick Wolfe, *Traces of History: Elementary Structures of Race* (London: Verso, 2016). Natsu Saito Taylor has suggested that in international law we define xenophobia to reference "both attitudes and actions that construct individuals and peoples as outsiders—often racialized outsiders—and then use that construction (i) to exclude them from benefits associated with an insider status that is often correlated, accurately or not, with a national or statist identity; (ii) to incite or excuse ideological or physical attacks on those deemed outsiders; or (iii) to facilitate the otherwise unlawful exclusion or removal of these groups or individuals from particular physical locations." Natsu Taylor Saito, "Why Xenophobia?" *La Raza Law Review* 31, no. 1 (2021): 1, 6.

14. See, e.g., Carol Mukhopadhyay et al., *How Real Is Race? A Sourcebook on Race, Culture, and Biology* (London: Rowman & Littlefield, 2007); Robert Wald Sussman, *The Myth of Race: The Troubling Persistence of an Unscientific Idea* (Cambridge: Harvard University Press, 2014); Michael Yudell, *Race Umasked: Biology and Race in the Twentieth Century* (New York: Columbia University Press, 2014).

15. Robert Jurmain et al., *Introduction to Physical Anthropology*, 15th ed. (Boston: Cengage Learning, 2018): 389–92.

16. Jurmain, *Physical Anthropology*, 417.

17. Kwame Anthony Appiah, *In My Father's House: Africa in the Philosophy of Culture* (New York: Oxford University Press, 1993), 45.

18. Appiah, *In My Father's House*, 45.

19. Walter Benn Michaels, *The Trouble with Diversity: How We Learned to Love Identity and Ignore Equality* (New York: Picador, 2006), 39.

20. Antonio Darder and Rodolfo Torres, *After Race: Racism after Multiculturalism* (New York: NYU Press, 2004), 12.

21. Darder and Torres, *After Race*, 23.

22. Neil Gotanda, "A Critique of 'Our Constitution is Colorblind,'" *Stanford Law Review* 44 (1991): 1.

23. *See* Daniel Zamora and Michael Behrent, eds., *Foucault and Neoliberalism* (Cambridge: Polity, 2015).

24. Desautels-Stein, *Right to Exclude*, 229–45.

25. Eduardo Bonilla-Silva, *Racism without Racists: Color-blind Racism and the Persistence of Racial Inequality in America* (London: Rowman & Littlefield, 2018), 2.

26. Wendy Brown, *Undoing the Demos: Neoliberalism's Stealth Revolution* (New York: Zone, 2015), 34.

27. Brown, *Undoing the Demos*, 22.

28. Brown, *Undoing the Demos*, 21.

29. David Theo Goldberg, *The Threat of Race: Reflections on Racial Neoliberalism* (Malden: Blackwell, 2009), 21.

30. Fredric Jameson, *Postmodernism, or, The Cultural Logic of Late Capitalism* (Durham: Duke University Press, 1991), 19.

31. Desautels-Stein, *Jurisprudence*, 239–61.

32. Kimberlé Crenshaw, "Twenty Years of Critical Race Theory: Looking Back to Move Forward," *Connecticut Law Review* 43 (2011): 1253, 1314.

33. Crenshaw, "Twenty Years of Critical Race Theory."

34. Wolfe, *Traces*, 7.

35. On the "constitutive outside," see Ernesto Laclau, *New Reflections on the Revolution of Our Time* (New York: Verso, 1990), 18.

36. On interpellation in general, see Louis Althusser, *Lenin and Philosophy and Other Essays*, (New York: NYU Press, 2001), 64–68.

37. See, e.g., Ian Haney Lopez, "Race, Ethnicity, Erasure: The Salience of Race to LatCrit Theory," *California Law Review* 85, no. 5 (1997): 1143.

38. For further discussion, see E. Tendayi Achiume, "Racial Borders," *Georgetown Law Journal* 110, no. 3 (2022): 445.

CHAPTER EIGHTEEN

TOWARD A TRANSNATIONAL CRITICAL RACE THEORY
Black Radicalism across the Oceans

JOEL MODIRI

> What divides the world is first and foremost what species, what race one belongs to.
>
> —FRANTZ FANON[1]

1. PREFACE: BRIDGING AND BREACHING DIVIDES

The concerns animating this chapter are not those of an international lawyer but of a scholar of jurisprudence based in "South Africa" working within the Black radical tradition.[2] The long and volatile relationship between race and law, as we know, receives its most sustained and serious theoretical treatment in the work of a group of Black legal scholars gathered together under the umbrella of "critical race theory" (CRT) in the twentieth-century American legal academy.[3] Seeking to critically re-interpret and expand the ideology of civil rights, the pioneering practitioners of critical race theory set out to insist through legal analysis and counternarrative on the analytic centrality of race, racialization, and racism to legal inquiry—and thereby developed a powerful anti-racist approach to the study, critique, and transformation of law and social structures. In their radical rewriting of the scripts of (American) law and legal history in light of the profound limits of civil rights ideology to redress the core structural roots of racial subordination and anti-Blackness, CRT drew its political and intellectual program from the philopraxis of the Black Power movement, which itself is part of the broader global Black radical tradition.[4]

This occasion to consider a "critical race approach to international law" intends to examine and amplify the relationship between CRT and Black radicalism against the commonplace identification of CRT with a certain American parochialism and legalism. Taking seriously the global, internationalist, and transnational visions of the Black radical tradition, especially in its African historicity and globality, provides an instructive angle to think critical race theory beyond its originary national and academic borders and precincts. The vital lodestar in this attempt to sketch an intellectual history of a transitional critical theory is the idea, concept, and framework of global white supremacy. Meant to denote the long historical processes—conquest, slavery, colonization, racial capitalism—by which the "European domination of the planet"[5] was installed and reinforced, and to signal the function of race as the structuring dynamic of the modern world,[6] global white supremacy has been conceptualized over centuries of Black political and intellectual struggle by a range of thinkers, actors, movements, and communities across the oceans.

For Charles Mills, global white supremacy is not simply an aggregation of national racial polities across the world but rather the formation and consolidation of a transitional, transcontinental, and systematized world order of Western racial rule anchored by a "dark ontology" or "metaphysical infrastructure" that produced a racially determined vertical hierarchy of peoples, lives, lands, and bodies. Both the unequal relationship between dominant First World powers and the so-called Third World, as well as local relations of racial stratification in white-dominated polities are linked to this process of global European power.[7] As Mills further explains, the global formation of white supremacy was assembled by way of common or shared political-economic, juridical, ideological, normative circuits, patterns, and arrangements "in which white rulers in different nations learnt from each other."[8]

In this sense, reading the concept of global white supremacy into the project of critical race theory would perform several critical ruptures in our dominant intellectual and political cartography or "sense of world."[9] Three specific ruptures are of relevance here: The first is a *rupture of geopolitical boundaries* that moves beyond domestic or national accounts of race and racial subjugation in order to apprehend the reproduction of race and racial ideology at the global and international level. Secondly, a *rupture of disciplinary boundaries* in terms of which law's specific role in constructing, rationalizing, mystifying, entrenching, and reproducing racism and white supremacy is co-located historically in the political and libidinal economies of racial power and violence. And bringing the first two together, a *rupture of methodological boundaries* by which a transnational apprehension of race proceeds not by way of comparison (and its protocols of context, similarity, and difference) but via interconnectedness, intimacy, and articulation. Whereas the study of comparative racializations presumes isolated local or regional contexts and thus tends to be faulted for either overstating similarities or downplaying differences, the transnational takes the global as the scene in which both transnational racializations and national articulations of racial structuring interact and intersect. This transnational modality takes its bearings from anti-colonial and anti-racist theorizations of the multi-century European colonial and imperial expansion across the continents as the primary source of the violent and inhumane predicaments of the global present. The corollary of this translational analytic is thus also that the resistance to global white supremacy and the site of its undoing would similarly take place at the global level through interconnected struggles for freedom and liberation.

2. INTRODUCTION: CRT BEYOND BORDERS?

The purpose of this chapter is to clear the ground for an international or more precisely transnational critical race theory by way of an intellectual history that aims to radicalize CRT by locating it within the much wider archive of Black radicalism. The effort being attempted here is to reanimate and restore the Black radical political underpinnings of CRT to its theoretical project of legal, social, political, and cultural critique. It poses an extended meditation on the problem of whether the experiences and horizons of Black people in Africa, and Black people and racialized communities in the diaspora (especially the United States and the Caribbean) are so incommensurable as to foreclose political and intellectual crossing between different traditions of Black political thought. Put more concretely, this entails an exploration of an oft-noted but rarely theorized contention that is raised when speaking of critical race theory outside of the North American legal academy, namely that critical race theory is a largely American import that is, for reasons of history, incompatible with other parts of the Black world. On this argument, critical race theory, its methods, assumptions, and overall procedures of analysis and writing are a product of the American historical experience of race and its emancipatory horizons are a function of the limitations of that experience. This chapter seeks to complicate that account.

The prolific social scientist Archie Mafeje may be the most vocal Africanist proponent of the "incommensurability thesis" as discussed above in his view that there is a historical, cultural, and sociological disjunction between the social realities of continental Africans and diasporic Africans so significant as to vitiate the assumption of a "common African identity."[10] In Mafeje's estimation, "culturally, socially, and historically the African Americans . . . have long ceased to be Africans."[11] He continues to state that "Black Americans are first Americans and second anything else they choose."[12] As evidence, Mafeje cites two instances in which African scholars "on home ground" interrogated and critiqued Black American scholars for what the former deem to be an inaccurate, exotic, and imperial misappropriation of African cultures and knowledges on the part of the latter. Olufemi Taiwo's critique of Henry Louis Gates, Jr., and Kwesi Prah's critique of Anthony Appiah are taken by Mafeje to signal a "rupture between black American notions of Africa and those of indigenous Africans."[13]

Extending this analysis, Mafeje recalls further examples of Black American arrogance towards Africa, stating plainly his discovery that continental Africans he had encountered "complained that black Americans behaved like whites."[14] Accordingly, Mafeje concludes that there can be no shared epistemic project between Africans and African Americans. Mafeje is characteristically uncompromising in cordoning off American Blacks from the larger project of "Africanity" and although his claims may have instinctive appeal, they are problematic for a number of reasons—not the least of which is the scholarly problem that they are made without sufficient evidence and lack any rigorous engagement with contending historical and theoretical materials. Indeed, Mafeje states these claims as incontrovertible truth and appears to be unaware of the unintended implication of according to Europeans born on the African continent a status of indigeneity or Africanness greater than that of African-descended peoples in other parts of the world. Although I will later dispute Mafeje's account insofar as it concerns the political, historical, and intellectual relationship between Black South Africans and African Americans, there is still great value in heeding his warning that drawing *unmodified* transcontinental analogies in social analysis may be misleading.[15]

One might even overlook Mafeje's overstated distinction between continental Africans and diasporic Africans in favor of an appreciation of the methodological and epistemological orientation that underlies it. Mafeje has throughout his work been vocal in his insistence on "endogeneity," which denotes the centering of local African ontological experiences and African conditions in the work of theory-building. For Mafeje, Africans should resist the "discursive alterity" imposed by Western and foreign conceptions of Africa and African realities by developing an "authentic interlocution" or "grounded theory"[16] of our own situation rather than subjecting local histories and contexts to what Mafeje scholar Jimi Adesina calls "the tyranny of received paradigms."[17] Mafeje's privileging of ideographic inquiry (which emphasizes the local and the particular) over "nomothetic inquiry" (which aspires to universality and generality)[18] as well as his scholarly counsel that Africans "should learn from their own experiences"[19] and should study local social phenomena *on their own terms* takes concrete form in Nkiru Nzegwu's opposition to analyses of colonial racism that "sweep out Africa using mother Europe's broom."[20]

In her essay, Nzegwu warns against importing into Africa theorizations and conceptions of race developed in the United States. For her, differences in experiences of European racism in Africa and the United States produce different "ontological and epistemological framework[s] of racialization."[21] Therefore, reducing the African encounter with race and racial domination to the American historical experience and grammar of race constitutes a violation of the "African conceptual scheme" and elides important and glaring contrasts between "the socio-cultural realities of the two geographical locations [namely, Africa and the New World]."[22] Although she speaks of Africa as a monolith, Nzegwu makes plain that she means to draw a distinction between the racial experience in West Africa and that in the New World (the Americas, including the Caribbean).[23] And for her the primary distinction lies in the modes of racism, and thus racialization, obtained in the two contexts: whereas racism in the United States was organized around the pathologization of Blackness and the Black body ("body-racism"), racism in West Africa—where there did not reside a significant white settler population—targeted the culture, language, facial markings, and modes of dress of Africans as a basis for racial dehumanization and oppression ("culture-racism").[24]

Notably, Nzegwu concedes that the South African case does not conform to this West African variant of racism and remarks that it is probably closer to the structure and ideology of American racism.[25] Indeed, due to its settler-colonial foundations, white racism in South Africa combines both "body-racism" and "culture-racism." In this respect, Nzegwu differs from Mafeje in that she regards the Black experience of racism in South Africa and the United States to bear important resonances worth studying. Her acknowledgment that different variants, modalities, and ideological expressions of racism may exist in the same continental space (such as in the case of West Africa and South Africa) does raise questions concerning the durability and solidity of the transcontinental divide she draws between the socio-political experiences of continental Africans and diasporic Africans, since it clearly does not exhaust differences in the context and operation of racial polities and ideologies. It is again more the methodological notes that Nzegwu offers that are instructive. Nzegwu argues that in order to produce "textured socio-historical understanding" of colonial racism, the concepts and vocabulary we employ to describe it must possess a degree of "empirical and historical specificity as well as geographical accuracy."[26] There is thus a clear danger that aspects of the one social reality of Blackness, race, and white supremacy may get lost if one works from the entirely *unreconstructed* theoretical frames from other times and places.

———

Finding our way out of the problem of an unreconstructed theoretical frame requires reflexive engagement. Attentiveness to historical and social context, grounding one's thinking in local realities and perspectives is a crucial scholarly imperative. Although it is the hallmark of scholarly endeavor for concepts to travel to and from different times and spaces in order to illuminate new and different contexts, and to enrich and complexify contemporary debates, the transplant of any theories, concepts, and paradigms must be historically sensitive and responsive to the particular context and character of their new site of application.

Because of the historical marginalization of knowledge produced by Black Africans in South Africa's still highly Eurocentric and northbound academy, these worries about the importation of critical race theory as developed in the United States cannot be merely dismissed as epistemically parochial, essentialist, nativist, and isolationist. There is a very real sense in which the continual flight to Black (and, quite recently, Latin) America may generate theoretical blindness to African and in particular Black South African intellectual traditions and vernaculars, or more problematically may produce a distorted analysis of South African histories and social realities by imposing ready-made conceptual frames and vocabularies drawn from without. Consequent to the massive power and wide reach of American imperialism, this transatlantic cultural exchange between South African and American Blacks tends to also be remarkably unidirectional, from North to South.[27]

This risk of an over-immersion in African American culture and discourse has the effect of further invisibilizing African and Black South African knowledges, histories, and literatures and thereby abetting continued South African ignorance about local cultural and intellectual productions in South Africa and the continent at large. Rather than jettisoning CRT as a political project within the academy, however, the present challenge to be grappled with is how to "retool" critical race theory for a transnational imaginary of critique and resistance, to "change the letters" of critical race theory, as Hortense Spillers would put it.[28]

Yet, the singular view of CRT as an American import is itself too reductive and simplistic. Although critical race theory as an analytic (and as with all knowledge) emerges from a particular context, it is not entirely reducible to its context as it mostly develops general, bendable, and contextually permeable concepts and frames of analysis that can travel to other contexts. What might be harder to transpose however may be the reconstructive dimension of the theory, the type of emancipation envisaged as a remedy for the political injustices of racism and attendant forms of political action chosen since these are more immediately circumscribed by their context.

To the extent that "critical race theory" is an umbrella term for multiple critical approaches that at minimum figure race as the central socio-political construct in the making and functioning of the modern world, it anticipates and makes room for such important differences at the level of geographical location, disciplinary context, and philosophical traditions among others.[29] Ultimately, I expect to contest this "fear" of critical race theory—which derives from the claim of rupture and incommensurability between the continent and the diaspora—through an appeal to a much deeper historical archaeology of the Black Radical Tradition with reference mainly to the works of George Fredrickson, Cedric Robinson, Bernard Magubane, and Malcolm X. This archaeology suggests deep symbolic, political, and ideological ties between African peoples (and the Third World more broadly) emanating from their shared historical and cultural realities and critical encounters with Western civilization in the modern world. It will turn out that a global system of white supremacy, a concomitant political ontology of race and the invention of Africa as the home of Blackness orders the racial logics of the modern world in ways that sustain diasporic ties between Blacks in (South) Africa and in the United States—ties not easily erased even in the face of sociological and empirical variations between the two contexts. This chapter proceeds on the argument that the African genealogy of the Black Radical Tradition underwrites the conceptual and historical basis of a transnational CRT, which would in turn inform a critical race approach to international law specifically.

3. CUTTING THE BORDER, CROSSING THE ATLANTIC

In a sequel to his comparative study of the development, structure, and ideology of white supremacy in American and South African history,[30] the historian George Fredrickson registers an important shift in his position from that previous study to the subsequent one on a comparative history of Black resistance movements in both countries.[31] In the earlier study, Fredrickson placed the analytic accent on variations and differences between the regimes of racial domination in South Africa and the United States. His discoveries on the nature of racial attitudes and policies in the two countries, Fredrickson noted at the time, led him "away from common cultural influences and toward differing environmental circumstances and political contingencies."[32] The three major variations that he highlighted as setting the racial histories of the two societies widely apart include:

(a) Demography.[33] Blacks in South Africa constituted then and still constitute an overwhelming indigenous majority while African Americans are a relatively small numerical and social minority in the United States. Blacks in the United States are descendants of enslaved Africans who were forcibly removed from mostly Central and West Africa. Whereas ethnic and linguistic diversity was not a problem for African Americans stripped from their roots, Blacks in South Africa were further sub-divided into ethnic, linguistic, and cultural groups that impacted their national consciousness, their sense of political Blackness, and racial unity. In addition, the composition of each society's population groups naturally resulted in layered modes of racial classification and categorization that generated differently complicated meanings and constructions of race. Whereas in South Africa, the predominant topology of race historically recognized four categories (Black African [previously Native and Bantu], Indian, Colored, and White [or European]— one could also add Asian), the United States recognizes at least five major racial

or ethnic groups (Whites, Blacks [first referred to as Negroes and then African Americans], Latinos, Asian Americans, and Native Americans). The specific historical and contextual arrangements in each country vastly affected the category of "Other" to which numerically smaller racial groups were consigned as well as the permeability or ambiguity of racial categories and the phenomenon of "passing," particularly in relation to "mixed race" (biracial) and "off-white" groups.

(b) Physical and geographical environment and their impact on economic development.[34] Unlike North America, the physical makeup of South Africa did not provide white settlers with as much opportunity to accumulate and exploit natural resources. Not only is South Africa just about a sixth of the size of the United States, it is also a largely arid or semi-arid country. White South Africa, and its economic, military, and social dominance, thus developed much slower during the first two centuries of settlement, whereas the system of white supremacy in the United States was emerging as the most developed given its reliance on a large slave economy. It was only after the Mineral Revolution and the installation of a system of cheap Black labor in the late 1800s in South Africa that whites here began to definitively consolidate power. These environmental differences affected the rates of economic and industrial development—and hence the "racial state formation"—in both countries.

(c) The modes of government and politics that structured each country.[35] Both settler-colonies or "racial states" were initially under the sovereign control of a European metropole. This considerably impacted the degree to which "natives" in South Africa and "slaves" in the United States could be controlled, and thus the legal mechanisms that were put in place. The internal conflicts between whites (such as the American Revolution and Civil War and the Great Trek and the Anglo–Boer Wars)—although always influenced by racial interests rooted in the ideology of white superiority—also impacted the role and status of Blacks in both countries. In other words, the forms of white nationalism that emerged in these countries determined the modes of statecraft and the attendant legal architecture of citizenship, civil rights, and political power.

These demographic, environment, and structural differences are crucial to the historical dynamics that unfold in the process of racialization and impact not only how the regimes of white domination are structured and develop over time but also shapes the emergent forms of Black resistance and opposition to those regimes. Among a few areas where notable differences flow from the above three key variations that Fredrickson identifies are: the racial consciousness of Blacks and whites including their analysis of and response to the racial situation in both countries; the nature, modality, and degree of white domination and the manner in which relations between whites and Blacks are negotiated legally and spatially; the political economy of race and class; the modes of control and repression employed by the State (including modalities by which law would be deployed for the purposes of racial domination); the content of cultural, media, and educational discourses; and, significantly, the strategies of resistance and emancipatory possibilities available to the oppressed Black population. Owing to what he viewed as "*fundamental differences*" in the two situations, Fredrickson concluded by insisting on a radical incongruence, on the impossibility of a shared or at least comparative model for analysis and emancipation between the two countries.[36]

It is notable that it was only in his study of Black resistance against white supremacy, that is, it was only when he entered the imagination of Black opposition to white domination, that Fredrickson noted "remarkable similarities" that cast doubt on his earlier conclusions concerning a deep transatlantic gulf between the racial histories of the United States and South Africa respectively.[37] In his own words, Fredrickson confesses to being "forced to retreat" from his earlier position.[38] While not claiming that the situations in both societies are identical, Fredrickson notes an important set of commonalities between the two contexts that suggest important ideological and political parallels. We might describe the shift in Fredrickson's conclusion as also a shift in historical perspective. Because he is now reading the racial histories of both countries from the perspective of the oppressed, he is now able to see more clearly an underlying logic of racial terror, ontological degradation, and epistemicide that lies behind the more obvious geographical differences. Although he lists them as four, Fredrickson in the updated study identifies five sources of "ideological parallelism" and "discursive congruence" between the racial experiences in South Africa and the United States:

(1) Similar modalities and rationalizations of white supremacy.[39] In both countries, Black people were constructed as intellectually and morally inferior, lacking in the critical faculty of reason/rationality and thus predestined to live under white rule and to serve white people and their interests. Because rationality in particular was a predicate for humanity proper, this construction of Blacks as inferior performed their expulsion from Humanity itself. Closely related to this was the fact that the white conquerors of both South Africa and the Americas in differing waves and numbers originated from the same or close parts of Europe (especially the British, the Dutch, the Germans, the French, the Portuguese, and the Spanish). This meant that they operated on the basis of a similar cultural code of a Christian-infused vision of European capitalism and ethnocentrism. Blacks in both societies thus encountered whites with quite similar beliefs, values, social mores, civilizational reflexes, ideological orientations, behaviors, and sensibilities.[40] In sum, the regimes of white supremacy that were fabricated and installed in both societies emanated from a near-uniform European racial consciousness and thus contained identical logics.

(2) A shared sense of minority status.[41] Irrespective of their numerical majority status, Black South Africans were treated and experienced life as social, cultural, and political minorities, non-citizens, powerless and marginalized in a manner not

entirely different from African Americans. It is on the premise that power in and over society overrides the numerical composition of racial groups that the Black condition in both countries becomes indistinguishable. In both contexts, Blacks experienced their status as one of non-belonging, non-being, and wretchedness.

(3) A Pan-African or "Black internationalist" frame of reference.[42] Because of Africa's place as the original site of the antagonism between Western and African civilization, which is the basis of the conflictual Black-white race relations in both countries, the struggles against white supremacy by Black South Africans and Black Americans proceeded, and were conceived in terms of, a much larger "global" struggle of Africans and African people against the efforts of Europeans to enslave, colonize, and subjugate them.

(4) The fact of interracial coexistence.[43] Both countries are notable for very pronounced divisions and social stratifications between their Black and white populations, with all other racial groups falling somewhere in between on a continuum that determines their relative status.[44] Importantly, the fact that whites and Blacks lived together (or perhaps "together-apart") in the same local and national space and would probably do so for the foreseeable future resulted in very similar modes of racial-social ordering (anti-miscegenation laws, Black labor exploitation, valorization of whiteness, and legalized segregation)—owing to a heightened conflict over resources, entitlements, and interests—and produced similar modes of resistance and disobedience to those social orders. The imagined future liberation postulated by Blacks in both countries had to also factor in the white segment of the population, which raised complications for what freedom from white supremacy, and in some ways, from white people as a group, entails.

(5) The comparable social and cultural position within Black communities of the intellectual and political leaders of Black liberation movements and organizations.[45] In both cases, especially after the nineteenth century, these struggles were led and articulated by literate, educated, middle-class, or "elite" Blacks. Their absorption of aspects of European and Euro-American cultures, lifestyles, and languages (such as French and English) shaped the type of thought and action formed but also posed problems for negotiating and building solidarities with working-class and illiterate Black communities. In South Africa, the language barrier was even more significant in a country where Black people are not first-language English speakers and thus unfamiliar with the central cluster of radical political keywords that make up the pantheon of Black political thought. Ideological and cultural tensions also emerged between the leaders (elites) and followers (masses) of these movements.

Because of these fundamental parallels identified by Fredrickson, the thought and politics that developed from Black communities and intellectuals in the racial polities of the United States and South Africa came to revolve around similar themes, and made border-crossing between those traditions possible. This was more so given that Black South Africans and African Americans had mutual awareness of each other's struggles and accordingly influenced each other through political, intellectual, and artistic interactions and exchanges.[46] A shared historical consciousness and existential reality of "being-Black-in-the-world"[47] generated deep resonances and linkages between Blacks in South Africa and in the United States to such a degree as to vitiate any argument of total incommensurability and incongruence between Black America and Black South Africa. The entire history of Black revolt not only on the African content and in North America but in South America and the Caribbean and stretching even to the Black world in Europe and colonized and indigenous communities in Australia, New Zealand, and the Middle East emanate from this consciousness and reality.

4. NOTES ON "THE TIES THAT BIND"

Bernard Magubane phrases this deep but no less complicated connection between the life-worlds and struggles of African Americans and Black South Africans as the *"ties that bind."*[48] In a book with the same name, Magubane proposes to examine the "African consciousness" that underlies the struggles and politics of American Blacks. His central thesis is that the social rejection and non-belonging that Black Americans experience as a result of their alienation from the Western and largely Judeo-Christian culture of the United States as well as their violent and forced dislocation from the African continent prompts in them a "search for roots" that leads to a symbolic (re)connection to Africa.[49] The subjugation and suffering they have had to (and still) endure is attached to the Blackness that bears the trace of their African origins and so reanimated an "ethnic and spiritual consciousness of Africa"[50] and activated a deep-rooted solidarity with the struggles of Africans against European colonization and racial oppression.[51] As Magubane writes: "The denial of social equality placed the American black in the same status position as his putative brother in colonized Africa."[52]

The "hegemonic dominance of the white world over the non-white world" thus placed the realities and experiences of Blacks in the United States and on the African continent on the same political and ideological plane.[53] In this regard, Magubane is aligned with Mills's definition of "global white supremacy" as *the* socio-political system that orders the modern world as a whole.[54] It has its historical basis in European conquest and expansionism—expropriation, slavery, colonialism, and settlement—which thereby "[brought] race into existence as a global social reality," with the most significant stratification being that between white and Black (or more broadly "non-white"), light and dark. Magubane and Mills here are not unique in their view that European modernity ushered in a world racial system. Their arguments are an echo of W.E.B. Du Bois's historically modest prediction that "the problem of the twentieth century is the problem of the color-line—the relation between the darker to lighter races of men in Asia, and Africa, in America and the islands of the sea"[55] (modest because all indications are that this problem has persisted into the twenty-first century), as well as Frantz Fanon's insight that "what parcels out this world is to begin with the fact of belonging to or not belonging to a given race, a given species."[56]

Within this global racial hierarchy, those marked as white generally acquire a civil, moral, and juridical standing that elevates them above the Other races such that wherever there is a *Manichean* divide or racial hierarchy, whites are at the top of the social pyramid and those racialized as Black or as not-white are at the bottom. Under global white supremacy, this pattern of hierarchy and domination reproduces itself globally, taking different (local) forms and evolving across time.[57] Blacks in South Africa and the United States therefore have had to confront different (national) iterations of the same (larger and global) structure and ideology of white domination that has its roots in European racism.[58] From this reading and as explained earlier, the thematic of *global* white supremacy implies more than that the struggles Blacks in different parts of the world face against racism are the same or similar, but that they are "transnational and inter*connected*" (my emphasis).[59]

Consequently, the forms of Black struggle that emerged in both the United States and on the African continent (especially South Africa) imagined, theorized, and understood these struggles as historically and symbolically (if not symbiotically) linked such that the emancipation of Blacks in the United States was joined to the liberation of Africans on the continent and other Third World peoples who were subjects of colonialism and imperialism.[60] Insofar as African peoples were arrayed against this system of global white supremacy and viewed it as having introduced a deep trauma in their identity *as Africans*, a certain desire for restoration of, and to, Africa, if not physically but spiritually and culturally, was at the heart of the internationalist emphasis in Black nationalist movements.[61] On this score, Magubane makes repeated reference to Malcolm X—a canonical figure in Black radical political thought.[62] Malcolm X frequently argued that racism was not "an American problem, but a world problem"[63] and that "the black revolution [is] international in nature."[64] Malcolm X cited the rise of African nationalism on the continent in the 1960s as a major impetus and inspiration for the emergence of US Black Nationalism. As he intimated, the gaining of independence by African states in the 1960s "affected the [political] mood of Black people in the Western Hemisphere"[65] and inspired Blacks in the Americas and the Caribbean to take a stand against the political oppression, economic exploitation, and social degradation they experienced "at the hands of the white man."[66] The spirit of African revolution did not remain on the African continent, as according to Malcolm X,

> it slipped into the Western Hemisphere and got into the heart and the mind and the soul of the Black man in the Western Hemisphere *who supposedly had been separate from the African continent for almost 400 years.*[67]

And true to Magubane's analysis, Malcolm X theorizes the disconnection of Blacks in the diaspora from their African roots as a crucial source of their subjugation and psychological suffering,[68] hence his oft-stated injunction that American Blacks should realize that "being born here in America doesn't make you an American"[69] and that they are instead Africans: "Africans who are in America. *Nothing but* Africans."[70] The decolonization of Africa and the liberation of Blacks in the New World were therefore bound together into a singular emancipatory impulse that Malcolm X himself named "the end of white-world supremacy."[71]

A reading of Magubane's text suggests that he regards his analysis of the "ties that bind" as especially true of the relationship between Black South Africans and African Americans.[72] He reads both as carrying the special markings of having borne the brunt of seventeenth-century European expansionism in which comparable systems of "total subjugation" were imposed by means of conquest in the South African case and enslavement in the United States. In this regard, Magubane is in the company of not only Fredrickson discussed above but also John Cell, who also selects the racial regimes of South Africa and the United States for having reached "the highest stage of white supremacy."[73] A spectacular array of colonization and enslavement, super-exploitation of Black labor, cultural decimation through Christianity and Western (mis)education, economic deprivation, social invisibilization, psychological warfare through among other things notorious racial slurs (the "Nigger" and the "Kaffir," respectively), spatial segregation, inferior public services, denial of basic human rights, massive state repression and anti-Communist propaganda, police brutality, and repeated rituals of humiliation and cruelty unfolded from the 1600s to the present and cemented the status of the United States and South Africa as two of the most powerful white supremacist states in the world. Since "center and periphery need not be *literally* located,"[74] the inescapable conclusion to be drawn at this point is that Black America although literally located in the Global North or Euro-Atlantic West is very much experientially and politically part of the Global South or more precisely what Black Consciousness prophet-intellectual Steve Biko calls "the black world."[75]

The "diasporic affinity," solidarity campaigns, and collaborative efforts between Black South Africans and African Americans emanates from this shared historical experience of social life and social death within the matrix of anti-Blackness.[76] The singularity of racial Blackness bound them together in ways that exceed the boundaries and strictures of geographical distance into a group that Lewis Gordon calls *"the blacks of everywhere, the black blacks, the blackest blacks."*[77] Gordon's evocation of the "everywhere" suggests an additional reading of "diaspora" itself as an ontological condition—activated by the colonization of Africa and the transatlantic slave trade—that names the displacement and dislocation of all Africans. Along these lines, Frank B. Wilderson writes:

> [Even] Africans who were not captured [during the Asian and European trade in Africans as slaves] are nonetheless repositioned as Slaves in relation to the rest of the world, the absence of chains and the distance from the middle passage notwithstanding. Though these "free" Africans may indeed still know themselves through coherent cultural accoutrements unavailable to the Black American, they are known by other positions within the global structure as beings unable to "attain to immanent differentiation or to the clarity of self-knowledge." They are recast as objects in a world of subjects.[78]

Magubane's notion of "the ties that bind" is an instructive historical metaphor for the diasporic connection that holds, or binds, African Americans and Black South Africans and provides a compelling basis on which to ground the traveling of intellectual and theoretical ideas between them. The relationship between Africa and the African diaspora is therefore built as much on affinity, solidarity, and connection as it is on difference, distance, and loss. As Paul Zeleza writes, diaspora—more than a spatio-temporal geographical marker—denotes a "culture and a consciousness ... a 'there' that is invoked as a rhetoric of self-affirmation, of belonging to 'here' differently."[79] On the ruins of the spatial and geographic dispersal of Africans, a deeper symbolic kinship *is retained*, making possible multidirectional political, cultural, and ideological flows of Pan-African transnational solidarities, of spiritual and aesthetic forms, and of ideas and ideologies.[80]

To be sure, this argument does not deny the significant consequences of the spatio-temporal ruptures and dispersals of Africans across the world.[81] Rather the argument is that the African roots of Blacks across the world has been central to their social identities and political outlook in important ways that cannot be overlooked. African diasporic encounters cannot be understood outside of the Pan-Africanist and Black internationalist conception of Black liberation as a collective, dialogic, and global project.[82]

5. AFRICA AS MEMORY AND SYMBOL OF BLACK RADICALISM

This historical frame for understanding the "diasporic ties that bind" Blacks in South Africa and in the United States that has been sketched so far turns on three impression points around which the intellectual and political impulse of Black radicalism revolves, and from which anti-colonial and anti-racist Black thought and praxis emerges, namely (1) the global character of white supremacy; (2) the shared existential reality and ontological status of Blackness; and (3) the African genealogy of Blacks in the United States and Blackness in general. This third point can be rendered with more depth through Cedric Robinson's historical archaeology of the Black Radical Tradition, thus resisting the spatial and ideological separation of continental Africa from Black America and in a way problematizing the view of CRT as an entirely foreign paradigm to the Black South African experience. Indeed, I would argue that the very sense of critical race theory as a separate American paradigm is called into question when placed into a much larger genealogy, namely the Black Radical Tradition.

In his magisterial text on the historical and intellectual relationship between Marxism and Black radicalism, Cedric Robinson locates the revolutionary impulse of the Black Radical Tradition in the history of African peoples against European domination, and the specific cultural meanings that formed the basis of African resistance.[83] Robinson sets out to draw out the "ideological connective" between the Amistad slave rebellion and other slave ship uprisings, the maroons who escaped slavery and formed independent settlements, the Haitian Revolution, African anti-colonial wars of resistance, slave insurrections in the Caribbean and the Americas, the freed slaves who emigrated back to Africa, and the successive movements of national liberation, Black power, self-determination, and civil rights.[84] Robinson notes that such a connection cannot be comprehended or anticipated within the Western historical imagination, which typically treats this wide array of struggles as "geographically and historically bounded" and connected only by the similarity of their sociological elements (i.e., being slave and colonial societies). Rarely if ever are they linked as part of a larger political current, movement, social ideology, or historical experience.[85]

In order to overturn this major historical oversight, which he attributes to two historicist tendencies, namely the "diminution of diaspora"[86] and the "destruction of the African past,"[87] Robinson proceeds to eschew the view that Black radicalism is merely a variant of Western radicalism (such as Marxism or anarchism) whose proponents happen to be Black.[88] Indeed, Robinson intends to theorize Black radicalism as a revolutionary tradition that cannot be fully contained within a Marxian imaginary of liberation. For Robinson, the epistemology of Marxism is a Western construction—by which he means a "conceptualisation of human affairs and historical developments" that emanates from the particular experiences of European peoples mediated by their civilizational outlook, their social orders, and their cultural perspectives.[89] Robinson argues that while its encounters with Western society is the cauldron from which Black radicalism emerged, Western society is not in itself the source of its ideological and political inspiration. The Black Radical Tradition proper takes its foundational task to be a critique of, and struggle against, Western civilization. As he writes, Black radicalism is

> a *specifically African* response to an oppression emergent from the immediate determinants of European development in the modern era and framed by orders of human exploitation woven into the interstices of European social life from the inception of Western civilisation.[90]

Thus in Robinson's historical archaeology, *Africa* is the "material, social and ideological foundation" of the Black Radical Tradition.[91] As he illustrates, African persons forcibly shipped from Africa to be enslaved in the New World "also contained African cultures, critical mixtures and admixtures of language and thought, of cosmology and metaphysics, of habits, beliefs and morality."[92] Thus Blacks who arrived in the United States as slaves were not decultured or intellectually bereft. The memory and symbol of Africa as their prior *episteme* gave them "a knowledge of freedom" and defined the terms of their humanity.[93] Robinson painstakingly highlights two important historical details: firstly that the Middle Passage did not produce a complete rupture in enslaved Africans with the previous African onto-episteme and universe they inhabited, and secondly, that this African onto-episteme was the collective unconscious that activated Black radicalism and confounded their European captors and colonizers.[94] In this regard, the analytic arc of Robinson's arguments moves in an opposite direction to, among others (1) Saidiya Hartman's reading of the Middle Passage as the production of an irreversible estrangement of American Blacks from Africa,[95] a "loss of the mother" that Jared Sexton augments further as the "loss of any self that could experience such loss;"[96] (2) Paul Gilroy's celebration of a post-African, hybridized Blackness, or a modern Black Atlantic culture *in the wake* of Africa, where Africa freezes into a conceptually irrelevant historical relic;[97] (3) Kwame Anthony Appiah's liberal-cosmopolitan critique of racial nationalism as regressive;[98] and (4) Achille Mbembe's aversion to African-centered historical discourses, which he derides as nativist racial mythologies steeped in essentialist notions of authenticity and victimhood.[99] In contrast to these thinkers, Robinson refuses to adopt a postmodern attitude of ambivalence and disavowal in relation to the African heritage that is the root *and route* of modern Black culture, politics, and theory.[100]

As he insightfully remarks, following Amilcar Cabral, the transport of African bodies to the mines and plantations of the Americas and the Caribbean also meant

> the transfer of African ontological and cosmological systems, African presumptions of the organisation and significance of the social structure, African codes embodying historical consciousness and social experience, and African ideological and behavioural constructions.[101]

It is generally within this material everyday culture derived from Africa that the seeds of Black opposition to white supremacy are to be found as these displaced Africans conducted and imagined themselves in accordance with forms of life incomprehensible to the European master class.[102] And so, from the moment of their arrival in the New World, rebellion came instinctively to Black slaves and laborers. Countering dominant accounts, Robinson also points out that the docility purportedly displayed by enslaved Africans was a mask that concealed a deeply felt political rage against what they clearly understood as the unnatural, which is to say unethical, social system and structure of bondage.[103] This is evidenced by historical surveys and accounts of slave resistance against domination that range from small acts of disobedience to major threats of rebellion such as, among other things, the breaking of tools, burning of crops, work slowdowns, assisting and protecting runaway slaves, stealing, escapes and maroonage, revolts and killing of European "masters," and general insurrections against slavery.[104] A less overt but powerful source of resistance was the turn by the enslaved Africans to spiritual and cosmological resources (vodou, African ancestral veneration, Black Christianity), which again kept alive their sense of themselves as human and African against the overwhelming force of racial terror, displacement, and dehumanization.

Robinson's account thus refutes any possibility that enslaved Africans (the ancestors of African Americans) ever accepted the terms of slavery or submitted to white supremacy. Put another way, Black Africans in the New World never became *slaves* as they always regarded their enslavement as a condition to be overcome. Thus, African people remained ontologically animate: "Slavery altered the conditions of their being, but it could not negate their being."[105] A core feature of the struggles of colonized and enslaved people not only in the Americas and the Caribbean but also in Brazil, Africa, and the British West Indies that prefigured Black radicalism was the battle of African peoples to preserve their "collective identity as African people."[106] It was as African people that Black women and men fought against the disruption of their material and spiritual being.[107]

The sense of Africanity, of Africa as a memory and symbol of life-affirming freedom, is thus lodged deeply at the epistemological and ontological sub-stratum of the Black Radical Tradition. And Robinson goes further to record the unique feature of the Black Radical Tradition that significantly departs from Western Marxism, namely the emphasis in Black radicalism on "structures of the mind": the privileging, that is, of the metaphysical over the material and the stress placed on the "mind, metaphysics, ideology and consciousness" and on the "supernatural, sacred and poetic" elements of human life.[108] The novelty and enduring legacy of Robinson's work is its restoration of Black radicalism to its interminable African roots. The consciousness and history of African civilization that was never fully ruptured by the interdictions of European invasions and violence thus formed the basis of Black radicalism as a world-historical revolutionary tradition. It also enlivens the deep historical and symbolic link—those ties that bind—between Black rebellions across the modern world in earlier centuries and the articulations of a theory and movement of Black radicalism in the twentieth and twenty-first centuries. The powerful trace of Africa that suffused struggles for Black liberation could not be accounted for in a Marxian paradigm precisely because it was outside of the signposts and markers of Western experience. Robinson writes that the political "outrage" expressed by the Black radical tradition against the racism of white European society

> was most certainly informed by the Africanity of our consciousness—some epistemological measure culturally embedded in our minds that deemed that the racial capitalism we have been witness to was an unacceptable standard of human conduct... The depths to which racialist behavior has fouled Western agencies transgressed against a world-consciousness rooted in our African past. Nevertheless, the sense of deep sadness at the spectacle of Western racial oppression is shared with other non-Western peoples.[109]

Robinson interprets Black radicalism as a fundamentally oppositional and utopian structure of feeling, a struggle by enslaved and colonized Africans who were extracted and displaced from their African social formations to re-create their lives:

> It was the ability to conserve their native consciousness of the world from alien intrusion, the ability to imaginatively re-create a precedent metaphysic while being subjected to enslavement, racial domination, and repression. This was the raw material of the Black radical tradition, the values, ideas, conceptions, and constructions of reality from which resistance was manufactured. And in each instance of resistance, the social and psychological dynamics that are shared by human communities in long-term crises resolved for the rebels the particular moment, the collective and personal chemistries that congealed into social movement. But it was the materials constructed from a shared philosophy developed in the African past and transmitted as culture, from which revolutionary consciousness was realized and the ideology of struggle formed.[110]

More than the revolutionary transformation of Westernized, capitalist society, the object of Black radicalism was and remains the preservation of the historical and social consciousness formed and evolved from the African past and the reconstitution of bonds of community and personhood assaulted by the racialism of Western society. This focus on the interior life, on de-linking from the European symbolic order and refusing its protocols of racial capitalism, domination, and cruelty was therefore vital.[111] The anchoring of the struggle for freedom and dignity in the consciousness of African civilization thus made Pan-Africanism and Black internationalism a natural and necessary development in Black radicalism given that the confrontation was with Western civilization itself and the racist, colonial, and capitalist modernity it had imposed on African peoples and not merely with particular forms or symptoms of this civilizational excess. Black radicalism from this view engages in a dialectical confrontation and total opposition to racial social orders and to the European imaginary that created and rationalizes those orders.[112] Near the closing of his book, Robinson also returns to the notion of diaspora, with the exhortation that Blacks "must be as one."[113] These are among his final prophetic and instructive musings:

> The Black radical tradition suggests a more complete contradiction. In social and political practice, it has acquired its immediate momentum from the necessity to respond to the persisting threats to African peoples characteristic of the modern world system. Over the many generations, the specificity of resistance—at best securing only a momentary respite—has given way to the imperatives of broader collectivities. Particular languages, cultures, and social sensibilities have evolved into world-historical consciousness. *The distinctions of political space and historical time have fallen away so that the making of one Black collective identity suffuses nationalisms.* Harbored in the African diaspora there is a single historical identity that is in opposition to the systemic privations of racial capitalism. Ideologically, it cements pain to purpose, experience to expectation, consciousness to collective action. It deepens with each disappointment at false mediation and reconciliation, and is crystallized into ever-increasing cores by betrayal and repression. The resoluteness of the Black radical tradition advances as each generation assembles the data of its experience to an ideology of liberation. The experimentation with Western political inventories of change, specifically nationalism and class struggle, is coming to a close. Black radicalism is transcending those traditions in order to adhere to its own authority. It will arrive as points of resistance here, rebellion there, and mass revolutionary movements still elsewhere. But each instance will be formed by the Black radical tradition in an awareness of the others and the consciousness that there remains nothing to which it may return. Molded by a long and brutal experience and rooted in a specifically African development, the tradition will provide for no compromise between liberation and annihilation.[114]

Robinson can be recalled here for his definitive dismissal of the claim that there exists an impenetrable wall between Black South Africa and Black America since they are part of one world in the much deeper historical, cosmological, and ontological sense he outlines. Such claims may themselves be the products of a Western historiographical imagination whose spatial boundaries and temporal periodizations also neglect to view Black radicalism through its longer and deeper African heritage. The fracturing and distance between Black traditions in South Africa and the United States may also result from the failure to self-consciously archive Black radicalism as a "tradition" of African people. It is plain that Robinson is not indulging a pre-colonial African romanticism (or a "nativist" mode of self-writing, as Mbembe might describe it). Rather he treats Africa as a historical consciousness and a repertoire of living cosmologies, epistemologies, and ontologies that is the symbolic and memorial inheritance of Blacks who generations after the first colonial encounters drew on this consciousness—directly and indirectly—as the raw material from which to fashion forms of Black resistance and Black critique appropriate to their time and space.

Through Robinson's intellectual cartography of the Black radical tradition, we may conclude that the dismissals, doubts, and ambivalences concerning critical race theory as an entirely foreign, North American, imported discourse are too simplistic when judged from a Black internationalist standpoint and in view of the existential status of Blackness under global white supremacy. When inflected through the specific historical context and social conditions of the Black world, critical race theory as an analytic paradigm is eminently available to a transnational, global, and international critical project.

Properly construed, critical race theory is a grammar of critique that takes up the historical burden or vocation of the Black Radical Tradition that Robinson identified as the negation and critique of Western civilization. In all its disciplinary instantiations, CRT aims to contend—theoretically and politically—with the historical results and afterlife of Western racialism and its productions of racial hierarchy from the standpoint of the Black experience. Costas Douzinas and Adam Gearey frame critical race theory as an approach to law, society, politics, and discourse that repeatedly stages a confrontation between "Black power" and "white law."[115] As a field of theory, it seeks to reckon with the history of Black people's "encounters with western law" and its entangled properties of enlightenment and exclusion, rationality and brutality, universalism and ethnocentrism, formality and indeterminacy.[116] As such, CRT presents itself as an instructive mode of analysis in transnational contexts where race, settler-colonialism, colonial histories, and racial capitalism signify the predominant social contradiction. In Douzinas and Gearey's words:

> CRT provides a critical thinking that is *not limited to a historical time and place* but confronts law's complicity in the perpetuation of a racially defined economic and social order.[117]

The critical dimension of CRT inheres in its search for "oppositionist accounts of race" or "counter-accounts of social reality"[118] that challenge mainstream legal-liberal and racial optimist understandings of race, law, power, equality, and justice. As scholars such as E. Tendayi Achiume[119] and Chris Gevers[120] have shown, these insights can be powerfully retooled into a critique of the international legal order, its universalist conceits, its racial silences, and its imperial disorders.

6. CODA

The most immediate associations we could draw to this type of unbounded globalist thinking is in the realm of music, jazz, and the arts. In his biography *Still Grazing*, Hugh Masekela describes his musical journey and that of his comrade and contemporary Fela Anikulapo Kuti as one of African diasporic encounters, resonances, and blending of sounds, voices, and styles.[121] Of Fela, he briefly narrates the story of an African child of "professional parents" who wished for him to study medicine. Arriving in London, the young Fela switched from medicine to music—and apparently achieved self-consciousness at the moment when he broke from European classical music and developed a "hybrid of Nigerian folk and urban dance music with a touch of jazz."[122] Fela's sound, we are told—and hopefully have also heard—is composed of what Masekela describes as a "diaspora's worth of influences": Ghanaian dance groove, big-band swing music, Afro-Caribbean calypso, Jamaican ska, and South African township mbaqanga. From these musical elements, Fela created his distinct "Afro-Beat" style, partly—Masekela intimates—as a critique of African performers who had completely "turned their back on their musical roots in order to emulate American pop music trends."[123]

For Both Fela and Masekela, every encounter with the world was to be shaped by their "Africanism."[124] Indeed, even while living in the States and experimenting with African American artistic forms, Masekela insisted on texturing his music with the "chants of [his] father's clan" and connecting this to "the suffering of impoverished or misplaced people of African origin all around the world."[125] Both Hugh Masekela's and Fela Kuti's musical styles underscore the centrality of Africa as a grounding of the Black historical and aesthetic experience, a source for diasporic affinity and resistance against purity.

The comparative historical studies of Fredrickson and Magubane illustrate a linkage between the deep structural homologies in the history, sociology, and political economy of race in South Africa and the United States and the ideological and political affinities that emerged from across the Atlantic that enabled a thinking-together of the problem of Black existence under white supremacy. We may understand these as the binding ties in the lived experience of race and Blackness between the two spaces. Robinson and Malcolm X added to this an appreciation of Africa—its ways of knowing and its cultures of resistance—as the ontological root of critical traditions of Black political thought and creative expression. Robinson's extensive genealogy of the emergence of the Black Radical Tradition as emanating out of revolts and rebellion based on the memory of Africa, its confrontation with the racialism of Western culture, and the inheritance of African epistemologies and spiritualities works against the tendency to associate critique exclusively with Western radical traditions. It also helps to resituate critical race theory within an African intellectual and political universe.

We can see the trace of the Black Radical Tradition in the driving impulse of CRT, which in effect concerns itself with studying the world, and the word of law, and its intersections with power and (in)justice from the vantage point of the critique of Western civilization. Through its radical race-conscious social critique and analysis, CRT postulates a revisionist narrative of law, modernity, and society that locates racial violence, coloniality, and Eurocentrism to be central to their development and functioning. It was mined in its early stages from a particular moment in the racial and political history of the United States where the promise of justice embodied in the 1964 Civil Rights Act turned out not only to be extremely hollow but created a legal, political, and social atmosphere in which the material and social significance of racism was being denied or ignored—celebrated as having been overcome—even while it was being reproduced. Yet, law's paradoxical rejection and affirmation of racism turns out not to be a paradox at all. The historical imbrications of Western legal modernity and its role in processes of European expansion that installed white racial domination in the United States and South Africa produced as well a moral economy in which the only true measure of humanity is the white European subject. According to the reading offered in this chapter, it is with these processes and this global reality that critical race theory was *always already* grappling.

NOTES

1. Frantz Fanon, *The Wretched of the Earth*, trans. Richard Philcox (London: Pluto 2004), 5.
2. On the placing of South Africa in quotation marks, and the general idea of the South African black radical tradition, see Joel Modiri, "Azanian Political Thought and the Undoing of South African Knowledges," *Theoria* 62 (2021): 42–85.
3. See in general Kimberle Crenshaw et al., eds., *Critical Race Theory: The Key Writings that Formed the Movement* (New York: New Press, 1995).
4. Gary Peller, "Race Consciousness," *Duke Law Journal* (1990): 758–847.
5. Charles Mills, *Blackness Visible: Essays on Philosophy and Race* (New York: Cornell University Press 1998), 98.
6. Charles Mills, *The Racial Contract* (New York: Cornell University Press, 1997).
7. Mills, *Blackness Visible,* 97, 98–99, 103; Charles Mills, "The Illumination of Blackness," in *Antiblackness,* ed. Moon-Kie Jung and João H. Costa Vargas, (North Carolina: Duke University Press, 2021), 20.
8. Charles Mills, "Global White Ignorance," in *Routledge International Handbook of Ignorance Studies,* 2nd ed., ed. Matthias Gross and Linzey McGoey (London: Routledge 2015), 223.
9. Nahum Dimitri Chandler, *"Beyond This Narrow Now" Or, Delimitations of W.E.B. Du Bois* (NC: Duke University Press 2021), 96.
10. Archie Mafeje, "Africanity: A Combative Ontology," in *The Postcolonial Turn: Reimagining Anthropology and Africa,* ed. Rene Devisch and Francis B. Nyamnjoh (Bemenda: Langaa RPCID, 2011), 39.
11. Mafeje, "Africanity: A Combative Ontology," 37.
12. Mafeje, "Africanity: A Combative Ontology," 37.
13. Mafeje, "Africanity: A Combative Ontology," 37.
14. Mafeje, "Africanity: A Combative Ontology," 38.
15. Archie Mafeje, "The Agrarian Question, Access to Land, and Peasant Responses in Sub-Saharan Africa," in *UNSRID Civil Society and Social Movements Programme*, no 6. (2003): 17 (although in this instance, Mafeje was referring to comparisons between Russia [Eurasia] and Africa).

16. Bongani Nyoka, "Mafeje and 'Authentic Interlocutors': An Appraisal of His Epistemology," *African Sociological Review* 16 (2012): 6.

17. Jimi Adesina, "Archie Mafeje and the Pursuit of Endogeny: Against Alterity and Extraversion," *Africa Development* 33 (2008): 134. See also Dani Nabudere, *Archie Mafeje: Scholar, Activist, Thinker* (Pretoria: AISA 2011), 7–13, 14–18, 51–56, 94–99.

18. Archie Mafeje, "On the Articulation of Modes of Production," *Journal of Southern African Studies* 8 (1981): 123–38.

19. Archie Mafeje, "African Socio-cultural Formations in the 21st Century," *African Development Review* 7 (1995): 154.

20. Nkiru Nzegwu, "Colonial Racism: Sweeping out Africa with Mother Europe's Broom," in *Racism and Philosophy*, ed. Susan Babbit and Sue Campbell (New York: Cornell University Press, 1999), 124–56.

21. Nzegwu, "Colonial Racism: Sweeping out Africa with Mother Europe's Broom," 126.

22. Nzegwu, "Colonial Racism: Sweeping out Africa with Mother Europe's Broom," 131–32.

23. Nzegwu, "Colonial Racism: Sweeping out Africa with Mother Europe's Broom," 135.

24. Nzegwu, "Colonial Racism: Sweeping out Africa with Mother Europe's Broom," 130–31.

25. Nzegwu, "Colonial Racism: Sweeping out Africa with Mother Europe's Broom," 128, 132.

26. Nzegwu, "Colonial Racism: Sweeping out Africa with Mother Europe's Broom," 126.

27. P. T. Zeleza "Diaspora Dialogues: Engagements Between Africa and its Diasporas," in *The New African Diaspora*, ed. Isisdore Okpewho and Nkiru Nzegwu (Bloomington: Indiana University Press, 2009), 48.

28. Hortense J. Spillers, *Black, White and in Color: Essays on American Literature and Culture* (Chicago: Chicago University Press, 2003), 176.

29. Charles Mills, "Critical Race Theory—A Reply to Mike Cole," *Ethnicities* 9 (2009): 270–71.

30. George Fredrickson, *White Supremacy: A Comparative Study in American and South African History* (New York: OUP, 1981).

31. George Fredrickson, *Black Liberation: A Comparative History of Black Ideologies in the United States and South Africa* (New York: OUP, 1995).

32. Fredrickson, *White Supremacy*, xvii.

33. Fredrickson, *White Supremacy*, xxi.

34. Fredrickson, *White Supremacy*, xxii.

35. Fredrickson, *White Supremacy*, xxiii.

36. Fredrickson, *White Supremacy*, xxv.

37. Fredrickson, *Black Liberation*, 5.

38. Fredrickson, *Black Liberation*, 6.

39. Fredrickson, *Black Liberation*, 5.

40. Fredrickson, *White Supremacy*, xviii.

41. Fredrickson, *Black Liberation*, 6.

42. Fredrickson, *Black Liberation*, 5–6.

43. Fredrickson, *Black Liberation*, 5.

44. The one complication in the American situation may be that European settlement and the installation of white supremacy there was made possible through native genocide, whereas in South Africa, land dispossession and labor exploitation were the primary

modes of consolidating white settlement. Moreover, unlike in South Africa, Blacks in the United States must reconcile their political demand for historical justice with those of Native Americans. A major limit of Black radical anti-racism in the United States is that its demands for reparations, redress, and recognition may not only fail to disrupt but inadvertently legitimize the settler-colonial foundations of North America. See Jared Sexton, "The *Vel* of Slavery: Tracking the Figure of The Unsovereign," *Critical Sociology* (2014): 5.

45. Fredrickson, *Black Liberation*, 7.

46. Fredrickson, *Black Liberation*, 6, 9.

47. Noel Chabani Manganyi, *Being-Black in the World* (Johannesburg: Ravan Press, 1973).

48. Bernard Magubane, *The Ties that Bind: Afro-American Consciousness of Africa* (New Jersey: Africa World Press, 1987).

49. Magubane, *Ties that Bind*, 1–3.

50. Magubane, *Ties that Bind*, 3.

51. Magubane, *Ties that Bind*, 4.

52. Magubane, *Ties that Bind*, 4.

53. Magubane, *Ties that Bind*, 5–7.

54. Mills, *Blackness Visible*, 98–99; Mills, *The Racial Contract*, 3, 20–30; Charles Mills, "Race and Global Justice," in *Domination and Global Justice: Conceptual, Historical and Institutional Perspectives*, ed. Barbara Buckinx et al. (New York: Routledge, 2015), 181–205. To be clear, Mills is arguing that race as a political category is fundamental to global history and to the political structure of the modern world. His theory of global white supremacy is not intended to be exhaustive of the political universe. Rather, its aim is to supplement—not replace—other theoretical paradigms and political categories. He means to use the term as a way of registering and making visible the usually ignored but massively significant "racial dimension" of the global political order.

55. W.E.B. Du Bois, *The Souls of Black Folk* (New York: Simon & Schuster [1903] 2009), 17–18.

56. Frantz Fanon, trans. C. Farrington, *The Wretched of the Earth* (New York: Grove Press, 1963), 39.

57. Mills, *Blackness Visible*, xiv, 101.

58. Mabogo More, "Biko and Douglass: Existential Conception of Death and Freedom," *Philosophia Africana* 17 (2015): 106: "Plantation slavery and Apartheid are the same form of racial violence."

59. Tyler Fleming, "Binding the Ties Together: A Reflection on Bernard Magubane and the Transnational Nature of South African Studies," *Safundi: The Journal on South African and American Studies* (2015): 236.

60. Magubane, *Ties that Bind*, 10.

61. Magubane, *Ties that Bind*, 10.

62. Magubane, *Ties that Bind*, 238. Another notable thinker who would shift from Black Power to Pan-Africanism, or from nationalism to internationalism, is Stokely Carmichael (Kwame Ture) in *Stokely Speaks: From Black Power to Pan-Africanism* (Chicago: Chicago Review Press, [1971] 2007).

63. Malcolm X, *Malcolm X: The Last Speeches*, ed. Bruce Perry (New York: Pathfinder, 1989), 151–81.

64. Malcolm X, ed. I Benjamin Karim, *The End of White World Supremacy: Four Speeches* (New York: Arcade Publishing, 2011), 138.

65. Malcolm X, *The Last Speeches*, 168.

66. Malcolm X, ed. George Breitman, *Malcolm X Speaks: Selected Speeches and Statements* (New York: Grove Press, 1965), 34.

67. Malcolm X, *The Last Speeches*, 168 (my emphasis).

68. Malcolm X, *Malcolm X Speaks*, 168.

69. Malcolm X, *Malcolm X Speaks*, 26.

70. Malcolm X, *Malcolm X Speaks*, 36.

71. Malcolm X, *The End of White World Supremacy*.

72. Magubane, *Ties that Bind*, 207–28.

73. John W. Cell, *Segregation: The Highest Stage of White Supremacy* (Cambridge: Cambridge University Press, 1982).

74. David Theo Goldberg, *Racist Culture: Philosophy and the Politics of Meaning* (Oxford: Blackwell, 1993), 203.

75. Steve Biko, *I Write What I Like: A Selection of His Writings*, ed. Aelred Stubbs (Johannesburg: Picador Africa [1978] 2012), 74.

76. Magubane, *Ties that Bind*, 211–21.

77. Lewis R. Gordon, *Her Majesty's Other Children: Sketches of Racism from a Neocolonial Age* (Lanham: Rowman & Littlefield, 1997), 53.

78. Frank B. Wilderson III, *Red, White & Black: Cinema and the Structure of US Antagonisms* (NC: Duke University Press, 2010), 95–96.

79. Paul Zeleza, "Diaspora Dialogues," 32.

80. Zeleza, "Diaspora Dialogues," 46.

81. On the construction and theorization of the African diaspora, and related debates concerning questions of race, nation, and history, see among others, Isidore Okpewho et al., eds., *The African Diaspora: African Origins and New World Identities* (Bloomington: Indiana University Press 1999); Michelle Wright *Becoming Black: Creating Identity in the African Diaspora* (NC: Duke University Press, 2003); Brent Edwards, *The Practice of Diaspora: Literature, Translation and the Rise of Black Internationalism* (Cambridge: Harvard University Press, 2003).

82. Paul Zeleza, "The Challenges of Studying the African Diasporas," *African Sociological Review* 12 (2008): 4.

83. Cedric Robinson, *Black Marxism: The Making of the Black Radical Tradition* (Chapel Hill: North Carolina Press,1983), 5.

84. Robinson, *Black Marxism*, 72.

85. Robinson, *Black Marxism*, 72.

86. Robinson, *Black Marxism*, 72.

87. Robinson, *Black Marxism*, 81.

88. Robinson, *Black Marxism*, 73.

89. Robinson, *Black Marxism*, 2.

90. Robinson, *Black Marxism*, 73 (my emphasis).

91. Robinson, *Black Marxism*, 112; also see 169.

92. Robinson, *Black Marxism*, 121–22.

93. Robinson, *Black Marxism*, 121–22.

94. Robinson, *Black Marxism*, 122.

95. Saidiya Hartman, *Lose Your Mother: A Journey Along the Atlantic Slave Route* (New York: Farrar, Strauss & Giroux, 2007).

96. Sexton, "The *Vel* of Slavery," 9.

97. Paul Gilroy, *The Black Atlantic: Modernity and Double Consciousness* (London: Verso, 1995).

98. Kwame Anthony Appiah, *In My Father's House: Africa in the Philosophy of Culture* (Oxford: Oxford University Press, 1992).

99. Achille Mbembe, "African Modes of Self-Writing," *Public Culture* 14 (2002): 239–73; Achille Mbembe, "On the Power of the False," *Public Culture* 14 (2002): 629–41; Achille Mbembe, "Ways of Seeing: Beyond the New Nativism," *African Studies Review* 44 (2001): 1–14.

100. Robinson's treatment of the relationship between Africa and Black identity is bound to be caught up in the polarity between on the one hand, postmodern, post-structural, and postcolonial theoretical projects aimed at decentering knowledge and language as well as deconstructing unities, foundations, and grand narratives, and on the other hand, pan-Africanist, Marxist, and nationalist endeavors to recuperate African history and culture and to recompose African identity, agency, and subjectivity. Whereas the former position takes its cue from a moment in European scholarship that announced the death of the Subject and performed a theoretical fragmentation of epistemic and ontological positions such as "Truth," the latter sought to assert African difference against colonial and imperial distortions, and defined its core mission as the recovery of epistemological and ontological integrity and presence for the African subject. To the extent that they are driven by divergent impulses—*decomposition* of fixed essences and group identities on the one hand, and *rebirth* of the African self and assertion of African difference on the other—these two trends were always bound to clash on how to theorize Africa, African history and culture, Black identity, and race in modernity. The ascendancy of the "posts" (postmodernism, post-structuralism, and postcolonialism) in African and Black studies introduced a language—cosmopolitanism, Afropolitanism, hybridity, mimicry, invention—that was hostile to any perceived postulations of a genetic *unity* of African people, a singular *essential* understanding of the world held by all Africans, racial Blackness as a marker of national (or transnational) belonging, and the fundamental alterity of Africanity as against Western and other identities. The charge from proponents of the "posts" in African, Black, and postcolonial studies (most notably represented by, among others, Achille Mbembe, Paul Gilroy, Kwame Anthony Appiah, Homi Bhabha, and Valentin Mudimbe) is that such postulations tend to generate nostalgic romanticizations of pre-colonial Africa; essentialist, rigid, and purist constructions of African and Black identity and nativist renderings of African history and culture. Although I do not read Robinson to be vulnerable to such critics given his insistence on African *agency* and the rich historical evidence he provides (see Robin Kelley, "Foreword," in Robinson, *Black Marxism,* xx), the methodological and scholarly weaknesses of the cultural postmodern critiques adumbrated above should be noted. These critiques are in the first place patently Eurocentric in their theorization of race, Blackness, and Africa through the philosophical instruments of white, Western thinkers (notably Michel Foucault, Jacques Derrida, Giles Deleuze, Jacques Lacan, Roland Barthes, Mikhail Bakhtin, and Walter Benjamin)—thinkers for whom Africa and Black existence were not primary objects of analysis. Secondly, such critiques tend to display a reductive and generalizing grasp of the African scholarship they charge with cultural essentialism, nativism, and regressive nationalism. Thirdly, since they mostly emanate from literary and cultural studies, they tend to fixate on the discursive and the cultural side of life to the almost complete neglect of material and political realities (especially violence and power). Finally, and most disturbingly, such critiques evince a spectacularly apologist orientation towards colonial oppression and its neocolonial persistence—and tend instead

to insist on a notion of "agency" centered on highlighting the complicity of Africans in their own political and economic malaise. Indeed, it appears that sympathy with the Western archive and intimacy with the West and with white subjects—even if this is phrased in terms of a resistance against singular origins and purity and affirmation of common humanity and relationality—is an underlying motivation of much of the postmodern and postcolonial critique of African nationalist, Pan-Africanist, and Marxist theories of Africanity and Blackness. A voluminous amount of ink has been spilled in debates across many disciplines on this issue and this very strained footnote could not settle those debates. For a short roadmap into these debates, see Sara Marzagora, "The Humanism of Reconstruction: African Intellectuals, Decolonial Critical Theory and the Opposition to the 'Posts' (Postmodernism, Poststructuralism, Postcolonialism)," *Journal of African Cultural Studies* 28 (2016): 161–78; and Godwin Murunga, "African Cultural Identity and Self-Writing," *African Review of Books* (2004): 15–16.

101. Robinson, *Black Marxism*, 122.
102. Robinson, *Black Marxism*, 122.
103. Robinson, *Black Marxism*, 123.
104. Robinson, *Black Marxism*, 123. See also C.L.R. James, *A History of Pan-African Revolt* (California: PM Press, [1938] 2012).
105. Robinson, *Black Marxism*, 125.
106. Robinson, *Black Marxism*, 132.
107. Robinson, *Black Marxism*, 146, 170–71.
108. Robinson, *Black Marxism*, 169.
109. Robinson, *Black Marxism*, 308.
110. Robinson, *Black Marxism*, 309.
111. Robinson, *Black Marxism*, 310–11.
112. One critical implication of this conception of Black radicalism is that it implies that African rebels forcibly transported to the New World resisted their Americanization (the erasure of their Africanity) and constructed and imagined themselves as part of the Third World and Global South. Not doing otherwise would align American Blacks with the "racial metaphysics" of Western civilization that resulted in, among other things, the genocidal clearing of Native Americans from their indigenous lands.
113. Robinson, *Black Marxism*, 318.
114. Robinson, *Black Marxism*, 317 (my emphasis).
115. Costas Douzinas and Adam Gearey, *Critical Jurisprudence: The Political Philosophy of Justice* (Oxford: Hart, 2005), 259.
116. Douzinas and Gearey, *Critical Jurisprudence*, 259.
117. Douzinas and Gearey, *Critical Jurisprudence*, 259 (my emphasis).
118. Crenshaw et al., "Introduction," in *Critical Race Theory: Key Writings*, xiv.
119. See E. Tendayi Achiume, "Racial Borders," *Georgetown Law Journal* 11 (2022): 445.
120. Christopher Gevers, "'Unwhitening the World': Rethinking Race and International Law," *UCLA Law Review* 67 (2021): 1652.
121. Hugh Masekela and D. Michael Cheers, *Still Grazing: The Musical Journey of Hugh Masekela* (Johannesburg: Jacana, 2015 [2004]).
122. Masekela and Cheers, *Still Grazing*, 242.
123. Masekela and Cheers, *Still Grazing*, 242.
124. Masekela and Cheers, *Still Grazing*, 243.
125. Masekela and Cheers, *Still Grazing*, 243.

CHAPTER NINETEEN

SHADES OF IGNORANCE

A Critique of the Epistemic Whiteness of International Law

Mohsen al Attar and Claire Smith[*]

1. INTRODUCTION

International law acts on the world in various ways. Only recently have mainstream scholars undertaken sustained consideration of its impact on race. As one of the defining features of the modern era—denoted by virulent practices of racialization and racism—the absence of race from mainstream debates about international law has always felt both strange and strategic. Or at least it did to those familiar with the white supremacist discourse that runs through the history of the regime.

From the early days of international law, race was central to its civilizational (and civilizing) mission. It played a key role in stratifying the world along hierarchical lines, bestowing cognitive agency to those racialized as white and denying both epistemology and humanity to everyone else. From Vitoria to Vattel, Grotius to Westlake, and Lorimer to Lauterpacht, key interlocutors developed and disseminated racialized tropes to advance a particular vision of international law, one that centered and safeguarded a white supremacist episteme.

Yet, as the currency of overt racism stumbles in the post-decolonization period, international legal scholars began retelling the story, now denuded of race. The rationale was simple: it would be difficult to instigate a normative commitment to international law from the decolonizing Third World or the insurrectionist Fourth World if the regime's history of white supremacy was acknowledged or, worse, problematized. As scholars suspended engagement with race in scholarship and teaching, white ignorance grew into another defining feature of the regime.

In the following chapter, we reflect on the interplay between race and international law. Foremost, we examine the part played by white ignorance in the advance of international law's epistemic violence. Our intent is to expose some ways international legal thinkers and pedagogues conceal the epistemic project they are engaged in, whitewashing the constitutive character of white supremacy from the Eurocentric project.

2. ICONOCLASM IN INTERNATIONAL LEGAL SCHOLARSHIP

How is thinking about international law and the knowledge it produces situated? Variations of this question are proliferating across legal academia. Despite the persistence of formalist and doctrinal viewpoints, scholars increasingly recognize that contemporary legal thought constitutes—and is constituted—by context, contingency, and standpoint. They are also contemplating how these factors combine to adumbrate the contours of a parochial epistemic frame.

When considering this question, we must account for both subjective and normative elements. First, it is normative since the starting point of most interlocutors includes a commitment to extant international law as a legitimate, even desirable frame with which to mediate human relations. Second, it is subjective since, despite our best efforts at critical detachment, it is impossible for scholars to extricate themselves from themselves. The prevalence of practices of domination in human relations means that legal academics have participated in these processes, and from a panoply of positions. Engagement and non-engagement with the oppressions that pervade the regime and our identities are also normative positions.

Notwithstanding the prominence of subjectivity and normativity in contemporary legal thought, various scholars insist on the universality of international law. However, we suggest their commitment is disingenuous. According to Pierre Schlag, publicists "sort of know" they operate within a truncated universality and that their efforts at knowledge production "might [equally] be understood as efforts not to know."[1] Schlag regards ignorance as a useful instrument in the study of law, helping scholars reconcile their theory of universality with the arbitrary choices they make about what and who to exclude from the discipline. A deliberate state of not knowing applies to scholars who identify as formalists as much as it does to a critical cohort.

For purposes of this argument, we will distinguish formalists from critical scholars with broad brushstrokes. While formalists opt to situate the social and economic outside their frame of examination, their critical counterparts embrace them, centering the impact of social forces on legality. Both groups may seek to understand ways in which the law impacts factor X or produces outcome Y, but they make distinct political choices about the locus of examination. The divide appears theoretical and political, but it is also epistemic as each trajectory privileges a way of knowing to the exclusion of others.

What motivates this approach? The world is complex, and shortcuts help a researcher make sense of it. Epistemic projects corralled by ontological boundaries are invaluable for narrowing our scope of vision and rendering the phenomena under observation more manageable. Schlag goes further, arguing we develop "elaborate academic strategies to avoid taking cognizance of career-arresting phenomena."[2] Knowledge production can become hostile to understanding, especially when the production seeks to convey "formalization, mastery, and authoritativeness."[3] Indeed, while disciplinary boundaries are reasonable—a "discipline would collapse under the weight of uncertainty were it otherwise"—they come at a high cost.

> Disciplinary boundaries exclude the viewpoints of those that do not fit the frame, do not conform to it, or reject received logic ... They protect a centre ground, allowing the inclusion of "non-orthodox" accounts in as far as they pass the "test of intelligibility"–implicitly measured against the yardstick of white western judgment, its sensibilities, assumptions, norms and conventions as the non-negotiable yardstick. [Critical accounts are] pushed to the periphery ... While academia masquerades as a form of safe space, it is neither democratic nor representative: the obvious consequence is that most research fields suffer from severe forms of misrecognition (status inequality) and misrepresentation (participatory inequality).[4]

As scholarly debates about international law have veered toward the epistemological, publicists are now weighing the impact of epistemology on the ways we think about our discipline and the ways we teach it. In an illuminating chapter, Ana Luísa Bernadino underlines the powerful space international legal scholars occupy. By deciding what to teach and, likewise, what not to teach, they construct "proven fact[s]" and integrate "self-evident truth[s]" about the world.[5] Because of the overlap between academia and practice, the pedagogy of international law plays a foundational role in international relations. Claiming the mantle of orthodoxy is an effective way of embedding premises, presumptions, and prejudices in the curriculum, *truths* that are contingent and cultural. As happens with any subjectivity that postures as objectivity, those with incongruent subjectivities are excluded from or rendered unintelligible in the conversation. Pedagogy is a virulent conduit for epistemic violence. Through the adoption of dubious and arbitrary barometers of inclusion and exclusion, disciplines privilege those who reproduce the status quo while delegitimizing alternative ways of knowing and their knowers.

When studying the path of this epistemic project in international legal pedagogy, we uncover the prejudices that guide the discipline.[6] As Bernadino observes, "there is thus merit to analysing what is ignored in the most influential contemporary textbooks of international law."[7] Especially elucidative is her use of Henry Giroux's concept of a hidden curriculum to illustrate "hierarchies of relevance."[8] Rather than an apolitical exercise, curricular choices are deliberate interventions in the advance of an epistemic project. Bernardino's observations cohere with al Attar's critique of Eurocentrism in the teaching of international law:

> A revealing exercise involves contrasting the original architects with today's engineers, the authors of the most widespread textbooks on international law: among others, Ian Brownlie, James Crawford, Malcolm Evans, Jan Klabbers, and Malcolm Shaw. The parallels are plain, at least to those who pay attention. The platitude of the European hold over textbooks on international law protects the ideological influence of Eurocentrism for, according to Rodolfo Acuna, "textbooks establish the paradigms for the disciplines within the area of study." In line with Acuna's cogent observation, the topics the authors of textbooks prefer to include in their respective treatises reflect their Eurocentric vision.[9]

al Attar provides numerous examples of the embedding of Eurocentrism in the most popular textbooks of international law. Perhaps the most damning aspect of these texts is the exclusion of themes that are constitutive of Eurocentrism and the modern order: capitalism, white supremacy, and racism. To illustrate, few textbooks on international law include TWAIL or CRT scholarship despite the value they provide in linking the discipline to the contentious historical and cultural contexts that manifested at the time of the regime's development. One can and should question which power structure the disciplinary reluctance to name racial oppression serves.[10]

Guided by an iconoclastic tautology, TWAIL and CRT scholars challenge the theory, ideology, and, occasionally, epistemology of international law. Iconoclasm is palpable as they reject the terms of order and knowledge reified by the discipline, recognizing them as both contingent and prejudiced. Rather than abstract truths, they root their research in social forces and lived experiences, derailing the ideal theories masquerading as neutrality that permeate journals and syllabi. They are critical in their conclusions, but equally of their starting points, aware the questions we ask shape the conclusions we draw. TWAIL and CRT compel us to reflect on the epistemic commitments of the discipline. TWAIL centers colonialism, neocolonialism, and anthropocentrism in the rise and operation of international law, while CRT brings race into sharp focus. Both show these transcendental events are in tension with representations of the discipline conveyed via its textbooks.

Despite their value in revealing international law's controversial character—perhaps because of this—CRT and TWAIL have experienced steady resistance to their critiques. According to E. Tendayi Achiume and Devon Carbado, orthodox scholars treat TWAIL and CRT as "second class scholarship," disparaging these traditions as "outside the boundaries of the presumptively neutral scholarly conventions."[11] To return to our rhetorical question about disciplinary reluctance, it is no accident the textbooks cohere with the racial proclivities of the field, constructing some and not others as legitimate knowers. By omitting white supremacy and racialized exploitation from deliberations about international law, orthodox scholars can claim to teach the subject in apolitical or pragmatic ways. For example, James Crawford demanded we "leave behind the glacial uplands of juristic abstraction" for "theoretical constructions have done much to obscure realities."[12] Hostility to critical theory coheres with the knowledge bubble Schlag laments, helping to preserve an exclusionary epistemic project. To paraphrase Schlag again, most authors of textbooks "sort of know" about international law's practices of domination but prefer to hide this knowledge from their students.[13]

It is international law's success as an epistemic project that poses the greatest conundrum for critical scholars. Consider this passage from Antony Anghie:

> I teach my introductory public international law [course] in the classical, positivist form... I think teaching the classical approach is an important part of the larger project of teaching what we might broadly term "critical international law"... I believe it is my duty towards my students, whatever their reasons for taking my course, to teach the classical perspective... the classical positivist approach, which presents international law in its own terms as it were... [This] seems indispensable for other inquiries, whether critical or philosophical; and it is the foundation of the practice of international law.[14]

While many critical scholars would endorse Anghie's impulse, his approach occludes more than it reveals. Once we endorse a Eurocentric epistemic frame, what is logical for scholars to critique? It is worth acknowledging that laws favored by Eurocentric international law align with the predatory anthropocentric episteme established during the colonial era. As scholars of racial capitalism demonstrated, racialized exploitation was instrumental to capitalism: colonialism, imperialism, slavery, and genocide remain the building blocks for our current order. An incongruity between international law and racialized exploitation does not provoke the dissatisfaction critical scholars suffer. Rather, it manifests for the scholar who endorses the underlying epistemology while rejecting the normative agenda. These are impossible to reconcile, generating a schizophrenic commitment to the same system they condemn.[15]

Having experienced the conundrum, we empathize with Anghie's premise. Still, to declare a positivist pedagogy for international law as indispensable reinforces the blind spots that permeate the frame. It implies that, irrespective of its shortcomings, it possesses value beyond mystification. By legitimizing the underlying epistemology, international legal scholars reproduce relations of power, implicating themselves in practices of domination.

In the following section, we extend our analysis to the relationship between colonialism, epistemology, and race.

3. THE ADVANCE OF A COLONIAL EPISTEME

Colonialism was both a world-making and world-ending project. European monarchies, eventually empires, ventured in search of worlds that lay beyond their own. There was a cultivated romanticism to the expeditions as peoples challenged material limits to navigation and psychology. However, it was not a sightseeing journey alone. A mercantilist impulse guided them, a subtext hidden in plain sight. They waylaid conquest, settlement, and expropriation in the cargo hold, oppressions that gradually rose to the level of leitmotif of the era.

The heights and effects of European imperialism were dramatic, spreading with pace across geography, bodies, and minds. Both the logic and dynamics of colonialism came to imbue the organization and normativity of the world in at least three interrelated ways. First, through varied processes of dispossession and expropriation, the colonial apparatus fused human existence with novel circuits of capital. Second, its proponents corralled perceptions of ecology within the epistemic borders of an anthropocentric worldview. A third logic complemented both the first and second: the development and circulation of modern racial categories. These relational and imbricated processes operated concurrently, translated through law and materializing internally and externally as they extended across societies.

Consider the term *resource*. We define it as "a stock or supply of money, materials, staff, and other assets that can be drawn on by a person or organization in order to function effectively."[16] Embedded within popular nomenclature, this conceptualization is epistemologically deterministic, codifying alienation, fetishism, and instrumentalism within our understanding of ecology. Of course, the concept is ahistorical and contingent, conflicting with the many non-anthropocentric worldviews that flourished prior to the colonial era. Yet, because "resource" is divorced from the underlying epistemic project, the term acquires a neutral character. The epistemic project that came to dominate during the colonial era suffocated non-European peoples, forcing them to adapt to a way of knowing of neither their making nor their preference. It was also contra-intellectual: Europeans no longer engaged the world as it was but only as they wanted it to be.

The circulation of European prejudice as universal knowledge was paramount to the ascendancy of Europe during and since the imperial-colonial period. The international was the "international society of the white race,"[17] as known publicist John Westlake declared. Such ascendancy required a two-part equation: the denial of local epistemes and the elevation of Eurocentrism as the singular bastion of rational thought, both of which were contingent on the de-humanization of non-Europeans.[18] Via this equation, the utility of whiteness and a corresponding Blackness emerged: context-specific, contingent, and malleable, co-constituted dialectically through the struggle for epistemic dominance.

The second half of the perverse epistemic equation required constant propagation. Nascent European states supported their world-making ambitions through exploitative economic activities and muscular politico-military apparatuses. Their efforts were brutal and effective. Still, neither would have enjoyed the success they did were it not for the accompanying epistemic framework. As Ngũgĩ wa Thiong'o observed, the morning of the chalk and the blackboard followed the night of the gunboat.[19] Through the former, Europe legitimized hierarchical constructs that naturalized the superiority of a white epistemic subject position, championing their way of knowing as the singular path toward the maximization of human potential. In the process, Europe established a firm yet "flexible positional superiority" as the universal paragon of humanity itself.[20]

Samir Amin further expounded on Eurocentrism in compelling ways, highlighting its substantive and aspirational characteristics. Perhaps Eurocentrism's most durable contribution to the trajectory of humanity is a linear vision of history. This was a precursor to the normalization of a juvenile classification of human societies: developed, developing, under-developed, or least-developed. Via a timeline and a template, Europe claimed both human apex and future, debasing entire societies in evolutionary terms. Other trappings of Eurocentrism relevant to international law include liberalism as civilizational theory, nation-state boundaries, capitalist economic ordering, enclosure, and many more. "Within the framework of Eurocentrism's impossible project, the ideology of the market—with its democratic complement, assumed to be almost a given—has become a veritable theology, bordering on the grotesque."[21] These trappings form a subjective epistemology with universalist pretensions.

> European Enlightenment philosophy . . . is founded on a tradition of mechanistic materialism that posits chains of causal determination. Principal among these is that science and technology determine by their autonomous progress the advance of all spheres of social life. Class struggle is removed from history and replaced by a mechanistic determination that imposes itself as an external force, a law of nature. This crude materialism, often opposed to idealism, is in fact its twin: these two ideologies are the two sides of the same coin.[22]

European states achieved these outcomes through processes of racialization of body but equally of space, place, and time. Despite its chauvinistic qualities, Amin did not reduce Eurocentrism to "a banal ethnocentrism." Rather, Europe's forceful deployment of the technologies of colonialism and capitalism rationalized and naturalized its ideology globally. By imposing itself at the level of science and universal laws, first, and in the articulation of these laws into a universal social project, second, Eurocentrism overcame the contextual limits of its partial epistemological predilections.

Paradoxically, Amin condemns Eurocentrism as an "anti-universalist" phenomenon, its disinterest in empiricism meaning it neither seeks to explain nor predict the logic that guides human societies. As the logic of a truncated universalism, its proponents leverage epistemological destruction to advance Eurocentrism. In this way, they advance a logic of human objectivity through epistemic conquest, excluding the flattened and racialized *other* from the cognitive sphere,[23] folded away to epistemic object rather than an epistemic subject. This is the way of Eurocentrism and the whiteness it birthed: to fashion a world of binaries, hierarchies, and subordination.[24] Through a process of epistemic foreclosure and disavowal, European powers imprinted their outlook on the world, codifying one way of knowing at the expense of all others.

Colonialism thus manifested two forms of genocide: material and epistemic. To make a home in a place inhabited by others, the settler could either pursue coexistence, involving assimilation, or conquest, achieved through eradication. Both approaches informed colonialism, with law used to devastate the epistemological consciousnesses of the populations encountered.[25] Colonialism's triumph was its future-proofing of Eurocentrism's ascendency, sabotaging counterchallenges and the potential for alternative world-making. To understand colonialism thus demands engagement with its destructive nature. However, since destruction clashes with the positive self-perception needed to justify the current order, the system's beneficiaries transmute colonialism from destruction to evolution: banished to a (sometimes) lamentable yet profoundly historical event.[26] Religion, the human rights framework, liberal race theory, industrial and technological development, and even mass consumption advance a positive view of the world colonialism birthed. Each technology naturalizes the exploitative and hierarchical dynamics established during the colonial era and the afterlives that persist today.

As we discuss next, international law represents one of these technologies.

4. COMMITTED TO COLONIAL INTERNATIONAL LAW

Colonialism was constituted by and is constitutive of international law. CRT and TWAIL have documented the role of the regime in promoting destruction and domination. Throughout modern international law's history, European states used it to validate, among others, conquest, settlement, expropriation, and slavery. For example, during the bicentennial celebration for Britain's role in restricting its participation in the transatlantic slave trade—an exercise in transnational gaslighting if there ever was one—former British Prime Minister Tony Blair captured the brutality of European international law. "It is hard to believe that what would today be regarded as a crime against humanity" Blair proclaimed, "was lawful at the time."[27]

This was a cunning rhetorical move. Exploiting international law's permissive character, he interpreted the absence of a prohibition against slavery in positive ways, rendering England's actions lawful. Of course, this presupposes the universality of a European conception of international legality, itself contingent on Eurocentrism and white supremacy. At least Blair was consistent. In an earlier turn of phrase, he declared: "Ours are not Western values. They are values of the human spirit."[28] That he was addressing the Congress of the US after the UK and the US breached international law to invade Iraq tells us much about who is competent to speak on behalf of the human spirit.

Blair's pronouncements were consistent with European international law. Tracking the regime's history, we learn that a breed of technocrat arose alongside conquistadors to manage relations between competing imperial powers. Francisco de Vitoria, Hugo Grotius, Emer de Vattel, John Westlake, and others developed an original system of jus gentium. Its initial function was to mediate encounters between European powers outside of Europe. More outer-state law than international, they customized rules to accommodate the activities Europeans might clash around. Doctrines of *terra nullius*, conquest, and native title facilitated settlement and exclusive possession, while others such as terra communis and the right to trade enabled the rise of mercantile, gradually capitalist economic relations. The law of nations' subsequent function was to universalize a vision of the world couched in what we defined above as Eurocentrism.

Outside its academic societies and textbooks, international law enjoys a vile history, with the volume of its violence bordering on the banal. As a technology of colonialism, European powers were less motivated in international law's capacity to regulate relations between equally sovereign states than in its ability to legitimize takings from non-Europeans. Like other technologies, international law advanced the causes of material expropriation and epistemic destruction. Examples are plenty. Under the doctrine of *uti possidetis*, Third World states were shackled to the artificial borders colonial powers established. Theories of statehood remain wedded to a vision of peoples articulated in Vienna in the early nineteenth century and codified in Montevideo a century later. That Indigenous peoples played no part in notions of sovereignty is inconvenient but immaterial. And the principle of inter-temporality ensures that victims of colonialism can never use international law to hold European states accountable for the barbarism they continue to benefit from.

As a vehicle for the universalization of Eurocentrism, international law normalized the colonial and racial hierarchies that now permeate our existence. To quote Westlake, international law is the purview of "fully sovereign states of the white society whose rules are that law."[29] International law was a conduit of white supremacy, disseminating a racial hierarchy through its construction of racial categories embedded in its civilizational discourses.[30] The epistemological character of these discourses is evident in the works of international law's *patrons*. Here, the epistemic subjectivity of non-European states and peoples was measured against their proximity to white rationality and personality. In this way, they predicated Eurocentric thought on epistemological and ontological premises that are themselves white supremacist, imbuing international law with what Gurminder K. Bhambra terms methodological whiteness: the assimilation of colonial and racist premises into international law's very methods and normativity.[31]

We return to the inclusion referenced above. Irrespective of mid-twentieth century "formal decolonization," racialized subject positions remain omnipresent in the functioning of international institutions and epistemic practices.[32] Epistemic enclosure ensures non-European states participate within the parameters established, extending from their racialized assumptions, evidence, and methodologies to the operation of Black and Indigenous bodies within racially hierarchical knowledge-producing spaces. Epistemic foreclosure delineates the type of social renewal international law tolerates and promotes. Through its language of inclusive universality, international law holds yet occludes the global color line: ongoing racial formations and their distributions and consequences continue to play out *within* and *through* international law. As Westlake volunteers, "the international society which develops international law... is composed of all the states of European blood."[33]

International legal scholars have only recently considered the epistemic violence endemic to a regime of international law devised to advance conquest. For example, Achiume and Carbado proclaim that an "epistemological legitimacy problem" prejudices international law.[34] Despite the frame's contingent, cultural, and ideological character, its proponents describe the knowledge upon which international law rests as universal and eternal. European states thus continue to posture as the singular cognizers of a planetary-wide, yet context-less, universality. International law facilitated the creation and export of knowledge to regions the frame subordinated, inhibiting the ability of racialized peoples to develop and champion their preferred ways of knowing and being. Like Westlake, James Lorimer is illustrative: "the right of undeveloped races, like the right of undeveloped individuals, is a right not to recognition as to what they are not, but to guardianship—that is, to guidance—in becoming that to which they are capable, in realising their special ideals."[35]

Notwithstanding the counternarratives that have refashioned contemporary understandings of international law, both orthodox and critical scholars remain entrapped within international law and its Eurocentric episteme. Luis Eslava and Sundhya Pahuja declare that "rather than replacement, TWAIL scholarship is more interested in overcoming international law's problems while still remaining committed to the idea of an international normative regime."[36] Anghie and Bhupinder Chimni make a similar argument.[37] While perhaps exercising a deeper awareness of the tension, critical race theorists also recognize the CRT critique is not a call to abandon law as a reconstructive project.[38]

One reason for the enduring commitment to international law is the fallacy that guides our understanding of the frame. Textbooks, journals, and institutions represent international law as a system of social order: how might we mediate relations among equally sovereign states? The essence of sovereignty is one of internal rather than external restraint. International law is a compromise between sovereigns' self-imposed limitations to a putatively natural state of autonomy. By assenting to reciprocal restrictions that corral state behavior, we avert the chaos made inevitable by sovereignty. Capitalist modes of social organization exacerbate the need for international law. In a world of scarce resources, capitalism spotlights the contradictions inherent to doctrines of nonintervention, self-determination, and self-help. Under these circumstances, a regime of international law is sensible, promising even. Unfortunately, it is also wrong.

The commitment of critical scholars raises questions about the mainstreaming of critique and the disciplinary boundaries in operation. Modern Europe sought to rationalize the world within its capitalist prism. Material and political inequality are endemic to the order, including its regulatory frame. Whether we account for formal inequality in the UN Security Council, plutocratic governance at the World Bank and IMF, or the unidirectional nature of intervention and violence under Article 1, international law is much more than a system of social order. Rather, it is a system of white supremacist structuring. The racial dynamics are part of this process, even if they began as instrumental rather than strictly teleological. Racism was another technology deployed to legitimize the exploitative dynamics at the core of the burgeoning global order.

This dynamic poses a fundamental problem for scholars of international law, at least those motivated by anti-racism. Commitment to and intelligibility in international law implicitly requires a commitment to a Eurocentric epistemology, including its particularized racialized thinking and articulations, upon which both historic and contemporary practices of racial domination sit.[39] By insisting—or at least accepting—that the prejudices of the past must guide our path into the future, we foreclose both imagination and aspiration. From this vantage point, international law as anti-racism becomes "unrealistic" or "unreasonable," allowing white ignorance to roam unchecked.

We turn to the interplay between race, ignorance, and international law.

5. WHITE IGNORANCE AND THE IMPOSSIBILITY OF RACIAL JUSTICE

Talk of structural domination, including cultural misrecognition, economic maldistribution, and political misrepresentation, is unwelcome in international legal circles. The academy has actively excluded debates about the consequences of class, race, and gender situatedness on both the structure and operation of the regime. While today's environment is less antagonistic, domination, exploitation, hegemony, mystification, and racism still receive short shrift in international legal textbooks. "Despite their enlightened beginnings, at no time [do authors of textbooks] account for the role of epistemology in framing their manner of thinking about international law or its role in organizing international relations."[40] Since publicists do not recognize let alone problematize either whiteness or white supremacy in international law, representations of the relationship between race, racism, and international law remain stunted.[41] How do we explain the resistance?

As corpus and ideology, international law is laden with what Charles Mills labels white ignorance.[42] Central to this phenomenon is a denial of the centrality of racial domination in our milieus and institutions. In contrast to conventional ignorance, understood as a lack of knowledge, white ignorance reveals both its false belief and racial privilege. It is less about "not knowing" of racial domination's prominence but of actively maintaining a "way of knowing" that refuses to acknowledge its presence. The rationale of cultivated ignorance is obvious. Acknowledging the legacies of racism that permeate modernity would both implicate and destabilize other social constructs upon which our epistemology relies: liberalism, meritocracy, and equality, putatively defining features of European societies and structures. White ignorance is a way of fighting back, of resisting enlightenment about racial injustice, and, as Mills affirms, of "refus[ing] to go quietly."[43]

White ignorance is useful in centering the epistemic violence of international law. At its core, international law naturalizes a contingent and contextual epistemology informed by an abstract cognitive agent, whether the sovereign state or the neutral publicist. Such abstraction serves an epistemic function. By shearing the state and scholar of their historic, geographic, and ideological specificity, the regime vanishes the origins, contours, and requirements of international law's episteme. Within this purportedly universal framework, we preserve Eurocentrism and white supremacy by obfuscating the epistemological commitments. European jurists mapped categories of savage, civilized, and human to advance imperialism. International law was a narrative rather than a concept, built upon presuppositions tailored to bolster European expansion. That publicists still speak of the doctrine of discovery when peoples inhabited the lands purportedly discovered verifies the irrelevance of empirical evidence to the story of international law.[44] White ignorance is thus an invaluable concept to better understand our continued loyalty to a myth of dubious origins.

Ignorance is a layered, impelling concept. "When reviewing the current literature in the epistemology of ignorance," Nadja El Kassar observes, we locate three conceptions: "(1) ignorance as lack of knowledge/true belief, (2) ignorance as actively upheld false outlooks and (3) ignorance as substantive epistemic practice."[45] Active ignorance and ignorance as epistemic practice are critical when reflecting on international law. We take them in turn.

Charles Mills and José Medina help us decipher the commitment of international legal scholars to a flawed frame. Active ignorance comprises the "participation of the subject . . . [in] a battery of defence mechanisms" designed to thwart any disturbance to the status quo.[46] Publicists, for example, are cognizant of the (racialized) colonial practices that undergird international law. However, such recognition occupies a range. Most common is a willingness to recognize colonialism as a historical fact. Less popular is any interest in exploring its contemporary consequences,[47] let alone to critique the colonial-laced partialities embedded in the regime. Irrespective of the position one holds—critical or orthodox—evangelical commitment to the project rarely falters.

In keeping with Mills, there is another level altogether. What El Kassar terms "agential" ignorance reveals something beyond disempowering psychology. Rather than dissonance as defense, we confront active support for the spread of ignorance. To preserve a fabricated reality, the epistemic agent deploys *offense* mechanisms to avoid confronting a situatedness that calls into question their epistemic frame. Eve Tuck and K. Wayne Yang describe these as "move[s] to white innocence."[48] Scholars seek to rescue their discipline and themselves from a rival perception or a *feel-bad* history. It involves a doubling down on contentious epistemic boundaries such as international law's intrinsic benevolence. These moves represent the peculiar shades of self-unknowing white ignorance, soothing white anxiety, while maintaining the positional superiority of methodological whiteness.[49] The result is an interpretive impoverishment that derails international law's emancipatory potential.[50]

We turn to Linda Alcoff to explain ignorance as "substantive epistemic practice." Like El Kassar, she introduces an agential component but adds to it a structural one. Much of the scholarship on epistemological ignorance adopts a complementary viewpoint: "there are identities and social locations and modes of belief formation, all produced by structural social conditions of a variety of sorts, that are in some cases epistemically disadvantaged or defective."[51] It is not only about a class of publicists ignoring the flaws within the regime, but of structures that actively cultivate ignorance. When seen through the lens of substantive epistemic practice, we appreciate the epistemic agent's "attitudes and habits" are informed by and merge with an epistemology of ignorance.[52] The result is a frame of international law that nurtures the identities of scholars—agents—who believe in it despite its contradictions.

Both forms of ignorance yield a system untroubled with the practices of domination propagated by international law. Beyond critical scholarship, itself peripheral, the picture most publicists hold is of an egalitarian, inclusive, and progressive regime. If they acknowledge racism, sexism, heteronormativity, able-bodiedness, or classism at all, they treat manifestations of partiality as deviant rather than systemic. This approach allows international legal scholars to disavow the regime's history and to disassociate it from the epistemology that produced it. For critical scholars like Anghie—and us—this is an enigma. While championing a radical reorientation of legal scholarship, we do so within an ideal rather than an actual framework. Because of this handicap, the illusion of the universality and legitimacy of international law disseminated by white ignorance preserves its validity.

The implications of white ignorance for questions about international law's relationship to the race debate are profound. While it would be disingenuous to think about the trajectory of international law without accounting for virulent patterns of racialization and racism, the academy has done just that, vanishing race from its agenda.[53]

> [Publicists] demonstrate a remarkable ability to overlook their ethno-chauvinism. That is the essence of epistemic and hermeneutical injustice. The AJIL excludes debates on race and international law. [AJIL] Unbound makes race invisible altogether. Non-Eurocentric perspectives enjoy diminished status, unless they are measured against the dominant one and preferably by a white scholar . . . [N]on-racialised scholars cannot appreciate how their approach toward racialised academics places [them] at an unfair disadvantage. Even in the face of crickets, we are compelled, over and over, to justify the relevance of our social experience.[54]

With the palpable links between international legal history and the transatlantic slave trade and with the countless critiques of international law's role in calcifying colonial legacies and a neocolonial future, white ignorance *gains revelatory* potential. Orthodox scholars are not ignorant in the lay sense but in the active and epistemic forms purported by Mills and Alcoff.[55] They actively ignore racial inequalities and subordination as they manifest within international law. "Self-deception, bad faith, evasion, and misrepresentation" ensure the preservation of the position of privilege they occupy.[56] Without the crutch of cognitive dissonance, we recognize our complicity in spreading ignorance in international law's move to white innocence.

This is neither an individual nor a group affliction alone. As Alcoff observes, epistemic blind spots are part of a substantive epistemic practice. Social milieus and institutions produce the identities of publicists, with many benefiting from the material and/or psychological wages of whiteness. While weary of scapegoating the system, the attitudes and habits of international legal scholars are intertwined with a structure saturated with white privilege and dependent on not knowing of its own racial predation. Liberal constructs such as color-blindness, meritocracy, and equality conspire to create an epistemology of ignorance that nurtures flawed cognition. Consider two seemingly infantile questions about international law: can we even describe it as international if its authors denied sovereignty to non-European peoples when developing it, and how do we account for the manifestations of its afterlives? When we perceive ignorance as a substantive epistemic practice, we recognize that international law as constituted could not exist without an epistemology of ignorance. A key consequence of this pattern of cognitive dysfunction is that the dominant group will lack understanding of the world they have made. Because of the "racial fantasyland" international legal scholars inhabit, they cannot account for either white supremacy or racial justice in their thinking. The cognitive model they have committed to "precludes self-transparency and genuine understanding of all social realities."[59] They can only maintain the frame by doubling down on the epistemological ignorance that entraps them.

To illustrate, in an essay published on the European Journal of International Law's virtual platform—EJIL Talk—Patryk Labuda chastises critical scholars, the authors included, for "false binaries" as they pertain to the relationship between race and international law:

> [There] have also been voices that situate the Ukraine war and international legal responses thereto in a wider context, including by criticising the role of human rights in inciting the war, the West's neglect of Global South crises, or international law's Euro-centrism. While these critiques are well intentioned, I want to offer some critical thoughts on these critical (and nominally progressive) responses—a critique of the critique, if you will. I argue that these calls for introspection on the part of some Western and Global South international lawyers inadvertently reproduce a Western-centric vision of the world.[60]

Labuda unpacks the situatedness of Ukrainians and other subaltern Europeans. He decries the false binary of white and Black proposed by critical scholars who bemoaned the academy's double standards in its response to Russia's invasion of Ukraine. Critical scholars have lamented the frenzy of academic initiatives launched in support of Ukrainian scholars with the meek solidarity afforded to other scholars following the invasions of Afghanistan, Iraq, Libya, Palestine, and many other Third World states. Most fascinating about Labuda's spirited riposte is his inability to contemplate the coexistence of multiple truths, or the necessity of relational modes of analysis in the understanding of race. We need not contest any of his claims about Eastern Europe, Ukraine, and their struggle for self-determination; frankly, it has little to do with the critique Third World scholars leveled against double standards.

> What has Russia's invasion of Ukraine reaffirmed for racialised scholars of international law? . . . Alongside the outpouring of sympathy, solidarity, and sundry demands for accountability, the international legal academy's response has again exposed the ontological parameters of international law, and the fundamental space whiteness occupies within it. To illustrate, consider the following scenario. We recently attended an expert panel at a leading British university, organised to deliberate the war. No less than ten (white) scholars spoke about assorted aspects of it, with only one alluding to the issue of race. During

the Q&A, we asked about its erasure from the debate—despite its prevalence in the war and the response thereto—and were met with a violent outburst from one (white) panelist who declared, with a mixture of entitlement and bile, that "the past failings of international law have no place in this discussion... none!" Seething at the suggestion that European sympathy was racially selective, he seemed to overlook the irony of his jingoism.[61]

The authors of this passage channeled W.E.B. Du Bois, pulling back the veil of white ignorance. They sought to expose scholars of international law to the racial injustices those on the sharp end of white supremacy suffer. Neither the panelists nor Labuda could accept the critique is not about past failings of international law but of a structural dynamic that erases truths that do not conform to the understandings of its dominant strata.

Labuda's response was consistent with both forms of white ignorance. First, he deployed a battery of defense mechanisms to safeguard the status quo. For example, while declaring his sympathy for the plight of "Africa"—incidentally, Africa's plight is situated apart from international law—he has no appetite for either epistemic blind spots or racial injustices. Delegitimizing Third World and racialized scholars' capacity for epistemic agency, he paternalistically accuses them of false consciousness, of blindly embracing Eurocentrism and committing the worst racial injustice of all: misrepresenting shades of whiteness.

Second, he also went on the offense. Endorsing the colonial logic that guided the development of international law, Labuda uses its structural prejudices to fight back. For example, instead of engaging with a critique of racial double standards, clear to scholars racialized as non-white and to laypeople alike, he rushes to deny their experience and to re-center whiteness. *Nominally progressive* Third World scholars, he tells us, have failed to appreciate the Eurocentrism of their critique. Next, he spotlights his background as a legal scholar who has "spent [his] adult life working in and on international law in Africa" as a preemptive against accusations of racial insensitivity or ignorance.[62] Like his predecessors, he sees no contradiction between a white European pontificating about the African continent as a collective mass while chastising non-Europeans for flattening discourse about Europe. Despite "most of [his] post-graduate academic affiliations [being] in the West,"[63] he believes his work on Africa has provided him with the competence to critique the racialized experiences of the native.

Shunting aside a truth about race situatedness and experiences of white supremacy in international law, he worried white victims would suffer the indignity of misrecognition. Labuda is not a lone wolf, and his intervention circulated approvingly among members of the European Society of International Law (ESIL). Like the enraged panelist, members of the ESIL were aggrieved at the proposition that there is something about international law they do not understand (or deny).

As Labuda's garden variety epistemic violence highlights, the maintenance of positional superiority of the white, western male as the ideal agent of international law's epistemology knows no bounds.[64] We paraphrase Mills's earlier quote: ignorance as epistemic practice prevents the dominant group from understanding the law they themselves made.

Because of white ignorance's prominence in international law, most publicists are ill-equipped to evaluate the crucial ways race influences its design and operation. This is the nature of ignorance as substantive epistemic practice: deliberating race is difficult because the structure nurtures our ignorance about its racial dynamics, generating flawed cognitive functions. White ignorance explodes the gaps in the conceptual frame that guides our thinking. Why are scholars of the Labuda variety—comfortable commenting on the racial dynamics of international law without engaging with scholarship on race—far more common than those who problematize its operation as a scholarly debate? We are thinking of E. Tendayi Achiume, Brenna Bhandar, Adelle Blackett, and Vasuki Nesiah, not to mention the editors of this collection. Recall the international legal academy has consistently excluded race from scrutiny.

Stated otherwise, an international legal frame steeped in white ignorance is purposefully inadequate to grasp racial injustice. Many white scholars—and some racialized ones—are content censoring and censuring race when the critique proves overly revealing of their racial privilege and incongruent with their outlook. International law is thus incapable of countering the racialized inequalities that corrupt our discipline, not to say our existence.

6. CONCLUSION

Derrick Bell observed that any true awareness of race requires an understanding of the Rules of Racial Standing:

> As an individual's understanding of these rules increases, there will be more and more instances where one can discern their workings. Using this knowledge, one gains the gift of knowing racism, its essence, its goals, even its remedies. The price of this knowledge is the frustration that follows recognition that no amount of public prophecy, no matter its accuracy, can either repeal the Rules of Racial Standing or prevent their operation.[65]

We end with Bell not because his pessimism feels familiar, but because he returns us to our starting point: what can critical scholars motivated by anti-racism logically challenge when operating within a frame of international law constituted by and constitutive of white supremacy? As Carbado and Achiume underscore, blunting the hard end of the system is necessary and timely anti-racist work. Racialized scholars and scholars of race and law are not naïve about international law's white supremacist epistemology.[66] They recognize the harm it commits to its racialized subjects, the corresponding effect on their knowledge production, and how law's epistemological violence formulated its trajectory and evolution.

Where we are less comfortable is negotiating our own scholarly entanglement in epistemologies of white ignorance. Besides "clear eyes," teaching the banality of racialized violence from the belly of the beast requires transparency about its effects on our knowledge. The internalization of white supremacy and its consequences, Saidiya Hartman tells us, remains a negotiation with racialized colonial violence inherent in our inherited knowledge.[67] We must counter the naturalization and flattening of racism and racialization, as well as our complicities in maintaining the "conceptual incoherence of the black framework of assumptions" within international law's white "dominant framework" and its knowledge-producing spaces.[68] Otherwise, we risk falling into a familiar trap: promoting white supremacy through the banality of white solipsism. Without the active pursuit of an anti-racist agenda, our research and pedagogy are at risk of perpetuating a state of cultivated ignorance, maintaining international law's operation as a metaphoric mastery over the world.

NOTES

* This chapter was written and finalised prior to the events of October 7 and the following attacks by Israel on Gaza and Occupied Palestinian Territories. These attacks remain continuing, and have resulted in allegations of genocide brought before the International Court of Justice.

1. Pierre Schlag, "The Knowledge Bubble - Something Amiss in Expertopia," in *In Search of Contemporary Legal Thought*, ed. Justin Desautels-Stein and Christian Tomlins (Cambridge: Cambridge University Press, 2017), 430.

2. Schlag, *Expertopia*, 429.

3. Schlag, *Expertopia*, 440.

4. Mohsen al Attar, "The Peculiar Double-Consciousness of TWAIL," *Indonesian Journal of International Law* 19, no. 2 (2022): 242.

5. Ana Luísa Bernardino, "Going by the Book: What International Law Textbooks Teach Us Not to Know," in *International Law's Invisible Frames*, ed. Andrea Bianchi and Moshe Hirsch (Oxford: Oxford University Press, 2021), 298.

6. Mohsen al Attar, "Must International Legal Pedagogy Remain Eurocentric?," *Asian Journal of International Law* 11, no. 1 (2021): 182.

7. Bernadino, *Going*, 300.

8. Bernadino, *Going*, 303.

9. al Attar, "Pedagogy," 182.

10. Olivia Umurerwa Rutazibwa, "From the Everyday to IR: In Defence of the Strategic Use of the R-Word," *Post-Colonial Studies* 19, no. 2 (2016): 192.

11. E. Tendayi Achiume and Devon Carbado, "Critical Race Theory Meets Third World Approaches to International Law," *UCLA Law Review* 67, no. 6 (2021): 1491.

12. Bernardino, *Going*, 299.

13. Schlag, *Expertopia*, 430.

14. Antony Anghie, "Critical Pedagogy Symposium: Critical Thinking and Teaching as Common Sense - Random Reflections," *Opinio Juris,* August 30, 2020. http://opiniojuris.org/2020/08/31/critical-pedagogy-symposium-critical-thinking-and-teaching-as-common-sense-random-reflections/.

15. Mohsen al Attar, "TWAIL: A Paradox within a Paradox," *International Community Law Review* 22 (2020): 191.

16. "Resource," Encyclopedia.com, accessed January 25, 2023, https://www.encyclopedia.com/science-and-technology/computers-and-electrical-engineering/computers-and-computing/resource.

17. John Westlake, *Chapters on the Principles of International Law* (Cambridge: Cambridge University Press, 1894), 198.

18. Nancy Tuana, "Feminist Epistemology: the Subject of Knowledge," in *The Routledge Handbook of Epistemic Injustice,* ed. Ian James Kidd et al. (London and New York: Routledge, 2017), 129.

19. Ngũgĩ wa Thiong'o, *Decolonizing the Mind The Politics of African Literature* (London: James Curry, 1986), 9.

20. Edward Said, *Orientalism* (New York: Penguin Press, 2019), 7.

21. Samir Amin, *Eurocentrism: Modernity, Religion and Democracy: A Critique of Eurocentrism and Culturalism* (New York: Monthly Review Press, 2009), 112.

22. Amin, *Eurocentrism,* 80.

23. Tuana, "Feminist," 129.

24. Achille Mbembé, "Necropolitics," *Public Culture* 15, no. 1 (2003): 24.

25. Attempted epistemicide has been met with the tenacious guarding and—where possible—reinvigoration of indigenous knowledge production and consciousness.

26. Manu Vimalassery et al., "Introduction - On Colonial Unknowing," *Theory and Event* 19, no. 4 (2016).

27. David Smith, "Blair: Britain's 'Sorrow' for Shame of Slave Trade," *The Guardian,* November 26, 2006, https://www.theguardian.com/politics/2006/nov/26/race.immigrationpolicy.

28. Smith, "Blair."

29. Westlake, *Chapters,* 190.

30. Chantal Thomas, "Racial Justice and International Law," in *The Oxford Handbook of Race and Law in the United States,* ed. Devon Carbado et al. (Oxford: Oxford University Press, forthcoming).

31. Gurminder K. Bhambra, "Brexit, Trump, and 'methodological whitenesss': on the misrecognition of race and class," *The British Journal of Sociology* 68, no. S1 (2017).

32. Francisco Valdes and Sumi Cho, "'Critical Race Materialism': Theorizing Justice in the Wake of Global Neoliberalism," *Connecticut Law Review* 43 (2011): 1568.

33. John Westlake, *International Law* (Cambridge: Cambridge University Press 1904), 40.

34. Achiume and Carbado, "Critical," 1491.

35. James Lorimer, *The Institutes of the Law of Nations; a Treatise of the Jural Relations of Separate Political Communities* (Edinburgh and London: William Blackwood & Sons, 1883), 157.

36. Luis Eslava and Sundhya Pahuja, "Beyond the (Post) Colonial: TWAIL and the Everyday Life of International Law," *Journal of Law and Politics in Africa, Asia and Latin America* 45 (2012): 206.

37. Antony Anghie, *Imperialism, Sovereignty and the Making of International Law* (Cambridge: Cambridge University Press, 2007), 317–18; Bhupinder Chimni, "Third World Approaches to International Law: A Manifesto" *International Community Law Review* 8, no. 1 (2006): 22–26.

38. Achiume and Carbado, "Critical," 1498.

39. Ramón Grosfugal, "Epistemic Racism/Sexism, Westernized Universities and the Four Genocides/Epistemicides of the Long Sixteenth Century," in *Eurocentrism, Racism and Knowledge: Debates on History and Power in Europe and the Americas,* ed. Marta Araújo and Silvia Rodríguez Maeso (New York: Palgrave Macmillan: 2015), 23.

40. al Attar, "Pedagogy," 185.

41. Brenna Bhandar, *Colonial Lives of Property: Law, Land, and Racial Regimes of Ownership* (Durham: Duke University Press, 2018), 15.

42. Charles Mills, "White Ignorance," in *Race and Epistemologies of Ignorance,* ed. Shannon Sullivan and Nancy Tuana (New York: New York University Press: 2007). We are, of course, not the first to explore the realm of white ignorance in international law; see Christopher Gevers, "'Unwhitening the World': Rethinking Race and International Law," *UCLA Law Review* 67, no. 6 (2021); E. Tendayi Achiume, "Transnational Racial (In)Justice in Liberal Democratic Empire," *Harvard Law Review Forum* 134 (2021).

43. Mills, "Ignorance," 13.

44. José Medina, *The Epistemology of Resistance Gender and Racial Oppression, Epistemic Injustice, and the Social Imagination* (Oxford: Oxford University Press, 2013), 35.

45. Nadja El Kassar, "What Ignorance Really Is: Examining the Foundations of Epistemology of Ignorance," *Social Epistemology* 32, no. 5 (2018): 301.

46. Medina, *Resistance,* 58.

47. Vimalassery et al., "Unknowing."

48. Eve Tuck and K. Wayne Yang, "Decolonization is Not a Metaphor," *Decolonization: Indigeneity, Education and Society* 1, no. 1 (2012): 3.

49. Charles Mills, *The Racial Contract* (Ithaca and London: Cornell University Press, 1997).

50. Medina, *Resistance,* 105.

51. Linda Martín Alcoff, "Epistemologies of Ignorance: Three Types," in *Race and Epistemologies of Ignorance,* ed. Shannon Sullivan and Nancy Tuana (New York: New York University Press, 2007): 39–40.

52. Medina, *Resistance,* 39.

53. See for example: James Thuo Gathii, "Studying Race in International Law Scholarship Using a Social Science Approach," *Chicago Journal of International Law* 22, no. 1 (2021); Mohsen al Attar and Claire Smith, "Racial Capitalism and the Dialectics of Development: Exposing the Limits and Lies of International Economic Law," *Law and Critique* (2022), https://doi.org/10.1007/s10978-022-09336-z.

54. Mohsen al Attar, "Subverting Racism in/through International Law Scholarship," *Opinio Juris,* March 3, 2021, http://opiniojuris.org/2021/03/03/subverting-racism-in-international-law-scholarship/.

55. Mills, "Ignorance," 17; Alcoff, "Epistemologies of Ignorance: Three Types," 39–40.

56. Mills, "Ignorance," 17.

57. Mills, *Contract*, 18–19.

58. Patryk Labuda, "On Eastern Europe, 'Whataboutism' and 'West(s)plaining': Some Thoughts on International Lawyers' Responses to Ukraine," *EJIL Talk,* April 12, 2022,

https://www.ejiltalk.org/on-eastern-europe-whataboutism-and-westsplaining-some-thoughts-on-international-lawyers-responses-to-ukraine/.

59. Mohsen al Attar et al., "Everybody Knows About Racism, Goddam! Pathways in the Struggle Against the Racialised Universe of International Law," *Opinio Juris*, April 5, 2022, https://opiniojuris.org/2022/04/05/a-corrective-methodology-pathways-in-the-struggle-against-the-racialised-universe-of-international-law/.

60. Labuda, "West(s)plaining."

61. Labuda, "West(s)plaining."

62. Said, speaking of positional superiority, notes the idea of European identity as a superior one in comparison with all the non-European peoples. "There is in addition the hegemony of European ideas about the Orient, themselves reiterating European superiority over Oriental backwardness, usually overriding the possibility that a more independent, or more skeptical, thinker might have had different views on the matter. In a quite constant way, Orientalism depends for its strategy on this flexible positional superiority, which puts the Westerner in a whole series of possible relationships with the Orient without ever losing him the relative upper hand." Said, *Orientalism*, 7.

63. Derrick Bell, *Faces at the Bottom of the Well: The Permanence of Racism* (New York: Basic Books, 1992), 125.

64. Achiume and Carbado, "Critical," 1492–96.

65. Saidiya Hartman, "Venus in Two Acts," *Small Axe* 12, no. 2 (2008).

66. Charles Mills, "Ideology," in *The Routledge Handbook of Epistemic Injustice*, ed. Ian James Kidd et al. (New York and London: Routledge, 2015), 108.

BIBLIOGRAPHY

Achiume, Tendayi. "Transnational Racial (In)Justice In Liberal Democratic Empire." *Harvard Law Review Forum* 134 (2021): 378–397.

Achiume, Tendayi and Devon Carbado. "Critical Race Theory Meets Third World Approaches to International Law." *UCLA Law Review* 67, no. 6 (2021): 1462–1503.

al Attar, Mohsen. "Must International Legal Pedagogy Remain Eurocentric?" *Asian Journal of International Law* 11, no. 1 (2021): 176–206.

al Attar, Mohsen. "The Peculiar Double-Consciousness of TWAIL." *Indonesian Journal of International Law* 19, no. 2 (2022): 239–262.

al Attar, Mohsen. "TWAIL: A Paradox within a Paradox." *International Community Law Review* 22 (2020): 163–196.

al Attar, Mohsen, Ata Hindi and Claire Smith. "Everybody Knows About Racism, Goddam! Pathways in the Struggle Against the Racialised Universe of International Law." *Opinio Juris*, April 5, 2022. https://opiniojuris.org/2022/04/05/a-corrective-methodology-pathways-in-the-struggle-against-the-racialised-universe-of-international-law/.

al Attar, Mohsen and Claire Smith. "Racial Capitalism and the Dialectics of Development: Exposing the Limits and Lies of International Economic Law." *Law and Critique* (2022). https://doi.org/10.1007/s10978-022-09336-z.

Alcoff, Linda Martín. "Epistemologies of Ignorance: Three Types." In *Race and Epistemologies of Ignorance*, edited by Shannon Sullivan and Nancy Tuana, 39–50. New York: New York University Press, 2007.

Amin, Samir. *Eurocentrism: Modernity, Religion and Democracy: A Critique of Eurocentrism and Culturalism*. New York: Monthly Review Press, 2009.

Anghie, Antony. "Critical Pedagogy Symposium: Critical Thinking and Teaching as Common Sense - Random Reflections." *Opinio Juris,* August 30, 2020. http://opiniojuris.org/2020/08/31/critical-pedagogy-symposium-critical-thinking-and-teaching-as-common-sense-random-reflections/.

Anghie, Antony. *Imperialism, Sovereignty, and the Making of International Law*. Cambridge: Cambridge University Press, 2005.

Bernardino, Ana Luísa. "Going by the Book: What International Law Textbooks Teach Us Not To Know." in *International Law's Invisible Frames*, edited by Andrea Bianchi and Moshe Hirsch, 293–308. Oxford: Oxford University Press, 2021.

Bell, Derrick. *Faces at the Bottom of the Well: The Permanence of Racism*. New York: Basic Books, 1992.

Bhandar, Breanna. *Colonial Lives of Property: Law, Land, and Racial Regimes of Ownership*. Durham: Duke University Press, 2018.

Chimni, Bhupinder. "Third World Approaches to International Law: A Manifesto." *International Community Law Review* 8, no. 1 (2006): 3–27.

El Kassar, Nadia. "What Ignorance Really Is. Examining the Foundations of Epistemology of Ignorance." *Social Epistemology* 32 no.5, (2018): 300–310.

Eslava, Luis and Sundhya Pahuja. "Beyond the (Post) Colonial: TWAIL and the Everyday Life of International Law." *Journal of Law and Politics in Africa, Asia and Latin America* 45, (2012): 195–221.

Lorimer, James. *The Institutes of the Law of Nations; a Treatise of the Jural Relations of Separate Political Communities*. Edinburgh and London: William Blackwood & Sons, 1883.

Gathii, James Thuo. "Studying Race in International Law Scholarship Using a Social Science Approach." *Chicago Journal of International Law* 22, no. 1 (2021): 71–109.

Gevers, Christopher. "Unwhitening the World": Rethinking Race and International Law. "*UCLA Law Review* 67, no.6 (2021): 1653–1685.

Grosfoguel, Ramón. "Epistemic Racism/Sexism, Westernized Universities and the Four Genocides/Epistemicides of the Long Sixteenth Century." In *Eurocentrism, Racism and Knowledge: Debates on History and Power in Europe and the Americas,* edited by Marta Araújo and Silvia Rodríguez Maeso, 23–46. New York: Palgrave Macmillan: 2015.

Hartman, Saidiya. "Venus in Two Acts." *Small Axe* 12, no.2 (2008): 1–14.

Labuda, Patryk. "On Eastern Europe, 'Whataboutism' and 'West(s)plaining': Some Thoughts on International Lawyers' Responses to Ukraine." *EJIL Talk*, April 12, 2022. https://www.ejiltalk.org/on-eastern-europe-whataboutism-and-westsplaining-some-thoughts-on-international-lawyers-responses-to-ukraine/.

Mbembé, Achille. "Necropolitics." *Public Culture* 15, no. 1 (2003): 11–40.

Medina, José. *The Epistemology of Resistance Gender and Racial Oppression, Epistemic Injustice, and the Social Imagination*. Oxford: Oxford University Press, 2013.

Mills, Charles. "Ideology." In *The Routledge Handbook of Epistemic Injustice*, edited by Ian James Kidd, José Medina and Gaile Pohlaus, Jr., 100–112. New York and London: Routledge, 2015.

Mills, Charles. *The Racial Contract*. Ithaca and London: Cornell University Press, 1997.

Mills, Charles. "White Ignorance." in *Race and Epistemologies of Ignorance,* edited by Shannon Sullivan and Nancy Tuana, 11–38. New York: New York University Press: 2007.

Rutazibwa, Olivia Umurerwa. "From the Everyday to IR: In Defence of the Strategic Use of the R-Word." *Post-Colonial Studies* 19, no. 2 (2016): 191–200.

Said, Edward. *Orientalism.* New York: Penguin Press, 2019.

Schlag, Pierre. "The Knowledge Bubble - Something Amiss in Expertopia." In *In Search of Contemporary Legal Thought,* edited by Justin Desautels-Stein and Christian Tomlins, 428–553. Cambridge: Cambridge University Press, 2017.

Smith, David. "Blair: Britain's 'sorrow' for shame of slave trade." *The Guardian,* November 26, 2006, https://www.theguardian.com/politics/2006/nov/26/race.immigrationpolicy.

Tuana, Nancy. "Feminist epistemology: the subject of knowledge." In *The Routledge Handbook of Epistemic Injustice,* edited by Ian James Kidd, Jose Medina, and Gaile Pohlaus, Jr., 125–138. London and New York: Routledge, 2017.

Tuck, Eve and K. Wayne Yang. "Decolonization is not a metaphor." *Decolonization: Indigeneity, Education and Society* 1, no.1 (2012): 1–40.

Valdes, Francisco and Sumi Cho. ""Critical Race Materialism" Theorizing Justice in the Wake of Global Neoliberalism." *Connecticut Law Review* 43, no 5. (2011): 1513–1572.

Venzke, Ingo and Kevin Jon Heller, eds. *Contingency in International Law: On the Possibility of Different Legal Histories.* Oxford: Oxford University Press, 2021.

Vimalassery, Manu, Juliana Hu Pegues and Alyosha Goldstein. "Introduction - On Colonial Unknowing." *Theory and Event* 19, no. 4 (2016). muse.jhu.edu/article/633283.

Westlake, John. *Chapters on the principles of International Law.* Cambridge: Cambridge University Press, 1894.

Westlake, John. *International Law.* Cambridge: Cambridge University Press, 1904.

CHAPTER TWENTY

A CRITICAL RACE THEORY OF GLOBAL COLORBLINDNESS

Racial Ideology and White Supremacy

MICHELLE CHRISTIAN

INTRODUCTION

When Russia invaded Ukraine in the spring of 2022, Western media coverage was full of imagery and commentary on terrified fleeing Ukrainians, brave Ukrainian fighters, and valiant civilians who sought shelter from Russian artillery in subway tunnels and basements. European countries were sympathetically opening their doors to provide food, shelter, and other necessary resources for refugees. In their analysis of media war coverage, Moustafa Bayoumi[1] and Rafia Zakaria[2] exposed how race at the global level was shaping white sympathies, foreign policy, and nation-building. There was less commentary, however, about how the invasion of Ukraine also highlighted the ways in which global racist actions, responses, and understandings are also cloaked by discourses and practices of global colorblindness.

Unfortunately, little scholarship addresses colorblindness as a global ideological force. This is striking since race was always a global phenomenon, what Debra Thompson calls a "transnational norm,"[3] and the movement away from race, what David Theo Goldberg labels "raceless racism,"[4] occurs across global scales and geographies in similar and distinct ways. Global colorblindness works contemporaneously with "planetary" global white supremacy to "whitewash [it] out of existence."[5] Thus, we need an analysis of global colorblindness that details a complex, overlapping structural ideological apparatus that interacts with national-local ideological schemas to mask how global and national racisms continue. Essentially, there is no geographic "outside" to racial ideology.[6] Every society is globally racialized, creates and adapts to racialized structures and discourses, but responds and negotiates racialization uniquely. An investigation into global colorblindness unearths how colorblind discursive and material forms travel, land, and maneuver in every region and country across the globe.

Identifying the theoretical construction of global colorblindness, however, is absent from mainstream international law and international relations scholarship where, as many of my co-contributors argue, race is either ignored, reduced in significance, or uncritically interpreted.[7] The underuse/misuse of race is particularly astonishing considering assumptions of white superiority, racial "geopolitical paranoia,"[8] and racialized constructions of "civilized" and "backward" historically centered analyses in international relations.[9] The "international" as a field, as Chris Gevers notes, was constituted in and through whiteness.[10] Whiteness historically shaped the global "racial imaginary," the "vocabulary of race" that normalized racial hierarchy, racial science, and conflict,[11] and was used to justify *de jure* legal techniques of global white supremacy.[12] Thus, the current "conceptual invisib[ility]"[13] of racial analyses, let alone colorblind analyses, in international law despite this history tells us something about academic acquiescence to global colorblindness and the necessity for further engagement.

With this call, I combine Critical Race Theory (CRT) precepts within critical international law,[14] world-systems sociological insights, and racial ideology conceptualizations to construct a Critical Race Theory of Global Colorblindness (CRTGC). As a sociologist, I find several points CRT and international law scholars outline particularly generative. These scholars call our attention to the current de-historicized and de-racialized global moment and the tension of formal state-sovereignty within a global order of vastly unequal states regulated by colorblind international law and global institutions.[15] They expose how global neoliberal discourses and practices of developmentalism, formal equality, and human rights were configured, produced, and forced upon newly independent, former colonized states[16] creating a veneer of "natural, inevitable, and therefore, immutable" logics.[17] These logics, nonetheless, display the continuity between historically overtly racist belief and perceivably non-racist doctrine. Hence, illusions of universal progress, change, and advancement fuel global racial forgetting, misinterpretation, and silences. Collectively these practices articulate and sustain a new regime of colorblindness beyond the nation state.[18] In the remaining pages I draw and expand these ideas to outline a Critical Race Theory of Global Colorblindness (CRTGC). Concretely, CRTGC functions through (1) a global erasure of the significance of racism; (2) the global policies, procedures, and discourses of neoliberalism that represent "human rights," "developmentalism," and "securitization"; (3) six geographically spread colorblind "politicultures"; (4) a global racial hierarchy between whiteness and anti-Blackness; and (5) global white knowledge production.

CRITICAL RACE THEORY OF GLOBAL COLORBLINDNESS (CRTGC) COMPONENTS

Before conceptualizing a CRTGC it is important to highlight how racial ideology forms and operates. For critical race scholars, racial ideology emerges and reproduces through a material racial structure that gives meaning and representation to the language of race.[19] The racial structure is vast, exists in layers and multitudes, and is configured through discreet, interlocking practices in apparatus.[20] A concentrated toolkit of an "ever-changing collection of components,"[21] such as racial frames, terms, discourses, narratives, representations, schemas, visuals, and emotions, helps construct a racial worldview.[22] Racial ideology is also always in process, reacts and responds to historical "racial events,"[23] is often unconscious and hegemonic,[24] but remains rooted in the "deep schemas"[25] of white superiority and anti-Blackness that secure white racial power and white knowledge.[26] The racial ideology of the late twentieth and early twenty-first century is colorblindness.

Despite thirty years of groundbreaking scholarship on colorblindness the dominant strands suffer from a lack of global expansion.[27] The "urgency for new frontiers" in colorblind theory is palpable.[28] Therefore, I propose we shift our analytic attention on colorblindness in several ways. First, the "break" from the overtly racist past, which colorblind scholars normally ground analyses in, is distinctive but also highlights the continuation of past colorblind techniques. CRT and international law scholars have documented how colorblind legal statutes and jurisprudence were mechanisms of racism during the "overt" era of U.S. and global white supremacy.[29] Unpacking continuities with change discloses how colorblindness, as Moon-Kie Jung attests, operates at relatively "shallow depths" in comparison to the deep schemas of anti-Blackness and white supremacy.[30] Second, most colorblind sociological scholars focus on the replication and patterns of frames and discourse, and CRT scholars focus on laws and procedures. We need to do both. Third, we need to scale up our identification of colorblind practices to cross multiple levels. Race as a "globalizing ideology"[31] calls for an analysis of multiscale, interconnected, hierarchical racial social systems that charge forward with colorblindness. Fourth, by scaling up we expose the *complexity, malleability*, and *stability* of colorblindness at a transnational level that is also embedded in specific regions and geographies.[32] Complexity, malleability, and stability underscore a multitude of overlapping global colorblind forms across geographies. Finally, national white racial power solidified through colorblindness is also white global power. The "moves and investments"[33] in colorblindness, and its markings as "post-intent racism,"[34] are transnationally broad, expansive, and deep, working to reinforce a global "possessive investment in whiteness" and white supremacy in a seemingly invisible fashion.[35]

Accordingly, with this analytic shift and an attention to scale, context, and elasticity I conceptualize a CRTGC as: (1) predicated on *racist erasure*; (2) produced

A Critical Race Theory of Global Colorblindness

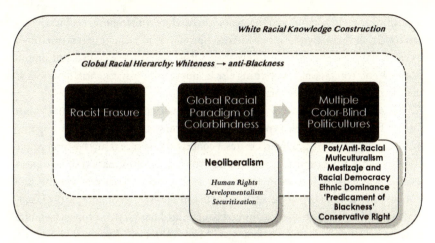

FIGURE 20.1   *A Critical Race Theory of Global Colorblindness*

through a *global racial paradigm of colorblindness* represented through the policies and practices of neoliberalism; (3) as embodying multiscale racial interactions that create complex, varying geographic *colorblind politicultures*; (4) but always reflecting a stable *global racial hierarchy*; and (5) anchored by the authority of *white racial knowledge* construction (see Figure 20.1).

RACIST ERASURE

The end of World War II, the passage of civil rights legislation in the U.S., perceived global decolonization, and the collapse of apartheid in South Africa, ushered in an era of racist erasure. Howard Winant describes this moment as a "break" from the overt racial orders of the past where now "the crisis of race and racism" embodies a "dualism:" a co-existence between commitments and discourses to formal racial equality while global white supremacy and the global racial system continues.[36] Therefore, the "racial events"[37] of the mid- to late twentieth century demanded new ways to manage and resolve "race," heightening its contradictions, but streamlining the most useful and perceivably anti-racist colorblind praxis: liberalism and capitalism. In the process, the "international retreat from race"[38] activated a deliberate erasure of racism as a global systemic force and its formation and production in European and European-influenced empire-making.

Global colorblindness forms from how the foundation of racism is erased and selectively curated and packaged to distance the past from the present. We remember what Alana Lentin labels "frozen racisms," those racisms such as the Holocaust, apartheid, and Jim Crow that act as both litmus tests for which to judge if something is racist today,[39] and incidents where white contemporary subjectivities can construct themselves as moral victors—producers of racial progress untainted by the racial prejudices of their forebearers. Other than these calcified and simplified views of "real racism," everything else is "not racism," what Lentin describes as the "denial and redefinition of racism."[40]

Racist erasure takes on further regional and national "states of denial."[41] For former European empires, expunging racist history, and the reality of ongoing European imperial geographies, creates a context where race is always somewhere else, beyond Europe, constituting an ever-evolving racial formation of European whiteness. For many post-colonial geographies there are differences between white settler societies and non-white settler societies in the avenues of how parts of colonial racial history are ignored, minimized, or denied but all point to, with empire states, a larger politics of epistemological historical racial "disavowal."[42] Overall, these racial myths created by omission of the past become hegemonic and shape how people contemporarily understand themselves, including their place in their nation and the world.

GLOBAL RACIAL PARADIGM OF COLORBLINDNESS, NEOLIBERALISM

Global colorblindness is produced by a global racial paradigm of colorblindness that embodies the politics and practices of neoliberalism. A global racial paradigm of colorblindness incorporates and scales up Vilna Bashi Treitler's conceptualization of "racial paradigms." Racial paradigms organize how "race works" and "are emblematic of the 'racial commonsense.'"[43] Paradigms tell societies "what is relevant, what we know," what is assured, and what is not that produces a racial "social structure based on racial thinking."[44] A global racial paradigm of colorblindness foregrounds racism as a global system displacing the typical emphasis on national boundaries.[45] With this focus racial practices and processes do not emerge in local/national vacuums but are entangled, in conversation, and in response to what Thompson describes as "racial transnationalism" and what Paola Bacchetta, Sunaina Maira, and Howard Winant label "global racialities": the discourses and practices bred from racialized enslavement, empire, capitalism, and post-coloniality.[46]

The global racial paradigm of global colorblindness calls our attention to the scale of transnational practice that intersects with regional, national, and local contexts but points to *continuities, similarities,* and *convergences*. There are "striking"[47] similarities across geographies in how race is categorized, structured, and understood because race was always constituted through a global hierarchical field between whiteness and anti-Blackness but which is now propelled by colorblindness. Colorblindness as a transnational, malleable discourse, according to Marzia Milazzo, "transcends national, historical, disciplinary, linguistic boundaries,"[48] and is seen in how race is "continuously absorbed into the political and social vicissitudes of the local space" but race is not "actively named."[49] Globally there are circulating "iconic racial meanings" "unfolding synchronically" across geographies that conjure perceived racial truths without ever evoking direct racist language.[50] Collectively, we find a "transnational assemblage" of global colorblind practices and discourses "that appear to be disconnected from one other across space and time, but which nonetheless flow and come together to sustain racialized power structures."[51]

Neoliberalism provides the rules, policies, logics, and beliefs that represent global colorblindness in practice. Racial neoliberalism is an amalgamation of practices to manage global and specific national racial "threats" that have formed out of racist erasure in a manner that continues to "confer legitimacy on white hegemonic global rule."[52] "Neoliberal projects" depict logics of individualism, privatization, unfettered markets, limited state intervention, free trade, democracy, and private freedoms.[53] Furthermore, the practices of neoliberalism efficaciously handle contradictions. Across the right-left political spectrum, neoliberalism is advanced, negotiated, and adapted (even in socialist-oriented regimes), as neoliberal thought shapes global policy within global institutions dictating and influencing national political maneuvers. In addition, it has space for multicultural forms and explicit racial attacks and expressions. Both fall under a veneer of "cultural" and "national identity" protections and individual, private "freedoms." Therefore, neoliberal projects find full hegemonic expression in global colorblindness.

The practices of neoliberalism embody the latest iteration of racial modernity, what Charles Mills labels "racial liberalism": the connections between racist liberalism and colorblind liberalism today.[54] Racial modernity exposes how the historical development of "personhood," "rights of man," and "human freedom" with racial enslavement, colonial expansion, and dispossession are not contradictions or outlier ideas but integral to the modern project. Following Lisa Lowe, I find racial modernity most poignant and pronounced when we view it as globally expansive and interconnected across scales and places. With a planetary view, the genealogy of liberalism shows how at different points, through divergent connections, liberalism always encompassed perception of progress with racial domination through demarcation, sanction, and control.[55] Liberal ideas of rights, political economy, property, and governance were used in conjunction to race to justify an evolving colonial enterprise, labor discipline, citizenship status, and metropole and settler security. In the process, essentialized notions of liberties, rights, capabilities, and civilization were fused with whiteness. Today, those ideas and practices linger within the production of neoliberalism without overt racial claims. Three specific projects across scales embedded in apparatus are particularly pronounced: human rights, developmentalism, and securitization.

HUMAN RIGHTS

Human rights encode humanity in a romanticized umbrella of universalism/sameness, individualism, and equity that decouples it from the centrality of race.[56] If we unpack each abstract convention in international law, however, we find how global human rights discourses are rooted in white Western logics and deployed politically to serve the interests of a white Western-dominated world. Feminist Ugandan legal scholar Sylvia Tamale explains how original Greek conceptions of human rights were rooted in beliefs of sameness between similar persons. Primacy was placed on the abstract autonomous individual where formal equality was to be protected by the state. The ideas that sanctioned the rights for those considered "members" of a body politic simultaneously withheld rights for those deemed not worthy, outside the confines of citizenship, specifically those racialized as non-white.[57] Therefore, the equality that is presumed and touted today was always rooted in beliefs of human difference where the default standard was a white, heterosexual, Christian male.[58]

When we use human rights standards in contemporary neoliberal practice through global institutions that seep into national formal modes, we ignore the "coloniality inherent in the human rights system" where Africans and those racialized non-white "were viewed as objects rather than subjects in international law." As Tamale notes, human rights terminologies sound righteous and inherently good but hold "no eternal truth or supreme value"[59] and are used in ways that sustain the continuation of Western powers and as weapons against groups and states labeled violators of human rights. Obiora Okafur describes the "western super gaze" of international human rights praxis as a "one way traffic paradigm" where the Western world continues to be framed as the standard-bearer.[60] Thus, expounding human rights as a default standard of equality throughout the globe produces global colorblindness by facilitating the illusion of a race-neutral equal global plain governed by de-racialized states protecting non-raced individual rights.

DEVELOPMENTALISM

"Universalist abstraction" and "formal equality" deeply embedded in the assuredness of a "laissez-faire" capitalist system also fuels the neoliberal project of "developmentalism." Developmental practices operate within a universalizing global capitalism ontology where the tools of capitalism need simply to be applied, captured, and advanced uniformly in geographies across the globe.[61] The modern global apparatus of global capitalism—the World Trade Organization (WTO), International Monetary Fund (IMF), World Bank, multinational corporations (MNCs), and a vast network of non-governmental organizations

(NGOs)—is dominated by a white Global North elite, and those who have captured a form of structural whiteness, who dictate the rules and procedures for capital incorporation inside and outside their borders.[62] This global capitalist power imbalance is naturalized, nonetheless, with the presumption that those countries and (white) subjectivities represent the pinnacle of modernization, industrial capitalism, and (mostly) liberal democracy and therefore are justifiable in setting the terms of global capital engagement.

The perceived universal good of global capitalism is entangled with the post-independence creation of "developing countries."[63] When former colonial geographies became "developing" with political formal independence, enslavement, empire, colonialism, and exploitation were left in the margins of history and countries merely needed to "develop" out of tradition, customs, and unproductivity for modern success. Specific development discourses, such as the need for "good governance," "capacity building," and "anti-corruption," provide the façade of colorblindness while being firmly rooted in the long historical racial arc of colonial "civilizing missions," the League of Nations Mandate System, and the United Nations Trusteeship System.[64] Hence, global white supremacy structures what Jemima Pierre calls the "racial vernacular of development." As a "racial vernacular," development discourses and the policy regimes they support, such as export-led growth, foreign direct investment, labor deregulation, land privatization, resource extraction, and commodity chain incorporation, "sustain racial thought, index particular, racial meanings, and prescribe social practices"[65] all without ever alluding specifically to race. Even twenty-first-century group multicultural policies of development coming out of global institutions like the World Bank erase race.[66] Altogether, developmentalism, whether espoused for the geographies of the "developing world" or embedded within the capitalist logics to help "poor" non-white communities, is continuously wrapped in the production and ideological work of global colorblindness.

SECURITIZATION

Discourses and practices of securitization work to protect national borders, demarcate the lines of deserved citizenship, and shape foreign policy and criminal statutes. They represent an abstract commitment to colorblindness while managing perceived internal and external "racial threats." Internal racial threats historically were colonial "natives," "mixed race" populations, indentured labor, enslaved individuals who sought freedom and the newly emancipated, migrant workers, and immigrant populations. External racial threats were symbolic and material. Historical racial discourses on so-called Yellow and Black Peril fears coalesced with the rise of Japan and a "resurgent East," Haiti's revolution,

African and Asian colonial resistance, and global flows of racially constructed "degenerate" populations.[67] Hence, historical securitization discourses and practices—broadly found in immigration, foreign policy, and criminal constructions—formed from acute global white racial anxiety.

Contemporary white racial anxiety informs securitization in profound ways. States enact, according to Catherine Baker, "racialized security regimes"[68] dictating who they allow in, who they target and police, who they support in foreign affairs, and who they frame as deserving immigrants, refugees, and asylum seekers. In Europe, and former white settler states, racialized security regimes are products of the "contingencies of whiteness"[69] and the "repertoires of whiteness"[70] where shoring up white racial national identity formation, and marking the boundaries of whiteness, is tantamount. But the contingencies of whiteness are also negotiated outside of Europe and white settler geographies. Global South nations negotiate their transnational racialization with their own national racial security projects. Thus, we find the Global War on Terror, refugee crises, and anti-immigrant and migrant worker global assemblages colliding with national racial orders that operate within the global racial paradigm of colorblindness. Security appeals are typically made with entreaties to common culture, ethnicity, and national security that discount any charge of racism and exhibits the continuation of overt and subtle racist practice under the umbrella of global colorblindness.

DIVERSE COLORBLIND POLITICULTURES

The practices of global neoliberalism, with the foundation of racist erasure, intersect and interact across geographies of the global racial system creating complex, varying colorblind "politicultures." Politicultures, according to Bashi Treitler, are the "politics and culture of race" within the racial paradigm of colorblindness and neoliberalism that grant how racial categories are interpreted, rewards and sanctions are structured, and hierarchies justified.[71] The multiscale neoliberal colorblind practices and discourses within the "multiplicity of [economic, political, social] structures"[72] are globally articulated and then interact with regional-national-local racial projects.[73] Crucially, countries and groups are incorporated into the global racial system unequally based upon the history of how race emerged and formed in their borders, its formation in political, economic, and social processes, and the arrangement of racial power dynamics between groups within and outside its borders.[74] Therefore, countries and regions tell their colorblind racial stories across an unequal global field between power and marginalization as products of transnational racialization and national-local racial adaptations.[75]

Formatively, "the [colorblind racial] logics of the global order"[76] are the hegemonic actions by "global white" countries, institutions, and actors dictating the conditions of local transformations. Across the globe we find a vast array of colorblind politicultures that appear with different racial significations, distinctions, and commonsense understandings. Colorblind politicultures are the locally adapted toolkits of racial frames, narratives, representations, and schemas and are emblematic of what Frank Dikötter signals as the "interactive model of interpretation."[77] Hence, colorblindness is not uniform but characteristic of the synergy between global racist erasure and global neoliberal projects that descend in geographies that have their own local worldviews and specific regional, national, and cultural stratification milieus. Different colorblind politicultures, while meaningful and compelling, however, are all "produced and circulated within a larger global framework of racialization [and colorblindness] and indeed are meaningless outside of this framework."[78] Thus, the complex, malleable, and similar patterns between politicultures are apparent.

I identify six colorblind politicultures within the global racial system (see Table 20.1 and the end section of this chapter). These politicultures are *post/anti-racialism, multiculturalism, mestizaje and racial democracy, ethnic dominance, "Predicament of Blackness,"* and *conservative right,* and while they are not exhaustive and exact, they are "ideal types" to categorize colorblind ideological phenomena across regions and geographies. These forms of colorblindness are also not static: some evolve from another, can take place simultaneously, and overlap. In some cases, regions and nations may have multiple forms of colorblindness occurring at the same time. For example, the U.S. can be described as a combination of "post/anti-racial," "multicultural," and "conservative right."

TABLE 20.1 *Politicultures of Global Colorblindness*

Colorblind Politiculture	Regions/Countries
Post/Anti-Racialism	Western Europe: France, Germany, Italy, Spain
Multiculturalism	U.S., Canada, Australia, New Zealand, Sweden, UK, Singapore, South Africa
Mestizaje and Racial Democracy	Mexico, Central and South America, Spanish Caribbean
Ethnic Dominance	East Asia, Eastern Europe, South Asia, Turkey, Middle East
"Predicament of Blackness"	Central, East/West, Southern Africa; British Caribbean
Conservative Right	U.S., Russia, Italy, Eastern Europe, Brazil

With overlaps, nonetheless, one form typically becomes more dominant. Consequently, a CRTGC disentangles and re-entangles each politiculture to uncover a comprehensive racial paradigm of global colorblindness.

GLOBAL RACIAL HIERARCHY

Despite differences all colorblind politicultures reflect a stable global racial architecture between whiteness and anti-Blackness. Racial architectures are the racial categories and hierarchies deployed and assigned in racial paradigms.[79] A global racial hierarchy between whiteness and anti-Blackness, regardless of geography, nationality, and locality, is testament to the historical ideological and structural emergence of race as only understood within a relational global hierarchy. Those "designated as 'white' use[d] their political and economic power to hoard privileges"[80] and those racialized as "Black" could be enslaved, abused, and exploited for white gain—the "antithesis"[81] to whiteness—while other racialized groups fell along and within the hierarchical poles. The white/Black hierarchy does not preclude racist exploitation of other non-white racialized groups. These groups, rather, experience and navigate global and national racial fields in various ways informed by their racial marginalization and structural proximity or distance to whiteness, or in solidarity with Blackness. Thus, the global "color line [is] inherently messy" but it is nonetheless built upon the foundation of white supremacy and anti-Blackness.

Poignantly, regardless if phenotypically or traditionally constructed Black and white bodies are present across geographies, Blackness in each colorblind politiculture is constructed as "the bottom"[82] with whiteness at the top. This exposes how markers of race always included non-phenotypical symbols such as geography, language, accent, clothes, citizenship, occupation, and political status that intersect with each area's stratification and colonial history shaping how groups and countries embody global and national racialization.[83] Markers also shift depending on history, geography, and local context. Individuals and groups can go up or down in racial status depending on time and when they leave geographies. For example, in Italy, Southern Italians were historically nationally constructed as "Black," which informed the U.S.'s racialization of Italians when they immigrated in the late nineteenth century. But Italians were also specifically targeted during this period in *blanqueamiento* (whitening) immigration policies to Latin America as a means for those countries to whiten. And today, southern Italians in Italy racialize African migrants as Black while Italian Americans are constructed as white.[84] This points to the flexibility and elasticity of whiteness and Blackness across the globe that continues to reproduce white supremacy and anti-Black racism.

Moreover, the racial architecture uncovers how different colorblind politicultures are not equal. Regional and country varieties of colorblindness emanating from former colonized geographic histories are not the same as former western empire and white-settler geographies that structure and dictate the global racial paradigm of colorblindness. Even former empire and European spaces exhibit their own hierarchies across their regions with Spain, Russia, and Eastern Europe occupying various lower rungs on the whiteness scale. For former colonial geographies, their politicultures are in response, negotiation, and navigation of the global racial order, and in the process, they create national local varieties. The tools of colorblind racism learned and adapted by semi-periphery and periphery geographies travel and take on new implications when they participate in global neoliberal projects, such as with Chinese investment in Africa, Russian military offenses across the former Soviet bloc, and Israeli settlements in the occupied West Bank. Yet, racialized nonwhite states, particularly those racialized as Black spaces, that reproduce colorblindness should not be mistaken as "consenting"[85] to or crafting of the ideology.

WHITE RACIAL KNOWLEDGE

Lastly, a CRTGC is anchored in the active global performance of white racial ignorance that facilitates white racial power that authoritatively controls, defines, and manages the knowledge of what race is across the globe.[86] Those racialized as "white" mandate the global rules, frames, and narratives of engagement of what is a contemporary racial matter that in turn produces an "epistemic regime"[87] of "legitimate knowledge"[88] activated by "structured blindness"[89] in support of white supremacy. The epistemic regime adroitly handles seeming contradictions. Racial hierarchical arrangements produced during the Enlightenment, which gave way to scientific racism, for example, are not inconsistent with liberal Enlightenment principles because within the epistemic regime at that time it was not constructed as racist but expert knowledge on difference. The contemporary epistemic regime has evolved to continue to handle contradictions. Within the current epistemic regime scientific racism is challenged but the underlying logics of racial difference remain.[90] Therefore, the racial paradigm of global colorblindness provides space for direct racial thought, belief in racial difference, and liberal principles to co-exist in a manner that minimizes, denies, and disavows racism and white supremacy—"an [updated] agreement to misinterpret the world."[91]

Global colorblindness is only possible because it embodies, according to Gloria Wekker, a "militant, aggressive ignorance, posing as knowledge."[92] Ignorance, however, is not passive. "It requires real effort and dedication in a world saturated with evidence of racism and the suffering, counter discourse, and resistance of People of Color," as Jennifer Mueller writes.[93] Thus, it is the "conscious refusal to acknowledge"[94] that shows ignorance as a "valuable resource"[95] in the collective investment in the morality and materiality of whiteness that propels the global racial paradigm of colorblindness forward. Global colorblind praxis is absorbed in politicultures as "tacit nonrecognition" of racism but with an "underlying racial logic that implicitly assumes racial differences [are natural] ... and renders the suffering of some incommensurable with and less worthy than the suffering of the"[96] dominant racial group. When non-white racialized countries reproduce colorblindness through their politicultures it is under the coercive influence of the epistemic regime and what Mueller describes as "corporate white agency":[97] the "unparalleled [global] collective power" of white actors and states. Thus, white racial knowledge fueling global colorblindness is far-reaching, forceful, and compliant for local adoption.

COLORBLIND POLITICULTURES ACROSS THE GLOBE

I use the remaining pages to address in more detail the six colorblind politicultures introduced above to highlight how global colorblindness comes to life across the globe in similar and distinct patterns.

POST/ANTI-RACIALISM

Post-racialism represents a form of colorblindness where, according to Sumi Cho, societies "transcend" race.[98] In Western Europe, where it is most dominant, it is not just that countries "transcend" the problem of race but for some race never really existed as a problem in the first place: an "anti-racialism."[99] More than racist erasure it is racist oblivion. What David Theo Goldberg describes as "racial Europeanization," post-racialism is found in the lack of acknowledging empire, enslavement, and colonialism and how it structured the political, economic, and social landscape of the metropole then and now and continues to shape power dynamics and policies with former colonies and current territories.[100] Obliteration is also found in how official statistical data are collected. Not only is race not present but "ethnic categories are rejected in order to promote national unity."[101] Thus, "the very possibility of naming facts, organizational logics, official discourses,"[102] and neoliberal practices abroad and at home as racist is virtually impossible if race does not exist, what Miguel Mellino terms as "the foreclosure of race and racism."[103] Notably, postracialism has specific national contours.

France is the quintessential case. The tradition of French "dissimulation, denial, and camouflage" goes back to the sixteenth and seventeenth centuries during the French Enlightenment and rise of Republicanism, where French universal principles dictated that enslavement and colonialism were "cleansed" from constructions of French nationhood while structuring its material and symbolic wealth.[104] Modern French neoliberal education, economic, housing, religious, and security policies police and culturally separate French Caribbean, North African, West African, and Asian populations under the guise of French universalism and a commitment to "*laïcité*" (separation between church and state)[105] while to be the "dreaded term" "*communitarste*" is to be discriminatory.[106]

In Italy, postracialism rose from the ashes of World War II and the politics of de-Fascistization, which included excising racism from fascism, ignoring ongoing colonialism, and presenting a modern Italy. Mackda Ghebremariam Tesfau' and Giovanni Picker document how contemporary Italian post-racial rationale justified the passage of draconian security and immigration laws, called for removing "*razza*" from law books and the Constitution, and demanded the continued persistence on the principle of *jus sanguinis* to define Italian citizenship.[107] Germany, similarly, emerged in the postwar era trying to distance itself from its Nazi past and any reference to race and racial classification. In its wake, the Holocaust is remembered, but as a lesson "against race," and German classification schemas around religion and migration status become proxy organizing terms for non-Germanness.

In the Netherlands, postracialism is enveloped in what Gloria Wekker describes as a Dutch identity of being a small, innocent, democratic nation with a fighting spirit.[108] Spanish post-racialism is riddled with overlapping contradictions. Spaniards see themselves as homogenous and white[109] but more open and tolerant because of their history. For centuries Europeans and later Americans saw Spaniards as not fully white because of centuries of "Moor" rule, and Spaniards became "obsessed" with controlling the purity of their ancestry through *limpieza de sangre* (blood purity) state mechanisms.[110] Spaniards racialized religious categorization; developed the rationale for the enslavement of Indigenous people in the "Americas," then only Africans; racialized Roma Spaniards as criminal; and continue to racialize immigrant populations through neoliberal economic and security policy.

MULTICULTURALISM

Multiculturalism rose to manage race, and the demands of anti-racism, by replacing racial discourses with those of culture and difference. Diversity, pluralism, and tolerance are celebrated but typically decoupled from the history of racial inequity and the need for justice and redistribution. It is found most dominantly in former white-settler societies (e.g., U.S., Canada, Australia, New Zealand, South Africa) and sparingly in Europe, for example in the UK and Sweden. In some multicultural landscapes, more emphasis is placed on policy and discourse as it pertains to equity, such as in the rise of Diversity and Inclusion initiatives post–civil rights and after the murder of George Floyd in the U.S., or at the end of apartheid in South Africa. Yet, in those cases, and in forms of multiculturalism lite—where there are limited or no direct policy changes, but symbolic calls for cultural diversity are proclaimed—there is also commonly a backlash. Thus, the politics of multiculturalism are layered.

Some localities use multiculturalism to superficially embrace the idea of culture and difference, others use it to initiate minor change, and others use it to appease racial group and global norm demands. Regardless of geography, however, multiculturalism as a form of global colorblindness represents a de-emphasis of hierarchy, power, and racial inequity that allows the racial dominant group to both proclaim ethnic progress and that multiculturalism has gone too far. The backlash to multiculturalism is most pronounced in European geographies where multiculturalism was never fully enacted, like in the Netherlands, the UK, and Sweden, but was still blamed for a slew of societal ills. In a post–9/11, post-ISIS climate, anti-Muslim racism is notably wrapped in counter-multicultural arguments. In these cases, Islamic cultural practices are framed as separatist, anti-democratic, anti-feminist, and antithetical to the "fundamental values"[111] or "national spirit" to national identities.

In contrast, in South Africa, we find a form of multiculturalism instructed by a racial order defined by minority white economic and social rule. After apartheid, Black South African political rule had to navigate the economic and political rules and discourses set by global institutions, the continued structural power of South African whiteness, and the legacy of racial group divide and rule. What emerged was a form of multiculturalism that works in tandem with white South African post-racialism, "non-racialism."[112] Non-racialism[113] represents much in South Africa: a focus on class, a focus on individual meritocracy, a focus on ethnic pluralism, and the embodiment of what Melissa Steyn and Don Foster call "white talk," the discourses around a *"new South Africa"* representative of democracy and social development.[114] Through a lens of non-racialism, policies of Black Economic Empowerment, affirmative action at universities, and land redistribution become unfair, misplaced, corrupt, and even discriminatory, and the devastating continuation of Black poverty and unemployment is deemed "acceptable because the terms of recognition now exclude the analytics of racial articulation."[115]

MESTIZAJE AND RACIAL DEMOCRACY

Unlike multiculturalism, which acknowledges separate group cultures, *mestizaje* and racial democracy are about group mixture, hybridity, and fluidity. *Mestizaje* is most associated with Mexico, Central America, and parts of South America and Spanish American–colonized Caribbean that had Indigenous, enslaved African, and racial indentured labor with European settler populations. Racial democracy is applied to Brazil, the country outside of Africa with the largest African-descendent population. *Mestizaje* formed as a nation-building strategy in the late nineteenth and early twentieth centuries after Spanish colonialism and the Mexican revolution.[116] The national projects were in negotiation with a global racial ideology that proclaimed Latin American countries were racially degenerate due to intermixture during colonialism.[117] *Mestizaje* was a way for elites, who saw themselves as "white" based on European ancestry, to redefine race, heralding the *"mestizo,"* or *"indio"* in the Dominican Republic or *"ladino"* in Guatemala, as national symbols while also pursuing liberal state-making policies of capitalist development, luring European immigration, and sustaining white aesthetic ideals.[118] With the heralding of *mestizaje*, and the lack of race being officially codified in legal structure post-colonialism yet present in *de facto* forms, the illusion of a perceived lack of racism became powerful state myths that allowed for European-descendent elites to sustain power, and essentially "control access to whiteness,"[119] all while denying the role of race. Similarly, in Brazil, *mestiçagem* was the base to the ideology of racial democracy that positioned Brazilians as colorblind and not racist because of the specificities of Portuguese colonialism and enslavement.[120]

These ideologies were always in dialogue with and in response to the global racial system. The U.S. heavily influences regional racial dynamics. The U.S. created the internal racial constructions of "Mexican/Hispanic/Latino," and ongoing U.S.-led country and regional racialization shapes country-specific neoliberal political, economic, and security policies.[121] The U.S. is also framed by state elites as the quintessential example of racism to deflect against national racial projects. *Mestizaje* and racial democracy use "the same logic of the [global] racial hierarchy as its premise," and Blackness and Asianness are commonly left out of the racial calculus of the "mestizo."[122] Anti-Black, anti-Indigenous, anti-Asian racism endures. More recently, after Indigenous and Afro-descendent activism, multiculturalism has emerged in the region but not surpassed *mestizaje* and racial democracy. Latin American multiculturalism, supported by global institutions with human rights discourses and development agendas, overlaps with *mestizaje* racial hierarchies. Racial politics separate indigeneity from Blackness,[123] and Black spaces are incorporated and stratified into global neoliberal economic extractive-service based industries. Even Latin American countries that eschewed *mestizaje* for a racial ideology of "white exceptionalism," such as Costa Rica, Argentina, and Chile have evolved into "white multiculturalism," a multicultural turn that continues to sustain investments in homogenous whiteness.[124]

ETHNIC DOMINANCE

Countries and regions that produce a colorblind politiculture of ethnic dominance center ethnic homogeneity in state formations divorced from race. Ethnic dominance is most pronounced in East Asia, Central Asia, Eastern Europe, Turkey, Israel, and the Middle East, but it is also seen in South Asia. Ethnicity in many cases merges with religious identities and lineage claims cementing group authority. Supposedly natural homogenous ethnic histories eclipse the specter of race and local ethno-racial diversity. Ethnic dominant state formation policies and discourses form in navigation with the global racial field between whiteness and anti-Blackness and the regional geopolitical markers that it informs.[125] Countries compete and position themselves along the field by negotiating their historical global racialization and adapting global racial cultural codes to their specific local geographies, producing essentialized ethnic national identities that are constructed as not about race but ethnicity.

In India, *Hindutva*, ethnic Hindu nationalism, is a product of British colonial racialization projects that constructed the "Hindu race" with Aryan roots, and the interaction with regional-local discourses and boundaries that produce racialized Muslim, regional, and caste identities.[126] In China, contemporary Han-superiority discourses and policies are informed by the history of binary constructions, China's response to scientific racism, and global geopolitics linking a Han racial identity and nation together.[127] Han superiority remains in communist-ruled, capitalist-oriented China, and China simultaneously experiences global anti-Chinese racism and reproduces racism in its borders with its treatment of *minzu* (minority) groups and through its global capital development projects outside China. Russia maneuvers a complex racial global landscape as well where it represents a peripheral white status in Western Europe, but also "Russianness is understood as a form of 'privileged whiteness,'"[128] a Slavic whiteness, vis-à-vis ethnic Eastern European nations, and Euro-Asian groups within and along its border. In all the country examples in various ways, anti-Black racism—heard in anti-Black epithets, assumptions, practices, and violence—act as a unifying boundary in which ethnic dominant identity claims are made against while proximity to and/or capturing of whiteness is unstably pursued.

"PREDICAMENT OF BLACKNESS"

The politiculture of the "Predicament of Blackness" alludes to the complexity of conceptualizing global colorblindness in geographies that experience global anti-Black racism. "The Predicament of Blackness" is the title of Jemima Pierre's[129] revelatory book on post-colonial African racial formations that are a product of global transnational racialization processes and national local histories. The Predicament of Blackness politiculture found across Africa, Haiti, Melanesia, and parts of the Caribbean is more about how racism is taken out of the equation by global actors in shaping local material experiences and racial formations today, and how local geographies respond and navigate what Achille Mbembe calls the "duality" of Blackness,[130] than about how these geographies enact forms of colorblindness. Global discourse and policies about Africa, Haiti, Melanesia, and parts of the Caribbean essentialize a calcified view of colorblind underdevelopment and historical cultural proclivities that render these societies ill prepared for democracy, rule of law, and capitalist development. Post-colonial conflict in Africa is also naturalized as "pre-colonial" antagonisms and further proof of essentialized cultural animosity rather than products of colonial-created racial identities.[131]

Countries respond to global anti-Blackness under the weight of colorblindness in dialectic ways. Black resistance, agency, and epistemologies are often centered as building upon Black nationalist liberation histories, Pan-Africanism, and a transnational Black diaspora community. These alternative ideological discourses counter colorblindness but also exhibit tensions around "national representations" and what Deborah Thomas, in an analysis of Jamaica, calls "modern blackness," "a subaltern aesthetic and politics from which to make claims upon earlier forms of nationalism."[132] Thus, pressures around national strategies and narratives occur when countries are tasked with confronting the structures of global white supremacy that dictate the rules of global participation and post-independence development success but are hidden by the racial paradigm of global colorblindness. The whiteness of "transnational capital, media, [and] seemingly progressive projects"[133] like development, humanitarianism, and conservation are negotiated within the legacy of colonial-crafted racial divisions that can be reproduced but also masked under a veneer of perceived ethnic and class absolutes.

Colorblindness is further found in the lack of scholarship on contemporary African racial matters not including South Africa. When racism is eliminated as an explanatory mechanism shaping the Continent, global processes, North/South divides, and racialized group power divisions are understood with class-reductionist or cultural, religious, and political arguments, and global anti-Blackness is reproduced and ignored.[134] Moreover, white African subjectivities are increasingly coalescing around notions of "victimhood or besiegement"[135] claiming that whites in Africa are now the victims of human rights violations and non-democratic practices.

CONSERVATIVE RIGHT

The conservative right as a colorblind politiculture runs parallel with other colorblind politicultures within geographies. Across the globe there is a rise of conservative right racist ideologies that practice a politics of what Casey Kelly labels "repressive victimhood."[136] Repressive victimhood turns whiteness and white subjectivities into an "oppressed majority" and uses a combination of colorblind liberal tenets and securitization discourses and policies to claim their victimhood. Claiming victimhood also includes redefining and upending, according to Nasar Meer, the "flagstones of anti-racism" and "in [the] wreckage fascists are renamed 'populists,' and white 'racial self-interest' is not racism."[137] Essentially, the politiculture at its core is profoundly racist and exceedingly violent but denies racism at every turn with an assemblage of liberal, seemingly "reasonable" discursive proclamations about preserving white Western cultural and material values. The card trick of the conservative right politiculture turns what once was considered classically racist not racist and embodies what Philomena Essed labels the new "entitlement racism"[138] and Dwanna McKay describes as "legitimized racism:"[139] the new acceptable patterns and standards of [white] thought and behavior that de-legitimize white racism as a reality.

The politiculture is also extraordinarily global, interconnected, and flexible with conservative groups—ranging from established political parties, avowed white nationalists, and anti-governmental organizations—who all traffic in a transnational collective toolkit of cultural reference points, discursive strategies, and appeals to aggrieved white precarity. From the U.S. to Italy, to Central Europe, to Russia, Brazil, Costa Rica, and many more, conservative right politicultures are found. The U.S., as a global reference point and transnational force, commonly serves as a centerpiece of global white identity maintenance and imagery, with locals from Brazil to Russia and across Europe consuming "transcultural dimensions to confederate"[140] iconography and other far-right appropriated insignia, like the Gadsden flag, in an interactive global-local process of white racial meaning-making. Anti-Black imagery also circulates and is locally produced in what Gloria Wekker, adopting Stuart Hall, calls "ritualized degradation."[141] Beyond imagery, specific policies centering policing and controlling immigration and non-white citizens (e.g., calls for citizenship entitlements, Constitutional rights, and jobs for "real" citizens) are embedded in the conservative right politiculture. Ultimately the global production of the conservative right politiculture represents the apex to the ascendancy of global colorblindness—nothing is racist, not even professed white superiority.

CONCLUSION

As the dominant global racial ideology of the twenty-first century, I argue a Critical Race Theory of Global Colorblindness makes four important contributions to the fields of Critical Race Theory and international law. The theory (1) centers global, interconnected power-laden processes in shaping national local racial understandings; (2) identifies how racial meaning-making is constructed across the globe in a relational hierarchical field between whiteness and anti-Blackness; (3) underscores neoliberal discourses and practices as productive colorblind engines; and (4) labels white knowledge production, and white interests and investments, as the anchor.

The question now is how do we challenge the racial ideology of global colorblindness? Racial ideology theorists note how dominant ideologies always contend with "subaltern ideologies,"[142] countering discourses, narratives, and brewing "cultures of resistance."[143] Stuart Hall argues that exposing and deconstructing the dominant racial ideology to question its assumptions is the first step to constructing an "anti-racist common sense."[144] But how do we do this when racial reasoning is rooted in abstract, universalistic forms of liberalism codified as colorblind? In his later writings, Charles Mills advocated for a form of "Black Radical Liberalism,"[145] while Sylvia Tamale argues we must search for "transformative alternatives to hegemonic liberalism."[146] In this regard, rights should be viewed as "integral, interconnected, indivisible" and "emanat[ing] from a social paradigm based on reciprocity, solidarity and inclusiveness, values that are far richer than the basis on which modern rights have been founded."[147] Thus, tensions and transformation points collide. Through it all, the urgent necessity of confronting global white supremacy and its complex colorblind ideological web remains.

NOTES

1. Moustafa Bayoumi, "They are 'Civilized,' and 'Look Like Us,' The Racist Coverage of Ukraine," *Guardian*, May 2, 2022, https://www.theguardian.com/commentisfree/2022/mar/02/civilised-european-look-like-us-racist-coverage-ukraine.

2. Rafia Zakaria, "White Russian Empire. The Racist Myths Behind Vladimir Putin's Power Grabs," *The Forum*, March 10, 2022, https://www.aapf.org/theforum-white-russian-empire.

3. Debra Thompson, "Through, Against, and Beyond the Racial State: The Transnational Stratum of Race," *Cambridge Review of International Affairs* 26, no. 1 (2013): 133.

4. David Theo Goldberg, *The Threat of Race: Reflections on Racial Neoliberalism* (Malden: John Wiley & Sons, 2009), 25.

5. Charles Mills, *Black Rights/White Wrongs: The Critique of Racial Liberalism* (New York: Oxford University Press, 2017), 3.

6. Zeus Leonardo, "The Multicultural Glass: Althusser, Ideology and Race Relations in Post-Civil Rights America," *Policy Futures in Education* 3, no. 4 (2005): 400, 407.

7. Justin Desautels-Stein, *The Right to Exclude: A Critical Race Approach to Sovereignty, Borders, and International Law* (Oxford: Oxford University Press, 2023); Erroll Henderson, "Hidden in Plain Sight: Racism in International Relations Theory," in *Race and Racism in International Relations,* ed. Alexander Anievas et al. (Routledge, 2014), 19–43; Duncan Bell, "Race and International Relations: Introduction," *Cambridge Review of International Affairs* 26, no. 1 (2013).

8. Bell, "Race and International Relations," 2.

9. Robert Vitalis, *White World Order, Black Power Politics: The Birth of American International Relations* (Ithaca: Cornell University Press, 2016), 1; Henderson, "Hidden in Plain Sight," 72.

10. Christopher Gevers, "Unwhitening the World: Rethinking Race and International Law," *UCLA Law Review* 67 (2020).

11. Alexander D. Barder, "Scientific Racism, Race War and the Global Racial Imaginary," *Third World Quarterly* 40, no. 2 (2019): 209.

12. Gevers, "Unwhitening the World," 1386.

13. Gevers, "Unwhitening the World," 1386.

14. See Third World Approaches to International Law (TWAIL) and Jeanne Woods, "Introduction: Theoretical Insights from the Cutting Edge," in *Proceedings of the ASIL Annual Meeting*, (Cambridge: Cambridge University Press, 2016), 389–93.

15. Sumi Cho and Francisco Valdes, "Critical Race Materialism: Theorizing Justice in the Wake of Global Neoliberalism," *Connecticut Law Review* 43 (2010): 1513; Justin Desautels-Stein, *The Right to Exclude*, 12–13.

16. Eslava et al. expose "the weakness of political formal independence in a world already crafted through the tools of imperial disciplines and economic interests." Luis Eslava et al., "The Spirit of Bandung," in *Bandung, Global History, and International Law: Critical Pasts and Pending Future*, ed. Luis Eslava et al. (Cambridge: Cambridge University Press, 2017), 3–32.

17. Chantal Thomas, "Critical Race Theory and Postcolonial Development Theory: Observations on Methodology," *Villanova Law Review* 45 (2000): 1195.

18. Cho and Valdes, "Critical Race Materialism," 1517.

19. Zeus Leonardo, "The Multicultural Glass: Althusser, Ideology and Race Relations in Post-Civil Rights America," *Policy Futures in Education* 3, no. 4 (2005); Stuart Hall, "The Whites of Their Eyes: Racist Ideologies and the Media," in *Selected Writings on Race and Difference*, ed. Paul Gilroy and Ruth Wilson Gilmore (Durham: Duke University Press), 97–120; Woody Doane, "Beyond Colorblindness: (Re:) Theorizing Racial Ideology," *Sociological Perspectives* 60, no. 5 (2017): 975–91; Moon-Kie Jung, *Beneath the Surface of White Supremacy: Denaturalizing U.S. Racisms Past and Present* (Palo Alto: Stanford University Press, 2015); Eduardo Bonilla-Silva, *White Supremacy and Racialism in the Post-Civil Rights Era* (Boulder: Lynn Reinner, 2000).

20. Achille Mbembe, *Critique of Black Reason* (Durham: Duke University Press, 2017).

21. Doane, "Beyond Colorblindness," 977.

22. Leonardo, "The Multicultural Glass," 401.

23. Doane, "Beyond Colorblindness," 981.

24. Leonardo, "The Multicultural Glass," 406.

25. Jung, *Beneath the Surface of White Supremacy*, 36.

26. Jodi Melamed, *Represent and Destroy, Rationalizing Violence in the New Racial Capitalism* (Minneapolis: University of Minnesota Press, 2011), 12.

27. Jean Beaman and Amy Petts, "Toward a Global Theory of Colorblindness: Comparing Racial Ideology in France and the United States," *Sociological Compass* 14, no. 4 (2020): e12774.

28. Meghan Burke, *Colorblind Racism* (Hoboken: John Wiley & Sons, 2018), 22.

29. Cho and Valdes, "Critical Race Materialism"; George Lipsitz, "The Sounds of Silence: How Race Neutrality Preserves White Supremacy," in *Seeing Race Again: Countering Colorblindness Across Disciplines*, ed. Kimberlé Crenshaw et al. (Berkeley: University of California Press, 2019), 23–51.

30. Jung, *Beneath the Surface of White Supremacy*, 45.

31. Peter Wade, *Race: An Introduction* (Cambridge: Cambridge University Press, 2015), 221.

32. Marzia Milazzo, "The Rhetorics of Racial Power: Enforcing Colorblindness in Post-Apartheid Scholarship on Race," *Journal of International and Intercultural Communications* 8, no. 1 (2015): 7–26.

33. Kimberlé Crenshaw et al., "Introduction," in *Seeing Race Again: Countering Colorblindness Across Disciplines*, ed. Kimberlé Crenshaw et al. (Berkeley: University of California Press, 2019), 5.

34. Imani Perry, "Post-Intent Racism: A New Framework for an Old Problem," *National Black Law Journal* 19 (2005): 113.

35. George Lipsitz, *Possessive Investment in Whiteness: How White People Profit from Identity Politics* (Philadelphia: Temple University Press, 2006); Cheryl I. Harris, "Whiteness as Property," *Harvard Law Review* (1993): 1707–91.

36. Howard Winant, "The Modern World Racial System," in *Transnational Blackness: Navigating the Global Color Line*, ed. Manning Marable (New York: Palgrave Macmillan, 2008), 41–53.

37. Doane, "Beyond Colorblindness," 981.

38. Saul Dubow, "Smuts, the United Nations and the Rhetoric of Race and Rights," *Journal of Contemporary History* 43, no. 1 (2008): 63.

39. Alana Lentin, "Beyond Denial: 'Not Racism' As Racist Violence," *Continuum* 32, no. 4 (2018): 8.

40. Lentin, "Beyond Denial," 3.

41. Mills, *Black Rights/White Wrongs*, 43.

42. Marzia Milazzo, "On the Transportability, Malleability, and Longevity of Colorblindness: Reproducing White Supremacy in Brazil and South Africa," in *Seeing Race Again: Countering Colorblindness Across Disciplines*, ed. Kimberlé Crenshaw at al. (Berkeley: University of California Press, 2019), 105–27.

43. Vilna Bashi Treitler, *The Ethnic Project: Transforming Racial Fiction into Ethnic Factions* (Palo Alto: Stanford University Press, 2013), 27.

44. Bashi Treitler, *The Ethnic Project*, 27–28.

45. Thompson, "Through, Against, and Beyond the Racial State," 141.

46. Thompson, "Through, Against, and Beyond the Racial State," 139–40; Paola Bacchetta et al., eds., *Global Raciality: Empire, PostColoniality, DeColoniality* (Routledge, 2019), 9.

47. Milazzo, "On the Transportability, Malleability, and Longevity of Colorblindness," 122.

48. Milazzo, "On the Transportability, Malleability, and Longevity of Colorblindness," 110.

49. Sivamohan Valluvan, "What Is 'Post-Race' and What Does it Reveal About Contemporary Racisms?" *Ethnic and Racial Studies* 39, no. 13 (2016): 2247.

50. Valluvan, "What Is 'Post-Race'?," 2247–48.

51. Vrushali Patil and Bandana Purkayastha, "The Transnational Assemblage of Indian Rape Culture," *Ethnic and Racial Studies* 41, no. 11 (2018): 1952–70.

52. Goldberg, *The Threat of Race*, 331.

53. Michael Omi and Howard Winant, *Racial Formation in the United States*, 3rd ed. (Routledge, 2015), 211.

54. Mills, *Black Rights/White Wrongs*, xv.

55. Lisa Lowe, *The Intimacies of Four Continents* (Durham: Duke University Press, 2015).

56. Eduardo Bonilla-Silva, "'Look, a Negro': Reflections on the Human Rights Approach to Racial Inequality," in *Globalization and America*, ed. Angela J. Hattery et al. (Lanham: Rowman & Littlefield, 2008), 9.

57. Bonilla-Silva, "'Look a Negro,'" 13.

58. Sylvia Tamale, *Decolonization and Afro-Feminism* (Ottawa: Daraja Press, 2020), 210–13.

59. Tamale, *Decolonization and Afro-Feminism* (Ottawa: Daraja Press, 2020), 203.

60. Obiora Okafor, "The Bandung Ethic and International Human Rights Praxis: Yesterday, Today and Tomorrow," in *Bandung, Global History, and International Law: Critical Pasts and Pending Futures*, ed. Luis Eslava et al. (Cambridge: Cambridge University Press, 2017), 522.

61. B. S. Chimni, "Anti-imperialism Then and Now," in *Bandung, Global History, and International Law: Critical Pasts and Pending Futures*, ed. Luis Eslava et al. (Cambridge: Cambridge University Press, 2017), 36.

62. Ruth E. Gordon and Jon H. Sylvester, "Deconstructing Development," *Wisconsin International Law Journal* 22 (2004); Keith Aoki, "Space Invaders: Critical Geography, The Third World in International Law and Critical Race Theory," *Villanova Law Review* 45 (2000): 913.

63. Luis Eslava et al., "The Spirit of Bandung," in *Bandung, Global History, and International Law: Critical Pasts and Pending Future*, ed. Luis Eslava et al. (Cambridge: Cambridge University Press, 2017), 22; Keith Aoki, "Space Invaders," 913.

64. Ediberto Román, "Race as the Missing Variable in Both the Neocolonial and Self-Determination Discourses," in *Proceedings of the ASIL Annual Meeting* 93 (Cambridge: Cambridge University Press, 1999), 226.

65. Jemima Pierre, "The Racial Vernaculars of Development: A View from West Africa," *American Anthropologist* 122, no. 1 (2020): 86.

66. Charles Hale, "Neoliberal Multiculturalism: The Remaking of Cultural Rights and Racial Dominance in Central America," *PoLAR* 28 (2005): 10.

67. Alexander D. Barder, "Scientific Racism, Race War and the Global Racial Imaginary," *Third World Quarterly* 40, no. 2 (2019): 207–23.

68. Catherine Baker, "The Contingencies of Whiteness: Gendered/Racialized Global Dynamics of Security Narratives," *Security Dialogue* 52, no. 1 (2021): 124–32.

69. Baker, "The Contingencies of Whiteness."

70. Damian Breen and Nasar Meer, "Securing Whiteness?: Critical Race Theory (CRT) and the Securitization of Muslims in Education," *Identities* 26, no. 5 (2019): 596.

71. Vilna Bashi Treitler, "Racialization and its Paradigms: From Ireland to North America," *Current Sociology* 64, no. 2 (2016): 213, 215.

72. Jung, *Beneath Surface of White Supremacy*, 26.

73. Leith Mullings, "Race and Globalization," in *Transnational Blackness: Navigating the Global Color Line*, ed. Manning Marable (New York: Palgrave Macmillan, 2008).

74. Michelle Christian, "A Global Critical Race and Racism Framework," *Sociology of Race and Ethnicity* 5, no. 2 (2019): 169–85.

75. Christian, "A Global Critical Race and Racism Framework."

76. Nikolay Zakharov, *Race and Racism in Russia* (Springer, 2015), 4.

77. Frank Dikötter, "The Racialization of the Globe: An Interactive Interpretation," *Ethnic and Racial Studies* 31, no. 8 (2008): 1478.

78. Vrushali Patil, "On Coloniality, Racialized Forgetting and the 'Group Effect': Interrogating Ethnic Studies' Meta-Narrative of Race," *Journal of Historical Sociology* 27, no. 3 (2014): 365.

79. Bashi Treitler, "Racialization and its Paradigms," 215.

80. Bashi Treitler, *The Ethnic Project*, 34.

81. George Yancey, ed., *What White Looks Like: African-American Philosophers on the Whiteness Question* (Routledge, 2004).

82. Devon Carbado, "Race to the Bottom," *UCLA Law Review* 49 (2001): 1283.

83. Imani Perry, "Of Desi, J. Lo and Color Matters: Law, Critical Race Theory the Architecture of Race," *Cleveland State Law Review* (2004): 139.

84. Sandro Mezzadra, "The New European Migratory Regime and the Shifting Patterns of Contemporary Racism" in *Postcolonial Italy*, ed. Christina Lombardi-Diop and Caterina Romeo (New York: Palgrave Macmillan, 2012), 44.

85. Kimberlé Crenshaw, "Race, Reform, and Retrenchment: Transformation and Legitimation in Antidiscrimination Law," *Harvard Law Review* 101 (1988): 1357.

86. Charles Mills, *The Racial Contract* (Ithaca: Cornell University Press, 2014).

87. George Lipsitz, "The Sounds of Silence: How Race Neutrality Preserves White Supremacy," in *Seeing Race Again: Countering Colorblindness Across Disciplines*, ed. Kimberlé Crenshaw et al. (Berkeley: University of California Press, 2019), 44.

88. Jodi Melamed, *Represent and Destroy: Rationalizing Violence in the New Racial Capitalism* (Minneapolis: University of Minnesota Press), 11.

89. Mills, *The Racial Contract*, 19.

90. Dorothy Roberts, *Fatal Invention: How Science, Politics, and Big Business Re-Create Race in the Twenty-First Century* (New York: New Press, 2011).

91. Mills quoted in George Lipsitz, "The Sounds of Silence: How Race Neutrality Preserves White Supremacy," in *Seeing Race Again: Countering Colorblindness Across Disciplines*, ed. Kimberlé Crenshaw et al. (Berkeley: University of California Press, 2019).

92. Gloria Wekker, *White Innocence: Paradoxes of Colonialism and Race* (Durham: Duke University Press, 2016), 172.

93. Jennifer Mueller, "Racial Ideology or Racial Ignorance? An Alternative Theory of Racial Cognition," *Sociological Theory* 38, no. 2 (2020): 142.

94. Jung, *Beneath the Surface of White Supremacy*, 41.

95. Mueller, "Racial Ideology or Racial Ignorance?," 149.

96. Jung, *Beneath the Surface of White Supremacy*, 143.

97. Mueller, "Racial Ideology or Racial Ignorance?," 152.

98. Cho and Valdes, "Critical Race Materialism," 1601.

99. Celeste Curington, *Laboring in the Shadow of Empire: Race, Gender and Care Work in Portugal* (New Brunswick: Rutgers University Press, 2024).

100. Goldberg, *The Threat of Race*, 152.

101. Ann Morning, "Ethnic Classification in Global Perspective: A Cross-National Survey of the 2000 Census Round," *Population Research Policy Review* 27 (2008): 239, 243.

102. Mackda Ghebremariam Tesfau' and Giovanni Picker, "The Italian Postracial Archive," *Ethnic and Racial Studies* 44, no. 2 (2021): 195, 197.

103. Miguel Mellino, "De-provincializing Italy: Notes on Race, Racialization, and Italy's Coloniality," in *Postcolonial Italy: Challenging National Homogeneity*, ed. Christina Lombardi-Diop and Caterina Romeo (New York: Palgrave Macmillan, 2012), 99.

104. Mbembe, *Critique of Black Reason*, 67.

105. Jean Beaman and Amy Petts, "Towards A Global Theory of Colorblindness: Comparing Colorblind Racial Ideology in France and the United States," *Sociology Compass* 14, no. 4 (2020): 6.

106. Beaman and Petts, "Towards a Global Theory of Colorblindness," 4.

107. Ghebremariam Tesfau' and Picker, "The Italian Postracial Archive."
108. Wekker, *White Innocence*.
109. Joshua Goode, "Race, Crime and Criminal Justice in Spain," in *Race, Crime and Criminal Justice: International Perspectives*, ed. Anita Kalunta-Crumpton (New York: Palgrave Macmillan, 2010), 162–84.
110. Baltasar Fra-Molinero, "The Suspect Whiteness of Spain," in *At Home and Abroad: Historicizing Twenty-First Century Whiteness in Literature and Performance*, ed. La Vinia Delois Jennings (Knoxville: University of Tennessee Press, 2009), 147, 149.
111. Damian Breen and Nasar Meer, "Securing Whiteness?: Critical Race Theory (CRT) and the Securitization of Muslims in Education," *Identities* 26, no. 5 (2019): 595, 599.
112. Milazzo, "The Rhetorics of Racial Power," 7.
113. Milazzo, "The Rhetorics of Racial Power," 7–26.
114. Melissa Steyn and Don Foster, "Repertoires for Talking White: Resistant Whiteness in Post-Apartheid South Africa," *Ethnic and Racial Studies* 31, no. 1 (2008): 25–51.
115. Goldberg, *The Threat of Race*, 314.
116. Edward Telles and Rene Flores, "Not Just Color: Whiteness, Nation, and Status in Latin America," *Hispanic American Historical Review* 93, no. 3 (2013): 411–49.
117. Bettina Ng'weno and Lok Siu, "Comparative Raciality: Erasure and Hypervisibility of Asian and Afro Mexicans," in *Global Raciality: Empire, PostColoniality, DeColoniality*, ed. Paola Bacchetta et al. (Routledge, 2019), 62.
118. Richard Graham, ed., *The Idea of Race in Latin America, 1870–1940* (Austin: University of Texas Press, 1990).
119. Laura E. Goméz, *Inventing Latinos: A New Story of American Racism* (New York: The New Press, 2020).
120. Milazzo, "On the Transportability, Malleability, and Longevity of Colorblindness."
121. Goméz, *Inventing Latinos*, 71.
122. Bettina Ng'weno and Lok Siu, "Comparative Raciality: Erasure and Hypervisibility of Asian and Afro Mexicans," in *Global Raciality: Empire, PostColoniality, DeColoniality*, ed. Paola Bacchetta et al. (Routledge, 2019), 69.
123. Juliet Hooker, "Indigenous Inclusion/Black Exclusion: Race, Ethnicity, and Multicultural Citizenship in Latin America," *Journal of Latin American Studies* 37, no. 2 (2005): 285–310.
124. Prisca Gayles and Marianela Muñoz-Muñoz, "Unveiling Latin American White Multiculturalism: Black Women's Politics in Argentina and Costa Rica," *Latin American and Caribbean Ethnic Studies* 18, no. 2 (2023): 200–16.
125. Michelle Christian, "A Global Critical Race and Racism Framework," *Sociology of Race and Ethnicity* 5, no. 2 (2019): 169–85.
126. Zaheer Baber, "'Race Might Be a Unicorn, but its Horn Could Draw Blood': Racialization, Class and Racism in a Non-Western Context," *Critical Sociology* 48, no. 1 (2022): 151–69.
127. Frank Dikötter, *The Discourse of Race in Modern China* (Oxford: Oxford University Press, 2015).
128. Zakharov, *Race and Racism in Russia*, 13.
129. Jemima Pierre, *The Predicament of Blackness: Postcolonial Ghana and the Politics of Race* (Chicago: University of Chicago Press, 2012)
130. Mbembe, *Critique of Black Reason*, 26–31.

131. Amina Mama, "Challenging Subjects: Gender and Power in African Contexts," *African Sociological Review* 5, no. 2 (2001): 63–73.

132. Deborah Thomas, *Modern Blackness: Nationalism, Globalization, and the Politics of Culture in Jamaica* (Durham: Duke University Press, 2004), 13.

133. Danelle van Zyl-Hermann and Jacob Boersema, "Introduction: The Politics of Whiteness in South Africa," *Africa* 87, no. 4 (2017): 651–61.

134. Jemima Pierre, "Race in Africa Today: A Commentary," *American Anthropological Association* 28, no. 3 (2013): 547–51.

135. Van Zyl-Hermann and Boersema, "Introduction: The Politics of Whiteness in South Africa," 658.

136. Casey Ryan Kelly, "Whiteness, Repressive Victimhood, and the Foil of the Intolerant Left," *First Amendment Studies* 55, no. 1 (2021): 59.

137. Nasar Meer, "'Race' and 'Post-Colonialism': Should One Come Before the Other?" *Ethnic and Racial Studies* 41, no. 6 (2018): 1163–81.

138. Philomena Essed and Sarah Louise Muhr, "Entitlement Racism and Its Intersections: An Interview with Philomena Essed, Social Justice Scholar," *Ephemera: Theory & Politics in Organization* 18, no. 1 (2018): 183.

139. Dwanna McKay, "Masking Legitimized Racism: Indigeneity, Colorblindness, and the Sociology of Race," in *Seeing Race Again: Countering Colorblindness Across Disciplines*, ed. Kimberlé Crenshaw et al. (Berkeley: University of California Press, 2019), 85–104.

140. Jordan Brasher, "The Crisis of Confederate Memory in the Interior of São Paulo, Brazil," *Memory Studies* 14, no. 6 (2021): 1317.

141. Wekker, *White Innocence*, 140.

142. Jung, *Beneath the Surface of White Supremacy*, 42.

143. Stuart Hall, "Race, Articulation and Societies Structured in Dominance," in *Selected Writings on Race and Difference*, ed. Paul Gilroy and Ruth Wilson Gilmore (Durham: Duke University Press, 2021), 241.

144. Stuart Hall, "The Whites of Their Eyes: Racist Ideologies and the Media." In *Selected Writings on Race and Difference*, ed. Paul Gilroy and Ruth Wilson Gilmore (Durham: Duke University Press, 2021), 97–120.

145. Mills, *Black Rights/White Wrongs*, xxi.

146. Tamale, *Decolonization and Afro-Feminism*, 201.

147. Tamale, *Decolonization and Afro-Feminism*, 201.

CHAPTER TWENTY-ONE

THE POST-RACIAL UNIVERSALIST FRAMEWORK

Colonial Logic in International Law and Relations

Kehinde Andrews

The end of the First World War ushered in a new era of international law. For the preceding three centuries European empires dominated the globe, plundering from the colonies and warring with each other. The war pitted the empire against empire in Europe, leading to unprecedented loss of European lives on the battlefields. There had been previous attempts at limited global standards of justice, for instance the Geneva conventions, but following the carnage an attempt was made to bring the world together under the auspices of the League of Nations. The League was extremely ineffective, lacking any real power to enforce global order, and could not prevent the outbreak of the Second World War in 1939.

The world was once again plunged into chaos, and seeing the horrors of the Holocaust and nuclear warfare in Japan provided the impetus for a more robust framework of international law. The United Nations replaced the failed League and established economic organizations like the International Monetary Fund (IMF) and World Trade Organization (WTF) to lay the ground for international cooperation. But the framework that was established managed to entirely avoid the issue of racism that had been the basis for the building of the modern world. Without genocide, slavery and colonialism the West could not have risen, and the underdeveloped world would not be as poor. But the framework of international law that emerged froze the world in the brutal colonial inequalities that still exist today. By avoiding the issue of racism, the legal framework ensured no measures would be taken to rebalance the scales of justice. To understand the nature of international law this chapter will first explore what Malcolm X called the era of "benevolent colonialism" that emerged in the postwar period, and how post-racialism is a necessary feature of the new age of empire. The intellectual foundation for this new era was in enlightenment figures like Immanuel Kant who created a universal set of rights that was deeply racist. We continue to live under that legacy today. The result of post-racial international law is that billions of those who were formerly colonized live in a state of subject citizenry.

BENEVOLENT COLONIALISM

The United Nations has been a beacon of hope for nations and activists in the Third World and oppressed minorities in countries like the United States.[1] The one nation, one vote General Assembly meant that it quickly became a space for anti-colonial rhetoric. Fidel Castro, Patrice Lumumba, Kwame Nkrumah, and a host of other revolutionary leaders denounced imperialist powers from the Assembly floor, and in 1960 the General Assembly Declaration on the Granting of Independence to Colonial Countries and Peoples. When Malcolm X founded the Organization of Afro-American Unity in 1964, he specifically cited the UN charter as a document that "represents the essence of mankind's hopes and good intentions."[2] He was also intent to take the US to the United Nations to answer for its racial crimes. He argued that it was pointless seeking redress through the American legal system because "you don't take your case to the criminal, you take the criminal to court."[3] Malcolm was following in a tradition of activists who had sought refuge in the UN. In 1951 a group of activists including Claudia Jones and W.E.B. Du Bois submitted *We Charge Genocide*, highlighting the racism of the United States, to the UN.[4] The faith of Black activists in the UN was misplaced, particularly in the case of Malcolm X.

Malcolm was a staunch supporter of revolutionary Pan-Africanist Patrice Lumumba, who was the first elected leader of the Democratic Republic of Congo. The UN had pledged to support his democratically elected regime against a range of illegitimate claims to the government, including the eventual dictatorship of Mobutu. The UN had troops stationed in Congo to keep the peace and protect Lumumba from being captured and assassinated. But the world watched as the USA worked its "diplomacy" within the UN to undermine the democratically elected government of the nation, and UN troops effectively stood by as Lumumba was captured, with the support of the CIA, and then murdered in January 1961.[5] Nevertheless Malcolm maintained his faith in the powers of the "world court" to deliver on racial justice. But that would change. In his final speech before being assassinated in 1965 Malcolm had lost faith in the global order, and most likely in the UN, when he perfectly diagnosed the postwar settlement as "benevolent colonialism." In his typically accessible style, Malcolm likened the problem that the European powers found themselves in Africa after the war to being like a basketball player "trapped" on a basketball court with nowhere to go. From Malcolm's vantage point, the European powers had raped and pillaged their way through the continent and then had to draw on African support in the war. The natives had now picked up arms to defend the mother country and were in no mood to return to the previous racist status quo. The wars had also largely bankrupted these once great empires and drained them of human resources so Europe simply could no longer sustain their colonial domination. So just like in basketball when a player is trapped, the Europeans had to find an open teammate, and so "they passed the ball to Uncle Sam."

It is no coincidence that the UN, IMF, and World Bank were all based in the United States; their location marked the shift in the seat of power in the new age of empire.[6] The US did not have the same colonial baggage as the European empires and used its revolution against the British to burnish its anti-imperialist credentials. Indeed, both Nkrumah and Lumumba gave speeches that indicated some faith in the US because of this history.[7] So the US took the pass from Europe and laid the framework for international cooperation and law. Malcolm explained that "they switched from the old, open colonial, imperialistic approach to the benevolent approach. They came up with some benevolent colonialism, philanthropic colonialism, humanitarianism, or dollarism."[8]

The US's new approach to imperialism is reminiscent of Malcolm's distinction between the racism of the Southern "bloody jawed wolf" and the Northern "smiling fox."[9] Malcolm preferred the wolf who would "show their teeth in a snarl that keeps the Negro always aware of where he stands with them." In this context the wolf is Europe. In all its naked brutality, European colonialism was very easy to see and therefore easy to target for resistance. Malcolm was more wary of the fox who would "show their teeth to the Negro but pretend that they are smiling." Just like Malcolm warned, "a fox and a wolf are both canine" so either way "you'll still be in the doghouse."[10] There is probably no better example of the fox at work than the UN, which offers hope and progressive resolutions but is a central pillar of maintaining the racist global order.

It is worth remembering the mission of the UN from the outset, in terms of understanding its limitations. It took two world wars that brought bloodshed and violence into Europe for the organization to come into being. The preamble of the charter opens with "We the peoples of the United Nations determined to save succeeding generations from the scourge of war, which twice in our lifetime has brought untold sorrow to mankind."[11] Sorrow to mankind only became relevant when the violence was being inflicted on White lives. The empires that collided during the wars were collectively responsible for the largest genocide in human history in the Americas from the fifteenth century; the barbarity of taking millions of Africans in chains across the Atlantic; and tens of millions of deaths around the globe in colonial conquest.[12] But none of this led to a breakthrough in international law. In fact, the UN aimed to bring together the violent empires in peace. The charter was specifically written so as not to give those living in colonial regimes the right to freedom.[13] Along with the US, Britain, the nation who presided over the largest empire in human history, was the key architect of the Atlantic charter. France, with a competing empire, was also given a seat on the security council, along with the USSR and China. Africa was not excluded by accident. Even if they had wanted to be there, few African independent countries existed at this time, and the British and French empire accounted for most of the continent. The real power in the UN lies in the permanent members of the security council who have the power of veto over binding resolutions. So whilst in theory the UN can declare a war illegal, if the US, France, China, Russia, or their allies want to invade a country, they are free to do so. Since the UN was founded, the US has waged major wars in Korea, Vietnam, Afghanistan, and Iraq, despite the US's ostensible commitment to global peace (we should never forget that the US still acts like a bloody jawed wolf when necessary).

POST-RACIAL FRAMEWORK

Post-racialism lies at the heart of the UN project. The original declarations fail to recognize the racism that was shaping the world at the time, and the organization has continued this trend in the present day. In fact, it was scholars brought together by the United Nations Educational, Scientific, and Cultural Organization (UNESCO) who officially declared the end of race in their 1950 statement, which reads:

> National, religious, geographic, linguistic and cultural groups do not necessarily coincide with racial groups: and the cultural traits of such groups have no demonstrated genetic connection with racial traits. Because serious errors of this kind are habitually committed when the term "race" is used in popular parlance, it would be better when speaking of human races to drop the term "race" altogether and speak of ethnic groups.[14]

The desire to abandon the concept of race was due to the horrors of the Holocaust, which shook Europe to the core. The systematic slaughter of Jewish people was seen as a unique horror, an historical aberration that could never be allowed to happen again. But nothing could be further from the truth: as Aimé Cesaire explained, the Holocaust was the "boomerang" effect of the logics of colonialism coming home to Europe.[15] The racial violence necessary to produce the Holocaust had long been practiced in the pursuit of empire. The concept of race that was mobilized by the Nazis was the same one used to justify genocide, slavery, and colonialism across the globe. Scholar Zygmunt Bauman argued that the Holocaust was therefore not only a "legitimate resident in the house of modernity" but it in fact "would not be at home in any other house."[16]

Often overlooked in understanding the Holocaust is that its precursor was the German genocide of the Herero and Nama people in what is now Namibia. Between 1904 and 1906 the Germans killed at least 70,000 Herero and 30,000 Nama people, representing 80 and 50 percent of the total populations, respectively.[17] From 1905 to 1907, the Germans killed up to 250,000 Africans in Tanzania in order to quell a rebellion.[18] German scientists took thousands of African skulls home with them and used them to prove Black supposed inferiority. It was not only the slaughter that was pioneered in Africa but the archive of knowledge for scientific racism was built off such macabre colonial exploits.

Notorious Nazi scientist Eugen Fischer, whose work influenced Hitler's Nuremberg laws, cut his teeth researching in Namibia in 1905 during the genocide. He created a device to categorize the "races," a box with thirty different strands of hair from blond to black, with color and texture often meaning the difference between "life and death."[19] He gave this device to Karl Pearson, who was one of the first leading researchers on statistics, at University College London in 1908. Pearson was the protégé of Francis Galton, who pioneered the study of eugenics, which was accepted as legitimate science until the horrors of the Holocaust.

In 2015 the German government recognized and apologized for the genocide after refusing to do so for decades. In 2021 (no doubt swept up in the post–George Floyd fervor) they also agreed to send an additional 1.1 billion euros to Namibia over a thirty-year period alongside their statement of regret.[20] But they refused to call the payment either compensation or reparations, and the Herero and Nama leaders strongly denounced the government for accepting the deal, and in fact filed suit against the agreement.[21] The leaders have been filing suit for compensation in the US courts since 2001 due to the Alien Tort Statute, which potentially makes those companies open to suit. The leaders were angered not only by the fact that the compensation was not marked as reparations, but also that it was directed generally to Namibia rather than to repair the Herero and Nama communities. The lack of success in the courts is one window on the problem with international law. The 2017 case was thrown out of the US courts because of a lack of jurisdiction, which reveals the degree to which international disputes have no traction in US courts. But in terms of taking the German government to court there is no court that holds jurisdiction. There is therefore no legal remedy to seek reparations within the framework of international law. Given the vastly different lives that people live across the globe due to racist exploitation, a system that guarantees only the basic rights will always support the unjust status quo. It bears remembering Malcolm X's observation: If a country commits an atrocity, it is pointless to try to take "the case to the criminal."[22]

The German negotiator with Namibia exposed another dimension of the problem. He explained that Germany had "no legal obligation because at that moment in time there was no legal framework that one could apply." Genocide simply wasn't illegal in the colonies in the early twentieth century; in fact, there wasn't even a name for it. Slaughtering the natives was one of the many necessary features of the colonial system.

The post-racial framework freezes the world in colonial injustice in two ways. Firstly, by refusing to apply contemporary standards to the past it ensures that the former colonial powers do not have to pay reparations for their past atrocities. We have moved beyond race now, so we apparently no longer need to account for how it has shaped the world. If the West were answerable for its past crimes the entire economic system would collapse due to the reparations due. Perhaps more disturbingly, however, is that conceptually the post-racial framework maintains the disregard for Black and Brown life of the original colonial period. Not only did historical colonial genocides not meet the criteria for recognition in the West, but even modern-day atrocities struggle to receive the designation in the underdeveloped world. The West was subject to stark criticism for delaying declaring the attempted annihilation of the Tutsis by the Hutus in Rwanda a genocide. Between April and July 1994 approximately a million Rwandans and 70 percent of the Tutsi population had been massacred,[23] but the West was hesitant to get involved. Bill Clinton, the US president at the time, later apologized to Rwanda, estimating that they could have saved a third of the lives lost had the nation acted sooner.[24] The truth is that the US and the West knew the full scale of the horror, but African lives are simply worth less. The West neglecting Africa should not be surprising, but it took until February 2014 for the UN to officially recognize the slaughter in Rwanda as a genocide through the International Criminal Tribunal for Rwanda.

The key with any post-racial framework is the pretense that racism is over whilst maintaining a system of racial oppression. When we look at the roots of the framework of international law in benevolent colonialism, we can see from the very conception that post-racialism was its basis.

UNIVERSALLY UNEQUAL RIGHTS

The intellectual ghost of Immanuel Kant haunts the framework of international law. His work on human rights lay at the foundation for contemporary understandings and supranational bodies like the UN.[25] This is often seen as a positive because Kant's work on moral philosophy remains at the foundation of mainstream understandings. But Kant is also the perfect example of the problems of the post-racial framework. The universal rights that Kant offers are in fact deeply racist and freeze the world in colonial inequality. The fact that Kant remains a hero of the West tells us just how deep racism is embedded within Western knowledge. Kant was an ugly racist who firmly believed that "humanity at its greatest perfection [is] in the race of the whites."[26] A large portion of his work was what he called "moral geography" where he used a frankly ridiculous climate theory to identify four races (White, Negro, Hun, and Hindu) and to place them in a hierarchy with White people firmly at the top.[27] He was so committed to his deluded ideas that he once gave advice to enslavers on how best to beat a so-called Negro:

> Use a split bamboo cane instead of a whip, so that the "negro" will suffer a great deal of pains (because of the "negro's" thick skin, he would not be racked with sufficient agonies through a whip) but without dying... the blood needs to find a way out of the Negro's thick skin to avoid festering.[28]

It is bizarre that anyone claiming to perpetuate inclusive knowledge could teach someone with such horrendous views, but it beggars belief that his theory would be used as a basis for a progressive set of universal rights. Towards the end of his life, Kant condemned both slavery (which was largely over by then) and colonialism, but to argue that a "superior" society does not have the right to take the land of a "savage" one they encounter is hardly an anti-racist commitment.[29] While Kant came to appreciate all human life, he did not view all humans as equal. I can say that gorillas have a right to roam freely in their terrain without arguing that they have the same rights as humans. By maintaining his racist moral geography, Kant's universal rights were never truly universal. What was universal about Kant's theory was the degree to which it reflected a central idea in Western thought—that Whites were on top of the racial hierarchy.

The UN, and international law more broadly, is the perfect example of this universalism. Only the most basic of rights are guaranteed under the UN charter, for instance the right to life, and the right not to be tortured or abused. There are more generic rights like the right to education, but again only on the most basic level. There is no right to prosperity, or a right to economic equality, enshrined in the UN. Nothing in the UN disrupts the racial hierarchy that colonialism produced. The rights, at best, ensure that people live relatively freely, without starving to death, provide some level of literacy, and promote formal gender equality. These are all laudable rights, but they do nothing to address the global inequality caused by racism. In fact, many of the rights are deeply paternalistic in the sense of reflecting the idea that the developed world needs to be ensuring the rights and freedoms of those it has underdeveloped.

One of the most notable absences from any of the UN discourse on global inequality is its most obvious feature. If you look at a map of GDP per capita, the racist nature of the globe is immediately apparent. The richest countries are where White people live (Europe, North America, Australia) and the poorest region is where the Black people reside (so-called sub-Saharan Africa). This is by no means a coincidence given the history of colonial exploitation. Although it is the most glaring feature of global inequality, you will not see any recognition of this in the UN development goals or mission against racism. In the post-racial framework "racial" inequality becomes "global" inequality and the oppressors are given the benevolent role of saving the former savages from themselves.

The idea that all nations could be treated the same under the law after centuries of colonial conquest cemented the existing inequalities. Economically, it should have been easy to predict that nations that did not have infrastructure or educated populations and had been made entirely dependent on their mother countries would struggle to survive, let alone compete.[30] But by adopting a nation state model of the world, this is exactly what was expected. In fact, there is no more damaging reality to those in the underdeveloped world than the nation state.

The West built its fortune as vast empires and decolonized her subjects into nation states. Particularly in Africa, these nations were the creation of European powers, taking little account of geography or ethnicity of the people contained within their borders. As individual, often small nations, these formerly colonized nations have very little power to resist their continued exploitation. The UN provides the perfect ruse of representation for each nation that is in reality meaningless. The dominant powers continue to shape the world in their interests while the underdeveloped countries survive on the scraps from the table. International law does nothing to disrupt this. Indeed, the development of international law has done nothing either to help ease the suffering created by historic wrongs or to address the problems of continued racial discrimination.

Malcolm X complained that the major limitation of the civil rights movement was that it kept the problem of racism "under the jurisdiction of Uncle Sam."[31] This was why he was keen to take the case before the UN and not any nation state government. If Malcolm had lived he would have taken the case of US racism to the world court of the UN. But if he had have lived to do so he would have found that there was very little that the UN could do, even if the body wanted to. The UN approach to racism has reduced the problem to one to be solved by individual nation states. There is a UN Special Rapporteur on Contemporary Forms of Racism, Racial Discrimination, Xenophobia, and Related Intolerance, with the convoluted name indicating just how diluted the problem of racism has become. The special rapporteur visits member states and writes stinging reports on the problems in various countries, making a series of recommendations. But they have absolutely no power to change the law. Thanks to the General Assembly there is also a panel of experts specifically dedicated to those of African descent, and we are in the tail end of the International Decade for People of African Descent, which started in 2015. Part of the remit of the decade is to call governments to recognize the impacts of their enslavement of African people and to consider paying reparations. But there is no money to support these endeavors and no obligation on member states to do anything for the decade, much less consider reparatory justice. The UN Decade for People of African Descent is just a rhetorical tool, something that may make us feel empowered but does nothing to empower us.

The power of the nation state in the framework of international law is so overwhelming that nations can often exempt themselves from international laws they do not want to follow. For example, in 1969 the UK ratified the International Convention on the Elimination of All Forms of Racial Discrimination (ICERD) but submitted a reservation to Article 4 that promises nations will "undertake to adopt immediate and positive measures designed to eradicate all incitement to, or acts of, such discrimination." The result of this is that the article is not incorporated into British law and therefore citizens have no recourse outside of the British courts for racial discrimination cases.[32] Nowhere in the UN is the structural role of racism recognized and it is certainly not addressed in any meaningful way in international law.

SUBJECT CITIZENRY

Prior to the supposedly progressive proclamations of international law from the West, there were frameworks of global governance. The empires that spread across the globe had to govern outside of their national borders. In fact, the very notion of the nation state is a fantasy when dealing with the last four centuries of history. One of the main principles that has been retained in the post-racial framework of international law is that different rules apply in the mother country than in the colonies. This was essential to ensure that the violence necessary for colonial conquest was not permitted on home soil. For example, although Britain was the premiere slave trading nation in the eighteenth century, slavery was outlawed in English law.

In 1772 James Somerset was taken to London from the plantation in the Caribbean by his enslaver, as was common practice. But he escaped and appealed to the English courts to prevent him from being forcibly removed back to the plantation. In what was seen as a landmark case Lord Chief Justice Mansfield ruled that Somerset could neither be detained by his enslaver in England nor forcibly returned to slavery. He remarked that:

> The state of slavery is of such a nature, that it is incapable of being introduced on any reasons, moral or political; but only positive law, which preserves its force long after the reasons, occasion, and the time itself from whence it was created, is erased from memory: It's so odious, that nothing can be suffered to support it, but positive law.[33]

Due to there being no "positive law" permitting slavery in England, Mansfield reasoned that there was no basis for the horrific practice and effectively determined it to be illegal to keep the enslaved in the country. However, this did nothing to stop plantation owners bringing their enslaved with them to the country. The police were not arresting enslavers and there was no punishment for the plantation owner who trafficked Somerset into Britain. The only recourse the enslaved had was if they could escape and file suit. The end result was that enslavers simply had to be more careful with their supposed property if they did not want to lose it. Somerset had been assisted by the veteran abolitionist Granville Sharp in his plight.[34] Even though slavery never technically took place in Britain, there were at least 15,000 Africans in Britain by 1785.[35]

Mansfield may have declared slavery illegal on the soil of England, but in another infamous case he firmly supported the "odious" institution in the colonies. In 1783, the case of the *Zong* slave ship came before his court, where the ship captain was claiming insurance for the 132 Africans he threw overboard during the voyage. The captain argued that it was due to circumstances out of his control that the "cargo" had to be jettisoned overboard, but the insurers did not want to pay out.[36] The case was later used by abolitionists to highlight the horrors of the slave trade, but at the time it went largely unremarked upon. Insurance claims and counterclaims were common, a feature of the brutal system.[37] Mansfield certainly did not treat this as a special case and refused to see it as anything other than an insurance claim. The notion that there might be criminal liability for the murder of 132 people never occurred to him. It was eventually discovered that the captain had been at fault for the lack of water on board and therefore Mansfield did not rule that the insurers had to pay out. Mansfield made it abundantly clear that

> the Case of Slaves was the same as if Horses had been thrown over board. The question was, whether there was not an Absolute Necessity for throwing them over board to save the rest.[38]

Remember this is the same Mansfield who had earlier ruled that slavery was "odious" and was not legal in England. But because maritime law made it perfectly legal to dispense of Africans as though they were chattel, Mansfield upheld the actions as merely an insurance dispute. It may sound like a contradictory position, but this distinction is what held the empire together.

In the post-racial framework of international law such openly racist reasoning no longer has a place, but the principles have remained intact. One of the main tools used to pillage the former colonies to keep them in a state of neo-colonial dependence are the conditions attached to IMF and World Bank loans. Nations won their independence but had no prospects for prosperity given their underdevelopment and balkanization. When they fell into debt, the West stepped in to provide loans. But their "help" came at a steep cost.

When the US bailed out Europe with the Marshall Plan after the war, there were no strings attached. The same is true originally of the IMF, which was initially set up to help get European countries back on their feet. But when loans were given to underdeveloped countries, they had to submit to the conditions of Western financial institutions. Dubbed the "Washington consensus" because of the location of both the IMF and World Bank, this typically involved opening up their markets to international free trade, removing state subsidies, privatizing state industries, and putting in place stark austerity measures to try to balance the budget.[39] This process is called "structural readjustment" to mold the economies to fit what the West needs from them. It is a devastating feature of the development industry that wreaks havoc on the lives of those in the underdeveloped world. It is also effectively a plank of international law in the sense that Western countries dictate economic legislation to the poorer parts of the world. A study of 135 recipient countries found that accepting money from the IMF significantly increased income inequality.[40] Structural adjustment has a negative effect on women's employment.[41] IMF loans lead to higher suicide rates in countries that accept them.[42] IMF policies also reduce human rights in a recipient country, specifically torture and extrajudicial killings.[43] The whole purpose of IMF intervention is meant to be to save struggling economies, but "two thirds of IMF members experienced a financial crisis after 1980, some more than twice."

The case of Ghana is instructive of devastation wrought and also the double standards enshrined in the policies. Rice farming was one of the successes of the post-independence economy, because it was supported by government subsidies and there was a ban on foreign imports of the product. In the eighties, the country wanted to improve its rice production by developing irrigation systems, so it turned to the West for a helping hand. The IMF and World Bank loaned Ghana the money but on the condition that the nation "liberalize" her markets to supposedly help boost the economy. Liberalizing here meant opening their market to free trade, and therefore ending governmental subsidies to rice farmers and prohibiting the banning of foreign imports.

The inevitable happened. Much cheaper and higher-quality, mostly American, rice flooded the Ghanaian market. The once booming rice farming industry has almost completely collapsed, bringing increased poverty into formerly flourishing rural areas. Demonstrating the same logic that applied in the colonial era, the laws in the mother country (in this case the United States) are different than those in the colonies. State subsidies were outlawed in Ghana, but the US rice flooding the market was heavily subsidized by the US government. In 2003 the US government paid $1.3 billion in subsidies to rice farmers, which accounted for 72 percent of the value of the crop.[44] The so-called free trade on the Ghanaian market was anything of the sort; local famers had no chance to compete and were forced into poverty by neo-colonial regulations. Ghana's rice production was destroyed by the loans it took out to support the industry ... and they are still paying back the money. The first president of Ghana, Kwame Nkrumah, was right when he said that the relationship between Africa and the West has an "Alice in wonderland craziness" about it.[45] It is through policies like the ones to which Ghana was subjected that those in the underdeveloped world live in a state of subject citizenry in their own countries.

Those children of the empire who live within the former mother countries also find themselves as subject citizens. Unlike in the settler colonies like the United States and Brazil, the vast majority of Black and Brown people living in Europe have a recent relative who was born in a former colony. One of the features of the new age of empire after the Second World War was the mass migration of those in European empires to the metropolis. The UK passed the British Nationalities Act in 1948, which was effectively a piece of international law, affirming the right of the hundreds of millions of colonial subjects to have apparently equal status as citizens of the United Kingdom and the Colonies. In principle, this was the case before the act; Britain was not a nation state but an empire with colonial subjects recognized under British law. But the government was keen to codify the fact in law to keep countries like Canada from leaving the empire. The act coincided with better access to transatlantic travel, which meant that those descended from the enslaved in the Caribbean could migrate to Europe.

The Caribbean is essentially the American South for nations like Britain and France, the part of the nation where slavery took place and the vast majority of Black people lived. But due to the ocean the migration to Europe (or North) was delayed until people were able to travel.[46] In 1948 the *Empire Windrush* left Jamaica with hundreds of colonial subjects seeking to find work in Britain. Even though they were subjects of the British crown, the left-wing British government at the time tried to stop the ship from docking in Britain.[47] But there was nothing the administration could do because the immigrants were effectively moving from one part of the nation to another.

The *Windrush* was not the first ship to bring colonial immigrants to Britain, but the period of mass migration after the war became synonymous with the ship and is known as the *Windrush* generation. In recent years, *Windrush* has become tied to scandal, as potentially thousands of people who migrated to Britain legally decades ago have found themselves declared illegal and lost their jobs, been detained in immigration centers, and even deported. The problem is that they had no documentation to prove they are in the country legally because they traveled as children on their parents' passports, which have been long lost. In 2012, the British government instituted the "hostile environment" policy that meant people needed to prove their immigration status for work, housing, and many routine practices in life for the first time, in a bid to root out the apparent scourge of illegal immigrants.[48]

Ironically, the scandal broke in the year that Britain was getting ready to celebrate seventy years after the *Windrush* had docked and all the supposed successes of building a multiracial society. In reality, the anniversary showed that for many in Britain they had only colonial citizenship, which could be revoked if they could not prove their status. This could be viewed as a case of racist domestic policy on behalf of Britain. But in order to make immigration from the Caribbean, African, and Asian colonies illegal, the regions first needed to be made independent of the mother country. It is no coincidence that the Commonwealth Immigrants Act of 1962, which laid the foundation for the subsequent tightening of immigration that led to the *Windrush* scandal, came into the law the very same year that Jamaica and Trinidad (Britain's largest Caribbean colonies) became so-called independent. Britain supported liberation movements to stop the influx of people into the nation. The current nation state framework that is the hallmark of the new age of empire and international law was partly brought into being to stop the chickens coming home to roost in the mother countries of Europe.

Restricting the movement of people from the underdeveloped to the developed world has become a feature of the global system. Britain has been at the forefront of this movement, as the largest former empire, and has gone to extremes to pull up the drawbridge. Theresa May, the same home secretary to introduce the hostile environment, who later became prime minister, seemed comfortable with letting migrants crossing the Mediterranean drown as a deterrent to others who might attempt the same. In 2022, Priti Patel, Britain's first female of color home secretary, introduced a plan to deport those crossing into Britain on small boats to Rwanda to be processed. The plan was so draconian that even Theresa May, architect of the hostile environment, declared she could not support it.[49] Apparently, neither government was dissuaded by the optics of a developed former colonizing country deporting those (often Black and Brown) to a former colony, albeit one that was not in the British Empire. They were also not perturbed by the criticism of Gillian Triggs, the assistant high commissioner at the UNHCR, who was clear that the plan "would not comply with the UK's international legal responsibilities."[50] But as is with much of the corpus of international law, when a rich country wants to ignore it, there is little to stop them. Subsequent administrations have doubled down on the plan even after it was declared illegal by the British supreme court.[51] The government subsequently changed the legislation and have even considered leaving the European Court of Human Rights to get around the illegality of the plan.[52]

The dawn of an international legal framework to ensure global rights and freedoms was a false one. Rather than representing a shift of power and a break with the colonial order, international law was just one manifestation of "benevolent colonialism." It may look progressive in theory but because of the post-racial nature of international law, the regime of international law has functioned to reinforce the racism that lies at the heart of the Western imperial project.

This is not by accident but design. The architects of universal rights and laws are the very same dead White men who provided the scholarship for racial science and justified the slaughter of hundreds of millions of people of color in the pursuit of White supremacy. Bodies like the UN, which are meant to make the world fairer, serve the opposite purpose. There can be no racial justice when individual nation states, or their citizens, try to fight for recognition and restitution from their former colonial masters. The unfortunate reality is that the majority of us are left in a state of "subject citizenry" or, as Malcolm X put it, "we are second class citizens,"[53] where we have rights but none that need to be respected.

NOTES

1. C. Anderson, *Eyes Off the Prize: The United Nations and the African American Struggle for Human Rights, 1944–1955* (Cambridge: Cambridge University Press, 2003).
2. Malcolm X, 2nd OAAU Founding Rally, Audubon Ballroom, New York, 1964.
3. Malcolm X, "The Ballot or the Bullet," speech at Cory Methodist Church in Cleveland, Ohio, April 3, 1964.
4. Civil Rights Congress, *We Charge Genocide: The Historic Petition to the United Nations for Relief from a Crime of the United States Government Against the Negro People* (1951).
5. S. Williams, *White Malice: The CIA and the Neocolonisation of Africa* (London: C. Hurst and Co., 2021).
6. K. Andrews, *The New Age of Empire: How Racism and Colonialism Still Rule the World* (London: Penguin, 2021).
7. Williams, *White Malice*.
8. Malcolm X, speech at Ford Auditorium, Detroit, Michigan, February 14, 1965.
9. Malcolm X, interview by Louis Lomax, Educational Video Group, Greenwood, IN, 1963.
10. Malcolm X, "The Ballot or the Bullet."
11. UN, United Nations Charter (full text), 1946. Available at: https://www.un.org/en/about-us/un-charter/full-text.
12. Andrews, *New Age*.
13. J. Pearson, "Defending Empire at the United Nations: The Politics of International Colonial Oversight in the Era of Decolonisation," *The Journal of Imperial and Commonwealth History* 45, no. 3 (2017): 525–49.
14. UNESCO, "Fallacies of Racism Exposed: UNESCO Publishes Declaration by World's Scientists," *UNESCO Courier*, 1950, https://unesdoc.unesco.org/ark:/48223/pf0000081475.nameddest=81490
15. A. Cesaire, *Discourse on Colonialism* (New York: Monthly Review Press, 2000).
16. Z. Bauman, *Modernity and the Holocaust* (Cambridge: Polity, 1989), 17.
17. B. Madley, "Patterns of Frontier Genocide 1803–1910: The Aboriginal Tasmanians, the Yuki of California, and the Herero of Namibia," *Journal of Genocide Research* 6, no. 2 (2004): 167–92, 168–69.
18. D. Schaller, "From Conquest to Genocide: Colonial Rule in German Southwest Africa and German East Africa," in *Empire, Colony and Genocide: Conquest, Occupation and Subaltern Resistance in World History*, ed. D. Moses (Oxford: Berghahn Books, 2008), 296–324, 309.
19. A. Saini, *Superior: The Return of Race Science* (Boston: Beacon Press, 2019), 47.
20. P. Oltermann, "Germany Agrees to Pay Namibia €1.1bn over Historical Herero-Nama Genocide," *The Guardian*, May 28, 2021.

21. D. Pelz, "Herero and Nama File Suit Against Genocide Agreement," *Politics Africa,* January 22, 2023, https://www.dw.com/en/herero-and-nama-dispute-genocide-agreement-with-germany/a-64476907#:~:text=Herero%20and%20Nama%20file%20suit%20against%20genocide%20agreement.

22. Malcolm X, "The Ballot or the Bullet."

23. J. Semujanga, *Origins of Rwandan Genocide* (Amherst, NY: Humanity Books, 2003).

24. B. Clinton, Rwanda Speech, Kigali International Airport, March 25, 1998.

25. C. J. Friedrich, "The Ideology of the United Nations Charter and the Philosophy of Peace of Immanuel Kant 1795–1945," *The Journal of Politics,* 9, no. 1 (1947): 10–30.

26. T. Hill and B. Boxill, "Kant and Race," in *Race and Racism,* ed. B. Boxill (Oxford: Oxford University Press, 2001), 448–72, 455.

27. I. Kant, "On the Different Races of Man," in *The Idea of Race: Readings in Philosophy,* ed. R. Bernasconi (Hackett Publishing Company, 2000).

28. E. Eze, "The Color of Reason: The Idea of 'Race' in Kant's Anthropology," in *Postcolonial African Philosophy: A Critical Reader,* ed. E. Eze (Oxford: Blackwell, 1997), 103–40, 116.

29. L. Allais, "Kant's Racism," *Philosophical Papers* 45, nos. 1–2 (2016): 1–36, 19.

30. K. Andrews, *Back to Black: Retelling Black Radicalism for the Twenty-first Century* (London: Zed Books, 2018).

31. Malcolm X, "Ballot or the Bullet."

32. J. Yorke et al., *Minorities and Deprivation of Liberty Report* (Birmingham: Birmingham City University, 2022). Available at: https://www.bcu.ac.uk/law/research/centre-for-human-rights/consultancy/upr-project-at-bcu/upr-project-at-bcu-uk.

33. P. Finkleman, "Let Justice Be Done, Though the Heavens May Fall: The Law and Freedom," *Chicago-Kent Law Review* 70, no. 2 (1994): 325.

34. D. Olusoga, *Black and British: A Forgotten History* (London: Macmillan, 2016).

35. Olusoga, *Black and British.*

36. D. Smith and S. H. Friedman, "'Let Justice Be Done Though the Heavens May Fall': The Zong in Amma Asante's Belle," *Journal of the American Academy of Psychiatry Law* 42 (2014): 530–32.

37. A. Rupprecht, "'A Very Uncommon Case': Representations of the Zong and the British Campaign to Abolish the Slave Trade," *Journal of Legal History* 28 (2007): 329–46.

38. J. Krikler, "The Zong and the Lord Chief Justice," *History Workshop Journal* 64 (2007): 29–47, 36.

39. R. Peet, *Unholy Trinity: The IMF, World Bank and WTO* (London: Zed, 2007).

40. T. Forstera et al., "How Structural Adjustment Programs Affect Inequality: A Disaggregated Analysis of IMF Conditionality, 1980–2014," *Social Science Research* 80 (2019): 83–113.

41. J. Ball, "The Effects of Neoliberal Structural Adjustment on Women's Relative Employment in Latin America," *International Journal of Social Economics* 31 (2004): 974–87.

42. E. Goulas and A. Zervoyianni, "IMF-Lending Programs and Suicide Mortality," *Social Science & Medicine* 153 (2016): 44–53.

43. M. Abouharb and D. Cingranelli, "IMF Programs and Human Rights 1981–2003," *Review of International Organisations* 4 (2009): 47–72.

44. C. Moore, "Ghana Pays Price for West's Rice Subsidies," *The Guardian,* April 11, 2005, https://www.theguardian.com/world/2005/apr/11/hearafrica05.development.

45. K. Nkrumah, *Africa Must Unite* (London: Panaf Books, 1998), 27.
46. Andrews, *Back to Black*.
47. Olusoga, *Black and British*.
48. M. Goodfellow, *Hostile Environment: How Immigrants Became Scapegoats* (London: Verso, 2020).
49. R. Syal, "Theresa May Questions 'Legality and Practicality' of Rwanda Asylum Plan," *The Guardian*, April 19, 2022.
50. A. Gentleman and A. Allegretti, "UN Refugee Agency Condemns Boris Johnson's Rwanda Asylum Plan," *The Guardian*, April 15, 2022, https://www.theguardian.com/uk-news/2022/apr/15/un-refugee-agency-condemns-johnsons-rwanda-asylum-plan.
51. AAA (Syria) and others vs. Secretary of State for the Home Department, November 15, 2023, On appeal from: [2023] EWCA Civ 745.
52. P. Crerar and K. Stacey, "Rishi Sunak Claims New Rwanda Asylum Bill Will Prevent Legal Challenges," *The Guardian,* December 7, 2023.
53. Malcolm X, "Message to the Grassroots," speech at the Negro␣Grass Roots Leadership Conference, Michigan, November 10, 1963.

CHAPTER TWENTY-TWO

CRITICAL RACE THEORY MEETS THIRD WORLD APPROACHES TO INTERNATIONAL LAW

E. Tendayi Achiume and Devon W. Carbado

INTRODUCTION

This chapter[1] articulates six important parallel thematic developments in Critical Race Theory (CRT)[2] and Third World Approaches to International Law (TWAIL).[3] The parallels we describe mark not only the continuities of ideas across CRT and TWAIL, but also the continuities in the historical, political, racial, and disciplinary forces against which those ideas have been articulated. Which is to say, we are interested in both the critical moves through which CRT and TWAIL are articulated and the resistance to, and obfuscation and delegitimization of, those moves, especially in scholarly arenas. For simplicity, we frame international law as the site of concern for TWAIL scholars and constitutional law as the site of concern for Critical Race Theorists.

We should note at the outset that this chapter is a critique of neither CRT nor TWAIL. One might, for example, reasonably ask the colonization question vis-à-vis CRT (why are the problems of empire, imperialism, and colonization largely absent from CRT?).[4] In a similar vein, one might reasonably ask the racialization question vis-à-vis TWAIL (why are problems of racialization—particularly of nations, global power, and international law and relations—not a more central part of TWAIL?).[5] These questions invite a CRT intervention into TWAIL and a TWAIL intervention into CRT, and there are rich examples of such work.[6] Interventions such as these are important, but are not our focus here. Instead, our aim is to draw out synergies between CRT and TWAIL on the view that a mapping of the normative, theoretical, and critical spaces where CRT meets TWAIL will also help to reveal precisely where an intervention into both fields might be warranted.

Needless to say, there are other axes along which one might fairly lodge critiques of TWAIL and CRT, including through interrogations of both fields' limited engagement with indigeneity and—sometimes—dichotomous representations of "the west and rest" (in the TWAIL literature)[7] and "the white and the nonwhite" (in the CRT literature).[8] For now, we put these concerns to one side as well and focus instead on some of the ways in which CRT and TWAIL are performing similar analytical and normative work.

Our final prefatory comment before turning to the substance of our argument is this: Articulating the boundaries of any theoretical movement is fraught with contingencies and reductionisms. Such a project is all the more contestable when those boundary delineations implicate two intellectual movements, both of which have their own internal disputes. In this respect, we should be clear to note that this chapter is a full articulation of neither CRT nor TWAIL. It is a preliminary effort to describe some of the parallel epistemological projects on which both CRT and TWAIL rest.

We have organized the chapter in six moments: Moment I: Foundational Racial Capitalism; Moment II: Formal Equality and Racial Inclusion; Moment III: Colorblindness; Moment IV: Social Responsibility and Agency; Moment V: Quasi and Second-Class Scholarship; and Moment VI: Reconstruction and Transformation. We discuss each moment in turn.

PARALLEL MOMENTS OF INEQUALITY AND INTERVENTIONS

A. MOMENT I: FOUNDATIONAL RACIAL CAPITALISM

The first moment we describe implicates what Cedric Robinson calls "racial capitalism."[9] Which is to say, here, both international law, on the TWAIL side, and constitutional law, on the CRT side, operate as regimes of power and violence that implicate racism, capitalism, and colonialism. In Moment I, there are profound questions under international law to which TWAIL scholars have attended concerning which nations belong to the "family of nations" (and therefore deserve sovereignty);[10] and profound questions under constitutional law to which CRT scholars have attended concerning which peoples belong to the "family of man" (and therefore deserve citizenship).[11] In other words, in Moment I, there are social meaning attributions to nations and peoples (and nations of peoples) that facilitate, legitimize, and entrench global and domestic orderings of white supremacy, whose entailments have included conquest, expansionism, militarism, economic extraction, slavery, and genocide. CRT scholars have highlighted the operation of this global ordering of white supremacy in constitutional law cases[12] and TWAIL scholars have highlighted its manifestation in positivist jurisprudence and its sanctioning of imperial practices.[13]

With respect to the constitutional law side of this engagement, consider the case of *Dred Scott v. Sandford*,[14] formally an anticanonical case in U.S. constitutional law. Explicit in that case is the idea that African Americans are "so far inferior, that they ha[ve] no rights which the white man was bound to respect."[15] Note that in this formulation, Black inferiority is articulated as a preexisting fact (Black people are "so far inferior") rather than the effect of the very regime of slavery on which the idea of Black inferiority rests. In other words, obscured in the articulation that Black people are "so far inferior" are the acts of racial violence (including but not limited to Middle Passage) through which Black people became inferiorized under conditions of economic extraction, racial domination, and involuntary servitude.

Importantly, the framing of Black subalternity as an effect of rather than an anterior to white supremacy is a central claim in CRT.[16] It is part of a broader contention in that literature that race is socially constructed through, among other sources of power, law.[17] With respect to *Dred Scott* specifically, the argument would be that in the context of constitutionalizing slavery (its racial dimensions, economic dimensions, and violent dimensions), the Court's construction of Black people as "so far inferior" positioned African Americans beyond the reach of liberal subjectivity and outside of "the family of man." Thus positioned, African Americans became socially unintelligible as citizens and constitutionally ineligible for citizenship. Understood in that way, the white supremacist ordering of slavery produced the subjugated status of Blackness that the regime purported merely to find. To put that another way still, and borrow from a point Simone de Beauvoir made about women, Black people were not born the appropriate subjects of slavery.[18] They were made the appropriate subjects of slavery through the racially naturalizing dimensions of that regime.[19]

If it is fair to say that CRT reflects an interrogation of which people belong to "the family of man" and therefore deserve citizenship, it is also fair to say that TWAIL reflects an interrogation of which nations belong to the "family of nations" and therefore deserve sovereignty. Since its inception, TWAIL has foregrounded the constitutive role of European colonialism in shaping international doctrine. In particular, TWAIL scholars have demonstrated how the imperial logics of nonwhite exclusion where embedded by a concept that sits at the very foundation of international law—sovereignty. In a pathbreaking contribution to the TWAIL canon, Antony Anghie details not only how membership in international society formed a prerequisite for sovereignty, but also how that membership was simultaneously racially and culturally restricted to European nations.[20] These racializing dimensions of international law generally do not figure into the conventional international law scholarship. According to Anghie, that body of work, which focuses on "order among sovereign states," elides the role of race and culture in shaping the very formation and formulations of concepts such as sovereignty.[21]

Conventional international legal scholarship is problematic in another way. It does not address how international legal doctrine and policies construct race. We have already hinted at the nexus between the social construction of race in the international arena and the instantiation of racialized global hierarchies. We will say more on this point further along in the chapter. For now, we simply want to note that inquiries about which nations belonged to the "family of nations" and therefore deserved sovereignty were never made or answered without recourse (at least implicitly) to racialized views about peoples and nations. As Christopher Gevers notes, the very idea of the international is always already racialized in the sense of being articulated against background assumptions about the necessity and naturalness of a white global order. It is crucial, then, to confront the "international" of international law as "a racial imaginary—a 'White World' . . . that emerges from and reinforces Global White Supremacy."[22]

TWAIL's racial critique of sovereignty specifically and the international legal order more generally is particularly attentive to positivism, the methodological means through which the racialization of sovereignty was achieved.[23] In a move analogous to the claims CRT scholars have rehearsed about the social construction of race, TWAIL scholars have long argued that non-European nations did not, a priori, lack sovereignty. Positivist jurisprudence produced that "lack" through ostensibly objective facts about racially inferior people, uncivilized cultures, and dysfunctional and backward governments.[24] TWAIL's interrogation of these representational contingencies reveals that non-European nations were not, in some pre-political sense, outside of the "family of nations." Colonization placed them there, in part by relying on the otherizing images of the Third World that positivist jurisprudence expressed. Understood in that way, the racial work positivist jurisprudence performed was never just discursive. It was also material in the sense of presaging and ultimately effectuating legalized racial domination.[25] To put these points another way still, if slavery was underwritten by the idea that African Americans had no rights that white people were bound to respect, colonization was underwritten by the idea that nonwhite nations had no claims to sovereignty that white nations were bound to respect. In short, the racial logics of colonialism rendered non-European nations not only available for domination but also the appropriate subjects for domination.[26] By effectively defining sovereignty as Europeanness, international law underwrote a white-dominated global order in which European nations exploited, dominated, and, in some instances, facilitated the genocide of Third World people.

James Gathii's work in this area speaks to the political and economic dimension of this white global hegemony. His study of the fusion of British imperial expansion in East Africa and British colonialism in the region offers a prototypical example of a TWAIL intervention delineating the link between positivist sovereignty jurisprudence and the political and economic exploitation it enabled. In Gathii's formulation, imperialism is defined to emphasize capitalist expansion and economic exploitation, and colonialism is defined to emphasize territorial conquest and acquisition.[27] Gathii demonstrates how British courts' positivist jurisprudence relied on racist conceptions of the Maasai and other East African peoples to ratify British expropriation of Maasai land.[28] In the relevant cases, British courts' characterization of the Maasai as variously uncivilized or semicivilized proved vital to the vitiation of the Maasai people's legal challenges to British expropriation of their land.[29] These courts employed formal positivist analysis to rule that the Maasai were sufficiently sovereign to enter into treaties ceding their territories to the British,[30] but insufficiently civilized to be protected as such. This sufficiently sovereign/insufficiently civilized construction of the Maasai provided the normative foundation on which British courts treated the expulsion of the Maasai people from their land as legitimate under both international and British law, notwithstanding that the expulsion unequivocally contravened various treaty agreements.[31]

As we have already said, and want to reemphasize here, the racialized determinations about the unfitness of Black people under U.S. constitutional law for citizenship and the unfitness of non-European nations under positivist jurisprudence for sovereignty were never made outside of economies of violence and economic exploitation. Domestically and globally, those determinations were part of a broader set of racial logics through which labor was extracted, genocide effectuated, territories confiscated, wars initiated, bodies subjugated, and capital accumulated.

B. MOMENT II: FORMAL EQUALITY AND RACIAL INCLUSION

In Moment II, CRT and TWAIL foreground the problem of racial inclusion, albeit at different scales. Here, TWAIL scholars focus on the formal inclusion of nonwhite peoples into the international society of sovereign nation states (under First World and white dominated international terms and norms), and CRT scholars focus on the formal inclusion of nonwhite peoples into citizenship (under white dominated domestic terms and norms).[32] For both CRT and TWAIL scholars, then, the preceding acts of inclusion, or incorporation, if you prefer, are not a fundamental reconfiguration of power but rather a particular technology through which to maintain, manage, and legitimize the prior hierarchical domestic and global racial orderings. Under this formulation, the old regimes of racial exclusion (sovereignty and citizenship) are repurposed to carry forward their subordinating work as new regimes of racial inclusion. Giorgio Agamben might describe this phenomenon as an example of an "inclusive exclusion."[33] Our point is that both TWAIL and CRT scholars have identified inclusion and recognition as means of perpetuating subordination. Within TWAIL, the analysis is of formal sovereign recognition in international law and the ways in which that recognition was structured to perpetuate quasi sovereign status in the global arena. Within CRT, the analysis is of formal citizenship recognition in constitutional law and the ways in which that recognition was structured to perpetuate second-class citizenship in the domestic arena.

A classic example from constitutional law of how processes of racial inclusion can be mechanisms through which to reproduce rather than undermine a prior hierarchical ordering is *Plessy v. Ferguson*,[34] the U.S. Supreme Court case that litigated the equality boundaries of the Fourteenth Amendment. Reflecting an express repudiation of *Dred Scott*, the Fourteenth Amendment is one of the Reconstruction Amendments that was designed to facilitate the inclusion of Black people into citizenship. The amendment includes a Citizenship Clause—"All persons born or naturalized in the United States, and subject to the jurisdiction thereof, are citizens of the United States and of the State wherein they reside"—and an Equal Protection Clause—"No state shall . . . deny to any person within its jurisdiction the equal protection of the laws."[35] A central question *Plessy* presented was whether separate-but-equal violated this latter clause, that is to say, ran afoul of the Fourteenth Amendment's guarantee of equal protection. Writing for the Majority, Justice Brown answered that question in the negative.[36] In so doing, he constitutionalized Jim Crow and ensured that Black people would be included into citizenship on racially subordinating terms. This feature of Jim Crow—that it performed its racially subordinating work *inside* of citizenship—is at least one sense in which *Plessy v. Ferguson* structuralized Black people's membership in and belonging to the United States society as an "inclusive exclusion." It is precisely because this inclusive exclusion carried forward substantive dimensions of the ideological and material apparatus of slavery that, borrowing from Saidiya Hartman, one might describe Jim Crow as an "afterlife of slavery."[37]

With respect to international law, one of TWAIL's pivotal examples of the subordinating inclusion of nonwhite nations into a terrain from which they had historically been excluded is the formal decolonization of the Third World. TWAIL characteristically marks this moment of incorporation into the "family of nations" as inclusion on terms that have ultimately ensured *neo*colonial domination, not substantive sovereignty for the former colonial nations. Indeed, as the former colonies gained seats at the international lawmaking table, they had to contend with the hard reality that the former colonial powers had neocolonial aspirations. Those aspirations manifested themselves in strategic mobilizations of international law and policy doctrines that were designed to maintain not only the subordinate status of Third World nations, but also the control First World nations had over the international legal system. The former colonies organized in various attempts to disrupt this reassertion of colonial power. But their efforts largely failed. The built-in historical headwinds of colonialism ushered in a colonial afterlife in which formal sovereignty, or equality of states, comfortably existed alongside the quasi sovereignty of the Third World.

While Third World nations did not experience their quasi sovereignty in precisely the same way, they all confronted the fact that the postcolonial world was not a departure from the racial hierarchy on which colonialism was based but rather a rearticulation of that hierarchy on neocolonial terms. Antony Anghie and Siba N'zatioula Grovogui's scholarship have advanced a version of this claim, extending the analysis of neocolonial scholars, such as Kwame Nkrumah and Walter Rodney,[38] to demonstrate how, following formal decolonization, First World nations deployed multiple dimensions of the international system, including sovereignty doctrine and international institutional arrangements, to reproduce the economic and political domination of the First World over the Third.[39] As just one example of this dynamic, Anghie details how the precursor regime to formal decolonization—the mandate system that the League of Nations oversaw—included design features that effectively ensured the postcolonial subordination of former colonial nations.[40] Consequently, even as First World nations shifted in their articulation of Third World countries from describing them as too insufficiently developed to merit sovereignty to describing them as sufficiently developed enough to warrant that designation, that rearticulation still presupposed that the newly independent and sovereign Third World would serve and be subordinate to First World interests and demands.[41]

The story we are telling about the inclusion of Third World nations into sovereignty on racially hierarchical terms transcends the boundaries of formal sovereignty doctrines. Neocolonial assertions of the international legal system implicate development doctrines, international economic law, international humanitarian law, and domestic legal regimes. To begin with development, TWAIL scholar Sundhya Pahuja has powerfully demonstrated how the racial logics through which formerly colonized nations were naturalized as sovereign under conditions of marginality and subordination were carried over into the contemporary development paradigm. Under the guise of benefiting the Third World, that paradigm reproduced some of the very colonial-era hierarchies that characterized the mandate system.[42]

With respect to international economic law, James Gathii's work illustrates how the First World's influence on international economic law stripped that juridical body of its progressive possibilities.[43] According to Gathii, the First World's overdetermination of the content of international economic law undermined that law's redistributive and reparative potential and preserved the economic agendas of hegemonic First World states and international financial institutions.[44]

In the field of international humanitarian law, TWAIL scholars have shown how formal sovereignty has failed to shield Third World states from First World and international coercive intervention. The absence of an international shield for the Third World in that regard is tied directly to the ways in which the First World can wield the international system as a sword with which to treat Third World sovereignty as provisional and contingent on First World interests and assessments. Consider, for example, Aslı Bâli and Aziz Rana's study of U.S.- and European-led coercive intervention into various parts of the Arab world in the wake of the 2011 uprisings in that region. Although that intervention included some instances of regime change and implicated numerous humanitarian concerns, those coercive intrusions did not create a problem for the international legal order because they occurred in nations whose sovereignty had been vitiated for failing "to support key international and regional arrangements."[45] A crucial takeaway from Bâli and Rana's analysis is that Third World sovereignty is both *provisional* and *contingent*. It is only capable of constraining coercive foreign intervention—which is supposed to be unlawful under international law—when practiced to converge with First World global and national interests.[46]

Finally, TWAIL scholars have also interrogated the manner in which international law operates *within* nation states as an inclusive exclusion, including through its interactions with domestic legal doctrine. For example, John Reynolds describes the Israeli government's deployment of emergency doctrine to manage Israel's colonial governance of Palestinians as a form of "repressive inclusion," a mechanism of subordination through which legal doctrine facilitates racially contingent inclusion within the juridical order.[47] In a related vein, Mohammad Shahabuddin's work foregrounds how international law operates in postcolonial states to enable forms of inclusion of ethnic minorities that ultimately result in the "assimilation and the extinction of group identity."[48] On this account, the terms and means of inclusion presuppose and effectuate the erasure of cognizable groups.

The preceding examples are a way of saying that a definitive contribution of TWAIL, shared in common with CRT, is attention to how formal inclusion into the international order and the sovereignty recognition it effectuated was not an achievement of substantive equality for Third World nation states. Instead, the very terms of inclusion ensured a persisting global hierarchy with First World nations on top and Third World nations on the bottom that belies the common equation of formal decolonization with the end of colonial relations between the First and the Third World.

C. MOMENT III: COLORBLINDNESS

In Moment III, CRT and TWAIL expose and contest various iterations of colorblindness, including the idea that race no longer matters in structuring society and lived experience. In this moment, the analytical and normative fight is about both the speakability of race and racism and whether the real and pressing issues of inequality are somewhere (anywhere) beyond the boundaries of race and racism—think class, think religion, think nationalism, think culture. On the CRT front, there are at least two salient ways in which colorblindness functions in constitutional law—the complete elision of race from the doctrinal analysis at hand, and the explicit treatment of race as a suspect basis for governmental decision-making, whether or not that decision-making is designed to mitigate racial inequality. Consider first the elision of race with reference to Fourth Amendment jurisprudence.

The Fourth Amendment, which is supposed to protect us from "unreasonable searches and seizures,"[49] is arguably the most important constitutional provision for regulating police conduct. Part of the Bill of Rights (the original ten amendments added to the U.S. Constitution in 1791), the Fourth Amendment is part of a larger body of constitutional criminal procedure that was promulgated to impose constraints on police power. Debates about excessive force, stop-and-frisk, and Driving While Black all implicate Fourth Amendment law. Yet, in virtually none of the cases in which the Supreme Court adjudicates Fourth Amendment issues does one see a robust—or, indeed, much of any— engagement with race.[50] A perfect example of what we mean is manifested in the Court's "seizure" jurisprudence.

Because, as previously mentioned, the Fourth Amendment protects us from unreasonable searches and seizures, a preliminary or threshold question in Fourth Amendment law is whether governmental conduct amounts to a search or seizure. If, for example, a police officer interacts with a person and that interaction is not a search or a seizure, the Fourth Amendment has nothing to say about it. In other words, nonsearches and nonseizures reside beyond the regulatory reach of the Fourth Amendment. We should add, parenthetically, that if the police conduct in question does amount to a search or a seizure, that conduct is not necessarily unconstitutional. The question would then become whether that search or seizure was reasonable.[51] It turns out that lots of searches and seizures are reasonable, even ones that are racially motivated.[52]

With respect to what counts as a seizure, the Supreme Court has said that the inquiry is whether a "reasonable person feels free to leave or otherwise terminate the encounter." To flip that inquiry around, if a reasonable person would not feel free to leave or terminate the encounter, then that person is seized. To appreciate how the Court has elided race in its seizure jurisprudence, imagine that an officer observes Marcia on the street corner. He has no reason to believe she has done anything wrong. Nevertheless, he proceeds to:

Follow her;

> Question her along the following lines:
> *What's your name? Where are you going? Where have you been? Where do you live?*

He then asks Marcia for her identification.

Because Marcia has a Jamaican accent, he asks her questions about her immigration status.

Those questions are followed by a request to search Marcia's bag.

After searching the bag, the officer asks Marcia whether she would mind accompanying him to the station for additional questioning.

At the station, the officer continues to question Marcia about a range of matters.[53]

None of the foregoing would trigger the Fourth Amendment in the sense of constituting a seizure.[54] The Court would rule that, throughout the entire encounter, Marcia was free to leave. Was the officer required to inform Marcia of her right in that respect? No. Does it matter whether Marcia knows she has that right? No. What about the fact that Marcia was questioned at the police station? Was she still free to leave? Yes—or, at least, she should have felt free to leave. What if Marcia subjectively did not feel free to leave? Does that matter? No. The test is (supposedly) an objective one, not a subjective one.

You are probably now wondering about Marcia's race and gender. She is, after all, a Black woman. Surely that matters. It does not. Nor, in the context of applying the Fourth Amendment's seizure doctrine, would the Court take note of the historical and contemporary manifestations of overpolicing and police violence in the Black community.

The Court's colorblind approach to the seizure analysis communicates two troubling ideas. First, that the so-called reasonable person has no race (or would not be invested in paying attention to race); and second, that taking race into account in the context of determining whether a person is seized would be jurisprudentially unreasonable. Both ideas obscure what ought to travel in Fourth Amendment law as uncontestable social realities—namely, that race could inform a police officer's decision to target an African American for questioning and that being an African American could shape how one experiences and negotiates an interaction with the police.[55] Our broader point is that, consistent with one of the imperatives of colorblindness, the Supreme Court's seizure analysis almost entirely elides the ways in which race intersects with policing.

Another way in which colorblindness works in constitutional law is to treat any reference to race as constitutionally suspect. Perhaps the clearest example of this dimension of colorblindness is the Supreme Court's equal protection jurisprudence. In a series of equal protection cases, the Court has explicitly stated that *any* use of race on the part of the government is constitutionally suspect.[56] To illustrate the implications of this jurisprudential approach, stipulate that the federal government has decided to racially target members of the Black Lives Matter (BLM) movement and incarcerate them on the view that they are a radical group whose political agenda threatens the very nature of the country's democracy.[57] Assume, meanwhile, that the state of California is concerned about the displacement of African Americans via gentrification and creates a housing voucher for which only African Americans living in the parts of Los Angeles undergoing gentrification may apply. The Supreme Court would employ the same constitutional standard to determine the constitutionality of both decisions. Which is to say, in both instances, the Court would apply "strict scrutiny," the most rigorous form of judicial review.[58] The Court would treat California's effort to mitigate the racialized housing displacement gentrification effectuates, and not just the federal government's effort to incarcerate BLM members, as presumptively constitutionally suspect because both violate the constitutional norms of colorblindness.[59]

"Colorblindness" as an umbrella term for critiquing legal and jurisprudential elisions of race is arguably a term more commonly used in CRT than in TWAIL. Yet from TWAIL's founding, TWAIL scholars have variously interrogated international law's role in racialized subordination, including through carefully crafted legal and judicial techniques shorn of any explicit reference to race.[60] In other words, even without explicit reference to colorblindness, TWAIL scholars have critiqued means of racial subordination that variously obscure or disavow the racial nature of the respective interventions. TWAIL scholars have analyzed, for example, the reliance of international legal doctrine on purported cultural differences that Europeans used to establish themselves as morally and legally superior to non-European peoples they colonized, exploited, and exterminated, cloaking imperial projects of racial subordination in the language of distinctions between the "civilized" and the "uncivilized."[61]

More recent TWAIL scholarship on race traces a colorblindness of sorts within mainstream international legal scholarship,[62] even among critical international legal scholars who otherwise spotlight the colonial trappings of the discipline. Some scholars in the field have been unwilling to name and confront the ways in which race has operated on the international landscape. Other scholars insufficiently distinguish between (and sometimes conflate) racial and cultural difference in ways that obfuscate how race has structured the global order and the treatment of nations and peoples within it.[63] Still other scholars "in effect, minimize the role that race plays in international law,"[64] elide the "sociopolitical system of Global White Supremacy,"[65] and reduce their conceptualization of racism to the individual prejudices of a small number of aberrant international law scholars and practitioners.[66] Each of the preceding scholarly approaches reflects a particular technique of colorblindness in the sense of avoiding or marginalizing concerns about race and racism or disappearing them altogether.

Scholars such as Hope Lewis have criticized the ubiquity and currency of colorblind approaches to international law. Lewis's scholarship is particularly important because it blurs the boundary between CRT and TWAIL by explicitly pursuing both approaches to expose various racially subordinating features and mobilizations of international law.[67] These mobilizations have included the instantiation of neocolonial land arrangements that entrench and normalize the racialized economic order on which colonialism rested. A striking example of what we mean is a 2008 ruling from the highest adjudicatory body for the South African Development Community (SADC)[68]—the SADC Tribunal. That ruling traded on colorblindness to effectively both "lock out" Black Zimbabweans' access to land and "lock in" the access colonialism granted to whites.[69]

The case centered on Mike Campbell, the lead plaintiff and a white Zimbabwean commercial farmer. Campbell alleged that the Zimbabwean government's controversial Fast Track Land Reform Program (FTLRP), which authorized the uncompensated, compulsory seizure of agricultural lands for redistribution, constituted unlawful racial discrimination under the applicable international human rights law.[70] The SADC Tribunal ruled in favor of the plaintiffs. To do so it applied the prohibition on racial discrimination provided by the International Convention on the Elimination of Racial Discrimination, which prohibits de facto and de jure forms of such discrimination. In its conclusion, the Tribunal found that although the FTLRP made no mention of race, it nonetheless constituted unlawful de facto discrimination because of its disproportionate impact on white Zimbabwean farmers.[71]

Understanding Zimbabwe's broader sociopolitical context—a product of its colonial past and neocolonial present—reveals how this decision manifests a particular iteration of colorblindness in international human rights jurisprudence. Ostensibly mobilized in the defense of equality, colorblindness functions to reinforce racial subordination by bluntly invalidating race-conscious remedies without which it is impossible to redress persisting neocolonial racial subordination. At the time of Zimbabwe's independence from British colonial rule in 1980, an estimated six thousand white commercial farmers owned 42 percent of the country, specifically, the most arable land. Whites had acquired that land through violent and nonviolent dispossession of the majority Black population under colonial rule.[72]

In the context of independence, the British government ensured that the *colonial* racial allocation of land would remain in place *postcolonially*. To do so, that government promulgated a time-restricted guarantee that prevented the newly independent Zimbabwean nation from undoing white people's illegitimate (but legalized under international law) access to and mass accumulation of land. This neocolonial arrangement brings to mind Cheryl Harris's claims about whiteness as property.[73] By that, we mean the time-restricted guarantee is an example of the ease with which political and legal actors are able to deploy law to settle and entrench, rather than unsettle and disrupt, white people's expectation of a *right* to benefit from the legacies of racism, including the legacies of colonial domination.

The Zimbabwean example is revelatory in another sense. It lays bare the co-constitutive relationship between international law and neocolonialism. Consistent with international law, Black people's freedom from colonial rule in Zimbabwe was predicated on white people's freedom to maintain the land grab that was a core feature of that rule. The end result was that the formal end of colonialization created a neocolonial racial order that left in place—as a matter of international law—the racialized dispossession of land colonialism had effectuated.[74]

Significantly, the end of the time-restricted land policy ended neither white control of Zimbabwe's land nor the ways in which that unjust enrichment structured Zimbabwean society. On the contrary, subsequent to the expiration of that policy, an ineffectual preoccupied postcolonial government failed to make any significant inroads into redistributing land on more racially equitable terms.

But in 2005, things changed. That same postcolonial regime, in a desperate bid to shore up popular support, instituted the FTLRP, which it proceeded to implement violently, targeting predominantly white commercial farms.[75] As one of us has stressed elsewhere, there was much that was flawed about the FTLRP, especially in its implementation.[76] Its flaw, however, was not its disparate racial impact on whites. It bears emphasizing that, by the year 2000, white commercial farmers still dominated Zimbabwe's primarily agrarian economy.[77] This racially unequal structuring of the economy was achieved through laws that explicitly excluded Black people from certain forms of land ownership—laws that were in full effect when Mike Campbell himself acquired the farm whose seizure he ultimately challenged as racially discriminatory.[78]

Against the background of Zimbabwe's colonial history in which land was systematically taken away from Black people and given to white people, any intervention to redress that land theft was bound to disproportionately affect white farmers, as ownership had been accrued to them on a de jure racial basis. The *Campbell* opinion ignored these basic insights. The tribunal's ruling traded on two central logics of colorblindness: (1) that formal sameness in treatment is necessarily racially egalitarian,[79] and (2) that historical forms of legalized racial subordination are irrelevant to contemporary assessments of racial inequality. At no point does *Campbell* meaningfully engage the critical question the case presents: How does treating Black people and white people the same in the present address the fact that

Black people and white people were treated differently in the past? This question is not simply about whether and to what extent the tribunal should have structured a remedy to make up for what happened "then" (in the context of colonialism). The question is also a way of asking: What should the tribunal do about the fact that the colonial dispossession of land continues to racially structure access to land "now" (in the context of neocolonialism)? Informing our analysis is the view that colonialism "then" was not a momentary accomplishment fixed within a particular time frame. It created trajectories of inequality for Black people, and trajectories of opportunity for white people, into the future that shape extant racial hierarchies "now." Thus understood, contemporary juridical approaches rooted in treating all racial groups formally the same make little sense (unless one's racial project is to entrench in the present the race-based hierarchies colonialism produced in the past). The sum of what we are saying is that the racial discrimination ruling of the SADC Tribunal was flawed not only for treating FTLRP effectively as a form of so-called reverse discrimination against whites, but also for failing to view land redistribution as a necessary form of racial remediation to undo the deeply entrenched vestiges of colonization in the present.[80]

D. MOMENT IV: SOCIAL RESPONSIBILITY AND AGENCY

In Moment IV, CRT and TWAIL scholars engage and repudiate neoliberal claims about social responsibility and agency. Often expressed in the form of rhetorical questions, those claims look something like this: What's wrong with Africa? What's wrong with Black people?[81] Why are Black people always rioting in their own communities?[82] Why are they always killing themselves?[83] Why are African nations always at war? Why are they so corrupt? Why are they so violent? Fundamentally, these questions are postcolonial, post-slavery, and post–Jim Crow—which is to say, racially modern—ways of rearticulating concerns about Black people's fitness for citizenship and nonwhite nations' fitness for sovereignty, to wit: Why can't Black people properly manage the citizenship they have been given (by white people),[84] and why can't nonwhite nations properly manage the sovereignty they have been given (by white nations)?

Against the background normality, legitimacy, and ubiquity of questions of the foregoing sort, it is no wonder that the interventionary table for both civil rights and international law is set largely with ideas about foreign aid, antidiscrimination, and "racial preferences," rather than ideas about reparations, redistribution, unjust enrichment, and disgorgement.[85] As Ngũgĩ wa Thiong'o once put it, writing in 1981, "Africa's natural and human resources continue to develop Europe and America but Africa is made to feel grateful for aid."[86] At the same time, this "aid," and the overall sense that Black people and nonwhite nations are not pulling their citizenship and sovereignty weight, fuels domestic and global expressions of white anxiety, white exasperation, and white anger. None of these expressions are principally about what "these nations" and "these peoples" are doing to themselves. They are more fundamentally about the externalities of their conduct on white nations and white people.

Part of the way in which TWAIL and CRT scholars contest Moment IV is through structural accounts of domestic and global inequalities. That is to say, both groups of scholars have foregrounded—in materialist ways—not only the contemporary manifestation of the colonial and slavery/Jim Crow pasts, but also the particular ways in which current legal structures in constitutional law and international law continue to produce "proper" subjects for racial inequality and domination. Consider this point with respect to constitutional law first. In the context of determining the constitutional parameters of state punishment, the Supreme Court, in *McCleskey v. Kemp*,[87] made Black people the "proper" subjects of the death penalty by refusing to permit a robust showing of disparate impact to establish an equal protection challenge to the administration of that violent and morally bankrupt regime. The Court's unwillingness to act on the mountain of empirical evidence demonstrating that Black people are more "death eligible" than white people[88] legitimizes the idea that there is something natural and normal—and again, one might add, "proper"—about the disproportionate rate at which the state kills African Americans.[89]

We would be remiss not to note that the Court's approach in *McCleskey* built on a broader normative view in equal protection doctrine that discrimination is a function of conscious racial intentionality.[90] The Court's legitimation of intent as the baseline against which equal protection claims are adjudicated creates a constitutional landscape on which the racially disparate positions in which Black people find themselves across multiple dimensions of social life (from access to housing,[91] education,[92] and employment[93] to exposure to police violence,[94] mass incarceration,[95] and more recently COVID-19[96]) are—under constitutional law—existential givens, forms of inequality that are "properly" constitutive of Black life.

A final example of the "properizing" of Black subordination that bears mention is manifested in affirmative action jurisprudence. There, the Supreme Court has rendered Black people the "proper subjects" of societal discrimination in the sense of ruling that societal discrimination is too "amorphous" a concept to function as a compelling justification for affirmative action.[97] There are other examples to which we could refer, including the heightened pleading standards in civil procedure (which make it difficult for plaintiffs to bring racial discrimination claims[98]) and the legalization of pretextual policing under Fourth Amendment law (which makes it easy for police officers to racially target African Americans[99]). The point is that the cramped space Black people have (and historically have had) within which to mobilize law and contest the racially subordinating features of their lives helps to "properize" those features as natural (and naturally occurring) incidents in the lives of Black people. It is precisely against the backdrop of this "properizing" of Black subalternity that the expression "Black Lives Matter" becomes a necessary articulation.

TWAIL scholars, too, have surfaced how international law and its implementations have racialized the Third World and its peoples as "proper" subjects of First World receivership.[100] For example, Makau Mutua contends that, as a historical matter, international law routinely depicted the Third World as culturally aberrant savages—corrupt, despotic, and violent[101]—and the populations of those states as "powerless, helpless innocent[s] whose naturalist attributes have been negated by the primitive and offensive actions of the [Third World] state."[102] According to Makau Mutua, these supposedly neutral and objective representations of Third World nations and their peoples helped to legitimize supposedly universal and objective international human rights norms and principles that were fundamentally Eurocentric in their substance and origins, and imperial in their ambitions. Which is to say, these norms and principles functioned not only to reform Third World nations into European likeness,[103] but also to create a broader discursive economy that licensed colonial domination in part by naturalizing a "white man's burden" imperative. Driving this imperative was a narrative in which First World states, their international institutions, and their nongovernmental actors and entities became global saviors with "super powers" to vindicate, civilize, modernize, and discipline (through violence if necessary) the savagery and victimhood ostensibly characterizing the Third World.[104] The ongoing global market for and traction of these discursive renderings—propagated and backed up by international law—continues to make Third World nations and their peoples vulnerable to First World interventions and global control.[105]

As an example of the relationship between First World representations of and interventions into the Third World, Katherine Fallah and Ntina Tzouvala analyze a particular racialized deployment of the United Nations Security Council Resolutions.[106] Those resolutions are the primary legal means through which international law authorizes foreign military interventions. Fallah and Tzouvala deftly show how the UN Security Council resolution justifying the First World–led NATO military intervention in Libya in 2011 adopted and relied upon a racialized narrative of the conflict that cast African mercenaries who supported the Qaddafi regime as especially brutal and sexually violent. This racialized narrative created a hierarchy in the context of the international law of mercenarism that positioned African/Black mercenaries as greater threats to international security than West-based/white mercenaries.

The circulation of those anti-Black tropes helped to produce a First-World-into-the-Third-World externality. More specifically, the particular problems of dangerousness and violence African/Black mercenaries were constructed to pose laid the foundation for the idea that because Black Libyans and African migrants in Libya were particularly vulnerable to violence and displacement, they were particularly in need of humanitarian intervention, including in the form of First World receivership. Viewed in that way, Fallah and Tzouvala's case study of Libya is an example of how international law internalizes colonial-era racialized ideas about victims, perpetrators, and saviors to shore up a global stage on which "savages and victims are generally nonwhite and non-Western, while the saviors are white."[107] This (savage) perpetrator/(uncivilized) victim positionality in which Third World nations find themselves continues to structuralize their availability for various forms of First World entanglements, including military intervention.

E. MOMENT V: QUASI AND SECOND-CLASS SCHOLARSHIP

In Moment V, attempts to articulate versions of Moments I through IV within the disciplinary context of international law and constitutional law raise an epistemological legitimacy problem. Here, both TWAIL and CRT engender pushback, contestations, and refusals that shore up a hegemonic basis of knowledge within which CRT and TWAIL become "quasi scholarship" or "second-class" scholarship. As a consequence of this positioning, CRT and TWAIL are always already under pressure to signal and supply intellectual credibility and to assimilate into, dare we say, the "civilized" conventions of constitutional law and international law, respectively. The perception that both literatures exist outside the boundaries of the presumptively neutral scholarly conventions of constitutional law and international law has engendered either criticism or willful disattention and nonengagement.[108] The classic articulation of these points within CRT is Richard Delgado's still relevant and compelling "The Imperial Scholar," a title that speaks volumes to the ways in which white male scholars have dominated the epistemological terrain of constitutional law.[109] With respect to TWAIL, James Gathii marks a different but related kind of intellectual imperialism, the marginalization of critical international law perspectives, such as TWAIL, within the *American Journal of International Law*, the flagship journal of the field in the United States.[110]

Crucially, then, the disciplinary problem CRT and TWAIL scholars confront is not just that race and racial inequality are marginalized in or read out of the juridical fields of constitutional and international law, it is also that CRT and TWAIL scholarship that contests this intellectual arrangement are falsifiable as modalities of intellectual production and therefore read out of the scholarly domains of international law and constitutional law.

F. MOMENT VI: RECONSTRUCTION AND TRANSFORMATION

Moment VI speaks to CRT's and TWAIL's reconstructive interventions. In neither CRT nor TWAIL is this interventionary sensibility predicated on the view that law, standing alone, can produce a racially emancipatory world. The point is rather that law as a site of power should not be ceded but rather mobilized progressively to move the social justice needle. That both CRT and TWAIL conceive of law in this way is not to say that either movement acquiesces in regnant notions of exceptionalism. On the contrary, CRT and TWAIL's reconstructive moves are effectuated in opposition to, rather than in alignment with, claims about U.S. exceptionalism, or liberal democratic exceptionalism more broadly.

The reconstructive dimensions of CRT were written into the earliest articulations of the intellectual movement. Indeed, in one of the first CRT anthologies, Kimberlé Crenshaw, Neil Gotanda, Gary Peller, and Kendall Thomas identify reconstruction as one of two of CRT's minimalist commitments:

> The first is to understand how a regime of white supremacy and its subordination of people of color have been created and maintained in America, and, in particular, to examine the relationship between that social structure and professed ideals such as "the rule of law" and "equal protection." The second is a desire not merely to understand the vexed bond between law and racial power but to *change* it.[111]

CRT's investment in reconstruction (and not just deconstruction) engendered a vigorous debate between CRT and one of its intellectual allies: Critical Legal Studies (CLS), a largely white and male group of progressive intellectuals who had an insurgent presence in American law schools in the 1980s.[112] "CRT was aligned with the radicalizing dimensions of CLS, particularly the movement's trenchant critique of the legal ideology of law's neutrality, and its conceptualization of law as constitutive, and not simply reflective, of political and social relations."[113] As for the misalignment, CRT scholars differed with CLS scholars on the question of rights. According to CLS scholars, rights were not only "alienating" and "indeterminate," they were also a vehicle through which to effectuate social control.[114]

Critical Race Theorists did not disagree with the account of rights CLS scholars advanced. Instead, they foregrounded other crucial entailments of rights, especially for racially subordinated groups. In particular, Critical Race Theorists maintained that, with respect to groups that historically have been denied access to rights, the availability of rights can produce a sense of both political identity and political possibility ("*I* can mobilize rights to effectuate *positive social change*"). Patricia Williams's engagement with rights evidences this CRT sensibility. According to Williams:

> To say that [B]lacks never fully believed in rights is true. Yet it is also true that [B]lacks believed in them so much and so hard that we gave them life where there was none before; we held onto them, put the hope of them into our wombs, mothered them and not the notion of them. And this was not the dry process of reification, from which life is drained and reality fades as the cement of conceptual determinism hardens round— but its opposite. This was the resurrection of life from ashes four hundred years old. The making of something out of nothing took immense alchemical fire—the fusion of a whole nation and the kindling of several generations.[115]

More recently, Dorothy Roberts has articulated a version of this point in the context of theorizing the possibility for constitutional law to reflect an abolitionist orientation. According to Roberts, "The tension between recognizing the relentless anti[B]lack violence of constitutional doctrine, on one hand, and demanding the legal recognition of [B]lack people's freedom and equal citizenship, on the other, animates" her interventions into juridical arenas.[116] Roberts goes on to note that "despite my disgust with the perpetual defense of oppression in the name of constitutional principles, I am inspired by the possibility of an abolition constitutionalism emerging from the struggle to demolish prisons and create a society where they are obsolete."[117]

Part of what informs CRT's view that people of color should not cede rights as a domain of power is the claim that law is a site for the production, instantiation, and legitimation of racial hierarchy.[118] Precisely because law plays a role in structuring racial subordination, Critical Race Theorists see in law the possibility of structuring at least some measure of social change.[119] Consistent with that view, CRT scholars have staged numerous doctrinal interventions, including, but not limited to, the following ten examples:

1. Contestations of the intentional model of discrimination that governs equal protection law in favor of disparate impact[120] or other approaches.[121]
2. Arguments against the application of strict scrutiny to racial remediation and insisting instead that intermediate scrutiny or rational basis should apply.[122]
3. Expansive conceptualization of diversity and robust defenses of the rationale beyond the "robust exchange of ideas."[123]
4. Claims that defend affirmative action on terms other than diversity.[124]
5. Resistance to the conflation of desegregation efforts that began with *Brown v. Board of Education* with affirmative action case law.[125]
6. Arguments promoting the express consideration of race in constitutional criminal procedure cases, including Fourth Amendment jurisprudence, to account for the ways in which race interacts with every dimension of our criminal justice system.[126]
7. Interventions incorporating race into various articulations of the reasonable person standard across different bodies of law, including criminal law and criminal procedure.[127]
8. Proposals that courts adopt an intersectional approach to antidiscrimination claims that recognizes that people's vulnerability to discrimination might turn on more than one aspect of their identity.[128]
9. Repudiation of the same actor doctrine inference in Title VII law that creates a presumption that, for example, a person who hires an African American as an employee would not subsequently racially discriminate against that person in other contexts—for example, with respect to promotion.[129]

10. Expansions of the conceptualization of discrimination on the basis of race to include performative conceptions of race or the fact that people might experience discrimination "on the basis of racial orientation."[130]

To repeat, none of the preceding interventions reflect the naivete that law, standing alone, is the antiracist solution to extant forms of racial inequality. Moreover, some of them are quite clearly more radical than others. We could, of course, assess whether any of the interventions we have described should count as "non-reformist reforms."[131] But that question is beyond the scope of our project and should not elide the central claim we mean to advance here: namely, that the doctrinal reconstructions CRT scholars have proposed are (an admittedly limited) window into an investment on the part of Critical Race Theorists to abolish, disrupt, or mitigate the various ways in which law effectuates and maintains racial inequality. From that vantage point, at least some of the reconstructive moves CRT scholars have made align with precisely what Dorothy Roberts suggests is a worthwhile antiracist project—to infuse law with an abolitionist sensibility[132] that includes (but is not limited to) the dismantling of *anti*-abolitionist doctrines, such as colorblindness and the intentional discrimination paradigm.[133]

As a further indication of the doctrinal reconstruction efforts to which CRT is being put, we reference as well two texts on which one of us serves as a coeditor. The first, *Critical Race Judgments: Rewritten U.S. Court Opinions on Race and Law*, figures rewritten (mostly Supreme Court) cases from a CRT perspective.[134] The second, *The Oxford Handbook of Race and the Law in the United States* comprises a series of essays that perform racial analyses of central law school courses, including every first-year course and a range of second-year courses, such as Tax, Corporations, Evidence, and Professional Responsibility.[135] Both of these texts are ways of navigating the tension between CRT's deconstructive sensibilities and its reconstructive investments.[136]

To be clear, CRT's interventions in the domain of rights do not exhaust the transformative work CRT scholars mobilize their scholarship to perform. The field of CRT is enormously diverse, with some scholarly expressions more squarely within the modalities of conventional legal argumentation than others.[137] Thus, in addition to doctrinal interventions reflected in the examples we outlined above, one also finds CRT scholarship whose interventions are staged in relation to social movements[138] and in the register of abolitionism.[139] Our broader point is that the CRT critique of law is not a call for CRT scholars to abandon law as a reconstructive project.

TWAIL has been similarly reconstructive in its general orientation. While the critique of international law is a fundamental part of TWAIL's intellectual identity, the theory also reflects a commitment to rearticulate international law to achieve less subordinating and more liberatory ends. Here, too, one could assess whether

TWAIL's efforts in that regard should count as non-reformist reforms and, again, that project is beyond the scope of our engagement. The point we are emphasizing, to borrow from Luis Eslava and Sundhya Pahuja, is that "resistance and reform... come together in TWAIL to form a single process of destabilisation and renewal of international law's history and operation. Rather than replacement, TWAIL scholarship is more interested in overcoming international law's problems while still remaining committed to the idea of an international normative regime."[140] For many within TWAIL, international law retains transformative potential, and law remains a means of constraining power, notwithstanding the indeterminacy that inheres in international law and in law generally.[141] Thus, even while TWAIL scholars remain determined to confront and critique the imperial and colonial nature of international law, they view the abandonment of international law as a site of struggle as a luxury that many Third World peoples cannot afford.[142]

In their respective reconstructive projects, both CRT and TWAIL have had to attend to various forms of exceptionalism that serve to reify racial subordination within and through law. With respect to U.S. law, Aziz Rana describes the narrative of U.S. exceptionalism this way:

> From the founding the United States has always been committed to principles of freedom and equality... [that] the US is an exceptional nation because unlike Europe it's a place where feudalism never took hold. To the extent that the United States has had problems of native expropriation or African enslavement, these are really marginal to the basic identity of the country. We can think of the country as, fundamentally, if incompletely, liberal and on a steady path to fulfilling its essential project.[143]

Under U.S. exceptionalism, the very conditions of possibility for the establishment of the United States as a particular kind of racialized democracy—one that normalized and constitutionalized both slavery and the appropriation of Native lands—are at best footnotes. Those footnotes are subordinated to an easily falsifiable but nonetheless deeply entrenched text that posits the United States was always already a democracy that presupposed the availability of freedom and justice for all. The marginalization of the racial violence on which U.S. history rests, and the denial of contemporary forms of racial inequality, help to explain why the *New York Times'* 1619 Project has engendered so much controversy and contestation.[144]

Crucially, CRT's advocacy for legal change does not downplay the historical racialized features of U.S. democracy, or what one might call the democratization of racism. It is precisely because of the normal and constitutional ways in which racism in the United States historically functioned as an everyday democratic practice in which judges and legislatures, school educators and administers, bank officials and neighborhood associations, and public and private employers routinely engaged that leads CRT to recognize that, across different historical periods in the United States—and certainly in the context of slavery and Jim Crow—racism functioned as an unexceptional feature of American society whose contemporary impacts transcend intentional forms of discrimination.

Exceptionalism is an international phenomenon as well, and a TWAIL analysis reveals that exceptionalism at the international stage can mirror exceptionalism on the U.S. domestic stage to similar effect, in that U.S. exceptionalism—as one front of liberal democratic exceptionalism—can serve to reify racial subordination through international human rights mechanisms.[145] A recent example is illustrative.

Following the murder of George Floyd and the transnational racial justice uprising that followed, a coalition of over six hundred movement and NGO human rights activists mounted a campaign for a special session of the UN's primary human rights body (the UN Human Rights Council) to address the situation in the United States.[146] Among other demands, they requested that such a session authorize an independent international commission of inquiry to investigate the ongoing human rights abuses wrought by systemic, anti-Black racism.[147] Following this and other developments, the Africa Group—the Third World regional formation comprising African nations on the UN Human Rights Council—drove a process that ultimately resulted in precisely such an unprecedented session of the Council: an urgent debate on systemic anti-Black racism in U.S. law enforcement.[148]

During the session, however, the initial proposal for an independent international commission of inquiry for the United States was ultimately defeated, in part as a result of naked, behind-the-scenes geopolitical bullying of Third World nation states by their First World counterparts.[149] But this was only one tool in the arsenal that killed the possibility of an international legal mechanism to help tackle racism in the United States. The official justifications articulated by First World nation states and their allies during the debates on the resolution to oppose the commission plainly relied on U.S. exceptionalism specifically,[150] and liberal democratic exceptionalism generally. This exceptionalism in effect shielded systemic, anti-Black racism from the scrutiny of the international human rights system. U.S. opposition to international human rights accountability was articulated in precisely the terms of Aziz Rana's description above. In his official statement, the U.S. Secretary of State asserted:

> Americans work through difficult societal problems openly, knowing their freedoms are protected by the Constitution and a strong rule of law. We are serious about holding individuals and institutions accountable, and our democracy allows us to do so. If the Council were honest, it would recognize the strengths of American democracy and urge authoritarian regimes around the world to model American democracy and to hold their nations to the same high standards of accountability and transparency that we Americans apply to ourselves.[151]

Australia, among others, supported the U.S position, noting that "the United States is an open, liberal democracy, governed by the rule of law. Open and transparent democracies are well-placed to tackle such issues."[152] Such liberal democracies then, are not the appropriate subjects of international human rights interventions, which, as Makau Mutua would likely remind us, are reserved for savage, Third World nation states. As one of us has pointed out elsewhere, this exceptionalism flies in the face of the very reality that triggered the special session in the first place: the anti-Black racism of U.S. law enforcement as a *systemic* feature of U.S. liberal democracy, and which its liberal democratic institutions have proved incapable of redressing.[153] Here we see how narratives of U.S. and liberal democratic exceptionalism dissipate the possibility of international human rights intervention regularly deployed in the Third World, with the effect of shielding the systemic operation of anti-Black racism within liberal democratic society.

CONCLUSION

Our aim in this chapter has been decidedly limited: to articulate parallel developments in CRT and TWAIL. As we stated in the introduction and want to repeat here, we do not purport to have mapped all the ways in which the interventions performed by CRT scholars track similar interventions in TWAIL (or vice versa). There are other "moments" in the story we have told that we invite other scholars to describe.

We should also say that we view our chapter, and the contributions to this volume more generally, as a predicate for a disciplinary turn in both CRT and TWAIL. Which is to say, notwithstanding the parallel developments we have described, it remains true that, by and large, as modalities of scholarly production, CRT and TWAIL exist in separate epistemic universes with far too few moments of cross-fertilization. Our hope is that by demonstrating that both projects are performing similar kinds of intellectual and normative work against a backdrop of similar kinds of hurdles and challenges, scholars in both fields will more intentionally and robustly engage each other's work.

NOTES

1. An earlier version of this chapter appears in the UCLA Law Review. See E. Tendayi Achiume and Devon W. Carbado, "Critical Race Theory Meets Third World Approaches to International Law," *UCLA Law Review* 67, no. 6 (2021): 1462–503.

2. For introductions to CRT, see generally Kimberlé Crenshaw et al., Introduction to *Critical Race Theory: The Key Writings that Formed the Movement* (New York: New Press, 1995), xiii; Richard Delgado and Jean Stefancic, *Critical Race Theory: an Introduction* (New York: New York University Press, 2001); Athena D. Mutua, "The Rise, Development and Future Directions of Critical Race Theory and Related Scholarship," *Denver University*

Law Review 84, no. 2 (2006): 329–94; Devon W. Carbado, "Critical What What?," *Connecticut Law Review* 43, no. 5 (July 2011): 1593–644.

3. For introductions to TWAIL, see Makau Mutua, "What is TWAIL?," *American Society of International Law Proceedings*, no. 94 (2000): 31–40.

4. For excellent work in this area, see Natsu Taylor Saito, *Settler Colonialism, Race, and the Law: Why Structural Racism Persists* (New York: New York University Press, 2020); see also Ediberto Román, *The Other American Colonies: an International and Constitutional Law Examination of the United States' Nineteenth and Twentieth Century Island Conquests* (United States: Carolina Academic Press, 2006).

5. See Justin Desautels-Stein, "A Prolegomenon to the Study of Racial Ideology in the Era of International Human Rights," *UCLA Law Review* 67, no. 6 (2021): 1536–79.

6. See James Thuo Gathii, "Writing Race and Identity in a Global Context: What CRT and TWAIL Can Learn From Each Other," *UCLA Law Review* 67, no. 6 (2021): 1610–51; see Ruth Gordon, "Critical Race Theory and International Law: Convergence and Divergence," *Villanova Law Review* 45, no. 5 (2000): 827.

7. See, e.g., Amar Bhatia, "The South of the North: Building on Critical Approaches to International Law with Lessons from the Fourth World," *Oregon Review of International Law* 14, no. 1 (2012): 131–76.

8. See generally Crenshaw et al., *Critical Race Theory*. We should be clear, at the same time, we are not calling for projects that describe their invention as moving "beyond" the "Black/White" paradigm, an articulation that sometimes carries with it the implicit assumptions that the work of anti-Black racism is finished business or that Black people's civil rights time has expired.

9. Cedric J. Robinson, *Black Marxism: The Making of the Black Radical Tradition* (United States: University of North Carolina Press, 2000), 2; see also Cheryl I. Harris, "Reflections on Whiteness as Property," *Harvard Law Review Forum* 134, no. 1 (2020): 1–10. Harris offers an even more direct engagement of capitalism.

10. See, e.g., Antony Anghie, *Imperialism, Sovereignty and the Making of International Law* (United Kingdom: Cambridge University Press, 2004), 32–100.

11. Cheryl I. Harris, "Whiteness as Property," *Harvard Law Review* 106, no. 8 (1993): 1707–91.

12. See, e.g., Neil Gotanda, "A Critique of 'Our Constitution Is Color-Blind,'" *Stanford Law Review* 44, no.1 (1991): 1–68; Charles R. Lawrence III, "The Id, the Ego, and Equal Protection: Reckoning with Unconscious Racism," *Stanford Law Review* 39, no. 2 (1987): 317–88.

13. For a thoughtful discussion of the intersection between positivist jurisprudence and race, see Antony Anghie, "The Evolution of International Law: Colonial and Postcolonial Realities," *Third World Quarterly* 27, no. 5 (2006): 739–53.

14. Dred Scott v. Sandford, 60 U.S. 393 (1857).

15. *Dred Scott*, 60 U.S. at 407. The decision describes the state of public opinion regarding African Americans at the time the Declaration of Independence and U.S. Constitution were framed and adopted, and justifying the failure to recognize formal citizenship for African Americans.

16. See Carbado, "Critical What What?" (describing the genesis, boundaries, and principles of Critical Race Theory).

17. See, e.g., Ian F. Haney López, "The Social Construction of Race: Some Observations on Illusion, Fabrication, and Choice," *Harvard Civil Rights-Civil Liberties Law Review* 29, no. 1 (1994): 1–62.

18. "One is not born, but rather becomes, a woman." Simone de Beauvoir, *The Second Sex*, trans. H. M. Parshley (United States: Vintage Books, 1974), 301.

19. Devon W. Carbado, "Racial Naturalization," *American Quarterly* 57, no. 3 (2005): 633–58.

20. See Anghie, *Imperialism, Sovereignty and the Making of International Law*, 32–100.

21. See Anghie, *Imperialism, Sovereignty and the Making of International Law*, 101–2.

22. Christopher Gevers, "Unwhitening the World: Rethinking Race and International Law," *UCLA Law Review* 67, no. 6 (2021): 1652–85.

23. See Anghie, *Imperialism, Sovereignty and the Making of International Law*, 32–100; James Thuo Gathii, "Imperialism, Colonialism, and International Law," *Buffalo Law Review* 54, no. 4 (2007): 1015, 1043–54; Antony Anghie and B. S. Chimni, "Third World Approaches to International Law and Individual Responsibility in Internal Conflicts," *Chinese Journal of International Law* 2, no. 1 (2003): 98.

24. For an analysis of this dynamic in the field of international human rights law, see Makau Mutua, "Savages, Victims, and Saviors: The Metaphor of Human Rights," *Harvard International Law Journal* 42, no. 1 (2001): 201–46.

25. See Anghie, *Imperialism, Sovereignty and the Making of International Law*, 38–39.

26. See, e.g., Antony Anghie, "Civilization and Commerce: The Concept of Governance in Historical Perspective," *Villanova Law Review* 45, no. 5 (2000): 887–88.

27. Gathii, "Imperialism, Colonialism, and International Law," 1019–20.

28. Gathii, "Imperialism, Colonialism, and International Law," 1033–63. Gathii also shows the role of British common law in this process, and links these doctrinal moves to those made by U.S. federal courts in the 2000s in the Guantanamo Bay Detainee cases, which he argues similarly ratify U.S. imperial exploitation.

29. Gathii, "Imperialism, Colonialism, and International Law," 1041–42.

30. Gathii, "Imperialism, Colonialism, and International Law," 1045–46.

31. Gathii, "Imperialism, Colonialism, and International Law," 1042.

32. Chantal Thomas has made this point elsewhere, noting the shared exploration by CRT and TWAIL scholars of subordination in legal systems that have shifted from treating racial others as "formally separate and subordinate to formally equal." See Chantal Thomas, "Critical Race Theory and Postcolonial Development Theory: Observations on Methodology," *Villanova Law Review* 45, no. 5 (2000): 1197.

33. See Giorgio Agamben, *Homo Sacer: Sovereign Power and Bare Life* (Stanford University Press, 1998); see also Devon W. Carbado, "Racial Naturalization," *American Quarterly* 57, no. 3 (2005): 633–58.

34. Plessy v. Ferguson, 163 U.S. 537 (1896).

35. The text of the Fourteenth Amendment reads: "All persons born or naturalized in the United States, and subject to the jurisdiction thereof, are citizens of the United States and of the State wherein they reside. No State shall make or enforce any law which shall abridge the privileges or immunities of citizens of the United States; nor shall any State deprive any person of life, liberty, or property, without due process of law; nor deny to any person within its jurisdiction the equal protection of the laws." U.S. CONST. amend. XIV, § 1.

36. *Plessy*, 163 U.S. at 551.

37. See, e.g., Saidiya Hartman, *Lose Your Mother: A Journey Along the Atlantic Slave Route* (United States: Farrar, Straus and Giroux, 2008), 6.

38. See Kwame Nkrumah, *Neo-colonialism: The Last Stage of Imperialism* (United States: International Publishers, 1966); Walter Rodney, *How Europe underdeveloped Africa* (United States: Howard University Press, 1981).

39. Siba N'Zatioula Grovogui, Sovereigns, *Quasi Sovereigns, and Africans: Race and Self-determination in International Law* (United States: University of Minnesota Press, 1996); see Anghie, *Imperialism, Sovereignty and the Making of International Law*, 11.

40. Antony Anghie, "The Evolution of International Law: Colonial and Postcolonial Realities," *Third World Quarterly* 27, no. 5 (2006): 746–49.

41. Anghie, "The Evolution of International Law," 746–49.

42. Sundhya Pahuja, *Decolonising International Law: Development, Economic Growth and the Politics of Universality* (United Kingdom: Cambridge University Press, 2011). Pahuja deploys this analysis through three examples.

43. See James Thuo Gathii, "Neoliberalism, Colonialism and International Governance: Decentering the International Law of Governmental Legitimacy," *Michigan Law Review* 98, no. 6 (2000): 2033–34.

44. See Gathii, "Neoliberalism, Colonialism and International Governance," 2033–34.

45. Aslı U. Bâli and Aziz Rana, "Pax Arabica: Provisional Sovereignty and Intervention in the Arab Uprisings," *California Western International Law Journal* 42, no. 2 (2012): 321–52.

46. Bali and Rana, "Pax Arabica," 321–52. Note how this claim aligns with CRT's claims about interest convergence; see Derrick A. Bell, Jr., "Brown v. Board of Education and the Interest-Convergence Dilemma," *Harvard Law Review* 93, no. 3 (1980): 518.

47. John Reynolds, *Empire, Emergency and International Law* (United Kingdom: Cambridge University Press, 2017), 210–11.

48. Mohammad Shahabuddin, "Minorities and the Making of Postcolonial States in International Law," *TWAILR: REFLECTIONS,* May 13, 2020, [https://perma.cc/BS3M-9LS7].

49. "The right of the people to be secure in their persons, houses, papers, and effects, against unreasonable searches and seizures, shall not be violated, and no Warrants shall issue, but upon probable cause, supported by Oath or affirmation, and particularly describing the place to be searched, and the persons or things to be seized." U.S. Const. amend. IV.

50. See Paul Butler, "The White Fourth Amendment," *Texas Tech Law Review* 43, no. 1 (2010): 245–54; Devon W. Carbado, "From Stopping Black People to Killing Black People: The Fourth Amendment Pathways to Police Violence," *California Law Review* 105, no. 1 (2017): 125–64; Devon W. Carbado, "From Stop and Frisk to Shoot and Kill: Terry v. Ohio's Pathway to Police Violence," *UCLA Law Review* 64, no. 6 (2017): 1508–53; Tracey Maclin, "The Central Meaning of the Fourth Amendment," *William and Mary Law Review* 35, no. 1 (1993): 197–250.

51. For an explanation of this analytical structure of the Fourth Amendment, see Carbado, "From Stopping Black People to Killing Black People," 125–64.

52. In discussing Whren v. U.S., 517 U.S. 806 (1996), the Court effectively turned probable cause that a person had committed a traffic infraction into a license for police officers to employ race as a basis for determining which people to stop to enforce those infractions. See Carbado, "From Stopping Black People to Killing Black People," 152.

53. For a more extended discussion of these examples, see Carbado, "From Stopping Black People to Killing Black People," 133, 137–38.

54. We will not, in this chapter, cite the relevant Fourth Amendment cases. They are discussed at length in one of our prior projects. See generally Carbado, "From Stopping Black People to Killing Black People."

55. For an explicit engagement of the role colorblindness plays in structuring Fourth Amendment jurisprudence, see Devon W. Carbado, "(E)racing the Fourth Amendment," *Michigan Law Review* 100, no. 5 (2002): 946–1044.

56. Adarand Constructors, Inc. v. Peña Sec'y Transp., 515 U.S. 200, 224 (1995); see also Grutter v. Bollinger, 539 U.S. 306, 326 (2003).

57. This is not entirely hypothetical. There is evidence that the FBI has systematically targeted so-called "Black Identity Extremists," which includes people who are perceived to be too closely associated with various Black Lives Matter formations. See Mike German, "The FBI Has a History of Targeting Black Activists. That's Still True Today," Opinion, *The Guardian*, June 26, 2020, https://perma.cc/ PSR5-MAAW.

58. "It should be noted, to begin with, that all legal restrictions which curtail the civil rights of a single racial group are immediately suspect. That is not to say that all such restrictions are unconstitutional. It is to say that courts must subject them to the most rigid scrutiny." See, e.g., Korematsu v. United States, 323 U.S. 214, 216 (1944).

59. "All racial classifications, imposed by whatever federal, state, or local government actor, must be analyzed by a reviewing court under strict scrutiny... [S]uch classifications are constitutional only if they are narrowly tailored measures that further compelling governmental interests." See, e.g., *Adarand*, 515 U.S. at 227; "absent searching judicial inquiry into the justification for such race-based measures, there is simply no way of determining what classifications are 'benign' or 'remedial' and what classifications are in fact motivated by illegitimate notions of racial inferiority or simple racial politics." City of Richmond v. J. A. Croson Co., 488 U.S. 469, 493 (1989).

60. Anghie, "Civilization and Commerce," 890–91.

61. See, e.g., Anghie, "The Evolution of International Law"; Gathii, "Imperialism, Colonialism, and International Law." In these examples, TWAIL scholars unmask parallel racial elisions in the service of racial subordination, to those that CRT scholars have engaged in, in the development of colorblindness critique.

62. Gevers, "Unwhitening the World," 1652–53.

63. Gevers, "Unwhitening the World," 1654–55. In our analysis, both Gevers and the TWAIL II scholarship of Anthony Anghie, which he charges with "reading down" racism, are engaged in critiques of racial subordination including through the elision of race, with Gevers representing momentum in TWAIL III that insists on greater analytical precision in race theory within TWAIL.

64. Gevers, "Unwhitening the World," 1654–55.

65. Gevers, "Unwhitening the World," 1654–55, 10n (defining Global White Supremacy as a "sociopolitical system that 'encompasses de facto as well as de jure white privilege and refers more broadly to the European domination of the planet that has left us with the racialized distributions of economic, political, and cultural power that we have today'") (citing Charles W. Mills, "Revisionist Ontologies: Theorizing White Supremacy," in *Blackness Visible: Essays on Philosophy and Race* [Cornell University Press, 1998], 97, 98).

66. Gevers, "Unwhitening the World," 1652–53.

67. Hope Lewis uses the term "BlackCrit Theory" to describe her work at the intersection of TWAIL, CRT, Critical Race Feminism, and several other critical traditions. See Hope Lewis, "Reflections on 'Blackcrit Theory': Human Rights," *Villanova Law Review* 45, no. 5 (2000): 1077.

68. See Mike Campbell (Pvt) Ltd v. Republic of Zim., Case No. 2/2007[2008] SADCT 2, 53 (Nov. 28, 2008), http://www.saflii.org/sa/cases/SADCT/2008/2.pdf. SADC is an economic community of sixteen countries in southern Africa. See "About SADC," South African Development Community, accessed Dec. 11, 2020 [https://perma.cc/ 2NP6-7P3P].

69. For a discussion of a "locked in" theory of inequality, see Daria Roithmayr, *Reproducing Racism: How Everyday Choices Lock In White Advantage* (United States: NYU Press, 2014).

70. E. Tendayi Achiume, "The SADC Tribunal: Sociopolitical Dissonance and the Authority of International Courts," in *International Court Authority*, ed. Karen J. Alter et al. (United Kingdom: OUP Oxford, 2018); see also E. Tendayi Achiume, "Transformative Vision in Liberal Rights Jurisprudence on Racial Equality: A Lesson from Justice Moseneke," in *A Warrior for Justice: Essays in Honor of Dikgang Moseneke*, ed. Penelope Andrews et al. (South Africa: Juta, 2018).

71. *Campbell*, Case No. 2/2007[2008], at 2, 53.

72. Achiume, "The SADC Tribunal," 131.

73. Harris, "Whiteness as Property," 1707–91.

74. Achiume, "The SADC Tribunal," 131.

75. For an analysis of the legitimate popular demands for land redistribution and the illegitimate means and political strategies pursued by the government, see Achiume, "The SADC Tribunal," 130–35.

76. See Achiume, "Transformative Vision in Liberal Rights Jurisprudence on Racial Equality: A Lesson from Justice Moseneke," 180–81.

77. Achiume, "The SADC Tribunal," 132.

78. Achiume, "Transformative Vision in Liberal Rights Jurisprudence on Racial Equality: A Lesson from Justice Moseneke," 190–91.

79. See Cheryl I. Harris, "Equal Treatment and the Reproduction of Inequality," *Fordham Law Review* 69, no. 5 (2001): 1753–84.

80. Achiume, "Transformative Vision in Liberal Rights Jurisprudence on Racial Equality: A Lesson from Justice Moseneke," 191–97.

81. Here, the matter is sometimes framed comparatively with respect to Asian Americans. The question then becomes: Why can't Africans be more like Asian Americans—that is to say, be a model minority? Frank H. Wu, "Neither Black Nor White: Asian Americans and Affirmative Action," *Boston College Third World Law Journal* 15, no. 2 (1995): 226.

82. This issue often surfaces against the backdrop of social unrest that includes looting and property destruction in the context of mass mobilization against police violence. See, e.g., Jonathan Peterson and Hector Tobar, "South L.A. Burns and Grieves: Life Has Been Hard in the Neglected Area for Years. But Now, as Self-Inflicted Wounds Mount, Residents Fear for the Future," *Los Angeles Times*, May 1, 1992, https://www.latimes.com/archives/la-xpm-1992-05-01-mn-1395-story.html [https://perma.cc/Y7T5-3YUG]; this narrative continues today. See, e.g., Katherine Kersten, "Racial Justice: The New Religion?," *StarTribune*, July 24, 2020, https://www.startribune.com/racial-justice-the-new-religion/571899352 [https://perma.cc/UPB7-N8LU]. The article accuses people of "torch[ing] whole neighborhoods" in response to the murder of George Floyd.

83. One sees versions of the foregoing claims manifested in debates about Black-on-Black crime. See Devon W. Carbado, "Blue-on-Black Violence: A Provisional Model of Some of the Causes," *Georgetown Law Journal* 104, no. 6 (2016): 1479–530; Sascha-Dominick Dov Bachmann and Naa A. Sowatey-Adjei, "The African Union-ICC Controversy Before the ICJ: A Way Forward to Strengthen International Criminal Justice?," *Washington International Law Journal* 29, no. 2 (2020): 247–302.

84. It must be remembered that denials of citizenship to Black people rested on, among other arguments, the claim that they could not manage the responsibilities and burdens of citizenship. See, e.g., Bryan v. Walton, 14 Ga. 185, 198–204 (1853).

85. For a critique of the racial preference frame in antidiscrimination law, see Luke Charles Harris, "Rethinking the Terms of the Affirmative Action Debate Established in the Regents of the University of California v. Bakke Decision," *Research in Politics and Society*, no. 6 (1999): 133; Devon W. Carbado and Cheryl I. Harris, "The New Racial Preferences," *California Law Review* 96, no. 5 (2008): 1139–214.

86. Ngũgĩ wa Thiong'o, "The Language of African Literature," in *Decolonising the Mind: The Politics of Launguage in African Literature* (Kenya: East African Educational Publishers, 1986), 4, 28.

87. McCleskey v. Kemp, 481 U.S. 279 (1987).

88. See Symposium, "Learning From Struggles," *Mercer Law Review* 67, no. 3 (2016): 529–44; Sherod Thaxton, "Disentangling Disparity: Exploring Racially Disparate Effect and Treatment in Capital Charging," *American Journal of Criminal Law* 45, no. 1 (2018): 95–166; Paul G. Davies et al., "Looking Deathworthy: Perceived Stereotypicality of Black Defendants Predicts Capital-Sentencing Outcomes," *Psychological Science* 17, no. 5 (2006): 383–86; Sheri Lynn Johnson, "Litigating for Racial Fairness After McCleskey v. Kemp," *Columbia Human Rights Law Review* 39, no. 1 (2007): 178–201.

89. We are not saying, to be clear, that the state should be in the business of punishing people via death. We think the death penalty is an abhorrent state practice that should be abolished. Our focus here is on its racially disparate impact.

90. See Washington v. Davis, 426 U.S. 229 (1976).

91. See Audrey G. McFarlane, "Race, Space and Place: The Geography of Economic Development," *San Diego Law Review* 36, no. 2 (1999): 295–354.

92. See LaToya Baldwin Clark, "Education as Property," *Virginia Law Review* 105, no. 2 (2019): 397–424.

93. Noah D. Zatz, "Disparate Impact and the Unity of Equality Law," *Boston University Law Review* 97, no. 4 (2017): 1357–426; Noah D. Zatz, "Special Treatment Everywhere, Special Treatment Nowhere," *Boston University Law Review* 95, no. 3 (2015): 1155–80.

94. See Carbado, "Blue-on-Black Violence," 1479–530.

95. Michelle Alexander, *The New Jim Crow: Mass Incarceration in the Age of Colorblindness*, (United States: New Press, 2012).

96. See The Atlantic and the Boston University Center for Antiracist Research, "The COVID Racial Data Tracker," *The Atlantic*, accessed July 17, 2020, https://covidtracking .com/race [https://perma.cc/JR9F-YRLK]; see also Harmeet Kaur and Naomi Thomas, "Black, Hispanic and Native American Workers and Their Families Face Greater Coronavirus Exposure Risks, Report Finds," CNN, December 3, 2020, https://www.cnn .com/2020/12/03/health/black-hispanic-native- american-workers-covid-risks-trnd/ index.html [https://perma.cc/VN6W-7HB4]; Daniel Wood, "As Pandemic Deaths Add Up, Racial Disparities Persist—and in Some Cases Worsen," NPR, September 23, 2020, https://www.npr.org/sections/health- shots/2020/09/23/914427907/as -pandemic-deaths-add-up-racial-disparities-persist-and-in- some-cases-worsen [https:// perma.cc/ QXQ4-JE7D.

97. Justice Powell first articulated this view in Regents of the University of California v. Bakke, disapproving of the idea that the state has a legitimate interest in combating "societal discrimination," and characterizing it as "an amorphous concept of injury that may

be ageless in its reach into the past." That idea remains a feature of contemporary affirmative action jurisprudence. Regents of the University of California v. Bakke, 438 U.S. 265, 307 (1978); the decision summarizes *Bakke* and concludes that diversity may function as a "compelling state interest" for affirmative action. See *Grutter*, 539 U.S. 306, 306–8, 325.

98. See Victor D. Quintanilla, "Beyond Common Sense: A Social Psychological Study of Iqbal's Effect on Claims of Race Discrimination," *Michigan Journal of Race & Law* 17, no. 1 (2011): 1–62.

99. See Carbado, "From Stopping Black People to Killing Black People," 125–64.

100. Aslı Bâli and Tendayi Achiume have described how the First World intervention that contributed to Libya's decimation relied in part and in different ways on racialization of Libyan territory and its inhabitants, rendering this intervention as a humanitarian pursuit, and belying a host of imperial interests. E. Tendayi Achiume and Aslı Bâli, "Race and Empire: Legal Theory Within, Through and Across National Borders," *UCLA Law Review* 67, no. 6 (2021): 1386–431.

101. Makau Mutua, "Savages, Victims, Saviors: The Metaphor of Human Rights," *Harvard International Law Journal* 42, no. 1 (2001): 202–3, 219–27.

102. Makau Mutua, "Savages, Victims, Saviors: The Metaphor of Human Rights," 227–33.

103. Makau Mutua, "Savages, Victims, Saviors: The Metaphor of Human Rights," 209–219.

104. Makau Mutua, "Savages, Victims, Saviors: The Metaphor of Human Rights," 204, 233–42.

105. Observing that "human rights law continues this tradition of universalizing Eurocentric norms by intervening in Third World cultures and societies to save them from the traditions and beliefs that it frames as permitting or promoting despotism and disrespect for human rights itself." Makau Mutua, "Savages, Victims, Saviors: The Metaphor of Human Rights," 235.

106. Katherine Fallah and Ntina Tzouvala, "Deploying Race, Employing Force: 'African Mercenaries' and the 2011 NATO Intervention in Libya," *UCLA Law Review* 67, no. 6 (2021): 1580–609.

107. Makau Mutua, "Savages, Victims, Saviors: The Metaphor of Human Rights," 207.

108. We limit ourselves to a few examples. First, Jeff Rosen attacks CRT scholars for failing to attain objectivity, before going on to describe CRT as akin to "play[ing] the race card" or engaging in "open race war." Jeffrey Rosen, "The Bloods and the Crits," *New Republic*, December 8, 1996, https://newrepublic.com/article/74070/the-bloods-and-the-crits [https:// perma.cc/2CEU-NZEM]; second, Daniel Farber and Suzanna Sherry wrote a book directed largely (though not entirely) at CRT in which they framed particular strands of CRT as "beyond all reason." Daniel A. Farber and Suzanna Sherry, *Beyond All Reason: The Radical Assault on Truth in American Law* (United Kingdom: Oxford University Press, 1997); in a review of the book, Richard Posner suggests CRT has a "lunatic core" that is rejecting objective reality and rational inquiry. Richard A. Posner, "The Skin Trade," review of *The Radical Assault on Truth in American Law*, by Daniel A. Farber and Suzanna Sherry, *New Republic*, October 13, 1997.

109. Richard Delgado, "The Imperial Scholar: Reflections on a Review of Civil Rights Literature," *University of Pennsylvania Law Review* 132, no. 3 (1984): 561–78.

110. Gathii, "Writing Race and Identity in a Global Context," 1621n39.

111. Crenshaw et al., *Critical Race Theory*, xiii.

112. See Kimberlé Williams Crenshaw, "Twenty Years of Critical Race Theory: Looking Back to Move Forward," *Connecticut Law Review* 43, no. 5 (2011): 1288–89; Mark Tushnet, "Critical Legal Studies: A Political History," *Yale Law Journal* 100, no. 5 (1991): 1519, 1541.

113. Devon W. Carbado and Cheryl I. Harris, "Intersectionality at 30: Mapping the Margins of Anti-Essentialism, Intersectionality, and Dominance Theory," *Harvard Law Review* 132, no. 8 (2019): 2212; see also Crenshaw, "Twenty Years of Critical Race Theory," 1288–89, 1294.

114. José A. Bracamonte, "Foreword: Minority Critiques of the Critical Legal Studies Movement," *Harvard Civil Rights-Civil Liberties Law Review* 22, no. 2 (1987): 298.

115. Patricia J. Williams, *The Alchemy of Race and Rights* (United States: Harvard University Press, 1991), 163.

116. Dorothy E. Roberts, "Foreword: Abolition Constitutionalism," *Harvard Law Review* 133, no. 1 (2019): 10.

117. Roberts, "Foreword: Abolition Constitutionalism," 10.

118. See Darren Lenard Hutchinson, "Critical Race Histories: In and Out," *American University Law Review* 53, no. 6 (2004): 1190; Athena D. Mutua, "The Rise, Development and Future Directions of Critical Race Theory and Related Scholarship," *Denver University Law Review* 84, no. 2 (2006): 333.

119. For two of the most powerful articulations of how CRT straddles the line between deconstruction and reconstruction, see Angela P. Harris, "Foreword: The Jurisprudence of Reconstruction," *California Law Review* 82, no. 4 (1987): 741–86; Mari J. Matsuda, "Looking to the Bottom: Critical Legal Studies and Reparations," *Harvard Civil Rights-Civil Liberties Law Review* 22, no. 2 (1987): 323–400.

120. See Angela Onwuachi-Willig, "From Loving v. Virginia to Washington v. Davis: The Erosion of the Supreme Court's Equal Protection Intent Analysis," *Virginia Journal of Social Policy & the Law* 25, no. 3 (2018): 308.

121. See Lawrence, "The Id, the Ego, and Equal Protection," 355–81.

122. Neil Gotanda, "A Critique of 'Our Constitution is Color-Blind,'" *Stanford Law Review* 44, no. 1 (1991): 1–68.

123. Devon W. Carbado, "Intraracial Diversity," *UCLA Law Review* 60, no. 5 (2013): 1149–57.

124. Jerry Kang and Mahzarin R. Banaji, "Fair Measures: A Behavioral Realist Revision of 'Affirmative Action,'" *California Law Review* 94, no. 4 (2006): 1070.

125. See, e.g., Lawrence, "The Id, the Ego, and Equal Protection," 379n294.

126. See, e.g., Carbado, "From Stopping Black People to Killing Black People," 125–64.

127. See Cynthia Kwei Yung Lee, "Race and Self-Defense: Toward a Normative Conception of Reasonableness," *Minnesota Law Review* 81, no. 2 (1996): 454.

128. For the classic articulation of intersectionality, see Kimberlé Crenshaw, "Demarginalizing the Intersection of Race and Sex: A Black Feminist Critique of Antidiscrimination Doctrine, Feminist Theory and Antiracist Politics," *University of Chicago Legal Forum*, no. 1989 (1989): 139–68; for a mobilization of the idea to equal protection doctrine, see Devon W. Carbado, and Kimberlé W. Crenshaw, "An Intersectional Critique of Tiers of Scrutiny: Beyond 'Either/Or' Approaches to Equal Protection," *Yale Law Journal Forum*, no. 129 (2019): 108–29.

129. Angela Onwuachi-Willig and Mario L. Barnes, "By Any Other Name?: On Being 'Regarded as' Black, and Why Title VII Should Apply Even if Lakisha and Jamal are White," *Wisconsin Law Review* 2005, no. 5 (2005): 1314.

130. Devon W. Carbado, "Discrimination on the Basis of Racial Orientation," unpublished manuscript, March 10, 2013 (on file with author); see also Devon W. Carbado and Mitu Gulati, "Working Identity," *Cornell Law Review* 85, no. 5 (2000): 1259–308.

131. For an example of one legal scholar's engagement with the idea of non-reformist reforms in the context of articulating a broader discussion of instantiating democratic power, see Amna A. Akbar, "Demands for a Democratic Political Economy," *Harvard Law Review Forum* 134, no. 2 (2020): 90–118.

132. Roberts, "Foreword: Abolition Constitutionalism."

133. Roberts, "Foreword: Abolition Constitutionalism," 77–90.

134. Bennett Capers et al., *Critical Race Judgments: Rewritten U.S. Court Opinions on Race and the Law* (United States: Cambridge University Press, 2022).

135. Devon W. Carbado et al., *The Oxford Handbook of Race and Law in the United States* (United Kingdom: Oxford University Press, 2022); Dorothy A. Brown, *Critical Race Theory: Cases, Materials, and Problems* (United States: West Academic Publishing, 2014).

136. For one of the most powerful articulations of this tension, see Angela P. Harris, "Foreword: The Jurisprudence of Reconstruction," *California Law Review* 82, no. 4 (1994): 741–86.

137. Kimberlé Williams Crenshaw, "The First Decade: Critical Reflections, or A Foot in the Closing Door," *UCLA Law Review* 49, no. 5 (2002): 1363.

138. See, e.g., Amna A. Akbar, "Toward a Radical Imagination of Law," *New York University Law Review* 93, no. 3 (2018): 405–79; see also Amna A. Akbar et al., "Movement Law," *Stanford Law Review* 73, no. 4 (2021): 821–84.

139. Roberts, "Foreword: Abolition Constitutionalism." Roberts argues that the abolition of the prison industrial complex is the only path to liberation; Paul Butler, "The System Is Working the Way It Is Supposed to: The Limits of Criminal Justice Reform," *Georgetown Law Journal* 104, no. 6 (2016): 1419, 1447.

140. Luis Eslava and Sundhya Pahuja, "Beyond the (Post)Colonial: TWAIL and the Everyday Life of International Law," *Verfassung und Recht in Übersee* 45, no. 2 (2012): 204; see also Anghie, "Civilization and Commerce," 891. Anghie describes that the study of history requires a critical engagement with the "existing histories of international law" and "telling . . . alternative histories"); but see John D. Haskell, "TRAIL-ing TWAIL: Arguments and Blind Spots in Third World Approaches to International Law," *Canadian Journal of Law and Jurisprudence*, no. 383 (2014). Haskell argues that "TWAIL unwittingly operates under the sway of a European capitalist orientation that produces some of the very problems TWAIL seeks to contest," in ways that constrain its emancipatory potential.

141. See Anghie and Chimni, "Third World Approaches to International Law and Individual Responsibility in Internal Conflicts," 101; see also James Thuo Gathii, "The Promise of International Law: A Third World View," Grotius Lecture Presented at the 2020 Virtual Annual Meeting of the American Society of International Law, *American University International Law Review* 36, no. 3 (2021): 377–478. Gathii cites the critical but reconstructive TWAIL scholarship of Alejandro Alvarez, R. P. Anand, Tieja Wang, Onuma Yasuki, George Abi-Saab, Mohammed Bedjaoui, Taslim O. Elias, Buphinder Chimni, Upendra Baxi, Christopher Weermantry, and Kamal Hosain.

142. See Anghie and Chimni, "Third World Approaches to International Law and Individual Responsibility in Internal Conflicts," 101.

143. Aziz Rana, "Keynote Speech, UCLA Law Review Symposium 2020: Law and Empire in the American Century," *UCLA Law Review* 67, no. 6 (2021): 1432–49.

144. "The 1619 Project," September 14, 2019, *New York Times Magazine,* https://www.nytimes.com/interactive/2019/08/14/magazine/1619-america-slavery.html [https://perma.cc/EYN2-7CM5].

145. See, e.g., E. Tendayi Achiume, "Black Lives Matter and the UN Human Rights System: Reflections on the Human Rights Council Urgent Debate," *European Journal of International Law: TALK,* December 15, 2020, https://www.ejiltalk.org/black-lives-matter-and-the-un-human-rights-system-reflections- on-the-human-rights-council-urgent-debate [https://perma.cc/7ZL8-GUFM].

146. "Coalition Letter—Request for U.N. Independent Inquiry into Escalating Situation of Police Violence and Repression of Protests in the United States," ACLU, June 8, 2020, https://www.aclu.org/letter/coalition-letter-request-un-independent-inquiry -escalating- situation-police-violence-and?redirect=letter/coalition-letter-request-un-investigation- escalating-situation-police-violence-and-repression [https:// perma.cc/D4H3-SYSB].

147. Independent experts within the UN human rights system also called for the establishment of such a commission. See "Statement From the UN Special Rapporteur on Contemporary Forms of Racism, Racial Discrimination, Xenophobia and Related Intolerance and the Working Group of Experts on People of African Descent," United Nations Human Rights Office of the High Commissioner, June 17, 2020, https://www.ohchr.org/en/NewsEvents/Pages/DisplayNews.aspx?NewsID=25969&LangI D=E [https://perma.cc/3CH5-VGPX]; for the rationale underpinning the request for the commission of inquiry, see E. Tendayi Achiume, "The UN Should Establish a Commission of Inquiry on Systemic Racism and Law Enforcement in the United States," *Just Security,* June 16, 2020, https://www.justsecurity.org/70811/the-un-human-rights-council-should-establish-a-commission-of-inquiry-on-systemic-racism-and-law-enforcement-in-the-united- states [https://perma.cc/W9B3-7U6C].

148. The debate was also intended to address the excessive use of force against and repression of peaceful protestors during the racial justice uprisings. It was unprecedented in that it was the first in the history of the Human Rights Council to focus on human rights violations within the territory of a liberal democratic hegemon, and also the first to center anti-Black racism.

149. Sejal Parmar, "The Internationalisation of Black Lives Matter at the Human Rights Council," *European Journal of International Law: TALK,* June 26, 2020, https://www.ejiltalk.org/the-internationalisation-of-black-lives-matter-at-the-human-rights-council [https://perma.cc/N9ZK-SN9J]; independent experts within the UN system, including one of us, issued a statement denouncing this geopolitical bullying. Ahmed Reid et al., "Statement on the Human Rights Council Urgent Debate Resolution," United Nations Human Rights Office of the High Commissioner, June 19, 2020, https://www.ohchr.org/en/NewsEvents/ Pages/DisplayNews.aspx?NewsID=25977&LangID=E [https://perma.cc/2S2G-NFSP].

150. Parmar remarks on different approaches within the session that shielded the United States from accountability through U.S. exceptionalism. Parmar, "The Internationalisation of Black Lives Matter at the Human Rights Council."

151. Michael R. Pompeo, "On the Hypocrisy of the UN Human Rights Council," June 20, 2020, https://www.state.gov/on-the-hypocrisy-of-un-human-rights-council [https://perma.cc/ GLT9-2DT2].

152. Lawrence Hill-Cawthorne, "Racism Will Not Pass," *European Journal of International Law: TALK!*, July 20, 2020, https://www.ejiltalk.org/racism-will-not-pass [https://perma.cc/K6LJ-LYLP].

153. See, e.g., E. Tendayi Achiume, "Black Lives Matter and the UN Human Rights System: Reflections on the Human Rights Council Urgent Debate."

INDEX

Abizadeh, Arash, 399
abolitionism, 77, 318, 487, 512, 513
Abrams, Kerry, 198
Achiume, Tendayi, 13, 19–20, 136n19, 259, 273n54, 421, 445, 523n100; on epistemological legitimacy problem, 438; "International Law and Racial Justice" conference, 12; on racial borders, 204–5; on SADC Tribunal, 370; on scholarly treatment of TWAIL and CRT, 433; on transnational life, 199; on United Nations, 261–62
ACT UP, 196
Adams, John, 54, 267
Adams, John Quincy, 54
Adams–Onís Treaty, 56, 71n57
Adesina, Jimi, 405
affirmative action, 1–2, 212, 466, 508, 523n97
Africa Command (AFRICOM), 34
Africa Group, 515
African exceptionalism, 130
Africanism, 422
African National Congress, 30
African nationalism, 413, 428n100, 507
African Union, 28–31, 155, 247
afromestizos, 288, 301n53
Agamben, Giorgio, 498–99
Ahmed, Aziza, 15

AIDS. *See* HIV/AIDS
al Attar, Mohsen, 18–19, 432
Alcoff, Linda, 441, 442
Al-Hammashi, Said, 243
Alston, Philip, 366–67, 377n18
"Amazing Grace" (song), 3
American Civil War, 88, 151, 158, 163–64, 409
American exceptionalism, 3, 8, 510–11, 514–16
American expansion, 46–47, 55–61, 64–65, 66, 281, 285, 297
American Journal of International Law, 108, 510
Amin, Rizgar Mohammed, 243
Amin, Samir, 435–36
Anderson, Benedict, 282
d'Andrade, Freire, 127, 132
Andrews, Kehinde, 19, 137n22
Anfal campaign, 242
Anghie, Antony, 8, 48, 433, 438–39, 442, 496–97, 500
Anglo-Iranian Oil Company, 86
anti-Blackness, 402, 414, 453–56, 462, 467–70, 515–16
anti-racialism, 397, 464–65
anti-racism, 27, 76, 78; borders and, 282; conservative right and, 469; CRT, TWAIL, and, 513; depoliticization of

anti-racism (*cont.*)
  race and, 110; geopolitics of welcome and, 268; international economic law and, 366, 374; international law scholarship and, 439, 445, 446; multiculturalism and, 465; neoliberalism and, 396–97; postracial xenophobia and, 384–85, 391, 399; racial contract and, 266; racial panics and, 95, 96; right of *dominium* and, 391; transnational critical race theory and, 402, 404, 415
Anzaldúa, Gloria, 289
apartheid, 105–6, 107, 391, 455, 465; boycotts against, 9; Convention on the Elimination of All Forms of Racial Discrimination and, 112–15, 121n87, 327; Du Bois on, 111; medical apartheid, 206; New International Economic Order and, 326–30, 346; spectacularization of, 122n112
Apess, William, 149–50
Appiah, Kwame Anthony, 395, 405, 417
Arab League, 29, 30–31
Arab Spring, 30–31, 338
Árbenz, Jacobo, 293
Aristide, Jean-Bertrand, 193
assimilation: "civilized by," 47, 66; knowledge production and, 359; *mestizaje* and, 289; nationalism and, 154, 288; in postcolonial states, 501; races considered incapable of, 94; settler colonialism and, 436, 438
Atanasova, Dafina, 367
Australia: multiculturalism in, 465; "White Australia Policy," 92, 93
Azikiwe, Nnamdi, 149
Aziz, Sahar, 241

Bacchetta, Paola, 456
Bach, Renee, 221–22
Baja California, Mexico, 47, 52

Baker, Catherine, 460
Bâli, Aslı, 12, 13, 501, 523n100
Bandung Conference, 327–29
Bashford, Alison, 146
Bashir, Omar al-, 241, 247–49, 250
Bashi Treitler, Vilna, 456, 460
Bathes, Roland, 386
Bauman, Zygmunt, 481
Bayoumi, Moustafa, 452
Beck, Ulrich, 194
Belgium, 84, 86, 106
Bell, Derrick, 1, 258, 271n22, 445
Bellegarde, Dantès: Du Bois on, 128; legacy of, 124–26, 133; role on Temporary Slavery Commission, 126–27; universalist strategy of, 129–33
Bellegarde-Smith, Patrick, 124–25
Benghazi attack of 2012, 32, 33
Benton, Lauren, 78
Berlin Act, 89
Berlin Conference, 208, 384
Berlusconi, Silvio, 36
Bernadino, Ana Luisa, 431
Bhandar, Brenna, 445
Biden, Joseph, 214, 232n117, 260
Bilbao, Francisco, 64–66, 67
Black AIDS Mobilization, 196
Black codes, 288, 317
Blackett, Adelle, 14, 445
Blackhawk, Ned, 157, 158
Black Lives Matter movement, 504, 509
Black Nationalism, 413
Black Panthers, 151, 159, 165
Black Power movement, 97, 402, 416, 421
Black Radical Tradition, 112, 402–3, 407–8, 416–22
Blair, Tony, 437
Bluntschli, Johann Kaspar, 49, 67
Bolivar, Simón, 54
Bonilla-Silva, Eduardo, 396
Borchard, Edwin, 62–63, 73n92

border imperialism, 277, 290–91, 303n81
border nationalism, 279–84
Boston Trades' Union, 163
boycotts, 9
Boyer, Jean-Pierre, 84–85
Brexit, 153
Broude, Tomer, 373
Brown, Henry, 499
Brown, Michael, 106
Brown, Wendy, 396
Brown v. Board of Education, 512
Brussels Act, 133
Bruyneel, Kevin, 289
Butler, Judith, 294

Caal Maquín, Jakelin, 292, 293
Cabral, Amilcar, 417
Cabrera Lopez, Juanita, 292
Calhoun, John, 61
Calvo, Carlos, 66
Calvo Doctrine, 65–66
Campbell, Mike, 368, 370–71, 374, 505–6
Canada: anti-Chinese policies, 93; multiculturalism in, 465; U.S.-Canadian border, 283; in Western European and Others Group, 256
Candace, Gratien, 129, 139n45
Cantonments Acts, 317
Carbado, Devon, 19–20, 136n19, 433, 438, 445
Carmichael, Stokely, 97
Carter, Jimmy, 260
Cassese, Antonio, 245
caste systems, racial, 316, 318, 468
Castile, Philando, 106
Cavafy, C. P., 325
Cell, John, 414
Center for Constitutional Rights, 196
Centers for Disease Control (CDC), 194, 199
Chan, Shuk Ying, 149, 155

Chandler, Nahum Demetri, 386
Chang, Ha-Joon, 309
Charles X of France, 84–85
Chatterjee, Partha, 31–32, 327, 329
Cherokee people, 157, 162
Chickasaw people, 157
Chimni, Bhupinder, 438–39
China: anti-Chinese policies and sentiment, 93, 164, 198, 468; borders and, 92–93; COVID-19 pandemic and, 174, 214, 236n166; Han identity, 468; United Nations and, 481
Chinese Exclusion Act, 93, 164
Chinese nationalism, 153
Cho, Sumi, 464
Choctaw people, 157
Christian, Michelle, 19
"civilizing mission," 31, 47, 97, 205, 339, 459
Civil Rights Act of 1964, 164, 423
Clarke, Kamari, 248
Clay, Henry, 289
Clinton, Bill, 180, 196, 197, 261, 483
Coalition Provisional Authority (CPA), 242–43
Cobiella, Kelly, 258
Cohen, Cathy, 198
Cohen, Stanley, 76
Cold War, 165, 308, 327, 332
colonial expansion, 147, 208, 264, 290, 414, 457, 497–98
colonial mentality, 221–22, 237n174
colorblindness, 2–5, 50; CRT, TWAIL, and, 502–7; neoliberal colorblindness, 396–98. *See also* Critical Race Theory of Global Colorblindness
Columbus, Christopher, 295
Comanche people, 156, 288
commodity production, 307–10
Common But Differentiated Responsibility (CBDR), 224–25

Commonwealth v. Jennison, 162
Constitution of South Africa, 105
Constitution of United States, 7–8; anti-slavery constitutionalists and, 163; Bill of Rights, 502; Declaration of Independence and, 149–50, 159; Fifteenth Amendment, 163–64; Fourteenth Amendment, 157, 163–64, 499, 518n35; Fourth Amendment, 502, 512; National Conservatives and, 154; Thirteenth Amendment, 159, 163–64
Contagious Diseases Acts, 317
Convention for the Elimination of Discrimination against Women (CEDAW), 179, 181–82
Convention on Rights of Persons with Disabilities (CRPD), 179, 182
Convention on the Elimination of All Forms of Racial Discrimination (CERD), 112–15, 121n87, 179, 182, 231n96, 327, 370–73, 486
Convention on the Rights of the Child (CRC), 179, 182
Cook, Joseph, 82
Corea, Gamani, 331–32
Corwine, Amos, 51–52, 53
counterterrorism, 28, 29, 32–35, 37–38
COVID-19 pandemic, 12; cases and deaths, 174; CEDAW and, 181–82; COVAX, 217, 218; early history of, 174; gender-based violence (GBV) and, 176–77, 180, 181–82, 184, 185; IACHR resolutions and, 183–84; ICCPR and, 179–80; ICESCR and, 180–81; IHR and, 182–83; impact on global economy, 174; impact on women of color, 176–85; international law and, 178–84; intersectionality and, 178–84; personal protective equipment (PPE), 176; Public Health Emergency of International Concern (PHEIC) declaration, 182, 212; racial inequality and, 508; racialization of, 213–15; sexual and reproductive health and, 177, 181, 182; Trump administration and, 260; World Health Organization and, 182, 212, 213–18, 225–26
COVID Capitalism, 174–75
Crawford, James, 433
Crenshaw, Kimberlé W., 175, 386, 398, 511
Critical Race Theory (CRT): Bellegarde and, 125, 126; colonial international law and, 436, 439; contemporary international law scholarship and, 1–2, 4–10, 340; Global Critical Race Feminist (GCRF) theory, 173–84; goals of, 5; international law scholarship and, 432–33; postracial xenophobia and, 392; transnational, 402–23
Critical Race Theory (CRT), TWAIL and, 494–95; colorblindness, 502–7; CR•TWAIL, 45, 47–51; formal equality and racial inclusion, 498–501; post-racial technocracy and, 333–34; public health and, 193–94, 198; quasi and second-class scholarship, 509; race and empire, 27–28, 38; racial capitalism, 495–98; reconstruction and transformation, 509–16; social responsibility and agency, 507–9
Critical Race Theory of Global Colorblindness (CRTGC), 453, 470–71; components of, 454–55; developmentalism and, 458–59; human rights and, 458; neoliberalism and, 456–60; politicultures and, 460–70; racial hierarchy and, 462–63; racist erasure and, 455–56; securitization and, 459–60; white racial knowledge and, 463–64
Cuba, 132, 206, 260–61, 291. *See also* Guantanamo Bay, Cuba
Cushing, William, 162

Index

Dahl, Adam, 149–50, 156, 159, 161, 162
Dakar, 207
Darder, Antonio, 395
Darfur, 240–41, 247–49
Declaration of Alma-Alta, 220–21, 224
Declaration of Independence, 90, 149–50, 157, 159–66
De Genova, Nicholas, 278
de-historicization, 106, 107, 113, 453, 1110
Delafosse, Maurice, 127, 132–33
de León Gutiérrez, Juan, 292
Delgado, Richard, 175, 333, 510
DeMint, Jim, 153
DeMuth, Christopher, 153–54
depoliticization, 109–10, 114, 122
de Pombo, Lino, 52–53
deracialization, 388, 389, 390, 391–93, 396
Desautels-Stein, Justin, 12, 13, 18, 151
diasporic affinity, 414
Díaz, Porfirio, 61
Dikköter, Frank, 461
disease: cholera, 207, 209, 210, 211; dengue, 207, 209; Ebola, 214, 221, 233n123, 236n167; leprosy, 206, 207; malaria, 207, 209; plague, 207, 208, 209, 210, 211; polio, 219; smallpox, 208, 210; typhus, 209, 210; yellow fever, 206, 209, 211, 229n43. *See also* COVID-19 pandemic; health justice; HIV/AIDS
dispositif, 321–22n26
domestication of race, 105–16
domestic violence, 176–77. *See also* gender-based violence
Domingo, Deirdre, 177
dominium, right to, 387–93, 398
Douglass, Frederick, 159–60, 163
Douzinas, Costas, 421
Drago Doctrine, 66
Dred Scott v. Sandford, 496, 499

Du Bois, W. E. B., 107, 132, 151, 444, 479; on apartheid, 111; on Bellegarde, 126; on the color line, 130–31, 412–13; on culture of white folk, 110, 115–16; on the Great Migration, 295; International Labor Organization and, 128–29; pan-Africanism and, 67; on the wage of whiteness, 337n29
Dunbar-Ortiz, Roxanne, 146–47, 149, 153, 159
Durkheim, Emile, 359
Duvalier, Jean-Claude, 193, 260

Eagleton, Terry, 357
El Kassar, Nadja, 440–41
El Salvador, 291, 292
Elsheikh, Elsadig, 249
Empire Windrush scandal, 489–90
Enlightenment, European, 149, 157–58, 161, 255–56, 435, 463, 464
epidemics. *See* disease
Eslava, Luis, 438, 514
Essed, Philomena, 470
essentialism, 6, 175, 177, 184, 208, 287, 407, 417, 468–69
Estes, Nick, 297–98
Ethiopia, 82, 83, 90, 111, 126, 131, 136–37n20, 394
eugenics, 92–93, 301n53, 390, 482
Eurocentrism, 407, 423, 509; contemporary international law scholarship and, 339, 346, 432–33; epistemic whiteness and, 432–33, 435–40, 444; New International Economic Order and, 325, 330, 336
European Convention on Human Rights, 36–37, 91
European Court of Human Rights, 36, 368, 490
European Society of International Law (ESIL), 444–45

exceptionalism: African exceptionalism, 130; American exceptionalism, 3, 8, 510–11, 514–16; liberal democratic exceptionalism, 511, 515–16; Trump exceptionalism, 296; white exceptionalism, 268, 467
expansionism: American, 46–47, 55–61, 64–65, 66, 281, 285, 297; colonial, 147, 208, 264, 290, 414, 457, 497–98

Fallah, Katherine, 509–10
Fanon, Frantz, 88, 108, 109, 115–16, 329, 402, 413
Farmer, Paul, 198
Fast Track Land Reform Program (FTLRP), 505–7
Fauchille, Paul, 94
Feeman, Alan David, 3
Ferguson, James, 286
Ferreira da Silva, Denise, 386
Feuerbach, Ludwig, 356
Fifteenth Amendment, 163–64
First Universal Races Congress (1911), 67
Fischer, Eugen, 482
Flagg, Barbara, 356, 357, 359
Floyd, George, 106, 107, 465, 482, 515
Ford, Lisa, 78
Fortner, Michael Javen, 148
Foucault, Michel, 150, 322n26, 348, 353
Fouron, Georges, 196
Fourteenth Amendment, 157, 163–64, 499, 518n35
Fourth Amendment, 502, 512
Fredrickson, George, 408, 409–10, 411, 414, 422
freedom of movement: anti-colonial, 296; borders and, 282–83; civilization and, 92; gender-based violence and, 180; history of international law and, 94–95; Whiteness and, 262, 263, 266, 267
French Revolution, 79–80

Friedman, Milton, 131–32
Fromm, Erich, 356

Gabrial, Brian, 76
Gadsden Purchase, 60, 71n57, 290
Gage, Thomas, 162
Gallant, Yoav, 248, 253n58
Gandhi, Indira, 332
Garrison, William Lloyd, 163
Gates, Henry Louis, Jr., 405
Gathii, James Thuo, 67n1, 68n10, 108, 111, 135n11, 145–46, 157, 372, 497–98, 500–501, 510
Gaza, 219
Gbedemah, Hilary, 179
Gearey, Adam, 421
gender-based violence (GBV), 176–77, 180, 181–82, 184, 185
General Agreement on Tariffs and Trade (GATT), 307, 309
Geneva conventions, 88, 90–91, 478
genocide: charges against Omar al-Bashir, 247; charges against Saddam Hussein, 242; colonialism and, 433, 436, 480, 481–83, 495, 497, 498; against Indigenous Americans, 292; International Health Regulations and, 215–16; in Palestine, 219; post-racialism and, 481–83; reparations for, 149; "white genocide," 95, 369–70
George III of Great Britain, 87–88, 90
Geronimo, 297
Getachew, Adom, 125, 126, 136–37n20, 146, 148–49, 151, 155
Gevers, Christopher, 13–14, 49, 62, 421, 453, 497, 520n63
Ghana, 488
Ghebremariam Tesfau', Mackda, 465
Gilmore, Ruthie, 333
Gilroy, Paul, 417
Giroux, Henry, 432

globalization, 5; backlash against, 308; labor migration and, 312; migration and, 312; neoliberalism and, 330, 332, 396; public health and, 208; race as globalizing ideology, 454

Global Value Chain (GVC), 347

global Whiteness, 267

Global White Supremacy, 117n7, 497, 504–5; Black radical tradition and, 421; colorblindness and, 452–55, 459–60, 469–71; CRT and, 107; definition of, 520n65; transnational critical race theory and, 403–4, 412–13; as worldmaking project, 108, 111, 112

Gohr, Albrecht, 127, 132

Goldberg, David Theo, 396–97, 452, 464

Golder, Ben, 374

Gómez Alonzo, Felipe, 292, 294

Gómez-Barris, Macarena, 278

Gonzalez, Juan, 291

Gordon, Hannah, 146, 159

Gordon, Lewis, 116, 414–15

Gordon, Ruth, 9

Gorgas, William Crawford, 206

Gotanda, Neil, 1, 511

Graeber, David, 157–58, 161, 166

Grandin, Greg, 293

Grant, Madison, 93

Grimshaw, Harold, 129, 131–33

Grotius, Hugo, 59, 437

Guantanamo Bay, Cuba, 193–99, 260–61

Guatemala, 291–94, 467

Gulick, Sidney L., 87

Gupta, Akhil, 286

Guterres, António, 176–77

Haftar, Khalifa, 35

Haitian coup d'éta (1991), 193, 195–96

Haitian Revolution, 78, 125, 416

Haitian Services Center, 196

Hall, Stuart, 386, 470–71

Hämäläinen, Pekka, 155–59

Hannah-Jones, Nikole, 165

Hariri, Rakif al-, 241, 244–47, 250

Harney, Stefano, 284

Harris, Cheryl, 3, 313, 386, 506

Hartman, Saidiya, 295–96, 386, 417, 446, 499

Hathaway, James, 262

Hayek, Friedrich, 131–32, 330, 368

Hazony, Yoram, 153

health justice: coloniality and, 220–22; Declaration of Alma-Alta, 220–21, 224; global health, 208–10, 222–26; racialized states and public health, 204–6; tropical and colonial medicine, 206–8; World Health Organization and, 210–20

Henckels, Caroline, 373

Hernández Vásquez, Carlos Gregorio, 292

Hezbollah, 245, 246, 253n51

Hindu nationalism, 153, 468

Hirsi Jamaa v. Italy, 36–37

HIV/AIDS, 176, 193–99, 260–61

Hoar, George, 164

Holocaust, 465, 478, 481–82

Honduras, 291, 292, 295

Huntington, Samuel P., 144–46, 153, 166

Hussein, Saddam, 240–44, 249, 250

hybridity: hybridized Blackness, 417; hybrid tribunals and courts, 245–46, 249, 253n51; *mestizaje* and, 466; of modern peoples, 156–57

iconoclasm, 430–32

Immerwahr, Daniel, 284–85

Immigration and Naturalization Service (INS), 195, 197

Immigration Quota Act, 93

Immigration Restriction League, 93

imperium, right of, 387–93, 398

Ina, Satsuki, 297
India, 82, 209, 215, 317, 318, 468
Indian Declaration of Independence and, 149
Ingersoll, Jared, 73n87
Institut de Droit International (IDI), 91, 94
Insular Cases, 286
InterAmerican Commission on Human Rights (IACHR) resolutions, 179, 183, 184
International Commission on Epidemics, 209
International Conference on Primary Health Care (1978), 220
International Convention for Mutual Protection against Dengue Fever, 209
International Convention on the Suppression and Publishment of the Crime of Apartheid, 114
International Court of Justice (ICJ), 9, 111, 112, 326
International Covenant on Civil and Political Rights (ICCPR), 179–80
International Criminal Court (ICC), 241, 247–49
International Health Regulations (IHR), 179, 182–83, 211–19, 235n154
International Labor Organization (ILO), 127–29, 132–33, 139n46
"International Law and Racial Justice" (Boulder conference), 12
international law scholarship (ILS), contemporary, 338–40, 360; added value and, 341–45, 347, 350, 361n9; as economy of knowledge production, 341–45; global division of labor and, 345–56; quality assurance protocols and, 353–56, 359; race consciousness in, 356–60
International Monetary Fund (IMF), 216, 307, 330, 439, 458, 478, 480, 487–88

International Sanitary Agency of Notification, 209–10
International Sanitary Bureau (later Pan American Sanitary Bureau), 210
intersectionality, 175, 178–84, 512
Iran, 86, 242
Iran–Iraq War, 242
Iraq, 34, 240–44, 248–50; de-Baathification policy, 242–43; Dujail incident and trial, 242, 243, 247, 249; Special Iraqi Criminal Tribunal, 240–41, 242–43, 247, 248, 249; United States invasion of, 437, 481. *See also* Hussein, Saddam
Iraqi Special Tribunal (IST), 242
Isay, Ernst, 92
Islamic State (ISIS), 33–34, 466
Islamophobia, 247
Israel, 114, 219, 248, 253n51, 280, 294, 463. 467, 501
Italy: colorblindness and, 462, 465, 470; *Hirsi Jamaa v. Italy,* 36–37; Partnership Treaty (with Libya), 36

Jackson, Andrew, 58
Jackson, Jesse, 196, 197
Jackson Sow, Marissa, 16
James, C. L. R., 125
Jameson, Fredric, 397
Jay, John, 161
Jay Treaty, 283
Jefferson, Thomas, 80
Jim Crow policies, 2, 5, 206, 295, 317, 355, 396, 455–56, 499, 507–8, 515
Johnson, Lyndon, 164
Johnson, Sterling, 197
Jones, Claudia, 479
Jones, Howard, 88
Joseph, Chief, 164
Jung, Moon-Kie, 454
Jurmain, Robert, 394–95

Kandiaronk, 157
Kant, Immanuel, 479, 483–84
Kashyap, Monika Batra, 146, 159
Kelly, Casey, 469
Kennedy, David, 358
Kennedy, Duncan, 358, 386
King, Martin Luther, Jr., 164
Kinsella, Helen, 90
Kirk, Charlie, 153
Know Nothing movement, 163
Knox, Robert, 83
Koskenniemi, Martti, 366
Kundnani, Arun, 368
Kuti, Fela Anikulapo, 421–22
Kuwait, 242
Kymlicka, Will, 399

labor migration, 311–14
Labuda, Patryk, 443–45
Lakota people, 156, 159
Latin-Americanism, 47
Latin-American race, 63–66
"Latin America," origins of the term, 64
Latin race, 46, 65–66
League of Arab States, 30
League of Nations, 74n107; Bellegarde and, 124, 126–28, 130; Health Organization of the League of Nations, 210; mandate system, 459, 478, 500; Minority Rights Treaty System, 384; pan-Africanism and, 107; postracial xenophobia and, 384, 389; Selassie and, 83; white ordering and, 108
Lebanon, 241, 244–46, 248, 250, 252n45
legal panics, 77–78
Lentin, Alana, 455–56
Leong, Nancy, 148
Léopold II of Belgium, 84
Levenson, Zachary, 148
Levinas, Emmanuel, 291

Levi-Strauss, Claude, 386
Lewis, Hope, 505
Li, Darryl, 130
liberal democratic exceptionalism, 511, 515–16
Liberator, The, 163
Liberia, 30, 81, 83–84, 126, 129, 130, 131, 136–37n20, 136n18
Liberia & Ethiopia v. South Africa, 111
Libya, military intervention in: counterterrorism and, 32–34; CRT-TWAIL analysis and, 27–28, 38; European migrant interdiction and, 35–37; Government of National Accord, 32–33; NATO and, 28–38, 509; Partnership Treaty and, 36; racial framing of, 28–29; rebuilding and, 31–32, 37; Tajoura Detention Center airstrike, 35, 36, 37, 38; United Nations and, 28–32, 35–38; UN Security Council Resolution 1973, 31
Libyan Coast Guard (LCG), 37
Libyan National Army (LNA), 35
Libyan uprising, 30
Lieber, Francis, 90
Lincoln, Abraham, 87–88, 159, 163, 285, 287
Locke, John, 150, 162, 265
Logan, George, 80
Long, Huey, 206
Longan, John P., 293
López, Rachel, 248
Lorca, Arnulf Becker, 13
Lorde, Audre, 158
Lord's Resistance Army, 249
Lorimer, James, 49, 429, 438
Lowe, Lisa, 457
Lugard, Frederick, 127, 132–33, 136n19, 140n55, 142n81, 143n88
Luhmann, Niklas, 366
Lumumba, Patrice, 479–80
Luna, José Manuel, 51–52

Machel, Graça, 177, 184
Mafeje, Archie, 404–5, 406
Magubane, Bernard, 408, 412–15, 422
Mahmud, Tayyab, 316
Maira, Sunaina, 456
Malcolm X, 106, 107, 111, 115, 408, 413–14, 422, 479, 482, 485, 491
Mamdani, Mahmood, 147, 241, 244, 249
manifest destiny, 55–61, 65, 266, 285
Manley, Michael, 148
Marshall, John, 166
Marshall Plan, 487
Masekela, Hugh, 421–22
Massachusetts Constitution, 149, 162
Mathur, Rita, 78
May, Theresa, 490
Maya Q'eqchi', 293
Mbembe, Achille, 287, 330, 417, 420, 468
McCleskey v. Kemp, 508
McIlhenny, John Avery, 124
McKay, Dwanna, 470
McLane–Ocampo Treaty, 60
Meadows, Mark, 153
Medina, José, 441
Meeker, Royal, 128–29, 139n46
Meer, Nasar, 469
Mégret, Frédéric, 13
Mercier, Washington Henri, 88
mestizaje, 97, 288, 289, 301n53, 461, 466–67
mestizo, 49–50, 60, 285, 288, 301n53, 467
Metraux, Alfred, 110
Mexican-American War, 51, 55–57, 279, 285, 287. *See also* Treaty of Guadalupe Hidalgo
Michaels, Walter Benn, 395
Middle Passage, 417, 496
Mignolo, Walter, 278
migration laws and policies, 94–95, 146, 176, 198, 261, 287, 390–91, 393
Mike Campbell v. Zimbabwe, 368, 370–71, 374, 505–6
Milazzo, Marzia, 456–57
Mill, John Stuart, 264, 265
Miller, David, 399
Mills, Charles, 4, 49, 108, 109–10, 114–16, 263, 265, 403, 412, 440–42, 457
Miranda, Francisco de, 54
Mlambo-Ngcuka, Phumzile, 173
Modi, Narendra, 153
Modiri, Joel, 18
Mongia, Radhika, 321n24
Monroe Doctrine, 65, 293
Moore, William, 164
moral panics, 76–78
Moreton-Robinson, Aileen, 283
Morgan, Jennifer L., 148
Morrison, Toni, 109
Moten, Fred, 284
movement. *See* freedom of movement
Moyn, Samuel, 367
Moyo, Admark, 370–71
Mueller, Jennifer, 463–64
Mugabe, Robert, 369, 370, 371
multiculturalism, 465–66
Munshi, Sherally, 16
Museveni, Yoweri, 249
Mutua, Makau, 509, 516

NAFTA, 308
Namibia, 326, 328, 482–83
Napoleonic Wars, 388
Nasser, Gamal Abde, 329
NatCons, 153–54, 161, 166
National Association for the Advancement of Colored People (NAACP), 126, 132, 164, 196
National Conservatism movement, 153–54, 161, 166
"National Conservatism Statement of Principles," 153, 154
Nazi Germany, 336n17, 465, 481–82

Nehru, Jawaharlal, 329, 336n17
neocolonialism, 216, 256–57, 261–62, 265, 267, 499–500, 505–6
neoliberalism: anti-racism and, 396–97; colorblindness and, 396–98; Critical Race Theory of Global Colorblindness and, 456–60; definition of, 319n5; globalization and, 330, 332, 396
Nesiah, Vasuki, 17, 445
Netanyahu, Benjamin, 248, 253n58
New Granada, 51–53, 55
New International Economic Order (NIEO), 86, 149, 212, 220, 226, 325–34
Newton, John, 3
Nez Perce people, 164
Ngũgĩ wa Thiong'o, 435, 507
Nicaragua, 52, 291
Nietzsche, Friedrich, 356
1926 Slavery Convention, 132, 133
Nkosi, Lewis, 106
Nkrumah, Kwame, 149, 327, 479, 480, 488, 500
Non-Aligned Movement of States, 211–12, 327, 332
North Atlantic Treaty Organization (NATO): intervention in Libya, 28–38, 509; Ukraine and, 263, 271n23
North Korea, 178
Nuremberg laws, 90, 482
Nyere, Julius, 149
Nzegwu, Nkiru, 405–6

Occum, Samson, 162
Office International d'Hygiène Publique (OHIP), 210
O'Higgins, Bernardo, 54
Okafur, Obiora, 458
one-drop rule, 316
Onitositah (Corn Tassel), 162
O'odham peoples, 279–81

Oppenheimer, Gerald, 198
Orbán, Viktor, 153
Organisation of African Unity (OAU), 106, 107, 114
Organization of Afro-American Unity, 468
O'Sullivan, John, 55–60, 65, 67, 72–73n85, 72n83
Other and Othering, 49, 96, 108, 291, 294, 352, 409, 413

Padmore, George, 149
Pahuja, Sundhya, 438, 514
Paik, A. Naomi, 194, 199
Painter, Nell, 281
Palestine and Palestinian people, 114, 219, 226, 252n45, 271n17, 326, 329, 501
Pan-African Congress, 107
pan-Africanism, 125, 126, 128–29, 469; First Pan-African Conference (1900), 67; of Lumumba, 479; of Qaddafi, 30; Second Pan-African Congress (1921), 128; transnational CRT and, 411, 415, 419
Panama (Watermelon Incident), 47, 51–53, 55, 64
pandemics. *See* COVID-19 pandemic; disease
Paret, Marcel, 148
Partnership Treaty (Libya and Italy), 36
Patel, Priti, 490
Pearson, Karl, 482
Peller, Gary, 1, 511
People of the Global Majority, 203, 219, 226
perpetrator perspective, 2, 3, 5, 8, 109
Petersmann, Ernst-Ulrich, 366–67
Phelan, Edward, 128
Picker, Giovanni, 465
Pierre, Jemima, 459, 468
Pirtle, Whitney N. Laster, 174
plenary power, 145, 285, 389, 391, 393

Plessy v. Ferguson, 499
pogroms, 83
politicultures, 460–70
Polk, James, 55, 58–59, 61
post-racialism, 388, 393, 397, 398, 464–65, 466, 481, 483
postracial xenophobia, 383–84, 391, 392–95, 398, 399
Prah, Kwesi, 405
Prebisch, Raúl, 331
presidential election of 2024, U.S., 153
Proclamation Line of 1763, 290
"professional Arab," 338, 351–52
Proust, Adrien, 209
Public Health Emergency of International Concern (PHEIC), 174, 182–83, 213
Putin, Vladimir, 248

Qaddafi, Muammar, 30–31, 36, 509
Quijano, Anibal, 203, 278

race consciousness, 339–40, 356–60
"race question," 10
racial authoritarianism, 95
racial borders, 29, 36, 44n107, 146–47, 204–5, 399; definition of, 44n107; mobility and, 92–93
racial capitalism, 125, 147–48, 174, 205, 228, 315, 419–21, 495–98
racial contract, 10–11, 49–50, 67, 107, 108, 256–58, 261–68, 276
racial formalism, 79
racialization of diseases, 204, 205, 213, 214
racialized classifications, 10
racialized mobility, 79, 91–95
racialized sovereignty, 78, 79–86
racialized violence, 78–79, 86–92, 446
racialized world order, 5
racial panics, 76–79, 84, 91, 95–97; definition of, 77
racial polity, 10

racial privilege, 205, 313, 440, 445
Ramírez Vásquez, Wilmer Josué, 292
Rana, Aziz, 150–51, 157, 159, 161, 501, 514, 515
Rappard, William, 131–32
Rasulov, Akbar, 17
Ratner, Michael, 196–97
Reed, James A., 83
Refugee Convention, 261
reparative history, 337n32
responsibility to protect (R2P) doctrine, 29, 31, 32
Reynolds, John, 501
Rhodesia, 97, 369
Richardson, Henry J., III, 9, 125, 133
Riell, Henry E., 163
Roberts, Dorothy, 512, 513
Robinson, Cedric, 105, 115, 147–48, 151, 228n23, 386, 408, 416–22, 495
Rodney, Walter, 332, 500
Rodogno, Celestina, 183
Romulo, Carlos, 329
Roncagli, Giovanni, 130
Röpke, Wilhelm, 325, 329, 333
Rousseau, Jean-Jacques, 265, 268
Rufo, Christopher, 153
Russia, 248; invasion of Ukraine, 255–59, 263, 265, 443, 452; whiteness and, 463, 468
Russo-Japanese War, 86–87
Rutledge, John, 161

Said, Edward, 332, 449n63
Said, Wadie, 15–16
Saldaña-Portillo, María Josefina, 287, 289–90
Sanitary Conventions, 209–10
Sartre, Jean-Paul, 356, 358
Saudi Arabia, 30, 246
Saul, Ben, 245
Saussure, Ferdinand de, 386

"savages," 86–92, 198, 289, 509–10
Saviano, Roberto, 295
Scelle, Georges, 74n107
Schlag, Pierre, 354, 430–31, 433
Schoultz, Lars, 54
Schücking, Walther, 67
Schwaller, Robert C., 324n46
scientific racism, 96–97, 205, 463, 468, 482
Selassie, Haile, 83
Seneca Falls "Declaration of Sentiments," 163
Senegal, 207
settler empire, 150, 156
Sexton, Jared, 301n53, 417
sexual and reproductive health, 177, 181, 182, 223
Sharp, Granville, 487
Shilliam, Robbie, 107, 109, 118n28
shock doctrine, 82
Sierra Leone, 30, 207, 208, 246
Simpson, Audra, 282–83
Sirleaf, Matiangai, 15, 260–61
1619 Project, 165, 514
slave trade, 3–4, 7, 89, 110, 318, 417, 496
Slobodian, Quinn, 330, 332
Sloterdijk, Peter, 356
Smith, Caleb, 59
Smith, Claire, 18–19
Smith, Ian, 369
Smith, Rogers, 14
social Darwinism, 96
Société du Mont-Pèlerin, 131–32, 329
Somerset, James, 486–87
South Africa: African National Congress, 30, 117n4; SADC Treaty, 370. *See also* apartheid
Southern African Development Community Tribunal (SADC Tribunal), 368–71, 505, 507
sovereignty doctrine, 29–30
Spanish-American War, 164, 286

Special Iraqi Criminal Tribunal (SICT), 240–41, 242–43, 247, 248, 249
Special Tribunal for Lebanon (STL), 241, 244–47, 248, 249, 250, 253n51
Spender, Percy, 111
Spooner, Lysander, 163
Sraffa, Piero, 342, 343, 350
Stefancic, Jean, 333
St. John, Spencer, 131
Stoddard, Lothrop, 93
Stoler, Ann Laura, 277, 279, 290
Suez Canal, 209
Sukarno, 328, 329
Surkis, Judith, 323n34
Sustainable Development Goals (SDG), 223
Swain, Carol, 153
Syria, 244–46

Taiwo, Olufemi, 405
Tamale, Sylvia, 458
Taylor, Breonna, 106
technocracy, 332–33, 437
technology, definition of, 319n1
technology, race as, 314–19; of economic production, 318; of empires, 315–17; of legal rule, 317
Tehranian, John, 241
Temporary Slavery Commission, 124, 126–27, 129–30, 132–33
Thiel, Peter, 153
Third World Approaches to International Law (TWAIL), 7–8; health justice and, 193–94, 198; hybridity and, 157; international law scholarship and, 145–46, 157, 333–34, 339; slavery and, 125. *See also* Critical Race Theory (CRT), TWAIL and
Thirteenth Amendment, 159, 163–64
Thomas, Albert, 127–29
Thomas, Chantal, 16–17, 198, 264, 518n32
Thomas, Deborah, 469

Thomas, Kendall, 1, 511
Thompson, Debra, 452, 456
Tomba, Massimiliano, 295
Torres, Guillermo, 291–92
Torres, Rodolfo, 395
Torres Caicedo, José María, 65–66
TransAfrica, 196
"Transnational Legal Discourse on Race and Empire" (Los Angeles symposium), 12
Treaty of Brussels, 89
Treaty of Guadalupe Hidalgo, 51, 56, 60, 71n57, 288, 289–90, 302n65
Treaty of Peace, Amity, Navigation, and Commerce, 51
Treaty of Saint-Germain, 126, 133
Treaty of Versailles, 82, 93, 127, 129
Treichler, Paula, 198
Triggs, Gillian, 490
tropical and colonial medicine, 207–8
Trump, Donald, 166; border wall and immigration policies, 146, 153, 277–-281, 282, 291–92, 297, 321n24; COVID-19 pandemic and, 214, 232n117, 260; migrant caravan and, 291–92; "Muslim ban," 278, 297; Title 42 public health restrictions, 232n117, 260
Trump exceptionalism, 296
Tuck, Eve, 441
Tydings–McDuffie Act, 93
Tzouvala, Ntina, 17–18, 509–10

Uganda, 221–22, 249
Ukraine, 2022 Russian invasion of, 255–59, 263, 265–68, 443, 452; racial contract theory and, 263–66; refugee law and, 261–63; White right to protection and, 258–61
under-historicization, 49
Unger, Roberto, 386
Union Minière du Haut-Katanga (UMHK), 86

United Nations (UN): Achiume on, 261–62; China and, 481; Committee on Economic, Social, and Cultural Rights, 180–81; Convention for the Elimination of Discrimination against Women, 179, 181–82; Human Rights Council, 106–7, 515; International Covenant on Economic, Social, and Cultural Rights, 179, 180–81; intervention in Libya, 28–32, 35–38; responsibility to protect (R2P) doctrine, 29, 31, 32; Sustainable Development Goals, 223; Western European and Others Group (WEOG), 256
United Nations Children Fund, 220
United Nations Conference on Trade and Development (UNCTAD), 327, 331–32
United Nations Decade for People of African Descent, 485
United Nations Economic Commission for Latin America (CEPAL), 331–32
United Nations Educational, Scientific, and Cultural Organization (UNESCO), 110, 481
Universal Declaration of Human Rights, 269n4
U.S. Citizenship and Immigration Services, 153

Van Den Meerssche, Dimitri, 379n71
Van Rees, M., 127
Vattel, Emer de, 57–58, 59, 81, 92, 429, 437
Venezuela, 54, 113
Venta de La Mesilla (Gadsden Purchase), 60, 71n57, 290
Vermont Constitution, 159
Villa, Francisco (Pancho), 85
Vitoria, Francisco de, 389, 437
von Pezold and others v. Zimbabwe, 86, 366, 368–74
Voting Rights Act, 164

Waldron-Ramsey, Waldo, 112–13
Walia, Harsha, 290–91, 303n81
Walker, William, 47, 52
Washington, George, 80
Washington consensus, 82, 487–88
Watermelon Incident (Panama), 47, 51–53, 55, 64
waywardness, 295–96
Wekker, Gloria, 463, 465, 470
Wengrow, David, 157–58, 161, 166
Westlake, John, 49, 62, 67, 108, 429, 434, 437–38
Wheatley, Phillis, 162
Whigs, 58–59, 73n90, 163
White, Hayden, 386
White, Samuel, 80–81
white exceptionalism, 268, 467
"white genocide," 95, 369–70
White health, 203–4; coloniality and, 220–22; Declaration of Alma-Alta, 220–21, 224; global health, 208–10, 222–26; racialized states and public health, 204–6; tropical and colonial medicine, 206–8; World Health Organization and, 210–20
white ignorance, 439–45
"white man's burden," 92, 221, 509
white nationalism, 147, 277–78, 281–82, 287, 409, 470
White saviorism, 221, 222
"white slavery," 95
white supremacy. *See* Global White Supremacy
white transparency phenomenon, 356, 359
Whitman, Walt, 159
Whyte, Jessica, 334n2, 367–68
Wilderson, Frank B., 415
Wiley, Lindsay, 206
Williams, Eric, 149
Williams, Patricia, 6, 511

Winant, Howard, 455, 456
Wing, Adrien, 14–15
Winthrop, Robert, 59, 72n76
"woke" ideologies, 160
Wolfe, Patrick, 398
"Working Man's Declaration of Independence, The" (New York), 163
World Bank, 216, 307, 330, 439, 458, 459, 480, 487–88
World Health Organization (WHO): Constitution, 211, 220; COVID-19 pandemic and, 182, 212, 213–18, 225–26; creation and principles of, 210–13; health justice and, 210–20; International Health Regulations (IHR), 179, 182–83, 211–19, 235n154; Pandemic Influenza Preparedness Framework, 218; White health and, 210–20; World Health Assembly, 211, 213, 215, 224, 234n149
World Trade Organization (WTO), 215, 307, 308, 309, 366–67, 458, 478
World War I, 90–91, 384, 478, 480
World War II, 272n34, 297, 307, 384, 465, 480, 489
Wright, Richard, 328–29, 335n15
Wynter, Sylvia, 130

Xi, Jinping, 153

Yang, K. Wayne, 441
Yazzie, Melanie, 297
Yearby, Ruqaiijah, 206
"Yellow peril," 91
Younis, Musab, 76
Yusuf, Hakeem, 185

Zakaria, Rafia, 452
Zeleza, Paul, 415
Zimbabwe, 86, 369–75, 505–6
zones of sacrifice, 204, 219, 222